The Java® Tutorial

Sixth Edition

The Java® Series

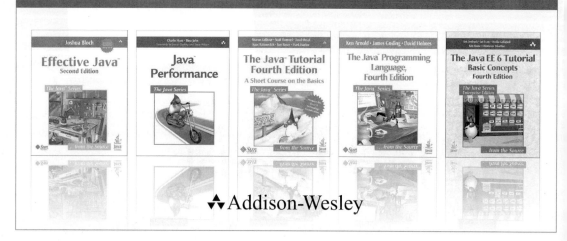

Effective Java Second Edition — Joshua Bloch

Java Performance — Charlie Hunt · Binu John

The Java Tutorial Fourth Edition A Short Course on the Basics — Sharon Zakhour · Scott Hommel · Jacob Royal · Isaac Robinson · Tom Risser · Mark Hoeber

The Java Programming Language, Fourth Edition — Ken Arnold · James Gosling · David Holmes

The Java EE 6 Tutorial Basic Concepts Fourth Edition

♦♦ **Addison-Wesley**

Visit informit.com/thejavaseries for a complete list of available publications.

Since 1996, when Addison-Wesley published the first edition of *The Java Programming Language* by Ken Arnold and James Gosling, this series has been the place to go for complete, expert, and definitive information on Java technology. The books in this series provide the detailed information developers need to build effective, robust, and portable applications and are an indispensable resource for anyone using the Java platform.

Make sure to connect with us!
informit.com/socialconnect

 | |

The Java® Tutorial

A Short Course on the Basics

Sixth Edition

Raymond Gallardo
Scott Hommel
Sowmya Kannan
Joni Gordon
Sharon Biocca Zakhour

✦✦ Addison-Wesley

Upper Saddle River, NJ • Boston • Indianapolis • San Francisco
New York • Toronto • Montreal • London • Munich • Paris • Madrid
Capetown • Sydney • Tokyo • Singapore • Mexico City

Library of Congress Cataloging-in-Publication Data
Gallardo, Raymond.
The Java tutorial : a short course on the basics / Raymond Gallardo, Scott Hommel, Sowmya Kannan,
    Joni Gordon, Sharon Biocca Zakhour.—Sixth edition.
       pages cm
Previous edition: The Java tutorial : a short course on the basics / Sharon Zakhour, Sowmya Kannan,
    Raymond Gallardo. 2013, which was originally based on The Java tutorial / by Mary Campione.
Includes index.
ISBN 978-0-13-403408-9 (pbk. : alk. paper)—ISBN 0-13-403408-2 (pbk. : alk. paper)
1. Java (Computer program language) I. Title.
QA76.73.J38Z35 2015
005.13'3—dc23

                                                 2014035811

ISBN-13: 978-0-13-403408-9
ISBN-10: 0-13-403408-2

Text printed in the United States on recycled paper at Edwards Brothers Malloy in Ann Arbor, Michigan.
First printing, December 2014

Contents

Preface   xxiii
About the Authors   xxvii

Chapter 1   Getting Started   1
                 The Java Technology Phenomenon   1
                     The Java Programming Language   2
                     The Java Platform   2
                     What Can Java Technology Do?   4
                     How Will Java Technology Change My Life?   4
                 The "Hello World!" Application   5
                     "Hello World!" for the NetBeans IDE   6
                     "Hello World!" for Microsoft Windows   15
                     "Hello World!" for Solaris and Linux   20
                 A Closer Look at the "Hello World!" Application   23
                     Source Code Comments   24
                     The HelloWorldApp Class Definition   25
                     The main Method   25
                 Common Problems (and Their Solutions)   27
                     Compiler Problems   27
                     Runtime Problems   29
                 Questions and Exercises: Getting Started   31

	Questions	31
	Exercises	32
	Answers	32
Chapter 2	Object-Oriented Programming Concepts	33
	What Is an Object?	34
	What Is a Class?	36
	What Is Inheritance?	38
	What Is an Interface?	39
	What Is a Package?	40
	Questions and Exercises: Object-Oriented Programming Concepts	41
	Questions	41
	Exercises	41
	Answers	41
Chapter 3	Language Basics	43
	Variables	44
	Naming	45
	Primitive Data Types	46
	Arrays	51
	Summary of Variables	57
	Questions and Exercises: Variables	57
	Operators	58
	Assignment, Arithmetic, and Unary Operators	59
	Equality, Relational, and Conditional Operators	62
	Bitwise and Bit Shift Operators	65
	Summary of Operators	66
	Questions and Exercises: Operators	67
	Expressions, Statements, and Blocks	68
	Expressions	68
	Statements	70
	Blocks	71
	Questions and Exercises: Expressions, Statements, and Blocks	71
	Control Flow Statements	72
	The if-then and if-then-else Statements	72
	The switch Statement	74
	The while and do-while Statements	79
	The for Statement	80
	Branching Statements	82
	Summary of Control Flow Statements	85
	Questions and Exercises: Control Flow Statements	86

Chapter 4   Classes and Objects   87
                  Classes   88
                      Declaring Classes   89
                      Declaring Member Variables   90
                      Defining Methods   92
                      Providing Constructors for Your Classes   94
                      Passing Information to a Method or a Constructor   95
                  Objects   99
                      Creating Objects   100
                      Using Objects   104
                  More on Classes   107
                      Returning a Value from a Method   107
                      Using the this Keyword   109
                      Controlling Access to Members of a Class   110
                      Understanding Class Members   112
                      Initializing Fields   116
                      Summary of Creating and Using Classes and Objects   118
                      Questions and Exercises: Classes   119
                      Questions and Exercises: Objects   120
                  Nested Classes   121
                      Why Use Nested Classes?   122
                      Static Nested Classes   122
                      Inner Classes   123
                      Shadowing   123
                      Serialization   124
                      Inner Class Example   125
                      Local and Anonymous Classes   127
                      Modifiers   127
                      Local Classes   127
                      Anonymous Classes   131
                      Lambda Expressions   136
                      When to Use Nested Classes, Local Classes,
                      Anonymous Classes, and Lambda Expressions   155
                      Questions and Exercises: Nested Classes   156
                  Enum Types   157
                      Questions and Exercises: Enum Types   161
Chapter 5   Annotations   163
                  Annotations Basics   164
                      The Format of an Annotation   164

Where Annotations Can Be Used   165
Declaring an Annotation Type   165
Predefined Annotation Types   167
    Annotation Types Used by the Java Language   167
    Annotations That Apply to Other Annotations   169
Type Annotations and Pluggable Type Systems   170
Repeating Annotations   171
    Step 1: Declare a Repeatable Annotation Type   172
    Step 2: Declare the Containing Annotation Type   172
    Retrieving Annotations   173
    Design Considerations   173
Questions and Exercises: Annotations   173
    Questions   173
    Exercise   174
    Answers   174

Chapter 6   Interfaces and Inheritance   175
Interfaces   175
    Interfaces in Java   176
    Interfaces as APIs   177
    Defining an Interface   177
    Implementing an Interface   178
    Using an Interface as a Type   180
    Evolving Interfaces   181
    Default Methods   182
    Summary of Interfaces   192
    Questions and Exercises: Interfaces   193
Inheritance   193
    The Java Platform Class Hierarchy   194
    An Example of Inheritance   195
    What You Can Do in a Subclass   196
    Private Members in a Superclass   196
    Casting Objects   197
    Multiple Inheritance of State, Implementation, and Type   198
    Overriding and Hiding Methods   199
    Polymorphism   203
    Hiding Fields   206
    Using the Keyword super   206
    Object as a Superclass   208
    Writing Final Classes and Methods   212
    Abstract Methods and Classes   212

	Summary of Inheritance	216
	Questions and Exercises: Inheritance	216
Chapter 7	Generics	219
	Why Use Generics?	220
	Generic Types	220
	A Simple Box Class	220
	A Generic Version of the Box Class	221
	Type Parameter Naming Conventions	221
	Invoking and Instantiating a Generic Type	222
	The Diamond	223
	Multiple Type Parameters	223
	Parameterized Types	224
	Raw Types	224
	Generic Methods	226
	Bounded Type Parameters	227
	Multiple Bounds	228
	Generic Methods and Bounded Type Parameters	229
	Generics, Inheritance, and Subtypes	229
	Generic Classes and Subtyping	230
	Type Inference	232
	Type Inference and Generic Methods	232
	Type Inference and Instantiation of Generic Classes	233
	Type Inference and Generic Constructors of Generic and Nongeneric Classes	234
	Target Types	235
	Wildcards	236
	Upper-Bounded Wildcards	236
	Unbounded Wildcards	237
	Lower-Bounded Wildcards	238
	Wildcards and Subtyping	239
	Wildcard Capture and Helper Methods	240
	Guidelines for Wildcard Use	243
	Type Erasure	244
	Erasure of Generic Types	245
	Erasure of Generic Methods	246
	Effects of Type Erasure and Bridge Methods	247
	Nonreifiable Types and Varargs Methods	249
	Restrictions on Generics	252
	Cannot Instantiate Generic Types with Primitive Types	252
	Cannot Create Instances of Type Parameters	253

                  Cannot Declare Static Fields Whose Types Are Type Parameters 254

                  Cannot Use Casts or instanceof with Parameterized Types 254

                  Cannot Create Arrays of Parameterized Types 255

                  Cannot Create, Catch, or Throw

                  Objects of Parameterized Types 255

                  Cannot Overload a Method Where the Formal Parameter

                  Types of Each Overload Erase to the Same Raw Type 256

         Questions and Exercises: Generics 256

                  Answers 258

Chapter 8   Packages 259

         Creating and Using Packages 259

                  Creating a Package 261

                  Naming a Package 262

                  Using Package Members 263

                  Managing Source and Class Files 267

                  Summary of Creating and Using Packages 269

         Questions and Exercises: Creating and Using Packages 269

                  Questions 269

                  Exercises 270

                  Answers 270

Chapter 9   Numbers and Strings 271

         Numbers 271

                  The Numbers Classes 272

                  Formatting Numeric Print Output 274

                  Beyond Basic Arithmetic 279

                  Autoboxing and Unboxing 283

                  Summary of Numbers 286

                  Questions and Exercises: Numbers 286

         Characters 287

                  Escape Sequences 288

         Strings 288

                  Creating Strings 289

                  String Length 290

                  Concatenating Strings 291

                  Creating Format Strings 292

                  Converting between Numbers and Strings 292

                  Manipulating Characters in a String 295

                  Comparing Strings and Portions of Strings 300

                  The StringBuilder Class 302

                  Summary of Characters and Strings 306

                  Questions and Exercises: Characters and Strings 307

Chapter 10	Exceptions	309
	What Is an Exception?	310
	The Catch or Specify Requirement	311
	The Three Kinds of Exceptions	311
	Bypassing Catch or Specify	312
	Catching and Handling Exceptions	313
	The try Block	314
	The catch Blocks	315
	The finally Block	316
	The try-with-resources Statement	317
	Putting It All Together	320
	Specifying the Exceptions Thrown by a Method	323
	How to Throw Exceptions	324
	The throw Statement	325
	Throwable Class and Its Subclasses	325
	Error Class	326
	Exception Class	326
	Chained Exceptions	326
	Creating Exception Classes	328
	Unchecked Exceptions: The Controversy	329
	Advantages of Exceptions	330
	Advantage 1: Separating Error-Handling	
	Code from "Regular" Code	331
	Advantage 2: Propagating Errors Up the Call Stack	332
	Advantage 3: Grouping and Differentiating Error Types	334
	Summary	335
	Questions and Exercises: Exceptions	336
	Questions	336
	Exercises	337
	Answers	337
Chapter 11	Basic I/O and NIO.2	339
	I/O Streams	339
	Byte Streams	340
	Character Streams	342
	Buffered Streams	345
	Scanning and Formatting	346
	I/O from the Command Line	352
	Data Streams	354
	Object Streams	357
	File I/O (Featuring NIO.2)	359
	What Is a Path? (And Other File System Facts)	359

The Path Class   362
File Operations   370
Checking a File or Directory   374
Deleting a File or Directory   375
Copying a File or Directory   376
Moving a File or Directory   377
Managing Metadata (File and File Store Attributes)   378
Reading, Writing, and Creating Files   386
Random Access Files   393
Creating and Reading Directories   395
Links, Symbolic or Otherwise   399
Walking the File Tree   401
Finding Files   407
Watching a Directory for Changes   410
Other Useful Methods   416
Legacy File I/O Code   418
Summary   421
Questions and Exercises: Basic I/O   422
Questions   422
Exercises   422
Answers   422

Chapter 12   Collections   423
Introduction to Collections   424
What Is a Collections Framework?   424
Benefits of the Java Collections Framework   425
Interfaces   426
The Collection Interface   428
Traversing Collections   429
Collection Interface Bulk Operations   432
Collection Interface Array Operations   432
The Set Interface   433
The List Interface   438
The Queue Interface   446
The Deque Interface   448
The Map Interface   449
Object Ordering   458
The SortedSet Interface   464
The SortedMap Interface   467
Summary of Interfaces   469
Questions and Exercises: Interfaces   470

Aggregate Operations   471
    Pipelines and Streams   472
    Differences between Aggregate Operations and Iterators   474
    Reduction   474
    Parallelism   480
    Side Effects   484
    Questions and Exercises: Aggregate Operations   487
Implementations   489
    Set Implementations   492
    List Implementations   493
    Map Implementations   495
    Queue Implementations   496
    Deque Implementations   498
    Wrapper Implementations   499
    Convenience Implementations   502
    Summary of Implementations   504
    Questions and Exercises: Implementations   504
Algorithms   505
    Sorting   505
    Shuffling   508
    Routine Data Manipulation   508
    Searching   508
    Composition   509
    Finding Extreme Values   509
Custom Collection Implementations   509
    Reasons to Write an Implementation   510
    How to Write a Custom Implementation   511
Interoperability   513
    Compatibility   513
    API Design   515

Chapter 13   Concurrency   519
Processes and Threads   520
    Processes   520
    Threads   520
Thread Objects   521
    Defining and Starting a Thread   521
    Pausing Execution with Sleep   522
    Interrupts   523
    Joins   525
    The SimpleThreads Example   525

Synchronization   527
    Thread Interference   527
    Memory Consistency Errors   528
    Synchronized Methods   529
    Intrinsic Locks and Synchronization   531
    Atomic Access   533
Liveness   533
    Deadlock   534
    Starvation and Livelock   535
Guarded Blocks   535
Immutable Objects   539
    A Synchronized Class Example   540
    A Strategy for Defining Immutable Objects   541
High-Level Concurrency Objects   543
    Lock Objects   544
    Executors   546
    Concurrent Collections   552
    Atomic Variables   553
    Concurrent Random Numbers   554
Questions and Exercises: Concurrency   555
    Question   555
    Exercises   555
    Answers   556

Chapter 14   Regular Expressions   557
Introduction   558
    What Are Regular Expressions?   558
    How Are Regular Expressions Represented in This Package?   558
Test Harness   559
String Literals   560
    Metacharacters   561
Character Classes   562
    Simple Classes   562
Predefined Character Classes   566
Quantifiers   568
    Zero-Length Matches   569
    Capturing Groups and Character Classes with Quantifiers   572
    Differences among Greedy, Reluctant,
    and Possessive Quantifiers   573
Capturing Groups   574
    Numbering   574
    Backreferences   575

Boundary Matchers   576
Methods of the Pattern Class   578
    Creating a Pattern with Flags   578
    Embedded Flag Expressions   580
    Using the matches(String,CharSequence) Method   580
    Using the split(String) Method   581
    Other Utility Methods   582
    Pattern Method Equivalents in java.lang.String   582
Methods of the Matcher Class   583
    Index Methods   583
    Study Methods   584
    Replacement Methods   584
    Using the start and end Methods   585
    Using the matches and lookingAt Methods   586
    Using replaceFirst(String) and replaceAll(String)   587
    Using appendReplacement(StringBuffer,String)
    and appendTail(StringBuffer)   588
    Matcher Method Equivalents in java.lang.String   589
Methods of the PatternSyntaxException Class   589
Unicode Support   591
    Matching a Specific Code Point   591
    Unicode Character Properties   591
Questions and Exercises: Regular Expressions   592
    Questions   592
    Exercise   593
    Answers   593

Chapter 15   The Platform Environment   595
Configuration Utilities   595
    Properties   596
    Command-Line Arguments   600
    Environment Variables   601
    Other Configuration Utilities   602
System Utilities   603
    Command-Line I/O Objects   603
    System Properties   604
    The Security Manager   607
    Miscellaneous Methods in System   608
PATH and CLASSPATH   609
    Update the PATH Environment Variable (Microsoft Windows)   609
    Update the PATH Variable (Solaris, Linux, and OS X)   611
    Checking the CLASSPATH Variable (All Platforms)   612

Questions and Exercises: The Platform Environment   613
    Question   613
    Exercise   614
    Answers   614

Chapter 16   Packaging Programs in JAR Files   615
Using JAR Files: The Basics   616
    Creating a JAR File   616
    Viewing the Contents of a JAR File   620
    Extracting the Contents of a JAR File   622
    Updating a JAR File   623
    Running JAR-Packaged Software   625
Working with Manifest Files: The Basics   627
    Understanding the Default Manifest   627
    Modifying a Manifest File   628
    Setting an Application's Entry Point   629
    Adding Classes to the JAR File's Class Path   630
    Setting Package Version Information   631
    Sealing Packages within a JAR File   633
    Enhancing Security with Manifest Attributes   634
Signing and Verifying JAR Files   635
    Understanding Signing and Verification   636
    Signing JAR Files   639
    Verifying Signed JAR Files   641
Using JAR-Related APIs   642
    An Example: The JarRunner Application   643
    The JarClassLoader Class   643
    The JarRunner Class   646
Questions and Exercises: Packaging Programs in JAR Files   648
    Questions   648
    Answers   648

Chapter 17   Java Web Start   649
    Additional References   650
Developing a Java Web Start Application   650
    Creating the Top JPanel Class   651
    Creating the Application   652
    Benefits of Separating Core Functionality
    from the Final Deployment Mechanism   652
    Retrieving Resources   653
Deploying a Java Web Start Application   653
    Setting Up a Web Server   656

Displaying a Customized Loading Progress Indicator   656
   Developing a Customized Loading Progress Indicator   657
   Specifying a Customized Loading Progress
   Indicator for a Java Web Start Application   659
Running a Java Web Start Application   660
   Running a Java Web Start Application from a Browser   660
   Running a Java Web Start Application
   from the Java Cache Viewer   660
   Running a Java Web Start Application from the Desktop   661
Java Web Start and Security   661
   Dynamic Downloading of HTTPS Certificates   662
Common Java Web Start Problems   662
   "My Browser Shows the Java Network Launch
   Protocol (JNLP) File for My Application as Plain Text"   663
   "When I Try to Launch My JNLP File, I Get the Following Error" 663
Questions and Exercises: Java Web Start   663
   Questions   663
   Exercises   664
   Answers   664

Chapter 18   Applets   665
Getting Started with Applets   666
   Defining an Applet Subclass   666
   Methods for Milestones   667
   Life Cycle of an Applet   668
   Applet's Execution Environment   670
   Developing an Applet   670
   Deploying an Applet   673
Doing More with Applets   677
   Finding and Loading Data Files   677
   Defining and Using Applet Parameters   678
   Displaying Short Status Strings   681
   Displaying Documents in the Browser   682
   Invoking JavaScript Code from an Applet   683
   Invoking Applet Methods from JavaScript Code   686
   Handling Initialization Status with Event Handlers   689
   Manipulating DOM of Applet's Web Page   691
   Displaying a Customized Loading Progress Indicator   693
   Writing Diagnostics to Standard Output and Error Streams   698
   Developing Draggable Applets   698
   Communicating with Other Applets   701

Working with a Server-Side Application   703
What Applets Can and Cannot Do   705
Solving Common Applet Problems   707
"My Applet Does Not Display"   707
"The Java Console Log Displays
java.lang.ClassNotFoundException"   708
"I Was Able to Build the Code Once, but Now the Build
Fails Even Though There Are No Compilation Errors"   708
"When I Try to Load a Web Page That Has an Applet,
My Browser Redirects Me to www.java.com without
Any Warning"   708
"I Fixed Some Bugs and Rebuilt My Applet's
Source Code. When I Reload the Applet's Web Page,
My Fixes Are Not Showing Up"   708
Questions and Exercises: Applets   708
Questions   708
Exercises   709
Answers   709

Chapter 19 Doing More with Java Rich Internet Applications   711
Setting Trusted Arguments and Secure Properties   711
System Properties   713
JNLP API   714
Accessing the Client Using the JNLP API   715
Cookies   719
Types of Cookies   719
Cookie Support in RIAs   719
Accessing Cookies   720
Customizing the Loading Experience   722
Security in Rich Internet Applications   722
Guidelines for Securing RIAs   724
Follow Secure Coding Guidelines   724
Test with the Latest Version of the JRE   724
Include Manifest Attributes   725
Use a Signed JNLP File   725
Sign and Time Stamp JAR Files   725
Use the HTTPS Protocol   726
Avoid Local RIAs   726
Questions and Exercises: Doing More with
Rich Internet Applications   726
Questions   726

	Exercise	726
	Answers	727
Chapter 20	Deployment in Depth	729
	User Acceptance of RIAs	729
	Deployment Toolkit	731
	Location of Deployment Toolkit Script	731
	Deploying an Applet	732
	Deploying a Java Web Start Application	735
	Checking the Client JRE Software Version	738
	Java Network Launch Protocol	739
	Structure of the JNLP File	739
	Deployment Best Practices	748
	Reducing the Download Time	748
	Avoiding Unnecessary Update Checks	749
	Ensuring the Presence of the JRE Software	751
	Questions and Exercises: Deployment in Depth	753
	Questions	753
	Exercise	753
	Answers	753
Chapter 21	Date-Time	755
	Date-Time Overview	756
	Date-Time Design Principles	756
	Clear	756
	Fluent	757
	Immutable	757
	Extensible	757
	The Date-Time Packages	757
	Method Naming Conventions	758
	Standard Calendar	759
	Overview	759
	DayOfWeek and Month Enums	760
	DayOfWeek	760
	Month	762
	Date Classes	762
	LocalDate	763
	YearMonth	763
	MonthDay	764
	Year	764
	Date and Time Classes	764
	LocalTime	764

LocalDateTime   765
Time Zone and Offset Classes   766
    ZoneId and ZoneOffset   766
    The Date-Time Classes   767
Instant Class   770
Parsing and Formatting   772
    Parsing   772
    Formatting   773
The Temporal Package   774
    Temporal and TemporalAccessor   774
    ChronoField and IsoFields   775
    ChronoUnit   775
    Temporal Adjuster   776
    Temporal Query   778
Period and Duration   780
    Duration   781
    ChronoUnit   781
    Period   782
Clock   783
Non-ISO Date Conversion   784
    Converting to a Non-ISO-Based Date   784
    Converting to an ISO-Based Date   786
Legacy Date-Time Code   787
    Interoperability with Legacy Code   787
    Mapping java.util Date and Time
    Functionality to java.time   788
    Date and Time Formatting   789
Summary   789
Questions and Exercises: Date-Time   791
    Questions   791
    Exercises   791
    Answers   791

Chapter 22   Introduction to JavaFX   793
Appendix   Preparation for Java Programming Language Certification   795
Programmer Level I Exam   795
    Section 1: Java Basics   795
    Section 2: Working with Java Data Types   796
    Section 3: Using Operators and Decision Constructs 797
    Section 4: Creating and Using Arrays   797
    Section 5: Using Loop Constructs   798

Section 6: Working with Methods and Encapsulation   798
Section 7: Working with Inheritance   799
Section 8: Handling Exceptions   799
Section 9: Working with Selected Classes
from the Java API   800
Programmer Level II Exam   801
Java SE 8 Upgrade Exam   801
Section 1: Lambda Expressions   801
Section 2: Using Built-In Lambda Types   801
Section 3: Filtering Collections with Lambdas   802
Section 4: Collection Operations with Lambda   803
Section 5: Parallel Streams   803
Section 6: Lambda Cookbook   804
Section 7: Method Enhancements   804
Section 8: Use Java SE 8 Date/Time API   804
Section 9: JavaScript on Java with Nashorn   805

Index   807

Preface

Since the acquisition of Sun Microsystems by Oracle Corporation in early 2010, it has been an exciting time for the Java language. As evidenced by the activities of the Java Community Process program, the Java language continues to evolve. The publication of this sixth edition of *The Java® Tutorial* reflects version 8 of the Java Platform Standard Edition (Java SE) and references the Application Programming Interface (API) of that release.

This edition introduces new features added to the platform since the publication of the fifth edition (under release 7):

- Lambda expressions enable you to treat functionality as a method argument or code as data. Lambda expressions let you express instances of single-method interfaces (referred to as functional interfaces) more compactly. See the new section in Chapter 4, "Lambda Expressions."

- Type annotations can be used in conjunction with pluggable type systems for improved type checking, and repeating annotations enable the application of the same annotation to a declaration or type use. See the new sections in Chapter 5, "Type Annotations and Pluggable Type Systems" and "Repeating Annotations."

- Default methods are methods in an interface that have an implementation. They enable new functionality to be added to the interfaces of libraries and ensure binary compatibility with code written for older versions of those interfaces. See the new section in Chapter 6, "Default Methods."

- Aggregate operations enable you to perform functional-style operations on streams of elements—in particular, bulk operations on collections such as sequential or parallel map-reduce transformations. See the new section in Chapter 12, "Aggregate Operations."
- Improvements have been added that focus on limiting attackers from using malicious applets and rich Internet applications (RIAs). See the following new and updated sections:
  - Chapter 16, "Packaging Programs in JAR Files"
  - Chapter 19, "Security in Rich Internet Applications" and "Guidelines for Securing Rich Internet Applications"
  - Chapter 20, "Deployment Best Practices"
- Date-Time APIs enable you to represent dates and times and manipulate date and time values. They support the International Organization for Standardization (ISO) calendar system as well as other commonly used global calendars. See the new Chapter 21.

If you plan to take one of the Java SE 8 certification exams, this book can help. The appendix, "Preparation for Java Programming Language Certification," lists the three exams that are available, detailing the items covered by each exam, cross-referenced to places in the book where you can find more information about each topic. Note that this is one source, among others, that you will want to use to prepare for your exam. Check the online tutorial for the latest certification objectives and cross-references to sections of the tutorial.

All of the material has been thoroughly reviewed by members of Oracle Java engineering to ensure that the information is accurate and up to date. This book is based on the online tutorial hosted on Oracle Corporation's web site at the following URL:

```
http://docs.oracle.com/javase/tutorial/
```

The information in this book, often referred to as "the core tutorial," is required by most beginning to intermediate programmers. Once you have mastered this material, you can explore the rest of the Java platform documentation on the web site. If you are interested in developing sophisticated RIAs, check out JavaFX, the Java graphical user interface (GUI) toolkit, which comes with the Java SE Development Kit (JDK). To learn more, see Chapter 22, "Introduction to JavaFX."

As always, our goal is to create an easy-to-read, practical programmers' guide to help you learn how to use the rich environment provided by Java to build applications, applets, and components. Go forth and program!

Who Should Read This Book?

This book is geared toward both novice and experienced programmers:

- *New programmers* can benefit most from reading the book from beginning to end, including the step-by-step instructions for compiling and running your first program in Chapter 1, "Getting Started."
- *Programmers experienced with procedural languages* such as C may want to start with the material on object-oriented concepts and features of the Java programming language.
- *Experienced programmers* may want to jump feet first into the more advanced topics, such as generics, concurrency, or deployment.

This book contains information to address the learning needs of programmers with various levels of experience.

How to Use This Book

This book is designed so you can read it straight through or skip around from topic to topic. The information is presented in a logical order, and forward references are avoided wherever possible.

The examples in this book are compiled against the JDK 8 release. *You need to download this release (or later) in order to compile and run most examples.*

Some material referenced in this book is available online—for example, the downloadable examples, the solutions to the questions and exercises, the JDK 8 guides, and the API specification.

You will see footnotes like the following:

```
8/docs/api/java/lang/Class.html
```

and

```
tutorial/java/generics/examples/BoxDemo.java
```

The Java documentation home on the Oracle web site is at the following location:

```
http://docs.oracle.com/javase/
```

To locate the footnoted files online, prepend the URL for the Java documentation home:

```
http://docs.oracle.com/javase/8/docs/api/java/lang/Class.html
```

```
http://docs.oracle.com/javase/tutorial/java/generics/examples/BoxDemo.java
```

The Java Tutorials are also available in two eBook formats:

- mobi eBook files for Kindle
- ePub eBook files for iPad, Nook, and other devices that support the ePub format

Each eBook contains a single trail that is equivalent to several related chapters in this book. You can download the eBooks via the link "In Book Form" on the home page for the Java Tutorials:

```
http://docs.oracle.com/javase/tutorial/index.html
```

We welcome feedback on this edition. To contact us, please see the tutorial feedback page:

```
http://docs.oracle.com/javase/feedback.html
```

Acknowledgments

This book would not be what it is without the Oracle Java engineering team who tirelessly reviews the technical content of our writing. For this edition of the book, we especially want to thank Alan Bateman, Alex Buckley, Stephen Colebourne, Joe Darcy, Jeff Dinkins, Mike Duigou, Brian Goetz, Andy Herrick, Stuart Marks, Thomas Ng, Roger Riggs, Leif Samuelsson, and Daniel Smith.

Illustrators Jordan Douglas and Dawn Tyler created our professional graphics quickly and efficiently.

Editors Janet Blowney, Deborah Owens, and Susan Shepard provided careful and thorough copyedits of our JDK 8 work.

Thanks for the support of our team: Devika Gollapudi, Ram Goyal, and Alexey Zhebel.

Last but not least, thanks for the support of our management: Sowmya Kannan, Sophia Mikulinsky, Alan Sommerer, and Barbara Ramsey.

About the Authors

Raymond Gallardo is a senior technical writer at Oracle Corporation. His previous engagements include college instructor, technical writer for IBM, and bicycle courier. He obtained his BSc in computer science and English from the University of Toronto and MA in creative writing from the City College of New York.

Scott Hommel is a senior technical writer at Oracle Corporation, where he documents Java SE. For the past fifteen years, he has written tutorials, technical articles, and core release documentation for Java SE and related technologies.

Sowmya Kannan wears many hats on the Java SE documentation team, including planning, writing, communicating with developer audiences, and tinkering with production tools. She has more than fifteen years of experience in the design, development, and documentation of the Java platform, Java-based middleware, and web applications.

Joni Gordon is a principal technical writer at Oracle Corporation. She has contributed to the documentation for Java SE and JavaFX. She has been a technical writer for more than fifteen years and has a background in enterprise application development.

Sharon Biocca Zakhour was previously a principal technical writer on staff at Oracle Corporation and formerly at Sun Microsystems. She has contributed to Java SE documentation for more than twelve years, including *The Java™ Tutorial, Fourth Edition,* and *The JFC Swing Tutorial, Second Edition.* She graduated from UC Berkeley with a BA in computer science and has worked as a programmer, developer support engineer, and technical writer for thirty years.

1

Getting Started

Chapter Contents

The Java Technology Phenomenon   1
The "Hello World!" Application   5
A Closer Look at the "Hello World!" Application   23
Common Problems (and Their Solutions)   27
Questions and Exercises: Getting Started   31

This chapter provides everything you'll need to know about getting started with the Java programming language. The first section provides an overview of Java technology as a whole. It discusses both the Java programming language and platform, providing a broad overview of what this technology can do and how it will make your life easier. The second section provides information on the "Hello World!" application. This hands-on approach describes what to download, what to install, and what to type when creating a simple "Hello World!" application. It provides separate instructions for the NetBeans integrated development environment (NetBeans IDE), Microsoft Windows, Solaris, Linux, and OS X users. The third section discusses the "Hello World!" application, describing each section of code in detail. It covers source code comments, the `HelloWorldApp` class definition block, and the `main` method. The fourth section presents common problems and solutions. This is the place to go if you have trouble compiling or running the programs in this chapter. The chapter ends with questions and exercises to test your understanding.

The Java Technology Phenomenon

Talk about Java technology seems to be everywhere, but what exactly is it? This section explains how Java technology is both a programming language and a platform and provides an overview of what this technology can do for you.

1

1 The Java Programming Language

The Java programming language is a high-level language that can be characterized by the following buzzwords:

- Simple
- Object oriented
- Distributed
- Multithreaded
- Dynamic
- Architecture neutral
- Portable
- High performance
- Robust
- Secure

Each of the preceding buzzwords is explained in *The Java Language Environment*, a white paper written by James Gosling and Henry McGilton.[1]

In the Java programming language, all source code is first written in plain text files ending with the `.java` extension. Those source files are then compiled into `.class` files by the `javac` compiler. A `.class` file does not contain code that is native to your processor; it instead contains *bytecodes*—the machine language of the Java Virtual Machine (Java VM).[2] The `java` launcher tool then runs your application with an instance of the Java VM.

Because the Java VM is available on many different operating systems, the same `.class` files are capable of running on Microsoft Windows, Solaris, Linux, or OS X. Some virtual machines, such as the Java HotSpot Virtual Machine, perform additional steps at runtime to give your application a performance boost.[3] This includes various tasks such as finding performance bottlenecks and recompiling (to native code) frequently used sections of code.

The Java Platform

A *platform* is the hardware or software environment in which a program runs. We've already mentioned some of the most popular platforms like Microsoft Windows,

---

1.   `http://www.oracle.com/technetwork/java/langenv-140151.html`

2.   The terms *Java Virtual Machine* and *Java VM* indicate a virtual machine for the Java platform.

3.   `http://www.oracle.com/technetwork/java/javase/tech/index-jsp-136373.html`

Linux, Solaris, and OS X. Most platforms can be described as a combination of the operating system and underlying hardware. The Java platform differs from most other platforms in that it's a software-only platform that runs on top of other hardware-based platforms.

The Java platform has two components:

- The Java Virtual Machine (Java VM)
- The Java Application Programming Interface (API)

You've already been introduced to the Java VM; it's the base for the Java platform and is ported onto various hardware-based platforms.

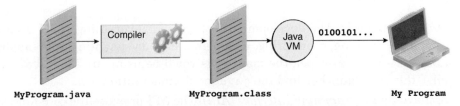

MyProgram.java   MyProgram.class   My Program

Figure 1.1 An Overview of the Software Development Process

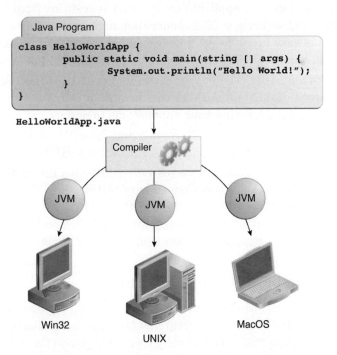

Figure 1.2 Through the Java VM, the Same Application
Is Capable of Running on Multiple Platforms

1

The API is a large collection of ready-made software components that provide many useful capabilities. It is grouped into libraries of related classes and interfaces; these libraries are known as *packages*. The next section highlights some of the functionality provided by the API.

As a platform-independent environment, the Java platform can be a bit slower than native code. However, advances in compiler and virtual machine technologies are bringing performance close to that of native code without threatening portability.

What Can Java Technology Do?

The general-purpose, high-level Java programming language is a powerful software platform. Every full implementation of the Java platform gives you the following features:

- *Development tools.* The development tools provide everything you'll need for compiling, running, monitoring, debugging, and documenting your applications. As a new developer, the main tools you'll be using are the `javac` compiler, the `java` launcher, and the `javadoc` documentation tool.
- *Application Programming Interface (API).* The API provides the core functionality of the Java programming language. It offers a wide array of useful classes ready for use in your own applications. It spans everything from basic objects, to networking and security, to XML generation and database access, and more. The core API is very large; to get an overview of what it contains, consult the Java Platform Standard Edition 8 Documentation.[4]
- *Deployment technologies.* The Java SE Development Kit (JDK) software provides standard mechanisms such as the Java Web Start software and Java Plug-In software for deploying your applications to end users.
- *User interface toolkits.* The JavaFX, Swing, and Java 2D toolkits make it possible to create sophisticated graphical user interfaces (GUIs).
- *Integration libraries.* Integration libraries such as the Java Interactive Data Language (IDL) API, Java Database Connectivity (JDBC) API, Java Naming and Directory Interface (JNDI) API, Java Remote Method Invocation (RMI), and Java Remote Method Invocation over Internet Inter-ORB Protocol (Java RMI-IIOP) Technology enable database access and manipulation of remote objects.

How Will Java Technology Change My Life?

We can't promise you fame, fortune, or even a job if you learn the Java programming language. Still, it is likely to make your programs better and requires less effort than other languages. We believe that Java technology will help you do the following:

---

4.   `8/docs/index.html`

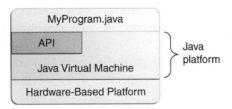

Figure 1.3 The API and Java VM Insulate the Program from the Underlying Hardware

- *Get started quickly.* Although the Java programming language is a powerful object-oriented language, it's easy to learn, especially for programmers already familiar with C or C++.

- *Write less code.* Comparisons of program metrics (class counts, method counts, and so on) suggest that a program written in the Java programming language can be four times smaller than the same program written in C++.

- *Write better code.* The Java programming language encourages good coding practices, and automatic garbage collection helps you avoid memory leaks. Its object orientation, its JavaBeans component architecture, and its wide-ranging, easily extendible API let you reuse existing, tested code and introduce fewer bugs.

- *Develop programs more quickly.* The Java programming language is simpler than C++, and as such, your development time could be up to twice as fast when writing in it. Your programs will also require fewer lines of code.

- *Avoid platform dependencies.* You can keep your program portable by avoiding the use of libraries written in other languages.

- *Write once; run anywhere.* Because applications written in the Java programming language are compiled into machine-independent bytecodes, they run consistently on any Java platform.

- *Distribute software more easily.* With Java Web Start, users will be able to launch your applications with a single click of the mouse. An automatic version check at start-up ensures that users are always up to date with the latest version of your software. If an update is available, Java Web Start will automatically update their installation.

The "Hello World!" Application

This section provides detailed instructions for compiling and running a simple "Hello World!" application. The first section provides information on getting started with the NetBeans IDE, an integrated development environment that greatly simplifies the software development process. The NetBeans IDE runs on the Java platform,

1

which means that you can use it with any operating system for which there is a JDK available. These operating systems include Microsoft Windows, Solaris, Linux, and OS X. We recommend using the NetBeans IDE instead of the command line whenever possible. The remaining sections provide platform-specific instructions for getting started without an integrated development environment. These instructions are provided for users of Windows, Solaris, and Linux, respectively. (For more information about which operating system versions are supported, see Oracle JDK 8 and JRE 8 Certified System Configurations.[5]) If you run into problems, be sure to consult the common problems section; it provides solutions for many issues encountered by new users.

"Hello World!" for the NetBeans IDE

It's time to write your first application! These detailed instructions are for users of the NetBeans IDE. The NetBeans IDE runs on the Java platform, which means that you can use it with any operating system for which there is a JDK available. These operating systems include Microsoft Windows, Solaris, Linux, and OS X.

A Checklist

To write your first program, you'll need the following:

1. *The Java SE Development Kit*. Consult the Java SE Downloads Index.[6]
2. *The NetBeans IDE*. To obtain this for all platforms, consult the NetBeans IDE Downloads Index.[7]

Creating Your First Application

Your first application, `HelloWorldApp`, will simply display the greeting "Hello World!" To create this program, do the following:

1. *Create an IDE project*. When you create an IDE project, you create an environment in which to build and run your applications. Using IDE projects eliminates configuration issues normally associated with developing on the command line. You can build or run your application by choosing a single menu item within the IDE.
2. *Add code to the generated source file*. A source file contains code, written in the Java programming language, that you and other programmers can understand.

---

5. http://www.oracle.com/technetwork/java/javase/certconfig-2095354
    .html
6. http://www.oracle.com/technetwork/java/javase/downloads/index.html
7. http://netbeans.org/downloads/index.html

As part of creating an IDE project, a skeleton source file will be automatically generated. You will then modify the source file to add the "Hello World!" message.

3. *Compile the source file into a* `.class` *file.* The IDE invokes the Java programming language *compiler* (`javac`), which takes your source file and translates its text into instructions that the Java VM can understand. The instructions contained within this file are known as *bytecodes*.

4. *Run the program.* The IDE invokes the Java application *launcher tool* (`java`), which uses the Java VM to run your application.

Create an IDE Project

To create an IDE project, do the following:

1. Launch the NetBeans IDE.
   - On Microsoft Windows systems, you can use the NetBeans IDE item in the Start menu.
   - On Solaris and Linux systems, you execute the IDE launcher script by navigating to the IDE's `bin` directory and typing `./netbeans`.
   - On OS X systems, click the NetBeans IDE application icon.

2. In the NetBeans IDE, choose **File | New Project** (Figure 1.4).

3. In the **New Project** wizard, expand the **Java** category, select **Java Application**, and then click **Next** (Figure 1.5).

4. In the **Name and Location** page of the wizard, do the following (Figure 1.6):
   - In the **Project Name** field, type `Hello World App`.
   - In the **Create Main Class** field, type `helloworldapp.HelloWorldApp`.

5. Click **Finish**.

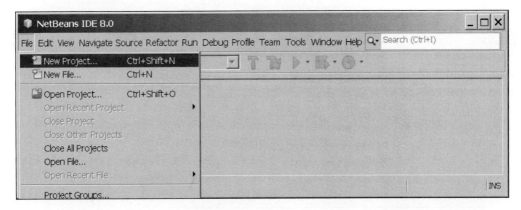

Figure 1.4 NetBeans IDE with the New Project Menu Item Selected

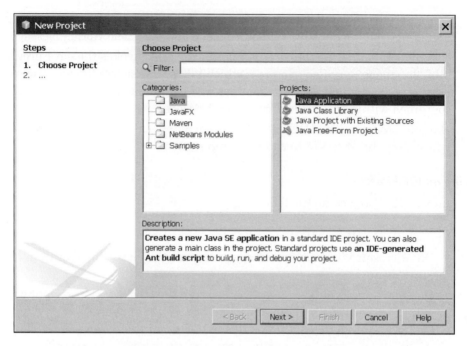

Figure 1.5 NetBeans IDE, New Project Wizard, Choose Project Page

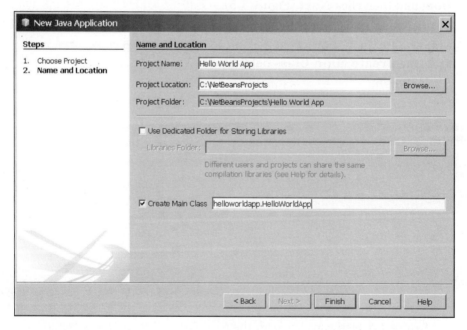

Figure 1.6 NetBeans IDE, New Project Wizard, Name and Location Page

The project is created and opened in the IDE (Figure 1.7). You should see the following components:

- The **Projects** window, which contains a tree view of the components of the project, including source files, libraries that your code depends on, and so on
- The **Source Editor** window with a file called `HelloWorldApp.java` open
- The **Navigator** window, which you can use to quickly navigate between elements within the selected class

Add JDK 8 to the Platform List (If Necessary)

It may be necessary to add JDK 8 to the IDE's list of available platforms. To do this, choose **Tools | Java Platforms**, as shown in Figure 1.8.

If you don't see JDK 8 (which might appear as 1.8 or 1.8.0) in the list of installed platforms, click **Add Platform**, navigate to your JDK 8 install directory, and click **Finish**. You should now see this newly added platform.

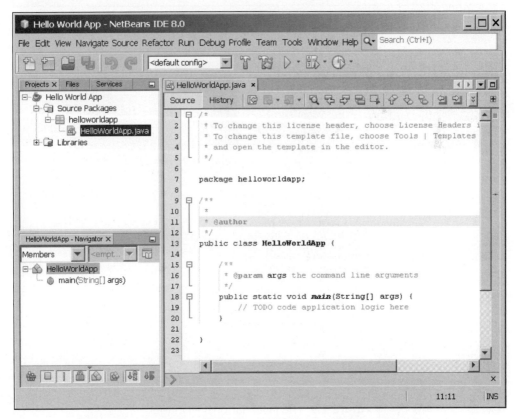

Figure 1.7 NetBeans IDE with the HelloWorldApp Project Open

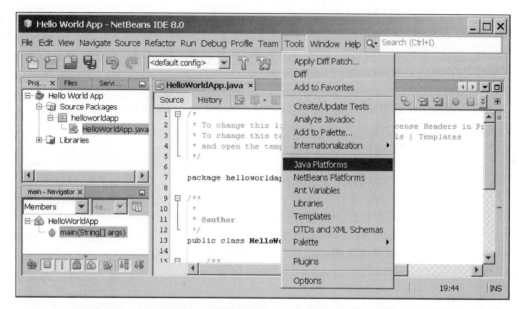

Figure 1.8 Selecting the Java Platform Manager from the Tools Menu

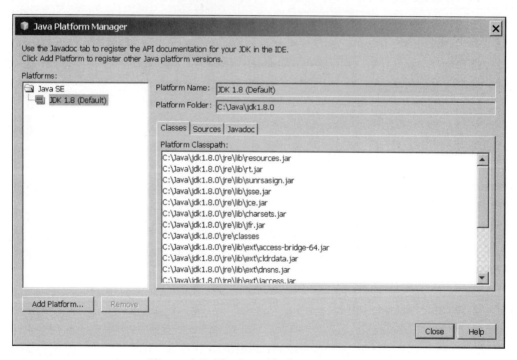

Figure 1.9 The Java Platform Manager

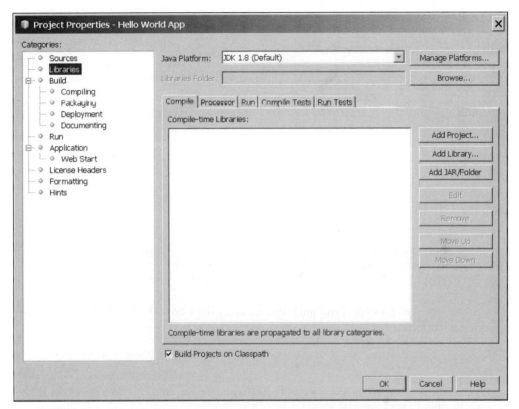

Figure 1.10 The Libraries Category in the Hello World App Project Properties

To set this JDK as the default for all projects, you can run the IDE with the `--jdkhome` switch on the command line or by entering the path to the JDK in the `netbeans_j2sdkhome` property of your `INSTALLATION_DIRECTORY/etc/netbeans.conf` file.

To specify this JDK for the current project only, select **Hello World App** in the **Projects** pane, choose **File | Project Properties (Hello World App)**, click **Libraries**, then select **JDK 1.8** in the **Java Platform** pull-down menu. You should see a screen similar to Figure 1.10. The IDE is now configured for JDK 8.

Add Code to the Generated Source File

When you created this project, you left the **Create Main Class** check box selected in the **New Project** wizard. The IDE has therefore created a skeleton class for you. You can add the "Hello World!" message to the skeleton code by replacing

1

```
// TODO code application logic here
```

with

```
System.out.println("Hello World!"); // Display the string.
```

Optionally, you can replace these four lines of generated code

```
/**
 *
 * @author
 */
```

with these lines

```
/**
 * The HelloWorldApp class implements an application that
 * simply prints "Hello World!" to standard output.
 */
```

These four lines are a code comment and do not affect how the program runs. Later sections of this chapter explain the use and format of code comments.

Note

Type all code, commands, and file names exactly as shown. Both the compiler (`javac`) and launcher (`java`) are *case sensitive*, so you must capitalize consistently. For example, `HelloWorldApp` is *not* the same as `helloworldapp`.

Save your changes by choosing **File | Save**. The file should look something like the following:

```
/*
 * To change this template, choose Tools | Templates
 * and open the template in the editor.
 */
package helloworldapp;
/**
 * The HelloWorldApp class implements an application that
 * simply prints "Hello World!" to standard output.
 */
public class HelloWorldApp {

    /**
     * @param args the command line arguments
     */
    public static void main(String[] args) {
        System.out.println("Hello World!"); // Display the string.
```

```
    }

}
```

Compile the Source File into a .class File

To compile your source file, choose **Run | Build Project (Hello World App)** from the IDE's main menu. The Output window opens and displays output similar to what you see in Figure 1.11.

If the build output concludes with the statement BUILD SUCCESSFUL, congratulations! You have successfully compiled your program!

If the build output concludes with the statement BUILD FAILED, you probably have a syntax error in your code. Errors are reported in the Output window as hyperlinked text. You double click such a hyperlink to navigate to the source of an error. You can then fix the error and once again choose **Run | Build Project**.

When you build the project, the bytecode file HelloWorldApp.class is generated. You can see where the new file is generated by opening the **Files** window and expanding the Hello World App/build/classes/helloworldapp node, as shown in Figure 1.12. Now that you have built the project, you can run your program.

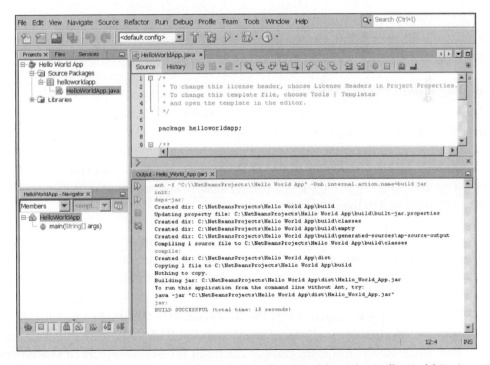

Figure 1.11 Output Window, Showing Results of Building the HelloWorld Project

1

Figure 1.12 Files Window, Showing the Generated .class File

Run the Program

From the IDE's menu bar, choose **Run | Run Main Project**. Figure 1.13 shows what you should now see. Congratulations! Your program works!

Continuing with the NetBeans IDE

The next few pages of the chapter explain the code in this simple application. After that, the sections go deeper into core language features and provide many more examples. Although the rest of the chapters do not give specific instructions about using the NetBeans IDE, you can easily use the IDE to write and run the sample code. The following are some tips on using the IDE and explanations of some IDE behavior that you are likely to see:

- Once you have created a project in the IDE, you can add files to the project using the **New File** wizard. Choose **File | New File**, and then select a template in the wizard, such as the Empty Java File template.

- You can compile and run an individual file (as opposed to a whole project) using the IDE's **Compile File (F9)** and **Run File (Shift+F6)** commands. If you use the **Run Main Project** command, the IDE will run the file that the IDE associates as the main class of the main project. Therefore, if you create an additional class in your HelloWorldApp project and then try to run that file

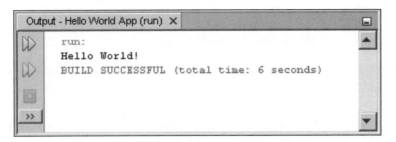

Figure 1.13 The Program Prints "Hello World!" to the Output Window
(along with Other Output from the Build Script)

with the **Run Main Project** command, the IDE will run the `HelloWorldApp`
file instead.

- You might want to create separate IDE projects for sample applications that
  include more than one source file.

- As you are typing in the IDE, a code completion box might periodically appear.
  You can either ignore the code completion box and keep typing or select one
  of the suggested expressions. If you would prefer not to have the code completion box automatically appear, you can turn off the feature. Choose **Tools
  | Options | Editor**, click the **Code Completion** tab, and clear the **Auto
  Popup Completion Window** check box.

- If you want to rename the node for a source file in the **Projects** window, choose
  Refactor from IDE's main menu. The IDE prompts you with the **Rename**
  dialog box to lead you through the options of renaming the class and updating
  code that refers to that class. Make the changes and click **Refactor** to apply
  the changes. This sequence of clicks might seem unnecessary if you have just a
  single class in your project, but it is very useful when your changes affect other
  parts of your code in larger projects.

- For a more thorough guide to the features of the NetBeans IDE, see the Net-
  Beans Documentation page.[8]

"Hello World!" for Microsoft Windows

The following instructions are for users of Windows. (For more information about
which operating system versions are supported, see Oracle JDK 8 and JRE 8 Certified System Configurations.[9])

---

8.   `https://netbeans.org/kb/`

9.   `http://www.oracle.com/technetwork/java/javase/certconfig-2095354`
     `.html`

1

A Checklist

To write your first program, you'll need the following:

1. *The Java SE Development Kit 8 (JDK 8)*. You can download the Windows version now.[10] (Make sure you download the JDK, *not* the JRE.) Consult the installation instructions.[11]

2. *A text editor*. In this example, we'll use Notepad, a simple editor included with Windows platforms. You can easily adapt these instructions if you use a different text editor.

These two items are all you'll need to write your first application.

Creating Your First Application

Your first application, `HelloWorldApp`, will simply display the greeting "Hello world!" To create this program, do the following:

1. *Create a source file*. A source file contains code, written in the Java programming language, that you and other programmers can understand. You can use any text editor to create and edit source files.

2. *Compile the source file into a .class file*. The Java programming language *compiler* (`javac`) takes your source file and translates its text into instructions that the Java VM can understand. The instructions contained within this file are known as *bytecodes*.

3. *Run the program*. The Java application *launcher tool* (`java`) uses the Java VM to run your application.

Create a Source File

To create a source file, you have two options: You can save the file `HelloWorldApp.java`[12] on your computer and avoid a lot of typing, or you can use the following (longer) instructions.

First, start your editor. You can launch the Notepad editor from the **Start** menu by selecting **Programs | Accessories | Notepad**. In a new document, type in the following code:

```
/**
 * The HelloWorldApp class implements an application that
 * simply prints "Hello World!" to standard output.
```

---

10. `http://www.oracle.com/technetwork/java/javase/downloads/index.html`

11. `8/docs/technotes/guides/install/install_overview.html`

12. `tutorial/getStarted/application/examples/HelloWorldApp.java`

```
*/
class HelloWorldApp {
    public static void main(String[] args) {
        System.out.println("Hello World!"); // Display the string.
    }
}
```

> **Note**
>
> Type all code, commands, and file names exactly as shown. Both the compiler (`javac`) and launcher (`java`) are *case sensitive*, so you must capitalize consistently. For example, `HelloWorldApp` is *not* the same as `helloworldapp`.

Save the code in a file with the name `HelloWorldApp.java`. To do this in Notepad, first choose the **File | Save As** menu item. Then, in the **Save As** dialog box, do the following:

1. Using the **Save In** combo box, specify the folder (directory) where you'll save your file. In this example, the directory is `myapplication` on the C drive.
2. In the **File Name** text field, type `"HelloWorldApp.java"`, including the quotation marks.
3. From the **Save As Type** combo box, choose **Text Documents (*.txt)**.
4. In the **Encoding** combo box, leave the encoding as ANSI.

When you're finished, the dialog box should look like Figure 1.14. Now click **Save** and exit Notepad.

Compile the Source File into a .class File

To compile your source file into a `.class` file, bring up a shell, or "command," window. You can do this from the **Start** menu by choosing **Run** and then entering `cmd`. The shell window should look similar to Figure 1.15.

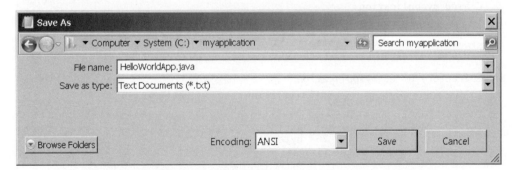

Figure 1.14 The Save As Dialog Just before You Click Save

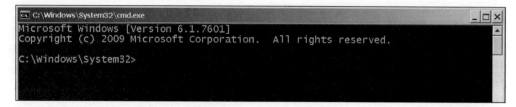

Figure 1.15 A Shell Window

The prompt shows your *current directory*. When you bring up the prompt, your current directory is usually your home directory for Windows (as shown in Figure 1.15).

To compile your source file, change your current directory to the directory where your file is located. For example, if your source directory is `myapplication` on the C drive, type the following command at the prompt and press **Enter**:

```
cd C:\myapplication
```

Now the prompt should change to `C:\myapplication>`.

Note

To change to a directory on a different drive, you must type an extra command: the name of the drive. For example, to change to the `myapplication` directory on the D drive, you must enter `D:`, as follows:

```
C:\>D:

D:\>cd myapplication

D:\myapplication>
```

If you enter `dir` at the prompt, you should see your source file, as follows:

```
C:\>cd myapplication

C:\myapplication>dir
 Volume in drive C is System
 Volume Serial Number is F2E8-C8CC

 Directory of C:\myapplication

2014-04-24 01:34 PM <DIR> .
2014-04-24 01:34 PM <DIR> ..
2014-04-24 01:34 PM 267 HelloWorldApp.java
               1 File(s) 267 bytes
```

```
               2 Dir(s) 93,297,991,680 bytes free

C:\myapplication>
```

Now you are ready to compile. At the prompt, type the following command and press **Enter**:

```
javac HelloWorldApp.java
```

The compiler has generated a bytecode file, `HelloWorldApp.class`. At the prompt, type `dir` to see the new file that was generated as follows:

```
C:\myapplication>javac HelloWorldApp.java

C:\myapplication>dir
 Volume in drive C is System
 Volume Serial Number is F2E8-C8CC

 Directory of C:\myapplication

2014-04-24 02:07 PM <DIR> .
2014-04-24 02:07 PM <DIR> ..
2014-04-24 02:07 PM 432 HelloWorldApp.class
2014-04-24 01:34 PM 267 HelloWorldApp.java
               2 File(s) 699 bytes
               2 Dir(s) 93,298,032,640 bytes free

C:\myapplication>
```

Now that you have a `.class` file, you can run your program.

Run the Program

In the same directory, enter the following command at the prompt:

```
java -cp . HelloWorldApp
```

You should see the following on your screen:

```
C:\myapplication>java -cp . HelloWorldApp
Hello World!

C:\myapplication>
```

Congratulations! Your program works! If you encounter problems with the instructions in this section, consult "Common Problems (and Their Solutions)" at the end of this chapter.

1

"Hello World!" for Solaris and Linux

The following instructions are for users of Solaris and Linux.

A Checklist

To write your first program, you'll need the following:

1. *The Java SE Development Kit 8 (JDK 8).* You can download the Solaris or Linux version now.[13] (Make sure you download the JDK, *not* the JRE.) Consult the installation instructions.[14]

2. *A text editor.* In this example, we'll use Pico, an editor typically available for Solaris and Linux. You can easily adapt these instructions if you use a different text editor, such as `vi` or `emacs`.

These two items are all you'll need to write your first application.

Creating Your First Application

Your first application, `HelloWorldApp`, will simply display the greeting "Hello world!" To create this program, do the following:

1. *Create a source file.* A source file contains code, written in the Java programming language, that you and other programmers can understand. You can use any text editor to create and edit source files.

2. *Compile the source file into a .class file.* The Java programming language *compiler* (`javac`) takes your source file and translates its text into instructions that the Java VM can understand. The instructions contained within this `.class` file are known as *bytecodes*.

3. *Run the program.* The Java application *launcher tool* (`java`) uses the Java VM to run your application.

Create a Source File

To create a source file, you have two options: You can save the file `HelloWorldApp.java`[15] on your computer and avoid a lot of typing, or you can use the following (longer) instructions.

---

13. http://www.oracle.com/technetwork/java/javase/downloads/index.html
14. 8/docs/technotes/guides/install/install_overview.html
15. tutorial/getStarted/application/examples/HelloWorldApp.java

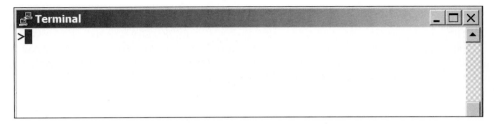

Figure 1.16 A New Terminal Window

First, open a shell, or "terminal," window. When you first bring up the prompt, your *current directory* will usually be your *home directory*. You can change your current directory to your home directory at any time by typing cd at the prompt and then pressing **Enter**.

The source files you create should be kept in a separate directory. You can create a directory by using the command mkdir. For example, to create the directory examples/java in the /tmp directory, use the following commands:

```
cd /tmp
mkdir examples
cd examples
mkdir java
```

To change your current directory to this new directory, you then enter

```
cd /tmp/examples/java
```

Now you can start creating your source file.

Start the Pico editor by typing pico at the prompt and pressing **Enter**. If the system responds with the message pico: command not found, then Pico is most likely unavailable. Consult your system administrator for more information, or use another editor.

When you start Pico, it'll display a new, blank *buffer*. This is the area in which you will type your code. Type the following code into the new buffer:

```
/**
 * The HelloWorldApp class implements an application that
 * simply prints "Hello World!" to standard output.
 */
class HelloWorldApp {
    public static void main(String[] args) {
        System.out.println("Hello World!"); // Display the string.
    }
}
```

Note

Type all code, commands, and file names exactly as shown. Both the compiler (`javac`) and launcher (`java`) are *case sensitive*, so you must capitalize consistently. For example, `HelloWorldApp` is *not* the same as `helloworldapp`.

Save the code in a file with the name `HelloWorldApp.java`. In the Pico editor, you do this by typing **Ctrl+O** and then, at the bottom where you see the prompt `File Name to write:`, entering the directory in which you wish to create the file, followed by `HelloWorldApp.java`. For example, if you wish to save `Hello-WorldApp.java` in the directory `/tmp/examples/java`, then you type `/tmp/examples/java/HelloWorldApp.java` and press **Enter**. You can type **Ctrl+X** to exit Pico.

Compile the Source File into a .class File

Bring up another shell window. To compile your source file, change your current directory to the directory where your file is located. For example, if your source directory is `/tmp/examples/java`, type the following command at the prompt and press **Enter**:

```
cd /tmp/examples/java
```

If you enter `pwd` at the prompt, you should see the current directory, which in this example has been changed to `/tmp/examples/java`. If you enter `ls` at the prompt, you should see your file.

Now are ready to compile the source file. At the prompt, type the following command and press **Enter**:

```
javac HelloWorldApp.java
```

The compiler has generated a bytecode file, `HelloWorldApp.class`. At the prompt, type `ls` to see the new file that was generated, as shown in Figure 1.18. Now that you have a `.class` file, you can run your program.

Run the Program

In the same directory, enter at the prompt:

```
java HelloWorldApp
```

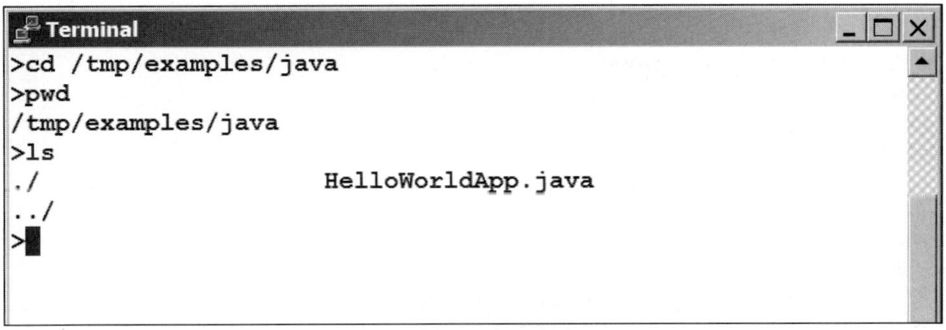

```
Terminal                                                    _ □ X
>cd /tmp/examples/java
>pwd
/tmp/examples/java
>ls
./                      HelloWorldApp.java
../
>
```

Figure 1.17 Results of the ls Command, Showing the .java Source File

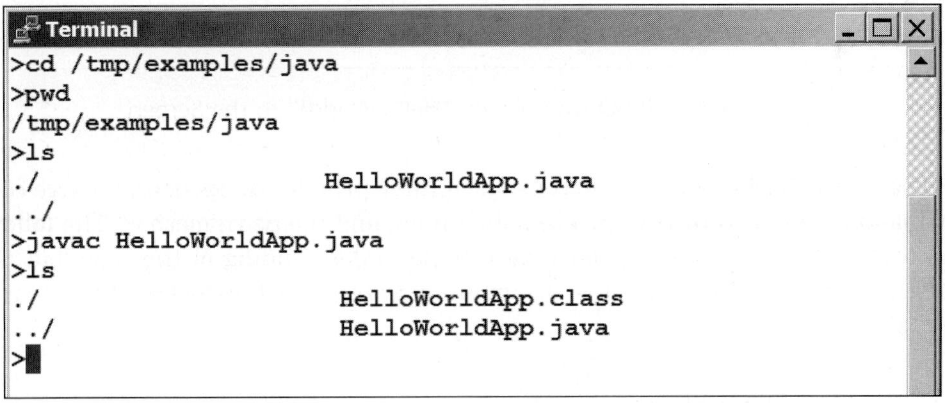

```
Terminal                                                    _ □ X
>cd /tmp/examples/java
>pwd
/tmp/examples/java
>ls
./                      HelloWorldApp.java
../
>javac HelloWorldApp.java
>ls
./                      HelloWorldApp.class
../                     HelloWorldApp.java
>
```

Figure 1.18 Results of the ls Command, Showing the Generated .class File

Figure 1.19 shows what you should now see. Congratulations! Your program works! If you encounter problems with the instructions in this section, consult "Common Problems (and Their Solutions)" at the end of the chapter.

A Closer Look at the "Hello World!" Application

Now that you've seen the "Hello World!" application (and perhaps even compiled and run it), you might be wondering how it works. Here again is its code:

```
class HelloWorldApp {
    public static void main(String[] args) {
        System.out.println("Hello World!"); // Display the string.
    }
}
```

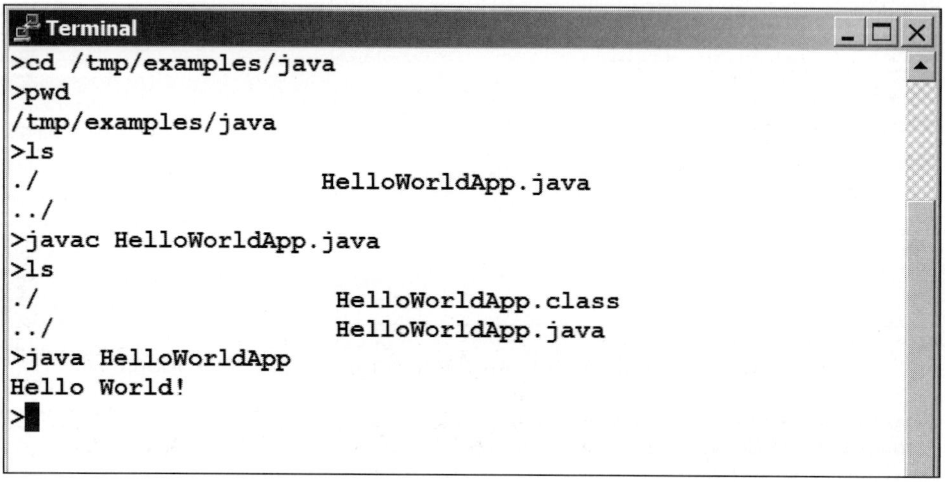

```
Terminal                                                          _ □ X
>cd /tmp/examples/java
>pwd
/tmp/examples/java
>ls
./                      HelloWorldApp.java
../
>javac HelloWorldApp.java
>ls
./                      HelloWorldApp.class
../                     HelloWorldApp.java
>java HelloWorldApp
Hello World!
>█
```

Figure 1.19 The Output Prints "Hello World!" to the Screen

The "Hello World!" application consists of three primary components: source code comments, the `HelloWorldApp` class definition, and the `main` method. The following explanation will provide you with a basic understanding of the code, but the deeper implications will only become apparent after you've finished reading the rest of book.

Source Code Comments

The following bold text indicates the *comments* of the "Hello World!" application:

```
/**
 * The HelloWorldApp class implements an application that
 * simply prints "Hello World!" to standard output.
 */
class HelloWorldApp {
    public static void main(String[] args) {
        System.out.println("Hello World!"); // Display the string.
    }
}
```

Comments are ignored by the compiler but are useful to other programmers. The Java programming language supports three kinds of comments:

1. `/* text */`. The compiler ignores everything from `/*` to `*/`.
2. `/** documentation */`. This indicates a documentation comment (*doc comment*, for short). The compiler ignores this kind of comment, just like it ignores comments that use `/*` and `*/`. The Javadoc tool uses doc comments when

preparing automatically generated documentation. For more information on javadoc, see the Javadoc tool documentation.[16]

3. `// text`. The compiler ignores everything from `//` to the end of the line.

The HelloWorldApp Class Definition

The following bold text begins the class definition block for the "Hello World!" application:

```
/**
 * The HelloWorldApp class implements an application that
 * simply displays "Hello World!" to the standard output.
 */
class HelloWorldApp {
    public static void main(String[] args) {
        System.out.println("Hello World!"); // Display the string.
    }
}
```

As shown above, the most basic form of a class definition is as follows:

```
class name {
    ...
}
```

The keyword `class` begins the class definition for a class named name, and the code for each class appears between the opening and closing curly braces marked in bold above. Chapter 2 provides an overview of classes in general, and Chapter 4 discusses classes in detail. For now, it is enough to know that every application begins with a class definition.

The main Method

The following bold text begins the definition of the `main` method:

```
/**
 * The HelloWorldApp class implements an application that
 * simply displays "Hello World!" to the standard output.
 */
class HelloWorldApp {
    public static void main(String[] args) {
        System.out.println("Hello World!"); //Display the string.
    }
}
```

---

16. `8/docs/technotes/guides/javadoc/index.html`

1

In the Java programming language, every application must contain a `main` method whose signature is as follows:

```
public static void main(String[] args)
```

The modifiers `public` and `static` can be written in either order (`public static` or `static public`), but the convention is to use `public  static` as shown above. You can name the argument anything you want, but most programmers choose `args` or `argv`.

The `main` method is similar to the `main` function in C and C++; it's the entry point for your application and will subsequently invoke all the other methods required by your program. The `main` method accepts a single argument: an array of elements of type `String`.

```
public static void main(String[] args)
```

This array is the mechanism through which the runtime system passes information to your application. For example,

```
java MyApp arg1 arg2
```

Each string in the array is called a *command-line argument*. Command-line arguments let users affect the operation of the application without recompiling it. For example, a sorting program might allow the user to specify that the data be sorted in descending order with this command-line argument:

```
-descending
```

The "Hello World!" application ignores its command-line arguments, but you should be aware of the fact that such arguments do exist.

Finally, the line

```
System.out.println("Hello World!");
```

uses the `System` class from the core library to print the "Hello World!" message to standard output. Portions of this library (also known as the *Application Programming Interface*, or *API*) will be discussed in later chapters.

Common Problems (and Their Solutions)

1

Compiler Problems

Common Error Messages on Microsoft Windows Systems

`'javac' is not recognized as an internal or external command, operable program or batch file`

If you receive this error, Windows cannot find the compiler (`javac`). Here's one way to tell Windows where to find `javac`. Suppose you installed the JDK in `C:\jdk1.8.0`. At the prompt, you would type the following command and press **Enter**:

```
C:\jdk1.8.0\bin\javac HelloWorldApp.java
```

If you choose this option, you'll have to precede your `javac` and `java` commands with `C:\jdk1.8.0\bin\` each time you compile or run a program. To avoid this extra typing, consult the section on updating the `PATH` variable in the JDK 8 installation instructions.[17]

`Class names, 'HelloWorldApp', are only accepted if annotation processing is explicitly requested`

If you receive this error, you forgot to include the `.java` suffix when compiling the program. Remember, the command is `javac HelloWorldApp.java`, not `javac HelloWorldApp`.

Common Error Messages on Solaris and Linux

`javac: Command not found`

If you receive this error, the operating system cannot find the compiler, `javac`. Here's one way to tell Solaris and Linux where to find `javac`. Suppose you installed the JDK in `/usr/local/jdk1.8.0`. At the prompt, you would type the following command and press **Enter**:

```
/usr/local/jdk1.8.0/javac HelloWorldApp.java
```

> **Note**
>
> If you choose this option, each time you compile or run a program, you'll have to precede your `javac` and `java` commands with `/usr/local/jdk1.8.0/`. To avoid this extra typing, you could add this information to your `PATH` variable. The steps for doing so will vary depending on which shell you are currently running.

---

17. 8/docs/webnotes/install/windows/jdk-installation-windows.html#path

Class names, 'HelloWorldApp', are only accepted if annotation processing is explicitly requested

If you receive this error, you forgot to include the `.java` suffix when compiling the program. Remember, the command is `javac HelloWorldApp.java`, not `javac HelloWorldApp`.

Syntax Errors (All Platforms)

If you mistype part of a program, the compiler may issue a *syntax* error. The message usually displays the type of the error, the line number where the error was detected, the code on that line, and the position of the error within the code. Here's an error caused by omitting a semicolon (`;`) at the end of a statement:

```
testing.java:14: ';' expected.
System.out.println("Input has " + count + " chars.")
                                                     ^
1 error
```

Sometimes the compiler can't guess your intent and prints a confusing error message or multiple error messages if the error cascades over several lines. For example, the following code snippet omits a semicolon (`;`) from the bold line:

```
while (System.in.read() != -1)
    count++
System.out.println("Input has " + count + " chars.");
```

When processing this code, the compiler issues two error messages:

```
testing.java:13: Invalid type expression.
        count++
              ^
testing.java:14: Invalid declaration.
    System.out.println("Input has " + count + " chars.");
                      ^
2 errors
```

The compiler issues two error messages because, after it processes `count++`, the compiler's state indicates that it's in the middle of an expression. Without the semicolon, the compiler has no way of knowing that the statement is complete. If you see any compiler errors, then your program did not successfully compile, and the compiler did not create a `.class` file. Carefully verify the program, fix any errors that you detect, and try again.

Semantic Errors

In addition to verifying that your program is syntactically correct, the compiler checks for other basic correctness. For example, the compiler warns you each time you use a variable that has not been initialized:

```
testing.java:13: Variable count may not have been initialized.
        count++;
        ^
testing.java:14: Variable count may not have been initialized.
    System.out.println("Input has " + count + " chars.");
                                       ^
2 errors
```

Again, your program did not successfully compile, and the compiler did not create a .class file. Fix the error and try again.

Runtime Problems

Error Messages on Microsoft Windows Systems

Exception in thread "main" java.lang.NoClassDefFoundError: HelloWorldApp

If you receive this error, java cannot find your bytecode file, HelloWorldApp.class. One of the places java tries to find your .class file is your current directory. So if your .class file is in C:\java, you should change your current directory to that. To change your directory, type the following command at the prompt and press **Enter**:

```
cd c:\java
```

The prompt should change to C:\java>. If you enter dir at the prompt, you should see your .java and .class files. Now enter java HelloWorldApp again.

If you still have problems, you might have to change your CLASSPATH variable. To see if this is necessary, try clobbering the class path with the following command:

```
set CLASSPATH=
```

Now enter java HelloWorldApp again. If the program works now, you'll have to change your CLASSPATH variable. To set this variable, consult the section on updating the PATH variable in the JDK 8 installation instructions.[18] The CLASSPATH variable is set in the same manner.

18. 8/docs/technotes/guides/install/windows_jdk_install.html#BABGDJFH

1

Could not find or load main class `HelloWorldApp.class`

A common mistake made by beginner programmers is to try to run the `java` launcher on the `.class` file that was created by the compiler. For example, you'll get this error if you try to run your program with `java HelloWorldApp.class` instead of `java HelloWorldApp`. Remember, the argument is the *name of the class* that you want to use, *not* the file name.

Exception in thread "main" `java.lang.NoSuchMethodError: main`

The Java VM requires that the class you execute with it has a `main` method at which to begin the execution of your application. The section "A Closer Look at the 'Hello World!' Application" discusses the `main` method in detail.

Error Messages on Solaris and Linux

Exception in thread "main" `java.lang.NoClassDefFoundError: HelloWorldApp`

If you receive this error, `java` cannot find your bytecode file, `HelloWorldApp. class`. One of the places `java` tries to find your bytecode file is your current directory. So, for example, if your bytecode file is in `/home/jdoe/java`, you should change your current directory to that. To change your directory, type the following command at the prompt and press **Enter**:

```
cd /home/jdoe/java
```

If you enter `pwd` at the prompt, you should see `/home/jdoe/java`. If you enter `ls` at the prompt, you should see your `.java` and `.class` files. Now enter `java HelloWorldApp` again.

If you still have problems, you might have to change your `CLASSPATH` environment variable. To see if this is necessary, try clobbering the class path with the following command:

```
unset CLASSPATH
```

Now enter `java HelloWorldApp` again. If the program works now, you'll have to change your `CLASSPATH` variable in the same manner as the `PATH` variable above.

Exception in thread "main" `java.lang.NoClassDefFoundError: HelloWorldApp/class`

A common mistake made by beginner programmers is to try to run the `java` launcher on the `.class` file that was created by the compiler. For example, you'll get this error if you try to run your program with `java HelloWorldApp.class` instead of `java HelloWorldApp`. Remember, the argument is the *name of the class* that you want to use, *not* the file name.

`Exception in thread "main" java.lang.NoSuchMethodError: main`

The Java VM requires that the class you execute with it has a `main` method at which to begin execution of your application. The section "A Closer Look at the 'Hello World!' Application" discusses the `main` method in detail.

Applet or Java Web Start Application Is Blocked

If you are running an application through a browser and get security warnings that say the application is blocked, check the following items:

- Verify that the attributes in the JAR file manifest are set correctly for the environment in which the application is running. The `Permissions` attribute is required. In a NetBeans project, you can open the manifest file from the **Files** tab of the NetBeans IDE by expanding the project folder and double clicking `manifest.mf`.
- Verify that the application is signed by a valid certificate and that the certificate is located in the Signer Certificate Authority (CA) keystore.
- If you are running a local applet, set up a web server to use for testing. You can also add your application to the exception site list, which is managed in the **Security** tab of the Java Control Panel.

Questions and Exercises: Getting Started

Questions

1. When you compile a program written in the Java programming language, the compiler converts the human-readable source file into platform-independent code that a Java VM can understand. What is this platform-independent code called?

2. Which of the following is *not* a valid comment?

   a. `/** comment */`

   b. `/* comment */`

   c. `/* comment`

   d. `// comment`

3. What is the first thing you should check if you see the following error at runtime?

```
Exception in thread "main" java.lang.NoClassDefFoundError:
HelloWorldApp.java.
```

4. What is the correct signature of the `main` method?

5. When declaring the `main` method, which modifier must come first—`public` or `static`?

6. What parameters does the `main` method define?

Exercises

1. Change the `HelloWorldApp.java` program so that it displays `Hola Mundo!` instead of `Hello World!`.

2. Here is a slightly modified version of the `HelloWorldApp`:

    ```
    // HelloWorldApp2.java
    // INTENTIONALLY UNCOMPILABLE!
    /**
     * The HelloWorldApp class implements an application that
     * simply prints "Hello World!" to standard output.
     */
    class HelloWorldApp2 {
      public static void main(String[] args) {
        System.out.println("Hello World!); // Display the string.
      }                                  ↑
    }                                   |(
    ```

    The program has an error. Define the error and fix it so that the program successfully compiles and runs.

Answers

You can find answers to these questions and exercises at `http://docs.oracle.com/javase/tutorial/getStarted/QandE/answers.html`.

2

Object-Oriented Programming Concepts

Chapter Contents

What Is an Object?   34
What Is a Class?   36
What Is Inheritance?   38
What Is an Interface?   39
What Is a Package?   40
Questions and Exercises: Object-Oriented Programming Concepts   41

If you've never used an object-oriented programming language before, you'll need to learn a few basic concepts before you can begin writing any code. This chapter will introduce you to objects, classes, inheritance, interfaces, and packages. Each section focuses on how these concepts relate to the real world while simultaneously providing an introduction to the syntax of the Java programming language.

The first section focuses on objects. An object is a software bundle of related state and behavior. Software objects are often used to model the real-world objects that you find in everyday life. This section explains how state and behavior are represented within an object, introduces the concept of data encapsulation, and explains the benefits of designing your software in this manner.

The second section discusses classes. A class is a blueprint or prototype from which objects are created. This section defines a class that models the state and behavior of a real-world object. It intentionally focuses on the basics, showing how even a simple class can cleanly model state and behavior.

The third section focuses on inheritance. Inheritance provides a powerful and natural mechanism for organizing and structuring your software. This section explains how classes inherit state and behavior from their superclasses and explains how to derive one class from another using the simple syntax provided by the Java programming language.

The fourth section discusses interfaces. An interface is a contract between a class and the outside world. When a class implements an interface, it promises to provide the behavior published by that interface. This section defines a simple interface and explains the necessary changes for any class that implements it.

The fifth section describes packages. A package is a namespace for organizing classes and interfaces in a logical manner. Placing your code into packages makes large software projects easier to manage. This section explains why this is useful and introduces you to the Application Programming Interface (API) provided by the Java platform.

The chapter ends with questions and exercises to test your understanding of objects, classes, inheritance, interfaces, and packages.

What Is an Object?

Objects are key to understanding *object-oriented* technology. Look around right now and you'll find many examples of real-world objects: your dog, your desk, your television set, your bicycle.

Real-world objects share two characteristics: They all have *state* and *behavior*. Dogs have state (name, color, breed, hungry) and behavior (barking, fetching, wagging tail). Bicycles also have state (current gear, current pedal cadence, current speed) and behavior (changing gear, changing pedal cadence, applying brakes). Identifying state and behavior for real-world objects is a great way to begin thinking in terms of object-oriented programming.

Take a minute right now to observe the real-world objects that are in your immediate area. For each object that you see, ask yourself two questions: "What possible states can this object be in?" and "What possible behavior can this object perform?" Make sure to write down your observations. As you do, you'll notice that real-world objects vary in complexity; your desktop lamp may have only two possible states (on and off) and two possible behaviors (turn on, turn off), but your desktop radio might have additional states (on, off, current volume, current station) and behavior (turn on, turn off, increase volume, decrease volume, seek, scan, and tune). You may also notice that some objects, in turn, will also contain other objects. These real-world observations all translate into the world of object-oriented programming.

Software objects are conceptually similar to real-world objects: they too consist of state and related behavior (Figure 2.1). An object stores its state in *fields* (variables in some programming languages) and exposes its behavior through *methods* (functions in some programming languages). Methods operate on an object's internal state and serve as the primary mechanism for object-to-object communication. The

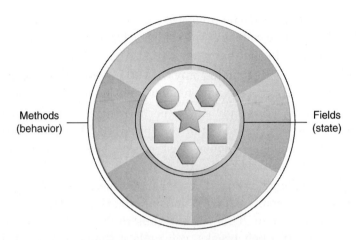

Figure 2.1 A Software Object

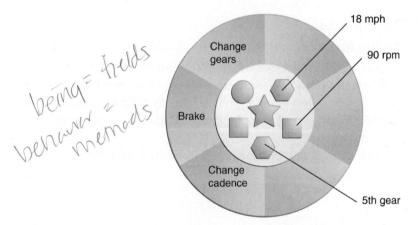

Figure 2.2 A Bicycle Modeled as a Software Object

act of hiding internal state and requiring all interaction to be performed through an object's methods is known as *data encapsulation*—a fundamental principle of object-oriented programming.

For example, let's consider a bicycle (Figure 2.2). By attributing state (current speed, current pedal cadence, and current gear) and providing methods for changing that state, the object remains in control of how the outside world is allowed to use it. For example, if the bicycle only has six gears, a method to change gears could reject any value that is less than one or greater than six.

Bundling code into individual software objects provides a number of benefits, including the following:

1. *Modularity.* The source code for an object can be written and maintained independently of the source code for other objects. Once created, an object can be easily passed around inside the system.

2. *Information hiding.* By interacting only with an object's methods, the details of its internal implementation remain hidden from the outside world.

3. *Code reuse.* If an object already exists (perhaps written by another software developer), you can use that object in your program. This allows specialists to implement, test, and debug complex, task-specific objects, which you can then trust to run in your own code.

4. *Pluggability and debugging ease.* If a particular object turns out to be problematic, you can simply remove it from your application and plug in a different object as its replacement. This is analogous to fixing mechanical problems in the real world. If a bolt breaks, you replace that particular bolt, not the entire machine.

What Is a Class?

In the real world, you'll often find many individual objects, all of the same kind. There may be thousands of other bicycles in existence, all of the same make and model. Each bicycle was built from the same set of blueprints and therefore contains the same components. In object-oriented terms, we say that your bicycle is an *instance* of the *class of objects* known as bicycles. A *class* is the blueprint from which individual objects are created.

The following `Bicycle` class is one possible implementation of a bicycle:

```
class Bicycle {

    int cadence = 0;
    int speed = 0;
    int gear = 1;

    void changeCadence(int newValue) {
        cadence = newValue;
    }

    void changeGear(int newValue) {
        gear = newValue;
    }

    void speedUp(int increment) {
        speed = speed + increment;
    }

    void applyBrakes(int decrement) {
        speed = speed - decrement;
    }
```

```
    void printStates() {
        System.out.println("cadence:" +
            cadence + " speed:" +
            speed + " gear:" + gear);
    }
}
```

2

The syntax of the Java programming language will look new to you, but the design of this class is based on the previous discussion of bicycle objects. The fields cadence, speed, and gear represent the object's state, and the methods (such as changeCadence, changeGear, and speedUp) define its interaction with the outside world.

You may have noticed that the Bicycle class does not contain a main method. That's because it's not a complete application; it's just the blueprint for bicycles that might be *used* in an application. The responsibility of creating and using new Bicycle objects belongs to some other class in your application.

Here's a BicycleDemo class that creates two separate Bicycle objects and invokes their methods:

```
class BicycleDemo {
    public static void main(String[] args) {

        // Create two different
        // Bicycle objects
        Bicycle bike1 = new Bicycle();
        Bicycle bike2 = new Bicycle();

        // Invoke methods on
        // those objects
        bike1.changeCadence(50);
        bike1.speedUp(10);
        bike1.changeGear(2);
        bike1.printStates();

        bike2.changeCadence(50);
        bike2.speedUp(10);
        bike2.changeGear(2);
        bike2.changeCadence(40);
        bike2.speedUp(10);
        bike2.changeGear(3);
        bike2.printStates();
    }
}
```

The output of this test prints the ending pedal cadence, speed, and gear for the two bicycles:

```
cadence:50 speed:10 gear:2
cadence:40 speed:20 gear:3
```

What Is Inheritance?

Different kinds of objects often have a certain amount in common with each other. Mountain bikes, road bikes, and tandem bikes, for example, all share the characteristics of bicycles (current speed, current pedal cadence, current gear). Yet each also has additional features that make it different: tandem bicycles have two seats and two sets of handlebars; road bikes have drop handlebars; and some mountain bikes have an additional chain ring, giving them a lower gear ratio.

Object-oriented programming allows classes to *inherit* commonly used state and behavior from other classes. In this example, Bicycle now becomes the *superclass* of MountainBike, RoadBike, and TandemBike. In the Java programming language, each class is allowed to have one direct superclass and each superclass has the potential for an unlimited number of *subclasses* (Figure 2.3).

The syntax for creating a subclass is simple. At the beginning of your class declaration, use the extends keyword, followed by the name of the class to inherit from:

```
class MountainBike extends Bicycle {

    // new fields and methods defining
    // a mountain bike would go here

}
```

This gives MountainBike all the same fields and methods as Bicycle yet allows its code to focus exclusively on the features that make it unique. This makes code

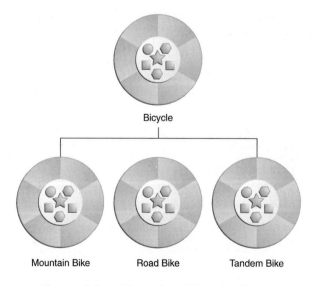

Figure 2.3 A Hierarchy of Bicycle Classes

for your subclasses easy to read. However, you must take care to properly document the state and behavior that each superclass defines, since that code will not appear in the source file of each subclass.

What Is an Interface?

As you've already learned, objects define their interaction with the outside world through the methods they expose. Methods form the object's *interface* with the outside world; the buttons on the front of your television set, for example, are the interface between you and the electrical wiring on the other side of its plastic casing. You press the power button to turn the television on and off.

In its most common form, an interface is a group of related methods with empty bodies. A bicycle's behavior, if specified as an interface, might appear as follows:

```
interface Bicycle {

    // wheel revolutions per minute
    void changeCadence(int newValue);

    void changeGear(int newValue);

    void speedUp(int increment);

    void applyBrakes(int decrement);
}
```

To implement this interface, the name of your class would change (to a particular brand of bicycle, for example, such as ACMEBicycle) and you'd use the implements keyword in the class declaration:

```
class ACMEBicycle implements Bicycle {

    int cadence = 0;
    int speed = 0;
    int gear = 1;

    // The compiler will now require that methods
    // changeCadence, changeGear, speedUp, and applyBrakes
    // all be implemented. Compilation will fail if those
    // methods are missing from this class.

    void changeCadence(int newValue) {
        cadence = newValue;
    }

    void changeGear(int newValue) {
        gear = newValue;
    }

    void speedUp(int increment) {
```

2

```
            speed = speed + increment;
    }

    void applyBrakes(int decrement) {
            speed = speed - decrement;
    }

    void printStates() {
            System.out.println("cadence:" +
                cadence + " speed:" +
                speed + " gear:" + gear);
    }
}
```

Implementing an interface allows a class to become more formal about the behavior it promises to provide. Interfaces form a contract between the class and the outside world, and this contract is enforced at build time by the compiler. If your class claims to implement an interface, all methods defined by that interface must appear in its source code before the class will successfully compile.

> **Note**
>
> To actually compile the ACMEBicycle class, you'll need to add the public keyword to the beginning of the implemented interface methods. You'll learn the reasons for this later, in Chapters 4 and 6.

What Is a Package?

A package is a namespace that organizes a set of related classes and interfaces. Conceptually, you can think of packages as being similar to different folders on your computer. You might keep HTML pages in one folder, images in another, and scripts or applications in yet another. Because software written in the Java programming language can be composed of hundreds or *thousands* of individual classes, it makes sense to keep things organized by placing related classes and interfaces into packages.

The Java platform provides an enormous class library (a set of packages) suitable for use in your own applications. This library is known as the *Application Programming Interface*, or *API* for short. Its packages represent the tasks most commonly associated with general-purpose programming. For example, a String object contains state and behavior for character strings; a File object allows a programmer to easily create, delete, inspect, compare, or modify a file on the file system; a Socket object allows for the creation and use of network sockets; various graphical user interface (GUI) objects control buttons and check boxes and anything else related to GUIs. There are literally thousands of classes to choose from. This allows you, the programmer, to focus on the design of your particular application, rather than the infrastructure required to make it work.

The Java Platform API Specification contains the complete listing for all packages, interfaces, classes, fields, and methods supplied by the Java SE platform.[1] Open the page in your browser and bookmark it. As a programmer, it will become your single most important piece of reference documentation.

Questions and Exercises: Object-Oriented Programming Concepts

Questions

1. Real-world objects contain ___ and ___. *state behavior*
2. A software object's state is stored in ___. *field*
3. A software object's behavior is exposed through ___. *methods*
4. Hiding internal data from the outside world and accessing it only through publicly exposed methods is known as data ___ *encapsulation*
5. A blueprint for a software object is called a ___ *class*
6. Common behavior can be defined in a ___ and inherited into a ___ using the ___ keyword. *extends* *superclass* *subclass*
7. A collection of methods with no implementation is called an ___ *interface*
8. A namespace that organizes classes and interfaces by functionality is called a ___ *package*
9. The term API stands for ___. *application programming interface*

Exercises

1. Create new classes for each real-world object that you observed at the beginning of this chapter. Refer to the `Bicycle` class if you forget the required syntax.
2. For each new class that you've created above, create an interface that defines its behavior and then require your class to implement it. Omit one or two methods and try compiling. What does the error look like?

Answers

You can find answers to these questions and exercises at `http://docs.oracle.com/javase/tutorial/java/concepts/QandE/answers.html`.

---

1. `8/docs/api/index.html`

3

Language Basics

Chapter Contents

Variables   44
Operators   58
Expressions, Statements, and Blocks   68
Control Flow Statements   72

You've already learned that objects store their state in fields. However, the Java programming language uses the term *variable* as well. The first section of this chapter discusses this relationship, plus variable naming rules and conventions, basic data types (primitive types, character strings, and arrays), default values, and literals.

The second section describes the operators of the Java programming language. It presents the most commonly used operators first and the less commonly used operators last. Each discussion includes code samples that you can compile and run.

Operators may be used for building expressions, which compute values; expressions are the core components of statements, and statements may be grouped into blocks. The third section discusses expressions, statements, and blocks using example code that you've already seen.

The final section describes the control flow statements supported by the Java programming language. It covers the decision-making, looping, and branching statements that enable your programs to conditionally execute particular blocks of code.

Note that each section contains its own questions and exercises to test your understanding.

Variables

As you learned in the previous chapter, an object stores its state in *fields*:

```
int cadence = 0;
int speed = 0;
int gear = 1;
```

In Chapter 2, the section "What Is an Object?" introduced you to fields, but you probably have still a few questions, such as, What are the rules and conventions for naming a field? Besides int, what other data types are there? Do fields have to be initialized when they are declared? Are fields assigned a default value if they are not explicitly initialized? We'll explore the answers to such questions in this chapter, but before we do, there are a few technical distinctions you must first become aware of. In the Java programming language, the terms *field* and *variable* are both used; this is a common source of confusion among new developers because both often seem to refer to the same thing. The Java programming language defines the following kinds of variables:

- *Instance variables (nonstatic fields).* Technically speaking, objects store their individual states in "nonstatic fields"—that is, fields declared without the static keyword. Nonstatic fields are also known as *instance variables* because their values are unique to each *instance* of a class (to each object, in other words); for example, the currentSpeed of one bicycle is independent of the currentSpeed of another.

- *Class variables (static fields).* A *class variable* is any field declared with the static modifier; this tells the compiler that there is exactly one copy of this variable in existence, regardless of how many times the class has been instantiated. For example, a field defining the number of gears for a particular kind of bicycle could be marked as static since conceptually the same number of gears will apply to all instances. The code static int numGears = 6; would create such a static field. Additionally, the keyword final could be added to indicate that the number of gears will never change.

- *Local variables.* Similar to how an object stores its state in fields, a method will often store its temporary state in *local variables*. The syntax for declaring a local variable is similar to declaring a field (e.g., int count = 0;). There is no special keyword designating a variable as local; that determination comes entirely from the location in which the variable is declared—which is between the opening and closing braces of a method. As such, local variables are only visible to the methods in which they are declared; they are not accessible from the rest of the class.

- *Parameters.* You've already seen examples of parameters, both in the `Bicycle` class and in the `main` method of the "Hello World!" application. Recall that the signature for the `main` method is `public static void main(String[] args)`. Here, the `args` variable is the parameter to this method. The important thing to remember is that parameters are always classified as *variables*, not *fields*. This applies to other parameter-accepting constructs as well (such as constructors and exception handlers) that you'll learn about later in the chapter.

3

That said, the remainder of the chapters use the following general guidelines when discussing fields and variables. If we are talking about *fields in general* (excluding local variables and parameters), we may simply use the term *fields*. If the discussion applies to *all of the above*, we may simply use the term *variables*. If the context calls for a distinction, we will use specific terms (such as *static field* or *local variables*) as appropriate. You may also occasionally see the term *member* used as well. A type's fields, methods, and nested types are collectively called its *members*.

Naming

Every programming language has its own set of rules and conventions for the kinds of names that you're allowed to use, and the Java programming language is no different. The rules and conventions for naming your variables can be summarized as follows:

- Variable names are case sensitive. A variable's name can be any legal identifier—an unlimited-length sequence of Unicode letters and digits, beginning with a letter, the dollar sign (`$`), or the underscore character (`_`). The convention, however, is to always begin your variable names with a letter, not `$` or `_`. Additionally, the dollar sign character, by convention, is never used at all. You may find some situations where autogenerated names will contain the dollar sign, but your variable names should always avoid using it. A similar convention exists for the underscore character; while it's technically legal to begin your variable's name with `_`, this practice is discouraged. White space is not permitted.

- Subsequent characters may be letters, digits, dollar signs, or underscore characters. Conventions (and common sense) apply to this rule as well. When choosing a name for your variables, use full words instead of cryptic abbreviations. Doing so will make your code easier to read and understand. In many cases, it will also make your code self-documenting; fields named `cadence`, `speed`, and `gear`, for example, are much more intuitive than abbreviated versions, such as s, c, and g. Also keep in mind that the name you choose must not be a keyword or reserved word.

- If the name you choose consists of only one word, spell that word in all lower-case letters. If it consists of more than one word, capitalize the first letter of each subsequent word. The names gearRatio and currentGear are prime examples of this convention. If your variable stores a constant value, such as static final int NUM_GEARS = 6, the convention changes slightly, capi-talizing every letter and separating subsequent words with the underscore character. By convention, the underscore character is never used elsewhere.

Primitive Data Types

The Java programming language is statically typed, which means that all variables must first be declared before they can be used. This involves stating the variable's type and name, as you've already seen:

```
int gear = 1;
```

Doing so tells your program that a field named *gear* exists, holds numerical data, and has an initial value of 1. A variable's data type determines the values it may contain plus the operations that may be performed on it. In addition to int, the Java programming language supports seven other *primitive data types*. A primitive type is predefined by the language and is named by a reserved keyword. Primitive values do not share state with other primitive values. The eight primitive data types supported by the Java programming language are as follows:

1. The **byte** data type is an 8-bit signed two's complement integer. It has a mini-mum value of −128 and a maximum value of 127 (inclusive). The byte data type can be useful for saving memory in large arrays, where the memory sav-ings actually matters. It can also be used in place of int where its limits help clarify your code; the fact that a variable's range is limited can serve as a form of documentation.

2. The **short** data type is a 16-bit signed two's complement integer. It has a minimum value of −32,768 and a maximum value of 32,767 (inclusive). As with byte, the same guidelines apply: you can use a short to save memory in large arrays in situations where the memory savings actually matter.

3. By default, the **int** data type is a 32-bit signed two's complement integer, which has a minimum value of -2^{31} and a maximum value of $2^{31} - 1$. In Java SE 8 and later, you can use the int data type to represent an unsigned 32-bit integer, which has a minimum value of 0 and a maximum value of $2^{32} - 1$. The Integer class also supports unsigned 32-bit integers. Static methods like

compareUnsigned and divideUnsigned have been added to the Integer class to support arithmetic operations for unsigned integers.[1]

4. The **long** data type is a 64-bit two's complement integer. The signed long has a minimum value of -2^{63} and a maximum value of $2^{63} - 1$. In Java SE 8 and later, you can use the long data type to represent an unsigned 64-bit long, which has a minimum value of 0 and a maximum value of $2^{64} - 1$. Use this data type when you need a range of values wider than those provided by the int data type. The Long class also contains methods like compareUnsigned and divideUnsigned to support arithmetic operations for unsigned long values.[2]

5. The **float** data type is a single-precision 32-bit IEEE 754 floating-point value. Its range of values is beyond the scope of this discussion but is specified in the Floating-Point Types, Formats, and Values section of the Java Language Specification.[3] As with the recommendations for the byte and short data types, use a float (instead of double) value if you need to save memory in large arrays of floating-point numbers. This data type should never be used for precise values, such as currency. For that, you will need to use the java.math.BigDecimal class instead.[4] Chapter 9 covers BigDecimal and other useful classes provided by the Java platform.

6. The **double** data type is a double-precision 64-bit IEEE 754 floating-point value. Its range of values is beyond the scope of this discussion but is specified in the Floating-Point Types, Formats, and Values section of the Java Language Specification.[5] For decimal values, this data type is generally the default choice. As mentioned previously, this data type should never be used for precise values, such as currency.

7. The **boolean** data type has only two possible values: true and false. Use this data type for simple flags that track true/false conditions. This data type represents one bit of information, but its "size" isn't something that's precisely defined.

8. The **char** data type is a single 16-bit Unicode character. It has a minimum value of '\u0000' (or 0) and a maximum value of '\uffff' (or 65,535 inclusive).

In addition to the eight primitive data types, the Java programming language also provides special support for character strings through the java.lang.String

---

1. 8/docs/api/java/lang/Integer.html
2. 8/docs/api/java/lang/Long.html
3. specs/jls/se7/html/jls-4.html#jls-4.2.3
4. 8/docs/api/java/math/BigDecimal.html
5. specs/jls/se7/html/jls-4.html#jls-4.2.3

class.[6] Enclosing your character string within double quotes will automatically create a new `String` object—for example, `String s = "this is a string";`. `String` objects are *immutable*, which means that, once created, their values cannot be changed. The `String` class is not technically a primitive data type, but considering the special support given to it by the language, you'll probably tend to think of it as such. You'll learn more about the `String` class in Chapter 9.

Default Values

It's not always necessary to assign a value when a field is declared. Fields that are declared but not initialized will be set to a reasonable default by the compiler. Generally speaking, this default will be zero or `null`, depending on the data type. Relying on such default values, however, is generally considered bad programming style. Table 3.1 summarizes the default values for the above data types.

Local variables are slightly different; the compiler never assigns a default value to an uninitialized local variable. If you cannot initialize your local variable where it is declared, make sure to assign it a value before you attempt to use it. Accessing an uninitialized local variable will result in a compile-time error.

Literals

You may have noticed that the `new` keyword isn't used when initializing a variable of a primitive type. Primitive types are special data types built into the language; they are not objects created from a class. A *literal* is the source code representation of a fixed value; literals are represented directly in your code without requiring computation. As shown here, it's possible to assign a literal to a variable of a primitive type:

```
boolean result = true;
char capitalC = 'C';
byte b = 100;
short s = 10000;
int i = 100000;
```

Integer Literals

An integer literal is of type `long` if it ends with the letter `L` or `l`; otherwise, it is of type `int`. It is recommended that you use the uppercase letter `L` because the lowercase letter `l` is hard to distinguish from the digit 1.

Values of the integral types `byte`, `short`, `int`, and `long` can be created from `int` literals. Values of type `long` that exceed the range of `int` can be created from `long` literals. Integer literals can be expressed by these number systems:

---

6.   `8/docs/api/java/lang/String.html`

Table 3.1 Default Values for Data Types

Data type	Default value (for fields)
byte	0
short	0
int	0
long	0L
float	0.0f
double	0.0d
boolean	false
char	'\u0000'
String (or any object)	null

- *Decimal.* Base 10, whose digits consist of the numbers 0 through 9 (This is the number system you use every day.)
- *Hexadecimal.* Base 16, whose digits consist of the numbers 0 through 9 and the letters A through F
- *Binary.* Base 2, whose digits consists of the numbers 0 and 1

For general-purpose programming, the decimal system is likely to be the only number system you'll ever use. However, if you need to use another number system, the following example shows the correct syntax. The prefix 0x indicates hexadecimal and 0b indicates binary:

```
// The number 26, in decimal
int decVal = 26;
// The number 26, in hexadecimal
int hexVal = 0x1a;
// The number 26, in binary
int binVal = 0b11010;
```

Floating-Point Literals

A floating-point literal is of type float if it ends with the letter F or f; otherwise, its type is double and it can optionally end with the letter D or d. The floating-point types (float and double) can also be expressed using E or e (for scientific notation), F or f (32-bit float literal), and D or d (64-bit double literal, which is the default and by convention is omitted).

```
double d1 = 123.4;
// same value as d1, but in scientific notation
double d2 = 1.234e2;
float f1 = 123.4f;
```

Character and String Literals

Literals of types char and String may contain any Unicode (UTF-16) characters. If your editor and file system allow it, you can use such characters directly in your code. If not, you can use a *Unicode escape*, such as `'\u0108'` (for a capital C with circumflex, Ĉ) or `"S\u00ED Se\u00F1or"` (for *Sí Señor* in Spanish). Always use 'single quotes' for char literals and "double quotes" for String literals. Unicode escape sequences may be used elsewhere in a program (such as in field names, for example), not just in char or String literals.

The Java programming language also supports a few special escape sequences for char and String literals: \b (backspace), \t (tab), \n (line feed), \f (form feed), \r (carriage return), \" (double quote), \' (single quote), and \\ (backslash).

There's also a special null literal that can be used as a value for any reference type. You may assign null to any variable except variables of primitive types. There's little you can do with a null value beyond testing for its presence. Therefore, null is often used in programs as a marker to indicate that some object is unavailable.

Finally, there's also a special kind of literal called a *class literal*, formed by taking a type name and appending .class (e.g., String.class). This refers to the object (of type Class) that represents the type itself.

Using Underscore Characters in Numeric Literals

Any number of underscore characters (_) can appear anywhere between digits in a numerical literal. This feature enables you, for example, to separate groups of digits in numeric literals, which can improve the readability of your code.

For instance, if your code contains numbers with many digits, you can use an underscore character to separate digits in groups of three, similar to how you would use a punctuation mark like a comma or a space as a separator.

The following example shows other ways you can use the underscore in numeric literals:

```
long creditCardNumber = 1234_5678_9012_3456L;
long socialSecurityNumber = 999_99_9999L;
float pi = 3.14_15F;
long hexBytes = 0xFF_EC_DE_5E;
long hexWords = 0xCAFE_BABE;
long maxLong = 0x7fff_ffff_ffff_ffffL;
byte nybbles = 0b0010_0101;
long bytes = 0b11010010_01101001_10010100_10010010;
```

You can place underscores only between digits; you cannot place underscores in the following places:

- At the beginning or end of a number
- Adjacent to a decimal point in a floating-point literal
- Prior to an F or L suffix
- In positions where a string of digits is expected

The following examples demonstrate valid and invalid underscore placements (which are bold) in numeric literals:

```
// Invalid: cannot put underscores
// adjacent to a decimal point
float pi1 = 3_.1415F;
// Invalid: cannot put underscores
// adjacent to a decimal point
float pi2 = 3._1415F;
// Invalid: cannot put underscores
// prior to an L suffix
long socialSecurityNumber1 = 999_99_9999_L;

// OK (decimal literal)
int x1 = 5_2;
// Invalid: cannot put underscores
// At the end of a literal
int x2 = 52_;
// OK (decimal literal)
int x3 = 5_____2;

// Invalid: cannot put underscores
// in the 0x radix prefix
int x4 = 0_x52;
// Invalid: cannot put underscores
// at the beginning of a number
int x5 = 0x_52;
// OK (hexadecimal literal)
int x6 = 0x5_2;
// Invalid: cannot put underscores
// at the end of a number
int x7 = 0x52_;
```

Arrays

An *array* is a container object that holds a fixed number of values of a single type. The length of an array is established when the array is created. After creation, its length is fixed. You have seen an example of arrays already, in the main method of the "Hello World!" application. This section discusses arrays in greater detail.

Each item in an array is called an *element*, and each element is accessed by its numerical *index*. As shown in the preceding illustration, numbering begins with 0. The ninth element, for example, would therefore be accessed at index 8.

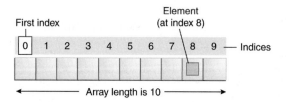

Figure 3.1 An Array of Ten Elements

The following program, `ArrayDemo`, creates an array of integers, puts some values in the array, and prints each value to standard output:

```
class ArrayDemo {
    public static void main(String[] args) {
        // declares an array of integers
        int[] anArray;

        // allocates memory for 10 integers
        anArray = new int[10];

        // initialize first element
        anArray[0] = 100;
        // initialize second element
        anArray[1] = 200;
        // and so forth
        anArray[2] = 300;
        anArray[3] = 400;
        anArray[4] = 500;
        anArray[5] = 600;
        anArray[6] = 700;
        anArray[7] = 800;
        anArray[8] = 900;
        anArray[9] = 1000;

        System.out.println("Element at index 0: "
                        + anArray[0]);
        System.out.println("Element at index 1: "
                        + anArray[1]);
        System.out.println("Element at index 2: "
                        + anArray[2]);
        System.out.println("Element at index 3: "
                        + anArray[3]);
        System.out.println("Element at index 4: "
                        + anArray[4]);
        System.out.println("Element at index 5: "
                        + anArray[5]);
        System.out.println("Element at index 6: "
                        + anArray[6]);
        System.out.println("Element at index 7: "
                        + anArray[7]);
        System.out.println("Element at index 8: "
                        + anArray[8]);
        System.out.println("Element at index 9: "
                        + anArray[9]);
    }
}
```

Here is the output from this program:

```
Element at index 0: 100
Element at index 1: 200
Element at index 2: 300
Element at index 3: 400
Element at index 4: 500
Element at index 5: 600
Element at index 6: 700
Element at index 7: 800
Element at index 8: 900
Element at index 9: 1000
```

3

In a real-world programming situation, you would probably use one of the supported *looping constructs* to iterate through each element of the array, rather than write each line individually as in the preceding example. However, the example clearly illustrates the array syntax. You will learn about the various looping constructs (`for`, `while`, and `do-while`) later in the "Control Flow" section.

Declaring a Variable to Refer to an Array

The preceding program declares an array (named `anArray`) with the following code:

```
// declares an array of integers
int[] anArray;
```

Like declarations for variables of other types, an array declaration has two components: the array's type and the array's name. An array's type is written as *type* [ ], where *type* is the data type of the contained elements; the brackets are special symbols indicating that this variable holds an array. The size of the array is not part of its type (which is why the brackets are empty). An array's name can be anything you want, provided that it follows the rules and conventions as previously discussed in the "Naming" section. As with variables of other types, the declaration does not actually create an array; it simply tells the compiler that this variable will hold an array of the specified type. Similarly, you can declare arrays of other types:

```
byte[] anArrayOfBytes;
short[] anArrayOfShorts;
long[] anArrayOfLongs;
float[] anArrayOfFloats;
double[] anArrayOfDoubles;
boolean[] anArrayOfBooleans;
char[] anArrayOfChars;
String[] anArrayOfStrings;
```

You can also place the brackets after the array's name:

```
// this form is discouraged
float anArrayOfFloats[];
```

However, convention discourages this form; the brackets identify the array type and should appear with the type designation.

Creating, Initializing, and Accessing an Array

One way to create an array is with the new operator. The next statement in the ArrayDemo program allocates an array with enough memory for ten integer elements and assigns the array to the anArray variable:

```
// create an array of integers
anArray = new int[10];
```

If this statement is missing, then the compiler prints an error like the following and compilation fails:

```
ArrayDemo.java:4: Variable anArray may not have been initialized.
```

The next few lines assign values to each element of the array:

```
anArray[0] = 100; // initialize first element
anArray[1] = 200; // initialize second element
anArray[2] = 300; // and so forth
```

Each array element is accessed by its numerical index:

```
System.out.println("Element 1 at index 0: " + anArray[0]);
System.out.println("Element 2 at index 1: " + anArray[1]);
System.out.println("Element 3 at index 2: " + anArray[2]);
```

Alternatively, you can use the shortcut syntax to create and initialize an array:

```
int[] anArray = {
    100, 200, 300,
    400, 500, 600,
    700, 800, 900, 1000
};
```

Here the length of the array is determined by the number of values provided between braces and separated by commas.

You can also declare an array of arrays (also known as a *multidimensional* array) by using two or more sets of brackets, such as String[][] names. Each element, therefore, must be accessed by a corresponding number of index values.

In the Java programming language, a multidimensional array is an array whose components are themselves arrays. This is unlike arrays in C or Fortran. A consequence of this is that the rows are allowed to vary in length, as shown in the following MultiDimArrayDemo program:

```
class MultiDimArrayDemo {
    public static void main(String[] args) {
        String[][] names = {
            {"Mr. ", "Mrs. ", "Ms. "},
            {"Smith", "Jones"}
        };
        // Mr. Smith
        System.out.println(names[0][0] + names[1][0]);
        // Ms. Jones
        System.out.println(names[0][2] + names[1][1]);
    }
}
```

3

Here is the output from this program:

```
Mr. Smith
Ms. Jones
```

Finally, you can use the built-in `length` property to determine the size of any array. The following code prints the array's size to standard output:

```
System.out.println(anArray.length);
```

Copying Arrays

The `System` class has an `arraycopy()` method that you can use to efficiently copy data from one array into another:

```
public static void arraycopy(Object src, int srcPos,
                             Object dest, int destPos, int length)
```

The two `Object` arguments specify the array to copy *from* and the array to copy *to*. The three `int` arguments specify the starting position in the source array, the starting position in the destination array, and the number of array elements to copy.

The following program, `ArrayCopyDemo`, declares an array of `char` elements, spelling the word *decaffeinated*. It uses the `System.arraycopy()` method to copy a subsequence of array components into a second array:

```
class ArrayCopyDemo {
    public static void main(String[] args) {
        char[] copyFrom = { 'd', 'e', 'c', 'a', 'f', 'f', 'e',
                            'i', 'n', 'a', 't', 'e', 'd' };
        char[] copyTo = new char[7];

        System.arraycopy(copyFrom, 2, copyTo, 0, 7);
        System.out.println(new String(copyTo));
    }
}
```

Here is output from this program:

```
caffein
```

Array Manipulations

Arrays are a powerful and useful concept in programming. Java SE provides methods to perform some of the most common manipulations related to arrays. For instance, the `ArrayCopyDemo` example uses the `arraycopy()` method of the `System` class instead of manually iterating through the elements of the source array and placing each one into the destination array. This is performed behind the scenes, enabling the developer to use just one line of code to call the method.

For your convenience, Java SE provides several methods for performing array manipulations (common tasks such as copying, sorting, and searching arrays) in the `java.util.Arrays` class.[7] For instance, the previous example can be modified to use the `copyOfRange()` method of the `java.util.Arrays` class, as you can see in the `ArrayCopyOfDemo` example. The difference is that using the `copyOfRange()` method does not require you to create the destination array before calling the method because the destination array is returned by the method:

```java
class ArrayCopyOfDemo {
    public static void main(String[] args) {

        char[] copyFrom = {'d', 'e', 'c', 'a', 'f', 'f', 'e',
            'i', 'n', 'a', 't', 'e', 'd'};

        char[] copyTo = java.util.Arrays.copyOfRange(copyFrom, 2, 9);

        System.out.println(new String(copyTo));
    }
}
```

As you can see, the output from this program is the same (`caffein`), although it requires fewer lines of code.

Some other useful operations provided by methods in the `java.util.Arrays` class are as follows:

- Search an array for a specific value to get the index at which it is placed (the `binarySearch()` method).
- Compare two arrays to determine if they are equal or not (the `equals()` method).
- Fill an array to place a specific value at each index (the `fill()` method).

---

7.   8/docs/api/java/util/Arrays.html

- Sort an array into ascending order. This can be done either sequentially, using the `sort()` method, or concurrently, using the `parallelSort()` method introduced in Java SE 8. Parallel sorting of large arrays on multiprocessor systems is faster than sequential array sorting.

3

Summary of Variables

The Java programming language uses both *fields* and *variables* as part of its terminology. Instance variables (nonstatic fields) are unique to each instance of a class. Class variables (static fields) are fields declared with the `static` modifier; there is exactly one copy of a class variable, regardless of how many times the class has been instantiated. Local variables store temporary state inside a method. Parameters are variables that provide extra information to a method; both local variables and parameters are always classified as *variables* (not *fields*). When naming your fields or variables, there are rules and conventions that you should (or must) follow.

The eight primitive data types are `byte`, `short`, `int`, `long`, `float`, `double`, `boolean`, and `char`. The `java.lang.String` class represents character strings.[8] The compiler will assign a reasonable default value for fields of these types; for local variables, a default value is never assigned. A literal is the source code representation of a fixed value. An array is a container object that holds a fixed number of values of a single type. The length of an array is established when the array is created. After creation, its length is fixed.

Questions and Exercises: Variables

Questions

1. The term *instance variable* is another name for ___.
2. The term *class variable* is another name for ___.
3. A local variable stores temporary state; it is declared inside a ___.
4. A variable declared within the opening and closing parenthesis of a method signature is called a ___.
5. What are the eight primitive data types supported by the Java programming language?
6. Character strings are represented by the class ___.
7. An ___ is a container object that holds a fixed number of values of a single type.

---

8.   `8/docs/api/java/lang/String.html`

Exercises

1. Create a small program that defines some fields. Try creating some illegal field names and see what kind of error the compiler produces. Use the naming rules and conventions as a guide.

2. In the program you created in Exercise 1, try leaving the fields uninitialized and print out their values. Try the same with a local variable and see what kind of compiler errors you can produce. Becoming familiar with common compiler errors will make it easier to recognize bugs in your code.

Answers

You can find answers to these questions and exercises at `http://docs.oracle .com/javase/tutorial/java/nutsandbolts/QandE/answers_variables .html`.

Operators

Now that you've learned how to declare and initialize variables, you probably want to know how to *do something* with them. Learning the operators of the Java programming language is a good place to start. Operators are special symbols that perform specific operations on one, two, or three *operands* and then return a result.

As we explore the operators of the Java programming language, it may be helpful for you to know ahead of time which operators have the highest precedence. The operators in Table 3.2 are listed according to precedence order. The closer to the top of the table an operator appears, the higher its precedence. Operators with higher precedence are evaluated before operators with relatively lower precedence. Operators on the same line have equal precedence. When operators of equal precedence appear in the same expression, a rule must govern which is evaluated first. All binary operators except for the assignment operators are evaluated from left to right; assignment operators are evaluated right to left.

In general-purpose programming, certain operators tend to appear more frequently than others; for example, the assignment operator (=) is far more common than the unsigned right shift operator (>>>). With that in mind, the following discussion focuses first on the operators that you're most likely to use on a regular basis and ends focusing on those that are less common. Each discussion is accompanied by sample code that you can compile and run. Studying its output will help reinforce what you've just learned.

Table 3.2 Operator Precedence

Operators	Precedence
Postfix	*expr* ++ *expr* --
unary	++*expr* --*expr* +*expr* -*expr* ~ !
multiplicative	* / %
additive	+ -
shift	<< >> >>>
relational	< > <= >= instanceof
equality	== !=
bitwise AND	&
bitwise exclusive OR	^
bitwise inclusive OR	|
logical AND	&&
logical OR	||
ternary	? :
assignment	= += -= *= /= %= &= ^= |= <<= >>= >>>=

Assignment, Arithmetic, and Unary Operators

The Simple Assignment Operator

One of the most common operators that you'll encounter is the simple assignment operator, =. You saw this operator in the `Bicycle` class; it assigns the value on its right to the operand on its left:

```
int cadence = 0;
int speed = 0;
int gear = 1;
```

This operator can also be used on objects to assign *object references*, as discussed in Chapter 4, "Creating Objects."

The Arithmetic Operators

The Java programming language provides operators that perform addition, subtraction, multiplication, and division. There's a good chance you'll recognize them by their counterparts in basic mathematics. The only symbol that might look new to you is %, which divides one operand by another and returns the remainder as its result.

Table 3.3 Arithmetic Operators

Operator	Description
+	Additive operator (also used for String concatenation)
–	Subtraction operator
*	Multiplication operator
/	Division operator
%	Remainder operator

The following program, `ArithmeticDemo`, tests the arithmetic operators:

```java
class ArithmeticDemo {

    public static void main (String[] args) {
        int result = 1 + 2;
        // result is now 3
        System.out.println("1 + 2 = " + result);
        int original_result = result;

        result = result - 1;
        // result is now 2
        System.out.println(original_result + " - 1 = " + result);
        original_result = result;

        result = result * 2;
        // result is now 4
        System.out.println(original_result + " * 2 = " + result);
        original_result = result;

        result = result / 2;
        // result is now 2
        System.out.println(original_result + " / 2 = " + result);
        original_result = result;

        result = result + 8;
        // result is now 10
        System.out.println(original_result + " + 8 = " + result);
        original_result = result;

        result = result % 7;
        // result is now 3
        System.out.println(original_result + " % 7 = " + result);
    }
}
```

This program prints the following:

```
1 + 2 = 3
3 - 1 = 2
2 * 2 = 4
4 / 2 = 2
2 + 8 = 10
10 % 7 = 3
```

You can also combine the arithmetic operators with the simple assignment operator to create *compound assignments*. For example, x+=1; and x=x+1; both increment the value of x by 1.

The + operator can also be used for concatenating (joining) two strings together, as shown in the following `ConcatDemo` program:

3

```
class ConcatDemo {
    public static void main(String[] args){
        String firstString = "This is";
        String secondString = " a concatenated string.";
        String thirdString = firstString + secondString;
        System.out.println(thirdString);
    }
}
```

By the end of this program, the variable `thirdString` contains "This is a concatenated string.", which gets printed to standard output.

The Unary Operators

The unary operators require only one operand; they perform various operations such as incrementing/decrementing a value by one, negating an expression, or inverting the value of a boolean.

The following program, `UnaryDemo`, tests the unary operators:

```
class UnaryDemo {

    public static void main(String[] args) {

        int result = +1;
        // result is now 1
        System.out.println(result);

        result--;
        // result is now 0
        System.out.println(result);

        result++;
        // result is now 1
        System.out.println(result);

        result = -result;
        // result is now -1
        System.out.println(result);

        boolean success = false;
        // false
        System.out.println(success);
        // true
        System.out.println(!success);
    }
}
```

Table 3.4 Unary Operators

Operator	Description
+	Unary plus operator; indicates positive value (numbers are positive without this, however)
–	Unary minus operator; negates an expression
++	Increment operator; increments a value by 1
– –	Decrement operator; decrements a value by 1
!	Logical complement operator; inverts the value of a `boolean`

The increment/decrement operators can be applied before (prefix) or after (postfix) the operand. The code `result++;` and `++result;` will both end in `result` being incremented by one. The only difference is that the prefix version (`++result`) evaluates to the incremented value, whereas the postfix version (`result++`) evaluates to the original value. If you are just performing a simple increment/decrement operation, it doesn't really matter which version you choose. But if you use this operator in part of a larger expression, the one you choose may make a significant difference.

The following program, `PrePostDemo`, illustrates the prefix/postfix unary increment operator:

```
class PrePostDemo {
    public static void main(String[] args){
        int i = 3;
        i++;
        // prints 4
        System.out.println(i);
        ++i;
        // prints 5
        System.out.println(i);
        // prints 6
        System.out.println(++i);
        // prints 6
        System.out.println(i++);
        // prints 7
        System.out.println(i);
    }
}
```

Equality, Relational, and Conditional Operators

The Equality and Relational Operators

The equality and relational operators determine if one operand is greater than, less than, equal to, or not equal to another operand. The majority of these operators will probably look familiar to you as well. Keep in mind that you must use ==, not =, when testing if two primitive values are equal:

```
== equal to
!= not equal to
> greater than
>= greater than or equal to
< less than
<= less than or equal to
```

The following program, `ComparisonDemo`, tests the comparison operators:

```
class ComparisonDemo {

    public static void main(String[] args){
        int value1 = 1;
        int value2 = 2;
        if(value1 == value2)
            System.out.println("value1 == value2");
        if(value1 != value2)
            System.out.println("value1 != value2");
        if(value1 > value2)
            System.out.println("value1 > value2");
        if(value1 < value2)
            System.out.println("value1 < value2");
        if(value1 <= value2)
            System.out.println("value1 <= value2");
    }
}
```

Here is the output:

```
value1 != value2
value1 < value2
value1 <= value2
```

The Conditional Operators

The `&&` and `||` operators perform *Conditional-AND* and *Conditional-OR* operations on two `boolean` expressions. These operators exhibit *short-circuiting* behavior, which means that the second operand is evaluated only if needed:

```
&& Conditional-AND
|| Conditional-OR
```

The following program, `ConditionalDemo1`, tests these operators:

```
class ConditionalDemo1 {

    public static void main(String[] args){
        int value1 = 1;
        int value2 = 2;
        if((value1 == 1) && (value2 == 2))
            System.out.println("value1 is 1 AND value2 is 2");
        if((value1 == 1) || (value2 == 1))
```

```
                        System.out.println("value1 is 1 OR value2 is 1");
          }
    }
```

Another conditional operator is ?:, which can be thought of as shorthand for an if-then-else statement (discussed in the "Control Flow Statements" section of this chapter). This operator is also known as the *ternary operator* because it uses three operands. In the following example, this operator should be read as follows: "If someCondition is true, assign the value of value1 to result. Otherwise, assign the value of value2 to result."

The following program, ConditionalDemo2, tests the ?: operator:

```
class ConditionalDemo2 {

    public static void main(String[] args){
        int value1 = 1;
        int value2 = 2;
        int result;
        boolean someCondition = true;
        result = someCondition ? value1 : value2;

        System.out.println(result);
    }
}
```

Because someCondition is true, this program prints 1 to the screen. Use the ?: operator instead of an if-then-else statement if it makes your code more readable (e.g., when the expressions are compact and without side effects, such as in assignments).

The Type Comparison Operator instanceof

The instanceof operator compares an object to a specified type. You can use it to test if an object is an instance of a class, an instance of a subclass, or an instance of a class that implements a particular interface.

The following program, InstanceofDemo, defines a parent class (named Parent), a simple interface (named MyInterface), and a child class (named Child) that inherits from the parent and implements the interface.

```
class InstanceofDemo {
    public static void main(String[] args) {

        Parent obj1 = new Parent();
        Parent obj2 = new Child();

        System.out.println("obj1 instanceof Parent: "
            + (obj1 instanceof Parent));
        System.out.println("obj1 instanceof Child: "
            + (obj1 instanceof Child));
```

```
        System.out.println("obj1 instanceof MyInterface: "
            + (obj1 instanceof MyInterface));
        System.out.println("obj2 instanceof Parent: "
            + (obj2 instanceof Parent));
        System.out.println("obj2 instanceof Child: "
            + (obj2 instanceof Child));
        System.out.println("obj2 instanceof MyInterface: "
            + (obj2 instanceof MyInterface));
    }
}

class Parent {}
class Child extends Parent implements MyInterface {}
interface MyInterface {}
```

Here is the output:

```
obj1 instanceof Parent: true
obj1 instanceof Child: false
obj1 instanceof MyInterface: false
obj2 instanceof Parent: true
obj2 instanceof Child: true
obj2 instanceof MyInterface: true
```

When using the `instanceof` operator, keep in mind that `null` is not an instance of anything.

Bitwise and Bit Shift Operators

The Java programming language also provides operators that perform bitwise and bit shift operations on integral types. The operators discussed in this section are less commonly used. Therefore their coverage is brief; the intent is to simply make you aware that these operators exist.

The unary bitwise complement operator (~) inverts a bit pattern; it can be applied to any of the integral types, making every 0 a 1 and every 1 a 0. For example, a `byte` contains 8 bits; applying this operator to a value whose bit pattern is 00000000 would change its pattern to 11111111.

The signed left shift operator (<<) shifts a bit pattern to the left, and the signed right shift operator (>>) shifts a bit pattern to the right. The bit pattern is given by the left-hand operand, and the number of positions to shift is given by the right-hand operand. The unsigned right shift operator (>>>) shifts a zero into the leftmost position, while the leftmost position after >> depends on sign extension.

The bitwise & operator performs a bitwise AND operation. The bitwise ^ operator performs a bitwise exclusive OR operation. The bitwise | operator performs a bitwise inclusive OR operation.

The following program, `BitDemo`, uses the bitwise AND operator to print the number 2 to standard output:

```
class BitDemo {
    public static void main(String[] args) {
        int bitmask = 0x000F;
        int val = 0x2222;
        // prints "2"
        System.out.println(val & bitmask);
    }
}
```

Summary of Operators

The following quick reference summarizes the operators supported by the Java programming language.

Simple Assignment Operator

=   Simple assignment operator

Arithmetic Operators

+   Additive operator (also used for `String` concatenation)
–   Subtraction operator
*   Multiplication operator
/   Division operator
%   Remainder operator

Unary Operators

+   Unary plus operator; indicates positive value, although numbers can be positive without this
–   Unary minus operator; negates an expression
++   Increment operator; increments a value by 1
--   Decrement operator; decrements a value by 1
!   Logical complement operator; inverts the value of a `boolean`

Equality and Relational Operators

==   Equal to
!=   Not equal to
>   Greater than
>=   Greater than or equal to
<   Less than
<=   Less than or equal to

3

Conditional Operators

&&   Conditional AND

|| Conditional OR

?:   Ternary (shorthand for `if-then-else` statement)

Type Comparison Operator

`instanceof`   Compares an object to a specified type

Bitwise and Bit Shift Operators

~   Unary bitwise complement

<<   Signed left shift

>>   Signed right shift

>>>   Unsigned right shift

&   Bitwise AND

^   Bitwise exclusive OR

| Bitwise inclusive OR

Questions and Exercises: Operators

Questions

1. Consider the following code snippet:

   ```
   arrayOfInts[j] > arrayOfInts[j+1]
   ```

   Which operators does the code contain?

2. Consider the following code snippet.

   ```
   int i = 10;
   int n = i++%5;
   ```

   a. What are the values of i and n after the code is executed?

   b. What are the final values of i and n if instead of using the postfix increment operator (i++), you use the prefix version (++i)?

3. To invert the value of a `boolean`, which operator would you use?

4. Which operator is used to compare two values, = or == ?

5. Explain the following code sample: `result = someCondition ? value1 : value2;`

Exercises

1. Change the following program to use compound assignments:

3

```
class ArithmeticDemo {

    public static void main (String[] args){

        int result = 1 + 2; // result is now 3
        System.out.println(result);

        result = result - 1; // result is now 2
        System.out.println(result);

        result = result * 2; // result is now 4
        System.out.println(result);

        result = result / 2; // result is now 2
        System.out.println(result);

        result = result + 8; // result is now 10
        result = result % 7; // result is now 3
        System.out.println(result);
    }
}
```

2. In the following program, explain why the value 6 is printed twice in a row:

```
class PrePostDemo {
    public static void main(String[] args){
        int i = 3;
        i++;
        System.out.println(i); // "4"
        ++i;
        System.out.println(i); // "5"
        System.out.println(++i); // "6"
        System.out.println(i++); // "6"
        System.out.println(i); // "7"
    }
}
```

Answers

You can find answers to these questions and exercises at `http://docs.oracle.com/ javase/tutorial/java/nutsandbolts/QandE/answers_operators.html`.

Expressions, Statements, and Blocks

Now that you understand variables and operators, it's time to learn about *expressions*, *statements*, and *blocks*. Operators may be used in building expressions, which compute values. Expressions are the core components of statements, and statements may be grouped into blocks.

Expressions

An *expression* is a construct made up of variables, operators, and method invocations, which are constructed according to the syntax of the language that evaluates to a single value. You've already seen examples of expressions, illustrated in bold as follows:

```
int cadence = 0;
anArray[0] = 100;
System.out.println("Element 1 at index 0: " + anArray[0]);

int result = 1 + 2; // result is now 3
if (value1 == value2)
    System.out.println("value1 == value2");
```

The data type of the value returned by an expression depends on the elements used in the expression. The expression `cadence = 0` returns an `int` because the assignment operator returns a value of the same data type as its left-hand operand; in this case, `cadence` is an `int`. As you can see from the other expressions, an expression can return other types of values as well, such as `boolean` or `String`.

The Java programming language allows you to construct compound expressions from various smaller expressions as long as the data type required by one part of the expression matches the data type of the other. Here's an example of a compound expression:

```
1 * 2 * 3
```

In this particular example, the order in which the expression is evaluated is unimportant because the result of multiplication is independent of order; the outcome is always the same, regardless of the order of the numbers being multiplied. However, this is not true for all expressions. For example, the following expression gives different results, depending on whether you perform the addition or the division operation first:

```
x + y / 100 // ambiguous
```

You can specify exactly how an expression will be evaluated using balanced parentheses: (and). For example, to make the previous expression unambiguous, you could write the following:

```
(x + y) / 100 // unambiguous, recommended
```

If you don't explicitly indicate the order for the operations to be performed, the order is determined by the precedence assigned to the operators in use within the expression. Operators that have a higher precedence get evaluated first. For example, the division operator has a higher precedence than the addition operator. Therefore the following two statements are equivalent:

```
x + y / 100

x + (y / 100) // unambiguous, recommended
```

When writing compound expressions, be explicit and indicate with parentheses which operators should be evaluated first. This practice makes code easier to read and maintain.

Statements

Statements are roughly equivalent to sentences in natural languages. A *statement* forms a complete unit of execution. The following types of expressions can be made into a statement by terminating the expression with a semicolon (**;**):

- Assignment expressions
- Any use of ++ or --
- Method invocations
- Object creation expressions

Such statements are called *expression statements*. Here are some examples of expression statements:

```
// assignment statement
aValue = 8933.234;
// increment statement
aValue++;
// method invocation statement
System.out.println("Hello World!");
// object creation statement
Bicycle myBike = new Bicycle();
```

In addition to expression statements, there are two other kinds of statements: *declaration statements* and *control flow statements*. A *declaration statement* declares a variable. You've seen many examples of declaration statements already:

```
// declaration statement
double aValue = 8933.234;
```

Finally, *control flow statements* regulate the order in which statements get executed. You'll learn about control flow statements in the next section, "Control Flow Statements."

Blocks

A *block* is a group of zero or more statements between balanced braces and can be used anywhere a single statement is allowed. The following example, `BlockDemo`, illustrates the use of blocks:

```
class BlockDemo {
    public static void main(String[] args) {
        boolean condition = true;
        if (condition) { // begin block 1
            System.out.println("Condition is true.");
        } // end block one
        else { // begin block 2
            System.out.println("Condition is false.");
        } // end block 2
    }
}
```

Questions and Exercises: Expressions, Statements, and Blocks

Questions

1. Operators may be used in building ___, which compute values.

2. Expressions are the core components of ___.

3. Statements may be grouped into ___.

4. The following code snippet is an example of a ___ expression:

   ```
   1 * 2 * 3
   ```

5. Statements are roughly equivalent to sentences in natural languages, but instead of ending with a period, a statement ends with a ___.

6. A block is a group of zero or more statements between balanced ___ and can be used anywhere a single statement is allowed.

Exercise

1. Identify the following kinds of expression statements:

   - `aValue = 8933.234;`
   - `aValue++;`
   - `System.out.println("Hello World!");`
   - `Bicycle myBike = new Bicycle();`

Answers

You can find answers to these questions and exercises at `http://docs.oracle`
`.com/javase/tutorial/java/nutsandbolts/QandE/answers_expressions`
`.html`.

Control Flow Statements

The statements inside your source files are generally executed from top to bottom, in the order that they appear. *Control flow statements*, however, break up the flow of execution by employing decision making, looping, and branching, enabling your program to *conditionally* execute particular blocks of code. This section describes the decision-making statements (`if-then`, `if-then-else`, `switch`), the looping statements (`for`, `while`, `do-while`), and the branching statements (`break`, `continue`, `return`) supported by the Java programming language.

The if-then and if-then-else Statements

The if-then Statement

The `if-then` statement is the most basic of all the control flow statements. It tells your program to execute a certain section of code *only if* a particular test evaluates to `true`. For example, the `Bicycle` class could allow the brakes to decrease the bicycle's speed *only if* the bicycle is already in motion. One possible implementation of the `applyBrakes` method could be as follows:

```
void applyBrakes() {
    // the "if" clause: bicycle must be moving
    if (isMoving){
        // the "then" clause: decrease current speed
        currentSpeed--;
    }
}
```

If this test evaluates to `false` (meaning that the bicycle is not in motion), control jumps to the end of the `if-then` statement.

In addition, the opening and closing braces are optional, provided that the "then" clause contains only one statement:

```
void applyBrakes() {
    // same as above, but without braces
    if (isMoving)
        currentSpeed--;
}
```

Deciding when to omit the braces is a matter of personal taste. Omitting them can make the code more brittle. If a second statement is later added to the "then" clause, a common mistake would be forgetting to add the newly required braces. The compiler cannot catch this sort of error; you'll just get the wrong results.

The if-then-else Statement

The `if-then-else` statement provides a secondary path of execution when an "if" clause evaluates to `false`. You could use an `if-then-else` statement in the `applyBrakes` method to take some action if the brakes are applied when the bicycle is not in motion. In this case, the action is to simply print an error message stating that the bicycle has already stopped.

```
void applyBrakes() {
    if (isMoving) {
        currentSpeed--;
    } else {
        System.err.println("The bicycle has already stopped!");
    }
}
```

The following program, `IfElseDemo`, assigns a grade based on the value of a test score: an A for a score of 90% or above, a B for a score of 80% or above, and so on:

```
class IfElseDemo {
    public static void main(String[] args) {

        int testscore = 76;
        char grade;

        if (testscore >= 90) {
            grade = 'A';
        } else if (testscore >= 80) {
            grade = 'B';
        } else if (testscore >= 70) {
            grade = 'C';
        } else if (testscore >= 60) {
            grade = 'D';
        } else {
            grade = 'F';
        }
        System.out.println("Grade = " + grade);
    }
}
```

The output from the program is as follows:

```
Grade = C
```

You may have noticed that the value of `testscore` can satisfy more than one expression in the compound statement: 76 `>=` 70 and 76 `>=` 60. However, once a condition is satisfied, the appropriate statements are executed (`grade = 'C';`) and the remaining conditions are not evaluated.

The switch Statement

Unlike `if-then` and `if-then-else` statements, the `switch` statement can have a number of possible execution paths. A `switch` works with the `byte`, `short`, `char`, and `int` primitive data types. It also works with *enumerated types* (discussed in Chapter 4, "Enum Types"), the `String` class, and a few special classes that wrap certain primitive types: `Character`, `Byte`, `Short`, and `Integer` (discussed in Chapter 9).

The following code example, `SwitchDemo`, declares an `int` named `month` whose value represents a month. The code displays the name of the month, based on the value of `month`, using the `switch` statement:

```java
public class SwitchDemo {
    public static void main(String[] args) {

        int month = 8;
        String monthString;
        switch (month) {
            case 1: monthString = "January";
                    break;
            case 2: monthString = "February";
                    break;
            case 3: monthString = "March";
                    break;
            case 4: monthString = "April";
                    break;
            case 5: monthString = "May";
                    break;
            case 6: monthString = "June";
                    break;
            case 7: monthString = "July";
                    break;
            case 8: monthString = "August";
                    break;
            case 9: monthString = "September";
                    break;
            case 10: monthString = "October";
                    break;
            case 11: monthString = "November";
                    break;
            case 12: monthString = "December";
                    break;
            default: monthString = "Invalid month";
                    break;
        }
        System.out.println(monthString);
    }
}
```

In this case, `August` is printed to standard output.

The body of a `switch` statement is known as a *switch block*. A statement in the switch block can be labeled with one or more `case` or `default` labels. The `switch` statement evaluates its expression and then executes all statements that follow the matching `case` label.

You could also display the name of the month with `if-then-else` statements:

```java
int month = 8;
if (month == 1) {
    System.out.println("January");
} else if (month == 2) {
    System.out.println("February");
}
// ... and so on
```

The choice between `if-then-else` statements or a `switch` statement depends on readability and the expression that the statement is testing. An `if-then-else` statement can test expressions based on ranges of values or conditions, whereas a `switch` statement tests expressions based only on a single integer, enumerated value, or `String` object.

Another point of interest is the `break` statement. Each `break` statement terminates the enclosing `switch` statement. Control flow continues with the first statement following the `switch` block. The `break` statements are necessary because without them, statements in `switch` blocks *fall through*: All statements after the matching `case` label are executed in sequence, regardless of the expression of subsequent `case` labels, until a `break` statement is encountered. The program `SwitchDemoFallThrough` shows statements in a `switch` block that fall through; it displays the month corresponding to the integer `month` and the months that follow in the year:

```java
public class SwitchDemoFallThrough {
    public static void main(String[] args) {
        java.util.ArrayList<String> futureMonths =
            new java.util.ArrayList<String>();

        int month = 8;

        switch (month) {
            case 1: futureMonths.add("January");
            case 2: futureMonths.add("February");
            case 3: futureMonths.add("March");
            case 4: futureMonths.add("April");
            case 5: futureMonths.add("May");
            case 6: futureMonths.add("June");
            case 7: futureMonths.add("July");
            case 8: futureMonths.add("August");
            case 9: futureMonths.add("September");
            case 10: futureMonths.add("October");
            case 11: futureMonths.add("November");
            case 12: futureMonths.add("December");
                     break;
            default: break;
        }
```

```
            if (futureMonths.isEmpty()) {
                System.out.println("Invalid month number");
            } else {
                for (String monthName : futureMonths) {
                    System.out.println(monthName);
                }
            }
        }
    }
```

This is the output from the code:

```
August
September
October
November
December
```

Technically, the final `break` is not required because flow falls out of the `switch` statement. Using a `break` is recommended so that modifying the code is easier and less error prone. The `default` section handles all values that are not explicitly handled by one of the `case` sections.

The following code example, `SwitchDemo2`, shows how a statement can have multiple `case` labels. The code example calculates the number of days in a particular month:

```
class SwitchDemo2 {
    public static void main(String[] args) {

        int month = 2;
        int year = 2000;
        int numDays = 0;

        switch (month) {
            case 1: case 3: case 5:
            case 7: case 8: case 10:
            case 12:
                numDays = 31;
                break;
            case 4: case 6:
            case 9: case 11:
                numDays = 30;
                break;
            case 2:
                if (((year % 4 == 0) &&
                    !(year % 100 == 0))
                    || (year % 400 == 0))
                    numDays = 29;
                else
                    numDays = 28;
                break;
            default:
                System.out.println("Invalid month.");
```

```
            break;
        }
        System.out.println("Number of Days = "
                            + numDays);
    }
}
```

This is the output from the code:

```
Number of Days = 29
```

Using Strings in switch Statements

You can use a `String` object in the `switch` statement's expression. The following code example, `StringSwitchDemo`, displays the number of the month based on the value of the `String` named month:

```java
public class StringSwitchDemo {

    public static int getMonthNumber(String month) {

        int monthNumber = 0;

        if (month == null) {
            return monthNumber;
        }

        switch (month.toLowerCase()) {
            case "january":
                monthNumber = 1;
                break;
            case "february":
                monthNumber = 2;
                break;
            case "march":
                monthNumber = 3;
                break;
            case "april":
                monthNumber = 4;
                break;
            case "may":
                monthNumber = 5;
                break;
            case "june":
                monthNumber = 6;
                break;
            case "july":
                monthNumber = 7;
                break;
            case "august":
                monthNumber = 8;
                break;
            case "september":
                monthNumber = 9;
                break;
```

```
                case "october":
                    monthNumber = 10;
                    break;
                case "november":
                    monthNumber = 11;
                    break;
                case "december":
                    monthNumber = 12;
                    break;
                default:
                    monthNumber = 0;
                    break;
            }

            return monthNumber;
        }

    public static void main(String[] args) {

        String month = "August";

        int returnedMonthNumber =
            StringSwitchDemo.getMonthNumber(month);

        if (returnedMonthNumber == 0) {
            System.out.println("Invalid month");
        } else {
            System.out.println(returnedMonthNumber);
        }
    }
}
```

The output from this code is 8.

The `String` in the `switch` expression is compared with the expressions associated with each `case` label, as if the `String.equals`[9] method was being used. In order for the `StringSwitchDemo` example to accept any month regardless of case, `month` is converted to lowercase (with the `toLowerCase`[10] method) and all the strings associated with the `case` labels are in lowercase.

Note

This example checks if the expression in the `switch` statement is `null`. Ensure that the expression in any `switch` statement is not `null` to prevent a `NullPointerException` from being thrown.

---

9.   8/docs/api/java/lang/String.html#equals-java.lang.Object-

10.   8/docs/api/java/lang/String.html#toLowerCase--

The while and do-while Statements

The while statement continually executes a block of statements while a particular condition is true. Its syntax can be expressed as follows:

```
while (expression) {
    statement(s)
}
```

The while statement evaluates *expression*, which must return a boolean value. If the expression evaluates to true, the while statement executes the *statement(s)* in the while block. The while statement continues testing the expression and executing its block until the expression evaluates to false. Using the while statement to print the values from 1 through 10 can be accomplished via the following WhileDemo program:

```
class WhileDemo {
    public static void main(String[] args){
        int count = 1;
        while (count < 11) {
            System.out.println("Count is: " + count);
            count++;
        }
    }
}
```

You can implement an infinite loop using the while statement as follows:

```
while (true){
    // your code goes here
}
```

The Java programming language also provides a do-while statement, which can be expressed as follows:

```
do {
    statement(s)
} while (expression);
```

The difference between do-while and while is that do-while evaluates its expression at the bottom of the loop instead of the top. Therefore, the statements within the do block are always executed at least once, as shown in the following DoWhileDemo program:

```
class DoWhileDemo {
    public static void main(String[] args){
        int count = 1;
        do {
```

```
        System.out.println("Count is: " + count);
        count++;
    } while (count < 11);
    }
}
```

The for Statement

The for statement provides a compact way to iterate over a range of values. Programmers often refer to it as the *for loop* because of the way it repeatedly loops until a particular condition is satisfied. The general form of the for statement can be expressed as follows:

```
for (initialization; termination; increment) {
    statement(s)
}
```

When using this version of the for statement, keep the following in mind:

- The *initialization* expression initializes the loop; it's executed once as the loop begins.
- When the *termination* expression evaluates to false, the loop terminates.
- The *increment* expression is invoked after each iteration through the loop; it is perfectly acceptable for this expression to increment *or* decrement a value.

The following program, ForDemo, uses the general form of the for statement to print the numbers 1 through 10 to standard output:

```
class ForDemo {
    public static void main(String[] args){
        for(int i=1; i<11; i++){
            System.out.println("Count is: " + i);
        }
    }
}
```

Here is the output of this program:

```
Count is: 1
Count is: 2
Count is: 3
Count is: 4
Count is: 5
Count is: 6
Count is: 7
Count is: 8
Count is: 9
Count is: 10
```

Notice how the code declares a variable within the initialization expression. The scope of this variable extends from its declaration to the end of the block governed by the `for` statement, so it can be used in the termination and increment expressions as well. If the variable that controls a `for` statement is not needed outside the loop, it's best to declare the variable in the initialization expression. The names i, j, and k are often used to control `for` loops; declaring them within the initialization expression limits their life span and reduces errors.

The three expressions of the `for` loop are optional; an infinite loop can be created as follows:

```
// infinite loop
for ( ; ; ) {

    // your code goes here
}
```

The `for` statement also has another form designed for iteration through collections and arrays. This form is sometimes referred to as the *enhanced for* statement and can be used to make your loops more compact and easier to read. To demonstrate, consider the following array, which holds the numbers 1 through 10:

```
int[] numbers = {1,2,3,4,5,6,7,8,9,10};
```

The following program, `EnhancedForDemo`, uses the enhanced `for` to loop through the array:

```
class EnhancedForDemo {
    public static void main(String[] args){
        int[] numbers =
            {1,2,3,4,5,6,7,8,9,10};
        for (int item : numbers) {
            System.out.println("Count is: " + item);
        }
    }
}
```

In this example, the variable `item` holds the current value from the numbers array. The output from this program is the same as before:

```
Count is: 1
Count is: 2
Count is: 3
Count is: 4
Count is: 5
Count is: 6
Count is: 7
Count is: 8
Count is: 9
Count is: 10
```

We recommend using this form of the `for` statement instead of the general form whenever possible.

Branching Statements

The break Statement

The `break` statement has two forms: labeled and unlabeled. You saw the unlabeled form in the previous discussion of the `switch` statement. You can also use an unlabeled `break` to terminate a `for`, `while`, or `do-while` loop, as shown in the following `BreakDemo` program:

```
class BreakDemo {
    public static void main(String[] args) {

        int[] arrayOfInts =
            { 32, 87, 3, 589,
              12, 1076, 2000,
              8, 622, 127 };
        int searchfor = 12;

        int i;
        boolean foundIt = false;

        for (i = 0; i < arrayOfInts.length; i++) {
            if (arrayOfInts[i] == searchfor) {
                foundIt = true;
                break;
            }
        }

        if (foundIt) {
            System.out.println("Found " + searchfor + " at index " + i);
        } else {
            System.out.println(searchfor + " not in the array");
        }
    }
}
```

This program searches for the number 12 in an array. The `break` statement, shown in boldface, terminates the `for` loop when that value is found. Control flow then transfers to the statement after the `for` loop. This program's output is as follows:

```
Found 12 at index 4
```

An unlabeled `break` statement terminates the innermost `switch`, `for`, `while`, or `do-while` statement, but a labeled `break` terminates an outer statement. The following program, `BreakWithLabelDemo`, is similar to the previous program but uses nested `for` loops to search for a value in a two-dimensional array. When the value is found, a labeled `break` terminates the outer `for` loop (labeled `search`):

```
class BreakWithLabelDemo {
    public static void main(String[] args) {

        int[][] arrayOfInts = {
            { 32, 87, 3, 589 },
            { 12, 1076, 2000, 8 },
            { 622, 127, 77, 955 }
        };
        int searchfor = 12;

        int i;
        int j = 0;
        boolean foundIt = false;

    search:
        for (i = 0; i < arrayOfInts.length; i++) {
            for (j = 0; j < arrayOfInts[i].length;
                 j++) {
                if (arrayOfInts[i][j] == searchfor) {
                    foundIt = true;
                    break search;
                }
            }
        }

        if (foundIt) {
            System.out.println("Found " + searchfor + " at " + i + ", " + j);
        } else {
            System.out.println(searchfor + " not in the array");
        }
    }
}
```

This is the output of the program:

```
Found 12 at 1, 0
```

The break statement terminates the labeled statement; it does not transfer the flow of control to the label. Control flow is transferred to the statement immediately following the labeled (terminated) statement.

The continue Statement

The continue statement skips the current iteration of a for, while, or do-while loop. The unlabeled form skips to the end of the innermost loop's body and evaluates the boolean expression that controls the loop. The following program, ContinueDemo, steps through a String, counting the occurrences of the letter p. If the current character is not a p, the continue statement skips the rest of the loop and proceeds to the next character. If it is a p, the program increments the letter count:

```
class ContinueDemo {
    public static void main(String[] args) {
```

```
        String searchMe = "peter piper picked a " + "peck of pickled peppers";
        int max = searchMe.length();
        int numPs = 0;

        for (int i = 0; i < max; i++) {
            // interested only in p's
            if (searchMe.charAt(i) != 'p')
                continue;

            // process p's
            numPs++;
        }
        System.out.println("Found " + numPs + " p's in the string.");
    }
}
```

Here is the output of this program:

```
Found 9 p's in the string.
```

To see this effect more clearly, try removing the `continue` statement and recompiling. When you run the program again, the count will be wrong, saying that it found 35 *p*'s instead of 9.

A labeled `continue` statement skips the current iteration of an outer loop marked with the given label. The following example program, `ContinueWithLabelDemo`, uses nested loops to search for a substring within another string. Two nested loops are required: one to iterate over the substring and another to iterate over the string being searched. The following program, `ContinueWithLabelDemo`, uses the labeled form of the `continue` statement to skip an iteration in the outer loop:

```
class ContinueWithLabelDemo {
    public static void main(String[] args) {

        String searchMe = "Look for a substring in me";
        String substring = "sub";
        boolean foundIt = false;

        int max = searchMe.length() -
                substring.length();

    test:
        for (int i = 0; i <= max; i++) {
            int n = substring.length();
            int j = i;
            int k = 0;
            while (n-- != 0) {
                if (searchMe.charAt(j++) != substring.charAt(k++)) {
                    continue test;
                }
            }
```

```
                foundIt = true;
                    break test;
            }
            System.out.println(foundIt ? "Found it" : "Didn't find it");
        }
    }
```

Here is the output from this program:

```
Found it
```

The return Statement

The last of the branching statements is the `return` statement. The `return` statement exits from the current method, and control flow returns to where the method was invoked. The `return` statement has two forms: one that returns a value and another that doesn't. To return a value, simply put the value (or an expression that calculates the value) after the `return` keyword:

```
return ++count;
```

The data type of the returned value must match the type of the method's declared return value. When a method is declared `void`, use the form of `return` that doesn't return a value:

```
return;
```

Chapter 4 covers everything you need to know about writing methods.

Summary of Control Flow Statements

The `if-then` statement is the most basic of all the control flow statements. It tells your program to execute a certain section of code *only if* a particular test evaluates to `true`. The `if-then-else` statement provides a secondary path of execution when an "if" clause evaluates to `false`. Unlike `if-then` and `if-then-else`, the `switch` statement allows for any number of possible execution paths. The `while` and `do-while` statements continually execute a block of statements while a particular condition is `true`. The difference between `do-while` and `while` is that `do-while` evaluates its expression at the bottom of the loop instead of the top. Therefore, the statements within the do block are always executed at least once. The `for` statement provides a compact way to iterate over a range of values. It has two forms, one of which was designed for looping through collections and arrays.

3

Questions and Exercises: Control Flow Statements

Questions

1. The most basic control flow statement supported by the Java programming language is the ___ statement.

2. The ___ statement allows for any number of possible execution paths.

3. The ___ statement is similar to the `while` statement but evaluates its expression at the ___ of the loop.

4. How do you write an infinite loop using the `for` statement?

5. How do you write an infinite loop using the `while` statement?

Exercises

1. Consider the following code snippet:

```
if (aNumber >= 0)
    if (aNumber == 0)
        System.out.println("first string");
else System.out.println("second string");
System.out.println("third string");
```

   a. What output do you think the code will produce if aNumber is 3?

   b. Write a test program containing the previous code snippet; make aNumber 3. What is the output of the program? Is it what you predicted? Explain why the output is what it is; in other words, what is the control flow for the code snippet?

   c. Using only spaces and line breaks, reformat the code snippet to make the control flow easier to understand.

   d. Use braces, { and }, to further clarify the code.

Answers

You can find answers to these questions and exercises at `http://docs.oracle` `.com/javase/tutorial/java/nutsandbolts/QandE/answers_flow.html`.

4

Classes and Objects

Chapter Contents

Classes   88
Objects   99
More on Classes   107
Nested Classes   121
Enum Types   157

With the knowledge you now have of the basics of the Java programming language, you can learn to write your own classes. In this chapter, you will find information about defining your own classes, including declaring member variables, methods, and constructors. You will learn to use your classes to create objects and how to use the objects you create. This chapter also covers nesting classes within other classes and enumerations

The first section shows you the anatomy of a class and how to declare fields, methods, and constructors. The second section covers creating and using objects. You will learn how to create an object by instantiating a class and, once instantiated, how to use the dot operator to access the object's instance variables and methods. The third section covers more aspects of classes that depend on object references and the dot operator: returning values from methods, the this keyword, class versus instance members, and access control. The fourth section discusses static nested classes, inner classes, anonymous inner classes, local classes, and lambda expressions. There is also a discussion on when to use which kind of class or lambda expression. The final section covers enumerations, specialized classes that allow you to define and use sets of constants. Selected sections contain questions and exercises to test your understanding.

Classes

The introduction to object-oriented concepts in Chapter 2 used a `Bicycle` class as an example, with racing bikes, mountain bikes, and tandem bikes as subclasses. Here is sample code for a possible implementation of a `Bicycle` class, to give you an overview of a class declaration. Subsequent sections of this chapter will back up and explain class declarations step by step. For the moment, don't concern yourself with the details:

```
public class Bicycle {

    // the Bicycle class has
    // three fields
    public int cadence;
    public int gear;
    public int speed;
    // the Bicycle class has
    // one constructor
    public Bicycle(int startCadence, int startSpeed, int startGear) {
        gear = startGear;
        cadence = startCadence;
        speed = startSpeed;
    }

    // the Bicycle class has
    // four methods
    public void setCadence(int newValue) {
        cadence = newValue;
    }

    public void setGear(int newValue) {
        gear = newValue;
    }

    public void applyBrake(int decrement) {
        speed -= decrement;
    }

    public void speedUp(int increment) {
        speed += increment;
    }
}
```

A class declaration for a `MountainBike` class that is a subclass of `Bicycle` might look like this:

```
public class MountainBike extends Bicycle {

    // the MountainBike subclass has
    // one field
    public int seatHeight;

    // the MountainBike subclass has
    // one constructor
```

```
    public MountainBike(int startHeight, int startCadence,
                        int startSpeed, int startGear) {
        super(startCadence, startSpeed, startGear);
        seatHeight = startHeight;
    }

    // the MountainBike subclass has
    // one method
    public void setHeight(int newValue) {
        seatHeight = newValue;
    }

}
```

4

MountainBike inherits all the fields and methods of Bicycle and adds the field seatHeight and a method to set it (since mountain bikes have seats that can be moved up and down as the terrain demands).

Declaring Classes

You've seen classes defined in the following way:

```
class MyClass {
    // field, constructor, and
    // method declarations
}
```

This is a *class declaration*. The *class body* (the area between the braces) contains all the code that provides for the life cycle of the objects created from the class: constructors for initializing new objects, declarations for the fields that provide the state of the class and its objects, and methods to implement the behavior of the class and its objects.

The preceding class declaration is a minimal one. It contains only those components of a class declaration that are required. You can provide more information about the class, such as the name of its superclass, whether it implements any interfaces, and so on, at the start of the class declaration. For example,

```
class MyClass extends MySuperClass implements YourInterface {
    // field, constructor, and
    // method declarations
}
```

means that MyClass is a subclass of MySuperClass and that it implements the YourInterface interface.

You can also add modifiers like public or private at the very beginning—so you can see that the opening line of a class declaration can become quite complicated. The modifiers public and private, which determine what other classes can access MyClass, are discussed later in this chapter. Chapter 6 will explain how and why you would use the extends and implements keywords in a class declaration. For the moment, you do not need to worry about these extra complications.

In general, class declarations can include the following components, in order:

1. Modifiers such as public, private, and a number of others that you will encounter later.
2. The class name, with the initial letter capitalized by convention.
3. The name of the class's parent (superclass), if any, preceded by the keyword *extends*. A class can only extend (subclass) one parent.
4. A comma-separated list of interfaces implemented by the class, if any, preceded by the keyword implements. A class can implement more than one interface.
5. The class body, surrounded by braces, {}.

Declaring Member Variables

There are several kinds of variables:

- *Member variables in a class*. These are called *fields*.
- *Variables in a method or block of code*. These are called *local variables*.
- *Variables in method declarations*. These are called *parameters*.

The Bicycle class uses the following lines of code to define its fields:

```
public int cadence;
public int gear;
public int speed;
```

Field declarations are composed of three components, in order:

1. Zero or more modifiers, such as public or private
2. The field's type
3. The field's name

The fields of Bicycle are named cadence, gear, and speed and are all of data type integer (int). The public keyword identifies these fields as public members, accessible by any object that can access the class.

Access Modifiers

The first (leftmost) modifier used lets you control which other classes have access to a member field. For the moment, consider only public and private. Other access modifiers will be discussed later:

- `public` *modifier*. The field is accessible from all classes.
- `private` *modifier*. The field is accessible only within its own class.

In the spirit of encapsulation, it is common to make fields private. This means that they can only be *directly* accessed from the `Bicycle` class. We still need access to these values, however. This can be done *indirectly* by adding public methods that obtain the field values for us:

```java
public class Bicycle {

    private int cadence;
    private int gear;
    private int speed;

    public Bicycle(int startCadence, int startSpeed, int startGear) {
        gear = startGear;
        cadence = startCadence;
        speed = startSpeed;
    }

    public int getCadence() {
        return cadence;
    }

    public void setCadence(int newValue) {
        cadence = newValue;
    }

    public int getGear() {
        return gear;
    }

    public void setGear(int newValue) {
        gear = newValue;
    }

    public int getSpeed() {
        return speed;
    }

    public void applyBrake(int decrement) {
        speed -= decrement;
    }

    public void speedUp(int increment) {
        speed += increment;
    }
}
```

Types

All variables must have a type. You can use primitive types such as `int`, `float`, and `boolean`. Alternatively, you can use reference types, such as strings, arrays, or objects.

Variable Names

All variables, whether they are fields, local variables, or parameters, follow the same naming rules and conventions that were covered in Chapter 3, "Variables." Be aware that the same naming rules and conventions are used for method and class names, with the following exceptions:

- The first letter of a class name should be capitalized.
- The first (or only) word in a method name should be a verb.

Defining Methods

Here is an example of a typical method declaration:

```
public double calculateAnswer(double wingSpan, int numberOfEngines,
                              double length, double grossTons) {
    //do the calculation here
}
```

The only required elements in a method declaration are the method's return type and name; a pair of parentheses, ( ); and a body between braces, { }.

More generally, method declarations have six components, in order:

1. *Modifiers.* Some examples include `public` and `private`; you will learn about others later.
2. *The return type.* This is the data type of the value returned by the method (or `void` if the method does not return a value).
3. *The method name.* The rules for field names apply to method names as well, but the convention is a little different.
4. *The parameter list in parentheses.* This is a comma-delimited list of input parameters, preceded by their data types, enclosed by parentheses. If there are no parameters, you must use empty parentheses.
5. *An exception list.* This will be discussed later.
6. *The method body, enclosed between braces.* The method's code, including the declaration of local variables, goes here.

Modifiers, return types, and parameters are discussed later in this chapter. Exceptions are discussed in Chapter 10.

Definition

Two of the components of a method declaration comprise the *method signature*—the method's name and the parameter types.

Here is the signature of the method declared previously:

```
calculateAnswer(double, int, double, double)
```

Naming a Method

Although a method name can be any legal identifier, code conventions generally restrict method names. By convention, method names should be a verb in lowercase or a multiword name that begins with a verb in lowercase, followed by adjectives, nouns, and other words to describe what the method does. In multiword names, the first letter of each of the second and following words should be capitalized. Here are some examples:

```
run
runFast
getBackground
getFinalData
compareTo
setX
isEmpty
```

Typically, a method has a unique name within its class. However, a method might have the same name as other methods due to *method overloading*.

Overloading Methods

The Java programming language supports method *overloading*, and Java can distinguish between methods with different *method signatures*. This means that methods within a class can have the same name if they have different parameter lists. (There are some qualifications to this that will be discussed in Chapter 6.)

Suppose you have a class that can use calligraphy to draw various types of data (strings, integers, and so on) and contains a method for drawing each data type. It is cumbersome to use a new name for each method—for example, drawString, drawInteger, drawFloat, and so on. In the Java programming language, you can use the same name for all the drawing methods but pass a different argument list to each method. Thus the data drawing class might declare four methods named draw, each of which has a different parameter list:

```
public class DataArtist {
    ...
    public void draw(String s) {
        ...
    }
    public void draw(int i) {
        ...
    }
    public void draw(double f) {
        ...
    }
```

```
    public void draw(int i, double f) {
        ...
    }
}
```

Overloaded methods are differentiated by the number and type of arguments passed into the method. In the code sample, draw(String s) and draw(int i) are distinct and unique methods because they require different argument types. You cannot declare more than one method with the same name and the same number and type of arguments, because the compiler cannot tell them apart. The compiler does not consider return type when differentiating methods, so you cannot declare two methods with the same signature even if they have a different return type.

Note

Overloaded methods should be used sparingly, as they can make code much less readable.

Providing Constructors for Your Classes

A class contains constructors that are invoked to create objects from the class blueprint. Constructor declarations look like method declarations, except they use the name of the class and have no return type. For example, Bicycle has one constructor:

```
public Bicycle(int startCadence, int startSpeed, int startGear) {
    gear = startGear;
    cadence = startCadence;
    speed = startSpeed;
}
```

To create a new Bicycle object called myBike, a constructor is called by the new operator:

```
Bicycle myBike = new Bicycle(30, 0, 8);
```

new Bicycle(30, 0, 8) creates space in memory for the object and initializes its fields.

Although Bicycle only has one constructor, it could have others, including a no-argument constructor:

```
public Bicycle() {
    gear = 1;
    cadence = 10;
    speed = 0;
}
```

`Bicycle yourBike = new Bicycle();` invokes the no-argument constructor to create a new `Bicycle` object called `yourBike`.

Both constructors could have been declared in `Bicycle` because they have different argument lists. As with methods, the Java platform differentiates constructors on the basis of the number of arguments in the list and their types. You cannot write two constructors that have the same number and type of arguments for the same class, because the platform would not be able to tell them apart. Doing so causes a compile-time error.

You don't have to provide any constructors for your class, but you must be careful when doing this. The compiler automatically provides a no-argument, default constructor for any class without constructors. This default constructor will call the no-argument constructor of the superclass. In this situation, the compiler will complain if the superclass doesn't have a no-argument constructor, so you must verify that it does. If your class has no explicit superclass, then it has an implicit superclass of `Object`, which *does* have a no-argument constructor.

You can use a superclass constructor yourself. The `MountainBike` class at the beginning of the chapter did just that. This will be discussed later, in Chapter 6. You can use access modifiers in a constructor's declaration to control which other classes can call the constructor.

> **Note**
>
> If another class cannot call a `MyClass` constructor, it cannot directly create `MyClass` objects.

Passing Information to a Method or a Constructor

The declaration for a method or a constructor declares the number and type of arguments for that method or constructor. For example, the following is a method that computes the monthly payments for a home loan, based on the amount of the loan, the interest rate, the length of the loan (the number of periods), and the future value of the loan:

```
public double computePayment(
    double loanAmt,
    double rate,
    double futureValue,
    int numPeriods) {
    double interest = rate / 100.0;
    double partial1 = Math.pow((1 + interest), -numPeriods);
    double denominator = (1 - partial1) / interest;
    double answer = (-loanAmt / denominator)
                    - ((futureValue * partial1) / denominator);
    return answer;
}
```

This method has four parameters: the loan amount, the interest rate, the future value, and the number of periods. The first three are double-precision floating-point numbers and the fourth is an integer. The parameters are used in the method body and at runtime will take on the values of the arguments that are passed in.

> **Note**
>
> *Parameters* refers to the list of variables in a method declaration. *Arguments* are the actual values that are passed in when the method is invoked. When you invoke a method, the arguments used must match the declaration's parameters in type and order.

Parameter Types

You can use any data type for a parameter of a method or a constructor. This includes primitive data types, such as doubles, floats, and integers, as you saw in the computePayment method, and reference data types, such as objects and arrays.

Here's an example of a method that accepts an array as an argument. In this example, the method creates a new Polygon object and initializes it from an array of Point objects (assume that Point is a class that represents an x, y coordinate and see the "Initializing an Object" section for the source code of the Point class):

```
public Polygon polygonFrom(Point[] corners) {
    // method body goes here
}
```

> **Note**
>
> If you want to pass a method into a method, then use a lambda expression or a method reference.

Arbitrary Number of Arguments

You can use a construct called *varargs* to pass an arbitrary number of values to a method. You use varargs when you don't know how many of a particular type of argument will be passed to the method. It's a shortcut to creating an array manually. (The previous method could have used varargs rather than an array.)

To use varargs, you follow the type of the last parameter by an ellipsis (. . .), then a space, and the parameter name. The method can then be called with any number of that parameter, including zero:

```
public Polygon polygonFrom(Point... corners) {
    int numberOfSides = corners.length;
    double squareOfSide1, lengthOfSide1;
    squareOfSide1 = (corners[1].x - corners[0].x)
```

```
                              *  (corners[1].x - corners[0].x)
                              +  (corners[1].y - corners[0].y)
                              *  (corners[1].y - corners[0].y);
        lengthOfSide1 = Math.sqrt(squareOfSide1);

        // more method body code follows that creates and returns a
        // polygon connecting the Points
    }
```

You can see that, inside the method, `corners` is treated like an array. The method can be called either with an array or with a sequence of arguments. The code in the method body will treat the parameter as an array in either case.

You will most commonly see varargs with the printing methods. For example, the following `printf` method allows you to print an arbitrary number of objects:

```
public PrintStream printf(String format, Object... args)
```

It can be called like this

```
System.out.printf("%s: %d, %s%n", name, idnum, address);
```

or like this

```
System.out.printf("%s: %d, %s, %s, %s%n", name, idnum, address, phone, email);
```

or with a different number of arguments.

Parameter Names

When you declare a parameter to a method or a constructor, you provide a name for that parameter. This name is used within the method body to refer to the passed-in argument.

The name of a parameter must be unique in its scope. It cannot be the same as the name of another parameter for the same method or constructor, and it cannot be the name of a local variable within the method or constructor.

A parameter can have the same name as one of the class's fields. If this is the case, the parameter is said to *shadow* the field. Shadowing fields can make your code difficult to read and is conventionally used only within constructors and methods that set a particular field. For example, consider the following `Circle` class and its `setOrigin` method:

```
public class Circle {
    private int x, y, radius;
    public void setOrigin(int x, int y) {
        ...
```

```
        }
    }
```

The `Circle` class has three fields: `x`, `y`, and `radius`. The `setOrigin` method has two parameters, each of which has the same name as one of the fields. Each method parameter shadows the field that shares its name. So using the simple names `x` or `y` within the body of the method refers to the parameter, *not* the field. To access the field, you must use a qualified name. This will be discussed later in the "Using the `this` Keyword" section.

Passing Primitive Data Type Arguments

Primitive arguments, such as an `int` or a `double`, are passed into methods *by value*. This means that any changes to the values of the parameters exist only within the scope of the method. When the method returns, the parameters are gone and any changes to them are lost. Here is an example:

```
public class PassPrimitiveByValue {

    public static void main(String[] args) {

        int x = 3;

        // invoke passMethod() with
        // x as argument
        passMethod(x);

        // print x to see if its
        // value has changed
        System.out.println("After invoking passMethod, x = " + x);

    }

    // change parameter in passMethod()
    public static void passMethod(int p) {
        p = 10;
    }
}
```

When you run this program, the output is as follows:

```
After invoking passMethod, x = 3
```

Passing Reference Data Type Arguments

Reference data type parameters, such as objects, are also passed into methods *by value*. This means that when the method returns, the passed-in reference still references the same object as before. *However*, the values of the object's fields *can* be changed in the method if they have the proper access level.

For example, consider a method in an arbitrary class that moves `Circle` objects:

```
public void moveCircle(Circle circle, int deltaX, int deltaY) {
    // code to move origin of circle to x+deltaX, y+deltaY
    circle.setX(circle.getX() + deltaX);
    circle.setY(circle.getY() + deltaY);

    // code to assign a new reference to circle
    circle = new Circle(0, 0);
}
```

Let the method be invoked with these arguments:

```
moveCircle(myCircle, 23, 56)
```

Inside the method, `circle` initially refers to `myCircle`. The method changes the x and y coordinates of the object that `circle` references (in this example, `myCircle`) by 23 and 56, respectively. These changes will persist when the method returns. Then `circle` is assigned a reference to a new `Circle` object with x = y = 0. This reassignment has no permanence, however, because the reference was passed in by value and cannot change. Within the method, the object pointed to by `circle` has changed, but when the method returns, `myCircle` still references the same `Circle` object it did before the method was called.

Objects

A typical Java program creates many objects, which as you know, interact by invoking methods. Through these object interactions, a program can carry out various tasks, such as implementing a graphical user interface (GUI), running an animation, or sending and receiving information over a network. Once an object has completed the work for which it was created, its resources are recycled for use by other objects.

Here's a small program called `CreateObjectDemo` that creates three objects: one `Point` object and two `Rectangle` objects (see the "Initializing an Object" section for the source code of the `Point` and `Rectangle` classes). You will need all three source files to compile this program:

```
public class CreateObjectDemo {

    public static void main(String[] args) {

        // Declare and create a point object and two rectangle objects.
        Point originOne = new Point(23, 94);
        Rectangle rectOne = new Rectangle(originOne, 100, 200);
        Rectangle rectTwo = new Rectangle(50, 100);

        // display rectOne's width, height, and area
```

```
System.out.println("Width of rectOne: " + rectOne.width);
System.out.println("Height of rectOne: " + rectOne.height);
System.out.println("Area of rectOne: " + rectOne.getArea());

// set rectTwo's position
rectTwo.origin = originOne;

// display rectTwo's position
System.out.println("X Position of rectTwo: " + rectTwo.origin.x);
System.out.println("Y Position of rectTwo: " + rectTwo.origin.y);

// move rectTwo and display its new position
rectTwo.move(40, 72);
System.out.println("X Position of rectTwo: " + rectTwo.origin.x);
System.out.println("Y Position of rectTwo: " + rectTwo.origin.y);
    }
  }
```

This program creates, manipulates, and displays information about various objects. Here's the output:

```
Width of rectOne: 100
Height of rectOne: 200
Area of rectOne: 20000
X Position of rectTwo: 23
Y Position of rectTwo: 94
X Position of rectTwo: 40
Y Position of rectTwo: 72
```

The following three sections use the above example to describe the life cycle of an object within a program. From them, you will learn how to write code that creates and uses objects in your own programs. You will also learn how the system cleans up after an object when its life has ended.

Creating Objects

As you know, a class provides the blueprint for objects; you create an object from a class. Each of the following statements taken from the CreateObjectDemo program creates an object and assigns it to a variable:

```
Point originOne = new Point(23, 94);
Rectangle rectOne = new Rectangle(originOne, 100, 200);
Rectangle rectTwo = new Rectangle(50, 100);
```

The first line creates an object of the Point class, and the second and third lines each create an object of the Rectangle class.

Each of these statements has three parts (discussed in detail later):

1. *Declaration.* The code set in **bold** are all variable declarations that associate a variable name with an object type.

2. *Instantiation.* The new keyword is a Java operator that creates the object.

3. *Initialization.* The new operator is followed by a call to a constructor, which initializes the new object.

Declaring a Variable to Refer to an Object

Previously, you learned that to declare a variable, you write the following:

```
type name;
```

This notifies the compiler that you will use *name* to refer to data whose type is *type*. With a primitive variable, this declaration also reserves the proper amount of memory for the variable. You can also declare a reference variable on its own line:

```
Point originOne;
```

If you declare originOne like this, its value will be undetermined until an object is actually created and assigned to it. Simply declaring a reference variable does not create an object. For that, you need to use the new operator, as described in the next section. You must assign an object to originOne before you use it in your code. Otherwise, you will get a compiler error. A variable in this state, which currently references no object, can be illustrated as shown in Figure 4.1 (the variable name, originOne, plus a reference pointing to nothing).

Instantiating a Class

The new operator instantiates a class by allocating memory for a new object and returning a reference to that memory. The new operator also invokes the object constructor.

> **Note**
>
> The phrase *instantiating a class* means the same thing as *creating an object.* When you create an object, you are creating an *instance* of a class, therefore *instantiating* a class.

The new operator requires a single, postfix argument: a call to a constructor. The name of the constructor provides the name of the class to instantiate. The new operator returns a reference to the object it created. This reference is usually assigned to a variable of the appropriate type:

```
Point originOne = new Point(23, 94);
```

originOne

Figure 4.1 When Declared as Point originOne, the Variable Has No Initial Value

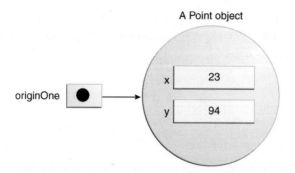

Figure 4.2 The originOne Variable Is Initialized

The reference returned by the new operator does not have to be assigned to a variable. It can also be used directly in an expression:

```
int height = new Rectangle().height;
```

This statement will be discussed in the next section.

Initializing an Object

Here's the code for the `Point` class:

```
public class Point {
    public int x = 0;
    public int y = 0;
    //constructor
    public Point(int a, int b) {
        x = a;
        y = b;
    }
}
```

This class contains a single constructor. You can recognize a constructor because its declaration uses the same name as the class and it has no return type. The constructor in the `Point` class takes two integer arguments, as declared by the code `(int a, int b)`. The following statement provides 23 and 94 as values for those arguments:

```
Point originOne = new Point(23, 94);
```

The result of executing this statement can be illustrated in Figure 4.2.

Here's the code for the `Rectangle` class, which contains four constructors:

```
public class Rectangle {
```

```
        public int width = 0;
        public int height = 0;
        public Point origin;

        // four constructors
        public Rectangle() {
            origin = new Point(0, 0);
        }
        public Rectangle(Point p) {
            origin = p;
        }
        public Rectangle(int w, int h) {
            origin = new Point(0, 0);
            width = w;
            height = h;
        }
        public Rectangle(Point p, int w, int h) {
            origin = p;
            width = w;
            height = h;
        }

        // a method for moving the rectangle
        public void move(int x, int y) {
            origin.x = x;
            origin.y = y;
        }

        // a method for computing the area of the rectangle
        public int getArea() {
            return width * height;
        }
}
```

Each constructor lets you provide initial values for the rectangle's origin, width, and height, using both primitive and reference types. If a class has multiple constructors, they must have different signatures. The Java compiler differentiates the constructors based on the number and type of arguments. When the Java compiler encounters the following code, it knows to call the constructor in the `Rectangle` class that requires a `Point` argument followed by two integer arguments:

```
Rectangle rectOne = new Rectangle(originOne, 100, 200);
```

This calls one of `Rectangle`'s constructors that initializes `origin` to `originOne`. Also, the constructor sets `width` to 100 and `height` to 200. Now there are two references to the same `Point` object. An object can have multiple references to it, as shown in Figure 4.3.

The following line of code calls the `Rectangle` constructor that requires two integer arguments, which provide the initial values for `width` and `height`. If you inspect the code within the constructor, you will see that it creates a new `Point` object whose x and y values are initialized to 0:

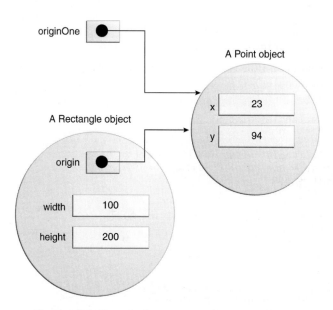

Figure 4.3 Two References to the Point Object

```
Rectangle rectTwo = new Rectangle(50, 100);
```

The `Rectangle` constructor used in the following statement doesn't take any arguments, so it's called a *no-argument constructor*:

```
Rectangle rect = new Rectangle();
```

All classes have at least one constructor. If a class does not explicitly declare any, the Java compiler automatically provides a no-argument constructor, called the *default constructor*. This default constructor calls the class parent's no-argument constructor or the `Object` constructor if the class has no other parent. If the parent has no constructor (`Object` does have one), the compiler will reject the program.

Using Objects

Once you've created an object, you probably want to use it for something. You may need to use the value of one of its fields, change one of its fields, or call one of its methods to perform an action.

Referencing an Object's Fields

Object fields are accessed by their names. You must use a name that is unambiguous. You may use a simple name for a field within its own class. For example, we can add a statement *within* the `Rectangle` class that prints the `width` and `height`:

```
System.out.println("Width and height are: " + width + ", " + height);
```

In this case, `width` and `height` are simple names.

Code that is outside the object's class must use an object reference or expression, followed by the dot (`.`) operator, followed by a simple field name:

```
objectReference.fieldName
```

4

For example, the code in the `CreateObjectDemo` class is outside the code for the `Rectangle` class. So to refer to the `origin`, `width`, and `height` fields within the `Rectangle` object named `rectOne`, the `CreateObjectDemo` class must use the names `rectOne.origin`, `rectOne.width`, and `rectOne.height`, respectively. The program uses two of these names to display the `width` and the `height` of `rectOne`:

```
System.out.println("Width of rectOne: " + rectOne.width);
System.out.println("Height of rectOne: " + rectOne.height);
```

Attempting to use the simple names `width` and `height` from the code in the `CreateObjectDemo` class doesn't make sense. These fields exist only within an object, and using them results in a compiler error.

Later, the program uses similar code to display information about `rectTwo`. Objects of the same type have their own copy of the same instance fields. Thus each `Rectangle` object has fields named `origin`, `width`, and `height`. When you access an instance field through an object reference, you reference that particular object's field. The two objects `rectOne` and `rectTwo` in the `CreateObjectDemo` program have different `origin`, `width`, and `height` fields.

To access a field, you can use a named reference to an object, as in the previous examples, or you can use any expression that returns an object reference. Recall that the new operator returns a reference to an object. So you could use the value returned from the new operator to access a new object's fields:

```
int height = new Rectangle().height;
```

This statement creates a new `Rectangle` object and immediately gets its height. In essence, the statement calculates the default height of a `Rectangle`. Note that after this statement has been executed, the program no longer has a reference to the created `Rectangle` because the program never stored the reference anywhere. The object is unreferenced, and its resources are free to be recycled by the Java Virtual Machine (Java VM).

Calling an Object's Methods

You also use an object reference to invoke an object's method. You append the method's simple name to the object reference with an intervening dot operator (`.`). Also, you provide, within enclosing parentheses, any arguments to the method. If the method does not require any arguments, use empty parentheses:

```
objectReference.methodName(argumentList);
```

or

```
objectReference.methodName();
```

The Rectangle class has two methods: getArea to compute the rectangle's area and move to change the rectangle's origin. Here's the CreateObjectDemo code that invokes these two methods:

```
System.out.println("Area of rectOne: " + rectOne.getArea());
...
rectTwo.move(40, 72);
```

The first statement invokes rectOne's getArea method and displays the results. The second line moves rectTwo because the move method assigns new values to the object's origin.x and origin.y.

As with instance fields, *objectReference* must be a reference to an object. You can use a variable name, but you can also use any expression that returns an object reference. The new operator returns an object reference, so you can use the value returned from new to invoke a new object's methods:

```
new Rectangle(100, 50).getArea()
```

The expression new Rectangle(100, 50) returns an object reference that refers to a Rectangle object. As shown, you can use the dot notation to invoke the new Rectangle's getArea() method to compute the area of the new rectangle.

Some methods, such as getArea(), return a value. For methods that return a value, you can use the method invocation in expressions. You can assign the return value to a variable, use it to make decisions, or control a loop. This code assigns the value returned by getArea to the variable areaOfRectangle:

```
int areaOfRectangle = new Rectangle(100, 50).getArea();
```

Remember, invoking a method on a particular object is the same as sending a message to that object. In this case, the object that getArea is invoked on is the rectangle returned by the constructor.

The Garbage Collector

Some object-oriented languages require that you keep track of all the objects you create and that you explicitly destroy them when they are no longer needed. Managing memory explicitly is tedious and error prone. The Java platform allows you to create as many objects as you want (limited, of course, by what your system can handle), and you don't have to worry about destroying them. The Java Runtime Environment (JRE) deletes objects when it determines that they are no longer being used. This process is called *garbage collection*.

An object is eligible for garbage collection when there are no more references to that object. References that are held in a variable are usually dropped when the variable goes out of scope. Or you can explicitly drop an object reference by setting the variable to the special value `null`. Remember that a program can have multiple references to the same object; all references to an object must be dropped before the object is eligible for garbage collection.

The JRE has a garbage collector that periodically frees the memory used by objects that are no longer referenced. The garbage collector does its job automatically when it determines that the time is right.

More on Classes

This section covers more aspects of classes that depend on using object references and the dot operator.

Returning a Value from a Method

A method returns to the code that invoked it when it completes all the statements in the method, reaches a `return` statement, or throws an exception (covered later)—whichever occurs first. You declare a method's return type in its method declaration. Within the body of the method, you use the `return` statement to return the value.

Any method declared `void` doesn't return a value. It does not need to contain a `return` statement, but it may do so. In such a case, a `return` statement can be used to branch out of a control flow block and exit the method and is simply used like this:

```
return;
```

If you try to return a value from a method that is declared `void`, you will get a compiler error. Any method that is not declared `void` must contain a `return` statement with a corresponding return value:

```
return returnValue;
```

The data type of the return value must match the method's declared return type; you can't return an integer value from a method declared to return a `boolean`.

The `getArea` method in the `Rectangle` class that was discussed in the sections on objects returns an integer:

```
    // a method for computing the area of the rectangle
    public int getArea() {
        return width * height;
    }
```

This method returns the integer that the expression `width * height` evaluates to.

The `getArea` method returns a primitive type. A method can also return a reference type. For example, in a program to manipulate `Bicycle` objects, we might have a method like this:

```
    public Bicycle seeWhosFastest(Bicycle myBike, Bicycle yourBike,
                                  Environment env) {
        Bicycle fastest;
        // code to calculate which bike is
        // faster, given each bike's gear
        // and cadence and given the
        // environment (terrain and wind)
        return fastest;
    }
```

Returning a Class or Interface

If this section confuses you, skip it and return to it after you have finished Chapter 6. When a method uses a class name as its return type, such as `whosFastest` does, the class of the type of the returned object must be either a subclass of or the exact class of the return type. Suppose that you have a class hierarchy in which `ImaginaryNumber` is a subclass of `java.lang.Number`, which is in turn a subclass of `Object`, as illustrated in Figure 4.4.

Now suppose you have a method declared to return a `Number`:

```
    public Number returnANumber() {
        ...
    }
```

The `returnANumber` method can return an `ImaginaryNumber` but not an `Object`. `ImaginaryNumber` is a `Number` because it's a subclass of `Number`. However, an `Object` is not necessarily a `Number`—it could be a `String` or another type.

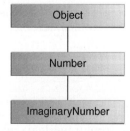

Figure 4.4 The Class Hierarchy for ImaginaryNumber

You can override a method and define it to return a subclass of the original method, like this:

```
public ImaginaryNumber returnANumber() {
    ...
}
```

4

This technique, called *covariant return type*, means that the return type is allowed to vary in the same direction as the subclass.

> **Note**
>
> You also can use interface names as return types. In this case, the object returned must implement the specified interface.

Using the this Keyword

Within an instance method or a constructor, this is a reference to the *current object*—the object whose method or constructor is being called. You can refer to any member of the current object from within an instance method or a constructor by using this.

Using this with a Field

The most common reason for using the this keyword is because a field is shadowed by a method or constructor parameter. For example, the Point class was written like this:

```
public class Point {
    public int x = 0;
    public int y = 0;

    //constructor
    public Point(int a, int b) {
        x = a;
        y = b;
    }
}
```

However, it could have been written like this:

```
public class Point {
    public int x = 0;
    public int y = 0;

    //constructor
    public Point(int x, int y) {
        this.x = x;
```

```
        this.y = y;
    }
}
```

Each argument to the constructor shadows one of the object's fields—inside the constructor **x** is a local copy of the constructor's first argument. To refer to the `Point` field **x**, the constructor must use **this.x**.

Using this with a Constructor

From within a constructor, you can also use the `this` keyword to call another constructor in the same class. Doing so is called an *explicit constructor invocation*. Here's another `Rectangle` class, with a different implementation than the one in the "Objects" section of this chapter:

```
public class Rectangle {
    private int x, y;
    private int width, height;

    public Rectangle() {
        this(0, 0, 1, 1);
    }
    public Rectangle(int width, int height) {
        this(0, 0, width, height);
    }
    public Rectangle(int x, int y, int width, int height) {
        this.x = x;
        this.y = y;
        this.width = width;
        this.height = height;
    }
    ...
}
```

This class contains a set of constructors. Each constructor initializes some or all of the rectangle's member variables. The constructors provide a default value for any member variable whose initial value is not provided by an argument. For example, the no-argument constructor creates a 1-by-1 `Rectangle` at coordinates 0,0. The two-argument constructor calls the four-argument constructor, passing in the width and height but always using the 0,0 coordinates. As before, the compiler determines which constructor to call based on the number and type of arguments. If present, the invocation of another constructor must be the first line in the constructor.

Controlling Access to Members of a Class

Access-level modifiers determine whether other classes can use a particular field or invoke a particular method. There are two levels of access control:

- *At the top level.* public or package-private (no explicit modifier)
- *At the member level.* public, private, protected, or package-private (no explicit modifier)

A class may be declared with the modifier public, in which case that class is visible to all classes everywhere. If a class has no modifier (the default, also known as *package-private*), it is visible only within its own package. (*Packages* are named groups of related classes—you will learn about them in Chapter 8.)

At the member level, you can also use the public modifier or no modifier (package-private), just as with top-level classes, and with the same meaning. For members, there are two additional access modifiers: private and protected. The private modifier specifies that the member can only be accessed in its own class. The protected modifier specifies that the member can only be accessed within its own package (as with package-private) and, in addition, by a subclass of its class in another package. Table 4.1 shows the access to members permitted by each modifier.

The first data column indicates whether the class itself has access to the member defined by the access level. As you can see, a class always has access to its own members. The second column indicates whether classes in the same package as the class (regardless of their parentage) have access to the member. The third column indicates whether subclasses of the class declared outside this package have access to the member. The fourth column indicates whether all classes have access to the member.

Access levels affect you in two ways. First, when you use classes that come from another source, such as the classes in the Java platform, access levels determine which members of those classes your own classes can use. Second, when you write a class, you need to decide which access level every member variable and every method in your class should have.

Let's look at a collection of classes and see how access levels affect visibility. Figure 4.5 shows the four classes in this example and how they are related. Table 4.2 shows where the members of the Alpha class are visible for each of the access modifiers that can be applied to them.

Table 4.1 Access Levels

Modifier	Class	Package	Subclass	World
public	Y	Y	Y	Y
protected	Y	Y	Y	N
no modifier	Y	Y	N	N
private	Y	N	N	N

4

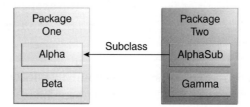

Figure 4.5 Classes and Packages of the Example Used to Illustrate Access Levels

Table 4.2 Visibility

Modifier	Alpha	Beta	Alphasub	Gamma
public	Y	Y	Y	Y
protected	Y	Y	Y	N
no modifier	Y	Y	N	N
private	Y	N	N	N

Note

If other programmers use your class, you want to ensure that errors from misuse cannot happen. Access levels can help you do this:

- Use the most restrictive access level that makes sense for a particular member. Use `private` unless you have a good reason not to.
- Avoid `public` fields except for constants. (Many of the examples in this book use public fields. This may help illustrate some points concisely but is not recommended for production code.) Public fields tend to link you to a particular implementation and limit your flexibility for changing your code.

Understanding Class Members

In this section, we discuss the use of the `static` keyword to create fields and methods that belong to the class rather than to an instance of the class.

Class Variables

When a number of objects are created from the same class blueprint, they each have their own distinct copies of *instance variables*. In the case of the `Bicycle` class, the instance variables are `cadence`, `gear`, and `speed`. Each `Bicycle` object has its own values for these variables, stored in different memory locations.

Sometimes you want to have variables that are common to all objects. This is accomplished with the `static` modifier. Fields that have the `static` modifier in their declaration are called *static fields* or *class variables*. They are associated with the class, rather than with any object. Every instance of the class shares a class variable, which is in one fixed location in memory. Any object can change the value of a class variable, but class variables can also be manipulated without creating an instance of the class.

For example, suppose you want to create a number of `Bicycle` objects and assign each a serial number, beginning with 1 for the first object. This ID number is unique to each object and is therefore an instance variable. At the same time, you need a field to keep track of how many `Bicycle` objects have been created so that you know which ID to assign to the next one. Such a field is not related to any individual object but to the class as a whole. For this, you need a class variable, `numberOfBicycles`, as follows:

```java
public class Bicycle {

    private int cadence;
    private int gear;
    private int speed;

    // add an instance variable for the object ID
    private int id;

    // add a class variable for the
    // number of Bicycle objects instantiated
    private static int numberOfBicycles = 0;
        ...
}
```

Class variables are referenced by the class name itself:

```java
Bicycle.numberOfBicycles
```

This makes it clear that they are class variables.

> **Note**
> You can also refer to static fields with an object reference like `myBike.numberOfBicycles`, but this is discouraged because it does not make it clear that they are class variables.

You can use the `Bicycle` constructor to set the `id` instance variable and increment the `numberOfBicycles` class variable:

```java
public class Bicycle {

    private int cadence;
    private int gear;
    private int speed;
    private int id;
    private static int numberOfBicycles = 0;

    public Bicycle(int startCadence, int startSpeed, int startGear){
```

4

```
        gear = startGear;
        cadence = startCadence;
        speed = startSpeed;

        // increment number of Bicycles
        // and assign ID number
        id = ++numberOfBicycles;
    }

    // new method to return the ID instance variable
    public int getID() {
        return id;
    }
        ...
}
```

Class Methods

The Java programming language supports static methods as well as static variables. Static methods, which have the `static` modifier in their declarations, should be invoked with the class name, without the need for creating an instance of the class:

```
ClassName.methodName(args)
```

> **Note**
>
> You can also refer to static methods with an object reference like `instanceName`
> `.methodName(args)`, but this is discouraged because it does not make it clear that they
> are class methods.

A common use for static methods is to access static fields. For example, we could add a static method to the `Bicycle` class to access the `numberOfBicycles` static field:

```
public static int getNumberOfBicycles() {
    return numberOfBicycles;
}
```

Not all combinations of instance and class variables and methods are allowed:

- Instance methods can access instance variables and instance methods directly.
- Instance methods can access class variables and class methods directly.
- Class methods can access class variables and class methods directly.
- Class methods *cannot* access instance variables or instance methods directly— they must use an object reference. Also, class methods cannot use the `this` keyword, as there is no instance for `this` to refer to.

Constants

The `static` modifier, in combination with the `final` modifier, is also used to define constants. The `final` modifier indicates that the value of this field cannot change.

For example, the following variable declaration defines a constant named `PI`, whose value is an approximation of pi (the ratio of the circumference of a circle to its diameter):

```
static final double PI = 3.141592653589793;
```

Constants defined in this way cannot be reassigned, and it is a compile-time error if your program tries to do so. By convention, the names of constant values are spelled in uppercase letters. If the name is composed of more than one word, the words are separated by an underscore (_).

> **Note**
>
> If a primitive type or a string is defined as a constant and the value is known at compile time, the compiler replaces the constant name everywhere in the code with its value. This is called a *compile-time constant*. If the value of the constant in the outside world changes (e.g., if it is legislated that pi actually should be 3.975), you will need to recompile any classes that use this constant to get the current value.

The Bicycle Class

After all the modifications made in this section, the `Bicycle` class is now as follows:

```java
public class Bicycle {

    private int cadence;
    private int gear;
    private int speed;

    private int id;

    private static int numberOfBicycles = 0;

    public Bicycle(int startCadence,
                   int startSpeed,
                   int startGear){
        gear = startGear;
        cadence = startCadence;
        speed = startSpeed;

        id = ++numberOfBicycles;
    }

    public int getID() {
```

```
        return id;
    }

    public static int getNumberOfBicycles() {
        return numberOfBicycles;
    }

    public int getCadence() {
        return cadence;
    }

    public void setCadence(int newValue) {
        cadence = newValue;
    }

    public int getGear(){
        return gear;
    }

    public void setGear(int newValue) {
        gear = newValue;
    }

    public int getSpeed() {
        return speed;
    }

    public void applyBrake(int decrement) {
        speed -= decrement;
    }

    public void speedUp(int increment) {
        speed += increment;
    }
}
```

Initializing Fields

As you have seen, you can often provide an initial value for a field in its declaration:

```
public class BedAndBreakfast {

    // initialize to 10
    public static int capacity = 10;

    // initialize to false
    private boolean full = false;
}
```

This works well when the initialization value is available and the initialization can be put on one line. However, this form of initialization has limitations because of its simplicity. If initialization requires some logic (e.g., error handling or a `for` loop to fill a complex array), simple assignment is inadequate. Instance variables can be initialized in constructors where error handling or other logic can be used. To provide the same capability for class variables, the Java programming language includes *static initialization blocks*.

> **Note**
>
> It is not necessary to declare fields at the beginning of the class definition, although this is the most common practice. It is only necessary that they be declared and initialized before they are used.

4

Static Initialization Blocks

A *static initialization block* is a normal block of code enclosed in braces, { }, and preceded by the `static` keyword. Here is an example:

```
static {
    // whatever code is needed for initialization goes here
}
```

A class can have any number of static initialization blocks, and they can appear anywhere in the class body. The runtime system guarantees that static initialization blocks are called in the order that they appear in the source code.

There is an alternative to static blocks—you can write a private static method:

```
class Whatever {
    public static varType myVar = initializeClassVariable();

    private static varType initializeClassVariable() {
        // initialization code goes here
    }
}
```

The advantage of private static methods is that they can be reused later if you need to reinitialize the class variable.

Initializing Instance Members

Normally, you would put code to initialize an instance variable in a constructor. There are two alternatives to using a constructor to initialize instance variables: initializer blocks and final methods.

Initializer blocks for instance variables look just like static initializer blocks but without the `static` keyword:

```
{
    // whatever code is needed for initialization goes here
}
```

The Java compiler copies initializer blocks into every constructor. Therefore, this approach can be used to share a block of code between multiple constructors.

A *final method* cannot be overridden in a subclass. This is discussed in Chapter 6. Here is an example of using a final method for initializing an instance variable:

```java
class Whatever {
    private varType myVar = initializeInstanceVariable();

    protected final varType initializeInstanceVariable() {
        // initialization code goes here
    }
}
```

This is especially useful if subclasses might want to reuse the initialization method. The method is final because calling nonfinal methods during instance initialization can cause problems.

Summary of Creating and Using Classes and Objects

A class declaration names the class and encloses the class body between braces. The class name can be preceded by modifiers. The class body contains fields, methods, and constructors for the class. A class uses fields to contain state information and uses methods to implement behavior. Constructors that initialize a new instance of a class use the name of the class and look like methods without a return type.

You control access to classes and members in the same way—by using an access modifier such as `public` in their declaration.

You specify a class variable or a class method by using the `static` keyword in the member's declaration. A member that is not declared as `static` is implicitly an instance member. Class variables are shared by all instances of a class and can be accessed through the class name as well as an instance reference. Instances of a class get their own copy of each instance variable, which must be accessed through an instance reference.

You create an object from a class by using the new operator and a constructor. The new operator returns a reference to the object that was created. You can assign the reference to a variable or use it directly.

Instance variables and methods that are accessible to code outside the class that they are declared in can be referred to by using a qualified name. The qualified name of an instance variable looks like this:

```
objectReference.variableName
```

The qualified name of a method looks like this:

```
objectReference.methodName(argumentList)
```

or

```
objectReference.methodName()
```

4

The garbage collector automatically cleans up unused objects. An object is unused if the program holds no more references to it. You can explicitly drop a reference by setting the variable holding the reference to null.

Questions and Exercises: Classes

Questions

1. Consider the following class:

```
public class IdentifyMyParts {
    public static int x = 7;
    public int y = 3;
}
```

a. What are the class variables?

b. What are the instance variables?

c. What is the output from the following code?

```
IdentifyMyParts a = new IdentifyMyParts();
IdentifyMyParts b = new IdentifyMyParts();
a.y = 5;
b.y = 6;
a.x = 1;
b.x = 2;
System.out.println("a.y = " + a.y);
System.out.println("b.y = " + b.y);
System.out.println("a.x = " + a.x);
System.out.println("b.x = " + b.x);
System.out.println("IdentifyMyParts.x = " + IdentifyMyParts.x);
```

Exercises

1. Write a class whose instances represent a single playing card from a deck of cards. Keep in mind that playing cards have two distinguishing properties: rank and suit. (Be sure to keep your solution, as you will be asked to rewrite it in the "Enum Types" sections.)

4

> **Note**
> You can use the `assert` statement to check your assignments. The following is the syntax of the `assert` statement:
>
> ```
> assert (boolean expression to test);
> ```
>
> If the `boolean` expression is false, you will get an error message. For example,
>
> ```
> assert (6 * 7) == (40 + 2);
> ```
>
> This statement should return `true`, so there will be no error message. If you use the `assert` statement, you must run your program with the ea flag:
>
> ```
> java -ea YourProgram.class
> ```

2. Write a class whose instances represent a *full* deck of cards. You should also keep this solution.

3. Write a small program to test your deck and card classes. The program can be as simple as creating a deck of cards and displaying its cards.

Answers

You can find answers to these questions and exercises at `http://docs.oracle` `.com/javase/tutorial/java/javaOO/QandE/creating-answers.html`.

Questions and Exercises: Objects

Questions

1. What's wrong with the following program?

```java
public class SomethingIsWrong {
    public static void main(String[] args) {
        Rectangle myRect;
        myRect.width = 40;
        myRect.height = 50;
        System.out.println("myRect's area is " + myRect.area());
    }
}
```

2. The following code creates one array and one string object. How many references to those objects exist after the code executes? Is either object eligible for garbage collection?

```java
...
String[] students = new String[10];
String studentName = "Peter Parker";
```

```
        students[0] = studentName;
        studentName = null;
        ...
```

3. How does a program destroy an object that it creates?

Exercises

1. Fix the program called SomethingIsWrong from question 1.
2. Given the following class, called NumberHolder, write some code that creates
    an instance of the class, initializes its two member variables, and then displays
    the value of each member variable:

```
        public class NumberHolder {
            public int anInt;
            public float aFloat;
        }
```

Answers

You can find answers to these questions and exercises at `http://docs.oracle`
`.com/javase/tutorial/java/javaOO/QandE/objects-answers.html`.

Nested Classes

The Java programming language allows you to define a class within another class.
Such a class is called a *nested class* and is illustrated here:

```
    class OuterClass {
        ...
        class NestedClass {
            ...
        }
    }
```

> **Definition**
>
> Nested classes are divided into two categories: static and nonstatic. Nested classes that
> are declared static are called *static nested classes*. Nonstatic nested classes are called *inner*
> *classes*.
>
> ```
>         class OuterClass {
>             ...
>             static class StaticNestedClass {
>                 ...
>             }
>             class InnerClass {
>                 ...
>             }
>         }
> ```

A nested class is a member of its enclosing class, or *outer class*. Nonstatic nested classes (inner classes) have access to other members of the enclosing class, even if they are declared private. Static nested classes do not have access to other members of the enclosing class. As a member of a class, a nested class can be declared `private`, `public`, `protected`, or *package private*. (Recall that, as detailed in the section "Controlling Access to Members of a Class," a class declared at the top level can only be declared `public` or *package private*.)

Why Use Nested Classes?

Here are some compelling reasons for the use of nested classes:

- *It is a way of logically grouping classes that are only used in one place.* If a class is useful to only one other class, then it is logical to embed it in that class and keep the two together. Nesting such "helper classes" makes their package more streamlined.
- *It increases encapsulation.* Consider two top-level classes, A and B, where B needs access to members of A that would otherwise be declared `private`. By hiding class B within class A, A's members can be declared private and B can access them. In addition, B itself can be hidden from the outside world.
- *It can lead to more readable and maintainable code.* Nesting small classes within top-level classes places the code closer to where it is used.

Static Nested Classes

As with class methods and variables, a static nested class is associated with its outer class. And like static class methods, a static nested class cannot refer directly to instance variables or methods defined in its enclosing class: it can use them only through an object reference.

> **Note**
>
> A static nested class interacts with the instance members of its outer class (and other classes) just like any other top-level class. In effect, a static nested class is behaviorally a top-level class that has been nested in another top-level class for packaging convenience.

Static nested classes are accessed using the enclosing class name:

```
OuterClass.StaticNestedClass
```

For example, to create an object for the static nested class, use this syntax:

```
OuterClass.StaticNestedClass nestedObject =
    new OuterClass.StaticNestedClass();
```

Inner Classes

As with instance methods and variables, an inner class is associated with an instance of its enclosing class and has direct access to that object's methods and fields. Also, because an inner class is associated with an instance, it cannot define any static members itself.

Objects that are instances of an inner class exist *within* an instance of the outer class. Consider the following classes:

```
class OuterClass {
    ...
    class InnerClass {
        ...
    }
}
```

An instance of `InnerClass` can exist only within an instance of `OuterClass` and has direct access to the methods and fields of its enclosing instance.

To instantiate an inner class, you must first instantiate the outer class. Then create the inner object within the outer object with this syntax:

```
OuterClass.InnerClass innerObject = outerObject.new InnerClass();
```

There are two special kinds of inner classes: local classes and anonymous classes.

Shadowing

If a declaration of a type (such as a member variable or a parameter name) in a particular scope (such as an inner class or a method definition) has the same name as another declaration in the enclosing scope, then the declaration *shadows* the declaration of the enclosing scope. You cannot refer to a shadowed declaration by its name alone. The following example, `ShadowTest`, demonstrates this:

```
public class ShadowTest {

    public int x = 0;

    class FirstLevel {
```

```
        public int x = 1;

        void methodInFirstLevel(int x) {
            System.out.println("x = " + x);
            System.out.println("this.x = " + this.x);
            System.out.println("ShadowTest.this.x = " + ShadowTest.this.x);
        }
    }

    public static void main(String... args) {
        ShadowTest st = new ShadowTest();
        ShadowTest.FirstLevel fl = st.new FirstLevel();
        fl.methodInFirstLevel(23);
    }
}
```

The following is the output of this example:

```
x = 23
this.x = 1
ShadowTest.this.x = 0
```

This example defines three variables named x: the member variable of the class ShadowTest, the member variable of the inner class FirstLevel, and the parameter in the method methodInFirstLevel. The variable x defined as a parameter of the method methodInFirstLevel shadows the variable of the inner class First-Level. Consequently, when you use the variable x in the method methodInFirst-Level, it refers to the method parameter. To refer to the member variable of the inner class FirstLevel, use the keyword this to represent the enclosing scope:

```
System.out.println("this.x = " + this.x);
```

Refer to member variables that enclose larger scopes by the class name to which they belong. For example, the following statement accesses the member variable of the class ShadowTest from the method methodInFirstLevel:

```
System.out.println("ShadowTest.this.x = " + ShadowTest.this.x);
```

Serialization

Serialization of inner classes, including local and anonymous classes, is strongly discouraged.[1] When the Java compiler compiles certain constructs, such as inner classes, it creates *synthetic constructs*; these are classes, methods, fields, and other constructs that do not have a corresponding construct in the source code. Synthetic constructs enable Java compilers to implement new Java language features

---

1.   tutorial/jndi/objects/serial.html

without changes to the Java VM. However, synthetic constructs can vary among different Java compiler implementations, which means that .class files can vary among different implementations as well. Consequently, you may have compatibility issues if you serialize an inner class and then deserialize it with a different JRE implementation.[2]

Inner Class Example

To see an inner class in use, first consider an array. In the following DataStructure.java example, you create an array, fill it with integer values, and then output only values of even indices of the array in ascending order. This example consists of the following:

- *The* DataStructure *outer class.* This includes a constructor to create an instance of DataStructure containing an array filled with consecutive integer values (0, 1, 2, 3, and so on) and a method that prints elements of the array that have an even index value.
- *The* EvenIterator *inner class.* This implements the DataStructureIterator interface, which extends the Iterator[3] <Integer> interface. Iterators are used to step through a data structure and typically have methods to test for the last element, retrieve the current element, and move to the next element.
- A main *method that instantiates a* DataStructure *object* (ds). This invokes the printEven method to print elements of the array arrayOfInts that have an even index value.

```
public class DataStructure {

    // Create an array
    private final static int SIZE = 15;
    private int[] arrayOfInts = new int[SIZE];

    public DataStructure() {
        // fill the array with ascending integer values
        for (int i = 0; i < SIZE; i++) {
            arrayOfInts[i] = i;
        }
    }

    public void printEven() {
```

---

2.   See "Implicit and Synthetic Parameters" for more information about the synthetic constructs generated when an inner class is compiled: tutorial/reflect/member/methodparameterreflection.html#implcit_and_synthetic

3.   8/docs/api/java/util/Iterator.html

```
        // Print out values of even indices of the array
        DataStructureIterator iterator = this.new EvenIterator();
        while (iterator.hasNext()) {
            System.out.print(iterator.next() + " ");
        }
        System.out.println();
    }

    interface DataStructureIterator extends java.util.Iterator<Integer> { }

    // Inner class implements the DataStructureIterator interface,
    // which extends the Iterator<Integer> interface

    private class EvenIterator implements DataStructureIterator {

        // Start stepping through the array from the beginning
        private int nextIndex = 0;

        public boolean hasNext() {

            // Check if the current element is the last in the array
            return (nextIndex <= SIZE - 1);
        }

        public Integer next() {

            // Record a value of an even index of the array
            Integer retValue = Integer.valueOf(arrayOfInts[nextIndex]);

            // Get the next even element
            nextIndex += 2;
            return retValue;
        }
    }

    public static void main(String s[]) {

        // Fill the array with integer values and print out only
        // values of even indices
        DataStructure ds = new DataStructure();
        ds.printEven();
    }
}
```

Here is the output:

```
0 2 4 6 8 10 12 14
```

Note that the EvenIterator class refers directly to the arrayOfInts instance variable of the DataStructure object.

You can use inner classes to implement helper classes such as the one shown in this example. To handle user-interface events, you must know how to use inner classes, because the event-handling mechanism makes extensive use of them.

Local and Anonymous Classes

There are two additional types of inner classes. You can declare an inner class within the body of a method. These classes are known as *local classes*. You can also declare an inner class within the body of a method without naming the class. These classes are known as *anonymous classes*.

4

Modifiers

You can use the same modifiers for inner classes that you use for other members of the outer class. For example, you can use the access specifiers `private`, `public`, and `protected` to restrict access to inner classes, just as you use them to restrict access to other class members.

Local Classes

Local classes are classes that are defined in a *block*, which is a group of zero or more statements between balanced braces. You typically find local classes defined in the body of a method.

Declaring Local Classes

You can define a local class inside any block. (See Chapter 3, "Expressions, Statements, and Blocks," for more information.) For example, you can define a local class in a method body, a `for` loop, or an `if` clause.

The following example, `LocalClassExample`, validates two phone numbers. It defines the local class `PhoneNumber` in the method `validatePhoneNumber`:

```
public class LocalClassExample {

    static String regularExpression = "[^0-9]";

    public static void validatePhoneNumber(
        String phoneNumber1, String phoneNumber2) {

        final int numberLength = 10;

        // Valid in JDK 8 and later:

        // int numberLength = 10;

        class PhoneNumber {

            String formattedPhoneNumber = null;

            PhoneNumber(String phoneNumber){
                // numberLength = 7;
```

```
                    String currentNumber = phoneNumber.replaceAll(
                        regularExpression, "");
                    if (currentNumber.length() == numberLength)
                        formattedPhoneNumber = currentNumber;
                    else
                        formattedPhoneNumber = null;
                }

                public String getNumber() {
                    return formattedPhoneNumber;
                }

                // Valid in JDK 8 and later:
//              public void printOriginalNumbers() {
//                  System.out.println("Original numbers are " + phoneNumber1 +
//                      " and " + phoneNumber2);
//              }
            }

            PhoneNumber myNumber1 = new PhoneNumber(phoneNumber1);
            PhoneNumber myNumber2 = new PhoneNumber(phoneNumber2);

            // Valid in JDK 8 and later:
//          myNumber1.printOriginalNumbers();

            if (myNumber1.getNumber() == null)
                System.out.println("First number is invalid");
            else
                System.out.println("First number is " + myNumber1.getNumber());
            if (myNumber2.getNumber() == null)
                System.out.println("Second number is invalid");
            else
                System.out.println("Second number is " + myNumber2.getNumber());

        }

        public static void main(String... args) {
            validatePhoneNumber("123-456-7890", "456-7890");
        }
    }
```

The example validates a phone number by first removing all characters from the phone number except the digits 0 through 9. After, it checks whether the phone number contains exactly ten digits (the length of a phone number in North America). This example prints the following:

```
First number is 1234567890
Second number is invalid
```

Accessing Members of an Enclosing Class

A local class has access to the members of its enclosing class. In the previous example, the PhoneNumber constructor accesses the member LocalClassExample .regularExpression.

In addition, a local class has access to local variables. However, a local class can only access local variables that are declared final. When a local class accesses a local variable or parameter of the enclosing block, it *captures* that variable or parameter. For example, the `PhoneNumber` constructor can access the local variable `numberLength` because it is declared final; `numberLength` is a *captured variable*.

However, starting in Java SE 8, a local class can access local variables and parameters of the enclosing block that are final or *effectively final*. A variable or parameter whose value is never changed after it is initialized is effectively final. For example, suppose that the variable `numberLength` is not declared final and you add the bold-face assignment statement in the `PhoneNumber` constructor:

```
PhoneNumber(String phoneNumber) {
    numberLength = 7;
    String currentNumber = phoneNumber.replaceAll(
        regularExpression, "");
    if (currentNumber.length() == numberLength)
        formattedPhoneNumber = currentNumber;
    else
        formattedPhoneNumber = null;
}
```

Because of this assignment statement, the variable `numberLength` is not effectively final anymore. As a result, the Java compiler generates an error message similar to "local variables referenced from an inner class must be final or effectively final" where the inner class `PhoneNumber` tries to access the number-Length variable:

```
if (currentNumber.length() == numberLength)
```

Starting in Java SE 8, if you declare the local class in a method, it can access the method's parameters. For example, you can define the following method in the `PhoneNumber` local class:

```
public void printOriginalNumbers() {
    System.out.println("Original numbers are " + phoneNumber1 +
        " and " + phoneNumber2);
}
```

The method `printOriginalNumbers` accesses the parameters `phoneNumber1` and `phoneNumber2` of the method `validatePhoneNumber`.

Shadowing and Local Classes

Declarations of a type (such as a variable) in a local class shadow declarations in the enclosing scope that have the same name. See the "Shadowing" section in this chapter for more information.

Local Classes Are Similar to Inner Classes

Local classes are similar to inner classes because they cannot define or declare any static members. Local classes in static methods, such as the class `PhoneNumber` that is defined in the static method `validatePhoneNumber`, can only refer to static members of the enclosing class. For example, if you do not define the member variable `regularExpression` as static, then the Java compiler generates an error similar to "nonstatic variable `regularExpression` cannot be referenced from a static context."

Local classes are nonstatic because they have access to instance members of the enclosing block. Consequently, they cannot contain most kinds of static declarations.

You cannot declare an interface inside a block; interfaces are inherently static. For example, the following code excerpt does not compile because the interface `HelloThere` is defined inside the body of the method `greetInEnglish`:

```java
public void greetInEnglish() {
    interface HelloThere {
        public void greet();
    }
    class EnglishHelloThere implements HelloThere {
        public void greet() {
            System.out.println("Hello " + name);
        }
    }
    HelloThere myGreeting = new EnglishHelloThere();
    myGreeting.greet();
}
```

You cannot declare static initializers or member interfaces in a local class. The following code excerpt does not compile because the method `EnglishGoodbye.sayGoodbye` is declared `static`. The compiler generates an error similar to "modifier 'static' is only allowed in constant variable declaration" when it encounters this method definition:

```java
public void sayGoodbyeInEnglish() {
    class EnglishGoodbye {
        public static void sayGoodbye() {
            System.out.println("Bye bye");
        }
    }
    EnglishGoodbye.sayGoodbye();
}
```

A local class can have static members, provided that they are constant variables. A *constant variable* is a variable of primitive type or type `String` that is declared final and initialized with a compile-time constant expression. A compile-time constant expression is typically a string or an arithmetic expression that can be evaluated at compile time. (See "Understanding Class Members" in this chapter for more

information.) The following code excerpt compiles because the static member
`EnglishGoodbye.farewell` is a constant variable:

```java
public void sayGoodbyeInEnglish() {
    class EnglishGoodbye {
        public static final String farewell = "Bye bye";
        public void sayGoodbye() {
            System.out.println(farewell);
        }
    }
    EnglishGoodbye myEnglishGoodbye = new EnglishGoodbye();
    myEnglishGoodbye.sayGoodbye();
}
```

Anonymous Classes

Anonymous classes enable you to make your code more concise. They enable you to
declare and instantiate a class at the same time. They are like local classes, except
they do not have a name. Use them if you need to use a local class only once.

Declaring Anonymous Classes

While local classes are class declarations, anonymous classes are expressions,
which means that you define the class in another expression. The following
example, `HelloWorldAnonymousClasses`, uses anonymous classes in the initialization statements of the local variables `frenchGreeting` and `spanishGreeting`
but uses a local class for the initialization of the variable `englishGreeting`:

```java
public class HelloWorldAnonymousClasses {

    interface HelloWorld {
        public void greet();
        public void greetSomeone(String someone);
    }

    public void sayHello() {

        class EnglishGreeting implements HelloWorld {
            String name = "world";
            public void greet() {
                greetSomeone("world");
            }
            public void greetSomeone(String someone) {
                name = someone;
                System.out.println("Hello " + name);
            }
        }

        HelloWorld englishGreeting = new EnglishGreeting();

        HelloWorld frenchGreeting = new HelloWorld() {
            String name = "tout le monde";
```

```
            public void greet() {
                greetSomeone("tout le monde");
            }
            public void greetSomeone(String someone) {
                name = someone;
                System.out.println("Salut " + name);
            }
        };

        HelloWorld spanishGreeting = new HelloWorld() {
            String name = "mundo";
            public void greet() {
                greetSomeone("mundo");
            }
            public void greetSomeone(String someone) {
                name = someone;
                System.out.println("Hola, " + name);
            }
        };
        englishGreeting.greet();
        frenchGreeting.greetSomeone("Fred");
        spanishGreeting.greet();
    }

    public static void main(String... args) {
        HelloWorldAnonymousClasses myApp =
            new HelloWorldAnonymousClasses();
        myApp.sayHello();
    }
}
```

Syntax of Anonymous Classes

As mentioned previously, an anonymous class is an expression. The syntax of an anonymous class expression is like the invocation of a constructor, except there is a class definition contained in a block of code.

Consider the instantiation of the frenchGreeting object:

```
HelloWorld frenchGreeting = new HelloWorld() {
    String name = "tout le monde";
    public void greet() {
        greetSomeone("tout le monde");
    }
    public void greetSomeone(String someone) {
        name = someone;
        System.out.println("Salut " + name);
    }
};
```

The anonymous class expression consists of the following:

- The new operator
- The name of an interface to implement or a class to extend (In this example, the anonymous class is implementing the interface HelloWorld.)

- Parentheses that contain the arguments to a constructor, just like a normal class instance creation expression
- A body, which is a class declaration body (More specifically, in the body, method declarations are allowed but statements are not.)

> **Note**
>
> When you implement an interface, there is no constructor, so you use an empty pair of parentheses, as in this example.

Because an anonymous class definition is an expression, it must be part of a statement. In this example, the anonymous class expression is part of the statement that instantiates the `frenchGreeting` object. (This explains why there is a semicolon after the closing brace.)

Accessing Local Variables of the Enclosing Scope and Declaring and Accessing Members of the Anonymous Class

Like local classes, anonymous classes can capture variables; they have the same access to local variables of the enclosing scope:

- An anonymous class has access to the members of its enclosing class.
- An anonymous class cannot access local variables in its enclosing scope that are not declared as `final` or effectively final.
- Like a nested class, a declaration of a type (such as a variable) in an anonymous class shadows any other declarations in the enclosing scope that have the same name. See the "Shadowing" section for more information.

Anonymous classes also have the same restrictions as local classes with respect to their members:

- You cannot declare static initializers or member interfaces in an anonymous class.
- An anonymous class can have static members, provided that they are constant variables.

Note that you can declare the following in anonymous classes:

- Fields
- Extra methods (even if they do not implement any methods of the supertype)
- Instance initializers
- Local classes

However, you cannot declare constructors in an anonymous class.

Examples of Anonymous Classes

Anonymous classes are often used in GUI applications. Consider the JavaFX example ple HelloWorld.java[4] (from the online tutorial's Hello World, JavaFX Style[5] from Getting Started with JavaFX[6]). This sample creates a frame that contains a **Say "Hello World"** button. The anonymous class expression is boldface:

```java
import javafx.event.ActionEvent;
import javafx.event.EventHandler;
import javafx.scene.Scene;
import javafx.scene.control.Button;
import javafx.scene.layout.StackPane;
import javafx.stage.Stage;

public class HelloWorld extends Application {
    public static void main(String[] args) {
        launch(args);
    }

    @Override
    public void start(Stage primaryStage) {
        primaryStage.setTitle("Hello World!");
        Button btn = new Button();
        btn.setText("Say 'Hello World'");
        btn.setOnAction(new EventHandler<ActionEvent>() {

            @Override
            public void handle(ActionEvent event) {
                System.out.println("Hello World!");
            }
        });

        StackPane root = new StackPane();
        root.getChildren().add(btn);
        primaryStage.setScene(new Scene(root, 300, 250));
        primaryStage.show();
    }
}
```

In this example, the method invocation `btn.setOnAction` specifies what happens when you select the **Say "Hello World"** button. This method requires an object of type `EventHandler<ActionEvent>`. The `EventHandler<ActionEvent>` interface contains only one method, `handle`. Instead of implementing this method with a new class, the example uses an anonymous class expression. Notice that this expression is the argument passed to the `btn.setOnAction` method.

---

4.   8/javafx/get-started-tutorial/hello_world.htm

5.   8/javafx/get-started-tutorial/hello_world.htm

6.   8/javafx/get-started-tutorial/javafx_get_started.htm

Because the `EventHandler<ActionEvent>` interface contains only one method, you can use a lambda expression instead of an anonymous class expression. See the "Lambda Expressions" section for more information.

Anonymous classes are ideal for implementing an interface that contains two or more methods. The following JavaFX example is from the online tutorial's Customization of UI Controls.[7] The boldface code creates a text field that only accepts numeric values. It redefines the default implementation of the `TextField` class with an anonymous class by overriding the `replaceText` and `replaceSelection` methods inherited from the `TextInputControl` class:

```java
import javafx.application.Application;
import javafx.event.ActionEvent;
import javafx.event.EventHandler;
import javafx.geometry.Insets;
import javafx.scene.Group;
import javafx.scene.Scene;
import javafx.scene.control.*;
import javafx.scene.layout.GridPane;
import javafx.scene.layout.HBox;
import javafx.stage.Stage;

public class CustomTextFieldSample extends Application {

    final static Label label = new Label();

    @Override
    public void start(Stage stage) {
        Group root = new Group();
        Scene scene = new Scene(root, 300, 150);
        stage.setScene(scene);
        stage.setTitle("Text Field Sample");

        GridPane grid = new GridPane();
        grid.setPadding(new Insets(10, 10, 10, 10));
        grid.setVgap(5);
        grid.setHgap(5);

        scene.setRoot(grid);
        final Label dollar = new Label("$");
        GridPane.setConstraints(dollar, 0, 0);
        grid.getChildren().add(dollar);

        final TextField sum = new TextField() {
            @Override
            public void replaceText(int start, int end, String text) {
                if (!text.matches("[a-z, A-Z]")) {
                    super.replaceText(start, end, text);
                }
                label.setText("Enter a numeric value");
            }
```

---

7.   8/javafx/user-interface-tutorial/custom.htm

4

```java
        @Override
        public void replaceSelection(String text) {
            if (!text.matches("[a-z, A-Z]")) {
                super.replaceSelection(text);
            }
        }
    };

    sum.setPromptText("Enter the total");
    sum.setPrefColumnCount(10);
    GridPane.setConstraints(sum, 1, 0);
    grid.getChildren().add(sum);

    Button submit = new Button("Submit");
    GridPane.setConstraints(submit, 2, 0);
    grid.getChildren().add(submit);

    submit.setOnAction(new EventHandler<ActionEvent>() {
        @Override
        public void handle(ActionEvent e) {
            label.setText(null);
        }
    });

    GridPane.setConstraints(label, 0, 1);
    GridPane.setColumnSpan(label, 3);
    grid.getChildren().add(label);

    scene.setRoot(grid);
    stage.show();
}

public static void main(String[] args) {
    launch(args);
}
}
```

Lambda Expressions

One issue with anonymous classes is that if the implementation of your anonymous class is very simple, such as an interface that contains only one method, then the syntax of anonymous classes may seem unwieldy and unclear. In these cases, you're usually trying to pass functionality as an argument to another method, such as which action should be taken when someone clicks a button. Lambda expressions enable you to do this—to treat functionality as method argument or code as data.

The previous section, "Anonymous Classes," shows you how to implement a base class without giving it a name. Although this is often more concise than a named class, for classes with only one method, even an anonymous class seems a bit excessive and cumbersome. Lambda expressions let you express instances of single-method classes more compactly.

Table 4.3 Use Case: Feature to Enable Administrator to Perform
Action on Selected Members

Field	Description
Name	Perform action on selected members
Primary actor	Administrator
Preconditions	Administrator is logged in to the system
Postconditions	Action is performed only on members that fit the specified criteria:
Main success scenario	1. Administrator specifies criteria of members on which to perform a certain action. 2. Administrator specifies an action to perform on those selected members. 3. Administrator selects the **Submit** button. 4. The system finds all members that match the specified criteria. 5. The system performs the specified action on all matching members.
Extensions	Administrator has an option to preview those members who match the specified criteria before he or she specifies the action to be performed or before selecting the **Submit** button.
Frequency of occurrence	Many times during the day

Ideal Use Case for Lambda Expressions

Suppose that you are creating a social-networking application. You want to create a feature that enables an administrator to perform any kind of action, such as sending a message, on members of the social-networking application that satisfy certain criteria. Table 4.3 describes this use case in detail.

Suppose that members of this social-networking application are represented by the following Person[8] class:

```java
public class Person {

    public enum Sex {
        MALE, FEMALE
    }

    String name;
    LocalDate birthday;
    Sex gender;
    String emailAddress;

    public int getAge() {
        // ...
    }
```

---

8.   `tutorial/java/javaOO/examples/Person.java`

```
        public void printPerson() {
            // ...
        }
    }
```

Also, suppose that the members of your social-networking application are stored in a `List<Person>` instance.

This section begins with a naive approach to this use case. It improves upon this approach with local and anonymous classes and then finishes with an efficient and concise approach using lambda expressions. Find the code excerpts described in this section in the example `RosterTest`.[9]

Approach 1: Create Methods That Search for Members That Match One Characteristic

One simplistic approach is to create several methods; each method searches for members that match one characteristic, such as gender or age. The following method prints members that are older than a specified age:

```
public static void printPersonsOlderThan(List<Person> roster, int age) {
    for (Person p : roster) {
        if (p.getAge() >= age) {
            p.printPerson();
        }
    }
}
```

> **Note**
>
> A `List`[10] is an ordered `Collection`.[11] A *collection* is an object that groups multiple elements into a single unit. Collections are used to store, retrieve, manipulate, and communicate aggregate data. For more information about collections, see Chapter 12.

This approach can potentially make your application *brittle*, which is the likelihood of an application not working because of the introduction of updates (such as newer data types). Suppose that you upgrade your application and change the structure of the `Person` class so that it contains different member variables; perhaps the class records and measures ages with a different data type or algorithm. You would have to rewrite a lot of your Application Programming Interface (API) to accommodate this change. In addition, this approach is unnecessarily restrictive; what if you wanted to print members younger than a certain age, for example?

---

9.   `tutorial/java/javaOO/examples/RosterTest.java`

10. `8/docs/api/java/util/List.html`

11. `8/docs/api/java/util/Collection.html`

Approach 2: Create More Generalized Search Methods

The following method is more generic than `printPersonsOlderThan`; it prints members within a specified range of ages:

```
public static void printPersonsWithinAgeRange(
    List<Person> roster, int low, int high) {
    for (Person p : roster) {
        if (low <= p.getAge() && p.getAge() < high) {
            p.printPerson();
        }
    }
}
```

What if you want to print members of a specified gender or a combination of a specified gender and age range? What if you decide to change the `Person` class and add other attributes such as relationship status or geographical location? Although this method is more generic than `printPersonsOlderThan`, trying to create a separate method for each possible search query can still lead to brittle code. You can instead separate the code that specifies the criteria for which you want to search into a different class.

Approach 3: Specify Search Criteria Code in a Local Class

The following method prints members that match search criteria that you specify:

```
public static void printPersons(
    List<Person> roster, CheckPerson tester) {
    for (Person p : roster) {
        if (tester.test(p)) {
            p.printPerson();
        }
    }
}
```

This method checks each `Person` instance contained in the `List` parameter `roster` to see if it satisfies the search criteria specified in the `CheckPerson` parameter `tester` by invoking the method `tester.test`. If the method `tester.test` returns a `true` value, then the method `printPersons` is invoked on the `Person` instance.

To specify the search criteria, you implement the `CheckPerson` interface:

```
interface CheckPerson {
    boolean test(Person p);
}
```

The following class implements the `CheckPerson` interface by specifying an implementation for the method `test`. This method filters members that are eligible for

Selective Service in the United States. It returns a `true` value if its `Person` parameter is male and between the ages of eighteen and twenty-five:

```
class CheckPersonEligibleForSelectiveService implements CheckPerson {
    public boolean test(Person p) {
        return p.gender == Person.Sex.MALE &&
            p.getAge() >= 18 &&
            p.getAge() <= 25;
    }
}
```

To use this class, you create a new instance of it and invoke the `printPersons` method:

```
printPersons(
    roster, new CheckPersonEligibleForSelectiveService());
```

   Although this approach is less brittle (e.g., you don't have to rewrite methods if you change the structure of the `Person`), you still have additional code: a new interface and a local class for each search you plan to perform in your application. Because `CheckPersonEligibleForSelectiveService` implements an interface, you can use an anonymous class instead of a local class and bypass the need to declare a new class for each search.

Approach 4: Specify Search Criteria Code in an Anonymous Class

One of the arguments of the following invocation of the method `printPersons` is an anonymous class that filters members that are eligible for Selective Service in the United States—those who are male and between the ages of eighteen and twenty-five:

```
printPersons(
    roster,
    new CheckPerson() {
        public boolean test(Person p) {
            return p.getGender() == Person.Sex.MALE
                && p.getAge() >= 18
                && p.getAge() <= 25;
        }
    }
);
```

This approach reduces the amount of code required because you don't have to create a new class for each search that you want to perform. However, the syntax of anonymous classes is bulky considering that the `CheckPerson` interface contains only one method. In this case, you can use a lambda expression instead of an anonymous class, as described in the next section.

Approach 5: Specify Search Criteria Code with a Lambda Expression

The CheckPerson interface is a *functional interface*. A functional interface is any interface that contains only one abstract method. (A functional interface may contain one or more default method or static method.) Because a functional interface contains only one abstract method, you can omit the name of that method when you implement it. To do this, instead of using an anonymous class expression, you use a *lambda expression*, which is boldface in the following method invocation:

```
printPersons(
    roster,
    (Person p) -> p.getGender() == Person.Sex.MALE
        && p.getAge() >= 18
        && p.getAge() <= 25
);
```

See the "Syntax of Lambda Expressions" section for information about how to define lambda expressions. You can use a standard functional interface in place of the interface CheckPerson, which reduces the amount of code required even further.

Approach 6: Use Standard Functional Interfaces with Lambda Expressions

Reconsider the CheckPerson interface:

```
interface CheckPerson {
    boolean test(Person p);
}
```

This is a very simple interface. It's a functional interface because it contains only one abstract method. This method takes one parameter and returns a boolean value. The method is so simple that it might not be worth it to define one in your application. Consequently, the JDK defines several standard functional interfaces, which you can find in the package java.util.function.[12]

For example, you can use the Predicate<T> interface in place of CheckPerson. This interface contains the method boolean test(T t):

```
interface Predicate<T> {
    boolean test(T t);
}
```

The interface Predicate<T> is an example of a generic interface. (For more information about generics, see Chapter 7.) Generic types (such as generic interfaces) specify one or more type parameters within angle brackets (<>). This interface contains only one type parameter, T. When you declare or instantiate a generic

------

12. 8/docs/api/java/util/function/package-summary.html

type with actual type arguments, you have a parameterized type. For example, the parameterized type `Predicate<Person>` is as follows:

```
interface Predicate<Person> {
    boolean test(Person t);
}
```

4

This parameterized type contains a method that has the same return type and parameters as `CheckPerson.boolean test(Person p)`. Consequently, you can use `Predicate<T>` in place of `CheckPerson`, as the following method demonstrates:

```
public static void printPersonsWithPredicate(
    List<Person> roster, Predicate<Person> tester) {
    for (Person p : roster) {
        if (tester.test(p)) {
            p.printPerson();
        }
    }
}
```

As a result, the following method invocation is the same as when you invoked `printPersons` in approach 3 to obtain members who are eligible for Selective Service:

```
printPersonsWithPredicate(
    roster,
    p -> p.getGender() == Person.Sex.MALE
        && p.getAge() >= 18
        && p.getAge() <= 25
);
```

This is not the only possible place in this method to use a lambda expression. The following approach suggests other ways to use lambda expressions.

Approach 7: Use Lambda Expressions throughout Your Application

Reconsider the method `printPersonsWithPredicate` to see where else you could use lambda expressions:

```
public static void printPersonsWithPredicate(
    List<Person> roster, Predicate<Person> tester) {
    for (Person p : roster) {
        if (tester.test(p)) {
            p.printPerson();
        }
    }
}
```

This method checks each `Person` instance contained in the `List` parameter `roster` to see if it satisfies the criteria specified in the `Predicate` parameter `tester`. If the

Person instance does satisfy the criteria specified by `tester`, the method `print-Person` is invoked on the `Person` instance.

Instead of invoking the method `printPerson`, you can specify a different action to perform on those `Person` instances that satisfy the criteria specified by `tester`. You can specify this action with a lambda expression. Suppose you want a lambda expression similar to `printPerson`—one that takes one argument (an object of type `Person`) and returns void. Remember, to use a lambda expression, you need to implement a functional interface. In this case, you need a functional interface that contains an abstract method that can take one argument of type `Person` and return void. The `Consumer<T>` interface contains the method void `accept(T t)`, which has these characteristics. The following method replaces the invocation `p.printPerson()` with an instance of `Consumer<Person>` that invokes the method accept:

```
public static void processPersons(
    List<Person> roster,
    Predicate<Person> tester,
    Consumer<Person> block) {
        for (Person p : roster) {
            if (tester.test(p)) {
                block.accept(p);
            }
        }
}
```

As a result, the following method invocation is the same as when you invoked `printPersons` in approach 3 to obtain members who are eligible for Selective Service. The lambda expression used to print members is boldface:

```
processPersons(
    roster,
    p -> p.getGender() == Person.Sex.MALE
        && p.getAge() >= 18
        && p.getAge() <= 25,
    p -> p.printPerson()
);
```

What if you want to do more with your members' profiles than printing them out? Suppose that you want to validate the members' profiles or retrieve their contact information. In this case, you need a functional interface that contains an abstract method that returns a value. The `Function<T,R>` interface contains the method R `apply(T t)`. The following method retrieves the data specified by the parameter `mapper` and then performs an action on it specified by the parameter `block`:

```
public static void processPersonsWithFunction(
    List<Person> roster,
    Predicate<Person> tester,
```

```
        Function<Person, String> mapper,
        Consumer<String> block) {
        for (Person p : roster) {
            if (tester.test(p)) {
                String data = mapper.apply(p);
                block.accept(data);
            }
        }
    }
```

The following method retrieves the email address from each member contained in roster who is eligible for Selective Service and then prints it:

```
processPersonsWithFunction(
    roster,
    p -> p.getGender() == Person.Sex.MALE
        && p.getAge() >= 18
        && p.getAge() <= 25,
    p -> p.getEmailAddress(),
    email -> System.out.println(email)
);
```

Approach 8: Use Generics More Extensively

Reconsider the method processPersonsWithFunction. The following is a generic version of it that accepts, as a parameter, a collection that contains elements of any data type:

```
public static <X, Y> void processElements(
    Iterable<X> source,
    Predicate<X> tester,
    Function <X, Y> mapper,
    Consumer<Y> block) {
    for (X p : source) {
        if (tester.test(p)) {
            Y data = mapper.apply(p);
            block.accept(data);
        }
    }
}
```

To print the email address of members who are eligible for Selective Service, invoke the processElements method as follows:

```
processElements(
    roster,
    p -> p.getGender() == Person.Sex.MALE
        && p.getAge() >= 18
        && p.getAge() <= 25,
    p -> p.getEmailAddress(),
    email -> System.out.println(email)
);
```

This method invocation performs the following actions:

1. *Obtains a source of objects from the collection* source. In this example, it obtains a source of Person objects from the collection roster. Notice that the collection roster, which is a collection of type List, is also an object of type Iterable.

2. *Filters objects that match the* Predicate *object* tester. In this example, the Predicate object is a lambda expression that specifies which members would be eligible for Selective Service.

3. *Maps each filtered object to a value as specified by the* Function *object* mapper. In this example, the Function object is a lambda expression that returns the email address of a member.

4. *Performs an action on each mapped object as specified by the* Consumer *object* block. In this example, the Consumer object is a lambda expression that prints a string, which is the email address returned by the Function object.

You can replace each of these actions with an aggregate operation.

Approach 9: Use Aggregate Operations That Accept Lambda Expressions as Parameters

The following example uses aggregate operations to print the email addresses of those members contained in the collection roster who are eligible for Selective Service:

```
roster
    .stream()
    .filter(
        p -> p.getGender() == Person.Sex.MALE
            && p.getAge() >= 18
            && p.getAge() <= 25)
    .map(p -> p.getEmailAddress())
    .forEach(email -> System.out.println(email));
```

Table 4.4 maps each of the operations the method processElements performs with the corresponding aggregate operation. The operations filter, map, and forEach are *aggregate operations*. Aggregate operations process elements from a stream, not directly from a collection (which is the reason why the first method invoked in this example is stream). A *stream* is a sequence of elements. Unlike a collection, it is not a data structure that stores elements. Instead, a stream carries values from a source, such as collection, through a pipeline. A *pipeline* is a sequence of stream operations, which in this example is filter-map-forEach. In addition, aggregate operations typically accept lambda expressions as parameters, enabling you to customize how they behave. For a more thorough discussion of aggregate operations, see Chapter 12, "Aggregate Operations."

Table 4.4 Action from processElements Method and
Corresponding Aggregate Operation

processElements action	Aggregate operation
Obtain a source of objects	Stream<E> **stream** ()
Filter objects that match a Predicate object	Stream<T> **filter** (Predicate<? super T> predicate)
Map objects to another value as specified by a Function object	<R> Stream<R> **map** (Function<? super T,? extends R> mapper)
Perform an action as specified by a Consumer object	void **forEach** (Consumer<? super T> action)

Lambda Expressions in GUI Applications

To process events in a GUI application, such as keyboard actions, mouse actions, and scroll actions, you typically create event handlers, which usually involves implementing a particular interface. Often event handler interfaces are functional interfaces; they tend to have only one method.

In the JavaFX example HelloWorld.java[13] (discussed in the previous section), you can replace the anonymous class in boldface with a lambda expression in this statement:

```
btn.setOnAction(new EventHandler<ActionEvent>() {

    @Override
    public void handle(ActionEvent event) {
        System.out.println("Hello World!");
    }
});
```

The method invocation btn.setOnAction specifies what happens when you select the button represented by the btn object. This method requires an object of type EventHandler<ActionEvent>. The EventHandler<ActionEvent> interface contains only one method, void handle(T event). This interface is a functional interface, so you could use the following boldface lambda expression to replace it:

13. 8/javafx/get-started-tutorial/hello_world.htm

```
btn.setOnAction(
    event -> System.out.println("Hello World!")
);
```

Syntax of Lambda Expressions

A lambda expression consists of the following:

- A comma-separated list of formal parameters enclosed in parentheses. The `CheckPerson.test` method contains one parameter, p, which represents an instance of the `Person` class.

> **Note**
>
> You can omit the data type of the parameters in a lambda expression. In addition, you can omit the parentheses if there is only one parameter. For example, the following lambda expression is also valid:
>
> ```
> p -> p.getGender() == Person.Sex.MALE
>     && p.getAge() >= 18
>     && p.getAge() <= 25
> ```

- The arrow token, ->
- A body, which consists of a single expression or a statement block. This example uses the following expression:

    ```
    p.getGender() == Person.Sex.MALE
        && p.getAge() >= 18
        && p.getAge() <= 25
    ```

If you specify a single expression, then the Java runtime evaluates the expression and then returns its value. Alternatively, you can use a return statement:

```
p -> {
    return p.getGender() == Person.Sex.MALE
        && p.getAge() >= 18
        && p.getAge() <= 25;
}
```

A return statement is not an expression; in a lambda expression, you must enclose statements in braces, { }. However, you do not have to enclose a void method invocation in braces. For example, the following is a valid lambda expression:

```
email -> System.out.println(email)
```

Note that a lambda expression looks a lot like a method declaration; you can consider lambda expressions as anonymous methods—methods without a name. The following example, `Calculator`, is an example of lambda expressions that take more than one formal parameter:

```
public class Calculator {

    interface IntegerMath {
        int operation(int a, int b);
    }

    public int operateBinary(int a, int b, IntegerMath op) {
        return op.operation(a, b);
    }

    public static void main(String... args) {

        Calculator myApp = new Calculator();
        IntegerMath addition = (a, b) -> a + b;
        IntegerMath subtraction = (a, b) -> a - b;
        System.out.println("40 + 2 = " +
            myApp.operateBinary(40, 2, addition));
        System.out.println("20 - 10 = " +
            myApp.operateBinary(20, 10, subtraction));
    }
}
```

The method `operateBinary` performs a mathematical operation on two integer operands. The operation itself is specified by an instance of `IntegerMath`. The example defines two operations with lambda expressions, `addition` and `subtraction`. The example prints the following:

```
40 + 2 = 42
20 - 10 = 10
```

Accessing Local Variables of the Enclosing Scope

Like local and anonymous classes, lambda expressions can capture variables; they have the same access to local variables of the enclosing scope. However, unlike local and anonymous classes, lambda expressions do not have any shadowing issues (see the "Shadowing" section for more information). Lambda expressions are lexically scoped. This means that they do not inherit any names from a supertype or introduce a new level of scoping. Declarations in a lambda expression are interpreted just as they are in the enclosing environment. The following example, `LambdaScopeTest`, demonstrates this:

```
import java.util.function.Consumer;

public class LambdaScopeTest {

    public int x = 0;

    class FirstLevel {

        public int x = 1;

        void methodInFirstLevel(int x) {
```

```
                    // The following statement causes the compiler to generate
                    // the error "local variables referenced from a lambda expression
                    // must be final or effectively final" in statement A:
                    //
                    // x = 99;

                    Consumer<Integer> myConsumer = (y) ->
                    {
                        System.out.println("x = " + x); // Statement A
                        System.out.println("y = " + y);
                        System.out.println("this.x = " + this.x);
                        System.out.println("LambdaScopeTest.this.x = " +
                            LambdaScopeTest.this.x);
                    };

                    myConsumer.accept(x);

                }
            }

        public static void main(String... args) {
            LambdaScopeTest st = new LambdaScopeTest();
            LambdaScopeTest.FirstLevel fl = st.new FirstLevel();
            fl.methodInFirstLevel(23);
        }
    }
```

This example generates the following output:

```
x = 23
y = 23
this.x = 1
LambdaScopeTest.this.x = 0
```

If you substitute the parameter x in place of y in the declaration of the lambda expression myConsumer, then the compiler generates an error:

```
Consumer<Integer> myConsumer = (x) -> {
    // ...
}
```

The compiler generates the error variable x is already defined in method methodInFirstLevel(int) because the lambda expression does not introduce a new level of scoping. Consequently, you can directly access fields, methods, and local variables of the enclosing scope. For example, the lambda expression directly accesses the parameter x of the method methodInFirstLevel. To access variables in the enclosing class, use the keyword this. In this example, this.x refers to the member variable FirstLevel.x.

However, like local and anonymous classes, a lambda expression can only access local variables and parameters of the enclosing block that are final or effectively final. For example, suppose that you add the following assignment statement imme-diately after the `methodInFirstLevel` definition statement:

```
void methodInFirstLevel(int x) {
    x = 99;
    // ...
}
```

4

Because of this assignment statement, the variable `FirstLevel.x` is not effec-tively final anymore. As a result, the Java compiler generates an error message similar to "local variables referenced from a lambda expression must be final or effectively final," where the lambda expression `myConsumer` tries to access the `FirstLevel.x` variable:

```
System.out.println("x = " + x);
```

Target Typing

How do you determine the type of a lambda expression? Recall the lambda expres-sion that selected members who are male and between the ages of eighteen and twenty-five:

```
p -> p.getGender() == Person.Sex.MALE
    && p.getAge() >= 18
    && p.getAge() <= 25
```

This lambda expression was used in the following two methods:

- `public static void printPersons(List<Person> roster, CheckPerson tester)` in approach 3
- `public void printPersonsWithPredicate(List<Person> roster, Predicate<Person> tester)` in approach 6

When the Java runtime invokes the method `printPersons`, it's expecting a data type of `CheckPerson`, so the lambda expression is of this type. However, when the Java runtime invokes the method `printPersonsWithPredicate`, it's expecting a data type of `Predicate<Person>`, so the lambda expression is of this type. The data type that these methods expect is called the *target type*. To determine the type of a lambda expression, the Java compiler uses the target type of the context or situation in which the lambda expression was found. It follows that you can only use lambda expressions in situations in which the Java compiler can determine a target type:

- Variable declarations
- Assignments

- Return statements
- Array initializers
- Method or constructor arguments
- Lambda expression bodies
- Conditional expressions, such as ? :
- Cast expressions

4

Target Types and Method Arguments

For method arguments, the Java compiler determines the target type with two other language features: overload resolution and type argument inference. Consider the following two functional interfaces (java.lang.Runnable[14] and java.util. concurrent.Callable<V>[15]):

```java
public interface Runnable {
    void run();
}

public interface Callable<V> {
    V call();
}
```

The method Runnable.run does not return a value, whereas Callable<V>.call does.

Suppose that you have overloaded the method invoke as follows (see "Defining Methods" for more information about overloading methods):

```java
void invoke(Runnable r) {
    r.run();
}

<T> T invoke(Callable<T> c) {
    return c.call();
}
```

Which method will be invoked in the following statement?

```java
String s = invoke(() -> "done");
```

The method invoke(Callable<T>) will be invoked because that method returns a value; the method invoke(Runnable) does not. In this case, the type of the lambda expression () -> "done" is Callable<T>.

---

14. 8/docs/api/java/lang/Runnable.html

15. 8/docs/api/java/util/concurrent/Callable.html

Serialization

You can serialize a lambda expression if its target type and its captured arguments are serializable. However, like inner classes, the serialization of lambda expressions is strongly discouraged.

Method References

You use lambda expressions to create anonymous methods. Sometimes, however, a lambda expression does nothing but call an existing method. In those cases, it's often clearer to refer to the existing method by name. Method references enable you to do this; they are compact, easy-to-read lambda expressions for methods that already have a name.

Consider again the `Person` class discussed previously:

```java
public class Person {

    public enum Sex {
        MALE, FEMALE
    }

    String name;
    LocalDate birthday;
    Sex gender;
    String emailAddress;

    public int getAge() {
        // ...
    }

    public Calendar getBirthday() {
        return birthday;
    }

    public static int compareByAge(Person a, Person b) {
        return a.birthday.compareTo(b.birthday);
    }}
```

Suppose that the members of your social-networking application are contained in an array and you want to sort the array by age. You could use the following code (and for the code excerpts described in this section, see the example MethodReferencesTest[16]):

```java
Person[] rosterAsArray = roster.toArray(new Person[roster.size()]);

class PersonAgeComparator implements Comparator<Person> {
    public int compare(Person a, Person b) {
```

---

16. `tutorial/java/javaOO/examples/MethodReferencesTest.java`

```
            return a.getBirthday().compareTo(b.getBirthday());
        }
    }

    Arrays.sort(rosterAsArray, new PersonAgeComparator());
```

The method signature of this invocation of `sort` is the following:

```
static <T> void sort(T[] a, Comparator<? super T> c)
```

4

Notice that the interface `Comparator` is a functional interface. Therefore, you could use a lambda expression instead of defining and then creating a new instance of a class that implements `Comparator`:

```
Arrays.sort(rosterAsArray,
    (Person a, Person b) -> {
        return a.getBirthday().compareTo(b.getBirthday());
    }
);
```

However, this method to compare the birth dates of two `Person` instances already exists as `Person.compareByAge`. You can invoke this method instead in the body of the lambda expression:

```
Arrays.sort(rosterAsArray,
    (a, b) -> Person.compareByAge(a, b)
);
```

Because this lambda expression invokes an existing method, you can use a method reference instead of a lambda expression:

```
Arrays.sort(rosterAsArray, Person::compareByAge);
```

The method reference `Person::compareByAge` is semantically the same as the lambda expression `(a, b) -> Person.compareByAge(a, b)`. Each has the following characteristics:

- Its formal parameter list is copied from `Comparator<Person>.compare`, which is `(Person, Person)`.
- Its body calls the method `Person.compareByAge`.

Kinds of Method References

There are four kinds of method references. Table 4.5 lists some examples.

Table 4.5 Kinds of Method References and Examples

Kind	Example
Reference to a static method	`ContainingClass::staticMethodName`
Reference to an instance method of a particular object	`containingObject::instanceMethodName`
Reference to an instance method of an arbitrary object of a particular type	`ContainingType::methodName`
Reference to a constructor	`ClassName::new`

Reference to a Static Method

The method reference `Person::compareByAge` is a reference to a static method.

Reference to an Instance Method of a Particular Object

The following is an example of a reference to an instance method of a particular object:

```
class ComparisonProvider {
    public int compareByName(Person a, Person b) {
        return a.getName().compareTo(b.getName());
    }

    public int compareByAge(Person a, Person b) {
        return a.getBirthday().compareTo(b.getBirthday());
    }
}
ComparisonProvider myComparisonProvider = new ComparisonProvider();
Arrays.sort(rosterAsArray, myComparisonProvider::compareByName);
```

The method reference `myComparisonProvider::compareByName` invokes the method `compareByName` that is part of the object `myComparisonProvider`. The JRE infers the method type arguments, which in this case are (`Person`, `Person`).

Reference to an Instance Method of an Arbitrary Object of a Particular Type

The following is an example of a reference to an instance method of an arbitrary object of a particular type:

```
String[] stringArray = { "Barbara", "James", "Mary", "John",
    "Patricia", "Robert", "Michael", "Linda" };
Arrays.sort(stringArray, String::compareToIgnoreCase);
```

The equivalent lambda expression for the method reference `String::compareToIgnoreCase` would have the formal parameter list (`String a, String b`), where a and b are arbitrary names used to better describe this example. The method reference would invoke the method `a.compareToIgnoreCase(b)`.

Reference to a Constructor

You can reference a constructor in the same way as a static method by using the name new. The following method copies elements from one collection to another:

```
public static <T, SOURCE extends Collection<T>, DEST extends Collection<T>>
    DEST transferElements(
        SOURCE sourceCollection,
        Supplier<DEST> collectionFactory) {

        DEST result = collectionFactory.get();
        for (T t : sourceCollection) {
            result.add(t);
        }
        return result;
}
```

The functional interface Supplier contains one method get that takes no arguments and returns an object. Consequently, you can invoke the method transfer-Elements with a lambda expression as follows:

```
Set<Person> rosterSetLambda =
    transferElements(roster, () -> { return new HashSet<>(); });
```

You can use a constructor reference in place of the lambda expression as follows:

```
Set<Person> rosterSet = transferElements(roster, HashSet::new);
```

The Java compiler infers that you want to create a HashSet collection that contains elements of type Person. Alternatively, you can specify this as follows:

```
Set<Person> rosterSet = transferElements(roster, HashSet<Person>::new);
```

When to Use Nested Classes, Local Classes, Anonymous Classes, and Lambda Expressions

Nested classes enable you to logically group classes that are only used in one place, increase the use of encapsulation, and create more readable and maintainable code. Local classes, anonymous classes, and lambda expressions also impart these advantages; however, they are intended to be used for more specific situations:

- *Local class.* Use it if you need to create more than one instance of a class, access its constructor, or introduce a new, named type (because, for example, you need to invoke additional methods later).
- *Anonymous class.* Use it if you need to declare fields or additional methods.
- *Lambda expression.* Use it under the following circumstances:

❏ You are encapsulating a single unit of behavior that you want to pass to other code. For example, you would use a lambda expression if you want a certain action performed on each element of a collection, when a process is completed, or when a process encounters an error.

❏ You need a simple instance of a functional interface and none of the preceding criteria apply (e.g., you do not need a constructor, a named type, fields, or additional methods).

▪ *Nested class.* Use it if your requirements are similar to those of a local class, you want to make the type more widely available, and you don't require access to local variables or method parameters. Use a nonstatic nested class (or inner class) if you require access to an enclosing instance's nonpublic fields and methods. Use a static nested class if you don't require this access.

Questions and Exercises: Nested Classes

Questions

1. The program `Problem.java` doesn't compile. What do you need to do to make it compile? Why?

```java
public class Problem {
    String s;
    static class Inner {
        void testMethod() {
            s = "Set from Inner";
        }
    }
}
```

2. Use the Java API documentation for the `Box`[17] class (in the `javax.swing` package) to help answer the following questions:

   a. What static nested class does `Box` define?

   b. What inner class does `Box` define?

   c. What is the superclass of `Box`'s inner class?

   d. Which of `Box`'s nested classes can you use from any class?

   e. How do you create an instance of `Box`'s `Filler` class?

Exercises

1. Get the file `Class1.java`.[18] Compile and run `Class1`. What is the output?

---

17. `8/docs/api/javax/swing/Box.html`

18. `tutorial/java/javaOO/QandE/Class1.java`

2. The following exercises involve modifying the class `DataStructure.java`, which the section "Inner Class Example" discusses.

   a. Define a method named `print(DataStructureIterator iterator)`. Invoke this method with an instance of the class `EvenIterator` so that it performs the same function as the method `printEven`.

   b. Invoke the method `print(DataStructureIterator iterator)` so that it prints elements that have an odd index value. Use an anonymous class as the method's argument instead of an instance of the interface `DataStructureIterator`.

   c. Define a method named `print(java.util.Function<Integer, Boolean> iterator)` that performs the same function as `print(DataStructure-Iterator iterator)`. Invoke this method with a lambda expression to print elements that have an even index value. Invoke this method again with a lambda expression to print elements that have an odd index value.

   d. Define two methods so that the following two statements print elements that have an even index value and elements that have an odd index value:

   ```
   DataStructure ds = new DataStructure()
   // ...
   ds.print(DataStructure::isEvenIndex);
   ds.print(DataStructure::isOddIndex);
   ```

Answers

You can find answers to these questions and exercises at `http://docs.oracle .com/javase/tutorial/java/javaOO/QandE/nested-answers.html`.

Enum Types

An *enum type* is a special data type that allows for a variable to be a set of pre-defined constants. The variable must be equal to one of the values that have been predefined for it. Common examples include compass directions (values of NORTH, SOUTH, EAST, and WEST) and the days of the week. Because they are constants, the names of an enum type's fields are in uppercase letters. In the Java programming language, you define an enum type by using the enum keyword. For example, you would specify a days-of-the-week enum type as follows:

```
public enum Day {
    SUNDAY, MONDAY, TUESDAY, WEDNESDAY,
    THURSDAY, FRIDAY, SATURDAY
}
```

You should use enum types any time you need to represent a fixed set of constants. That includes natural enum types such as the planets in our solar system and data sets where you know all possible values at compile time—for example, the choices on a menu, command-line flags, and so on.

Here is some code that shows you how to use the Day enum defined above:

```
public class EnumTest {
    Day day;

    public EnumTest(Day day) {
        this.day = day;
    }

    public void tellItLikeItIs() {
        switch (day) {
            case MONDAY:
                System.out.println("Mondays are bad.");
                break;

            case FRIDAY:
                System.out.println("Fridays are better.");
                break;

            case SATURDAY: case SUNDAY:
                System.out.println("Weekends are best.");
                break;

            default:
                System.out.println("Midweek days are so-so.");
                break;
        }
    }

    public static void main(String[] args) {
        EnumTest firstDay = new EnumTest(Day.MONDAY);
        firstDay.tellItLikeItIs();
        EnumTest thirdDay = new EnumTest(Day.WEDNESDAY);
        thirdDay.tellItLikeItIs();
        EnumTest fifthDay = new EnumTest(Day.FRIDAY);
        fifthDay.tellItLikeItIs();
        EnumTest sixthDay = new EnumTest(Day.SATURDAY);
        sixthDay.tellItLikeItIs();
        EnumTest seventhDay = new EnumTest(Day.SUNDAY);
        seventhDay.tellItLikeItIs();
    }
}
```

The output is as follows:

```
Mondays are bad.
Midweek days are so-so.
Fridays are better.
Weekends are best.
Weekends are best.
```

Java programming language enum types are much more powerful than their counterparts in other languages. The enum declaration defines a *class* (called an *enum type*). The enum class body can include methods and other fields. The compiler automatically adds some special methods when it creates an enum. For example, there is a static `values` method that returns an array containing all values of the enum in the order they are declared. This method is commonly used in combination with the `for-each` construct to iterate over the values of an enum type. For example, this code from the `Planet` class example below iterates over all the planets in the solar system:

```
for (Planet p : Planet.values()) {
    System.out.printf("Your weight on %s is %f%n",
                        p, p.surfaceWeight(mass));
}
```

> **Note**
>
> *All* enums implicitly extend `java.lang.Enum`. Because a class can only extend one parent (see the section "Declaring Classes"), the Java language does not support multiple inheritance of state (see the section "Multiple Inheritance of State, Implementation, and Type"), and therefore an enum cannot extend anything else.

In the following example, `Planet` is an enum type that represents the planets in the solar system. They are defined with constant mass and radius properties. Each enum constant is declared with values for the mass and radius parameters. These values are passed to the constructor when the constant is created. Java requires that the constants be defined first, prior to any fields or methods. Also, when there are fields and methods, the list of enum constants must end with a semicolon.

> **Note**
>
> The constructor for an enum type must be package-private or private access. It automatically creates the constants that are defined at the beginning of the enum body. You cannot invoke an enum constructor yourself.

In addition to its properties and constructor, `Planet` has methods that allow you to retrieve the surface gravity and weight of an object on each planet. Here is a sample program that takes your weight on earth (in any unit) and calculates and prints your weight on all planets (in the same unit):

```
public enum Planet {
    MERCURY (3.303e+23, 2.4397e6),
    VENUS (4.869e+24, 6.0518e6),
```

```
    EARTH   (5.976e+24, 6.37814e6),
    MARS    (6.421e+23, 3.3972e6),
    JUPITER (1.9e+27, 7.1492e7),
    SATURN  (5.688e+26, 6.0268e7),
    URANUS  (8.686e+25, 2.5559e7),
    NEPTUNE (1.024e+26, 2.4746e7);

    private final double mass;   // in kilograms
    private final double radius; // in meters
    Planet(double mass, double radius) {
        this.mass = mass;
        this.radius = radius;
    }
    private double mass()   { return mass; }
    private double radius() { return radius; }

    // universal gravitational constant (m3 kg-1 s-2)
    public static final double G = 6.67300E-11;

    double surfaceGravity() {
        return G * mass / (radius * radius);
    }
    double surfaceWeight(double otherMass) {
        return otherMass * surfaceGravity();
    }
    public static void main(String[] args) {
        if (args.length != 1) {
            System.err.println("Usage: java Planet <earth_weight>");
            System.exit(-1);
        }
        double earthWeight = Double.parseDouble(args[0]);
        double mass = earthWeight/EARTH.surfaceGravity();
        for (Planet p : Planet.values())
            System.out.printf("Your weight on %s is %f%n",
                              p, p.surfaceWeight(mass));
    }
}
```

If you run `Planet.class` from the command line with an argument of 175, you get this output:

```
$ java Planet 175
Your weight on MERCURY is 66.107583
Your weight on VENUS is 158.374842
Your weight on EARTH is 175.000000
Your weight on MARS is 66.279007
Your weight on JUPITER is 442.847567
Your weight on SATURN is 186.552719
Your weight on URANUS is 158.397260
Your weight on NEPTUNE is 199.207413
```

Questions and Exercises: Enum Types

Question

1. True or false: An Enum type can be a subclass of java.lang.String.

Exercises

1. Rewrite the class Card from the exercise in the "Questions and Exercises: Classes" section so that it represents the rank and suit of a card with enum types.
2. Rewrite the Deck class.

Answers

You can find answers to these questions and exercises at http://docs.oracle .com/javase/tutorial/java/javaOO/QandE/enum-answers.html.

5

Annotations

Chapter Contents

Annotations Basics   164
Declaring an Annotation Type   165
Predefined Annotation Types   167
Type Annotations and Pluggable Type Systems   170
Repeating Annotations   171
Questions and Exercises: Annotations   173

Annotations, a form of metadata, provide data about a program that is not part of the program itself. Annotations have no direct effect on the operation of the code they annotate. Annotations have a number of uses, such as the following:

- *Information for the compiler*. Annotations can be used by the compiler to detect errors or suppress warnings.
- *Compile-time and deployment-time processing*. Software tools can process annotation information to generate code, XML files, and so forth.
- *Runtime processing*. Some annotations are available to be examined at runtime.

This chapter explains where annotations can be used, how to apply annotations, what predefined annotation types are available in the Java SE Application Programming Interface (API), how type annotations can be used in conjunction with pluggable type systems to write code with stronger type checking, and how to implement repeating annotations.

Annotations Basics

The Format of an Annotation

In its simplest form, an annotation looks like the following:

```
@Entity
```

The at sign character (@) indicates to the compiler that what follows is an annotation. In the following example, the annotation's name is `Override`:

```
@Override
void mySuperMethod() { ... }
```

The annotation can include *elements*, which can be named or unnamed, and there are values for those elements:

```
@Author(
    name = "Benjamin Franklin",
    date = "3/27/2014"
)
class MyClass() { ... }
```

or

```
@SuppressWarnings(value = "unchecked")
void myMethod() { ... }
```

If there is just one element named `value`, then the name can be omitted:

```
@SuppressWarnings("unchecked")
void myMethod() { ... }
```

If the annotation has no elements, then the parentheses can be omitted, as shown in the previous `@Override` example. It is also possible to use multiple annotations on the same declaration:

```
@Author(name = "Jane Doe")
@EBook
class MyClass { ... }
```

If the annotations have the same type, then this is called a repeating annotation:

```
@Author(name = "Jane Doe")
@Author(name = "John Smith")
class MyClass { ... }
```

Repeating annotations are supported as of the Java SE 8 release. For more information, see the "Repeating Annotations" section.

The annotation type can be one of the types that are defined in the `java.lang` or `java.lang.annotation` packages of the Java SE API. In the previous examples, `Override` and `SuppressWarnings` are predefined Java annotations. It is also possible to define your own annotation type. The `Author` and `Ebook` annotations in the previous example are custom annotation types.

Where Annotations Can Be Used

Annotations can be applied to declarations: declarations of classes, fields, methods, and other program elements. When used on a declaration, each annotation often appears, by convention, on its own line.

As of the Java SE 8 release, annotations can also be applied to the *use* of types. Here are some examples:

- Class instance creation expression:

  ```
  new @Interned MyObject();
  ```

- Type cast:

  ```
  myString = (@NonNull String) str;
  ```

- `implements` clause:

  ```
  class UnmodifiableList<T> implements
      @Readonly List<@Readonly T> { ... }
  ```

- Thrown exception declaration:

  ```
  void monitorTemperature() throws
      @Critical TemperatureException { ... }
  ```

This form of annotation is called a *type annotation*. For more information, see the "Type Annotations and Pluggable Type Systems" section.

Declaring an Annotation Type

Many annotations replace comments in code. Suppose that a software group traditionally starts the body of every class with comments providing important information:

```
public class Generation3List extends Generation2List {

    // Author: John Doe
```

```
// Date: 3/17/2002
// Current revision: 6
// Last modified: 4/12/2004
// By: Jane Doe
// Reviewers: Alice, Bill, Cindy

// class code goes here

}
```

To add this same metadata with an annotation, you must first define the *annotation type*. The syntax for doing this is as follows:

```
@interface ClassPreamble {
    String author();
    String date();
    int currentRevision() default 1;
    String lastModified() default "N/A";
    String lastModifiedBy() default "N/A";
    // Note use of array
    String[] reviewers();
}
```

The annotation type definition looks similar to an interface definition where the keyword `interface` is preceded by the at sign (@, which is short for AT, as in annotation type). Annotation types are a form of *interface*, which will be covered later. For the moment, you do not need to understand interfaces.

The body of the previous annotation definition contains *annotation type element* declarations, which look a lot like methods. Note that they can define optional default values.

After the annotation type is defined, you can use annotations of that type, with the values filled in:

```
@ClassPreamble (
    author = "John Doe",
    date = "3/17/2002",
    currentRevision = 6,
    lastModified = "4/12/2004",
    lastModifiedBy = "Jane Doe",
    // Note array notation
    reviewers = {"Alice", "Bob", "Cindy"}
)
public class Generation3List extends Generation2List {

// class code goes here

}
```

> **Note**
>
> To make the information in `@ClassPreamble` appear in Javadoc-generated documenta-
> tion, you must annotate the `@ClassPreamble` definition with the `@Documented` an-
> notation:
>
> ```
> // import this to use @Documented
> import java.lang.annotation.*;
>
> @Documented
> @interface ClassPreamble {
>
>     // Annotation element definitions
>
> }
> ```

Predefined Annotation Types

A set of annotation types are predefined in the Java SE API. Some annotation types
are used by the Java compiler, and some apply to other annotations.

Annotation Types Used by the Java Language

The predefined annotation types defined in `java.lang` are `@Deprecated`, `@Over-`
`ride`, and `@SuppressWarnings`.

@Deprecated

The `@Deprecated` annotation indicates that the marked element is *deprecated* and
should no longer be used.[1] The compiler generates a warning whenever a program
uses a method, class, or field with the `@Deprecated` annotation. When an element
is deprecated, it should also be documented using the Javadoc `@deprecated` tag,
as shown in the following example. The use of the at sign (`@`) in both Javadoc comments and annotations is not coincidental: they are related conceptually. Also, note
that the Javadoc tag starts with a lowercase *d* and the annotation starts with an
uppercase *D*:

```
// Javadoc comment follows
/**
 * @deprecated
```

---

1.   8/docs/api/java/lang/Deprecated.html

```
 * explanation of why it was deprecated
 */
@Deprecated
static void deprecatedMethod() { }
}
```

@Override

The @Override annotation informs the compiler that the element is meant to override an element declared in a superclass.[2] Overriding methods will be discussed in Chapter 6:

```
// mark method as a superclass method
// that has been overridden
@Override
int overriddenMethod() { }
```

While it is not a requirement to use this annotation when overriding a method, it helps prevent errors. If a method marked with @Override fails to correctly override a method in one of its superclasses, the compiler generates an error.

@SuppressWarnings

The @SuppressWarnings annotation tells the compiler to suppress specific warnings that it would otherwise generate.[3] In the following example, a deprecated method is used. The compiler would typically generate a warning; in this case, however, the annotation causes the warning to be suppressed:

```
// use a deprecated method and tell
// compiler not to generate a warning
@SuppressWarnings("deprecation")
 void useDeprecatedMethod() {
     // deprecation warning
     // - suppressed
     objectOne.deprecatedMethod();
 }
```

Every compiler warning belongs to a category. The Java Language Specification lists two categories: deprecation and unchecked. The unchecked warning can occur when interfacing with legacy code written before the advent of generics. To suppress multiple categories of warnings, use the following syntax:

```
@SuppressWarnings({"unchecked", "deprecation"})
```

---

2.   8/docs/api/java/lang/Override.html

3.   8/docs/api/java/lang/SuppressWarnings.html

@SafeVarargs

The @SafeVarargs annotation, when applied to a method or constructor, asserts that the code does not perform potentially unsafe operations on its varargs parameter.[4] When this annotation type is used, unchecked warnings relating to varargs usage are suppressed.

@FunctionalInterface

The @FunctionalInterface annotation, introduced in Java SE 8, indicates that the type declaration is intended to be a functional interface, as defined by the Java Language Specification.[5]

Annotations That Apply to Other Annotations

Annotations that apply to other annotations are called *meta-annotations*. There are several meta-annotation types defined in java.lang.annotation.

@Retention

The @Retention annotation specifies how the marked annotation is stored:[6]

- RetentionPolicy.SOURCE. The marked annotation is retained only in the source level and is ignored by the compiler.
- RetentionPolicy.CLASS. The marked annotation is retained by the compiler at compile time but is ignored by the Java Virtual Machine (Java VM).
- RetentionPolicy.RUNTIME. The marked annotation is retained by the Java VM so it can be used by the runtime environment.

@Documented

The @Documented annotation indicates that whenever the specified annotation is used, those elements should be documented using the Javadoc tool.[7] (By default, annotations are not included in Javadoc.) For more information, see the Javadoc tools page.[8]

---

4. 8/docs/api/java/lang/SafeVarargs.html
5. 8/docs/api/java/lang/FunctionalInterface.html
6. 8/docs/api/java/lang/annotation/Retention.html
7. 8/docs/api/java/lang/annotation/Documented.html
8. 8/docs/technotes/guides/javadoc/index.html

@Target

The `@Target` annotation marks another annotation to restrict which kinds of Java elements the annotation can be applied to.[9] A target annotation specifies one of the following element types as its value:

- `ElementType.ANNOTATION_TYPE` can be applied to an annotation type.
- `ElementType.CONSTRUCTOR` can be applied to a constructor.
- `ElementType.FIELD` can be applied to a field or property.
- `ElementType.LOCAL_VARIABLE` can be applied to a local variable.
- `ElementType.METHOD` can be applied to a method-level annotation.
- `ElementType.PACKAGE` can be applied to a package declaration.
- `ElementType.PARAMETER` can be applied to the parameters of a method.
- `ElementType.TYPE` can be applied to any element of a class.

@Inherited

The `@Inherited` annotation indicates that the annotation type can be inherited from the super class.[10] (This is not true by default.) When the user queries the annotation type and the class has no annotation for this type, the class's superclass is queried for the annotation type. This annotation applies only to class declarations.

@Repeatable

The `@Repeatable` annotation, introduced in Java SE 8, indicates that the marked annotation can be applied more than once to the same declaration or type use.[11] For more information, see the "Repeating Annotations" section.

Type Annotations and Pluggable Type Systems

Before the Java SE 8 release, annotations could only be applied to declarations. As of the Java SE 8 release, annotations can also be applied to any *type use*. This means that annotations can be used anywhere you use a type. A few examples of where types are used are class instance creation expressions (`new`), casts, `implements` clauses, and `throws` clauses. This form of annotation is called a *type annotation*, and several examples are provided in "Annotations Basics."

Type annotations were created to support improved analysis of Java programs' way of ensuring stronger type checking. The Java SE 8 release does not provide a

---

9.   8/docs/api/java/lang/annotation/Target.html
10.   8/docs/api/java/lang/annotation/Inherited.html
11.   8/docs/api/java/lang/annotation/Repeatable.html

type-checking framework, but it allows you to write (or download) a type-checking framework that is implemented as one or more pluggable modules that are used in conjunction with the Java compiler.

For example, you want to ensure that a particular variable in your program is never assigned to null, and you want to avoid triggering a `NullPointerException`. You can write a custom plug-in to check for this. You would then modify your code to annotate that particular variable, indicating that it is never assigned to null. The variable declaration might look like this:

```
@NonNull String str;
```

When you compile the code, including the `NonNull` module at the command line, the compiler prints a warning if it detects a potential problem, allowing you to modify the code to avoid the error. After you correct the code to remove all warnings, this particular error will not occur when the program runs.

You can use multiple type-checking modules where each module checks for a different kind of error. In this way, you can build on top of the Java type system, adding specific checks when and where you want them.

With the judicious use of type annotations and the presence of pluggable type checkers, you can write code that is stronger and less prone to error. In many cases, you do not have to write your own type-checking modules. There are third parties who have done the work for you. For example, you might want to take advantage of the Checker Framework[12] created by the University of Washington. This framework includes a `NonNull` module, as well as a regular expression module, and a mutex lock module.

Repeating Annotations

There are some situations where you want to apply the same annotation to a declaration or type use. As of the Java SE 8 release, *repeating annotations* enable you to do this.

For example, you are writing code to use a timer service that enables you to run a method at a given time or on a certain schedule, similar to the `cron` service typically found on Solaris and Linux. Now you want to set a timer to run a method, `doPeriodicCleanup`, on the last day of the month and on every Friday at 11:00 p.m. To set the timer to run, create an `@Schedule` annotation and apply it twice to the `doPeriodicCleanup` method. The first use specifies the last day of the month, and the second use specifies Friday at 11 p.m., as shown in the following code example:

---

12.   `http://types.cs.washington.edu/checker-framework`

```
@Schedule(dayOfMonth="last")
@Schedule(dayOfWeek="Fri", hour="23")
public void doPeriodicCleanup() { ... }
```

The previous example applies an annotation to a method. You can repeat an annotation anywhere that you would use a standard annotation. For example, you have a class for handling unauthorized access exceptions. You annotate the class with one `@Alert` annotation for managers and another for admins:

```
@Alert(role="Manager")
@Alert(role="Administrator")
public class UnauthorizedAccessException extends SecurityException { ... }
```

For compatibility reasons, repeating annotations are stored in a *container annotation* that is automatically generated by the Java compiler. In order for the compiler to do this, two declarations are required in your code.

Step 1: Declare a Repeatable Annotation Type

The annotation type must be marked with the `@Repeatable` meta-annotation. The following example defines a custom `@Schedule` repeatable annotation type:

```
import java.lang.annotation.Repeatable;

@Repeatable(Schedules.class)
public @interface Schedule {
  String dayOfMonth() default "first";
  String dayOfWeek() default "Mon";
  int hour() default 12;
}
```

The value of the `@Repeatable` meta-annotation, in parentheses, is the type of container annotation that the Java compiler generates to store repeating annotations. In this example, the containing annotation type is `Schedules`, so repeating `@Schedule` annotations are stored in an `@Schedules` annotation. Applying the same annotation to a declaration without first declaring it to be repeatable results in a compile-time error.

Step 2: Declare the Containing Annotation Type

The containing annotation type must have a `value` element with an array type. The component type of the array type must be the repeatable annotation type. The declaration for the `Schedules` containing annotation type is the following:

```
public @interface Schedules {
    Schedule[] value();
}
```

Retrieving Annotations

There are several methods available in the Reflection API[13] that can be used to retrieve annotations. The behavior of the methods that return a single annotation, such as `AnnotatedElement.getAnnotationByType(Class<T>)`, are unchanged in that they only return a single annotation if *one* annotation of the requested type is present.[14] If more than one annotation of the requested type is present, you can obtain them by first getting their container annotation. In this way, legacy code continues to work. Other methods were introduced in Java SE 8 that scan through the container annotation to return multiple annotations at once, such as `AnnotatedElement.getAnnotations(Class<T>)`.[15] See the `AnnotatedElement` class specification for information on all the available methods.[16]

Design Considerations

When designing an annotation type, you must consider the *cardinality* of annotations of that type. It is now possible to use an annotation zero times, once, or, if the annotation's type is marked as `@Repeatable`, more than once. It is also possible to restrict where an annotation type can be used by using the `@Target` meta-annotation. For example, you can create a repeatable annotation type that can only be used on methods and fields. It is important to design your annotation type carefully to ensure that the programmer *using* the annotation finds it as flexible and powerful as possible.

Questions and Exercises: Annotations

Questions

1. What is wrong with the following interface?

```java
public interface House {
    @Deprecated
    void open();
    void openFrontDoor();
    void openBackDoor();
}
```

2. Consider this implementation of the `House` interface, shown in question 1.

---

13. `tutorial/reflect`

14. `8/docs/api/java/lang/reflect/AnnotatedElement.html#getAnnotationByType
    -java.lang.Class-`

15. `8/docs/api/java/lang/reflect/AnnotatedElement.html#getAnnotations
    -java.lang.Class-`

16. `8/docs/api/java/lang/reflect/AnnotatedElement.html`

```
public class MyHouse implements House {
    public void open() {}
    public void openFrontDoor() {}
    public void openBackDoor() {}
}
```

If you compile this program, the compiler produces a warning because open was deprecated (in the interface). What can you do to get rid of that warning?

3. Will the following code compile without error? Why or why not?

```
public @interface Meal { ... }

@Meal("breakfast", mainDish="cereal")
@Meal("lunch", mainDish="pizza")
@Meal("dinner", mainDish="salad")
public void evaluateDiet() { ... }
```

Exercise

1. Define an annotation type for an enhancement request with elements id, synopsis, engineer, and date. Specify the default value as unassigned for engineer and unknown for date.

Answers

You can find answers to these questions and exercises at http://docs.oracle .com/javase/tutorial/java/annotations/QandE/answers.html.

6

Interfaces and Inheritance

Chapter Contents
Interfaces   175
Inheritance   193

You saw an example of implementing an interface in the previous chapters. You can read more about interfaces in the first section of this chapter—what they are for, why you might want to write one, and how to write one. The second section of this chapter describes the way in which you can derive one class from another—that is, how a *subclass* can inherit fields and methods from a *superclass*. You will learn that all classes are derived from the Object class and how to modify the methods that a subclass inherits from superclasses. This section also covers interface-like *abstract classes*. Each section ends with questions and exercises to test your understanding.

Interfaces

There are a number of situations in software engineering when it is important for disparate groups of programmers to agree to a "contract" that spells out how their software interacts. Each group should be able to write their code without any knowledge of how the other group's code is written. Generally speaking, *interfaces* are such contracts.

For example, imagine a futuristic society where computer-controlled robotic cars transport passengers through city streets without a human operator. Automobile manufacturers write software (Java, of course) that operates the automobile—stop, start, accelerate, turn left, and so forth. Another industrial group, electronic guidance instrument manufacturers, makes computer systems that receive GPS (global positioning system) position data and wireless transmission of traffic conditions and use that information to drive the car.

The auto manufacturers must publish an industry standard interface that spells out in detail which methods can be invoked to make the car move (any car, from any manufacturer). The guidance manufacturers can then write software that invokes the methods described in the interface to command the car. Neither industrial group needs to know *how* the other group's software is implemented. In fact, each group considers its software highly proprietary and reserves the right to modify it at any time, as long as it continues to adhere to the published interface.

6

Interfaces in Java

In the Java programming language, an *interface* is a reference type, similar to a class, that can contain *only* constants, method signatures, default methods, static methods, and nested types. Method bodies exist only for default methods and static methods. Interfaces cannot be instantiated—they can only be *implemented* by classes or *extended* by other interfaces. Extension is discussed later in this chapter.

Defining an interface is similar to creating a new class:

```
public interface OperateCar {

    // constant declarations, if any

    // method signatures

    // An enum with values RIGHT, LEFT
    int turn(Direction direction,
            double radius,
            double startSpeed,
            double endSpeed);
    int changeLanes(Direction direction,
                   double startSpeed,
                   double endSpeed);
    int signalTurn(Direction direction,
                  boolean signalOn);
    int getRadarFront(double distanceToCar,
                     double speedOfCar);
    int getRadarRear(double distanceToCar,
                    double speedOfCar);
        ......
    // more method signatures
}
```

Note that the method signatures have no braces and are terminated with a semicolon.

To use an interface, you write a class that *implements* the interface. When an instantiable class implements an interface, it provides a method body for each of the methods declared in the interface. For example,

```
public class OperateBMW760i implements OperateCar {

    // the OperateCar method signatures, with implementation --
    // for example:
    int signalTurn(Direction direction, boolean signalOn) {
        // code to turn BMW's LEFT turn indicator lights on
        // code to turn BMW's LEFT turn indicator lights off
        // code to turn BMW's RIGHT turn indicator lights on
        // code to turn BMW's RIGHT turn indicator lights off
    }

    // other members, as needed -- for example, helper classes not
    // visible to clients of the interface
}
```

6

In the robotic car example above, it is the automobile manufacturers who will implement the interface. Chevrolet's implementation will be substantially different from that of Toyota, of course, but both manufacturers will adhere to the same interface. The guidance manufacturers, who are the clients of the interface, will build systems that use GPS data on a car's location, digital street maps, and traffic data to drive the car. In so doing, the guidance systems will invoke the interface methods: turn, change lanes, brake, accelerate, and so forth.

Interfaces as APIs

The robotic car example shows an interface being used as an industry standard Application Programming Interface (API). APIs are also common in commercial software products. Typically, a company sells a software package that contains complex methods that another company wants to use in its own software product. An example would be a package of digital image processing methods that are sold to companies making end-user graphics programs. The image processing company writes its classes to implement an interface, which it makes public to its customers. The graphics company then invokes the image processing methods using the signatures and return types defined in the interface. While the image processing company's API is made public (to its customers), its implementation of the API is kept as a closely guarded secret—in fact, it may revise the implementation at a later date as long as it continues to implement the original interface that its customers have relied on.

Defining an Interface

An interface declaration consists of modifiers, the keyword interface, the interface name, a comma-separated list of parent interfaces (if any), and the interface body. Here is an example:

```
public interface GroupedInterface extends Interface1, Interface2, Interface3 {

    // constant declarations

    // base of natural logarithms
    double E = 2.718282;

    // method signatures
    void doSomething (int i, double x);
    int doSomethingElse(String s);
}
```

6

The `public` access specifier indicates that the interface can be used by any class in any package. If you do not specify that the interface is public, then your interface is accessible only to classes defined in the same package as the interface.

An interface can extend other interfaces, just as a class can extend or subclass another class. However, whereas a class can extend only one other class, an interface can extend any number of interfaces. The interface declaration includes a comma-separated list of all the interfaces that it extends.

The Interface Body

The interface body can contain abstract methods, default methods, and static methods. An abstract method within an interface is followed by a semicolon but no braces (because an abstract method does not contain an implementation). Default methods are defined with the `default` modifier, and static methods are defined with the `static` keyword. All abstract, default, and static methods in an interface are implicitly `public`, so you can omit the `public` modifier.

In addition, an interface can contain constant declarations. All constant values defined in an interface are implicitly `public`, `static`, and `final`. Once again, you can omit these modifiers.

Implementing an Interface

To declare a class that implements an interface, you include an `implements` clause in the class declaration. Your class can implement more than one interface, so the `implements` keyword is followed by a comma-separated list of the interfaces implemented by the class. By convention, the `implements` clause follows the `extends` clause, if there is one.

A Sample Interface, Relatable

Consider an interface that defines how to compare the size of objects:

```
public interface Relatable {

    // this (object calling isLargerThan)
```

```
    // and other must be instances of
    // the same class returns 1, 0, -1
    // if this is greater than,
    // equal to, or less than other
    public int isLargerThan(Relatable other);
}
```

If you want to be able to compare the size of similar objects, no matter what they are, the class that instantiates them should implement `Relatable`.

Any class can implement `Relatable` if there is some way to compare the relative "size" of objects instantiated from the class. For strings, it could be number of characters; for books, it could be number of pages; for students, it could be weight; and so forth. For planar geometric objects, area would be a good choice (see the `RectanglePlus` class that follows), while volume would work for three-dimensional geometric objects. All such classes can implement the `isLarger-Than()` method.

If you know that a class implements `Relatable`, then you know that you can compare the size of the objects instantiated from that class.

Implementing the Relatable Interface

Here is the `Rectangle` class that was presented in Chapter 4, "Creating Objects," rewritten to implement `Relatable`:

```
public class RectanglePlus
    implements Relatable {
    public int width = 0;
    public int height = 0;
    public Point origin;

    // four constructors
    public RectanglePlus() {
        origin = new Point(0, 0);
    }
    public RectanglePlus(Point p) {
        origin = p;
    }
    public RectanglePlus(int w, int h) {
        origin = new Point(0, 0);
        width = w;
        height = h;
    }
    public RectanglePlus(Point p, int w, int h) {
        origin = p;
        width = w;
        height = h;
    }

    // a method for moving the rectangle
    public void move(int x, int y) {
        origin.x = x;
        origin.y = y;
    }
```

```
        // a method for computing
        // the area of the rectangle
        public int getArea() {
            return width * height;
        }

        // a method required to implement
        // the Relatable interface
        public int isLargerThan(Relatable other) {
            RectanglePlus otherRect
                = (RectanglePlus)other;
            if (this.getArea() < otherRect.getArea())
                return -1;
            else if (this.getArea() > otherRect.getArea())
                return 1;
            else
                return 0;
        }
    }
```

Because `RectanglePlus` implements `Relatable`, the size of any two `RectanglePlus` objects can be compared.

> **Note**
>
> The `isLargerThan` method, as defined in the `Relatable` interface, takes an object of type `Relatable`. The line of code, shown in bold in the previous example, casts `other` to a `RectanglePlus` instance. Type casting (see the "Casting Objects" section for more information) tells the compiler what the object really is. Invoking `getArea` directly on the `other` instance (`other.getArea()`) would fail to compile because the compiler does not understand that `other` is actually an instance of `RectanglePlus`.

Using an Interface as a Type

When you define a new interface, you are defining a new reference data type. You can use interface names anywhere you can use any other data type name. If you define a reference variable whose type is an interface, any object you assign to it *must* be an instance of a class that implements the interface.

As an example, here is a method for finding the largest object in a pair of objects, for *any* objects that are instantiated from a class that implements `Relatable`:

```
    public Object findLargest(Object object1, Object object2) {
        Relatable obj1 = (Relatable)object1;
        Relatable obj2 = (Relatable)object2;
        if ((obj1).isLargerThan(obj2) > 0)
            return object1;
        else
            return object2;
    }
```

Casting object1 to a Relatable type (see the "Casting Objects" section for more information) can invoke the isLargerThan method.

If you make a point of implementing Relatable in a wide variety of classes, the objects instantiated from *any* of those classes can be compared with the findLargest() method—provided that both objects are of the same class. Similarly, they can all be compared with the following methods:

```
public Object findSmallest(Object object1, Object object2) {
    Relatable obj1 = (Relatable)object1;
    Relatable obj2 = (Relatable)object2;
    if ((obj1).isLargerThan(obj2) < 0)
        return object1;
    else
        return object2;
}

public boolean isEqual(Object object1, Object object2) {
    Relatable obj1 = (Relatable)object1;
    Relatable obj2 = (Relatable)object2;
    if ( (obj1).isLargerThan(obj2) == 0)
        return true;
    else
        return false;
}
```

These methods work for any "relatable" objects, no matter what their class inheritance is. When they implement Relatable, they can be of both their own class (or superclass) type and a Relatable type. This gives them some of the advantages of multiple inheritance, where they can have behavior from both a superclass and an interface.

Evolving Interfaces

Consider an interface that you have developed called DoIt:

```
public interface DoIt {
    void doSomething(int i, double x);
    int doSomethingElse(String s);
}
```

Suppose that, at a later time, you want to add a third method to DoIt so that the interface is as follows:

```
public interface DoIt {

    void doSomething(int i, double x);
    int doSomethingElse(String s);
    boolean didItWork(int i, double x, String s);

}
```

If you make this change, then all classes that implement the old `DoIt` interface will break because they no longer implement the old interface. Programmers relying on this interface will protest loudly.

Try to anticipate all uses for your interface and specify it completely from the beginning. If you want to add additional methods to an interface, you have several options. You could create a `DoItPlus` interface that extends `DoIt`:

```
public interface DoItPlus extends DoIt {

    boolean didItWork(int i, double x, String s);

}
```

Now users of your code can choose to continue to use the old interface or upgrade to the new interface.

Alternatively, you can define your new methods as default methods. The following example defines a default method named `didItWork`:

```
public interface DoIt {

    void doSomething(int i, double x);
    int doSomethingElse(String s);
    default boolean didItWork(int i, double x, String s) {
        // Method body
    }

}
```

Note that you must provide an implementation for default methods. You could also define new static methods to existing interfaces. Users who have classes that implement interfaces enhanced with new default or static methods do not have to modify or recompile them to accommodate the additional methods.

Default Methods

The beginning of this section includes an example that involves manufacturers of computer-controlled cars who publish industry-standard interfaces that describe which methods can be invoked to operate their cars. What if those computer-controlled car manufacturers add new functionality, such as flight, to their cars? These manufacturers would need to specify new methods to enable other companies (such as electronic guidance instrument manufacturers) to adapt their software to flying cars. Where would these car manufacturers declare these new flight-related methods? If they add them to their original interfaces, then programmers who have implemented those interfaces would have to rewrite their implementations. If they add them as static methods, then programmers would regard them as utility methods, not as essential, core methods.

Default methods enable you to add new functionality to the interfaces of your libraries and ensure binary compatibility with code written for older versions of those interfaces.

Consider the following interface, `TimeClient`:[1]

```java
import java.time.*;

public interface TimeClient {
    void setTime(int hour, int minute, int second);
    void setDate(int day, int month, int year);
    void setDateAndTime(int day, int month, int year,
                            int hour, int minute, int second);
    LocalDateTime getLocalDateTime();
}
```

The following class, `SimpleTimeClient`, implements `TimeClient`:

```java
package defaultmethods;

import java.time.*;
import java.lang.*;
import java.util.*;

public class SimpleTimeClient implements TimeClient {

    private LocalDateTime dateAndTime;

    public SimpleTimeClient() {
        dateAndTime = LocalDateTime.now();
    }

    public void setTime(int hour, int minute, int second) {
        LocalDate currentDate = LocalDate.from(dateAndTime);
        LocalTime timeToSet = LocalTime.of(hour, minute, second);
        dateAndTime = LocalDateTime.of(currentDate, timeToSet);
    }

    public void setDate(int day, int month, int year) {
        LocalDate dateToSet = LocalDate.of(day, month, year);
        LocalTime currentTime = LocalTime.from(dateAndTime);
        dateAndTime = LocalDateTime.of(dateToSet, currentTime);
    }

    public void setDateAndTime(int day, int month, int year,
                            int hour, int minute, int second) {
        LocalDate dateToSet = LocalDate.of(day, month, year);
        LocalTime timeToSet = LocalTime.of(hour, minute, second);
        dateAndTime = LocalDateTime.of(dateToSet, timeToSet);
    }
```

---

1.   tutorial/java/IandI/QandE/interfaces-answers.html

```
        public LocalDateTime getLocalDateTime() {
            return dateAndTime;
        }

        public String toString() {
            return dateAndTime.toString();
        }

        public static void main(String... args) {
            TimeClient myTimeClient = new SimpleTimeClient();
            System.out.println(myTimeClient.toString());
        }
    }
```

6

Suppose that you want to add new functionality to the `TimeClient` interface, such as the ability to specify a time zone through a `ZonedDateTime`[2] object (which is like a `LocalDateTime`[3] object, except it stores time zone information):

```
public interface TimeClient {
    void setTime(int hour, int minute, int second);
    void setDate(int day, int month, int year);
    void setDateAndTime(int day, int month, int year,
        int hour, int minute, int second);
    LocalDateTime getLocalDateTime();
    ZonedDateTime getZonedDateTime(String zoneString);
}
```

Following this modification to the `TimeClient` interface, you would also have to modify the class `SimpleTimeClient` and implement the method `getZonedDateTime`. However, rather than leaving `getZonedDateTime` as `abstract` (as in the previous example), you can instead define a *default implementation*. (Remember that an abstract method is a method declared without an implementation.)

```
package defaultmethods;

import java.time.*;

public interface TimeClient {
    void setTime(int hour, int minute, int second);
    void setDate(int day, int month, int year);
    void setDateAndTime(int day, int month, int year,
                        int hour, int minute, int second);
    LocalDateTime getLocalDateTime();

    static ZoneId getZoneId (String zoneString) {
        try {
            return ZoneId.of(zoneString);
        } catch (DateTimeException e) {
```

---

2.   8/docs/api/java/time/ZonedDateTime.html

3.   8/docs/api/java/time/LocalDateTime.html

```
            System.err.println("Invalid time zone: " + zoneString +
                "; using default time zone instead.");
            return ZoneId.systemDefault();
        }
    }

    default ZonedDateTime getZonedDateTime(String zoneString) {
        return ZonedDateTime.of(getLocalDateTime(), getZoneId(zoneString));
    }
}
```

You specify that a method definition in an interface is a default method with the default keyword at the beginning of the method signature. All method declarations in an interface, including default methods, are implicitly public, so you can omit the public modifier.

With this interface, you do not have to modify the class SimpleTimeClient, and this class (and any class that implements the interface TimeClient) will have the method getZonedDateTime already defined. The following example, TestSimpleTimeClient, invokes the method getZonedDateTime from an instance of SimpleTimeClient:

```
package defaultmethods;

import java.time.*;
import java.lang.*;
import java.util.*;

public class TestSimpleTimeClient {
    public static void main(String... args) {
        TimeClient myTimeClient = new SimpleTimeClient();
        System.out.println("Current time: " + myTimeClient.toString());
        System.out.println("Time in California: " +
            myTimeClient.getZonedDateTime("Blah blah").toString());
    }
}
```

Extending Interfaces That Contain Default Methods

When you extend an interface that contains a default method, you can do the following:

- Not mention the default method at all, which lets your extended interface inherit the default method.
- Redeclare the default method, which makes it abstract.
- Redefine the default method, which overrides it.

Suppose that you extend the interface TimeClient as follows:

```
public interface AnotherTimeClient extends TimeClient { }
```

Any class that implements the interface `AnotherTimeClient` will have the implementation specified by the default method `TimeClient.getZonedDateTime`.

Suppose that you extend the interface `TimeClient` as follows:

```
public interface AbstractZoneTimeClient extends TimeClient {
    public ZonedDateTime getZonedDateTime(String zoneString);
}
```

Any class that implements the interface `AbstractZoneTimeClient` will have to implement the method `getZonedDateTime`; this method is an `abstract` method like all other nondefault (and nonstatic) methods in an interface.

Suppose that you extend the interface `TimeClient` as follows:

```
public interface HandleInvalidTimeZoneClient extends TimeClient {
    default public ZonedDateTime getZonedDateTime(String zoneString) {
        try {
            return ZonedDateTime.of(getLocalDateTime(),ZoneId.of(zoneString));
        } catch (DateTimeException e) {
            System.err.println("Invalid zone ID: " + zoneString +
                "; using the default time zone instead.");
            return ZonedDateTime.of(getLocalDateTime(),ZoneId.systemDefault());
        }
    }
}
```

Any class that implements the interface `HandleInvalidTimeZoneClient` will use the implementation of `getZonedDateTime` specified by this interface instead of the one specified by the interface `TimeClient`.

Static Methods

In addition to default methods, you can define static methods in interfaces. (A static method is a method that is associated with the class in which it is defined rather than with any object. Every instance of the class shares its static methods.) This makes it easier for you to organize helper methods in your libraries; you can keep static methods specific to an interface in the same interface rather than in a separate class. The following example defines a static method that retrieves a `ZoneId` object corresponding to a time zone identifier; it uses the system default time zone if there is no `ZoneId` object corresponding to the given identifier.[4] (As a result, you can simplify the method `getZonedDateTime`):

---

4.   8/docs/api/java/time/ZoneId.html

```
public interface TimeClient {
    // ...
    static public ZoneId getZoneId (String zoneString) {
        try {
            return ZoneId.of(zoneString);
        } catch (DateTimeException e) {
            System.err.println("Invalid time zone: " + zoneString +
                "; using default time zone instead.");
            return ZoneId.systemDefault();
        }
    }

    default public ZonedDateTime getZonedDateTime(String zoneString) {
        return ZonedDateTime.of(getLocalDateTime(), getZoneId(zoneString));
    }
}
```

Like static methods in classes, you specify that a method definition in an interface is a static method with the static keyword at the beginning of the method signature. All method declarations in an interface, including static methods, are implicitly public, so you can omit the public modifier.

Integrating Default Methods into Existing Libraries

Default methods enable you to add new functionality to existing interfaces and ensure binary compatibility with code written for older versions of those interfaces. In particular, default methods enable you to add methods that accept lambda expressions as parameters to existing interfaces. This section demonstrates how the Comparator[5] interface has been enhanced with default and static methods.

Consider the Card and Deck classes described in Chapter 4, "Questions and Exercises: Classes." This example rewrites the Card and Deck classes as interfaces. The Card interface contains two enum types (Suit and Rank) and two abstract methods (getSuit and getRank):

```
package defaultmethods;

public interface Card extends Comparable<Card> {

    public enum Suit {
        DIAMONDS (1, "Diamonds"),
        CLUBS    (2, "Clubs"   ),
        HEARTS   (3, "Hearts"  ),
        SPADES   (4, "Spades"  );

        private final int value;
        private final String text;
        Suit(int value, String text) {
            this.value = value;
            this.text = text;
```

---

5.   8/docs/api/java/util/Comparator.html

```
        }
        public int value() {return value;}
        public String text() {return text;}
    }

    public enum Rank {
        DEUCE   (2 , "Two"  ),
        THREE   (3 , "Three"),
        FOUR    (4 , "Four" ),
        FIVE    (5 , "Five" ),
        SIX     (6 , "Six"  ),
        SEVEN   (7 , "Seven"),
        EIGHT   (8 , "Eight"),
        NINE    (9 , "Nine" ),
        TEN     (10, "Ten"  ),
        JACK    (11, "Jack" ),
        QUEEN   (12, "Queen"),
        KING    (13, "King" ),
        ACE     (14, "Ace"  );
        private final int value;
        private final String text;
        Rank(int value, String text) {
            this.value = value;
            this.text = text;
        }
        public int value() {return value;}
        public String text() {return text;}
    }

    public Card.Suit getSuit();
    public Card.Rank getRank();
}
```

The Deck interface contains various methods that manipulate cards in a deck:

```
package defaultmethods;

import java.util.*;
import java.util.stream.*;
import java.lang.*;

public interface Deck {

    List<Card> getCards();
    Deck deckFactory();
    int size();
    void addCard(Card card);
    void addCards(List<Card> cards);
    void addDeck(Deck deck);
    void shuffle();
    void sort();
    void sort(Comparator<Card> c);
    String deckToString();

    Map<Integer, Deck> deal(int players, int numberOfCards)
        throws IllegalArgumentException;

}
```

The class `PlayingCard` implements the interface `Card`, and the class `StandardDeck` implements the interface `Deck`. The class `StandardDeck` implements the abstract method `Deck.sort` as follows:

```
public class StandardDeck implements Deck {

    private List<Card> entireDeck;
    // ...
    // ...

    public void sort() {
        Collections.sort(entireDeck);
    }

    // ...
}
```

The method `Collections.sort` sorts an instance of `List` whose element type implements the interface `Comparable`.[6] The member `entireDeck` is an instance of `List`, whose elements are of the type `Card`, which extends `Comparable`. The class `PlayingCard` implements the `Comparable.compareTo`[7] method as follows:

```
public int hashCode() {
    return ((suit.value()-1)*13)+rank.value();
}

public int compareTo(Card o) {
    return this.hashCode() - o.hashCode();
}
```

The method `compareTo` causes the method `StandardDeck.sort()` to sort the deck of cards first by suit and then by rank.

What if you want to sort the deck first by rank and then by suit? You would need to implement the `Comparator`[8] interface to specify new sorting criteria and use the method `sort(List<T> list, Comparator<? super T> c)`[9] (the version of the sort method that includes a `Comparator` parameter). You can define the following method in the class `StandardDeck`:

```
public void sort(Comparator<Card> c) {
    Collections.sort(entireDeck, c);
}
```

---

6.   8/docs/api/java/lang/Comparable.html

7.   8/docs/api/java/lang/Comparable.html#compareTo-T-

8.   8/docs/api/java/util/Comparator.html

9.   8/docs/api/java/util/Collections.html#sort-java.util.List-java.util
      .Comparator-

With this method, you can specify how the method `Collections.sort` sorts instances of the `Card` class. One way to do this is to implement the `Comparator` interface to specify how you want the cards sorted. The example `SortByRankThenSuit` does this:

```
package defaultmethods;

import java.util.*;
import java.util.stream.*;
import java.lang.*;

public class SortByRankThenSuit implements Comparator<Card> {
    public int compare(Card firstCard, Card secondCard) {
        int compVal =
            firstCard.getRank().value() - secondCard.getRank().value();
        if (compVal != 0)
            return compVal;
        else
            return firstCard.getSuit().value() - secondCard.getSuit().value();
    }
}
```

The following invocation sorts the deck of playing cards first by rank and then by suit:

```
StandardDeck myDeck = new StandardDeck();
myDeck.shuffle();
myDeck.sort(new SortByRankThenSuit());
```

However, this approach is too verbose; it would be better if you could specify *what* you want to sort, not *how* you want to sort. Suppose that you are the developer who wrote the `Comparator` interface. What default or static methods could you add to the `Comparator` interface to enable other developers to more easily specify sort criteria?

To start, suppose that you want to sort the deck of playing cards by rank, regardless of suit. You can invoke the `StandardDeck.sort` method as follows:

```
StandardDeck myDeck = new StandardDeck();
myDeck.shuffle();
myDeck.sort(
    (firstCard, secondCard) ->
        firstCard.getRank().value() - secondCard.getRank().value()
);
```

Because the interface `Comparator` is a functional interface, you can use a lambda expression as an argument for the `sort` method. In this example, the lambda expression compares two integer values.

It would be simpler for your developers if they could create a `Comparator` instance by invoking the method `Card.getRank` only. In particular, it would be helpful if your developers could create a `Comparator` instance that compares any object that can return a numerical value from a method such as getValue or hashCode. The Comparator interface has been enhanced with this ability with the static method comparing:[10]

```
myDeck.sort(Comparator.comparing((card) -> card.getRank()));
```

In this example, you can use a method reference instead:

```
myDeck.sort(Comparator.comparing(Card::getRank));
```

This invocation better demonstrates *what* to sort rather than *how* to do it.

The Comparator interface has been enhanced with other versions of the static method comparing, such as comparingDouble[11] and comparingLong,[12] that enable you to create Comparator instances that compare other data types.

Suppose that your developers would like to create a Comparator instance that could compare objects with multiple criteria. For example, how would you sort the deck of playing cards first by rank and then by suit? As before, you could use a lambda expression to specify these criteria for sorting the cards:

```
StandardDeck myDeck = new StandardDeck();
myDeck.shuffle();
myDeck.sort(
    (firstCard, secondCard) -> {
        int compare =
            firstCard.getRank().value() - secondCard.getRank().value();
        if (compare != 0)
            return compare;
        else
            return firstCard.getSuit().value() - secondCard.getSuit().value();
    }
);
```

It would be simpler for your developers if they could build a Comparator instance from a series of Comparator instances. The Comparator interface has been enhanced with this ability with the default method thenComparing:[13]

```
myDeck.sort(
    Comparator
```

---

10. 8/docs/api/java/util/Comparator.html#comparing-java.util.function
     .Function-java.util.Comparator-

11. 8/docs/api/java/util/Comparator.html#comparingDouble-java.util
     .function.ToDoubleFunction-java.util.Comparator-

12. 8/docs/api/java/util/Comparator.html#comparingLong-java.util.function
     .ToLongFunction-

13. 8/docs/api/java/util/Comparator.html#thenComparing-java.util
     .Comparator-

```
.comparing(Card::getRank)
.thenComparing(Comparator.comparing(Card::getSuit)));
```

The `Comparator` interface has been enhanced with other versions of the default method `thenComparing` (such as `thenComparingDouble`[14] and `thenComparing-Long`[15]) that enable you to build `Comparator` instances that compare other data types.

Suppose that your developers would like to create a `Comparator` instance that enables them to sort a collection of objects in reverse order. For example, how would you sort the deck of playing cards by descending order of rank, from ace to two (instead of from two to ace)? As before, you could specify another lambda expression. However, it would be simpler for your developers if they could reverse an existing `Comparator` by invoking a method. The `Comparator` interface has been enhanced with this ability with the default method `reversed`:[16]

```
myDeck.sort(
    Comparator.comparing(Card::getRank)
        .reversed()
        .thenComparing(Comparator.comparing(Card::getSuit)));
```

This example demonstrates how the `Comparator` interface has been enhanced with default methods, static methods, lambda expressions, and method references to create more expressive library methods whose functionality programmers can quickly deduce by looking at how they are invoked. Use these constructs to enhance the interfaces in your libraries.

Summary of Interfaces

An interface declaration can contain method signatures, default methods, static methods, and constant definitions. The only methods that have implementations are default and static methods. A class that implements an interface must implement all the methods declared in the interface. An interface name can be used anywhere a type can be used.

Questions and Exercises: Interfaces

Questions

1. What methods would a class that implements the `java.lang.CharSequence` interface have to implement?

---

14. `8/docs/api/java/util/Comparator.html#thenComparingDouble-java.util.function.ToDoubleFunction-`

15. `8/docs/api/java/util/Comparator.html#thenComparingLong-java.util.function.ToLongFunction-`

16. `8/docs/api/java/util/Comparator.html#reversed--`

2. What is wrong with the following interface?

```java
public interface SomethingIsWrong {
    void aMethod(int aValue){
        System.out.println("Hi Mom");
    }
}
```

3. Fix the interface in question 2.

4. Is the following interface valid?

```java
public interface Marker {
}
```

6

Exercises

1. Write a class that implements the `CharSequence` interface found in the `java.lang` package. Your implementation should return the string backward. Select one of the sentences from this book to use as the data. Write a small `main` method to test your class; make sure to call all four methods.

2. Suppose you have written a time server that periodically notifies its clients of the current date and time. Write an interface the server could use to enforce a particular protocol on its clients.

Answers

You can find answers to these questions and exercises at `http://docs.oracle` `.com/javase/tutorial/java/IandI/QandE/interfaces-answers.html`.

Inheritance

In the preceding sections, you have seen *inheritance* mentioned several times. In the Java language, classes can be *derived* from other classes, thereby *inheriting* fields and methods from those classes.

Definition

A class that is derived from another class is called a *subclass* (also a *derived class*, *extended class*, or *child class*). The class from which the subclass is derived is called a *superclass* (also a *base class* or a *parent class*). Except for `Object`, which has no superclass, every class has one and only one direct superclass (single inheritance). In the absence of any other explicit superclass, every class is implicitly a subclass of `Object`. Classes can be derived from classes that are derived from classes that are derived from classes, and so on, ultimately derived from the topmost class, `Object`. Such a class is said to be *descended* from all the classes in the inheritance chain stretching back to `Object`.

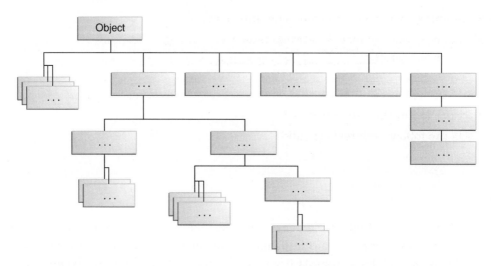

Figure 6.1 All Classes in the Java Platform Are Descendants of Object

The idea of inheritance is simple but powerful: When you want to create a new class and there is already a class that includes some of the code that you want, you can derive your new class from the existing class. In doing this, you can reuse the fields and methods of the existing class without having to write (and debug!) them yourself.

A subclass inherits all the *members* (fields, methods, and nested classes) from its superclass. Constructors are not members, so they are not inherited by subclasses, but the constructor of the superclass can be invoked from the subclass.

The Java Platform Class Hierarchy

The Object[17] class, defined in the `java.lang` package, defines and implements behavior common to all classes—including the ones that you write. In the Java platform, many classes derive directly from `Object`, other classes derive from some of those classes, and so on, forming a hierarchy of classes.

At the top of the hierarchy, `Object` is the most general of all classes. Classes near the bottom of the hierarchy provide more specialized behavior.

---

17. `8/docs/api/java/lang/Object.html`

An Example of Inheritance

Here is the sample code for a possible implementation of a `Bicycle` class that was presented in Chapter 4:

```java
public class Bicycle {

    // the Bicycle class has three fields
    public int cadence;
    public int gear;
    public int speed;

    // the Bicycle class has one constructor
    public Bicycle(int startCadence, int startSpeed, int startGear) {
        gear = startGear;
        cadence = startCadence;
        speed = startSpeed;
    }

    // the Bicycle class has four methods
    public void setCadence(int newValue) {
        cadence = newValue;
    }

    public void setGear(int newValue) {
        gear = newValue;
    }

    public void applyBrake(int decrement) {
        speed -= decrement;
    }

    public void speedUp(int increment) {
        speed += increment;
    }

}
```

A class declaration for a `MountainBike` class that is a subclass of `Bicycle` might look like this:

```java
public class MountainBike extends Bicycle {

    // the MountainBike subclass adds one field
    public int seatHeight;

    // the MountainBike subclass has one constructor
    public MountainBike(int startHeight,
                        int startCadence,
                        int startSpeed,
                        int startGear) {
        super(startCadence, startSpeed, startGear);
        seatHeight = startHeight;
```

```
    }
    // the MountainBike subclass adds one method
    public void setHeight(int newValue) {
        seatHeight = newValue;
    }
}
```

MountainBike inherits all the fields and methods of Bicycle and adds the field seatHeight and a method to set it. Except for the constructor, it is as if you had written a new MountainBike class entirely from scratch, with four fields and five methods. However, you didn't have to do all the work. This would be especially valuable if the methods in the Bicycle class were complex and had taken substantial time to debug.

What You Can Do in a Subclass

A subclass inherits all the *public* and *protected* members of its parent, no matter which package the subclass is in. If the subclass is in the same package as its parent, it also inherits the *package-private* members of the parent. You can use the inherited members as is, replace them, hide them, or supplement them with new members:

- The inherited fields can be used directly, just like any other fields.
- You can declare a field in the subclass with the same name as the one in the superclass, thus *hiding* it (not recommended).
- You can declare new fields in the subclass that are not in the superclass.
- The inherited methods can be used directly as they are.
- You can write a new *instance* method in the subclass that has the same signature as the one in the superclass, thus *overriding* it.
- You can write a new *static* method in the subclass that has the same signature as the one in the superclass, thus *hiding* it.
- You can declare new methods in the subclass that are not in the superclass.
- You can write a subclass constructor that invokes the constructor of the superclass, either implicitly or by using the keyword super.

The following sections will expand on these topics.

Private Members in a Superclass

A subclass does not inherit the private members of its parent class. However, if the superclass has public or protected methods for accessing its private fields, these can also be used by the subclass.

A nested class has access to all the private members of its enclosing class—both fields and methods. Therefore, a public or protected nested class inherited by a subclass has indirect access to all private members of the superclass.

Casting Objects

We have seen that an object is of the data type of the class from which it was instantiated. For example, if we write

```
public MountainBike myBike = new MountainBike();
```

6

then myBike is of type MountainBike.

MountainBike is descended from Bicycle and Object. Therefore, a MountainBike is a Bicycle and is also an Object, and it can be used wherever Bicycle or Object objects are called for.

The reverse is not necessarily true: a Bicycle *may be* a MountainBike, but it isn't necessarily. Similarly, an Object *may be* a Bicycle or a MountainBike, but it isn't necessarily.

Casting shows the use of an object of one type in place of another type among the objects permitted by inheritance and implementations. For example, if we write

```
Object obj = new MountainBike();
```

then obj is both an Object and a MountainBike (until such time as obj is assigned another object that is *not* a MountainBike). This is called *implicit casting*. If, on the other hand, we write

```
MountainBike myBike = obj;
```

we would get a compile-time error because obj is not known to the compiler to be a MountainBike. However, we can *tell* the compiler that we promise to assign a MountainBike to obj by *explicit casting*:

```
MountainBike myBike = (MountainBike)obj;
```

This cast inserts a runtime check that obj is assigned a MountainBike so that the compiler can safely assume that obj is a MountainBike. If obj is not a MountainBike at runtime, an exception will be thrown.

Note

You can make a logical test as to the type of a particular object using the `instanceof` operator. This can save you from a runtime error owing to an improper cast:

```
if (obj instanceof MountainBike) {
    MountainBike myBike = (MountainBike)obj;
}
```

Here the `instanceof` operator verifies that `obj` refers to a `MountainBike` so that we can make the cast with confidence that there will be no runtime exception thrown.

Multiple Inheritance of State, Implementation, and Type

One significant difference between classes and interfaces is that classes can have fields, whereas interfaces cannot. In addition, you can instantiate a class to create an object, which you cannot do with interfaces. As explained in Chapter 2, "What Is an Object?," an object stores its state in fields, which are defined in classes. One reason the Java programming language does not permit you to extend more than one class is to avoid the issues of *multiple inheritance of state*, which is the ability to inherit fields from multiple classes. For example, suppose that you are able to define a new class that extends multiple classes. When you create an object by instantiating that class, that object will inherit fields from all the class's superclasses. What if methods or constructors from different superclasses instantiate the same field? Which method or constructor will take precedence? Because interfaces do not contain fields, you do not have to worry about problems that result from multiple inheritance of state.

Multiple inheritance of implementation is the ability to inherit method definitions from multiple classes. Problems arise with this type of multiple inheritance, such as name conflicts and ambiguity. When compilers of programming languages that support this type of multiple inheritance encounter superclasses that contain methods with the same name, they sometimes cannot determine which member or method to access or invoke. In addition, a programmer can unwittingly introduce a name conflict by adding a new method to a superclass. Default methods introduce one form of multiple inheritance of implementation. A class can implement more than one interface, which can contain default methods that have the same name. The Java compiler provides some rules to determine which default method a particular class uses.

The Java programming language supports *multiple inheritance of type*, which is the ability of a class to implement more than one interface. An object can have multiple types: the type of its own class and the types of all the interfaces that the class implements. This means that if a variable is declared to be the type of an interface, then its value can reference any object that is instantiated from any class that implements the interface. This is discussed in the section "Using an Interface as a Type."

As with multiple inheritance of implementation, a class can inherit different implementations of a method defined (as default or static) in the interfaces that it extends. In this case, the compiler or the user must decide which one to use.

Overriding and Hiding Methods

Instance Methods

An instance method in a subclass with the same signature (name plus the number and the type of its parameters) and return type as an instance method in the superclass *overrides* the superclass's method. The ability of a subclass to override a method allows a class to inherit from a superclass whose behavior is "close enough" and then modify behavior as needed. The overriding method has the same name, number and type of parameters, and return type as the method it overrides. An overriding method can also return a subtype of the type returned by the overridden method. This subtype is called a *covariant return type*.

When overriding a method, you might want to use the @Override annotation that instructs the compiler that you intend to override a method in the superclass. If, for some reason, the compiler detects that the method does not exist in one of the superclasses, then it will generate an error. For more information on @Override, see Chapter 5.

Static Methods

If a subclass defines a static method with the same signature as a static method in the superclass, then the method in the subclass *hides* the one in the superclass. The distinction between hiding a static method and overriding an instance method has important implications:

- The version of the overridden instance method that gets invoked is the one in the subclass.
- The version of the hidden static method that gets invoked depends on whether it is invoked from the superclass or the subclass.

Consider an example that contains two classes. The first is Animal, which contains one instance method and one static method:

```
public class Animal {
    public static void testClassMethod() {
```

```
            System.out.println("The static method in Animal");
    }
    public void testInstanceMethod() {
        System.out.println("The instance method in Animal");
    }
}
```

The second class, a subclass of `Animal`, is called `Cat`:

```
public class Cat extends Animal {
    public static void testClassMethod() {
        System.out.println("The static method in Cat");
    }
    public void testInstanceMethod() {
        System.out.println("The instance method in Cat");
    }

    public static void main(String[] args) {
        Cat myCat = new Cat();
        Animal myAnimal = myCat;
        Animal.testClassMethod();
        myAnimal.testInstanceMethod();
    }
}
```

The `Cat` class overrides the instance method in `Animal` and hides the static method in `Animal`. The `main` method in this class creates an instance of `Cat` and invokes `testClassMethod()` on the class and `testInstanceMethod()` on the instance.

The output from this program is as follows:

```
The static method in Animal
The instance method in Cat
```

As promised, the version of the hidden static method that gets invoked is the one in the superclass, and the version of the overridden instance method that gets invoked is the one in the subclass.

Interface Methods

Default methods and abstract methods in interfaces are inherited like instance methods. However, when the supertypes of a class or interface provide multiple default methods with the same signature, the Java compiler follows inheritance rules to resolve the name conflict. These rules are driven by the following two principles:

1. *Instance methods are preferred over interface default methods.* Consider the following classes and interfaces:

   ```
   public class Horse {
       public String identifyMyself() {
           return "I am a horse.";
       }
   ```

```
    }
    public interface Flyer {
        default public String identifyMyself() {
            return "I am able to fly.";
        }
    }
    public interface Mythical {
        default public String identifyMyself() {
            return "I am a mythical creature.";
        }
    }
    public class Pegasus extends Horse implements Flyer, Mythical {
        public static void main(String... args) {
            Pegasus myApp = new Pegasus();
            System.out.println(myApp.identifyMyself());
        }
    }
```

6

The method `Pegasus.identifyMyself` returns the string `I am a horse.`

2. *Methods that are already overridden by other candidates are ignored.* This circumstance can arise when supertypes share a common ancestor. Consider the following interfaces and classes:

```
    public interface Animal {
        default public String identifyMyself() {
            return "I am an animal.";
        }
    }
    public interface EggLayer extends Animal {
        default public String identifyMyself() {
            return "I am able to lay eggs.";
        }
    }
    public interface FireBreather extends Animal { }

    public class Dragon implements EggLayer, FireBreather {
        public static void main (String... args) {
            Dragon myApp = new Dragon();
            System.out.println(myApp.identifyMyself());
        }
    }
```

The method `Dragon.identifyMyself` returns the string `I am able to lay eggs.`

If two or more independently defined default methods conflict or a default method conflicts with an abstract method, then the Java compiler produces a compiler error. You must explicitly override the supertype methods.

Consider the example about computer-controlled cars that can now fly. You have two interfaces (`OperateCar` and `FlyCar`) that provide default implementations for the same method (`startEngine`):

```
public interface OperateCar {
    // ...
    default public int startEngine(EncryptedKey key) {
        // Implementation
    }
}

public interface FlyCar {
    // ...
    default public int startEngine(EncryptedKey key) {
        // Implementation
    }
}
```

6

A class that implements both `OperateCar` and `FlyCar` must override the method `startEngine`. You can invoke any of the of the default implementations with the `super` keyword:

```
public class FlyingCar implements OperateCar, FlyCar {
    // ...
    public int startEngine(EncryptedKey key) {
        FlyCar.super.startEngine(key);
        OperateCar.super.startEngine(key);
    }
}
```

The name preceding `super` (in this example, `FlyCar` or `OperateCar`) must refer to a direct superinterface that defines or inherits a default for the invoked method. This form of method invocation is not restricted to differentiating between multiple implemented interfaces that contain default methods with the same signature. You can use the `super` keyword to invoke a default method in both classes and interfaces.

Inherited instance methods from classes can override abstract interface methods. Consider the following interfaces and classes:

```
public interface Mammal {
    String identifyMyself();
}

public class Horse {
    public String identifyMyself() {
        return "I am a horse.";
    }
}

public class Mustang extends Horse implements Mammal {
    public static void main(String... args) {
        Mustang myApp = new Mustang();
        System.out.println(myApp.identifyMyself());
    }
}
```

The method `Mustang.identifyMyself` returns the string `I am a horse`. The class `Mustang` inherits the method `identifyMyself` from the class `Horse`, which overrides the abstract method of the same name in the interface `Mammal`.

> **Note**
>
> Static methods in interfaces are never inherited.

Modifiers

The access specifier for an overriding method can allow more but not less access than the overridden method. For example, a protected instance method in the superclass can be made public but not private in the subclass. You will get a compile-time error if you attempt to change an instance method in the superclass to a static method in the subclass and vice versa.

Summary

Table 6.1 summarizes what happens when you define a method with the same signature as a method in a superclass.

> **Note**
>
> In a subclass, you can overload the methods inherited from the superclass. Such overloaded methods neither hide nor override the superclass instance methods—they are new methods, unique to the subclass.

Polymorphism

The dictionary definition of *polymorphism* refers to a principle in biology in which an organism or species can have many different forms or stages. This principle can also be applied to object-oriented programming and languages like the Java language. Subclasses of a class can define their own unique behaviors and yet share some of the same functionality of the parent class.

Table 6.1 Defining a Method with the Same Signature as a Superclass's Method

	Superclass Instance Method	Superclass Static Method
Subclass Instance Method	Overrides	Generates a compile-time error
Subclass Static Method	Generates a compile-time error	Hides

Polymorphism can be demonstrated with a minor modification to the `Bicycle` class. For example, a `printDescription` method could be added to the class that displays all the data currently stored in an instance:

```
public void printDescription(){
    System.out.println("\nBike is " + "in gear " + this.gear
        + " with a cadence of " + this.cadence +
        " and travelling at a speed of " + this.speed + ". ");
}
```

To demonstrate polymorphic features in the Java language, extend the `Bicycle` class with a `MountainBike` and a `RoadBike` class. For `MountainBike`, add a field for suspension, which is a `String` value that indicates if the bike has a front shock absorber, `Front`, or a front and back shock absorber, `Dual`. Here is the updated class:

```
public class MountainBike extends Bicycle {
    private String suspension;

    public MountainBike(
                int startCadence,
                int startSpeed,
                int startGear,
                String suspensionType){
        super(startCadence,
            startSpeed,
            startGear);
        this.setSuspension(suspensionType);
    }

    public String getSuspension(){
      return this.suspension;
    }

    public void setSuspension(String suspensionType) {
        this.suspension = suspensionType;
    }

    public void printDescription() {
        super.printDescription();
        System.out.println("The " + "MountainBike has a" +
            getSuspension() + " suspension.");
    }
}
```

Note the overridden `printDescription` method. In addition to the information provided before, additional data about the suspension is included in the output.

Next, create the `RoadBike` class. Because road or racing bikes have skinny tires, add an attribute to track the tire width. Here is the `RoadBike` class:

```
public class RoadBike extends Bicycle{
    // In millimeters (mm)
```

```
        private int tireWidth;

        public RoadBike(int startCadence,
                        int startSpeed,
                        int startGear,
                        int newTireWidth){
            super(startCadence,
                  startSpeed,
                  startGear);
            this.setTireWidth(newTireWidth);
        }

        public int getTireWidth(){
          return this.tireWidth;
        }

        public void setTireWidth(int newTireWidth){
            this.tireWidth = newTireWidth;
        }

        public void printDescription(){
            super.printDescription();
            System.out.println("The RoadBike" + " has " + getTireWidth() +
                " MM tires.");
        }
    }
```

Note that, once again, the `printDescription` method has been overridden. This time, information about the tire width is displayed.

To summarize, there are three classes: `Bicycle`, `MountainBike`, and `RoadBike`. The two subclasses override the `printDescription` method and print unique information.

Here is a test program that creates three `Bicycle` variables. Each variable is assigned to one of the three bicycle classes. Each variable is then printed:

```
public class TestBikes {
   public static void main(String[] args){
     Bicycle bike01, bike02, bike03;

     bike01 = new Bicycle(20, 10, 1);
     bike02 = new MountainBike(20, 10, 5, "Dual");
     bike03 = new RoadBike(40, 20, 8, 23);

     bike01.printDescription();
     bike02.printDescription();
     bike03.printDescription();
   }
}
```

The following is the output from the test program:

```
Bike is in gear 1 with a cadence of 20 and travelling at a speed of 10.

Bike is in gear 5 with a cadence of 20 and travelling at a speed of 10.
```

```
The MountainBike has a Dual suspension.

Bike is in gear 8 with a cadence of 40 and travelling at a speed of 20.
The RoadBike has 23 MM tires.
```

The Java Virtual Machine (Java VM) calls the appropriate method for the object that is referred to in each variable. It does not call the method that is defined by the variable's type. This behavior is referred to as *virtual method invocation* and demonstrates an aspect of the important polymorphism features in the Java language.

Hiding Fields

Within a class, a field that has the same name as a field in the superclass hides the superclass's field, even if their types are different. Within the subclass, the field in the superclass cannot be referenced by its simple name. Instead, the field must be accessed through super, which is covered in the next section. Generally, we don't recommend hiding fields, as it makes code difficult to read.

Using the Keyword super

Accessing Superclass Members

If your method overrides one of its superclass's methods, you can invoke the overridden method through the use of the keyword super. You can also use super to refer to a hidden field (although hiding fields is discouraged). Consider this class, Superclass:

```java
public class Superclass {

    public void printMethod() {
        System.out.println("Printed in Superclass.");
    }
}
```

Here is a subclass, called Subclass, that overrides printMethod():

```java
public class Subclass extends Superclass {

    // overrides printMethod in Superclass
    public void printMethod() {
        super.printMethod();
        System.out.println("Printed in Subclass");
    }
    public static void main(String[] args) {
        Subclass s = new Subclass();
        s.printMethod();
    }
}
```

Within `Subclass`, the simple name `printMethod()` refers to the one declared in `Subclass`, which overrides the one in `Superclass`. So, to refer to `printMethod()` inherited from `Superclass`, `Subclass` must use a qualified name, using `super` as shown. Compiling and executing `Subclass` prints the following:

```
Printed in Superclass.
Printed in Subclass
```

Subclass Constructors

The following example illustrates how to use the `super` keyword to invoke a super-class's constructor. Recall from the `Bicycle` example that `MountainBike` is a sub-class of `Bicycle`. Here is the `MountainBike` (subclass) constructor that calls the superclass constructor and then adds initialization code of its own:

```
public MountainBike(int startHeight,
                    int startCadence,
                    int startSpeed,
                    int startGear) {
    super(startCadence, startSpeed, startGear);
    seatHeight = startHeight;
}
```

Invocation of a superclass constructor must be the first line in the subclass con-structor. The syntax for calling a superclass constructor is

```
super();
```

or

```
super(parameter list);
```

With `super()`, the superclass no-argument constructor is called. With `super (parameter list)`, the superclass constructor with a matching parameter list is called.

Note

If a constructor does not explicitly invoke a superclass constructor, the Java compiler auto-matically inserts a call to the no-argument constructor of the superclass. If the super class does not have a no-argument constructor, you will get a compile-time error. `Object` *does* have such a constructor, so if `Object` is the only superclass, there is no problem.

If a subclass constructor invokes a constructor of its superclass, either explicitly or implicitly, you might think that there will be a whole chain of constructors called, all the way back to the constructor of `Object`. In fact, this is the case. It is called *constructor chaining*, and you need to be aware of it when there is a long line of class descent.

Object as a Superclass

The `Object`[18] class, in the `java.lang` package, sits at the top of the class hierarchy tree. Every class is a descendant, direct or indirect, of the `Object` class. Every class you use or write inherits the instance methods of `Object`. You need not use any of these methods, but if you choose to do so, you may need to override them with code that is specific to your class. The methods inherited from `Object` that are discussed in this section are as follows:

- `protected Object clone() throws CloneNotSupportedException`. This creates and returns a copy of this object.
- `public boolean equals(Object obj)`. This indicates whether some other object is "equal to" this one.
- `protected void finalize() throws Throwable`. This is called by the garbage collector on an object when garbage collection determines that there are no more references to the object.
- `public final Class getClass()`. This returns the runtime class of an object.
- `public int hashCode()`. This returns a hash code value for the object.
- `public String toString()`. This returns a string representation of the object.

The `notify`, `notifyAll`, and `wait` methods of `Object` all play a part in synchronizing the activities of independently running threads in a program, which is discussed in Chapter 13 and won't be covered here. There are five of these methods:

- `public final void notify()`
- `public final void notifyAll()`
- `public final void wait()`
- `public final void wait(long timeout)`
- `public final void wait(long timeout, int nanos)`

---

18.   8/docs/api/java/lang/Object.html

Note
There are some subtle aspects to a number of these methods, especially the `clone` method.

The clone() Method

If a class or one of its superclasses implements the `Cloneable` interface, you can use the `clone()` method to create a copy from an existing object. To create a clone, you write the following:

```
aCloneableObject.clone();
```

Object's implementation of this method checks to see whether the object on which `clone()` was invoked implements the `Cloneable` interface. If the object does not, the method throws a `CloneNotSupportedException` exception. Exception handling will be covered in Chapter 10. For the moment, you need to know that `clone()` must be declared as

```
protected Object clone() throws CloneNotSupportedException
```

or

```
public Object clone() throws CloneNotSupportedException
```

if you are going to write a `clone()` method to override the one in `Object`.

If the object on which `clone()` was invoked does implement the `Cloneable` interface, `Object`'s implementation of the `clone()` method creates an object of the same class as the original object and initializes the new object's member variables to have the same values as the original object's corresponding member variables.

The simplest way to make your class cloneable is to add `implements Cloneable` to your class's declaration. Your objects can then invoke the `clone()` method.

For some classes, the default behavior of `Object`'s `clone()` method works just fine. If, however, an object contains a reference to an external object, say `ObjExternal`, you may need to override `clone()` to get correct behavior. Otherwise, a change in `ObjExternal` made by one object will be visible in its clone also. This means that the original object and its clone are not independent—to decouple them, you must override `clone()` so that it clones the object *and* `ObjExternal`. Then the original object references `ObjExternal` and the clone references a clone of `ObjExternal` so that the object and its clone are truly independent.

The equals() Method

The equals() method compares two objects for equality and returns true if they are equal. The equals() method provided in the Object class uses the identity operator (==) to determine whether two objects are equal. For primitive data types, this gives the correct result. For objects, however, it does not. The equals() method provided by Object tests whether the object *references* are equal—that is, if the objects compared are the exact same object.

To test whether two objects are equal in the sense of *equivalency* (containing the same information), you must override the equals() method. Here is an example of a Book class that overrides equals():

```java
public class Book {
    ...
    public boolean equals(Object obj) {
        if (obj instanceof Book)
            return ISBN.equals((Book)obj.getISBN());
        else
            return false;
    }
}
```

Consider this code that tests two instances of the Book class for equality:

```java
// Swing Tutorial, 5th edition
Book firstBook  = new Book("0132761696");
Book secondBook = new Book("0132761696");
if (firstBook.equals(secondBook)) {
    System.out.println("objects are equal");
} else {
    System.out.println("objects are not equal");
}
```

This program displays objects are equal even though firstBook and secondBook reference two distinct objects. They are considered equal because the objects compared contain the same ISBN number. You should always override the equals() method if the identity operator is not appropriate for your class.

> **Note**
>
> If you override equals(), you must override hashCode() as well.

The finalize() Method

The Object class provides a callback method, finalize(), that *may be* invoked on an object when it becomes garbage. Object's implementation of finalize() does nothing—you can override finalize() to do cleanup, such as freeing resources.

The `finalize()` method *may be* called automatically by the system, but when it is called, or even if it is called, is uncertain. Therefore, you should not rely on this method to do your cleanup for you. For example, if you don't close file descriptors in your code after performing I/O and you expect `finalize()` to close them for you, you may run out of file descriptors.

The getClass() Method

You cannot override `getClass`. The `getClass()` method returns a `Class` object, which has methods you can use to get information about the class, such as its name (`getSimpleName()`), its superclass (`getSuperclass()`), and the interfaces it implements (`getInterfaces()`). For example, the following method gets and displays the class name of an object:

```
void printClassName(Object obj) {
    System.out.println("The object's" + " class is " +
        obj.getClass().getSimpleName());
}
```

The `Class`[19] class, in the `java.lang` package, has a large number of methods (more than fifty). For example, you can test to see if the class is an annotation (`isAnnotation()`), an interface (`isInterface()`), or an enumeration (`isEnum()`). You can see what the object's fields are (`getFields()`), what its methods are (`getMethods()`), and so on.

The hashCode() Method

The value returned by `hashCode()` is the object's hash code, which is the object's memory address in hexadecimal.

By definition, if two objects are equal, their hash code *must also* be equal. If you override the `equals()` method, you change the way two objects are equated and `Object`'s implementation of `hashCode()` is no longer valid. Therefore, if you override the `equals()` method, you must override the `hashCode()` method as well.

The toString() Method

You should always consider overriding the `toString()` method in your classes. The `Object`'s `toString()` method returns a `String` representation of the object, which is very useful for debugging. The `String` representation for an object depends entirely on the object, which is why you need to override `toString()` in your classes.

---

19. 8/docs/api/java/lang/Class.html

You can use `toString()` along with `System.out.println()` to display a text representation of an object, such as an instance of `Book`:

```
System.out.println(firstBook.toString());
```

For a properly overridden `toString()` method, this would print something useful, such as the following:

```
ISBN: 0132761696; The Swing Tutorial; A Guide to Constructing GUIs, 5th Edition
```

6

Writing Final Classes and Methods

You can declare some or all of a class's methods *final*. You use the `final` keyword in a method declaration to indicate that the method cannot be overridden by subclasses. The `Object` class does this—a number of its methods are `final`.

You might wish to make a method final if it has an implementation that should not be changed and it is critical to the consistent state of the object. For example, you might want to make the `getFirstPlayer` method in this `ChessAlgorithm` class final:

```
class ChessAlgorithm {
    enum ChessPlayer { WHITE, BLACK }
    ...
    final ChessPlayer getFirstPlayer() {
        return ChessPlayer.WHITE;
    }
    ...
}
```

Methods called from constructors should generally be declared final. If a constructor calls a nonfinal method, a subclass may redefine that method with surprising or undesirable results.

Note that you can also declare an entire class final. A class that is declared final cannot be subclassed. This is particularly useful, for example, when creating an immutable class like the `String` class.

Abstract Methods and Classes

An *abstract class* is a class that is declared `abstract`—it may or may not include abstract methods. Abstract classes cannot be instantiated but can be subclassed.

An *abstract method* is a method that is declared without an implementation (without braces and followed by a semicolon):

```
abstract void moveTo(double deltaX, double deltaY);
```

If a class includes abstract methods, then the class itself *must* be declared `abstract`:

```
public abstract class GraphicObject {
    // declare fields
    // declare nonabstract methods
    abstract void draw();
}
```

When an abstract class is subclassed, the subclass usually provides implementations for all abstract methods in its parent class. However, if it does not, then the subclass must also be declared `abstract`.

> **Note**
>
> Methods in an *interface* that are not declared as default or static are *implicitly* abstract, so the `abstract` modifier is not used with interface methods. (It can be used, but it is unnecessary.)

Abstract Classes Compared to Interfaces

Abstract classes are similar to interfaces. You cannot instantiate them, and they may contain a mix of methods declared with or without an implementation. However, with abstract classes, you can declare fields that are not static and final and define public, protected, and private concrete methods. With interfaces, all fields are automatically public, static, and final, and all methods that you declare or define (as default methods) are public. In addition, you can extend only one class, whether or not it is abstract, whereas you can implement any number of interfaces.

Which should you use, abstract classes or interfaces? Consider using abstract classes if any of these statements apply to your situation:

- You want to share code among several closely related classes.
- You expect that classes that extend your abstract class have many common methods or fields or require access modifiers other than `public` (such as `protected` and `private`).
- You want to declare nonstatic or nonfinal fields. This enables you to define methods that can access and modify the state of the object to which they belong.

Consider using interfaces if any of these statements apply to your situation:

- You expect that unrelated classes would implement your interface. For example, the interfaces `Comparable`[20] and `Cloneable`[21] are implemented by many unrelated classes.

---

20.   8/docs/api/java/lang/Comparable.html
21.   8/docs/api/java/lang/Cloneable.html

- You want to specify the behavior of a particular data type but are not concerned about who implements its behavior.
- You want to take advantage of multiple inheritance of type.

An example of an abstract class in the Java SE Development Kit (JDK) is `AbstractMap`, which is part of the collections framework.[22] Its subclasses (which include `HashMap`, `TreeMap`, and `ConcurrentHashMap`) share many methods (including `get`, `put`, `isEmpty`, `containsKey`, and `containsValue`) that `AbstractMap` defines.

An example of a class in the JDK that implements several interfaces is `HashMap`, which implements the interfaces `Serializable`, `Cloneable`, and `Map<K, V>`.[23] By reading this list of interfaces, you can infer that an instance of `HashMap` (regardless of the developer or company who implemented the class) can be cloned, is serializable (which means that it can be converted into a byte stream[24]), and has the functionality of a map. In addition, the `Map<K, V>` interface has been enhanced with many default methods, such as `merge` and `forEach`, that older classes that have implemented this interface do not have to define.

Note that many software libraries use both abstract classes and interfaces. The `HashMap` class implements several interfaces and also extends the abstract class `AbstractMap`.

An Abstract Class Example

In an object-oriented drawing application, you can draw circles, rectangles, lines, Bezier curves, and many other graphic objects. These objects all have certain states (e.g., position, orientation, line color, fill color) and behaviors (e.g., move to a new position, rotate, resize, draw) in common. Some of these states and behaviors are the same for all graphic objects (e.g., position, fill color, and move to a new position). Others require different implementations (e.g., resize or draw). All `GraphicObjects` must be able to draw or resize themselves; they just differ in how they do it. This is a perfect situation for an abstract superclass. You can take advantage of the similarities and declare all the graphic objects to inherit from the same abstract parent object (e.g., `GraphicObject`), as shown in Figure 6.2.

First, you declare an abstract class, `GraphicObject`, to provide member variables and methods that are wholly shared by all subclasses, such as the current position and the `moveTo` method. `GraphicObject` also declares abstract methods for methods, such as `draw` or `resize`, that need to be implemented by all subclasses

---

22.   8/docs/api/java/util/AbstractMap.html

23.   8/docs/api/java/util/HashMap.html

24.   tutorial/jndi/objects/serial.html

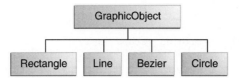

Figure 6.2 Classes Rectangle, Line, Bezier, and Circle Inherit from GraphicObject

but must be implemented in different ways. The `GraphicObject` class can look something like this:

```
abstract class GraphicObject {
    int x, y;
    ...
    void moveTo(int newX, int newY) {
        ...
    }
    abstract void draw();
    abstract void resize();
}
```

Each nonabstract subclass of `GraphicObject`, such as `Circle` and `Rectangle`, must provide implementations for the `draw` and `resize` methods:

```
class Circle extends GraphicObject {
    void draw() {
        ...
    }
    void resize() {
        ...
    }
}
class Rectangle extends GraphicObject {
    void draw() {
        ...
    }
    void resize() {
        ...
    }
}
```

When an Abstract Class Implements an Interface

In the previous section, it was noted that a class that implements an interface must implement *all* the interface's nondefault methods. It is possible, however, to define a class that does not implement all the interface's nondefault methods, provided the class is declared `abstract`:

```
abstract class X implements Y {
    // implements all but one method of Y
```

```
}
class XX extends X {
  // implements the remaining method in Y
}
```

In this case, class X must be `abstract` because it does not fully implement Y, but class XX does, in fact, implement Y.

Class Members

An abstract class may have `static` fields and `static` methods. You can use these static members with a class reference (e.g., `AbstractClass.staticMethod()`) as you would with any other class.

Summary of Inheritance

Except for the `Object` class, a class has exactly one direct superclass. A class inherits fields and methods from all its superclasses, whether direct or indirect. A subclass can override methods that it inherits or it can hide fields or methods that it inherits. (Note that hiding fields is generally bad programming practice.) Table 6.1 shows the effect of declaring a method with the same signature as a method in the superclass.

The `Object` class is the top of the class hierarchy. All classes are descendants from this class and inherit methods from it. Useful methods inherited from `Object` include `toString()`, `equals()`, `clone()`, and `getClass()`.

You can prevent a class from being subclassed by using the `final` keyword in the class's declaration. Similarly, you can prevent a method from being overridden by subclasses by declaring it a final method.

An abstract class can only be subclassed; it cannot be instantiated. An abstract class can contain abstract methods—methods that are declared but not implemented. Subclasses then provide the implementations for the abstract methods.

Questions and Exercises: Inheritance

Questions

1. Consider the following two classes:

```
public class ClassA {
    public void methodOne(int i) {
    }
    public void methodTwo(int i) {
    }
    public static void methodThree(int i) {
    }
    public static void methodFour(int i) {
```

```
        }
    }

    public class ClassB extends ClassA {
        public static void methodOne(int i) {
        }
        public void methodTwo(int i) {
        }
        public void methodThree(int i) {
        }
        public static void methodFour(int i) {
        }
    }
```

6

   a. Which method overrides a method in the superclass?

   b. Which method hides a method in the superclass?

   c. What do the other methods do?

2. Consider the `Card`, `Deck`, and `DisplayDeck` classes you wrote in Chapter 4, "Questions and Exercises: Classes." Which `Object` methods should each of these classes override?

Exercise

1. Write the implementations for the methods that you listed in response to question 2.

Answers

You can find answers to these questions and exercises at `http://docs.oracle.com/javase/tutorial/java/IandI/QandE/inherit-answers.html`.

7

Generics

Chapter Contents

Why Use Generics?   220
Generic Types   220
Generic Methods   226
Bounded Type Parameters   227
Generics, Inheritance, and Subtypes   229
Type Inference   232
Wildcards   236
Type Erasure   244
Restrictions on Generics   252
Questions and Exercises: Generics   256

In any nontrivial software project, bugs are simply a fact of life. Careful planning, programming, and testing can help reduce their pervasiveness, but somehow, somewhere, they'll always find a way to creep into your code. This becomes especially apparent as new features are introduced and your code base grows in size and complexity.

Fortunately, some bugs are easier to detect than others. Compile-time bugs, for example, can be detected early on; you can use the compiler's error messages to figure out what the problem is and fix it, right then and there. Runtime bugs, however, can be much more problematic; they don't always surface immediately, and when they do, it may be at a point in the program that is far removed from the actual cause of the problem.

Generics add stability to your code by making more of your bugs detectable at compile time. This chapter covers a range of topics related to generics, such as reasons for using them, types, methods, parameters, inheritance and subtypes, type interface, wildcards, type erasure, and restrictions. The chapter ends with questions and exercises to test your understanding.

Why Use Generics?

In a nutshell, generics enable *types* (classes and interfaces) to be parameters when defining classes, interfaces, and methods. Much like the more familiar *formal parameters* used in method declarations, type parameters provide a way for you to reuse the same code with different inputs. The difference is that the inputs to formal parameters are values, while the inputs to type parameters are types. Code that uses generics has many benefits over nongeneric code:

- *Stronger type checks at compile time*. A Java compiler applies strong type checking to generic code and issues errors if the code violates type safety. Fixing compile-time errors is easier than fixing runtime errors, which can be difficult to find.

- *Elimination of casts*. The following code snippet without generics requires casting:

```
List list = new ArrayList();
list.add("hello");
String s = (String) list.get(0);
```

When rewritten to use generics, the code does not require casting:

```
List<String> list = new ArrayList<String>();
list.add("hello");
String s = list.get(0);    // no cast
```

- *Enabling programmers to implement generic algorithms*. By using generics, programmers can implement generic algorithms that work on collections of different types, can be customized, and are type safe and easier to read.

Generic Types

A *generic type* is a generic class or interface that is parameterized over types. The following Box class will be modified to demonstrate the concept.

A Simple Box Class

We will begin by examining a nongeneric Box class that operates on objects of any type. It needs only to provide two methods: set, which adds an object to the box, and get, which retrieves it:

```
public class Box {
    private Object object;
```

```
        public void set(Object object) { this.object = object; }
        public Object get() { return object; }
    }
```

Since its methods accept or return an `Object`, you are free to pass in whatever you want, provided that it is not one of the primitive types. There is no way to verify, at compile time, how the class is used. One part of the code may place an `Integer` in the box and expect to get `Integers` out of it, while another part of the code may mistakenly pass in a `String`, resulting in a runtime error.

A Generic Version of the Box Class

A *generic class* is defined with the following format:

```
class name<T1, T2, ..., Tn> { /* ... */ }
```

The type parameter section, delimited by angle brackets (`<>`), follows the class name. It specifies the *type parameters* (also called *type variables*) `T1`, `T2`, ..., and `Tn`.

To update the `Box` class to use generics, you create a *generic type declaration* by changing the code `public class Box` to `public class Box<T>`. This introduces the type variable, `T`, that can be used anywhere inside the class.

With this change, the `Box` class becomes the following:

```
/**
 * Generic version of the Box class.
 * @param <T> the type of the value being boxed
 */
public class Box<T> {
    // T stands for "Type"
    private T t;

    public void set(T t) { this.t = t; }
    public T get() { return t; }
}
```

As you can see, all occurrences of `Object` are replaced by `T`. A type variable can be any *nonprimitive* type you specify: any class type, any interface type, any array type, or even another type variable. This same technique can be applied to create generic interfaces.

Type Parameter Naming Conventions

By convention, type parameter names are single, uppercase letters. This stands in sharp contrast to the variable naming conventions that you already know about, and with good reason: Without this convention, it would be difficult to tell the difference between a type variable and an ordinary class or interface name.

The most commonly used type parameter names are as follows:

- E—Element (used extensively by the Java collections framework)
- K—Key
- N—Number
- T—Type
- V—Value
- S, U, V, and so on—second, third, and fourth types

You'll see these names used throughout the Java SE Application Programming Interface (API) and the rest of this chapter.

Invoking and Instantiating a Generic Type

To reference the generic Box class from within your code, you must perform a *generic type invocation*, which replaces T with some concrete value, such as Integer:

```
Box<Integer> integerBox;
```

You can think of a generic type invocation as being similar to an ordinary method invocation, but instead of passing an argument to a method, you are passing a *type argument*—Integer, in this case—to the Box class itself.

> **Definition**
>
> Many developers use the terms *type parameter* and *type argument* interchangeably, but these terms are not the same. When coding, one provides type arguments in order to create a parameterized type. Therefore, the T in Foo<T> is a type parameter, and the String in Foo<String> f is a type argument. This chapter observes this definition when using these terms.

Like any other variable declaration, this code does not actually create a new Box object. It simply declares that integerBox will hold a reference to a "Box of Integer," which is how Box<Integer> is read.

An invocation of a generic type is generally known as a *parameterized type*. To instantiate this class, use the new keyword, as usual, but place <Integer> between the class name and the parentheses:

```
Box<Integer> integerBox = new Box<Integer>();
```

The Diamond

You can replace the type arguments required to invoke the constructor of a generic class with an empty set of type arguments (<>) as long as the compiler can determine, or infer, the type arguments from the context. This pair of angle brackets (<>) is informally called *the diamond*. For example, you can create an instance of Box<Integer> with the following statement:

```
Box<Integer> integerBox = new Box<>();
```

For more information on diamond notation and type inference, see the "Type Inference" section later on in this chapter.

Multiple Type Parameters

As mentioned previously, a generic class can have multiple type parameters. See, for example, the generic OrderedPair class, which implements the generic Pair interface:

```
public interface Pair<K, V> {
    public K getKey();
    public V getValue();
}

public class OrderedPair<K, V> implements Pair<K, V> {

    private K key;
    private V value;

    public OrderedPair(K key, V value) {
        this.key = key;
        this.value = value;
    }

    public K getKey() { return key; }
    public V getValue() { return value; }
}
```

The following statements create two instantiations of the OrderedPair class:

```
Pair<String, Integer> p1 = new OrderedPair<String, Integer>("Even", 8);
Pair<String, String> p2 = new OrderedPair<String, String>("hello", "world");
```

The code, new OrderedPair<String, Integer>, instantiates K as a String and V as an Integer. Therefore, the parameter types of OrderedPair's constructor are String and Integer, respectively. Due to autoboxing, it is valid to pass a String and an int to the class.

As mentioned previously, because a Java compiler can infer the K and V types from the declaration OrderedPair<String, Integer>, these statements can be shortened using diamond notation:

```
OrderedPair<String, Integer> p1 = new OrderedPair<>("Even", 8);
OrderedPair<String, String> p2 = new OrderedPair<>("hello", "world");
```

To create a generic interface, follow the conventions for creating a generic class.

Parameterized Types

You can also substitute a type parameter (such as K or V) with a parameterized type (such as List<String>). The following uses the OrderedPair<K, V> example:

```
OrderedPair<String, Box<Integer>> p = new OrderedPair<>("primes", new Box<Integer>(...));
```

Raw Types

A *raw type* is the name of a generic class or interface without any type arguments. Recall the generic Box class described previously:

```
public class Box<T> {
    public void set(T t) { /* ... */ }
    // ...
}
```

To create a parameterized type of Box<T>, you supply an actual type argument for the formal type parameter T:

```
Box<Integer> intBox = new Box<>();
```

If the actual type argument is omitted, you create a raw type of Box<T>:

```
Box rawBox = new Box();
```

Therefore, Box is the raw type of the generic type Box<T>. However, a nongeneric class or interface type is *not* a raw type.

Raw types show up in legacy code because lots of API classes (such as the Collections classes) were not generic prior to JDK 5.0. When using raw types, you essentially get pregenerics behavior—a Box gives you Objects. For backward compatibility, assigning a parameterized type to its raw type is allowed:

```
Box<String> stringBox = new Box<>();
Box rawBox = stringBox;                  // OK
```

But if you assign a raw type to a parameterized type, you get a warning:

```
Box rawBox = new Box();          // rawBox is a raw type of Box<T>
Box<Integer> intBox = rawBox;    // warning: unchecked conversion
```

You also get a warning if you use a raw type to invoke generic methods defined in the corresponding generic type:

```
Box<String> stringBox = new Box<>();
Box rawBox = stringBox;
rawBox.set(8);   // warning: unchecked invocation to set(T)
```

The warning shows that raw types bypass generic type checks, deferring the catch of unsafe code to runtime. Therefore, you should avoid using raw types. The "Type Erasure" section has more information on how the Java compiler uses raw types.

Unchecked Error Messages

As mentioned previously, when mixing legacy code with generic code, you may encounter warning messages similar to the following:

```
Note: Example.java uses unchecked or unsafe operations.
Note: Recompile with -Xlint:unchecked for details.
```

This can happen when using an older API that operates on raw types, as shown in the following example:

```
public class WarningDemo {
    public static void main(String[] args) {
        Box<Integer> bi;
        bi = createBox();
    }

    static Box createBox(){
        return new Box();
    }
}
```

The term *unchecked* means that the compiler does not have enough type information to perform all type checks necessary to ensure type safety. The unchecked warning is disabled, by default, though the compiler gives a hint. To see all unchecked warnings, recompile with -Xlint:unchecked.

Recompiling the previous example with -Xlint:unchecked reveals the following additional information:

```
WarningDemo.java:4: warning: [unchecked] unchecked conversion
found    : Box
```

```
required: Box<java.lang.Integer>
         bi = createBox();
                  ^
1 warning
```

To completely disable unchecked warnings, use the -Xlint:-unchecked flag. The @SuppressWarnings("unchecked") annotation suppresses unchecked warnings. If you are unfamiliar with the @SuppressWarnings syntax, see Chapter 5.

Generic Methods

Generic methods are methods that introduce their own type parameters. This is similar to declaring a generic type, but the type parameter's scope is limited to the method where it is declared. Static and nonstatic generic methods are allowed, as well as generic class constructors.

The syntax for a generic method includes a type parameter inside angle brackets that appears before the method's return type. For static generic methods, the type parameter section must appear before the method's return type.

The Util class includes a generic method, compare, which compares two Pair objects:

```
public class Util {
    // Generic static method
    public static <K, V> boolean compare(Pair<K, V> p1, Pair<K, V> p2) {
        return p1.getKey().equals(p2.getKey()) &&
                p1.getValue().equals(p2.getValue());
    }
}

public class Pair<K, V> {

    private K key;
    private V value;

    // Generic constructor
    public Pair(K key, V value) {
        this.key = key;
        this.value = value;
    }

    // Generic methods
    public void setKey(K key) { this.key = key; }
    public void setValue(V value) { this.value = value; }
    public K getKey()   { return key; }
    public V getValue() { return value; }
}
```

The complete syntax for invoking this method would be as follows:

```
Pair<Integer, String> p1 = new Pair<>(1, "apple");
Pair<Integer, String> p2 = new Pair<>(2, "pear");
boolean same = Util.<Integer, String>compare(p1, p2);
```

The type has been explicitly provided, as shown in bold. Generally, this can be left out and the compiler will infer the type that is needed:

```
Pair<Integer, String> p1 = new Pair<>(1, "apple");
Pair<Integer, String> p2 = new Pair<>(2, "pear");
boolean same = Util.compare(p1, p2);
```

This feature, known as *type inference*, allows you to invoke a generic method as an ordinary method without specifying a type between angle brackets. This topic is further discussed later in "Type Inference."

Bounded Type Parameters

There may be times when you want to restrict the types that can be used as type arguments in a parameterized type. For example, a method that operates on numbers might only want to accept instances of Number or its subclasses. This is what *bounded type parameters* are for.

To declare a bounded type parameter, list the type parameter's name, followed by the extends keyword, followed by its *upper bound*, which in this example is Number. Note that, in this context, extends is used in a general sense to mean either *extends* (as in classes) or *implements* (as in interfaces):

```
public class Box<T> {

    private T t;

    public void set(T t) {
        this.t = t;
    }

    public T get() {
        return t;
    }

    public <U extends Number> void inspect(U u){
        System.out.println("T: " + t.getClass().getName());
        System.out.println("U: " + u.getClass().getName());
    }

    public static void main(String[] args) {
        Box<Integer> integerBox = new Box<Integer>();
        integerBox.set(new Integer(10));
        integerBox.inspect("some text"); // error: this is still String!
    }
}
```

If we modify our generic method to include this bounded type parameter, compilation will now fail, since our invocation of inspect still includes a String:

```
Box.java:21: <U>inspect(U) in Box<java.lang.Integer> cannot
   be applied to (java.lang.String)
                          integerBox.inspect("10");
                          ^
1 error
```

In addition to limiting the types you can use to instantiate a generic type, bounded type parameters allow you to invoke methods defined in the bounds:

```
public class NaturalNumber<T extends Integer> {

    private T n;

    public NaturalNumber(T n) { this.n = n; }

    public boolean isEven() {
        return n.intValue() % 2 == 0;
    }

    // ...
}
```

The isEven method invokes the intValue method defined in the Integer class through n.

Multiple Bounds

The preceding example illustrates the use of a type parameter with a single bound, but a type parameter can have *multiple bounds*:

```
<T extends B1 & B2 & B3>
```

A type variable with multiple bounds is a subtype of all the types listed in the bound. If one of the bounds is a class, it must be specified first:

```
Class A { /* ... */ }
interface B { /* ... */ }
interface C { /* ... */ }

class D <T extends A & B & C> { /* ... */ }
```

If bound A is not specified first, you get a compile-time error:

```
class D <T extends B & A & C> { /* ... */ }  // compile-time error
```

Generic Methods and Bounded Type Parameters

Bounded type parameters are key to the implementation of generic algorithms. Consider the following method that counts the number of elements in an array T[ ] that are greater than a specified element elem:

```
public static <T> int countGreaterThan(T[] anArray, T elem) {
    int count = 0;
    for (T e : anArray)
        if (e > elem)   // compiler error
            ++count;
    return count;
}
```

7

The implementation of the method is straightforward, but it does not compile because the greater than operator (>) applies only to primitive types such as short, int, double, long, float, byte, and char. You cannot use the > operator to compare objects. To fix the problem, use a type parameter bounded by the Comparable<T> interface:

```
public interface Comparable<T> {
    public int compareTo(T o);
}
```

Here is the resulting code:

```
public static <T extends Comparable<T>> int countGreaterThan(T[] anArray, T elem) {
    int count = 0;
    for (T e : anArray)
        if (e.compareTo(elem) > 0)
            ++count;
    return count;
}
```

Generics, Inheritance, and Subtypes

As you already know, it is possible to assign an object of one type to an object of another type, provided that the types are compatible. For example, you can assign an Integer to an Object, since Object is one of Integer's supertypes:

```
Object someObject = new Object();
Integer someInteger = new Integer(10);
someObject = someInteger;   // OK
```

In object-oriented terminology, this is called an *is a* relationship. Since an `Integer` *is a* kind of `Object`, the assignment is allowed. But `Integer` is also a kind of `Number`, so the following code is valid as well:

```
public void someMethod(Number n) { /* ... */ }

someMethod(new Integer(10));    // OK
someMethod(new Double(10.1));   // OK
```

The same is also true with generics. You can perform a generic type invocation, passing `Number` as its type argument, and any subsequent invocation of add will be allowed if the argument is compatible with `Number`:

```
Box<Number> box = new Box<Number>();
box.add(new Integer(10));    // OK
box.add(new Double(10.1));   // OK
```

Now consider the following method:

```
public void boxTest(Box<Number> n) { /* ... */ }
```

What type of argument does it accept? By looking at its signature, you can see that it accepts a single argument whose type is `Box<Number>`. But what does that mean? Are you allowed to pass in `Box<Integer>` or `Box<Double>`, as you might expect? The answer is no because `Box<Integer>` and `Box<Double>` are not subtypes of `Box<Number>`. This is a common misunderstanding when it comes to programming with generics, but it is an important concept to learn.

> **Note**
>
> Given two concrete types A and B (e.g., `Number` and `Integer`), `MyClass<A>` has no relationship to `MyClass<B>`, regardless of whether or not A and B are related. The common parent of `MyClass<A>` and `MyClass<B>` is `Object`. For information on how to create a subtype-like relationship between two generic classes when the type parameters are related, see the "Wildcards and Subtyping" section.

Generic Classes and Subtyping

You can subtype a generic class or interface by extending or implementing it. The relationship between the type parameters of one class or interface and the type parameters of another is determined by the `extends` and `implements` clauses.

Using the `Collections` classes as an example, `ArrayList<E>` implements `List<E>`, and `List<E>` extends `Collection<E>`. So `ArrayList<String>` is a subtype of

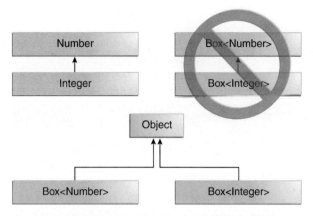

Figure 7.1 Box<Integer> Is Not a Subtype of Box<Number>
Even Though Integer Is a Subtype of Number

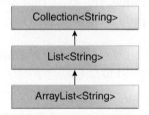

Figure 7.2 A Sample Collections Hierarchy

List<String>, which is a subtype of Collection<String>. So long as you do not vary
the type argument, the subtyping relationship is preserved between the types.

Now imagine we want to define our own list interface, PayloadList, that associates an optional value of generic type P with each element. Its declaration might
look like this:

```
interface PayloadList<E,P> extends List<E> {
  void setPayload(int index, P val);
  ...
}
```

The following parameterizations of PayloadList are subtypes of List<String>:

- PayloadList<String,String>
- PayloadList<String,Integer>
- PayloadList<String,Exception>

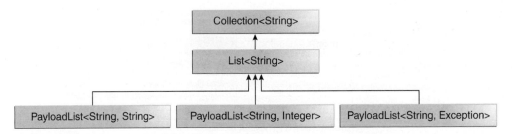

Figure 7.3 A Sample PayloadList Hierarchy

Type Inference

Type inference is a Java compiler's ability to look at each method invocation and corresponding declaration to determine the type argument (or arguments) that makes the invocation applicable. The inference algorithm determines the types of the arguments and, if available, the type that the result is being assigned or returned. Finally, the inference algorithm tries to find the *most specific* type that works with all the arguments.

To illustrate this last point, in the following example, inference determines that the second argument being passed to the `pick` method is of type `Serializable`:

```
static <T> T pick(T a1, T a2) { return a2; }
Serializable s = pick("d", new ArrayList<String>());
```

Type Inference and Generic Methods

The previous discussion of generic methods introduced you to type inference, which enables you to invoke a generic method as you would an ordinary method, without specifying a type between angle brackets. Consider the following example, `BoxDemo`, which requires the `Box` class:

```
public class BoxDemo {

    public static <U> void addBox(U u,
        java.util.List<Box<U>> boxes) {
      Box<U> box = new Box<>();
      box.set(u);
      boxes.add(box);
    }

    public static <U> void outputBoxes(java.util.List<Box<U>> boxes) {
      int counter = 0;
      for (Box<U> box: boxes) {
        U boxContents = box.get();
        System.out.println("Box #" + counter + " contains [" +
              boxContents.toString() + "]");
        counter++;
```

```
      }
    }
    public static void main(String[] args) {
      java.util.ArrayList<Box<Integer>> listOfIntegerBoxes =
        new java.util.ArrayList<>();
      BoxDemo.<Integer>addBox(Integer.valueOf(10), listOfIntegerBoxes);
      BoxDemo.addBox(Integer.valueOf(20), listOfIntegerBoxes);
      BoxDemo.addBox(Integer.valueOf(30), listOfIntegerBoxes);
      BoxDemo.outputBoxes(listOfIntegerBoxes);
    }
  }
```

The following is the output from this example:

```
Box #0 contains [10]
Box #1 contains [20]
Box #2 contains [30]
```

7

The generic method `addBox` defines one type parameter named U. Generally, a Java compiler can infer the type parameters of a generic method call. Consequently, in most cases, you do not have to specify them. For example, to invoke the generic method `addBox`, you can specify the type parameter with a *type witness* as follows:

```
BoxDemo.<Integer>addBox(Integer.valueOf(10), listOfIntegerBoxes);
```

Alternatively, if you omit the type witness, a Java compiler automatically infers (from the method's arguments) that the type parameter is `Integer`:

```
BoxDemo.addBox(Integer.valueOf(20), listOfIntegerBoxes);
```

Type Inference and Instantiation of Generic Classes

You can replace the type arguments required to invoke the constructor of a generic class with an empty set of type parameters (<>) as long as the compiler can infer the type arguments from the context. As mentioned previously, this pair of angle brackets is informally called *the diamond*. For example, consider the following variable declaration:

```
Map<String, List<String>> myMap = new HashMap<String, List<String>>();
```

You can substitute the parameterized type of the constructor with an empty set of type parameters (<>):

```
Map<String, List<String>> myMap = new HashMap<>();
```

Note that to take advantage of type inference during generic class instantiation, you must use the diamond. In the following example, the compiler generates an

unchecked conversion warning because the `HashMap()` constructor refers to the
`HashMap` raw type, not the `Map<String, List<String>>` type:

```
Map<String, List<String>> myMap = new HashMap(); // unchecked conversion warning
```

Type Inference and Generic Constructors of Generic and Nongeneric Classes

Note that constructors can be generic (in other words, declare their own formal type
parameters) in both generic and nongeneric classes. Consider the following example:

```
class MyClass<X> {
  <T> MyClass(T t) {
    // ...
  }
}
```

Now consider the following instantiation of the class `MyClass`:

```
new MyClass<Integer>("")
```

This statement creates an instance of the parameterized type `MyClass<Integer>`;
the statement explicitly specifies the type `Integer` for the formal type parameter,
`X`, of the generic class, `MyClass<X>`. Note that the constructor for this generic class
contains a formal type parameter, `T`. The compiler infers the type `String` for the
formal type parameter, `T`, of the constructor of this generic class (because the actual
parameter of this constructor is a `String` object).

Compilers can infer the actual type parameters of generic constructors, similar
to generic methods. However, compilers can also infer the actual type parameters
of the generic class being instantiated if you use the diamond (<>). Consider the
following example:

```
MyClass<Integer> myObject = new MyClass<>("");
```

In this example, the compiler infers the type `Integer` for the formal type parameter `X` of the generic class `MyClass<X>`. It infers the type `String` for the formal
type parameter `T` of the constructor of this generic class.

> **Note**
> It is important to note that the inference algorithm uses only invocation arguments, target
> types, and possibly an obvious expected return type to infer types. The inference algorithm
> does not use results from later in the program.

Target Types

The Java compiler takes advantage of target typing to infer the type parameters of a generic method invocation. The *target type* of an expression is the data type that the Java compiler expects, depending on where the expression appears. Consider the method `Collections.emptyList`, which is declared as follows:

```
static <T> List<T> emptyList();
```

Consider the following assignment statement:

```
List<String> listOne = Collections.emptyList();
```

This statement is expecting an instance of `List<String>`; this data type is the target type. Because the method `emptyList` returns a value of type `List<T>`, the compiler infers that the type argument `T` must be the value `String`. This works in both Java SE 7 and 8. Alternatively, you could use a type witness and specify the value of `T` as follows:

```
List<String> listOne = Collections.<String>emptyList();
```

However, this is not necessary in this context. It was necessary in other contexts, though. Consider the following method:

```
void processStringList(List<String> stringList) {
    // process stringList
}
```

Suppose you want to invoke the method `processStringList` with an empty list. In Java SE 7, the following statement does not compile:

```
processStringList(Collections.emptyList());
```

The Java SE 7 compiler generates an error message similar to the following:

```
List<Object> cannot be converted to List<String>
```

The compiler requires a value for the type argument `T` so it starts with the value `Object`. Consequently, the invocation of `Collections.emptyList` returns a value of type `List<Object>`, which is incompatible with the method `processString-List`. Thus, in Java SE 7, you must specify the value of the type argument as follows:

```
processStringList(Collections.<String>emptyList());
```

This is no longer necessary in Java SE 8. The notion of what constitutes a target type has been expanded to include method arguments, such as the argument to the method `processStringList`. In this case, `processStringList` requires an argument of type `List<String>`. The method `Collections.emptyList` returns a value of `List<T>`, so using the target type of `List<String>`, the compiler infers that the type argument `T` has a value of `String`. Thus, in Java SE 8, the following statement compiles:

```
processStringList(Collections.emptyList());
```

See Chapter 4, "Target Typing," for more information.

Wildcards

In generic code, the question mark (`?`), called the *wildcard*, represents an unknown type. The wildcard can be used in a variety of situations: as the type of a parameter, field, or local variable and sometimes as a return type (though it is better programming practice to be more specific). The wildcard is never used as a type argument for a generic method invocation, a generic class instance creation, or a supertype.

The following sections discuss wildcards in more detail, including upper-bounded wildcards, lower-bounded wildcards, and wildcard capture.

Upper-Bounded Wildcards

You can use an upper-bounded wildcard to relax the restrictions on a variable. For example, say you want to write a method that works on `List<Integer>`, `List<Double>`, *and* `List<Number>`; you can achieve this by using an upper-bounded wildcard.

To declare an upper-bounded wildcard, use the wildcard character (`?`), followed by the `extends` keyword, followed by its *upper bound*. Note that, in this context, extends is used in a general sense to mean either *extends* (as in classes) or *implements* (as in interfaces).

To write the method that works on lists of `Number` and the subtypes of `Number`, such as `Integer`, `Double`, and `Float`, you would specify `List<? extends Number>`. The term `List<Number>` is more restrictive than `List<? extends Number>` because the former matches a list of type `Number` only, whereas the latter matches a list of type `Number` or any of its subclasses.

Consider the following `process` method:

```
public static void process(List<? extends Foo> list) { /* ... */ }
```

The upper-bounded wildcard, <? extends Foo>, where Foo is any type, matches Foo and any subtype of Foo. The process method can access the list elements as type Foo:

```
public static void process(List<? extends Foo> list) {
    for (Foo elem : list) {
        // ...
    }
}
```

In the foreach clause, the elem variable iterates over each element in the list. Any method defined in the Foo class can now be used on elem.

The sumOfList method returns the sum of the numbers in a list:

```
public static double sumOfList(List<? extends Number> list) {
    double s = 0.0;
    for (Number n : list)
        s += n.doubleValue();
    return s;
}
```

The following code, using a list of Integer objects, prints sum = 6.0:

```
List<Integer> li = Arrays.asList(1, 2, 3);
System.out.println("sum = " + sumOfList(li));
```

A list of Double values can use the same sumOfList method. The following code prints sum = 7.0:

```
List<Double> ld = Arrays.asList(1.2, 2.3, 3.5);
System.out.println("sum = " + sumOfList(ld));
```

Unbounded Wildcards

The unbounded wildcard type is specified using the wildcard character (?; e.g., List<?>). This is called a *list of unknown type*. There are two scenarios where an unbounded wildcard is a useful approach:

- If you are writing a method that can be implemented using functionality provided in the Object class.
- When the code is using methods in the generic class that don't depend on the type parameter (e.g., List.size or List.clear). In fact, Class<?> is so often used because most of the methods in Class<T> do not depend on T.

Consider the following method, printList:

```
public static void printList(List<Object> list) {
    for (Object elem : list)
        System.out.println(elem + " ");
    System.out.println();
}
```

The goal of `printList` is to print a list of any type, but it fails to achieve that goal. It prints only a list of `Object` instances; it cannot print `List<Integer>`, `List<String>`, `List<Double>`, and so on, because they are not subtypes of `List<Object>`. To write a generic `printList` method, use `List<?>`:

```
public static void printList(List<?> list) {
    for (Object elem: list)
        System.out.print(elem + " ");
    System.out.println();
}
```

Because for any concrete type A, `List<A>` is a subtype of `List<?>`, you can use `printList` to print a list of any type:

```
List<Integer> li = Arrays.asList(1, 2, 3);
List<String> ls = Arrays.asList("one", "two", "three");
printList(li);
printList(ls);
```

> **Note**
>
> The `Arrays.asList`[1] method is used in examples throughout this chapter. This static factory method converts the specified array and returns a fixed-size list.

It's important to note that `List<Object>` and `List<?>` are not the same. You can insert an `Object`, or any subtype of `Object`, into a `List<Object>`. But you can only insert `null` into a `List<?>`. The "Guidelines for Wildcard Use" section has more information on how to determine what kind of wildcard, if any, should be used in a given situation.

Lower-Bounded Wildcards

The "Upper-Bounded Wildcards" section shows that an upper-bounded wildcard restricts the unknown type to be a specific type or a subtype of that type and is represented using the extends keyword. In a similar way, a *lower-bounded* wildcard restricts the unknown type to be a specific type or a *supertype* of that type. A lower-bounded wildcard is expressed using the wildcard character (?), followed by the super keyword, followed by its *lower bound*: `<? super A>`.

---

1.   8/docs/api/java/util/Arrays.html#asList-T...-

> **Note**
>
> You can specify an upper bound for a wildcard or you can specify a lower bound, but you cannot specify both.

Say you want to write a method that puts `Integer` objects into a list. To maximize flexibility, you would like the method to work on `List<Integer>`, `List<Number>`, and `List<Object>`—anything that can hold `Integer` values.

To write the method that works on lists of `Integer` and the supertypes of `Integer`, such as `Integer`, `Number`, and `Object`, you would specify `List<? super Integer>`. The term `List<Integer>` is more restrictive than `List<? super Integer>` because the former matches a list of type `Integer` only, whereas the latter matches a list of any type that is a supertype of `Integer`.

The following code adds the numbers 1 through 10 to the end of a list:

```
public static void addNumbers(List<? super Integer> list) {
    for (int i = 1; i <= 10; i++) {
        list.add(i);
    }
}
```

The "Guidelines for Wildcard Use" section provides guidance on when to use upper-bounded wildcards and when to use lower-bounded wildcards.

Wildcards and Subtyping

As described in "Generics, Inheritance, and Subtypes," generic classes or interfaces are not related merely because there is a relationship between their types. However, you can use wildcards to create a relationship between generic classes or interfaces.

Consider the following two regular (nongeneric) classes:

```
class A { /* ... */ }
class B extends A { /* ... */ }
```

Given these, it would be reasonable to write the following code:

```
B b = new B();
A a = b;
```

This example shows that inheritance of regular classes follows this rule of subtyping: class B is a subtype of class A if B extends A. This rule does not apply to generic types:

```
List<B> lb = new ArrayList<>();
List<A> la = lb;   // compile-time error
```

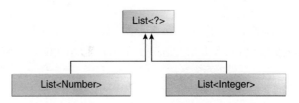

Figure 7.4 The Common Parent Is List<?>

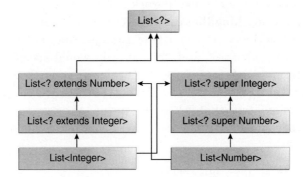

Figure 7.5 A Hierarchy of Several Generic List Class Declarations

Given that Integer is a subtype of Number, what is the relationship between List<Integer> and List<Number>? Although Integer is a subtype of Number, List<Integer> is not a subtype of List<Number> and, in fact, these two types are not related. The common parent of List<Number> and List<Integer> is List<?>.

In order to create a relationship between these classes so that the code can access Number's methods through List<Integer>'s elements, use an upper-bounded wildcard:

```
List<? extends Integer> intList = new ArrayList<>();
List<? extends Number> numList = intList;  // OK. List<? extends Integer> is
                                           // a subtype of List<? extends Number>
```

Because Integer is a subtype of Number and numList is a list of Number objects, a relationship now exists between intList (a list of Integer objects) and num-List. Figure 7.5 shows the relationships between several List classes declared with both upper- and lower-bounded wildcards.

The "Guidelines for Wildcard Use" section has more information about the ramifications of using upper- and lower-bounded wildcards.

Wildcard Capture and Helper Methods

In some cases, the compiler infers the type of a wildcard. For example, a list may be defined as List<?>, but when evaluating an expression, the compiler infers a particular type from the code. This scenario is known as *wildcard capture*.

For the most part, you don't need to worry about wildcard capture, except when you see an error message that contains the phrase *capture of*. The `WildcardError` example produces a capture error when compiled:

```
import java.util.List;

public class WildcardError {

    void foo(List<?> i) {
        i.set(0, i.get(0));
    }
}
```

In this example, the compiler processes the i input parameter as being of type `Object`. When the `foo` method invokes `List.set(int, E)`, the compiler is not able to confirm the type of object that is being inserted into the list and an error is produced. When this type of error occurs, it typically means that the compiler believes that you are assigning the wrong type to a variable. Generics were added to the Java language for this reason—to enforce type safety at compile time.

The `WildcardError` example generates the following error when compiled by Oracle's JDK `javac` implementation:

```
WildcardError.java:6: error: method set in interface List<E> cannot be applied to given types;
    i.set(0, i.get(0));
     ^
  required: int,CAP#1
  found: int,Object
  reason: actual argument Object cannot be converted to CAP#1 by method invocation conversion
  where E is a type-variable:
    E extends Object declared in interface List
  where CAP#1 is a fresh type-variable:
    CAP#1 extends Object from capture of ?
1 error
```

In this example, the code is attempting to perform a safe operation, so how can you work around the compiler error? You can fix it by writing a *private helper method* that captures the wildcard. In this case, you can work around the problem by creating the private helper method, `fooHelper`, as shown in `WildcardFixed`:

```
public class WildcardFixed {

    void foo(List<?> i) {
        fooHelper(i);
    }


    // Helper method created so that the wildcard can be captured
    // through type inference.
    private <T> void fooHelper(List<T> l) {
        l.set(0, l.get(0));
```

```
      }

  }
```

Thanks to the helper method, the compiler uses inference to determine that T is CAP#1, the capture variable, in the invocation. The example now compiles successfully.

By convention, helper methods are generally named *originalMethodName*Helper. Now consider a more complex example, WildcardErrorBad:

```java
import java.util.List;

public class WildcardErrorBad {

    void swapFirst(List<? extends Number> l1, List<? extends Number> l2) {
        Number temp = l1.get(0);
        l1.set(0, l2.get(0)); // expected a CAP#1 extends Number,
                              // got a CAP#2 extends Number;
                              // same bound, but different types
        l2.set(0, temp);      // expected a CAP#1 extends Number,
                              // got a Number
    }
}
```

In this example, the code is attempting an unsafe operation. For example, consider the following invocation of the swapFirst method:

```java
List<Integer> li = Arrays.asList(1, 2, 3);
List<Double> ld = Arrays.asList(10.10, 20.20, 30.30);
swapFirst(li, ld);
```

While List<Integer> and List<Double> both fulfill the criteria of List<? extends Number>, it is clearly incorrect to take an item from a list of Integer values and attempt to place it into a list of Double values.

Compiling the code with Oracle's JDK javac compiler produces the following error:

```
WildcardErrorBad.java:7: error: method set in interface List<E> cannot be applied to given types;
      l1.set(0, l2.get(0)); // expected a CAP#1 extends Number,
        ^
  required: int,CAP#1
  found: int,Number
  reason: actual argument Number cannot be converted to CAP#1 by method invocation conversion
  where E is a type-variable:
    E extends Object declared in interface List
  where CAP#1 is a fresh type-variable:
    CAP#1 extends Number from capture of ? extends Number
WildcardErrorBad.java:10: error: method set in interface List<E> cannot be applied to given types;
      l2.set(0, temp);      // expected a CAP#1 extends Number,
        ^
  required: int,CAP#1
  found: int,Number
  reason: actual argument Number cannot be converted to CAP#1 by method invocation conversion
  where E is a type-variable:
```

```
      E extends Object declared in interface List
    where CAP#1 is a fresh type-variable:
      CAP#1 extends Number from capture of ? extends Number
WildcardErrorBad.java:15: error: method set in interface List<E> cannot be applied to given types;
        i.set(0, i.get(0));
        ^
    required: int,CAP#1
    found:    int,Object
    reason: actual argument Object cannot be converted to CAP#1 by method invocation conversion
    where E is a type-variable:
      E extends Object declared in interface List
    where CAP#1 is a fresh type-variable:
      CAP#1 extends Object from capture of ?
3 errors
```

There is no helper method to work around the problem because the code is funda-
mentally wrong.

Guidelines for Wildcard Use

One of the more confusing aspects when learning to program with generics is deter-
mining when to use an upper-bounded wildcard and when to use a lower-bounded
wildcard. This page provides some guidelines to follow when designing your code.

For purposes of this discussion, it is helpful to think of variables as providing one
of two functions:

- An *in* variable serves up data to the code. Imagine a copy method with two
  arguments: copy(src, dest). The src argument provides the data to be
  copied, so it is the *in* parameter.
- An *out* variable holds data for use elsewhere. In the copy example, copy(src,
  dest), the dest argument accepts data, so it is the *out* parameter.

Of course, some variables are used for both *in* and *out* purposes—this scenario is
also addressed in the guidelines.

You can use the *in* and *out* principle when deciding whether to use a wildcard and
what type of wildcard is appropriate. The following list provides the guidelines to follow:

- An *in* variable is defined with an upper-bounded wildcard, using the extends
  keyword.
- An *out* variable is defined with a lower-bounded wildcard, using the super
  keyword.
- In the case where the *in* variable can be accessed using methods defined in the
  Object class, use an unbounded wildcard.
- In the case where the code needs to access the variable as both an *in* and an
  out variable, do not use a wildcard.

These guidelines do not apply to a method's return type. Using a wildcard as a return type should be avoided because it forces programmers using the code to deal with wildcards.

A list defined by List<? extends ...> can be informally thought of as read-only, but that is not a strict guarantee. Suppose you have the following two classes:

```
class NaturalNumber {

    private int i;

    public NaturalNumber(int i) { this.i = i; }
    // ...
}

class EvenNumber extends NaturalNumber {

    public EvenNumber(int i) { super(i); }
    // ...
}
```

Consider the following code:

```
List<EvenNumber> le = new ArrayList<>();
List<? extends NaturalNumber> ln = le;
ln.add(new NaturalNumber(35));  // compile-time error
```

Because List<EvenNumber> is a subtype of List<? extends NaturalNumber>, you can assign le to ln. But you cannot use ln to add a natural number to a list of even numbers. The following operations on the list are possible:

- You can add null.
- You can invoke clear.
- You can get the iterator and invoke remove.
- You can capture the wildcard and write elements that you've read from the list.

You can see that the list defined by List<? extends NaturalNumber> is not read-only in the strictest sense of the word, but you might think of it that way because you cannot store a new element or change an existing element in the list.

Type Erasure

Generics were introduced to the Java language to provide tighter type checks at compile time and to support generic programming. To implement generics, the Java compiler applies type erasure to do the following:

- Replace all type parameters in generic types with their bounds or `Object` if the type parameters are unbounded. The produced bytecode therefore contains only ordinary classes, interfaces, and methods.
- Insert type casts if necessary to preserve type safety.
- Generate bridge methods to preserve polymorphism in extended generic types.

Type erasure ensures that no new classes are created for parameterized types; consequently, generics incur no runtime overhead.

Erasure of Generic Types

During the type erasure process, the Java compiler erases all type parameters and replaces each with its first bound if the type parameter is bounded or `Object` if the type parameter is unbounded.

Consider the following generic class that represents a node in a singly linked list:

```java
public class Node<T> {

    private T data;
    private Node<T> next;

    public Node(T data, Node<T> next) }
        this.data = data;
        this.next = next;
    }

    public T getData() { return data; }
    // ...
}
```

Because the type parameter `T` is unbounded, the Java compiler replaces it with `Object`:

```java
public class Node {

    private Object data;
    private Node next;

    public Node(Object data, Node next) {
        this.data = data;
        this.next = next;
    }

    public Object getData() { return data; }
    // ...
}
```

In the following example, the generic `Node` class uses a bounded type parameter:

```
public class Node<T extends Comparable<T>> {

    private T data;
    private Node<T> next;

    public Node(T data, Node<T> next) {
        this.data = data;
        this.next = next;
    }

    public T getData() { return data; }
    // ...
}
```

7

The Java compiler replaces the bounded type parameter T with the first bound class, Comparable:

```
public class Node {

    private Comparable data;
    private Node next;

    public Node(Comparable data, Node next) {
        this.data = data;
        this.next = next;
    }

    public Comparable getData() { return data; }
    // ...
}
```

Erasure of Generic Methods

The Java compiler also erases type parameters in generic method arguments. Consider the following generic method:

```
// Counts the number of occurrences of elem in anArray.

public static <T> int count(T[] anArray, T elem) {
    int cnt = 0;
    for (T e : anArray)
        if (e.equals(elem))
            ++cnt;
        return cnt;
}
```

Because T is unbounded, the Java compiler replaces it with Object:

```
public static int count(Object[] anArray, Object elem) {
    int cnt = 0;
    for (Object e : anArray)
        if (e.equals(elem))
            ++cnt;
```

```
            return cnt;
    }
```

Suppose the following classes are defined:

```
class Shape { /* ... */ }
class Circle extends Shape { /* ... */ }
class Rectangle extends Shape { /* ... */ }
```

You can write a generic method to draw different shapes:

```
public static <T extends Shape> void draw(T shape) { /* ... */ }
```

The Java compiler replaces T with Shape:

```
public static void draw(Shape shape) { /* ... */ }
```

Effects of Type Erasure and Bridge Methods

Sometimes type erasure causes a situation that you may not have anticipated. The following example shows how this can occur. The example (described in the section "Bridge Methods") shows how a compiler sometimes creates a synthetic method, called a bridge method, as part of the type erasure process.

Consider the following two classes:

```
public class Node<T> {

    private T data;

    public Node(T data) { this.data = data; }

    public void setData(T data) {
        System.out.println("Node.setData");
        this.data = data;
    }
}

public class MyNode extends Node<Integer> {
    public MyNode(Integer data) { super(data); }

    public void setData(Integer data) {
        System.out.println("MyNode.setData");
        super.setData(data);
    }
}
```

Now, consider the following code:

```
MyNode mn = new MyNode(5);
```

```
Node n = mn;            // A raw type - compiler throws an unchecked warning
n.setData("Hello");     // Causes a ClassCastException to be thrown.
Integer x = mn.data;
```

After type erasure, this code is as follows:

```
MyNode mn = new MyNode(5);
Node n = (MyNode)mn;          // A raw type - compiler throws an unchecked warning
n.setData("Hello");
Integer x = (String)mn.data; // Causes a ClassCastException to be thrown.
```

Here is what happens as the code is executed:

- `n.setData("Hello");` causes the method `setData(Object)` to be executed on the object of class `MyNode`. (The `MyNode` class inherited `setData(Object)` from `Node`.)
- In the body of `setData(Object)`, the data field of the object referenced by n is assigned to a `String`.
- The data field of that same object, referenced via mn, can be accessed and is expected to be an integer (since mn is a `MyNode` which is a `Node<Integer>`).
- Trying to assign a `String` to an `Integer` causes a `ClassCastException` from a cast inserted at the assignment by a Java compiler.

Bridge Methods

When compiling a class or interface that extends a parameterized class or implements a parameterized interface, the compiler may need to create a synthetic method, called a *bridge method*, as part of the type erasure process. You normally don't need to worry about bridge methods, but you might be puzzled if one appears in a stack trace.

Here are the `Node` and `MyNode` classes after type erasure:

```
public class Node {

    private Object data;

    public Node(Object data) { this.data = data; }

    public void setData(Object data) {
        System.out.println("Node.setData");
        this.data = data;
    }
}

public class MyNode extends Node {

    public MyNode(Integer data) { super(data); }

    public void setData(Integer data) {
```

```
            System.out.println(Integer data);
            super.setData(data);
      }
   }
```

After type erasure, the method signatures do not match. The Node method becomes setData(Object) and the MyNode method becomes setData(Integer). Therefore, the MyNode setData method does not override the Node setData method.

To solve this problem and preserve the polymorphism of generic types after type erasure, a Java compiler generates a bridge method to ensure that subtyping works as expected. For the MyNode class, the compiler generates the following bridge method for setData:

```
class MyNode extends Node {

    // Bridge method generated by the compiler
    //
    public void setData(Object data) {
        setData((Integer) data);
    }

    public void setData(Integer data) {
        System.out.println("MyNode.setData");
        super.setData(data);
    }

    // ...
}
```

As you can see, the bridge method, which has the same method signature as the Node class's setData method after type erasure, delegates to the original setData method.

Nonreifiable Types and Varargs Methods

A *reifiable* type is a type whose type information is fully available at runtime. This includes primitives, nongeneric types, raw types, and invocations of unbound wildcards.

Nonreifiable types are types whose information has been removed at compile time by type erasure—invocations of generic types that are not defined as unbounded wildcards. (The section "Type Erasure" discusses the process where the compiler removes information related to type parameters and type arguments.) A nonreifiable type does not have all its information available at runtime. Examples of nonreifiable types are List<String> and List<Number>; the Java Virtual Machine (Java VM) cannot tell the difference between these types at runtime. As shown in "Restrictions on

Generics," there are certain situations where nonreifiable types cannot be used: in an `instanceof` expression, for example, or as an element in an array.

Type erasure has consequences for varargs methods whose varargs parameters have a nonrefiable type. (The varargs, or variable arguments, construct enables a method to accept any number of arguments of a particular type. See Chapter 4, "Arbitrary Number of Arguments," for more information about varargs methods.)

Heap Pollution

Heap pollution occurs when a variable of a parameterized type refers to an object that is not of that parameterized type. This situation occurs if the program performed some operation that gives rise to an unchecked warning at compile time. An *unchecked warning* is generated if either at compile time (within the limits of the compile-time type-checking rules) or at runtime the correctness of an operation involving a parameterized type (e.g., a cast or method call) cannot be verified. For example, heap pollution occurs when mixing raw types and parameterized types or when performing unchecked casts.

In normal situations, when all code is compiled at the same time, the compiler issues an unchecked warning to draw your attention to potential heap pollution. If you compile sections of your code separately, it is difficult to detect the potential risk of heap pollution. If you ensure that your code compiles without warnings, then no heap pollution can occur.

Potential Vulnerabilities of Varargs Methods with Nonreifiable Formal Parameters

Generic methods that include vararg input parameters can cause heap pollution. Consider the following `ArrayBuilder` class:

```java
public class ArrayBuilder {

  public static <T> void addToList (List<T> listArg, T... elements)
  {
    for (T x : elements) {
      listArg.add(x);
    }
  }

  public static void faultyMethod(List<String>... l) {
    Object[] objectArray = l;         // Valid
    objectArray[0] = Arrays.asList(42);
    String s = l[0].get(0);           // ClassCastException thrown here
  }

}
```

The following example, `HeapPollutionExample`, uses the `ArrayBuilder` class:

```
public class HeapPollutionExample {

  public static void main(String[] args) {

    List<String> stringListA = new ArrayList<String>();
    List<String> stringListB = new ArrayList<String>();

    ArrayBuilder.addToList(stringListA, "Seven", "Eight", "Nine");
    ArrayBuilder.addToList(stringListA, "Ten", "Eleven", "Twelve");
    List<List<String>> listOfStringLists =
      new ArrayList<List<String>>();
    ArrayBuilder.addToList(listOfStringLists,
      stringListA, stringListB);

    ArrayBuilder.faultyMethod(Arrays.asList("Hello!"), Arrays.asList("World!"));
  }
}
```

7

When compiled, the following warning is produced by the definition of the `ArrayBuilder.`
`addToList` method:

```
warning: [varargs] Possible heap pollution from parameterized vararg type T
```

When the compiler encounters a varargs method, it translates the varargs formal
parameter into an array. However, the Java programming language does not permit the creation of arrays of parameterized types. In the method `ArrayBuilder.`
`addToList`, the compiler translates the varargs formal parameter `T...` elements
to the formal parameter `T[]` elements, an array. However, because of type erasure, the compiler converts the varargs formal parameter to `Object[]` elements.
Consequently, there is a possibility of heap pollution.

The following statement assigns the varargs formal parameter `l` to the `Object`
array `objectArgs`:

```
Object[] objectArray = l;
```

This statement can potentially introduce heap pollution. A value that does match
the parameterized type of the varargs formal parameter `l` can be assigned to the
variable `objectArray` and thus can be assigned to `l`. However, the compiler does
not generate an unchecked warning at this statement. The compiler has already generated a warning when it translated the varargs formal parameter `List<String>... l`
to the formal parameter `List[] l`. This statement is valid; the variable `l` has the
type `List[]`, which is a subtype of `Object[]`.

Consequently, the compiler does not issue a warning or error if you assign a `List`
object of any type to any array component of the `objectArray` array, as shown by
this statement:

```
objectArray[0] = Arrays.asList(42);
```

This statement assigns to the first array component of the `objectArray` array with a `List` object that contains one object of type `Integer`.

Suppose you invoke `ArrayBuilder.faultyMethod` with the following statement:

```
ArrayBuilder.faultyMethod(Arrays.asList("Hello!"), Arrays.asList("World!"));
```

At runtime, the Java VM throws a `ClassCastException` at the following statement:

```
// ClassCastException thrown here
String s = l[0].get(0);
```

The object stored in the first array component of the variable `l` has the type `List<Integer>`, but this statement is expecting an object of type `List<String>`.

Prevent Warnings from Varargs Methods with Nonreifiable Formal Parameters

If you declare a varargs method that has parameters of a parameterized type and you ensure that the body of the method does not throw a `ClassCastException` or other similar exception due to improper handling of the varargs formal parameter, then you can prevent the warning that the compiler generates for these kinds of varargs methods by adding the following annotation to static and nonconstructor method declarations:

```
@SafeVarargs
```

The `@SafeVarargs` annotation is a documented part of the method's contract; this annotation asserts that the implementation of the method will not improperly handle the varargs formal parameter.

It is also possible, though less desirable, to suppress such warnings by adding the following to the method declaration:

```
@SuppressWarnings({"unchecked", "varargs"})
```

However, this approach does not suppress warnings generated from the method's call site. If you are unfamiliar with the `@SuppressWarnings` syntax, see Chapter 5.

Restrictions on Generics

To use Java generics effectively, you must consider the following restrictions.

Cannot Instantiate Generic Types with Primitive Types

Consider the following parameterized type:

```
class Pair<K, V> {

    private K key;
    private V value;

    public Pair(K key, V value) {
        this.key = key;
        this.value = value;
    }

    // ...
}
```

When creating a `Pair` object, you cannot substitute a primitive type for the type parameter K or V:

```
Pair<int, char> p = new Pair<>(8, 'a');   // compile-time error
```

You can substitute only nonprimitive types for the type parameters K and V:

```
Pair<Integer, Character> p = new Pair<>(8, 'a');
```

Note that the Java compiler autoboxes 8 to `Integer.valueOf(8)` and a to `Character('a')`:

```
Pair<Integer, Character> p = new Pair<>(Integer.valueOf(8), new Character('a'));
```

For more information on autoboxing, see Chapter 9, "Autoboxing and Unboxing."

Cannot Create Instances of Type Parameters

You cannot create an instance of a type parameter. For example, the following code causes a compile-time error:

```
public static <E> void append(List<E> list) {
    E elem = new E();   // compile-time error
    list.add(elem);
}
```

As a workaround, you can create an object of a type parameter through reflection:

```
public static <E> void append(List<E> list, Class<E> cls) throws Exception {
    E elem = cls.newInstance();    // OK
    list.add(elem);
}
```

You can invoke the append method as follows:

```
List<String> ls = new ArrayList<>();
append(ls, String.class);
```

Cannot Declare Static Fields Whose Types Are Type Parameters

A class's static field is a class-level variable shared by all nonstatic objects of the class. Hence static fields of type parameters are not allowed. Consider the following class:

```
public class MobileDevice<T> {
    private static T os;

    // ...
}
```

If static fields of type parameters were allowed, then the following code would be confusing:

```
MobileDevice<Smartphone> phone = new MobileDevice<>();
MobileDevice<Pager> pager = new MobileDevice<>();
MobileDevice<TabletPC> pc = new MobileDevice<>();
```

Because the static field os is shared by phone, pager, and pc, what is the actual type of os? It cannot be Smartphone, Pager, and TabletPC at the same time. You therefore cannot create static fields of type parameters.

Cannot Use Casts or instanceof with Parameterized Types

Because the Java compiler erases all type parameters in generic code, you cannot verify which parameterized type for a generic type is being used at runtime:

```
public static <E> void rtti(List<E> list) {
    if (list instanceof ArrayList<Integer>) {  // compile-time error
        // ...
    }
}
```

The set of parameterized types passed to the rtti method is as follows:

```
S = { ArrayList<Integer>, ArrayList<String> LinkedList<Character>, ... }
```

The runtime does not keep track of type parameters, so it cannot tell the difference between an ArrayList<Integer> and an ArrayList<String>. The most you can do is to use an unbounded wildcard to verify that the list is an ArrayList:

```
public static void rtti(List<?> list) {
    if (list instanceof ArrayList<?>) {  // OK; instanceof requires a reifiable type
        // ...
```

```
      }
   }
```

Typically, you cannot cast to a parameterized type unless it is parameterized by unbounded wildcards:

```
List<Integer> li = new ArrayList<>();
List<Number> ln = (List<Number>) li;  // compile-time error
```

However, in some cases, the compiler knows that a type parameter is always valid and allows the cast:

```
List<String> l1 = ...;
ArrayList<String> l2 = (ArrayList<String>)l1;  // OK
```

Cannot Create Arrays of Parameterized Types

You cannot create arrays of parameterized types. For example, the following code does not compile:

```
List<Integer>[] arrayOfLists = new List<Integer>[2];  // compile-time error
```

The following code illustrates what happens when different types are inserted into an array:

```
Object[] strings = new String[2];
strings[0] = "hi";   // OK
strings[1] = 100;    // An ArrayStoreException is thrown.
```

If you try the same thing with a generic list, there would be a problem:

```
Object[] stringLists = new List<String>[]; // compiler error, but pretend it's allowed
stringLists[0] = new ArrayList<String>();  // OK
stringLists[1] = new ArrayList<Integer>(); // An ArrayStoreException should be thrown,
                                           // but the runtime can't detect it.
```

If arrays of parameterized lists were allowed, the previous code would fail to throw the desired `ArrayStoreException`.

Cannot Create, Catch, or Throw Objects of Parameterized Types

A generic class cannot extend the `Throwable` class directly or indirectly. For example, the following classes will not compile:

```
// Extends Throwable indirectly
class MathException<T> extends Exception { /* ... */ }    // compile-time error
```

```
// Extends Throwable directly
class QueueFullException<T> extends Throwable { /* ... */ // compile-time error
```

A method cannot catch an instance of a type parameter:

```
public static <T extends Exception, J> void execute(List<J> jobs) {
    try {
        for (J job : jobs)
            // ...
    } catch (T e) {    // compile-time error
        // ...
    }
}
```

You can, however, use a type parameter in a throws clause:

```
class Parser<T extends Exception> {
    public void parse(File file) throws T {       // OK
        // ...
    }
}
```

Cannot Overload a Method Where the Formal Parameter Types of Each Overload Erase to the Same Raw Type

A class cannot have two overloaded methods that will have the same signature after type erasure.

```
public class Example {
    public void print(Set<String> strSet) { }
    public void print(Set<Integer> intSet) { }
}
```

The overloads would all share the same class file representation and generate a compile-time error.

Questions and Exercises: Generics

1. Write a generic method to count the number of elements in a collection that have a specific property (e.g., odd integers, prime numbers, palindromes).

2. Will the following class compile? If not, why?

```
public final class Algorithm {
    public static T max(T x, T y) {
        return x > y ? x : y;
    }
}
```

3. Write a generic method to exchange the positions of two different elements in an array.

4. If the compiler erases all type parameters at compile time, why should you use generics?

5. What is the following class converted to after type erasure?

```java
public class Pair<K, V> {

    public Pair(K key, V value) {
        this.key = key;
        this.value = value;
    }

    public K getKey(); { return key; }
    public V getValue(); { return value; }

    public void setKey(K key)     { this.key = key; }
    public void setValue(V value) { this.value = value; }

    private K key;
    private V value;
}
```

7

6. What is the following method converted to after type erasure?

```java
public static <T extends Comparable<T>>
    int findFirstGreaterThan(T[] at, T elem) {
    // ...
}
```

7. Will the following method compile? If not, why?

```java
public static void print(List<? extends Number> list) {
    for (Number n : list)
        System.out.print(n + " ");
    System.out.println();
}
```

8. Write a generic method to find the maximal element in the range [begin, end] of a list.

9. Will the following class compile? If not, why?

```java
public class Singleton<T> {

    public static T getInstance() {
        if (instance == null)
            instance = new Singleton<T>();

        return instance;
    }

    private static T instance = null;
}
```

10. Consider the following classes:

```
class Shape { /* ... */ }
class Circle extends Shape { /* ... */ }
class Rectangle extends Shape { /* ... */ }

class Node<T> { /* ... */ }
```

Will the following code compile? If not, why?

```
Node<Circle> nc = new Node<>();
Node<Shape> ns = nc;
```

11. Consider this class:

```
class Node<T> implements Comparable<T> {
    public int compareTo(T obj) { /* ... */ }
    // ...
}
```

Will the following code compile? If not, why?

```
Node<String> node = new Node<>();
Comparable<String> comp = node;
```

12. How do you invoke the following method to find the first integer in a list that is relatively prime to a list of specified integers?

```
public static <T>
    int findFirst(List<T> list, int begin, int end,
UnaryPredicate<T> p)
```

Note that two integers a and b are relatively prime if $gcd(a, b) = 1$, where gcd is short for *greatest common divisor*.

Answers

You can find answers to these questions and exercises at `http://docs.oracle` `.com/javase/tutorial/java/generics/QandE/generics-answers.html`.

8

Packages

Chapter Contents

Creating and Using Packages   259
Questions and Exercises: Creating and Using Packages   269

This chapter explains how to bundle classes and interfaces into packages, how to use classes that are in packages, and how to arrange your file system so that the compiler can find your source files.

Creating and Using Packages

To make types easier to find and use, to avoid naming conflicts, and to control access, programmers bundle groups of related types into packages.

> **Definition**
>
> A *package* is a grouping of related types providing access protection and namespace management. Note that *types* refers to classes, interfaces, enumerations, and annotation types. Enumerations and annotation types are special kinds of classes and interfaces, respectively, so *types* are often referred to in this chapter simply as *classes and interfaces*.

The types that are part of the Java platform are members of various packages that bundle classes by function: fundamental classes are in `java.lang`, classes for reading and writing (input and output) are in `java.io`, and so on. You can put your types in packages, too.

Suppose you write a group of classes that represent graphic objects, such as circles, rectangles, lines, and points. You also write an interface, `Draggable`, that classes implement if they can be dragged with the mouse.

```
//in the Draggable.java file
public interface Draggable {
    ...
}

//in the Graphic.java file
public abstract class Graphic {
    ...
}

//in the Circle.java file
public class Circle extends Graphic
    implements Draggable {
    ...
}

//in the Rectangle.java file
public class Rectangle extends Graphic
    implements Draggable {
    ...
}

//in the Point.java file
public class Point extends Graphic
    implements Draggable {
    ...
}

//in the Line.java file
public class Line extends Graphic
    implements Draggable {
    ...
}
```

You should bundle these classes and the interface in a package for several reasons, including the following:

- You and other programmers can easily determine that these types are related.
- You and other programmers know where to find types that can provide graphics-related functions.
- The names of your types won't conflict with the type names in other packages because the package creates a new namespace.
- You can allow types within the package to have unrestricted access to one another yet still restrict access for types outside the package.

Creating a Package

To create a package, you choose a name for the package (naming conventions are discussed in the next section) and put a package statement with that name at the top of *every source file* that contains the types (classes, interfaces, enumerations, and annotation types) that you want to include in the package.

The package statement (e.g., package graphics;) must be the first line in the source file. There can be only one package statement in each source file, and it applies to all types in the file.

> **Note**
>
> If you put multiple types in a single source file, only one can be public, and it must have the same name as the source file. For example, you can define public class Circle in the file Circle.java, define public interface Draggable in the file Draggable.java, define public enum Day in the file Day.java, and so forth. You can include nonpublic types in the same file as a public type (which is strongly discouraged, unless the nonpublic types are small and closely related to the public type), but only the public type will be accessible from outside the package. All the top-level, nonpublic types will be *package private*.

8

If you put the graphics interface and classes listed in the preceding section in a package called graphics, you would need six source files, like this:

```
//in the Draggable.java file
package graphics;
public interface Draggable {
    ...
}

//in the Graphic.java file
package graphics;
public abstract class Graphic {
    ...
}

//in the Circle.java file
package graphics;
public class Circle extends Graphic
    implements Draggable {
    ...
}

//in the Rectangle.java file
package graphics;
public class Rectangle extends Graphic
    implements Draggable {
    ...
```

```
    }

    //in the Point.java file
    package graphics;
    public class Point extends Graphic
        implements Draggable {
        ...
    }

    //in the Line.java file
    package graphics;
    public class Line extends Graphic
        implements Draggable {
        ...
    }
```

If you do not use a `package` statement, your type ends up in an unnamed package. Generally speaking, an unnamed package is only for small or temporary applications or when you are just beginning the development process. Otherwise, classes and interfaces belong in named packages.

Naming a Package

With programmers worldwide writing classes and interfaces using the Java programming language, it is likely that many programmers will use the same name for different types. In fact, the previous example does just that: it defines a `Rectangle` class when there is already a `Rectangle` class in the `java.awt` package. Still, the compiler allows both classes to have the same name if they are in different packages. The fully qualified name of each `Rectangle` class includes the package name—that is, the fully qualified name of the `Rectangle` class in the `graphics` package is `graphics.Rectangle` and the fully qualified name of the `Rectangle` class in the `java.awt` package is `java.awt.Rectangle`.

This works well unless two independent programmers use the same name for their packages. What prevents this problem? Naming conventions.

Naming Conventions

Package names are written in all lowercase to avoid conflict with the names of classes or interfaces. Companies use their reversed Internet domain name to begin their package names—for example, `com.example.mypackage` for a package named `mypackage` created by a programmer at `example.com`. Name collisions that occur within a single company need to be handled by convention within that company, perhaps by including the region or the project name after the company name (e.g., `com.example.region.mypackage`). Packages in the Java language itself begin with `java.` or `javax.`

Table 8.1 Legalizing Package Names

Domain name	Package name prefix
hyphenated-name.example.org	org.example.hyphenated_name
example.int	int_.example
123name.example.com	com.example._123name

In some cases, the Internet domain name may not be a valid package name. This can occur if the domain name contains a hyphen or other special character, if the package name begins with a digit or other character that is illegal to use as the beginning of a Java name, or if the package name contains a reserved Java keyword, such as `int`. In this event, the suggested convention is to add an underscore (Table 8.1).

Using Package Members

The types that comprise a package are known as the *package members*. To use a `public` package member from outside its package, you must do one of the following:

- Refer to the member by its fully qualified name.
- Import the package member.
- Import the member's entire package.

Each is appropriate for different situations, as explained in the sections that follow.

Referring to a Package Member by Its Qualified Name

So far, most of the examples in this book have referred to types by their simple names, such as `Rectangle` and `StackOfInts`. You can use a package member's simple name if the code you are writing is in the same package as that member or if that member has been imported.

However, if you are trying to use a member from a different package and that package has not been imported, you must use the member's fully qualified name, which includes the package name. Here is the fully qualified name for the `Rectangle` class declared in the `graphics` package in the previous example:

```
graphics.Rectangle
```

You could use this qualified name to create an instance of `graphics.Rectangle`:

```
graphics.Rectangle myRect = new graphics.Rectangle();
```

Qualified names are alright for infrequent use. When a name is used repetitively, however, typing the name repeatedly becomes tedious and the code becomes difficult to read. As an alternative, you can *import* the member or its package and then use its simple name.

Importing a Package Member

To import a specific member into the current file, put an `import` statement at the beginning of the file before any type definitions but after the `package` statement, if there is one. Here's how you would import the `Rectangle` class from the `graphics` package created in the previous section:

```
import graphics.Rectangle;
```

Now you can refer to the `Rectangle` class by its simple name:

```
Rectangle myRectangle = new Rectangle();
```

This approach works well if you use just a few members from the `graphics` package. But if you use many types from a package, you should import the entire package.

Importing an Entire Package

To import all the types contained in a particular package, use the `import` statement with the asterisk (`*`) wildcard character:

```
import graphics.*;
```

Now you can refer to any class or interface in the `graphics` package by its simple name:

```
Circle myCircle = new Circle();
Rectangle myRectangle = new Rectangle();
```

The asterisk in the `import` statement can be used only to specify all the classes within a package, as shown here. It cannot be used to match a subset of the classes in a package. For example, the following does not match all the classes in the `graphics` package that begin with `A`:

```
// does not work
import graphics.A*;
```

Instead, it generates a compiler error. With the `import` statement, you generally import only a single package member or an entire package.

> **Note**
>
> Another, less common form of `import` allows you to import the public nested classes of an enclosing class. For example, if the `graphics.Rectangle` class contained useful nested classes, such as `Rectangle.DoubleWide` and `Rectangle.Square`, you could import `Rectangle` and its nested classes by using the following *two* statements:
>
> ```
> import graphics.Rectangle;
> import graphics.Rectangle.*;
> ```
>
> Be aware that the second import statement will *not* import `Rectangle`. Another less common form of `import`, the *static import statement*, will be discussed at the end of this section.

For convenience, the Java compiler automatically imports two entire packages for each source file: (1) the `java.lang` package and (2) the current package (the package for the current file).

8

Apparent Hierarchies of Packages

At first, packages appear to be hierarchical, but they are not. For example, the Java Application Programming Interface (API) includes a `java.awt` package, a `java.awt.color` package, a `java.awt.font` package, and many others that begin with `java.awt`. However, the `java.awt.color` package, the `java.awt.font` package, and other `java.awt.xxxx` packages are *not included* in the `java.awt` package. The prefix `java.awt` (the Java Abstract Window Toolkit) is used for a number of related packages to make the relationship evident but not to show inclusion.

Importing `java.awt.*` imports all the types in the `java.awt` package, but it *does not import* `java.awt.color`, `java.awt.font`, or any other `java.awt.xxxx` packages. If you plan to use the classes and other types in `java.awt.color` as well as those in `java.awt`, you must import both packages with all their files:

```
import java.awt.*;
import java.awt.color.*;
```

Name Ambiguities

If a member in one package shares its name with a member in another package and both packages are imported, you must refer to each member by its qualified name. For example, the `graphics` package defined a class named `Rectangle`. The `java.awt` package also contains a `Rectangle` class. If both `graphics` and `java.awt` have been imported, the following is ambiguous:

```
Rectangle rect;
```

In such a situation, you have to use the member's fully qualified name to indicate exactly which `Rectangle` class you want. Here is an example:

```
graphics.Rectangle rect;
```

The Static Import Statement

There are situations where you need frequent access to static final fields (constants) and static methods from one or two classes. Prefixing the name of these classes over and over can result in cluttered code. The *static import* statement gives you a way to import the constants and static methods that you want to use so that you do not need to prefix the name of their class.

The `java.lang.Math` class defines the `PI` constant and many static methods, including methods for calculating sines, cosines, tangents, square roots, maxima, minima, exponents, and many more. Here's an example:

```
public static final double PI
    = 3.141592653589793;
public static double cos(double a)
{
    ...
}
```

Ordinarily, to use these objects from another class, you prefix the class name:

```
double r = Math.cos(Math.PI * theta);
```

You can use the static import statement to import the static members of `java.lang.Math` so that you don't need to prefix the class name, `Math`. The static members of `Math` can be imported either individually

```
import static java.lang.Math.PI;
```

or as a group

```
import static java.lang.Math.*;
```

Once they have been imported, the static members can be used without qualification. For example, the previous code snippet would become

```
double r = cos(PI * theta);
```

Obviously, you can write your own classes that contain constants and static methods that you use frequently and then use the static import statement. Here's an example:

```
import static mypackage.MyConstants.*;
```

> **Note**
>
> Use static import very sparingly. Overusing static import can result in code that is difficult to read and maintain because readers of the code won't know which class defines a particular static object. Used properly, static import makes code more readable by removing class name repetition.

Managing Source and Class Files

Many implementations of the Java platform rely on hierarchical file systems to manage source and class files, although the Java Language Specification does not require this. The strategy is as follows.

Put the source code for a class, interface, enumeration, or annotation type in a text file whose name is the simple name of the type and whose extension is `.java`:

```
//in the Rectangle.java file
package graphics;
public class Rectangle {
   ...
}
```

Then, put the source file in a directory whose name reflects the name of the package to which the type belongs:

```
.....\graphics\Rectangle.java
```

The qualified name of the package member and the path name to the file are parallel, assuming the Microsoft Windows file name separator backslash. (For Solaris, Linux, and OS X, use the forward slash.)

- Class name—`graphics.Rectangle`
- Pathname to file—`graphics\Rectangle.java`

As you should recall, by convention, a company uses its reversed Internet domain name for its package names. The Example company, whose Internet domain name is `example.com`, would precede all its package names with `com.example`. Each component of the package name corresponds to a subdirectory. So if the Example company had a `com.example.graphics` package that contained a `Rectangle.java` source file, it would be contained in a series of subdirectories like this:

```
....\com\example\graphics\Rectangle.java
```

When you compile a source file, the compiler creates a different output file for each type defined in it. The base name of the output file is the name of the type, and its extension is `.class`. For example, if the source file is like this

```
//in the Rectangle.java file
package com.example.graphics;
public class Rectangle {
    ...
}

class Helper {
    ...
}
```

then the compiled files will be located at

<path to the parent directory of the output files>\com\example\graphics\Rectangle.class
<path to the parent directory of the output files>\com\example\graphics\Helper.class

Like the `.java` source files, the compiled `.class` files should be in a series of directories that reflect the package name. However, the path to the `.class` files does not have to be the same as the path to the `.java` source files. You can arrange your source and class directories separately:

<path_one>\sources\com\example\graphics\Rectangle.java

<path_two>\classes\com\example\graphics\Rectangle.class

By doing this, you can give the `classes` directory to other programmers without revealing your sources. You also need to manage source and class files in this manner so that the compiler and the Java Virtual Machine (Java VM) can find all the types your program uses.

The full path to the `classes` directory, *<path_two>*\classes, is called the *class path* and is set with the `CLASSPATH` system variable. Both the compiler and the Java VM construct the path to your `.class` files by adding the package name to the class path. For example, if

<path_two>\classes

is your class path and the package name is

com.example.graphics

then the compiler and Java VM look for `.class files` in

<path_two>\classes\com\example\graphics

A class path may include several paths, separated by a semicolon (Windows) or colon (Solaris, Linux, or OS X). By default, the compiler and the Java VM search the current directory and the JAR file containing the Java platform classes so that these directories are automatically in your class path.

Setting the CLASSPATH System Variable

To display the current CLASSPATH variable, use these commands in Windows and Solaris, Linux, and OS X:

- Windows—`C:\> set CLASSPATH`
- Solaris, Linux, and OS X—`% echo $CLASSPATH`

To delete the current contents of the CLASSPATH variable, use these commands:

- Windows—`C:\> set CLASSPATH=`
- Solaris, Linux, and OS X—`unset CLASSPATH; export CLASSPATH`

To set the CLASSPATH variable, use these commands (for example):

- Windows—`C:\> set CLASSPATH=C:\users\george\java\classes`
- Solaris, Linux, and OS X—`% CLASSPATH=/home/george/java/classes; export CLASSPATH`

Summary of Creating and Using Packages

To create a package for a type, put a `package` statement as the first statement in the source file that contains the type (class, interface, enumeration, or annotation type). To use a public type that's in a different package, you have three choices: (1) use the fully qualified name of the type, (2) import the type, or (3) import the entire package of which the type is a member. The path names for a package's source and class files mirror the name of the package. You might have to set your CLASS-PATH so that the compiler and the Java VM can find the `.class` files for your types.

Questions and Exercises: Creating and Using Packages

Questions

Assume you have written some classes. Belatedly, you decide they should be split into three packages, as listed in Table 8.2. Furthermore, assume the classes are currently in the default package (and they have no `package` statements).

Table 8.2 Destination Packages

Package name	Class name
mygame.server	Server
mygame.shared	Utilities
mygame.client	Client

1. Which line of code will you need to add to each source file to put each class in the right package?
2. To adhere to the directory structure, you will need to create some subdirectories in the development directory and put source files in the correct subdirectories. Which subdirectories must you create? Which subdirectory does each source file go in?
3. Do you think you'll need to make any other changes to the source files to make them compile correctly? If so, describe these changes.

Exercises

Download the source files as listed here.

- `Client.java`[1]
- `Server.java`[2]
- `Utilities.java`[3]

1. Implement the changes you proposed in questions 1 through 3 using the source files you just downloaded.
2. Compile the revised source files. Note that if you're invoking the compiler from the command line (as opposed to using a builder), you should invoke the compiler from the directory that contains the `mygame` directory you just created.

Answers

You can find answers to these questions and exercises at `http://docs.oracle .com/javase/tutorial/java/package/QandE/packages-answers.html`.

---

1.   `tutorial/java/package/QandE/question/Client.java`
2.   `tutorial/java/package/QandE/question/Server.java`
3.   `tutorial/java/package/QandE/question/Utilities.java`

9

Numbers and Strings

Chapter Contents

Numbers   271
Characters   287
Strings   288

This chapter begins with a discussion of the Number class (in the java.lang package) and its subclasses. In particular, the first section talks about the situations where you would use instantiations of these classes rather than the primitive data types. Additionally, this section talks about other classes that format the output of numbers and perform more complex mathematical functions. Finally, there is a discussion on autoboxing and unboxing, a compiler feature that simplifies your code. The second section discusses characters, and the third section discusses strings, which are a sequence of characters and widely used in Java programming. In the Java programming language, strings are objects. This section describes using the String class to create and manipulate strings. It also compares the String and StringBuilder classes. There are questions and exercises throughout the chapter to test your knowledge.

Numbers

This section begins with a discussion of the Number[1] class in the java.lang package, its subclasses, and the situations where you would use instantiations of these

---

1.   8/docs/api/java/lang/Number.html

classes rather than the primitive number types. It also presents the `PrintStream`[2] and `DecimalFormat`[3] classes, which provide methods for writing formatted numerical output. Finally, the `Math`[4] class in the `java.lang` package is discussed. It contains mathematical functions to complement the operators built into the language. This class has methods for the trigonometric functions, exponential functions, and so forth.

The Numbers Classes

When working with numbers, most of the time you use the primitive types in your code:

```
int i = 500;
float gpa = 3.65f;
byte mask = 0xff;
```

There are, however, reasons to use objects in place of primitives, and the Java platform provides *wrapper* classes for each of the primitive data types. These classes "wrap" the primitive in an object. Often, the wrapping is done by the compiler—if you use a primitive where an object is expected, the compiler *boxes* the primitive in its wrapper class for you. Similarly, if you use a number object when a primitive is expected, the compiler *unboxes* the object for you. For more information, see the "Autoboxing and Unboxing" section. All numeric wrapper classes are subclasses of the abstract class `Number`.

> **Note**
>
> There are four other subclasses of `Number` that are not discussed here. `BigDecimal` and `BigInteger` are used for high-precision calculations. `AtomicInteger` and `AtomicLong` are used for multithreaded applications.

There are three reasons why you might use a `Number` object rather than a primitive:

1. As an argument of a method that expects an object (often used when manipulating collections of numbers)
2. To use constants defined by the class, such as `MIN_VALUE` and `MAX_VALUE`, that provide the upper and lower bounds of the data type

---

2.   8/docs/api/java/io/PrintStream.html

3.   8/docs/api/java/text/DecimalFormat.html

4.   8/docs/api/java/lang/Math.html

3. To use class methods for converting values to and from other primitive types, for converting to and from strings, and for converting between number systems (decimal, octal, hexadecimal, and binary)

Table 9.1 lists the instance methods that all the subclasses of the Number class implement. Each Number class contains other methods that are useful for converting numbers to and from strings and for converting between number systems. Table 9.2 lists these methods in the Integer class. Methods for the other Number subclasses are similar.

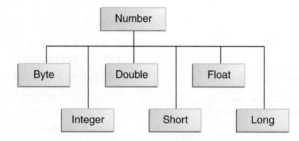

Figure 9.1 Subclasses of the Number Class

Table 9.1 Methods Implemented by All Subclasses of Number

Method	Description
byte byteValue() short shortValue() int intValue() long longValue() float floatValue() double doubleValue()	These methods convert the value of this Number object to the primitive data type returned.
int compareTo(Byte anotherByte) int compareTo(Double anotherDouble) int compareTo(Float anotherFloat) int compareTo(Integer anotherInteger) int compareTo(Long anotherLong) int compareTo(Short anotherShort)	These methods compare this Number object to the argument.
boolean equals(Object obj)	This method determines whether this number object is equal to the argument. The methods return true if the argument is not null and is an object of the same type and with the same numeric value. There are some extra requirements for Double and Float objects that are described in the Java Application Programming Interface (API) documentation.

Table 9.2 Conversion Methods, Integer Class

Method	Description
`static Integer decode(String s)`	Decodes a string into an integer and can accept string representations of decimal, octal, or hexadecimal numbers as input
`static int parseInt(String s)`	Returns an integer (decimal only)
`static int parseInt(String s, int radix)`	Returns an integer, given a string representation of decimal, binary, octal, or hexadecimal (`radix` equals 10, 2, 8, or 16, respectively) numbers as input
`String toString()`	Returns a `String` object representing the value of this `Integer`
`static String toString(int i)`	Returns a `String` object representing the specified integer
`static Integer valueOf(int i)`	Returns an `Integer` object holding the value of the specified primitive
`static Integer valueOf(String s)`	Returns an `Integer` object holding the value of the specified string representation
`static Integer valueOf(String s, int radix)`	Returns an `Integer` object holding the integer value of the specified string representation, parsed with the value of radix (e.g., if s equals 333 and radix equals 8, the method returns the base-ten integer equivalent of the octal number 333)

Formatting Numeric Print Output

Earlier you saw the use of the `print` and `println` methods for printing strings to standard output (`System.out`). Since all numbers can be converted to strings (as you will see later in this chapter), you can use these methods to print out an arbitrary mixture of strings and numbers. The Java programming language has other methods, however, that allow you to exercise much more control over your print output when numbers are included.

The printf and format Methods

The `java.io` package includes a `PrintStream` class that has two formatting methods that you can use to replace `print` and `println`. These methods, `format` and `printf`, are equivalent to one another. The familiar `System.out` that you have been using happens to be a `PrintStream` object, so you can invoke `PrintStream` methods on `System.out`. Thus you can use `format` or `printf` anywhere in your code where you have previously been using `print` or `println`:

```
System.out.format(...);
```

The syntax for these two `java.io.PrintStream`[5] methods is the same:

```
public PrintStream format(String format, Object... args)
```

Here, `format` is a string that specifies the formatting to be used and `args` is a list of the variables to be printed using that formatting. A simple example would be the following:

```
System.out.format("The value of " + "the float variable is " +
    "%f, while the value of the " + "integer variable is %d, " +
    "and the string is %s", floatVar, intVar, stringVar);
```

The first parameter, `format`, is a format string specifying how the objects in the second parameter, `args`, are to be formatted. The format string contains plain text as well as *format specifiers*, which are special characters that format the arguments of `Object...` `args`. (The notation `Object...` `args` is called *varargs*, which means that the number of arguments may vary; see Chapter 4, "Arbitrary Number of Arguments.")

Format specifiers begin with a percent sign (%) and end with a *converter*. The converter is a character indicating the type of argument to be formatted. In between the percent sign (%) and the converter, you can have optional flags and specifiers. There are many converters, flags, and specifiers, which are documented in `java.util.Formatter`.[6] Here is a basic example:

```
int i = 461012;
System.out.format("The value of i is: %d%n", i);
```

The `%d` specifies that the single variable is a decimal integer. The `%n` is a platform-independent newline character. This is the output:

```
The value of i is: 461012
```

The `printf` and `format` methods are overloaded. Each has a version with the following syntax:

```
public PrintStream format(Locale l, String format, Object... args)
```

---

5.   8/docs/api/java/io/PrintStream.html
6.   8/docs/api/java/util/Formatter.html

To print numbers in the French system (where a comma is used in place of the decimal place in the English representation of floating-point numbers), for example, you would use the following:

```
System.out.format(Locale.FRANCE,
    "The value of the float " + "variable is %f, while the " +
    "value of the integer variable " + "is %d, and the string is %s%n",
    floatVar, intVar, stringVar);
```

An Example

Tables 9.3 and 9.4 list some of the converters and flags that are used in the sample program, TestFormat.java, which shows some of the formatting that you can do with format. The output is shown within double quotes in the embedded comment:

Table 9.3 Converters Used in TestFormat.java

Converter	Explanation
D	A decimal integer
F	A float
N	A new line character appropriate to the platform running the application—always use %n, rather than \n
tB	A date and time conversion—locale-specific full name of month
td, te	A date and time conversion—two-digit day of month (Note that td has leading zeroes as needed; te does not.)
ty, tY	A date and time conversion—ty = two-digit year, tY = four-digit year
Tl	A date and time conversion—hour in twelve-hour clock.
tM	A date and time conversion—minutes in two digits, with leading zeroes as necessary
Tp	A date and time conversion—locale-specific am/pm (lowercase)
Tm	A date and time conversion—months in two digits, with leading zeroes as necessary
tD	A date and time conversion—date as %tm%td%ty

Table 9.4 Flags Used in TestFormat.java

Flag	Explanation
08	Eight characters in width, with leading zeroes as necessary
+	Includes sign, whether positive or negative
,	Includes locale-specific grouping characters
–	Left justified
.3	Three places after decimal point
10.3	Ten characters in width, right justified, with three places after decimal point

```
        import java.util.Calendar;
        import java.util.Locale;

        public class TestFormat {

            public static void main(String[] args) {
                long n = 461012;
                System.out.format("%d%n", n);      // --> "461012"
                System.out.format("%08d%n", n);    // --> "00461012"
                System.out.format("%+8d%n", n);    // -->  " +461012"
                System.out.format("%,8d%n", n);    // -->  " 461,012"
                System.out.format("%+,8d%n%n", n); // --> "+461,012"

                double pi = Math.PI;

                System.out.format("%f%n", pi);     // --> "3.141593"
                System.out.format("%.3f%n", pi);   // --> "3.142"
                System.out.format("%10.3f%n", pi); // -->  "     3.142"
                System.out.format("%-10.3f%n", pi); // --> "3.142"
                System.out.format(Locale.FRANCE,
                               "%-10.4f%n%n", pi); // --> "3,1416"

                Calendar c = Calendar.getInstance();
                System.out.format("%tB %te, %tY%n", c, c, c); // --> "May 29, 2006"

                System.out.format("%tl:%tM %tp%n", c, c, c);  // --> "2:34 am"

                System.out.format("%tD%n", c);     // --> "05/29/06"
            }
        }
```

9

> **Note**
>
> The discussion in this section covers just the basics of the `format` and `printf` methods. Further detail can be found in Chapter 11. Using `String.format` to create strings is covered in the "Strings" section.

The DecimalFormat Class

You can use the `java.text.DecimalFormat` class to control the display of leading and trailing zeroes, prefixes and suffixes, grouping (thousands) separators, and the decimal separator.[7] `DecimalFormat` offers a great deal of flexibility in the formatting of numbers, but it can make your code more complex.

The example that follows creates a `DecimalFormat` object, `myFormatter`, by passing a pattern string to the `DecimalFormat` constructor. The `format()` method, which `DecimalFormat` inherits from `NumberFormat`, is then invoked by `myFormatter`—it accepts a `double` value as an argument and returns the formatted number in a string:

---

7.   8/docs/api/java/text/DecimalFormat.html

Here is a sample program that illustrates the use of DecimalFormat:

```
import java.text.*;

public class DecimalFormatDemo {

    static public void customFormat(String pattern, double value ) {
        DecimalFormat myFormatter = new DecimalFormat(pattern);
        String output = myFormatter.format(value);
        System.out.println(value + "   " + pattern + "   " + output);
    }

    static public void main(String[] args) {

        customFormat("###,###.###", 123456.789);
        customFormat("###.##", 123456.789);
        customFormat("000000.000", 123.78);
        customFormat("$###,###.###", 12345.67);
    }
}
```

Here is the output:

```
123456.789  ###,###.###  123,456.789
123456.789  ###.##  123456.79
123.78  000000.000  000123.780
12345.67  $###,###.###  $12,345.67
```

Table 9.5 explains each line of output.

Table 9.5 DecimalFormat.java Output

Value	Pattern	Output	Explanation
123456.789	###,###.###	123,456.789	The pound sign (#) denotes a digit, the comma is a placeholder for the grouping separator, and the period is a placeholder for the decimal separator.
123456.789	###.##	123456.79	The value has three digits to the right of the decimal point, but the pattern has only two. The format method handles this by rounding up.
123.78	000000.000	000123.780	The pattern specifies leading and trailing zeroes because the 0 character is used instead of the pound sign (#).
12345.67	$###,###.###	$12,345.67	The first character in the pattern is the dollar sign ($). Note that it immediately precedes the leftmost digit in the formatted output.

Beyond Basic Arithmetic

The Java programming language supports basic arithmetic with its arithmetic operators: +, −, *, /, and %. The Math class in the `java.lang` package provides methods and constants for doing more advanced mathematical computation.[8]

The methods in the Math class are all static, so you call them directly from the class:

```
Math.cos(angle);
```

> **Note**
>
> Using the `static import` language feature, you don't have to write Math in front of every math function:
>
> ```
> import static java.lang.Math.*;
> ```
>
> This allows you to invoke the Math class methods by their simple names:
>
> ```
> cos(angle);
> ```

Constants and Basic Methods

The Math class includes two constants:

- Math.E, which is the base of natural logarithms
- Math.PI, which is the ratio of the circumference of a circle to its diameter

The Math class also includes more than forty static methods. Table 9.6 lists a number of the basic methods.

The following program, BasicMathDemo, illustrates how to use some of these methods:

```
public class BasicMathDemo {
    public static void main(String[] args) {
        double a = -191.635;
        double b = 43.74;
        int c = 16, d = 45;

        System.out.printf("The absolute value " + "of %.3f is %.3f%n",
                          a, Math.abs(a));
```

---

8.   8/docs/api/java/lang/Math.html

```
System.out.printf("The ceiling of " + "%.2f is %.0f%n",
                  b, Math.ceil(b));

System.out.printf("The floor of " + "%.2f is %.0f%n",
                  b, Math.floor(b));

System.out.printf("The rint of %.2f " + "is %.0f%n",
                  b, Math.rint(b));

System.out.printf("The max of %d and " + "%d is %d%n",
                  c, d, Math.max(c, d));

System.out.printf("The min of of %d " + "and %d is %d%n",
                  c, d, Math.min(c, d));
    }
}
```

Here's the output from this program:

```
The absolute value of -191.635 is 191.635
The ceiling of 43.74 is 44
```

Table 9.6 Basic Math Methods

Method	Description
`double abs(double d)` `float abs(float f)` `int abs(int i)` `long abs(long lng)`	Returns the absolute value of the argument
`double ceil(double d)`	Returns the smallest integer that is greater than or equal to the argument; returned as a double
`double floor(double d)`	Returns the largest integer that is less than or equal to the argument; returned as a double
`double rint(double d)`	Returns the integer that is closest in value to the argument; returned as a double
`long round(double d)` `int round(float f)`	Returns the closest long or int, as indicated by the method's return type, to the argument
`double min(double arg1, double arg2)` `float min(float arg1, float arg2)` `int min(int arg1, int arg2)` `long min(long arg1, long arg2)`	Returns the smaller of the two arguments
`double max(double arg1, double arg2)` `float max(float arg1, float arg2)` `int max(int arg1, int arg2)` `long max(long arg1, long arg2)`	Returns the larger of the two arguments

```
The floor of 43.74 is 43
The rint of 43.74 is 44
The max of 16 and 45 is 45
The min of 16 and 45 is 16
```

Exponential and Logarithmic Methods

Table 9.7 lists exponential and logarithmic methods of the Math class. The following program, ExponentialDemo, displays the value of *e* and then calls each of the methods listed in Table 9.7 on arbitrarily chosen numbers:

```
public class ExponentialDemo {
    public static void main(String[] args) {
        double x = 11.635;
        double y = 2.76;

        System.out.printf("The value of " + "e is %.4f%n",
                        Math.E);

        System.out.printf("exp(%.3f) " + "is %.3f%n",
                        x, Math.exp(x));

        System.out.printf("log(%.3f) is " + "%.3f%n",
                        x, Math.log(x));

        System.out.printf("pow(%.3f, %.3f) " + "is %.3f%n",
                        x, y, Math.pow(x, y));

        System.out.printf("sqrt(%.3f) is " + "%.3f%n",
                        x, Math.sqrt(x));
    }
}
```

Here's the output you'll see when you run ExponentialDemo:

```
The value of e is 2.7183
exp(11.635) is 112983.831
log(11.635) is 2.454
pow(11.635, 2.760) is 874.008
sqrt(11.635) is 3.411
```

Table 9.7 Exponential and Logarithmic Methods

Method	Description
double exp(double d)	Returns the base of the natural logarithms, *e*, to the power of the argument
double log(double d)	Returns the natural logarithm of the argument
double pow(double base, double exponent)	Returns the value of the first argument raised to the power of the second argument
double sqrt(double d)	Returns the square root of the argument

Trigonometric Methods

The `Math` class also provides a collection of trigonometric functions, which are summarized in Table 9.8. The value passed into each of these methods is an angle expressed in radians. You can use the `toRadians` method to convert from degrees to radians.

Here's a program, `TrigonometricDemo`, that uses each of these methods to compute various trigonometric values for a 45-degree angle:

```
public class TrigonometricDemo {
    public static void main(String[] args) {
        double degrees = 45.0;
        double radians = Math.toRadians(degrees);

        System.out.format("The value of pi " + "is %.4f%n",
                        Math.PI);

        System.out.format("The sine of %.1f " + "degrees is %.4f%n",
                        degrees, Math.sin(radians));

        System.out.format("The cosine of %.1f " + "degrees is %.4f%n",
                        degrees, Math.cos(radians));

        System.out.format("The tangent of %.1f " + "degrees is %.4f%n",
                        degrees, Math.tan(radians));

        System.out.format("The arcsine of %.4f " + "is %.4f degrees %n",
                        Math.sin(radians),
                        Math.toDegrees(Math.asin(Math.sin(radians))));

        System.out.format("The arccosine of %.4f " + "is %.4f degrees %n",
                        Math.cos(radians),
                        Math.toDegrees(Math.acos(Math.cos(radians))));

        System.out.format("The arctangent of %.4f " + "is %.4f degrees %n",
                        Math.tan(radians),
                        Math.toDegrees(Math.atan(Math.tan(radians))));
    }
}
```

The output of this program is as follows:

```
The value of pi is 3.1416
The sine of 45.0 degrees is 0.7071
The cosine of 45.0 degrees is 0.7071
The tangent of 45.0 degrees is 1.0000
The arcsine of 0.7071 is 45.0000 degrees
The arccosine of 0.7071 is 45.0000 degrees
The arctangent of 1.0000 is 45.0000 degrees
```

Table 9.8 Trigonometric Methods

Method	Description
`double sin(double d)`	Returns the sine of the specified double value
`double cos(double d)`	Returns the cosine of the specified double value
`double tan(double d)`	Returns the tangent of the specified double value
`double asin(double d)`	Returns the arcsine of the specified double value
`double acos(double d)`	Returns the arccosine of the specified double value
`double atan(double d)`	Returns the arctangent of the specified double value
`double atan2(double y, double x)`	Converts rectangular coordinates (x, y) to polar coordinate $(r, theta)$ and returns `theta`
`double toDegrees(double d)` `double toRadians(double d)`	Converts the argument to degrees or radians

Random Numbers

The `random()` method returns a pseudorandomly selected number between 0.0 and 1.0. The range includes 0.0 but not 1.0. In other words, `0.0 <= Math.random() < 1.0`. To get a number in a different range, you can perform arithmetic on the value returned by the random method. For example, to generate an integer between 0 and 9, you would write the following:

```
int number = (int)(Math.random() * 10);
```

By multiplying the value by 10, the range of possible values becomes `0.0 <= number < 10.0`.

Using `Math.random` works well when you need to generate a single random number. If you need to generate a series of random numbers, you should create an instance of `java.util.Random` and invoke methods on that object to generate numbers.

Autoboxing and Unboxing

Autoboxing is the automatic conversion that the Java compiler makes between the primitive types and their corresponding object wrapper classes (e.g., converting an `int` to an `Integer`, a `double` to a `Double`). If the conversion goes the other way, this is called *unboxing*.

Here is the simplest example of autoboxing:

```
Character ch = 'a';
```

The rest of the examples in this section use generics. If you are not yet familiar with the syntax of generics, see Chapter 7.

Consider the following code:

```
List<Integer> li = new ArrayList<>();
for (int i = 1; i < 50; i += 2)
    li.add(i);
```

Although you add the `int` values as primitive types, rather than `Integer` objects, to `li`, the code compiles. Because `li` is a list of `Integer` objects, not a list of `int` values, you may wonder why the Java compiler does not issue a compile-time error. The compiler does not generate an error because it creates an `Integer` object from `i` and adds the object to `li`. Thus the compiler converts the previous code to the following at runtime:

```
List<Integer> li = new ArrayList<>();
for (int i = 1; i < 50; i += 2)
    li.add(Integer.valueOf(i));
```

Converting a primitive value (an `int`, for example) into an object of the corresponding wrapper class (`Integer`) is called autoboxing. The Java compiler applies autoboxing when a primitive value is passed as a parameter to a method that expects an object of the corresponding wrapper class or assigned to a variable of the corresponding wrapper class. Consider the following method:

```
public static int sumEven(List<Integer> li) {
    int sum = 0;
    for (Integer i: li)
        if (i % 2 == 0)
            sum += i;
        return sum;
}
```

Because the remainder (`%`) and unary plus (`+=`) operators do not apply to `Integer` objects, you may wonder why the Java compiler compiles the method without issuing any errors. The compiler does not generate an error because it invokes the `intValue` method to convert an `Integer` to an `int` at runtime:

```
public static int sumEven(List<Integer> li) {
    int sum = 0;
    for (Integer i : li)
        if (i.intValue() % 2 == 0)
            sum += i.intValue();
        return sum;
}
```

Converting an object of a wrapper type (`Integer`) to its corresponding primitive (`int`) value is called unboxing. The Java compiler applies unboxing when an object of a wrapper class is passed as a parameter to a method that expects a value of the corresponding primitive type or assigned to a variable of the corresponding primitive type.

The Unboxing example shows how this works:

```java
import java.util.ArrayList;
import java.util.List;

public class Unboxing {

    public static void main(String[] args) {
        Integer i = new Integer(-8);

        // 1. Unboxing through method invocation
        int absVal = absoluteValue(i);
        System.out.println("absolute value of " + i + " = " + absVal);

        List<Double> ld = new ArrayList<>();
        ld.add(3.1416);     // Π is autoboxed through method invocation.

        // 2. Unboxing through assignment
        double pi = ld.get(0);
        System.out.println("pi = " + pi);
    }

    public static int absoluteValue(int i) {
        return (i < 0) ? -i : i;
    }
}
```

The program prints the following:

```
absolute value of -8 = 8
pi = 3.1416
```

Autoboxing and unboxing lets developers write cleaner code, making it easier to read. Table 9.9 lists the primitive types and their corresponding wrapper classes, which are used by the Java compiler for autoboxing and unboxing.

Table 9.9 Primitive Type and Equivalent Wrapper Class

Primitive type	Wrapper class
boolean	Boolean
byte	Byte
char	Character
float	Float
int	Integer
long	Long
short	Short
double	Double

Summary of Numbers

You use one of the wrapper classes—`Byte`, `Double`, `Float`, `Integer`, `Long`, or `Short`—to wrap a number of primitive type in an object. The Java compiler automatically wraps (boxes) primitives for you when necessary and unboxes them again when necessary.

The `Number` classes include constants and useful class methods. The `MIN_VALUE` and `MAX_VALUE` constants contain the smallest and largest values that can be contained by an object of that type. The `byteValue`, `shortValue`, and similar methods convert one numeric type to another. The `valueOf` method converts a string to a number, and the `toString` method converts a number to a string.

To format a string containing numbers for output, you can use the `printf()` or `format()` methods in the `PrintStream` class. Alternatively, you can use the `NumberFormat` class to customize numerical formats using patterns.

The `Math` class contains a variety of class methods for performing mathematical functions, including exponential, logarithmic, and trigonometric methods. `Math` also includes basic arithmetic functions, such as absolute value and rounding, and a method, `random()`, for generating random numbers.

Questions and Exercises: Numbers

Questions

1. Use the API documentation to find answers to the following questions:
    a. What `Integer` method can you use to convert an `int` into a string that expresses the number in hexadecimal? For example, what method converts the integer 65 into the string 41?
    b. What `Integer` method would you use to convert a string expressed in base 5 into the equivalent `int`? For example, how would you convert the string 230 into the integer value 65? Show the code you would use to accomplish this task.
    c. What `Double` method can you use to detect whether a floating-point number has the special value `Not a Number` (NaN)?

2. What is the value of the following expression and why?

    ```
    Integer.valueOf(1).equals(Long.valueOf(1))
    ```

Exercises

1. Change `MaxVariablesDemo` to show minimum values instead of maximum values. You can delete all code related to the variables `aChar` and `aBoolean`. What is the output?

2. Create a program that reads an unspecified number of integer arguments from the command line and adds them together. For example, suppose that you enter the following:

```
java Adder 1 3 2 10
```

The program should display 16 and then exit. The program should display an error message if the user enters only one argument. You can base your program on `ValueOfDemo`.

3. Create a program that is similar to the previous one but has the following differences:

- Instead of reading integer arguments, it reads floating-point arguments.
- It displays the sum of the arguments, using exactly two digits to the right of the decimal point.

For example, suppose that you enter the following:

```
java FPAdder 1 1e2 3.0 4.754
```

The program would display 108.75. Depending on your locale, the decimal point might be a comma (,) instead of a period (.).

Answers

You can find answers to these questions and exercises at `http://docs.oracle .com/javase/tutorial/java/data/QandE/numbers-answers.html`.

Characters

Most of the time, if you are using a single character value, you will use the primitive char type. Here is an example:

```
char ch = 'a';
// Unicode for uppercase Greek omega character
char uniChar = '\u03A9';
// an array of chars
char[] charArray = { 'a', 'b', 'c', 'd', 'e' };
```

There are times, however, when you need to use a char as an object—for example, as a method argument where an object is expected. The Java programming language provides a *wrapper* class that "wraps" the char in a Character object for this purpose. An object of type Character contains a single field whose type is char. This Character class also offers a number of useful class (i.e., static) methods for manipulating characters.[9]

---

9.   8/docs/api/java/lang/Character.html

You can create a `Character` object with the `Character` constructor:

```
Character ch = new Character('a');
```

The Java compiler will also create a `Character` object for you under some circumstances. For example, if you pass a primitive `char` into a method that expects an object, the compiler automatically converts the `char` to a `Character` for you. This feature is called *autoboxing*—or *unboxing*, if the conversion goes the other way. For more information on autoboxing and unboxing, see "Autoboxing and Unboxing."

> **Note**
>
> The `Character` class is immutable, so once it is created, a `Character` object cannot be changed.

Table 9.10 lists some of the most useful methods in the `Character` class but is not exhaustive. For a complete listing of all methods in this class (there are more than fifty), refer to the `java.lang.Character` API specification.[10]

Escape Sequences

A character preceded by a backslash (\) is an *escape sequence* and has special meaning to the compiler. Table 9.11 shows the Java escape sequences.

When an escape sequence is encountered in a print statement, the compiler interprets it accordingly. For example, if you want to put quotes within quotes, you must use the escape sequence, \", for the interior quotes. To print the sentence

```
She said "Hello!" to me.
```

you would write

```
System.out.println("She said \"Hello!\" to me.");
```

Strings

Strings, which are widely used in Java programming, are a sequence of characters. In the Java programming language, strings are objects. The Java platform provides the `String` class to create and manipulate strings.[11]

---

10.   8/docs/api/java/lang/Character.html

11.   8/docs/api/java/lang/String.html

Table 9.10 Useful Methods in the Character Class

Method	Description
`boolean isLetter(char ch)` `boolean isDigit(char ch)`	Determines whether the specified char value is a letter or a digit, respectively
`boolean isWhitespace(char ch)`	Determines whether the specified char value is white space
`boolean isUpperCase(char ch)` `boolean isLowerCase(char ch)`	Determines whether the specified char value is upper-case or lowercase, respectively
`char toUpperCase(char ch)` `char toLowerCase(char ch)`	Returns the uppercase or lowercase form of the specified char value
`toString(char ch)`	Returns a `String` object representing the specified character value—that is, a one-character string

Table 9.11 Escape Sequences

Escape sequence	Description
`\t`	Insert a tab in the text at this point
`\b`	Insert a backspace in the text at this point
`\n`	Insert a newline in the text at this point
`\r`	Insert a carriage return in the text at this point
`\f`	Insert a form feed in the text at this point
`\'`	Insert a single quote character in the text at this point
`\"`	Insert a double quote character in the text at this point
`\\`	Insert a backslash character in the text at this point

Creating Strings

The most direct way to create a string is to write

```
String greeting = "Hello world!";
```

In this case, `"Hello world!"` is a *string literal*—a series of characters in your code that is enclosed in double quotes. Whenever it encounters a string literal in your code, the compiler creates a `String` object with its value—in this case, `Hello world!`.

As with any other object, you can create `String` objects by using the `new` keyword and a constructor. The `String` class has thirteen constructors that allow you to provide the initial value of the string using different sources, such as an array of characters:

```
char[] helloArray = { 'h', 'e', 'l', 'l', 'o', '.' };
String helloString = new String(helloArray);
System.out.println(helloString);
```

The last line of this code snippet displays `hello`.

> **Note**
>
> The String class is immutable, so once it is created, a String object cannot be changed. The String class has a number of methods, some of which will be discussed later, that appear to modify strings. Since strings are immutable, what these methods really do is create and return a new string that contains the result of the operation.

String Length

Methods used to obtain information about an object are known as *accessor methods*. One accessor method that you can use with strings is the length() method, which returns the number of characters contained in the string object. After the following two lines of code have been executed, len equals 17:

```
String palindrome = "Dot saw I was Tod";
int len = palindrome.length();
```

A *palindrome* is a word or sentence that is symmetric—it is spelled the same forward and backward, ignoring case and punctuation. Here is a short but inefficient program to reverse a palindrome string. It invokes the String method charAt(int index), which returns the character at the specified index in the string. (Note the first character of a string is at index 0.)

```
public class StringDemo {
    public static void main(String[] args) {
        String palindrome = "Dot saw I was Tod";
        int len = palindrome.length();
        char[] tempCharArray = new char[len];
        char[] charArray = new char[len];

        // put original string in an
        // array of chars
        for (int i = 0; i < len; i++) {
            tempCharArray[i] =
                palindrome.charAt(i);
        }

        // reverse array of chars
        for (int j = 0; j < len; j++) {
            charArray[j] =
                tempCharArray[len - 1 - j];
        }

        String reversePalindrome =
            new String(charArray);
        System.out.println(reversePalindrome);
    }
}
```

Running the program produces this output:

```
doT saw I was toD
```

To accomplish the string reversal, the program had to convert the string to an array of characters (first `for` loop), reverse the array into a second array (second `for` loop), and then convert back to a string. The `String`[12] class includes a method, `getChars()`, to convert a string or a portion of a string into an array of characters so we could replace the first `for` loop in the program above with

```
palindrome.getChars(0, len, tempCharArray, 0);
```

Concatenating Strings

The `String` class includes a method for concatenating two strings:

```
string1.concat(string2);
```

This returns a new string that is `string1` with `string2` added to it at the end. You can also use the `concat()` method with string literals:

```
"My name is ".concat("Rumplestiltskin");
```

Strings are more commonly concatenated with the + operator:

```
"Hello," + " world" + "!"
```

This results in

```
"Hello, world!"
```

The + operator is widely used in `print` statements:

```
String string1 = "saw I was ";
System.out.println("Dot " + string1 + "Tod");
```

This prints

```
Dot saw I was Tod
```

12.   8/docs/api/java/lang/String.html

Such a concatenation can be a mixture of any objects. For each object that is not a `String`, its `toString()` method is called to convert it to a `String`.

> **Note**
>
> The Java programming language does not permit literal strings to span lines in source files, so you must use the + concatenation operator at the end of each line in a multiline string:
>
> ```
> String quote =
>     "Now is the time for all good " +
>     "men to come to the aid of their country.";
> ```
>
> Breaking strings between lines using the + concatenation operator is, once again, very common in print statements.

Creating Format Strings

You have seen the use of the `printf()` and `format()` methods to print output with formatted numbers. The `String` class has an equivalent class method, `format()`, that returns a `String` object rather than a `PrintStream` object.

Using `String`'s static `format()` method allows you to create a formatted string that you can reuse, as opposed to a one-time print statement. For example, instead of

```
System.out.printf("The value of the float " +
                  "variable is %f, while " +
                  "the value of the " +
                  "integer variable is %d, " +
                  "and the string is %s",
                  floatVar, intVar, stringVar);
```

you can write

```
String fs;
fs = String.format("The value of the float " +
                   "variable is %f, while " +
                   "the value of the " +
                   "integer variable is %d, " +
                   " and the string is %s",
                   floatVar, intVar, stringVar);
System.out.println(fs);
```

Converting between Numbers and Strings

Converting Strings to Numbers

Frequently, a program ends up with numeric data in a string object—a value entered by the user, for example. The `Number` subclasses that wrap primitive numeric types

(Byte,[13] Integer,[14] Double,[15] Float,[16] Long,[17] and Short[18]) each provide a class method named valueOf that converts a string to an object of that type. Here is an example, ValueOfDemo, that gets two strings from the command line, converts them to numbers, and performs arithmetic operations on the values:

```java
public class ValueOfDemo {
    public static void main(String[] args) {

        // this program requires two
        // arguments on the command line
        if (args.length == 2) {
            // convert strings to numbers
            float a = (Float.valueOf(args[0])).floatValue();
            float b = (Float.valueOf(args[1])).floatValue();

            // do some arithmetic
            System.out.println("a + b = " +
                               (a + b));
            System.out.println("a - b = " +
                               (a - b));
            System.out.println("a * b = " +
                               (a * b));
            System.out.println("a / b = " +
                               (a / b));
            System.out.println("a % b = " +
                               (a % b));
        } else {
            System.out.println("This program " +
                "requires two command-line arguments.");
        }
    }
}
```

The following is the output from the program when you use 4.5 and 87.2 for the command-line arguments:

```
a + b = 91.7
a - b = -82.7
a * b = 392.4
a / b = 0.0516055
a % b = 4.5
```

---

13.   8/docs/api/java/lang/Byte.html
14.   8/docs/api/java/lang/Integer.html
15.   8/docs/api/java/lang/Double.html
16.   8/docs/api/java/lang/Float.html
17.   8/docs/api/java/lang/Long.html
18.   8/docs/api/java/lang/Short.html

> **Note**
>
> Each of the `Number` subclasses that wrap primitive numeric types also provides a `parseXXXX()` method (e.g., `parseFloat()`) that can be used to convert strings to primitive numbers. Since a primitive type is returned instead of an object, the `parseFloat()` method is more direct than the `valueOf()` method. For example, in the `ValueOfDemo` program, we could use
>
> ```
> float a = Float.parseFloat(args[0]);
> float b = Float.parseFloat(args[1]);
> ```

Converting Numbers to Strings

Sometimes you need to convert a number to a string because you need to operate on the value in its string form. There are several easy ways to convert a number to a string:

```
int i;
// Concatenate "i" with an empty string; conversion is handled for you.
String s1 = "" + i;
```

or

```
// The valueOf class method.
String s2 = String.valueOf(i);
```

Each of the `Number` subclasses includes a class method, `toString()`, that will convert its primitive type to a string:

```
int i;
double d;
String s3 = Integer.toString(i);
String s4 = Double.toString(d);
```

The `ToStringDemo` example uses the `toString` method to convert a number to a string. The program then uses some string methods to compute the number of digits before and after the decimal point:

```
public class ToStringDemo {

    public static void main(String[] args) {
        double d = 858.48;
        String s = Double.toString(d);

        int dot = s.indexOf('.');

        System.out.println(dot + " digits " +
            "before decimal point.");
        System.out.println( (s.length() - dot - 1) +
            " digits after decimal point.");
```

```
    }
}
```

The output of this program is

```
3 digits before decimal point.
2 digits after decimal point.
```

Manipulating Characters in a String

The `String` class has a number of methods for examining the contents of strings, finding characters or substrings within a string, changing case, and other tasks.

Getting Characters and Substrings by Index

You can get the character at a particular index within a string by invoking the `charAt()` accessor method. The index of the first character is 0, while the index of the last character is `length()-1`. For example, the following code gets the character at index 9 in a string:

```
String anotherPalindrome = "Niagara. O roar again!";
char aChar = anotherPalindrome.charAt(9);
```

Indices begin at 0, so the character at index 9 is *O*, as illustrated in Figure 9.2.

If you want to get more than one consecutive character from a string, you can use the `substring` method. The `substring` method has two versions, as shown in Table 9.12.

Returning to the Niagara palindrome, the following code obtains the substring that extends from index 11 up to but not including index 15, which is the word *roar*:

```
String anotherPalindrome = "Niagara. O roar again!";
String roar = anotherPalindrome.substring(11, 15);
```

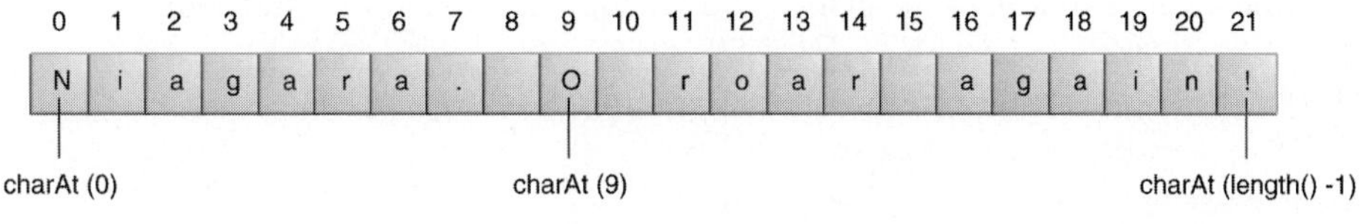

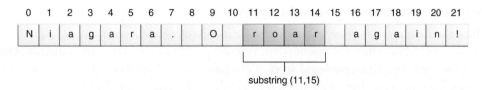

Figure 9.2 The Character at Index 9

Figure 9.3 Substring from Index 11 to 15

Table 9.12 The substring Methods in the String Class

Method	Description
`String substring(int beginIndex, int endIndex)`	This method returns a new string that is a substring of this string. The first integer argument specifies the index of the first character. The second integer argument is the index of the last character minus one.
`String substring(int beginIndex)`	This method returns a new string that is a substring of this string. The integer argument specifies the index of the first character. Here the returned substring extends to the end of the original string.

9

Other Methods for Manipulating Strings

Table 9.13 lists several other `String` methods for manipulating strings.

Searching for Characters and Substrings in a String

Here are some other `String` methods for finding characters or substrings within a string. The `String` class provides accessor methods that return the position within the string of a specific character or substring: `indexOf()` and `lastIndexOf()`. The `indexOf()` methods search forward from the beginning of the string, and the `lastIndexOf()` methods search backward from the end of the string. If a character or substring is not found, `indexOf()` and `lastIndexOf()` return −1.

The `String` class also provides a search method, `contains`, that returns true if the string contains a particular character sequence. Use this method when you only need to know that the string contains a character sequence but the precise location isn't important. Table 9.14 describes the various string search methods.

> **Note**
>
> `CharSequence` is an interface that is implemented by the `String` class. Therefore, you can use a string as an argument for the `contains()` method.

Replacing Characters and Substrings into a String

The `String` class has very few methods for inserting characters or substrings into a string. In general, they are not needed: You can create a new string by concatenation of substrings you have *removed* from a string with the substring that you want to insert. The `String` class does have four methods for *replacing* found characters or substrings, however; see Table 9.15.

Table 9.13 Other Methods in the String Class for Manipulating Strings

Method	Description
`String[] split(String regex)` `String[] split(String regex, int limit)`	These methods search for a match as specified by the string argument (which contains a regular expression) and split this string into an array of strings accordingly. The optional integer argument specifies the maximum size of the returned array. Regular expressions are covered in Chapter 14.
`CharSequence subSequence(int beginIndex, int endIndex)`	This method returns a new character sequence constructed from `beginIndex` index up until `endIndex` minus one.
`String trim()`	This method returns a copy of this string with leading and trailing white space removed.
`String toLowerCase()` `String toUpperCase()`	These methods return a copy of this string converted to lowercase or uppercase. If no conversions are necessary, these methods return the original string.

Table 9.14 The Search Methods in the String Class

Method	Description
`int indexOf(int ch)` `int lastIndexOf(int ch)`	Returns the index of the first (last) occurrence of the specified character
`int indexOf(int ch, int fromIndex)` `int lastIndexOf(int ch, int fromIndex)`	Returns the index of the first (last) occurrence of the specified character, searching forward (backward) from the specified index
`int indexOf(String str)` `int lastIndexOf(String str)`	Returns the index of the first (last) occurrence of the specified substring
`int indexOf(String str, int fromIndex)` `int lastIndexOf(String str, int fromIndex)`	Returns the index of the first (last) occurrence of the specified substring, searching forward (backward) from the specified index
`boolean contains(CharSequence s)`	Returns true if the string contains the specified character sequence

Table 9.15 Methods in the String Class for Manipulating Strings

Method	Description
`String replace(char oldChar, char newChar)`	Returns a new string resulting from replacing all occurrences of `oldChar` in this string with `newChar`
`String replace(CharSequence target, CharSequence replacement)`	Replaces each substring of this string that matches the literal target sequence with the specified literal replacement sequence
`String replaceAll(String regex, String replacement)`	Replaces each substring of this string that matches the given regular expression with the given replacement
`String replaceFirst(String regex, String replacement)`	Replaces the first substring of this string that matches the given regular expression with the given replacement

An Example

The following class, `Filename`, illustrates the use of `lastIndexOf()` and `substring()` to isolate different parts of a file name:

> **Note**
>
> The methods in the following `Filename` class don't do any error checking and assume that their argument contains a full directory path and a file name with an extension. If these methods were production code, they would verify that their arguments were properly constructed.

```java
public class Filename {
    private String fullPath;
    private char pathSeparator,
                 extensionSeparator;

    public Filename(String str, char sep, char ext) {
        fullPath = str;
```

```
            pathSeparator = sep;
            extensionSeparator = ext;
        }

        public String extension() {
            int dot = fullPath.lastIndexOf(extensionSeparator);
            return fullPath.substring(dot + 1);
        }

        // gets filename without extension
        public String filename() {
            int dot = fullPath.lastIndexOf(extensionSeparator);
            int sep = fullPath.lastIndexOf(pathSeparator);
            return fullPath.substring(sep + 1, dot);
        }

        public String path() {
            int sep = fullPath.lastIndexOf(pathSeparator);
            return fullPath.substring(0, sep);
        }
    }
```

9

Here is a program, `FilenameDemo`, that constructs a `Filename` object and calls all of its methods:

```
public class FilenameDemo {
    public static void main(String[] args) {
        final String FPATH = "/home/user/index.html";
        Filename myHomePage = new Filename(FPATH, '/', '.');
        System.out.println("Extension = " + myHomePage.extension());
        System.out.println("Filename = " + myHomePage.filename());
        System.out.println("Path = " + myHomePage.path());
    }
}
```

And here's the output from the program:

```
Extension = html
Filename = index
Path = /home/user
```

As shown in Figure 9.4, our `extension` method uses `lastIndexOf` to locate the last occurrence of the period (`.`) in the file name. Then `substring` uses the return value of `lastIndexOf` to extract the file name extension—that is, the substring from the period to the end of the string. This code assumes that the file name has a period in it; if the file name does not have a period, `lastIndexOf` returns –1 and the `substring` method throws a `StringIndexOutOfBoundsException`.

Also, notice that the `extension` method uses `dot + 1` as the argument to `substring`. If the period character (`.`) is the last character of the string, `dot + 1` is equal to the length of the string, which is one larger than the largest index into the string (because indices start at 0). This is a legal argument to `substring` because

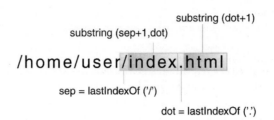

Figure 9.4 Isolating Different Parts of a File Name

that method accepts an index equal to but not greater than the length of the string and interprets it to mean *the end of the string*.

Comparing Strings and Portions of Strings

The `String` class has a number of methods for comparing strings and portions of strings. Table 9.16 lists these methods.

The following program, `RegionMatchesDemo`, uses the `regionMatches` method to search for a string within another string:

```
public class RegionMatchesDemo {
    public static void main(String[] args) {
        String searchMe = "Green Eggs and Ham";
        String findMe = "Eggs";
        int searchMeLength = searchMe.length();
        int findMeLength = findMe.length();
        boolean foundIt = false;
        for (int i = 0;
             i <= (searchMeLength - findMeLength);
             i++) {
            if (searchMe.regionMatches(i, findMe, 0, findMeLength)) {
                foundIt = true;
                System.out.println(searchMe.substring(i, i + findMeLength));
                break;
            }
        }
        if (!foundIt)
            System.out.println("No match found.");
    }
}
```

The output from this program is `Eggs`.

The program steps through the string referred to by `searchMe` one character at a time. For each character, the program calls the `regionMatches` method to determine whether the substring beginning with the current character matches the string the program is looking for.

Table 9.16 Methods for Comparing Strings

Method	Description
`boolean endsWith(String suffix)` `boolean startsWith(String prefix)`	These methods return `true` if the string ends with or begins with the substring specified as an argument to the method.
`boolean startsWith(String prefix, int offset)`	This method considers the string beginning at the index `offset` and returns `true` if it begins with the substring specified as an argument.
`int compareTo(String anotherString)`	This method compares two strings lexicographically and returns an integer indicating whether this string is greater than (result is > 0), equal to (result is = 0), or less than (result is < 0) the argument.
`int compareToIgnoreCase(String str)`	This method compares two strings lexicographically, ignoring differences in case, and returns an integer indicating whether this string is greater than (result is > 0), equal to (result is = 0), or less than (result is < 0) the argument.
`boolean equals(Object anObject)`	This method returns `true` if and only if the argument is a `String` object that represents the same sequence of characters as this object.
`boolean equalsIgnoreCase(String anotherString)`	This method returns `true` if and only if the argument is a `String` object that represents the same sequence of characters as this object, ignoring differences in case.
`boolean regionMatches(int toffset, String other, int ooffset, int len)`	This method tests whether the specified region of this string matches the specified region of the String argument. The region is of length `len` and begins at the index `toffset` for this string and `ooffset` for the other string.
`boolean regionMatches(boolean ignoreCase, int toffset, String other, int ooffset, int len)`	This method tests whether the specified region of this string matches the specified region of the String argument. The region is of length `len` and begins at the index `toffset` for this string and `ooffset` for the other string. The `boolean` argument indicates whether case should be ignored; if true, case is ignored when comparing characters.
`boolean matches(String regex)`	This method tests whether this string matches the specified regular expression. Regular expressions are discussed in Chapter 14.

9

The StringBuilder Class

StringBuilder[19] objects are like String[20] objects, except they can be modified. Internally, these objects are treated like variable-length arrays that contain a sequence of characters. At any point, the length and content of the sequence can be changed through method invocations.

Strings should always be used unless string builders offer an advantage in terms of simpler code (see the sample program described in the section "An Example Using the StringBuilder Class") or better performance. For example, if you need to concatenate a large number of strings, appending to a StringBuilder object is more efficient.

Length and Capacity

The StringBuilder class, like the String class, has a length() method that returns the length of the character sequence in the builder. Unlike strings, every string builder also has a *capacity*, the number of character spaces that have been allocated. The capacity, which is returned by the capacity() method, is always greater than or equal to the length (usually greater than) and will automatically expand as necessary to accommodate additions to the string builder.

For example, the following code will produce a string builder with a length of 9 and a capacity of 16:

```
// creates empty builder, capacity 16
StringBuilder sb = new StringBuilder();
// adds 9 character string at beginning
sb.append("Greetings");
```

The StringBuilder class has some methods related to length and capacity that the String class does not have (Table 9.18). A number of operations (e.g., append(), insert(), or setLength()) can increase the length of the character sequence in the string builder so that the resultant length() would be greater than the current capacity(). When this happens, the capacity is automatically increased.

StringBuilder Operations

The principal operations on a StringBuilder that are not available in String are the append() and insert() methods, which are overloaded so as to accept data of any type. Each converts its argument to a string and then appends or inserts the characters of that string to the character sequence in the string builder. The append() method always adds these characters at the end of the existing character sequence, while the insert() method adds the characters at a specified point. Table 9.19 lists a number of the methods of the StringBuilder class.

---

19. 8/docs/api/java/lang/StringBuilder.html
20. 8/docs/api/java/lang/String.html

> **Note**
> You can use any `String` method on a `StringBuilder` object by first converting the string builder to a string with the `toString()` method of the `StringBuilder` class. Then convert the string back into a string builder using the `StringBuilder(String str)` constructor.

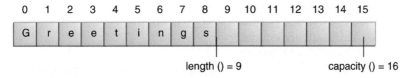

Figure 9.5 Creating a StringBuilder

9

Table 9.17 StringBuilder Constructors

Constructor	Description
`StringBuilder()`	Creates an empty string builder with a capacity of 16 (16 empty elements)
`StringBuilder(CharSequence cs)`	Constructs a string builder containing the same characters as the specified `CharSequence`, plus an extra 16 empty elements trailing the `CharSequence`
`StringBuilder(int initCapacity)`	Creates an empty string builder with the specified initial capacity
`StringBuilder(String s)`	Creates a string builder whose value is initialized by the specified string, plus an extra 16 empty elements trailing the string

Table 9.18 Length and Capacity Methods

Method	Description
`void setLength(int newLength)`	This method sets the length of the character sequence. If `newLength` is less than `length()`, the last characters in the character sequence are truncated. If `newLength` is greater than `length()`, null characters are added at the end of the character sequence.
`void ensureCapacity(int minCapacity)`	This method ensures that the capacity is at least equal to the specified minimum.

Table 9.19 Various StringBuilder Methods

Method	Description

`StringBuilder append(boolean b)`
`StringBuilder append(char c)`
`StringBuilder append(char[] str)`
`StringBuilder append(char[] str, int offset, int len)`
`StringBuilder append(double d)`
`StringBuilder append(float f)`
`StringBuilder append(int i)`
`StringBuilder append(long lng)`
`StringBuilder append(Object obj)`
`StringBuilder append(String s)`
	These methods append the argument to this string builder. The data is converted to a string before the append operation takes place.

`StringBuilder delete(int start, int end)` `StringBuilder deleteCharAt(int index)`	The first method deletes the subsequence from `start` to `end-1` (inclusive) in the `StringBuilder`'s char sequence. The second method deletes the character located at `index`.

`StringBuilder insert(int offset, boolean b)`
`StringBuilder insert(int offset, char c)`
`StringBuilder insert(int offset, char[] str)`
`StringBuilder insert(int index, char[] str,`
`   int offset, int len)`
`StringBuilder insert(int offset, double d)`
`StringBuilder insert(int offset, float f)`
`StringBuilder insert(int offset, int i)`
`StringBuilder insert(int offset, long lng)`
`StringBuilder insert(int offset, Object obj)`
`StringBuilder insert(int offset, String s)`
	These methods insert the second argument into the string builder. The first integer argument indicates the index before which the data is to be inserted. The data is converted to a string before the insert operation takes place.

`StringBuilder replace(int start, int end, String s)` `void setCharAt(int index, char c)`	This method replaces the specified character(s) in this string builder.
`StringBuilder reverse()`	This method reverses the sequence of characters in this string builder.
`String toString()`	This method returns a string that contains the character sequence in the builder.

9

An Example Using the StringBuilder Class

The `StringDemo` program that was listed in the section titled "Strings" is an example of a program that would be more efficient if a `StringBuilder` were used instead of a `String`. `StringDemo` reversed a palindrome. Here, once again, is its listing:

```java
public class StringDemo {
    public static void main(String[] args) {
        String palindrome = "Dot saw I was Tod";
        int len = palindrome.length();
        char[] tempCharArray = new char[len];
        char[] charArray = new char[len];

        // put original string in an
        // array of chars
        for (int i = 0; i < len; i++) {
            tempCharArray[i] =
                palindrome.charAt(i);
        }

        // reverse array of chars
        for (int j = 0; j < len; j++) {
            charArray[j] =
                tempCharArray[len - 1 - j];
        }

        String reversePalindrome =
            new String(charArray);
        System.out.println(reversePalindrome);
    }
}
```

Running the program produces this output:

```
doT saw I was toD
```

To accomplish the string reversal, the program converts the string to an array of characters (first `for` loop), reverses the array into a second array (second `for` loop), and then converts back to a string.

If you convert the `palindrome` string to a string builder, you can use the `reverse()` method in the `StringBuilder` class. It makes the code simpler and easier to read:

```java
public class StringBuilderDemo {
    public static void main(String[] args) {
        String palindrome = "Dot saw I was Tod";

        StringBuilder sb = new StringBuilder(palindrome);

        sb.reverse();  // reverse it

        System.out.println(sb);
```

```
    }
  }
```

Running this program produces the same output:

```
doT saw I was toD
```

Note that `println()` prints a string builder because `sb.toString()` is called implicitly, as it is with any other object in a `println()` invocation:

```
System.out.println(sb);
```

> **Note**
>
> There is also a `StringBuffer` class that is *exactly* the same as the `StringBuilder` class, except it is thread safe by virtue of having its methods synchronized. Threads will be discussed in Chapter 13.

Summary of Characters and Strings

Most of the time, if you are using a single character value, you will use the primitive `char` type. There are times, however, when you need to use a char as an object—for example, as a method argument where an object is expected. The Java programming language provides a *wrapper* class that "wraps" the char in a `Character` object for this purpose. An object of type `Character` contains a single field whose type is char. This `Character` class also offers a number of useful class (i.e., static) methods for manipulating characters.

Strings are a sequence of characters and are widely used in Java programming. In the Java programming language, strings are objects. The `String` class has more than sixty methods and thirteen constructors.[21] Most commonly, you create a string with a statement like this, rather than using one of the `String` constructors:

```
String s = "Hello world!";
```

The `String` class has many methods to find and retrieve substrings; these can then be easily reassembled into new strings using the + concatenation operator. The `String` class also includes a number of utility methods, among them `split()`, `toLowerCase()`, `toUpperCase()`, and `valueOf()`. The latter method is indispensable in converting user input strings to numbers. The `Number` subclasses also have methods for converting strings to numbers and vice versa.

---

21.   8/docs/api/java/lang/String.html

In addition to the `String` class, there is also a `StringBuilder`[22] class. Working with `StringBuilder` objects can sometimes be more efficient than working with strings. The `StringBuilder` class offers a few methods that can be useful for strings, among them `reverse()`. In general, however, the `String` class has a wider variety of methods.

A string can be converted to a string builder using a `StringBuilder` constructor. A string builder can be converted to a string with the `toString()` method.

Questions and Exercises: Characters and Strings

Questions

1. What is the initial capacity of the following string builder?

   ```
   StringBuilder sb = new StringBuilder("Able was I ere I saw Elba.");
   ```

2. Consider the following string:

   ```
   String hannah = "Did Hannah see bees? Hannah did.";
   ```

   a. What is the value displayed by the expression `hannah.length()`?

   b. What is the value returned by the method call `hannah.charAt(12)`?

   c. Write an expression that refers to the letter b in the string referred to by hannah.

3. How long is the string returned by the following expression? What is the string?

   ```
   "Was it a car or a cat I saw?".substring(9, 12)
   ```

4. In the following program, called `ComputeResult`, what is the value of `result` after each numbered line executes?

   ```
   public class ComputeResult {
       public static void main(String[] args) {
           String original = "software";
           StringBuilder result = new StringBuilder("hi");
           int index = original.indexOf('a');

   /*1*/   result.setCharAt(0, original.charAt(0));
   /*2*/   result.setCharAt(1, original.charAt(original.length()-1));
   /*3*/   result.insert(1, original.charAt(4));
   /*4*/   result.append(original.substring(1,4));
   /*5*/   result.insert(3, (original.substring(index, index+2) + " "));

           System.out.println(result);
       }
   }
   ```

22. 8/docs/api/java/lang/StringBuilder.html

Exercises

1. Show two ways to concatenate the following two strings together to get the string `"Hi, mom."`:

   ```
   String hi = "Hi, ";
   String mom = "mom.";
   ```

2. Write a program that computes your initials from your full name and displays them.

3. An anagram is a word or a phrase made by transposing the letters of another word or phrase; for example, "parliament" is an anagram of "partial men" and "software" is an anagram of "swear oft." Write a program that figures out whether one string is an anagram of another string. The program should ignore white space and punctuation.

Answers

You can find answers to these questions and exercises at `http://docs.oracle` `.com/javase/tutorial/java/data/QandE/characters-answers.html`.

10

Exceptions

Chapter Contents
What Is an Exception?   310
The Catch or Specify Requirement   311
Catching and Handling Exceptions   313
Specifying the Exceptions Thrown by a Method   323
How to Throw Exceptions   324
Unchecked Exceptions: The Controversy   329
Advantages of Exceptions   330
Summary   335
Questions and Exercises: Exceptions   336

The Java programming language uses *exceptions* to handle errors and other exceptional events. This chapter describes when and how to use exceptions. The first section defines an *exception*. An exception is an event that occurs during the execution of a program that disrupts the normal flow of instructions. The second section discusses the catch or specify requirement and describes the three kinds of exceptions. The third section covers how to catch and handle exceptions. The discussion includes the `try`, `catch`, and `finally` blocks. The fourth section covers how to specify the exceptions thrown by a method. The fifth section covers how to throw exceptions, how to chain exceptions, and how to create an exception class. The sixth section explains the correct and incorrect use of the unchecked exceptions indicated by subclasses of `RuntimeException`. The final section discusses the use of exceptions to manage errors, which has some advantages over traditional error-management techniques. The chapter ends with a summary and questions and exercises to test your knowledge.

What Is an Exception?

The term *exception* is shorthand for the phrase *exceptional event*.

> **Definition**
>
> An *exception* is an event that occurs during the execution of a program and disrupts the normal flow of the program's instructions.

When an error occurs within a method, the method creates an object and hands it off to the runtime system. The object, called an *exception object*, contains information about the error, including its type and the state of the program when the error occurred. Creating an exception object and handing it to the runtime system is called *throwing an exception*.

After a method throws an exception, the runtime system attempts to find something to handle it. This set of possible "somethings" to handle the exception is the ordered list of methods that had been called to get to the method where the error occurred. The list of methods is known as the *call stack* (see Figure 10.1).

The runtime system searches the call stack for a method that contains a block of code that can handle the exception. This block of code is called an *exception handler*. The search begins with the method in which the error occurred and proceeds through the call stack in the reverse order in which the methods were called. When an appropriate handler is found, the runtime system passes the exception to the handler. An exception handler is considered appropriate if the type of the exception object thrown matches the type that can be handled by the handler.

The exception handler chosen is said to *catch the exception*. If the runtime system exhaustively searches all the methods on the call stack without finding an appropriate exception handler, as shown in Figure 10.2, the runtime system (and consequently the program) terminates.

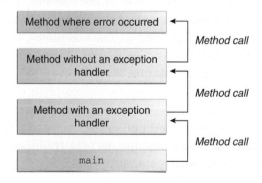

Figure 10.1 The Call Stack

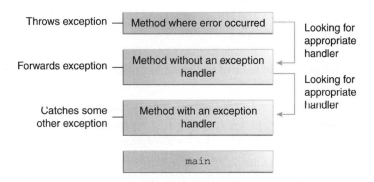

Figure 10.2 Searching the Call Stack for the Exception Handler

Using exceptions to manage errors has some advantages over traditional error-management techniques. You can learn more in the "Advantages of Exceptions" section.

The Catch or Specify Requirement

Valid Java programming language code must honor the *catch or specify requirement*. This means that code that might throw certain exceptions must be enclosed by either of the following:

- A `try` *statement that catches the exception*. The `try` must provide a handler for the exception, as described in "Catching and Handling Exceptions."
- A *method that specifies that it can throw the exception*. The method must provide a `throws` clause that lists the exception, as described in "Specifying the Exceptions Thrown by a Method."

Code that fails to honor the catch or specify requirement will not compile. Not all exceptions are subject to the catch or specify requirement. To understand why, we need to look at the three basic categories of exceptions, only one of which is subject to the requirement.

The Three Kinds of Exceptions

The first kind of exception is the *checked exception*. These are exceptional conditions that a well-written application should anticipate and recover from. For example, suppose an application prompts a user for an input file name and then opens the file by passing the name to the constructor for `java.io.FileReader`. Normally, the user provides the name of an existing, readable file, so the construction of the

`FileReader` object succeeds and the execution of the application proceeds normally. But sometimes the user supplies the name of a nonexistent file, and the constructor throws a `java.io.FileNotFoundException`. A well-written program will catch this exception and notify the user of the mistake, possibly prompting for a corrected file name.

Checked exceptions *are subject* to the catch or specify requirement. All exceptions are checked exceptions, except for those indicated by `Error`, `RuntimeException`, and their subclasses.

The second kind of exception is the *error*. These are exceptional conditions that are external to the application and that the application usually cannot anticipate or recover from. For example, suppose that an application successfully opens a file for input but is unable to read the file because of a hardware or system malfunction. The unsuccessful read will throw a `java.io.IOError`. An application might choose to catch this exception in order to notify the user of the problem, but it also might make sense for the program to print a stack trace and exit.

Errors *are not subject* to the catch or specify requirement. Errors are those exceptions indicated by `Error` and its subclasses.

The third kind of exception is the *runtime exception*. These are exceptional conditions that are internal to the application and that the application usually cannot anticipate or recover from. These usually indicate programming bugs, such as logic errors or improper use of an Application Programming Interface (API). For example, consider the application described previously that passes a file name to the constructor for `FileReader`. If a logic error causes a `null` to be passed to the constructor, the constructor will throw a `NullPointerException`. The application can catch this exception, but it probably makes more sense to eliminate the bug that caused the exception to occur. Runtime exceptions *are not subject* to the catch or specify requirement. Runtime exceptions are those indicated by `RuntimeException` and its subclasses.

Errors and runtime exceptions are collectively known as *unchecked exceptions*.

Bypassing Catch or Specify

Some programmers consider the catch or specify requirement a serious flaw in the exception mechanism and bypass it by using unchecked exceptions in place of checked exceptions. In general, this is not recommended. The section "Unchecked Exceptions: The Controversy" talks about when it is appropriate to use unchecked exceptions.

Catching and Handling Exceptions

This section describes how to use the three exception handler components—the `try`, `catch`, and `finally` blocks—to write an exception handler. After this, the `try`-with-resources statement is explained. This statement is particularly suited to situations that use `Closeable` resources, such as streams. The last part of this section walks through an example and analyzes what occurs during various scenarios.

The following example defines and implements a class named `ListOfNumbers`. When constructed, `ListOfNumbers` creates an `ArrayList` that contains 10 `Integer` elements with sequential values 0 through 9. The `ListOfNumbers` class also defines a method named `writeList`, which writes the list of numbers into a text file called `OutFile.txt`. This example uses output classes defined in `java.io`, which are covered in Chapter 11.

```java
// Note: This class will not compile yet.
import java.io.*;
import java.util.List;
import java.util.ArrayList;

public class ListOfNumbers {

    private List<Integer> list;
    private static final int SIZE = 10;

    public ListOfNumbers () {
        list = new ArrayList<Integer>(SIZE);
        for (int i = 0; i < SIZE; i++) {
            list.add(new Integer(i));
        }
    }

    public void writeList() {
        // The FileWriter constructor throws IOException, which must be caught.
        PrintWriter out = new PrintWriter(new FileWriter("OutFile.txt"));

        for (int i = 0; i < SIZE; i++) {
            // The get(int) method throws IndexOutOfBoundsException, which must be caught.
            out.println("Value at: " + i + " = " + list.get(i));
        }
        out.close();
    }
}
```

The first statement in boldface is a call to a constructor. The constructor initializes an output stream on a file. If the file cannot be opened, the constructor throws an `IOException`. The second boldface statement is a call to the `ArrayList` class's get method, which throws an `IndexOutOfBoundsException` if the value of its argument is too small (less than zero) or too large (more than the number of elements currently contained by the `ArrayList`).

If you try to compile the `ListOfNumbers` class, the compiler prints an error message about the exception thrown by the `FileWriter` constructor. However, it does not display an error message about the exception thrown by `get`. The reason is that the exception thrown by the constructor, `IOException`, is a checked exception and the one thrown by the `get` method, `IndexOutOfBoundsException`, is an unchecked exception.

Now that you're familiar with the `ListOfNumbers` class and where the exceptions can be thrown within it, you're ready to write exception handlers to catch and handle those exceptions.

The try Block

The first step in constructing an exception handler is to enclose the code that might throw an exception within a `try` block. In general, a `try` block looks like the following:

```
try {
    code
}
catch and finally blocks ...
```

The segment in the example labeled *code* contains one or more legal lines of code that could throw an exception. (The `catch` and `finally` blocks are explained in the next two sections.)

To construct an exception handler for the `writeList` method from the `ListOf-Numbers` class, enclose the exception-throwing statements of the `writeList` method within a `try` block. There is more than one way to do this. You can put each line of code that might throw an exception within its own `try` block and provide separate exception handlers for each, or you can put all the `writeList` code within a single `try` block and associate multiple handlers with it. The following listing uses one `try` block for the entire method because the code in question is very short:

```
private List<Integer> list;
private static final int SIZE = 10;

public void writeList() {
    PrintWriter out = null;
    try {
        System.out.println("Entered try statement");
        out = new PrintWriter(new FileWriter("OutFile.txt"));
        for (int i = 0; i < SIZE; i++) {
            out.println("Value at: " + i + " = " + list.get(i));
        }
```

```
        }
        catch and finally blocks  ...
    }
```

If an exception occurs within the `try` block, that exception is handled by an exception handler associated with it. To associate an exception handler with a `try` block, you must put a `catch` block after it; the next section shows you how.

The catch Blocks

You associate exception handlers with a `try` block by providing one or more `catch` blocks directly after the `try` block. No code can be between the end of the `try` block and the beginning of the first `catch` block.

```
try {

} catch (ExceptionType name) {

} catch (ExceptionType name) {

}
```

Each `catch` block is an exception handler that handles the type of exception indicated by its argument. The argument type, *ExceptionType*, declares the type of exception that the handler can handle and must be the name of a class that inherits from the `Throwable` class. The handler can refer to the exception with *name*.

The `catch` block contains code that is executed if and when the exception handler is invoked. The runtime system invokes the exception handler when the handler is the first one in the call stack whose *ExceptionType* matches the type of the exception thrown. The system considers it a match if the thrown object can legally be assigned to the exception handler's argument.

The following are two exception handlers for the `writeList` method:

```
try {

} catch (IndexOutOfBoundsException e) {
    System.err.println("IndexOutOfBoundsException: " + e.getMessage());
} catch (IOException e) {
    System.err.println("Caught IOException: " + e.getMessage());
}
```

Exception handlers can do more than just print error messages or halt the program. They can do error recovery, prompt the user to make a decision, or propagate the error up to a higher-level handler using chained exceptions, as described in the "Chained Exceptions" section.

Catching More Than One Type of Exception with One Exception Handler

A single `catch` block can handle more than one type of exception. This feature can reduce code duplication and lessen the temptation to catch an overly broad exception. In the `catch` clause, specify the types of exceptions that block can handle and separate each exception type with a vertical bar (|):

```
catch (IOException|SQLException ex) {
    logger.log(ex);
    throw ex;
}
```

> **Note**
>
> If a `catch` block handles more than one exception type, then the `catch` parameter is implicitly `final`. In this example, the `catch` parameter `ex` is `final`, and therefore you cannot assign any values to it within the `catch` block.

10

The finally Block

The `finally` block *always* executes when the `try` block exits. This ensures that the `finally` block is executed even if an unexpected exception occurs. But `finally` is useful for more than just exception handling—it allows the programmer to avoid having cleanup code accidentally bypassed by a `return`, `continue`, or `break`. Putting cleanup code in a `finally` block is always a good practice, even when no exceptions are anticipated.

> **Note**
>
> If the Java Virtual Machine (Java VM) exits while the `try` or `catch` code is being executed, then the `finally` block may not execute. Likewise, if the thread executing the `try` or `catch` code is interrupted or killed, the `finally` block may not execute even though the application as a whole continues.

The `try` block of the `writeList` method that you've been working with here opens a `PrintWriter`. The program should close that stream before exiting the `writeList` method. This poses a somewhat complicated problem because `writeList`'s `try` block can exit in one of three ways.

1. The new `FileWriter` statement fails and throws an `IOException`.
2. The `list.get(i)` statement fails and throws an `IndexOutOfBoundsException`.
3. Everything succeeds and the `try` block exits normally.

The runtime system always executes the statements within the `finally` block regardless of what happens within the `try` block, so it's the perfect place to perform cleanup.

The following `finally` block for the `writeList` method cleans up and then closes the `PrintWriter`:

```
finally {
    if (out != null) {
        System.out.println("Closing PrintWriter");
        out.close();
    } else {
        System.out.println("PrintWriter not open");
    }
}
```

> **Note**
>
> The `finally` block is a key tool for preventing resource leaks. When closing a file or otherwise recovering resources, place the code in a `finally` block to ensure that resource is *always* recovered. Consider using the try-with-resources statement in these situations, which automatically releases system resources when no longer needed. The next section has more information.

10

The try-with-resources Statement

The try-with-resources statement is a `try` statement that declares one or more resources. A *resource* is an object that must be closed after the program is finished with it. The try-with-resources statement ensures that each resource is closed at the end of the statement. Any object that implements `java.lang.AutoCloseable`, which includes all objects that implement `java.io.Closeable`, can be used as a resource.

The following example reads the first line from a file. It uses an instance of `BufferedReader` to read data from the file. `BufferedReader` is a resource that must be closed after the program is finished with it:

```
static String readFirstLineFromFile(String path) throws IOException {
    try (BufferedReader br =
                new BufferedReader(new FileReader(path))) {
        return br.readLine();
    }
}
```

In this example, the resource declared in the try-with-resources statement is a `BufferedReader`. The declaration statement appears within parentheses immediately after the `try` keyword. The class `BufferedReader` implements the interface `java.lang.AutoCloseable`. Because the `BufferedReader` instance is declared in a try-with-resource statement, it will be closed regardless of whether the `try` statement completes normally or abruptly (as a result of the method `BufferedReader.readLine` throwing an `IOException`).

Instead of a try-with-resources statement, you could use a `finally` block to ensure that a resource is closed regardless of whether the `try` statement completes normally or abruptly. The following example uses a `finally` block instead of a try-with-resources statement:

```
static String readFirstLineFromFileWithFinallyBlock(String path)
                                          throws IOException {
    BufferedReader br = new BufferedReader(new FileReader(path));
    try {
        return br.readLine();
    } finally {
        if (br != null) br.close();
    }
}
```

However, in this example, if the methods `readLine` and `close` both throw exceptions, then the method `readFirstLineFromFileWithFinallyBlock` throws the exception thrown from the `finally` block; the exception thrown from the `try` block is suppressed. In contrast, in the example `readFirstLineFromFile`, if exceptions are thrown from both the `try` block and the try-with-resources statement, then the method `readFirstLineFromFile` throws the exception thrown from the `try` block; the exception thrown from the try-with-resources block is suppressed. You can retrieve suppressed exceptions; see the "Suppressed Exceptions" section for more information.

You may declare one or more resources in a try-with-resources statement. The following example retrieves the names of the files packaged in the zip file `zipFileName` and creates a text file that contains the names of these files:

```
public static void writeToFileZipFileContents(String zipFileName,
                                     String outputFileName)
                                     throws java.io.IOException {

    java.nio.charset.Charset charset =
        java.nio.charset.StandardCharsets.US_ASCII;
    java.nio.file.Path outputFilePath =
        java.nio.file.Paths.get(outputFileName);

    // Open zip file and create output file with
    // try-with-resources statement

    try (
        java.util.zip.ZipFile zf =
            new java.util.zip.ZipFile(zipFileName);
        java.io.BufferedWriter writer =
            java.nio.file.Files.newBufferedWriter(outputFilePath, charset)
    ) {
        // Enumerate each entry
        for (java.util.Enumeration entries =
                        zf.entries(); entries.hasMoreElements();) {
            // Get the entry name and write it to the output file
            String newLine = System.getProperty("line.separator");
            String zipEntryName =
                ((java.util.zip.ZipEntry)entries.nextElement()).getName() +
```

```
                    newLine;
            writer.write(zipEntryName, 0, zipEntryName.length());
        }
    }
}
```

In this example, the `try-with-resources` statement contains two declarations that are separated by a semicolon: `ZipFile` and `BufferedWriter`. When the block of code that directly follows it terminates, either normally or because of an exception, the `close` methods of the `BufferedWriter` and `ZipFile` objects are automatically called in this order. Note that the `close` methods of resources are called in the *opposite* order of their creation.

The following example uses a `try-with-resources` statement to automatically close a `java.sql.Statement` object:

```
public static void viewTable(Connection con) throws SQLException {

    String query = "select COF_NAME, SUP_ID, PRICE, SALES, TOTAL from COFFEES";

    try (Statement stmt = con.createStatement()) {
        ResultSet rs = stmt.executeQuery(query);

        while (rs.next()) {
            String coffeeName = rs.getString("COF_NAME");
            int supplierID = rs.getInt("SUP_ID");
            float price = rs.getFloat("PRICE");
            int sales = rs.getInt("SALES");
            int total = rs.getInt("TOTAL");

            System.out.println(coffeeName + ", " + supplierID + ", " +
                                price + ", " + sales + ", " + total);
        }
    } catch (SQLException e) {
        JDBCTutorialUtilities.printSQLException(e);
    }
}
```

> **Note**
> A `try-with-resources` statement can have `catch` and `finally` blocks just like an ordinary `try` statement. In a `try-with-resources` statement, any `catch` or `finally` block is run after the resources declared have been closed.

Suppressed Exceptions

An exception can be thrown from the block of code associated with the `try-with-resources` statement. In the example `writeToFileZipFileContents`, an exception can be thrown from the `try` block, and up to two exceptions can be thrown from the `try-with-resources` statement when it tries to close the `ZipFile` and

BufferedWriter objects. If an exception is thrown from the try block and one or more exceptions are thrown from the try-with-resources statement, then those exceptions thrown from the try-with-resources statement are suppressed and the exception thrown by the block is the one that is thrown by the writeToFileZipFileContents method. You can retrieve these suppressed exceptions by calling the Throwable. getSuppressed method from the exception thrown by the try block.

Classes That Implement the AutoCloseable or Closeable Interface

See the Javadoc of the AutoCloseable[1] and Closeable[2] interfaces for a list of classes that implement either of these interfaces. The Closeable interface extends the AutoCloseable interface. The close method of the Closeable interface throws exceptions of type IOException, while the close method of the AutoCloseable interface throws exceptions of type Exception. Consequently, subclasses of the Auto-Closeable interface can override this behavior of the close method to throw specialized exceptions, such as IOException, or no exception at all.

Putting It All Together

The previous sections described how to construct the try, catch, and finally code blocks for the writeList method in the ListOfNumbers class. Now let's walk through the code and investigate what can happen.

When all the components are put together, the writeList method looks like the following.

```java
public void writeList() {
    PrintWriter out = null;

    try {
        System.out.println("Entering" + " try statement");

        out = new PrintWriter(new FileWriter("OutFile.txt"));
        for (int i = 0; i < SIZE; i++) {
            out.println("Value at: " + i + " = " + list.get(i));
        }
    } catch (IndexOutOfBoundsException e) {
        System.err.println("Caught IndexOutOfBoundsException: "
                        + e.getMessage());

    } catch (IOException e) {
        System.err.println("Caught IOException: " + e.getMessage());

    } finally {
        if (out != null) {
```

1.   8/docs/api/java/lang/AutoCloseable.html
2.   8/docs/api/java/io/Closeable.html

```
                    System.out.println("Closing PrintWriter");
                    out.close();
                }
                else {
                    System.out.println("PrintWriter not open");
                }
            }
        }
```

As mentioned previously, this method's `try` block has three different exit possibilities; here are two of them:

1. Code in the `try` statement fails and throws an exception. This could be an `IOException` caused by the new `FileWriter` statement or an `IndexOutOfBoundsException` caused by a wrong index value in the `for` loop.

2. Everything succeeds and the `try` statement exits normally.

Let's look at what happens in the `writeList` method during these two exit possibilities.

Scenario 1: An Exception Occurs

The statement that creates a `FileWriter` can fail for a number of reasons (e.g., the constructor for the `FileWriter` throws an `IOException` if the program cannot create or write to the file indicated).

When `FileWriter` throws an `IOException`, the runtime system immediately stops executing the `try` block; method calls being executed are not completed. The runtime system then starts searching at the top of the method call stack for an appropriate exception handler. In this example, when the `IOException` occurs, the `FileWriter` constructor is at the top of the call stack. However, the `FileWriter` constructor doesn't have an appropriate exception handler, so the runtime system checks the next method—the `writeList` method—in the method call stack. The `writeList` method has two exception handlers: one for `IOException` and one for `IndexOutOfBoundsException`.

The runtime system checks `writeList`'s handlers in the order in which they appear after the `try` statement. The argument to the first exception handler is `IndexOutOfBoundsException`. This does not match the type of exception thrown, so the runtime system checks the next exception handler—`IOException`. This matches the type of exception that was thrown, so the runtime system ends its search for an appropriate exception handler. Now that the runtime has found an appropriate handler, the code in that `catch` block is executed.

After the exception handler executes, the runtime system passes control to the `finally` block. Code in the `finally` block executes regardless of the exception caught above it. In this scenario, the `FileWriter` was never opened and doesn't need to be closed. After the `finally` block finishes executing, the program continues with the first statement after the `finally` block.

Here's the complete output from the `ListOfNumbers` program that appears when an `IOException` is thrown:

```
Entering try statement
Caught IOException: OutFile.txt
PrintWriter not open
```

The boldface code in the following listing shows the statements that get executed during this scenario:

```
public void writeList() {
    PrintWriter out = null;

    try {
        System.out.println("Entering try statement");
        out = new PrintWriter(new FileWriter("OutFile.txt"));
        for (int i = 0; i < SIZE; i++)
            out.println("Value at: " + i + " = " + list.get(i));

    } catch (IndexOutOfBoundsException e) {
        System.err.println("Caught IndexOutOfBoundsException: "
                             + e.getMessage());

    } catch (IOException e) {
        System.err.println("Caught IOException: " + e.getMessage());
    } finally {
        if (out != null) {
            System.out.println("Closing PrintWriter");
            out.close();
        }
        else {
            System.out.println("PrintWriter not open");
        }
    }
}
```

Scenario 2: The try Block Exits Normally

In this scenario, all the statements within the scope of the `try` block execute successfully and throw no exceptions. Execution falls off the end of the `try` block, and the runtime system passes control to the `finally` block. Because everything was successful, the `PrintWriter` is open when control reaches the `finally` block, which closes the `PrintWriter`. Again, after the `finally` block finishes executing, the program continues with the first statement after the `finally` block.

Here is the output from the `ListOfNumbers` program when no exceptions are thrown:

```
Entering try statement
Closing PrintWriter
```

The boldface code in the following sample shows the statements that get executed during this scenario:

```
public void writeList() {
    PrintWriter out = null;
    try {
        System.out.println("Entering try statement");
        out = new PrintWriter(new FileWriter("OutFile.txt"));
        for (int i = 0; i < SIZE; i++)
            out.println("Value at: " + i + " = " + list.get(i));

    } catch (IndexOutOfBoundsException e) {
        System.err.println("Caught IndexOutOfBoundsException: "
                                + e.getMessage());

    } catch (IOException e) {
        System.err.println("Caught IOException: " + e.getMessage());

    } finally {
        if (out != null) {
            System.out.println("Closing PrintWriter");
            out.close();
        }
        else {
            System.out.println("PrintWriter not open");
        }
    }
}
```

10

Specifying the Exceptions Thrown by a Method

The previous section showed how to write an exception handler for the writeList method in the ListOfNumbers class. Sometimes it's appropriate for code to catch exceptions that can occur within it. In other cases, however, it's better to let a method further up the call stack handle the exception. For example, if you were providing the ListOfNumbers class as part of a package of classes, you probably couldn't anticipate the needs of all the users of your package. In this case, it's better to *not* catch the exception and to allow a method further up the call stack to handle it.

If the writeList method doesn't catch the checked exceptions that can occur within it, the writeList method must specify that it can throw these exceptions. Let's modify the original writeList method to specify the exceptions it can throw instead of catching them. To remind you, here's the original version of the writeList method that won't compile:

```
public void writeList() {
    PrintWriter out = new PrintWriter(new FileWriter("OutFile.txt"));
```

```
        for (int i = 0; i < SIZE; i++) {
            out.println("Value at: " + i + " = " + list.get(i));
        }
        out.close();
    }
```

To specify that `writeList` can throw two exceptions, add a `throws` clause
to the method declaration for the `writeList` method. The `throws` clause
comprises the `throws` keyword followed by a comma-separated list of all the
exceptions thrown by that method. The clause goes after the method name and
argument list and before the brace that defines the scope of the method. Here's
an example:

```
public void writeList() throws IOException, IndexOutOfBoundsException {
```

Remember that `IndexOutOfBoundsException` is an unchecked exception; including it in the `throws` clause is not mandatory. You could just write the following:

```
public void writeList() throws IOException {
```

How to Throw Exceptions

Before you can catch an exception, some code somewhere must throw one. Any code
can throw an exception: your code or code from a package written by someone else,
such as the packages that come with the Java platform or the Java Runtime Environment (JRE). Regardless of what throws the exception, it's always thrown with
the `throw` statement.

As you have probably noticed, the Java platform provides numerous exception
classes. All the classes are descendants of the `Throwable`[3] class and all allow programs to differentiate among the various types of exceptions that can occur during
the execution of a program.

You can also create your own exception classes to represent problems that can
occur within the classes you write. In fact, if you are a package developer, you might
have to create your own set of exception classes to allow users to differentiate an
error that can occur in your package from errors that occur in the Java platform or
other packages.

You can also create *chained* exceptions. For more information, see the "Chained
Exceptions" section.

---

3.   8/docs/api/java/lang/Throwable.html

The throw Statement

All methods use the throw statement to throw an exception. The throw statement requires a single argument: a throwable object. Throwable objects are instances of any subclass of the Throwable class. Here's an example of a throw statement:

```
throw someThrowableObject;
```

Let's look at the throw statement in context. The following pop method is taken from a class that implements a common stack object. The method removes the top element from the stack and returns the object:

```java
public Object pop() {
    Object obj;

    if (size == 0) {
        throw new EmptyStackException();
    }

    obj = objectAt(size - 1);
    setObjectAt(size - 1, null);
    size--;
    return obj;
}
```

The pop method checks to see whether any elements are on the stack. If the stack is empty (its size is equal to zero), pop instantiates a new EmptyStackException object (a member of java.util) and throws it. The "Creating Exception Classes" section explains how to create your own exception classes. For now, all you need to remember is that you can throw only objects that inherit from the java.lang.Throwable class.

Note that the declaration of the pop method does not contain a throws clause. EmptyStackException is not a checked exception, so pop is not required to state that it might occur.

Throwable Class and Its Subclasses

The objects that inherit from the Throwable class include direct descendants (objects that inherit directly from the Throwable class) and indirect descendants (objects that inherit from children or grandchildren of the Throwable class). Figure 10.3 illustrates the class hierarchy of the Throwable class and its most significant subclasses. As you can see, Throwable has two direct descendants: Error[4] and Exception.[5]

---

4.   8/docs/api/java/lang/Error.html
5.   8/docs/api/java/lang/Exception.html

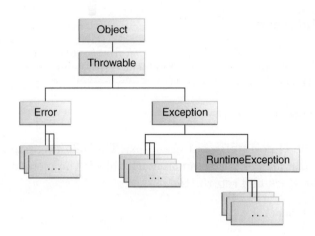

Figure 10.3 The Throwable Class

Error Class

When a dynamic linking failure or other hard failure in the Java VM occurs, the virtual machine throws an `Error`. Simple programs typically do *not* catch or throw `Error`s.

Exception Class

Most programs throw and catch objects that derive from the `Exception` class. An `Exception` indicates that a problem occurred, but it is not a serious system problem. Most programs you write will throw and catch `Exceptions` as opposed to `Errors`.

The Java platform defines the many descendants of the `Exception` class. These descendants indicate various types of exceptions that can occur. For example, `IllegalAccessException` signals that a particular method could not be found, and `NegativeArraySizeException` indicates that a program attempted to create an array with a negative size.

One `Exception` subclass, `RuntimeException`, is reserved for exceptions that indicate incorrect use of an API. An example of a runtime exception is `NullPointerException`, which occurs when a method tries to access a member of an object through a `null` reference. The section "Unchecked Exceptions: The Controversy" discusses why most applications shouldn't throw runtime exceptions or subclass `RuntimeException`.

Chained Exceptions

An application often responds to an exception by throwing another exception. In effect, the first exception *causes* the second exception. It can be very helpful to know when one exception causes another. *Chained Exceptions* help the programmer do this.

The following are the methods and constructors in `Throwable` that support chained exceptions:

```
Throwable getCause()
Throwable initCause(Throwable)
Throwable(String, Throwable)
Throwable(Throwable)
```

The `Throwable` argument to `initCause` and the `Throwable` constructors is the exception that caused the current exception. `getCause` returns the exception that caused the current exception, and `initCause` sets the current exception's cause.

The following example shows how to use a chained exception:

```
try {

} catch (IOException e) {
    throw new SampleException("Other IOException", e);
}
```

In this example, when an `IOException` is caught, a new `SampleException` exception is created with the original cause attached, and the chain of exceptions is thrown up to the next higher level exception handler.

Accessing Stack Trace Information

Now suppose that the higher-level exception handler wants to dump the stack trace in its own format.

> **Definition**
>
> A *stack trace* provides information on the execution history of the current thread and lists the names of the classes and methods that were called at the point when the exception occurred. A stack trace is a useful debugging tool that you'll normally take advantage of when an exception has been thrown.

The following code shows how to call the `getStackTrace` method on the exception object:

```
catch (Exception cause) {
    StackTraceElement elements[] = cause.getStackTrace();
    for (int i = 0, n = elements.length; i < n; i++) {
        System.err.println(elements[i].getFileName()
            + ":" + elements[i].getLineNumber()
            + ">> "
            + elements[i].getMethodName() + "()");
    }
}
```

Logging API

The next code snippet logs where an exception occurred from within the `catch` block. However, rather than manually parsing the stack trace and sending the output to `System.err()`, it sends the output to a file using the logging facility in the `java.util.logging` package:[6]

```
try {
    Handler handler = new FileHandler("OutFile.log");
    Logger.getLogger("").addHandler(handler);

} catch (IOException e) {
    Logger logger = Logger.getLogger("package.name");
    StackTraceElement elements[] = e.getStackTrace();
    for (int i = 0, n = elements.length; i < n; i++) {
        logger.log(Level.WARNING, elements[i].getMethodName());
    }
}
```

Creating Exception Classes

When faced with choosing the type of exception to throw, you can either use one written by someone else (since the Java platform provides a lot of exception classes you can use) or write one of your own. You should write your own exception classes if you answer yes to any of the following questions; otherwise, you can probably use someone else's:

- Do you need an exception type that isn't represented by those in the Java platform?
- Would it help users if they could differentiate your exceptions from those thrown by classes written by other vendors?
- Does your code throw more than one related exception?
- If you use someone else's exceptions, will users have access to those exceptions? A similar question is, should your package be independent and self-contained?

An Example

Suppose you are writing a linked list class. The class supports the following methods, among others:

- `objectAt(int n)`. This method returns the object in the nth position in the list and throws an exception if the argument is less than zero or more than the number of objects currently in the list.

---

6.   `8/docs/api/java/util/logging/package-summary.html`

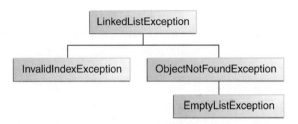

Figure 10.4 Example Exception Class Hierarchy

- `firstObject()`. This method returns the first object in the list and throws an exception if the list contains no objects.
- `indexOf(Object o)`. This method searches the list for the specified `Object` and returns its position in the list. It throws an exception if the object passed into the method is not in the list.

The linked list class can throw multiple exceptions, and it would be convenient to be able to catch all exceptions thrown by the linked list with one exception handler. Also, if you plan to distribute your linked list in a package, all related code should be packaged together. Thus the linked list should provide its own set of exception classes. Figure 10.4 illustrates one possible class hierarchy for the exceptions thrown by the linked list.

Choosing a Superclass

Any `Exception` subclass can be used as the parent class of `LinkedListException`. However, a quick perusal of those subclasses shows that they are inappropriate because they are either too specialized or completely unrelated to `LinkedListException`. Therefore, the parent class of `LinkedListException` should be `Exception`.

Most applets and applications you write will throw objects that are `Exceptions`. `Errors` are normally used for serious, hard errors in the system, such as those that prevent the Java VM from running.

> **Note**
>
> For readable code, it's good practice to append the string `Exception` to the names of all classes that inherit (directly or indirectly) from the `Exception` class.

Unchecked Exceptions: The Controversy

Because the Java programming language does not require methods to catch or to specify unchecked exceptions (`RuntimeException`, `Error`, and their subclasses), programmers may be tempted to write code that throws only unchecked exceptions or to make all their exception subclasses inherit from `RuntimeException`. Both shortcuts allow programmers to write code without bothering with compiler errors and without bothering to specify or to catch any exceptions. Although this may seem convenient to the programmer, it sidesteps the intent of the `catch` or `specify` requirement and can cause problems for others using your classes.

Why did the designers decide to force a method to specify all uncaught checked exceptions that can be thrown within its scope? Any `Exception` that can be thrown by a method is part of the method's public programming interface. Those who call a method must know about the exceptions that a method can throw so that they can decide what to do about them. These exceptions are as much a part of that method's programming interface as its parameters and return value.

The next question might be, "If it's so good to document a method's API, including the exceptions it can throw, why not specify runtime exceptions too?" Runtime exceptions represent problems that are the result of a programming problem, and as such, the API client code cannot reasonably be expected to recover from them or handle them in any way. Such problems include arithmetic exceptions, such as dividing by zero; pointer exceptions, such as trying to access an object through a null reference; and indexing exceptions, such as attempting to access an array element through an index that is too large or too small.

Runtime exceptions can occur anywhere in a program, and in a typical one, they can be very numerous. Having to add runtime exceptions in every method declaration would reduce a program's clarity. Thus the compiler does not require that you catch or specify runtime exceptions (although you can).

One case where it is common practice to throw a `RuntimeException` is when the user calls a method incorrectly. For example, a method can check if one of its arguments is incorrectly `null`. If an argument is `null`, the method might throw a `NullPointerException`, which is an *unchecked* exception. Generally speaking, do not throw a `RuntimeException` or create a subclass of `RuntimeException` simply because you don't want to be bothered with specifying the exceptions your methods can throw.

Here's the bottom line: If a client can reasonably be expected to recover from an exception, make it a checked exception. If a client cannot do anything to recover from the exception, make it an unchecked exception.

Advantages of Exceptions

Now that you know what exceptions are and how to use them, it's time to learn the advantages of using exceptions in your programs.

Advantage 1: Separating Error-Handling Code from "Regular" Code

Exceptions provide the means to separate the details of what to do when something out of the ordinary happens from the main logic of a program. In traditional programming, error detection, reporting, and handling often lead to confusing spaghetti code. For example, consider the pseudocode method here that reads an entire file into memory.

```
readFile {
    open the file;
    determine its size;
    allocate that much memory;
    read the file into memory;
    close the file;
}
```

At first glance, this function seems simple enough, but it ignores all the following potential errors:

- What happens if the file can't be opened?
- What happens if the length of the file can't be determined?
- What happens if enough memory can't be allocated?
- What happens if the read fails?
- What happens if the file can't be closed?

To handle such cases, the readFile function must have more code to do error detection, reporting, and handling. Here is an example of what the function might look like:

```
errorCodeType readFile {
    initialize errorCode = 0;

    open the file;
    if (theFileIsOpen) {
        determine the length of the file;
        if (gotTheFileLength) {
            allocate that much memory;
            if (gotEnoughMemory) {
                read the file into memory;
                if (readFailed) {
                    errorCode = -1;
                }
            } else {
                errorCode = -2;
            }
        } else {
            errorCode = -3;
        }
```

10

```
        close the file;
        if (theFileDidntClose && errorCode == 0) {
            errorCode = -4;
        } else {
            errorCode = errorCode and -4;
        }
    } else {
        errorCode = -5;
    }
    return errorCode;
}
```

There's so much error detection, reporting, and returning here that the original seven lines of code are lost in the clutter. Worse yet, the logical flow of the code has also been lost, thus making it difficult to tell whether the code is doing the right thing: Is the file really being closed if the function fails to allocate enough memory? It's even more difficult to ensure that the code continues to do the right thing when you modify the method three months after writing it. Many programmers solve this problem by simply ignoring it—errors are reported when their programs crash.

Exceptions enable you to write the main flow of your code and deal with the exceptional cases elsewhere. If the readFile function used exceptions instead of traditional error-management techniques, it would look more like the following.

```
readFile {
    try {
        open the file;
        determine its size;
        allocate that much memory;
        read the file into memory;
        close the file;
    } catch (fileOpenFailed) {
        doSomething;
    } catch (sizeDeterminationFailed) {
        doSomething;
    } catch (memoryAllocationFailed) {
        doSomething;
    } catch (readFailed) {
        doSomething;
    } catch (fileCloseFailed) {
        doSomething;
    }
}
```

Note that exceptions don't spare you the effort of doing the work of detecting, reporting, and handling errors, but they do help you organize the work more effectively.

Advantage 2: Propagating Errors Up the Call Stack

A second advantage of exceptions is the ability to propagate error reporting up the call stack of methods. Suppose that the readFile method is the fourth method in a series of nested method calls made by the main program: `method1` calls `method2`, which calls `method3`, which finally calls `readFile`:

```
method1 {
    call method2;
}

method2 {
    call method3;
}

method3 {
    call readFile;
}
```

Suppose also that `method1` is the only method interested in the errors that might occur within `readFile`. Traditional error-notification techniques force `method2` and `method3` to propagate the error codes returned by `readFile` up the call stack until the error codes finally reach `method1`—the only method that is interested in them:

```
method1 {
    errorCodeType error;
    error = call method2;
    if (error)
        doErrorProcessing;
    else
        proceed;
}

errorCodeType method2 {
    errorCodeType error;
    error = call method3;
    if (error)
        return error;
    else
        proceed;
}

errorCodeType method3 {
    errorCodeType error;
    error = call readFile;
    if (error)
        return error;
    else
        proceed;
}
```

Recall that the JRE searches backward through the call stack to find any methods that are interested in handling a particular exception. A method can duck any exceptions thrown within it, thereby allowing a method further up the call stack to catch it. Hence only the methods that care about errors have to worry about detecting errors:

```
method1 {
    try {
        call method2;
    } catch (exception e) {
        doErrorProcessing;
    }
}

method2 throws exception {
    call method3;
}

method3 throws exception {
    call readFile;
}
```

However, as the pseudocode shows, ducking an exception requires some effort on the part of the middleman methods. Any checked exceptions that can be thrown within a method must be specified in its `throws` clause.

Advantage 3: Grouping and Differentiating Error Types

Because all exceptions thrown within a program are objects, the grouping or categorizing of exceptions is a natural outcome of the class hierarchy. An example of a group of related exception classes in the Java platform are those defined in `java.io`—`IOException` and its descendants. `IOException` is the most general and represents any type of error that can occur when performing I/O operations. Its descendants represent more specific errors. For example, `FileNotFoundException` means that a file could not be located on disk.

A method can write specific handlers that can handle a very specific exception. The `FileNotFoundException` class has no descendants, so the following handler can handle only one type of exception:

```
catch (FileNotFoundException e) {
    ...
}
```

A method can catch an exception based on its group or general type by specifying any of the exception's superclasses in the `catch` statement. For example, to catch all I/O exceptions, regardless of their specific type, an exception handler specifies an `IOException` argument:

```
catch (IOException e) {
    ...
}
```

This handler will be able to catch all I/O exceptions, including `FileNotFound-Exception`, `EOFException`, and so on. You can find details about what occurred by querying the argument passed to the exception handler. For example, use the following to print the stack trace:

```
catch (IOException e) {
    // Output goes to System.err.
    e.printStackTrace();
    // Send trace to stdout.
    e.printStackTrace(System.out);
}
```

You could even set up an exception handler that handles any `Exception` with the following handler:

```
// A (too) general exception handler
catch (Exception e) {
    ...
}
```

The `Exception` class is close to the top of the `Throwable` class hierarchy. Therefore, this handler will catch many other exceptions in addition to those that the handler is intended to catch. You may want to handle exceptions this way if all you want your program to do, for example, is print out an error message for the user and then exit.

In most situations, however, you want exception handlers to be as specific as possible. The reason is that the first thing a handler must do is determine what type of exception occurred before it can decide on the best recovery strategy. In effect, by not catching specific errors, the handler must accommodate any possibility. Exception handlers that are too general can make code more error prone by catching and handling exceptions that weren't anticipated by the programmer and for which the handler was not intended.

As noted, you can create groups of exceptions and handle exceptions in a general fashion, or you can use the specific exception type to differentiate exceptions and handle exceptions in an exact fashion.

Summary

A program can use exceptions to indicate that an error occurred. To throw an exception, use the `throw` statement and provide it with an exception object—a descendant of `Throwable`—to provide information about the specific error that occurred. A method that throws an uncaught, checked exception must include a `throws` clause in its declaration.

A program can catch exceptions by using a combination of the `try`, `catch`, and `finally` blocks.

- The `try` block identifies a block of code in which an exception can occur.
- The `catch` block identifies a block of code, known as an exception handler, that can handle a particular type of exception.
- The `finally` block identifies a block of code that is guaranteed to execute and is the right place to close files, recover resources, and otherwise clean up after the code enclosed in the `try` block.

The `try` statement should contain at least one `catch` block or a `finally` block and may have multiple `catch` blocks.

The class of the exception object indicates the type of exception thrown. The exception object can contain further information about the error, including an error message. With exception chaining, an exception can point to the exception that caused it, which can in turn point to the exception that caused it, and so on.

Questions and Exercises: Exceptions

Questions

1. Is the following code legal?

   ```
   try {

   } finally {

   }
   ```

2. What exception types can be caught by the following handler?

   ```
   catch (Exception e) {

   }
   ```

   What is wrong with using this type of exception handler?

3. Is there anything wrong with the following exception handler as written? Will this code compile?

   ```
   try {

   } catch (Exception e) {

   } catch (ArithmeticException a) {

   }
   ```

4. Match each situation in the lettered list with an item in the numbered list:

  a. `int[] A;`

    `A[0] = 0;`

  b. The Java VM starts running your program, but the Java VM can't find the Java platform classes. (The Java platform classes reside in `classes.zip` or `rt.jar`.)

  c. A program is reading a stream and reaches the `end of stream` marker.

  d. Before closing the stream and after reaching the `end of stream` marker, a program tries to read the stream again.

1. __error

2. __checked exception

3. __compile error

4. __no exception

Exercises

10

1. Add a `readList` method to `ListOfNumbers.java`. This method should read in `int` values from a file, print each value, and append them to the end of the vector. You should catch all appropriate errors. You will also need a text file containing numbers to read in.

2. Modify the following `cat` method so that it will compile.

```
public static void cat(File file) {
    RandomAccessFile input = null;
    String line = null;

    try {
        input = new RandomAccessFile(file, "r");
        while ((line = input.readLine()) != null) {
            System.out.println(line);
        }
        return;
    } finally {
        if (input != null) {
            input.close();
        }
    }
}
```

Answers

You can find answers to these questions and exercises at `http://docs.oracle .com/javase/tutorial/essential/exceptions/QandE/answers.html`.

11

Basic I/O and NIO.2

Chapter Contents

I/O Streams   339
File I/O (Featuring NIO.2)   359
Summary   421
Questions and Exercises: Basic I/O   422

This chapter covers the Java platform classes used for basic input/output (I/O). It first focuses on *I/O streams*, a powerful concept that greatly simplifies I/O operations. The chapter also looks at serialization, which lets a program write whole objects out to streams and read them back again. Then the chapter looks at file I/O and file system operations, including random access files. Most of the classes covered in the "I/O streams" section are in the `java.io` package. Most of the classes covered in the "File I/O" section are in the `java.nio.file` package.

I/O Streams

An *I/O stream* represents an input source or an output destination. A stream can represent many different kinds of sources and destinations, including disk files, devices, other programs, and memory arrays.

Streams support many different kinds of data, including simple bytes, primitive data types, localized characters, and objects. Some streams simply pass on data; others manipulate and transform the data in useful ways.

No matter how they work internally, all streams present the same simple model to programs that use them: A stream is a sequence of data. A program uses an *input stream* to read data from a source, one item at a time, as indicated in Figure 11.1. A

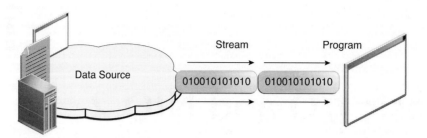

Figure 11.1 Reading Information into a Program

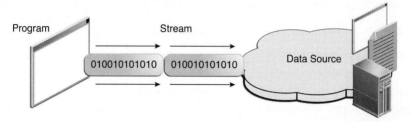

Figure 11.2 Writing Information from a Program

program uses an *output stream* to write data to a destination, one item at time, as indicated in Figure 11.2.

In this section, we'll see streams that can handle all kinds of data, from primitive values to advanced objects. The data source and data destination pictured in Figures 11.1 and 11.2 can be anything that holds, generates, or consumes data. Obviously this includes disk files, but a source or destination can also be another program, a peripheral device, a network socket, or an array.

In the next section, we'll use the most basic kind of streams, byte streams, to demonstrate the common operations of stream I/O. For sample input, we'll use the example file `xanadu.txt`, which contains the following verse:

```
In Xanadu did Kubla Khan
A stately pleasure-dome decree:
Where Alph, the sacred river, ran
Through caverns measureless to man
Down to a sunless sea.
```

Byte Streams

Programs use *byte streams* to perform input and output of 8-bit bytes. All byte stream classes are descended from `InputStream`[1] and `OutputStream`.[2]

---

1.   8/docs/api/java/io/InputStream.html

2.   8/docs/api/java/io/OutputStream.html

There are many byte stream classes. To demonstrate how byte streams work, we'll focus on the file I/O byte streams, `FileInputStream`[3] and `FileOutputStream`.[4] Other kinds of byte streams are used in much the same way; they differ mainly in the way they are constructed.

Using Byte Streams

We'll explore `FileInputStream` and `FileOutputStream` by examining an example program named `CopyBytes`, which uses byte streams to copy `xanadu.txt`, one byte at a time:

```
import java.io.FileInputStream;
import java.io.FileOutputStream;
import java.io.IOException;

public class CopyBytes {
    public static void main(String[] args) throws IOException {

        FileInputStream in = null;
        FileOutputStream out = null;

        try {
            in = new FileInputStream("xanadu.txt");
            out = new FileOutputStream("outagain.txt");
            int c;

            while ((c = in.read()) != -1) {
                out.write(c);
            }
        } finally {
            if (in != null) {
                in.close();
            }
            if (out != null) {
                out.close();
            }
        }
    }
}
```

`CopyBytes` spends most of its time in a simple loop that reads the input stream and writes the output stream, one byte at a time, as shown in Figure 11.3.

Always Close Streams

Closing a stream when it's no longer needed is very important—so important that `CopyBytes` uses a `finally` block to guarantee that both streams will be closed even if an error occurs. This practice helps avoid serious resource leaks.

---

3.   8/docs/api/java/io/FileInputStream.html
4.   8/docs/api/java/io/FileOutputStream.html

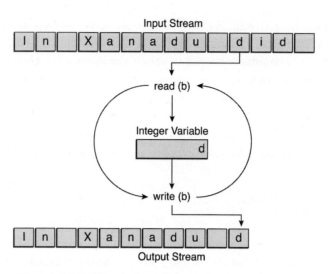

Figure 11.3 Simple Byte Stream Input and Output

One possible error is that `CopyBytes` was unable to open one or both files. When that happens, the stream variable corresponding to the file never changes from its initial `null` value. That's why `CopyBytes` makes sure that each stream variable contains an object reference before invoking `close`.

When Not to Use Byte Streams

`CopyBytes` seems like a normal program, but it actually represents a kind of low-level I/O that you should avoid. Since `xanadu.txt` contains character data, the best approach is to use character streams, as discussed in the next section. There are also streams for more complicated data types. Byte streams should only be used for the most primitive I/O.

So why talk about byte streams? Because all other stream types are built on byte streams.

Character Streams

The Java platform stores character values using Unicode conventions. Character stream I/O automatically translates this internal format to and from the local character set. In Western locales, the local character set is usually an 8-bit superset of ASCII.

For most applications, I/O with character streams is no more complicated than I/O with byte streams. Input and output done with stream classes automatically translates to and from the local character set. A program that uses character streams in place of byte streams automatically adapts to the local character set and is ready for internationalization—all without extra effort by the programmer.

If internationalization isn't a priority, you can simply use the character stream classes without paying much attention to character set issues. Later, if internationalization becomes a priority, your program can be adapted without extensive recoding.

Using Character Streams

All character stream classes are descended from Reader[5] and Writer.[6] As with byte streams, there are character stream classes that specialize in file I/O: FileReader[7] and FileWriter.[8] The CopyCharacters example illustrates these classes:

```java
import java.io.FileReader;
import java.io.FileWriter;
import java.io.IOException;

public class CopyCharacters {
    public static void main(String[] args) throws IOException {

        FileReader inputStream = null;
        FileWriter outputStream = null;

        try {
            inputStream = new FileReader("xanadu.txt");
            outputStream = new FileWriter("characteroutput.txt");

            int c;
            while ((c = inputStream.read()) != -1) {
                outputStream.write(c);
            }
        } finally {
            if (inputStream != null) {
                inputStream.close();
            }
            if (outputStream != null) {
                outputStream.close();
            }
        }
    }
}
```

11

CopyCharacters is very similar to CopyBytes. The most important difference is that CopyCharacters uses FileReader and FileWriter for input and output in place of FileInputStream and FileOutputStream. Notice that both CopyBytes and CopyCharacters read to and write from an int variable. However, in CopyCharacters, the int variable holds a character value in its last 16 bits; in CopyBytes, the int variable holds a byte value in its last 8 bits.

---

5.   8/docs/api/java/io/Reader.html

6.   8/docs/api/java/io/Writer.html

7.   8/docs/api/java/io/FileReader.html

8.   8/docs/api/java/io/FileWriter.html

Character Streams That Use Byte Streams

Character streams are often "wrappers" for byte streams. The character stream uses the byte stream to perform the physical I/O, while the character stream handles translation between characters and bytes. `FileReader`, for example, uses `FileInputStream`, while `FileWriter` uses `FileOutputStream`.

There are two general-purpose byte-to-character "bridge" streams: `InputStreamReader`[9] and `OutputStreamWriter`.[10] Use them to create character streams when there are no prepackaged character stream classes that meet your needs.

Line-Oriented I/O

Character I/O usually occurs in bigger units than single characters. One common unit is the line: a string of characters with a line terminator at the end. A line terminator can be a carriage-return/line-feed sequence (\r\n), a single carriage return (\r), or a single line feed (\n). Supporting all possible line terminators allows programs to read text files created on any of the widely used operating systems.

Let's modify the `CopyCharacters` example to use line-oriented I/O. To do this, we have to use two classes we haven't seen before, `BufferedReader`[11] and `PrintWriter`.[12] We'll explore these classes in greater depth in the sections "Buffered I/O Methods for Text Files" and "Formatting." Right now, we're just interested in their support for line-oriented I/O.

The `CopyLines` example invokes `BufferedReader.readLine` and `PrintWriter.println` to do input and output one line at a time:

```java
import java.io.FileReader;
import java.io.FileWriter;
import java.io.BufferedReader;
import java.io.PrintWriter;
import java.io.IOException;

public class CopyLines {
    public static void main(String[] args) throws IOException {

        BufferedReader inputStream = null;
        PrintWriter outputStream = null;

        try {
            inputStream = new BufferedReader(new FileReader("xanadu.txt"));
            outputStream = new PrintWriter(new FileWriter("characteroutput.txt"));

            String l;
```

---

9. 8/docs/api/java/io/InputStreamReader.html

10. 8/docs/api/java/io/OutputStreamWriter.html

11. 8/docs/api/java/io/BufferedReader.html

12. 8/docs/api/java/io/PrintWriter.html

```
                while ((l = inputStream.readLine()) != null) {
                    outputStream.println(l);
                }
            } finally {
                if (inputStream != null) {
                    inputStream.close();
                }
                if (outputStream != null) {
                    outputStream.close();
                }
            }
        }
    }
```

Invoking `readLine` returns a line of text with the line. `CopyLines` outputs each line using `println`, which appends the line terminator for the current operating system. This might not be the same line terminator that was used in the input file.

There are many ways to structure text input and output beyond characters and lines. For more information, see the section "Scanning and Formatting."

Buffered Streams

Most of the examples we've seen so far use *unbuffered* I/O. This means each read or write request is handled directly by the underlying operating system. This can make a program much less efficient, since each such request often triggers disk access, network activity, or some other operation that is relatively expensive.

To reduce this kind of overhead, the Java platform implements *buffered* I/O streams. Buffered input streams read data from a memory area known as a *buffer*; the native input Application Programming Interface (API) is called only when the buffer is empty. Similarly, buffered output streams write data to a buffer, and the native output API is called only when the buffer is full.

A program can convert an unbuffered stream into a buffered stream using the wrapping idiom we've used several times now, where the unbuffered stream object is passed to the constructor for a buffered stream class. Here's how you might modify the constructor invocations in the `CopyCharacters` example to use buffered I/O:

```
inputStream = new BufferedReader(new FileReader("xanadu.txt"));
outputStream = new BufferedWriter(new FileWriter("characteroutput.txt"));
```

There are four buffered stream classes used to wrap unbuffered streams: `BufferedInputStream`[13] and `BufferedOutputStream`[14] create buffered

---

13. 8/docs/api/java/io/BufferedInputStream.html

14. 8/docs/api/java/io/BufferedOutputStream.html

byte streams, while BufferedReader[15] and BufferedWriter[16] create buffered character streams.

Flushing Buffered Streams

It often makes sense to write out a buffer at critical points without waiting for it to fill. This is known as *flushing* the buffer.

Some buffered output classes support *autoflush*, specified by an optional constructor argument. When autoflush is enabled, certain key events cause the buffer to be flushed. For example, an autoflush PrintWriter object flushes the buffer on every invocation of println or format. See the section "Formatting" for more on these methods.

To flush a stream manually, invoke its flush method. The flush method is valid on any output stream but has no effect unless the stream is buffered.

Scanning and Formatting

Programming I/O often involves translating to and from the neatly formatted data humans like to work with. To assist you with these chores, the Java platform provides two APIs. The scanner API breaks input into individual tokens associated with bits of data. The formatting API assembles data into a nicely formatted, human-readable form.

Scanning

Objects of type Scanner[17] are useful for breaking down formatted input into tokens and translating individual tokens according to their data type.

Breaking Input into Tokens

By default, a scanner uses white space to separate tokens. (White space characters include blanks, tabs, and line terminators. For the full list, refer to the documentation for Character.isWhitespace.[18]) To see how scanning works, let's look at ScanXan, a program that reads the individual words in xanadu.txt and prints them out, one per line:

```java
import java.io.*;
import java.util.Scanner;
```

---

15.   8/docs/api/java/io/BufferedReader.html

16.   8/docs/api/java/io/BufferedWriter.html

17.   8/docs/api/java/util/Scanner.html

18.   8/docs/api/java/lang/Character.html#isWhitespace-char-

```
public class ScanXan {
    public static void main(String[] args) throws IOException {

        Scanner s = null;

        try {
            s = new Scanner(new BufferedReader(new FileReader("xanadu.txt")));

            while (s.hasNext()) {
                System.out.println(s.next());
            }
        } finally {
            if (s != null) {
                s.close();
            }
        }
    }
}
```

Notice that ScanXan invokes Scanner's close method when it is done with the scanner object. Even though a scanner is not a stream, you need to close it to indicate that you're done with its underlying stream.

The output of ScanXan looks like this:

```
In
Xanadu
did
Kubla
Khan
A
stately
pleasure-dome
...
```

To use a different token separator, invoke useDelimiter(), specifying a regular expression. For example, suppose you wanted the token separator to be a comma, optionally followed by white space. You would invoke the following:

```
s.useDelimiter(",\\s*");
```

Translating Individual Tokens

The ScanXan example treats all input tokens as simple String values. Scanner also supports tokens for all of the Java language's primitive types (except for char), as well as BigInteger and BigDecimal. Also, numeric values can use thousands separators. Thus, in a US locale, Scanner correctly reads the string "32,767" as representing an integer value.

We have to mention the locale because thousands separators and decimal symbols are locale specific. The following example would not work correctly in all locales if we didn't specify that the scanner should use the US locale. That's not something you usually have to worry about because your input data usually comes from sources that use the same locale as you do. But this example is part of the Java Tutorials and gets distributed all over the world.

The ScanSum example reads a list of double values and adds them up. Here's the source:

```java
import java.io.FileReader;
import java.io.BufferedReader;
import java.io.IOException;
import java.util.Scanner;
import java.util.Locale;

public class ScanSum {
    public static void main(String[] args) throws IOException {

        Scanner s = null;
        double sum = 0;

        try {
            s = new Scanner(new BufferedReader(new FileReader("usnumbers.txt")));
            s.useLocale(Locale.US);

            while (s.hasNext()) {
                if (s.hasNextDouble()) {
                    sum += s.nextDouble();
                } else {
                    s.next();
                }
            }
        } finally {
            s.close();
        }

        System.out.println(sum);
    }
}
```

Here is the sample input file, usnumbers.txt:

```
8.5
32,767
3.14159
1,000,000.1
```

The output string is 1032778.74159. The period will be a different character in some locales because System.out is a PrintStream object and that class doesn't provide a way to override the default locale. We could override the locale for the whole program, or we could just use formatting, as described in the next section.

11

Formatting

Stream objects that implement formatting are instances of either `PrintWriter`,[19] a character stream class, or `PrintStream`,[20] a byte stream class.

> ### Note
> The only `PrintStream` objects you are likely to need are `System.out`[21] and `System.err`.[22] (See the section "I/O from the Command Line" for more on these objects.) When you need to create a formatted output stream, instantiate `PrintWriter`, not `PrintStream`.

Like all byte and character stream objects, instances of `PrintStream` and `PrintWriter` implement a standard set of `write` methods for simple byte and character output. In addition, both `PrintStream` and `PrintWriter` implement the same set of methods for converting internal data into formatted output. Two levels of formatting are provided:

- `print` and `println` format individual values in a standard way.
- `format` formats almost any number of values based on a format string, with many options for precise formatting.

The print and println Methods

Invoking `print` or `println` outputs a single value after converting the value using the appropriate `toString` method. We can see this in the `Root` example:

```
public class Root {
    public static void main(String[] args) {
        int i = 2;
        double r = Math.sqrt(i);

        System.out.print("The square root of ");
        System.out.print(i);
        System.out.print(" is ");
        System.out.print(r);
        System.out.println(".");

        i = 5;
        r = Math.sqrt(i);
        System.out.println("The square root of " + i + " is " + r + ".");
    }
}
```

---

19. 8/docs/api/java/io/PrintWriter.html
20. 8/docs/api/java/io/PrintStream.html
21. 8/docs/api/java/lang/System.html#out
22. 8/docs/api/java/lang/System.html#err

Here is the output of Root:

```
The square root of 2 is 1.4142135623730951.
The square root of 5 is 2.23606797749979.
```

The i and r variables are formatted twice: the first time using code in an overload of print; the second time by conversion code automatically generated by the Java compiler, which also utilizes toString. You can format any value this way, but you don't have much control over the results.

The format Method

The format method formats multiple arguments based on a *format string*. The format string consists of static text embedded with *format specifiers*; except for the format specifiers, the format string is output unchanged.

Format strings support many features. In this section, we'll just cover some basics. For a complete description, see the section "Format String Syntax"[23] in the Formatter class API documentation.

The Root2 example formats two values with a single format invocation:

```java
public class Root2 {
    public static void main(String[] args) {
        int i = 2;
        double r = Math.sqrt(i);

        System.out.format("The square root of %d is %f.%n", i, r);
    }
}
```

Here is the output:

```
The square root of 2 is 1.414214.
```

Like the three used in this example, all format specifiers begin with a % and end with a one- or two-character *conversion* that specifies the kind of formatted output being generated. The following three conversions are used here:

- d formats an integer value as a decimal value.
- f formats a floating-point value as a decimal value.
- n outputs a platform-specific line terminator.

Here are some other conversions:

---

23.   8/docs/api/java/util/Formatter.html#syntax

- x formats an integer as a hexadecimal value.
- s formats any value as a string.
- tB formats an integer as a locale-specific month name.

There are many other conversions.

> **Note**
>
> Except for `%%` and `%n`, all format specifiers must match an argument. If they don't, an exception is thrown. In the Java programming language, the `\n` escape always generates the line-feed character (`\u000A`). Don't use `\n` unless you specifically want a line-feed character. To get the correct line separator for the local platform, use `%n`.

In addition to the conversion, a format specifier can contain several additional elements that further customize the formatted output. Here's an example, Format, that uses every possible kind of element:

```
public class Format {
    public static void main(String[] args) {
        System.out.format("%f, %1$+020.10f %n", Math.PI);
    }
}
```

Here is the output:

```
3.141593, +00000003.1415926536
```

The additional elements are all optional. Figure 11.4 shows how the longer specifier breaks down into elements.

The elements must appear in the order shown. Working from the right, the optional elements are as follows:

- *Precision.* For floating-point values, this is the mathematical precision of the formatted value. For s and other general conversions, this is the maximum width of the formatted value; the value is right-truncated if necessary.

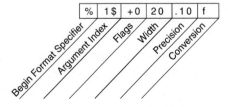

Figure 11.4 Elements of a Format Specifier

- *Width*. This is the minimum width of the formatted value; the value is padded if necessary. By default, the value is left-padded with blanks.

- *Flags*. These specify additional formatting options. In the `Format` example, the + flag specifies that the number should always be formatted with a sign and the 0 flag specifies that 0 is the padding character. Other flags include – (pad on the right) and , (format number with locale-specific thousands separators). Note that some flags cannot be used with certain other flags or with certain conversions.

- *Argument index*. This allows you to explicitly match a designated argument. You can also specify < to match the same argument as the previous specifier. Thus the example could have said `System.out.format("%f, %<+020.10f %n", Math.PI);`.

I/O from the Command Line

A program is often run from the command line and interacts with the user in the command-line environment. The Java platform supports this kind of interaction in two ways: through the standard streams and through the console.

Standard Streams

Standard streams are a feature of many operating systems. By default, they read input from the keyboard and write output to the display. They also support I/O on files and between programs, but that feature is controlled by the command-line interpreter, not the program.

The Java platform supports three standard streams: *standard input*, accessed through `System.in`; *standard output*, accessed through `System.out`; and *standard error*, accessed through `System.err`. These objects are defined automatically and do not need to be opened. Standard output and standard error are both for output; having error output separately allows the user to divert regular output to a file and still be able to read error messages. For more information, refer to the documentation for your command-line interpreter.

You might expect the standard streams to be character streams, but for historical reasons, they are byte streams. `System.out` and `System.err` are defined as `PrintStream` objects.[24] Although it is technically a byte stream, `PrintStream` utilizes an internal character stream object to emulate many of the features of character streams.

By contrast, `System.in` is a byte stream with no character stream features. To use standard input as a character stream, wrap `System.in` in `InputStreamReader`:

---

24.   8/docs/api/java/io/PrintStream.html

```
InputStreamReader cin = new InputStreamReader(System.in);
```

The Console

A more advanced alternative to the standard streams is the console. This is a single, predefined object of type `Console` that has most of the features provided by the standard streams and others besides.[25] The console is particularly useful for secure password entry. The console object also provides input and output streams that are true character streams through its `reader` and `writer` methods.

Before a program can use the console, it must attempt to retrieve the console object by invoking `System.console()`. If the console object is available, this method returns it. If `System.console` returns `NULL`, then console operations are not permitted, either because the operating system doesn't support them or because the program was launched in a noninteractive environment.

The console object supports secure password entry through its `readPassword` method. This method helps secure password entry in two ways. First, it suppresses echoing, so the password is not visible on the user's screen. Second, `readPassword` returns a character array, not a `String`, so the password can be overwritten, removing it from memory as soon as it is no longer needed.

The `Password` example is a prototype program for changing a user's password. It demonstrates several `Console` methods:

```
import java.io.Console;
import java.util.Arrays;
import java.io.IOException;

public class Password {

    public static void main (String args[]) throws IOException {

        Console c = System.console();
        if (c == null) {
            System.err.println("No console.");
            System.exit(1);
        }

        String login = c.readLine("Enter your login: ");
        char [] oldPassword = c.readPassword("Enter your old password: ");

        if (verify(login, oldPassword)) {
            boolean noMatch;
            do {
                char [] newPassword1 = c.readPassword("Enter your new password: ");
                char [] newPassword2 = c.readPassword("Enter new password again: ");
                noMatch = ! Arrays.equals(newPassword1, newPassword2);
                 if (noMatch) {
                     c.format("Passwords don't match. Try again.%n");
```

---

25.   8/docs/api/java/io/Console.html

```
            } else {
                change(login, newPassword1);
                c.format("Password for %s changed.%n", login);
            }
            Arrays.fill(newPassword1, ' ');
            Arrays.fill(newPassword2, ' ');
        } while (noMatch);
    }

    Arrays.fill(oldPassword, ' ');
}

// Dummy change method.
static boolean verify(String login, char[] password) {
    // This method always returns
    // true in this example.
    // Modify this method to verify
    // password according to your rules.
    return true;
}

// Dummy change method.
static void change(String login, char[] password) {
    // Modify this method to change
    // password according to your rules.
}
}
```

The `Password` class follows these steps:

1. Attempt to retrieve the console object. If the object is not available, abort.

2. Invoke `Console.readLine` to prompt for and read the user's login name.

3. Invoke `Console.readPassword` to prompt for and read the user's existing password.

4. Invoke `verify` to confirm that the user is authorized to change the password. (In this example, `verify` is a dummy method that always returns `true`.)

5. Repeat the following steps until the user enters the same password twice:

   a. Invoke `Console.readPassword` twice to prompt for and read a new password.

   b. If the user entered the same password both times, invoke `change` to change it. (Again, `change` is a dummy method.)

   c. Overwrite both passwords with blanks.

6. Overwrite the old password with blanks.

Data Streams

Data streams support binary I/O of primitive data type values (`boolean`, `char`, `byte`, `short`, `int`, `long`, `float`, and `double`) as well as `String` values. All data

Table 11.1 Data Used for the DataStreams Example

Order in record	Data type	Data description	Output method	Input method	Sample value
1	double	Item price	DataOutputStream. writeDouble	DataInputStream. readDouble	19.99
2	int	Unit count	DataOutputStream. writeInt	DataInputStream. readInt	12
3	String	Item description	DataOutputStream. writeUTF	DataInputStream. readUTF	"Java T-Shirt"

streams implement either the `DataInput`[26] interface or the `DataOutput`[27] interface. This section focuses on the most widely used implementations of these interfaces, `DataInputStream`[28] and `DataOutputStream`.[29]

The `DataStreams`[30] example demonstrates data streams by writing out a set of data records and then reading them in again. Each record consists of three values related to an item on an invoice, as shown in Table 11.1.

Let's examine crucial code in `DataStreams`. First, the program defines some constants containing the name of the data file and the data that will be written to it:

```
static final String dataFile = "invoicedata";

static final double[] prices = { 19.99, 9.99, 15.99, 3.99, 4.99 };
static final int[] units = { 12, 8, 13, 29, 50 };
static final String[] descs = {
    "Java T-shirt",
    "Java Mug",
    "Duke Juggling Dolls",
    "Java Pin",
    "Java Key Chain"
};
```

Then `DataStreams` opens an output stream. Since a `DataOutputStream` can only be created as a wrapper for an existing byte stream object, `DataStreams` provides a buffered file output byte stream:

```
out = new DataOutputStream(new BufferedOutputStream(
            new FileOutputStream(dataFile)));
```

`DataStreams` writes out the records and closes the output stream:

---

26.   8/docs/api/java/io/DataInput.html

27.   8/docs/api/java/io/DataOutput.html

28.   8/docs/api/java/io/DataInputStream.html

29.   8/docs/api/java/io/DataOutputStream.html

30.   tutorial/essential/io/examples/DataStreams.java

```
for (int i = 0; i < prices.length; i ++) {
    out.writeDouble(prices[i]);
    out.writeInt(units[i]);
    out.writeUTF(descs[i]);
}
```

The `writeUTF` method writes out `String` values in a modified form of UTF-8. This is a variable-width character encoding that only needs a single byte for common Western characters.

Now `DataStreams` reads the data back in again. First it must provide an input stream and variables to hold the input data. Like `DataOutputStream`, `DataInput-Stream` must be constructed as a wrapper for a byte stream:

```
in = new DataInputStream(new
            BufferedInputStream(new FileInputStream(dataFile)));

double price;
int unit;
String desc;
double total = 0.0;
```

Now `DataStreams` can read each record in the stream, reporting on the data it encounters:

```
try {
    while (true) {
        price = in.readDouble();
        unit = in.readInt();
        desc = in.readUTF();
        System.out.format("You ordered %d" + " units of %s at $%.2f%n",
            unit, desc, price);
        total += unit * price;
    }
} catch (EOFException e) {
}
```

Notice that `DataStreams` detects an end-of-file condition by catching `EOFEx-ception`[31] instead of testing for an invalid return value. All implementations of `DataInput` methods use `EOFException` instead of return values.

Also notice that each specialized `write` in `DataStreams` is exactly matched by the corresponding specialized `read`. It is up to the programmer to make sure that output types and input types are matched in this way: the input stream should consist of simple binary data, with nothing to indicate the type of individual values or where they begin in the stream.

---

31.   8/docs/api/java/io/EOFException.html

DataStreams uses one very bad programming technique: it uses floating-point numbers to represent monetary values. In general, floating point is bad for precise values. It's particularly bad for decimal fractions because common values (such as 0.1) do not have a binary representation.

The correct type to use for currency values is java.math.BigDecimal.[32] Unfortunately, BigDecimal is an object type, so it won't work with data streams. However, BigDecimal *will* work with object streams, which are covered in the next section.

Object Streams

Just as data streams support I/O of primitive data types, object streams support I/O of objects. Most but not all standard classes support serialization of their objects. Those that do implement the marker interface Serializable.[33]

The object stream classes are ObjectInputStream[34] and ObjectOutputStream.[35] These classes implement ObjectInput[36] and ObjectOutput,[37] which are subinterfaces of DataInput and DataOutput. This means that all the primitive data I/O methods covered in the "Data Streams" section are also implemented in object streams, so an object stream can contain a mixture of primitive and object values. The ObjectStreams[38] example illustrates this. ObjectStreams creates the same application as DataStreams, with a couple of changes. First, prices are now BigDecimal objects, to better represent fractional values.[39] Second, a Calendar object is written to the data file, indicating an invoice date.[40]

If readObject() doesn't return the object type expected, attempting to cast it to the correct type may throw a ClassNotFoundException.[41] In this simple example, that can't happen, so we don't try to catch the exception. Instead, we notify the compiler that we're aware of the issue by adding ClassNotFoundException to the main method's throws clause.

---

32. 8/docs/api/java/math/BigDecimal.html

33. 8/docs/api/java/io/Serializable.html

34. 8/docs/api/java/io/ObjectInputStream.html

35. 8/docs/api/java/io/ObjectOutputStream.html

36. 8/docs/api/java/io/ObjectInput.html

37. 8/docs/api/java/io/ObjectOutput.html

38. tutorial/essential/io/examples/ObjectStreams.java

39. 8/docs/api/java/math/BigDecimal.html

40. 8/docs/api/java/util/Calendar.html

41. 8/docs/api/java/lang/ClassNotFoundException.html

Output and Input of Complex Objects

The writeObject and readObject methods are simple to use, but they contain some very sophisticated object management logic. This isn't important for a class like Calendar, which just encapsulates primitive values, but many objects contain references to other objects. If readObject is to reconstitute an object from a stream, it has to be able to reconstitute all of the objects the original object referred to. These additional objects might have their own references and so on. In this situation, writeObject traverses the entire web of object references and writes all objects in that web onto the stream. Thus a single invocation of writeObject can cause a large number of objects to be written to the stream.

This is demonstrated in Figure 11.5, where writeObject is invoked to write a single object named a. This object contains references to objects b and c, while b contains references to d and e. Invoking writeobject(a) writes not just a but all the objects necessary to reconstitute a, so the other four objects in this web are written also. When a is read back by readObject, the other four objects are read back as well, and all the original object references are preserved.

You might wonder what happens if two objects on the same stream both contain references to a single object. Will they both refer to a single object when they're read back? The answer is yes. A stream can only contain one copy of an object, though it can contain any number of references to it. Thus if you explicitly write an object to a stream twice, you're really writing only the reference twice. For example, consider if the following code writes an object ob twice to a stream:

```
Object ob = new Object();
out.writeObject(ob);
out.writeObject(ob);
```

Each writeObject has to be matched by a readObject, so the code that reads the stream back will look something like this:

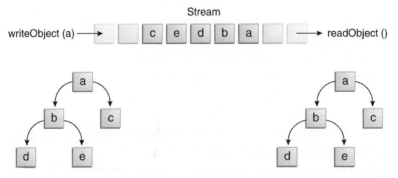

Figure 11.5 I/O of Objects Containing Multiple References to Other Objects

```
Object ob1 = in.readObject();
Object ob2 = in.readObject();
```

This results in two variables, ob1 and ob2, that are references to a single object. However, if a single object is written to two different streams, it is effectively duplicated; a single program reading both streams back will see two distinct objects.

File I/O (Featuring NIO.2)

The java.nio.file package and its related package, java.nio.file.attribute, provide comprehensive support for file I/O and for accessing the default file system. Though the API has many classes, you need to focus on only a few entry points. You will see that this API is very intuitive and easy to use.

This section starts by asking, what is a path? Then, the Path class, the primary entry point for the package, is introduced. Methods in the Path class relating to syntactic operations are explained. We then move on to the other primary class in the package, the Files class, which contains methods that deal with file operations. First, some concepts common to many file operations are introduced. We then cover methods for checking, deleting, copying, and moving files.

This section shows how metadata is managed before moving on to file I/O and directory I/O. Random access files are explained, and issues specific to symbolic and hard links are examined.

Next, some of the very powerful but more advanced topics are covered. First, the capability to recursively walk the file tree is demonstrated, followed by information about how to search for files using wildcards. Next, we explore how to watch a directory for changes. After this, methods that didn't fit elsewhere are given some attention.

Finally, if you have legacy file I/O code that uses the java.io.File class, there is a map from the functionality of this class to that of the java.nio.file package, as well as important information about the File.toPath method for developers who would like to leverage the java.nio.file package without rewriting existing code.

What Is a Path? (And Other File System Facts)

A file system stores and organizes files on some form of media, generally one or more hard drives, in such a way that they can be easily retrieved. Most file systems in use today store the files in a tree (or *hierarchical*) structure. At the top of the tree is one or more root nodes. Under the root node, there are files and directories (*folders* in Microsoft Windows). Each directory can contain files and subdirectories, which in turn can contain files and subdirectories and so on, potentially to an almost limitless depth.

What Is a Path?

Figure 11.6 shows a sample directory tree containing a single root node. Microsoft Windows supports multiple root nodes. Each root node maps to a volume, such as `C:\` or `D:\`. Solaris supports a single root node, which is denoted by the slash character, `/`.

A file is identified by its path through the file system, beginning from the root node. For example, the `statusReport` file in the previous figure is described by the following notation in Solaris:

```
/home/sally/statusReport
```

In Microsoft Windows, `statusReport` is described by the following notation:

```
C:\home\sally\statusReport
```

The character used to separate the directory names (also called the *delimiter*) is specific to the file system: Solaris uses the forward slash (`/`), and Microsoft Windows uses the backslash (`\`).

11

Relative or Absolute?

A path is either *relative* or *absolute*. An absolute path always contains the root element and the complete directory list required to locate the file. For example, `/home/sally/statusReport` is an absolute path. All the information needed to locate the file is contained in the path string.

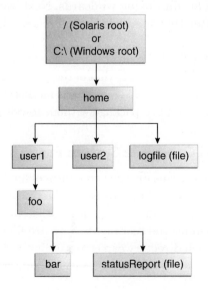

Figure 11.6 Sample Directory Structure

A relative path needs to be combined with another path in order to access a file. For example, `joe/foo` is a relative path. Without more information, a program cannot reliably locate the `joe/foo` directory in the file system.

Symbolic Links

File system objects are typically directories or files. Everyone is familiar with these objects. But some file systems also support the notion of symbolic links. A symbolic link is also referred to as a *symlink* or a *soft link*.

A *symbolic link* is a special file that serves as a reference to another file. For the most part, symbolic links are transparent to applications, and operations on symbolic links are automatically redirected to the target of the link. (The file or directory being pointed to is called the *target* of the link.) Exceptions are when a symbolic link is deleted or renamed, in which case the link itself is deleted or renamed and not the target of the link.

In Figure 11.7, `logFile` appears to be a regular file to the user, but it is actually a symbolic link to `dir/logs/HomeLogFile`. `HomeLogFile` is the target of the link. A symbolic link is usually transparent to the user. Reading or writing to a symbolic link is the same as reading or writing to any other file or directory. The phrase *resolving a link* means to substitute the actual location in the file system for the symbolic link. In the example, resolving `logFile` yields `dir/logs/HomeLogFile`.

In real-world scenarios, most file systems make liberal use of symbolic links. Occasionally, a carelessly created symbolic link can cause a circular reference. A circular reference occurs when the target of a link points back to the original link. The

11

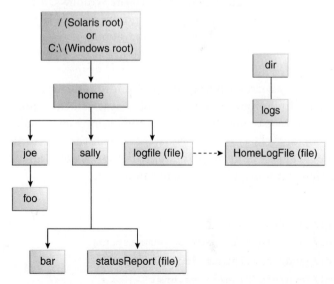

Figure 11.7 Example of a Symbolic Link

circular reference might be indirect: directory a points to directory b, which points to directory c, which contains a subdirectory pointing back to directory a. Circular references can cause havoc when a program is recursively walking a directory structure. However, this scenario has been accounted for and will not cause your program to loop infinitely.

The next section discusses the heart of file I/O support in the Java programming language, the Path class.

The Path Class

The Path[42] class is one of the primary entry points of the java.nio.file[43] package. If your application uses file I/O, you will want to learn about the powerful features of this class.

> **Note**
>
> If you have pre–JDK 7 code that uses java.io.File, you can still take advantage of the Path class functionality by using the File.toPath[44] method. See the section "Legacy File I/O Code" for more information.

As its name implies, the Path class is a programmatic representation of a path in the file system. A Path object contains the file name and directory list used to construct the path and is used to examine, locate, and manipulate files.

A Path instance reflects the underlying platform. In Solaris, a Path uses the Solaris syntax (/home/joe/foo), and in Microsoft Windows, a Path uses the Windows syntax (C:\home\joe\foo). A Path is not system independent. You cannot compare a Path from a Solaris file system and expect it to match a Path from a Windows file system, even if the directory structure is identical and both instances locate the same relative file.

The file or directory corresponding to the Path might not exist. You can create a Path instance and manipulate it in various ways: you can append to it, extract pieces of it, or compare it to another path. At the appropriate time, you can use the methods in the Files[45] class to check the existence of the file corresponding to the Path, create the file, open it, delete it, change its permissions, and so on.

The next section examines the Path class in detail.

---

42.   8/docs/api/java/nio/file/Path.html
43.   8/docs/api/java/nio/file/package-summary.html
44.   8/docs/api/java/io/File.html#toPath--
45.   8/docs/api/java/nio/file/Files.html

Path Operations

The `Path` class includes various methods that can be used to obtain information about the path, access elements of the path, convert the path to other forms, or extract portions of a path.[46] There are also methods for matching the path string and methods for removing redundancies in a path. This section addresses these `Path` methods, sometimes called *syntactic* operations, because they operate on the path itself and don't access the file system.

Creating a Path

A `Path` instance contains the information used to specify the location of a file or directory. At the time it is defined, a `Path` is provided with a series of one or more names. A root element or file name might be included, but neither are required. A `Path` might consist of just a single directory or file name.

You can easily create a `Path` object by using one of the following `get` methods from the `Paths` (note the plural) helper class:[47]

```
Path p1 = Paths.get("/tmp/foo");
Path p2 = Paths.get(args[0]);
Path p3 = Paths.get(URI.create("file:///Users/joe/FileTest.java"));
```

The `Paths.get` method is shorthand for the following code:

```
Path p4 = FileSystems.getDefault().getPath("/users/sally");
```

The following example creates /u/joe/logs/foo.log, assuming your home directory is /u/joe (or C:\joe\logs\foo.log if you are on Windows):

```
Path p5 = Paths.get(System.getProperty("user.home"),"logs", "foo.log");
```

Retrieving Information about a Path

You can think of the `Path` as storing these name elements as a sequence. The highest element in the directory structure would be located at index 0. The lowest element in the directory structure would be located at index [n-1], where n is the number of name elements in the `Path`. Methods are available for retrieving individual elements or a subsequence of the `Path` using these indexes.

The examples in this section use the structure shown in Figure 11.6. The following code snippet defines a `Path` instance and then invokes several methods to obtain information about the path:

---

46. 8/docs/api/java/nio/file/Path.html
47. 8/docs/api/java/nio/file/Paths.html

```
// None of these methods requires that the file corresponding
// to the Path exists.
// Microsoft Windows syntax
Path path = Paths.get("C:\\home\\joe\\foo");

// Solaris syntax
Path path = Paths.get("/home/joe/foo");

System.out.format("toString: %s%n", path.toString());
System.out.format("getFileName: %s%n", path.getFileName());
System.out.format("getName(0): %s%n", path.getName(0));
System.out.format("getNameCount: %d%n", path.getNameCount());
System.out.format("subpath(0,2): %s%n", path.subpath(0,2));
System.out.format("getParent: %s%n", path.getParent());
System.out.format("getRoot: %s%n", path.getRoot());
```

Table 11.2 shows the output for both Solaris and Windows.

The previous example shows the output for an absolute path. In the following example, a relative path is specified:

```
// Solaris syntax
Path path = Paths.get("sally/bar");
or
// Microsoft Windows syntax
Path path = Paths.get("sally\\bar");
```

Table 11.3 shows the output for Solaris and Windows.

Removing Redundancies from a Path

Many file systems use a period (.) to denote the current directory and two periods (..) to denote the parent directory. You might have a situation where a Path object contains redundant directory information. Perhaps a server is configured to save its log files in the /dir/logs/. directory and you want to delete the trailing /. notation from the path. The following examples both include redundancies:

```
/home/./joe/foo
/home/sally/../joe/foo
```

The normalize method removes any redundant elements, which includes any . or *directory* /.. occurrences. Both of the preceding examples normalize to / home/joe/foo.

It is important to note that normalize doesn't check the file system when it cleans up a path. It is a purely syntactic operation. In the second example, if sally were a symbolic link, removing sally/.. might result in a Path object that no longer locates the intended file.

To clean up a path while ensuring that the result locates the correct file, you can use the toRealPath method. This method is described in the next section.

Table 11.2 Output for Sample Code Using Absolute Path

Method invoked	Returns in Solaris	Returns in Microsoft Windows	Comment
toString	/home/joe/foo	C:\home\joe\foo	This method returns the string representation of the `Path`. If the path was created using `Filesystems.getDefault().getPath(String)` or `Paths.get` (the latter is a convenience method for `getPath`), the method performs minor syntactic cleanup. For example, in Solaris, it will correct the input string //home/joe/foo to /home/joe/foo.
getFileName	foo	foo	This method returns the file name or the last element of the sequence of name elements.
getName(0)	home	home	This method returns the path element corresponding to the specified index. The zeroth element is the path element closest to the root.
getNameCount	3	3	This method returns the number of elements in the path.
subpath(0,2)	home/joe	home\joe	This method returns the subsequence of the `Path` (not including a root element) as specified by the beginning and ending indexes.
getParent	/home/joe	\home\joe	This method returns the path of the parent directory.
getRoot	/	C:\	This method returns the root of the path.

Table 11.3 Output for Sample Code Using Relative Path

Method invoked	Returns in Solaris	Returns in Microsoft Windows
toString	sally/bar	sally\bar
getFileName	bar	bar
getName(0)	sally	sally
getNameCount	2	2
subpath(0,1)	sally	sally
getParent	sally	sally
getRoot	null	null

Converting a Path

You can use three methods to convert a `Path` object. If you need to convert a `Path` object to a string that can be opened from a browser, you can use `toUri`.[48] Here is an example:

```
Path p1 = Paths.get("/home/logfile");
// Result is file:///home/logfile
System.out.format("%s%n", p1.toUri());
```

The `toAbsolutePath` method converts a path to an absolute path.[49] If the passed-in path is already absolute, it returns the same `Path` object. The `toAbsolutePath` method can be very helpful when processing user-entered file names. Here is an example:

```
public class FileTest {
    public static void main(String[] args) {

        if (args.length < 1) {
            System.out.println("usage: FileTest file");
            System.exit(-1);
        }

        // Converts the input string to a Path object.
        Path inputPath = Paths.get(args[0]);

        // Converts the input Path
        // to an absolute path.
        // Generally, this means prepending
        // the current working
        // directory.  If this example
        // were called like this:
        //     java FileTest foo
        // the getRoot and getParent methods
        // would return null
        // on the original "inputPath"
        // instance.  Invoking getRoot and
        // getParent on the "fullPath"
        // instance returns expected values.
        Path fullPath = inputPath.toAbsolutePath();
    }
}
```

The `toAbsolutePath` method converts the user input and returns a `Path` object that returns useful values when queried. The file does not need to exist for this method to work.

---

48.   8/docs/api/java/nio/file/Path.html#toUri--

49.   8/docs/api/java/nio/file/Path.html#toAbsolutePath--

The `toRealPath`[50] method returns the *real* path of an existing file. This method performs several operations in one:

- If `true` is passed to this method and the file system supports symbolic links, then this method resolves any symbolic links in the path.
- If the path is relative, then it returns an absolute path.
- If the path contains any redundant elements, then it returns a path with those elements removed.

This method throws an exception if the file does not exist or cannot be accessed. You can catch the exception when you want to handle any of these cases:

```
try {
    Path fp = path.toRealPath();
} catch (NoSuchFileException x) {
    System.err.format("%s: no such" + " file or directory%n", path);
    // Logic for case when file doesn't exist.
} catch (IOException x) {
    System.err.format("%s%n", x);
    // Logic for other sort of file error.
}
```

Joining Two Paths

You can combine paths by using the `resolve` method. You pass in a *partial path*, which is a path that does not include a root element, and that partial path is appended to the original path.

For example, consider the following code snippet:

```
// Solaris
Path p1 = Paths.get("/home/joe/foo");
// Result is /home/joe/foo/bar
System.out.format("%s%n", p1.resolve("bar"));
```

or

```
// Microsoft Windows
Path p1 = Paths.get("C:\\home\\joe\\foo");
// Result is C:\home\joe\foo\bar
System.out.format("%s%n", p1.resolve("bar"));
```

Passing an absolute path to the `resolve` method returns the passed-in path:

```
// Result is /home/joe
Paths.get("foo").resolve("/home/joe");
```

---

50. 8/docs/api/java/nio/file/Path.html#toRealPath-java.nio.file.LinkOption...–

Creating a Path between Two Paths

A common requirement when you are writing file I/O code is the capability to construct a path from one location in the file system to another location. You can meet this using the `relativize` method. This method constructs a path originating from the original path and ending at the location specified by the passed-in path. The new path is *relative* to the original path.

For example, consider two relative paths defined as `joe` and `sally`:

```
Path p1 = Paths.get("joe");
Path p2 = Paths.get("sally");
```

In the absence of any other information, it is assumed that `joe` and `sally` are siblings, meaning nodes that reside at the same level in the tree structure. To navigate from `joe` to `sally`, you would expect to first navigate one level up to the parent node and then down to `sally`:

```
// Result is ../sally
Path p1_to_p2 = p1.relativize(p2);
// Result is ../joe
Path p2_to_p1 = p2.relativize(p1);
```

Consider a slightly more complicated example:

```
Path p1 = Paths.get("home");
Path p3 = Paths.get("home/sally/bar");
// Result is sally/bar
Path p1_to_p3 = p1.relativize(p3);
// Result is ../..
Path p3_to_p1 = p3.relativize(p1);
```

In this example, the two paths share the same node, home. To navigate from home to bar, you first navigate one level down to `sally` and then one more level down to bar. Navigating from bar to home requires moving up two levels.

A relative path cannot be constructed if only one of the paths includes a root element. If both paths include a root element, the capability to construct a relative path is system dependent. The recursive Copy[51] example uses the `relativize` and `resolve` methods.

---

51. tutorial/essential/io/examples/Copy.java

Comparing Two Paths

The `Path` class supports `equals`, enabling you to test two paths for equality.[52] The `startsWith`[53] and `endsWith`[54] methods enable you to test whether a path begins or ends with a particular string. These methods are easy to use:

```
Path path = ...;
Path otherPath = ...;
Path beginning = Paths.get("/home");
Path ending = Paths.get("foo");

if (path.equals(otherPath)) {
    // equality logic here
} else if (path.startsWith(beginning)) {
    // path begins with "/home"
} else if (path.endsWith(ending)) {
    // path ends with "foo"
}
```

The `Path` class implements the `Iterable` interface.[55] The `iterator` method returns an object that enables you to iterate over the name elements in the path.[56] The first element returned is that closest to the root in the directory tree. The following code snippet iterates over a path, printing each name element:

```
Path path = ...;
for (Path name: path) {
    System.out.println(name);
}
```

The `Path` class also implements the `Comparable` interface.[57] You can compare `Path` objects by using `compareTo`, which is useful for sorting. You can also put `Path` objects into a `Collection`. See Chapter 12 for more information about this powerful feature.

When you want to verify that two `Path` objects locate the same file, you can use the `isSameFile` method, as described in the section "Checking Whether Two Paths Locate the Same File."

---

52. 8/docs/api/java/nio/file/Path.html#equals-java.lang.Object-

53. 8/docs/api/java/nio/file/Path.html#startsWith-java.nio.file.Path-

54. 8/docs/api/java/nio/file/Path.html#endsWith-java.nio.file.Path-

55. 8/docs/api/java/lang/Iterable.html

56. 8/docs/api/java/nio/file/Path.html#iterator--

57. 8/docs/api/java/lang/Comparable.html

File Operations

The `Files` class is the other primary entry point of the `java.nio.file` package.[58] This class offers a rich set of static methods for reading, writing, and manipulating files and directories. The `Files` methods work on instances of `Path` objects. Before proceeding to the remaining sections, you should familiarize yourself with the following common concepts.

Releasing System Resources

Many of the resources that are used in this API, such as streams or channels, implement or extend the `java.io.Closeable` interface.[59] A requirement of a `Closeable` resource is that the `close` method must be invoked to release the resource when no longer required. Neglecting to close a resource can have a negative implication on an application's performance. The `try-with-resources` statement, described in the next section, handles this step for you.

Catching Exceptions

With file I/O, unexpected conditions are a fact of life: a file exists (or doesn't exist) when expected, the program doesn't have access to the file system, the default file system implementation does not support a particular function, and so on. Numerous errors can be encountered.

All methods that access the file system can throw an `IOException`. It is best practice to catch these exceptions by embedding these methods into a `try-with-resources` statement. The `try-with-resources` statement has the advantage that the compiler automatically generates the code to close the resource(s) when no longer required. The following code shows how this might look:

```
Charset charset = Charset.forName("US-ASCII");
String s = ...;
try (BufferedWriter writer = Files.newBufferedWriter(file, charset)) {
    writer.write(s, 0, s.length());
} catch (IOException x) {
    System.err.format("IOException: %s%n", x);
}
```

For more information, see Chapter 10, "The try-with-resources Statement."

Alternatively, you can embed the file I/O methods in a `try` block and then catch any exceptions in a `catch` block. If your code has opened any streams or channels, you should close them in a `finally` block. The previous example would look something like the following using the `try-catch-finally` approach:

---

58. 8/docs/api/java/nio/file/Files.html

59. 8/docs/api/java/io/Closeable.html

```
Charset charset = Charset.forName("US-ASCII");
String s = ...;
BufferedWriter writer = null;
try {
    writer = Files.newBufferedWriter(file, charset);
    writer.write(s, 0, s.length());
} catch (IOException x) {
    System.err.format("IOException: %s%n", x);
} finally {
    if (writer != null) writer.close();
}
```

For more information, see Chapter 10, "Catching and Handling Exceptions."

In addition to IOException, many specific exceptions extend FileSystemException.[60] This class has some useful methods that return the file involved (getFile),[61] the detailed message string (getMessage),[62] the reason why the file system operation failed (getReason),[63] and the "other" file involved, if any (getOtherFile).[64]

The following code snippet shows how the getFile method might be used:

```
try (...) {
    ...
} catch (NoSuchFileException x) {
    System.err.format("%s does not exist\n", x.getFile());
}
```

For purposes of clarity, the file I/O examples in this section may not show exception handling, but your code should always include it.

Varargs

Several Files methods accept an arbitrary number of arguments when flags are specified. For example, in the following method signature, the ellipsis notation after the CopyOption argument indicates that the method accepts a variable number of arguments, or *varargs*, as they are typically called:

```
Path Files.move(Path, Path, CopyOption...)
```

When a method accepts a varargs argument, you can pass it a comma-separated list of values or an array (CopyOption[ ]) of values.

In the move example, the method can be invoked as follows:

---

60. 8/docs/api/java/nio/file/FileSystemException.html

61. 8/docs/api/java/nio/file/FileSystemException.html#getFile--

62. 8/docs/api/java/nio/file/FileSystemException.html#getMessage--

63. 8/docs/api/java/nio/file/FileSystemException.html#getReason--

64. 8/docs/api/java/nio/file/FileSystemException.html#getOtherFile--

```
import static java.nio.file.StandardCopyOption.*;

Path source = ...;
Path target = ...;
Files.move(source,
           target,
           REPLACE_EXISTING,
           ATOMIC_MOVE);
```

For more information about varargs syntax, see Chapter 4, "Arbitrary Number of Arguments."

Atomic Operations

Several `Files` methods, such as `move`, can perform certain operations atomically in some file systems. An *atomic file operation* is an operation that cannot be interrupted or "partially" performed. Either the entire operation is performed or the operation fails. This is important when you have multiple processes operating on the same area of the file system, and you need to guarantee that each process accesses a complete file.

11

Method Chaining

Many of the file I/O methods support the concept of *method chaining*. You first invoke a method that returns an object. You then immediately invoke a method on *that* object, which returns yet another object, and so on. Many of the I/O examples use the following technique:

```
String value = Charset.defaultCharset().decode(buf).toString();
UserPrincipal group =
    file.getFileSystem().getUserPrincipalLookupService().
        lookupPrincipalByName("me");
```

This technique produces compact code and enables you to avoid declaring temporary variables that you don't need.

What Is a Glob?

Two methods in the `Files` class accept a glob argument, but what is a *glob*? You can use glob syntax to specify pattern-matching behavior. A glob pattern is specified as a string and is matched against other strings, such as directory or file names. Glob syntax follows several simple rules:

- An asterisk (`*`) matches any number of characters (including none).
- Two asterisks (`**`) work like `*` but cross directory boundaries. This syntax is generally used for matching complete paths.
- A question mark (`?`) matches exactly one character.

- Braces specify a collection of subpatterns:
  - `{sun,moon,stars}` matches `sun`, `moon`, or `stars`.
  - `{temp*,tmp*}` matches all strings beginning with `temp` or `tmp`.
- Square brackets convey a set of single characters or, when the hyphen character (–) is used, a range of characters:
  - `[aeiou]` matches any lowercase vowel.
  - `[0-9]` matches any digit.
  - `[A-Z]` matches any uppercase letter.
  - `[a-z,A-Z]` matches any uppercase or lowercase letter.
- Within the square brackets, *, ?, and \ match themselves. All other characters match themselves.
- To match *, ?, or the other special characters, you can escape them by using the backslash character (\). Here are some examples:
  - `\\` matches a single backslash.
  - `\?` matches the question mark.

Here are some examples of glob syntax:

- `*.html` matches all strings that end in `.html`.
- `???` matches all strings with exactly three letters or digits.
- `*[0-9]*` matches all strings containing a numeric value.
- `*.{htm,html,pdf}` matches any string ending with `.htm`, `.html`, or `.pdf`.
- `a?*.java` matches any string beginning with a, followed by at least one letter or digit, and ending with `.java`.
- `{foo*,*[0-9]*}` matches any string beginning with `foo` or any string containing a numeric value.

> **Note**
>
> If you are typing the glob pattern at the keyboard and it contains one of the special characters, you must put the pattern in quotes (`"*"`), use the backslash (`\*`), or use whatever escape mechanism is supported at the command line.

The glob syntax is powerful and easy to use. However, if it is not sufficient for your needs, you can also use a regular expression. For more information, see Chapter 14. For more information about the glob syntax, see the API specification for the `getPathMatcher`[65] method in the `FileSystem` class.

---

65. `8/docs/api/java/nio/file/FileSystem.html#getPathMatcher-java.lang .String-`

Link Awareness

The Files class is "link aware." Every Files method either detects what to do when a symbolic link is encountered or provides an option enabling you to configure the behavior when a symbolic link is encountered.

Checking a File or Directory

You have a Path instance representing a file or directory, but does that file exist on the file system? Is it readable? Writable? Executable?

Verifying the Existence of a File or Directory

The methods in the Path class are syntactic, meaning that they operate on the Path instance. But eventually you must access the file system to verify that a particular Path exists or does not exist. You can do so with the exists(Path, LinkOption...)[66] and the notExists(Path, LinkOption...)[67] methods. Note that !Files.exists(path) is not equivalent to Files.notExists(path). When you are testing a file's existence, three results are possible:

- The file is verified to exist.
- The file is verified to not exist.
- The file's status is unknown. This result can occur when the program does not have access to the file.

If both exists and notExists return false, the existence of the file cannot be verified.

Checking File Accessibility

To verify that the program can access a file as needed, you can use the isReadable(Path),[68] isWritable(Path),[69] and isExecutable(Path)[70] methods. The following code snippet verifies that a particular file exists and that the program has the ability to execute the file:

---

66. 8/docs/api/java/nio/file/Files.html#exists-java.nio.file.Path-java
     .nio.file.LinkOption...-

67. 8/docs/api/java/nio/file/Files.html#notExists-java.nio.file.Path-java
     .nio.file.LinkOption...-

68. 8/docs/api/java/nio/file/Files.html#isReadable-java.nio.file.Path-

69. 8/docs/api/java/nio/file/Files.html#isWritable-java.nio.file.Path-

70. 8/docs/api/java/nio/file/Files.html#isExecutable-java.nio.file.Path-

```
Path file = ...;
boolean isRegularExecutableFile = Files.isRegularFile(file) &
        Files.isReadable(file) & Files.isExecutable(file);
```

> **Note**
>
> Once any of these methods completes, there is no guarantee that the file can be accessed. A common security flaw in many applications is to perform a check and then access the file. For more information, use your favorite search engine to look up TOCTTOU (pronounced *TOCK-too*), which stands for *time of check to time of use*.

Checking Whether Two Paths Locate the Same File

When you have a file system that uses symbolic links, it is possible to have two different paths that locate the same file. The isSameFile(Path, Path) method compares two paths to determine if they locate the same file on the file system:[71]

```
Path p1 = ...;
Path p2 = ...;

if (Files.isSameFile(p1, p2)) {
    // Logic when the paths locate the same file
}
```

11

Deleting a File or Directory

You can delete files, directories, or links. With symbolic links, the link is deleted, not the target of the link. With directories, the directory must be empty or the deletion fails.

The Files class provides two deletion methods: delete(Path)[72] and deleteIfExists(Path).[73] The delete(Path) method deletes the file or throws an exception if the deletion fails. For example, if the file does not exist, a NoSuch-FileException is thrown. You can catch the exception to determine why the delete failed as follows:

```
try {
    Files.delete(path);
} catch (NoSuchFileException x) {
    System.err.format("%s: no such" + " file or directory%n", path);
} catch (DirectoryNotEmptyException x) {
    System.err.format("%s not empty%n", path);
```

---

71. 8/docs/api/java/nio/file/Files.html#isSameFile-java.nio.file.Path-java
     .nio.file.Path-

72. 8/docs/api/java/nio/file/Files.html#delete-java.nio.file.Path-

73. 8/docs/api/java/nio/file/Files.html#deleteIfExists-java.nio.file
     .Path-

```
} catch (IOException x) {
    // File permission problems are caught here.
    System.err.println(x);
}
```

The `deleteIfExists(Path)` method also deletes the file, but if the file does not exist, no exception is thrown. Failing silently is useful when you have multiple threads deleting files and you don't want to throw an exception just because one thread did so first.

Copying a File or Directory

You can copy a file or directory by using the `copy(Path, Path, CopyOption...)` method.[74] The copy fails if the target file exists, unless the REPLACE_EXISTING option is specified.

Directories can be copied. However, files inside the directory are not copied, so the new directory is empty even when the original directory contains files.

When copying a symbolic link, the target of the link is copied. If you want to copy the link itself and not the contents of the link, specify either the NOFOLLOW_LINKS or REPLACE_EXISTING option.

This method takes a varargs argument. The following `StandardCopyOption` and `LinkOption` enums are supported:

- REPLACE_EXISTING. This performs the copy even when the target file already exists. If the target is a symbolic link, the link itself is copied (and not the target of the link). If the target is a nonempty directory, the copy fails with the `FileAlreadyExistsException` exception.
- COPY_ATTRIBUTES. This copies the file attributes associated with the file to the target file. The exact file attributes supported are file system and platform dependent, but `last-modified-time` is supported across platforms and is copied to the target file.
- NOFOLLOW_LINKS. This indicates that symbolic links should not be followed. If the file to be copied is a symbolic link, the link is copied (and not the target of the link).

If you are not familiar with enums, see Chapter 4, "Enum Types." The following shows how to use the copy method:

---

74. 8/docs/api/java/nio/file/Files.html#copy-java.nio.file.Path-java
.nio.file.Path-java.nio.file.CopyOption...-

```
import static java.nio.file.StandardCopyOption.*;
...
Files.copy(source, target, REPLACE_EXISTING);
```

In addition to file copy, the `Files` class also defines methods that may be used to copy between a file and a stream. The `copy(InputStream, Path, CopyOptions...)`[75] method may be used to copy all bytes from an input stream to a file. The `copy(Path, OutputStream)`[76] method may be used to copy all bytes from a file to an output stream.

The `Copy`[77] example uses the `copy` and `Files.walkFileTree` methods to support a recursive copy. See the "Walking the File Tree" section for more information.

Moving a File or Directory

You can move a file or directory by using the `move(Path, Path, CopyOption...)` method.[78] The move fails if the target file exists, unless the `REPLACE_EXISTING` option is specified.

Empty directories can be moved. If the directory is not empty, the move is allowed when the directory can be moved without moving the contents of that directory. On Solaris, Linux, and OS X systems, moving a directory within the same partition generally consists of renaming the directory. In that situation, this method works even when the directory contains files.

This method takes a varargs argument. The following `StandardCopyOption` enums are supported:

- `REPLACE_EXISTING`. This performs the move even when the target file already exists. If the target is a symbolic link, the symbolic link is replaced but what it points to is not affected.
- `ATOMIC_MOVE`. This performs the move as an atomic file operation. If the file system does not support an atomic move, an exception is thrown. With an `ATOMIC_MOVE`, you can move a file into a directory and be guaranteed that any process watching the directory accesses a complete file.

---

75. `8/docs/api/java/nio/file/Files.html#copy-java.io.InputStream-java`
     `.nio.file.Path-java.nio.file.CopyOption...-`

76. `8/docs/api/java/nio/file/Files.html#copy-java.nio.file.Path-java`
     `.io.OutputStream-`

77. `tutorial/essential/io/examples/Copy.java`

78. `8/docs/api/java/nio/file/Files.html#move-java.nio.file.Path-java`
     `.nio.file.Path-java.nio.file.CopyOption...-`

The following shows how to use the move method:

```
import static java.nio.file.StandardCopyOption.*;
...
Files.move(source, target, REPLACE_EXISTING);
```

Though you can implement the move method on a single directory as shown, the method is most often used with the file tree recursion mechanism. For more information, see the "Walking the File Tree" section.

Managing Metadata (File and File Store Attributes)

The definition of *metadata* is "data about other data." With a file system, the data is contained in its files and directories and the metadata tracks information about each of these objects: is it a regular file, a directory, or a link? What is its size, creation date, last modified date, file owner, group owner, and access permissions?

A file system's metadata is typically referred to as its *file attributes*. The Files class includes methods that can be used to obtain a single attribute of a file or to set an attribute (Table 11.4).

If a program needs multiple file attributes around the same time, it can be inefficient to use methods that retrieve a single attribute. Repeatedly accessing the file system to retrieve a single attribute can adversely affect performance. For this reason, the Files class provides two readAttributes methods to fetch a file's attributes in one bulk operation (Table 11.5).

Before showing examples of the readAttributes methods, it should be mentioned that different file systems have different notions about which attributes should be tracked. For this reason, related file attributes are grouped together into views. A *view* maps to a particular file system implementation, such as POSIX or DOS, or to a common functionality, such as file ownership. The supported views are as follows:

- BasicFileAttributeView. This provides a view of basic attributes that are required to be supported by all file system implementations.[79]
- DosFileAttributeView. This extends the basic attribute view with the standard four bits supported on file systems that support the DOS attributes.[80]
- PosixFileAttributeView. This extends the basic attribute view with attributes supported on file systems that support the POSIX family of standards, such as Solaris. These attributes include file owner, group owner, and the nine related access permissions.[81]

79.   8/docs/api/java/nio/file/attribute/BasicFileAttributeView.html

80.   8/docs/api/java/nio/file/attribute/DosFileAttributeView.html

81.   8/docs/api/java/nio/file/attribute/PosixFileAttributeView.html

Table 11.4 BasicFileAttributes Methods

Methods	Comment
size(Path)[82]	This method returns the size of the specified file in bytes.
isDirectory(Path, LinkOption)[83]	This method returns true if the specified Path locates a file that is a directory.
isRegularFile(Path, LinkOption...)[84]	This method returns true if the specified Path locates a file that is a regular file.
isSymbolicLink(Path)[85]	This method returns true if the specified Path locates a file that is a symbolic link.
isHidden(Path)[86]	This method returns true if the specified Path locates a file that is considered hidden by the file system.
getLastModifiedTime(Path, LinkOption...)[87] setLastModifiedTime(Path, FileTime)[88]	These methods return or set the specified file's last modified time.
getOwner(Path, LinkOption...)[89] setOwner(Path, UserPrincipal)[90]	These methods return or set the owner of the file.

11

(continued)

---

82. 8/docs/api/java/nio/file/Files.html#size-java.nio.file.Path-

83. 8/docs/api/java/nio/file/Files.html#isDirectory-java.nio.file.Path -java.nio.file.LinkOption...-

84. 8/docs/api/java/nio/file/Files.html#isRegularFile-java.nio.file .Path-java.nio.file.LinkOption...-

85. 8/docs/api/java/nio/file/Files.html#isSymbolicLink-java.nio.file .Path-

86. 8/docs/api/java/nio/file/Files.html#isHidden-java.nio.file.Path-

87. 8/docs/api/java/nio/file/Files.html#getLastModifiedTime-java.nio .file.Path-java.nio.file.LinkOption...-

88. 8/docs/api/java/nio/file/Files.html#setLastModifiedTime-java.nio .file.Path-java.nio.file.attribute.FileTime-

89. 8/docs/api/java/nio/file/Files.html#getOwner-java.nio.file.Path -java.nio.file.LinkOption...-

90. 8/docs/api/java/nio/file/Files.html#setOwner-java.nio.file.Path -java.nio.file.attribute.UserPrincipal-

Table 11.4 BasicFileAttributes Methods (continued)

Methods	Comment
getPosixFilePermissions(Path, LinkOption...)[91] setPosixFilePermissions(Path, Set<PosixFilePermission>)[92]	These methods return or set a file's POSIX file permissions.
getAttribute(Path, String, LinkOption...)[93] setAttribute(Path, String, Object, LinkOption...)[94]	These methods return or set the value of a file attribute.

- `FileOwnerAttributeView`. This is supported by any file system implementation that supports the concept of a file owner.[95]

- `AclFileAttributeView`. This supports reading or updating a file's Access Control Lists (ACL). The NFSv4 ACL model is supported. Any ACL model, such as the Windows ACL model, that has a well-defined mapping to the NFSv4 model might also be supported.[96]

- `UserDefinedFileAttributeView`. This enables support of metadata that is user defined. This view can be mapped to any extension mechanisms that a system supports. In Solaris, for example, you can use this view to store the MIME type of a file.[97]

A specific file system implementation might support only the basic file attribute view, or it may support several of these file attribute views. A file system implementation might support other attribute views not included in this API.

In most instances, you should not have to deal directly with any of the `FileAttributeView` interfaces. (If you do need to work directly with the `FileAttributeView`, you can access it via the `getFileAttributeView(Path, Class<V>, LinkOption...)`[98] method.)

---

91. 8/docs/api/java/nio/file/Files.html#getPosixFilePermissions-java
     .nio.file.Path-java.nio.file.LinkOption...-

92. 8/docs/api/java/nio/file/Files.html#setPosixFilePermissions-java
     .nio.file.Path-java.util.Set-

93. 8/docs/api/java/nio/file/Files.html#getAttribute-java.nio.file.Path
     -java.lang.String-java.nio.file.LinkOption...-

94. 8/docs/api/java/nio/file/Files.html#setAttribute-java.nio.file.Path
     -java.lang.String-java.lang.Object-java.nio.file.LinkOption...-

95. 8/docs/api/java/nio/file/attribute/FileOwnerAttributeView.html

96. 8/docs/api/java/nio/file/attribute/AclFileAttributeView.html

97. 8/docs/api/java/nio/file/attribute/UserDefinedFileAttributeView.html

98. 8/docs/api/java/nio/file/Files.html#getFileAttributeView-java.nio
     .file.Path-java.lang.Class-java.nio.file.LinkOption...-

Table 11.5 Methods in Files Class for Reading Attributes

Method	Comment
readAttributes(Path, String, LinkOption...)[99]	This method reads a file's attributes as a bulk operation. The String parameter identifies the attributes to be read.
readAttributes(Path, Class<A>, LinkOption...)[100]	This method reads a file's attributes as a bulk operation. The Class<A> parameter is the type of attributes requested, and the method returns an object of that class.

The readAttributes methods use generics and can be used to read the attributes for any of the file attributes views. The examples in the rest of this page use the readAttributes methods.

Basic File Attributes

As mentioned previously, to read the basic attributes of a file, you can use one of the Files.readAttributes methods, which reads all the basic attributes in one bulk operation. This is far more efficient than accessing the file system separately to read each individual attribute. The varargs argument currently supports the LinkOption[101] enum, NOFOLLOW_LINKS. Use this option when you do not want symbolic links to be followed.

> **Note**
>
> The set of basic attributes includes three time stamps: creationTime, lastModifiedTime, and lastAccessTime. Any of these time stamps might not be supported in a particular implementation, in which case the corresponding accessor method returns an implementation-specific value. When supported, the time stamp is returned as a FileTime object.[102]

The following code snippet reads and prints the basic file attributes for a given file and uses the methods in the BasicFileAttributes class:[103]

---

99. 8/docs/api/java/nio/file/Files.html#readAttributes-java.nio.file
 .Path-java.lang.String-java.nio.file.LinkOption...-

100. 8/docs/api/java/nio/file/Files.html#readAttributes-java.nio.file
 .Path-java.lang.Class-java.nio.file.LinkOption...-

101. 8/docs/api/java/nio/file/LinkOption.html

102. 8/docs/api/java/nio/file/attribute/FileTime.html

103. 8/docs/api/java/nio/file/attribute/BasicFileAttributes.html

```
Path file = ...;
BasicFileAttributes attr = Files.readAttributes(file, BasicFileAttributes.class);

System.out.println("creationTime: " + attr.creationTime());
System.out.println("lastAccessTime: " + attr.lastAccessTime());
System.out.println("lastModifiedTime: " + attr.lastModifiedTime());

System.out.println("isDirectory: " + attr.isDirectory());
System.out.println("isOther: " + attr.isOther());
System.out.println("isRegularFile: " + attr.isRegularFile());
System.out.println("isSymbolicLink: " + attr.isSymbolicLink());
System.out.println("size: " + attr.size());
```

In addition to the accessor methods shown in this example, there is a `fileKey` method that returns either an object that uniquely identifies the file or `null` if no file key is available.

Setting Time Stamps

The following code snippet sets the last modified time in milliseconds:

```
Path file = ...;
BasicFileAttributes attr =
    Files.readAttributes(file, BasicFileAttributes.class);
long currentTime = System.currentTimeMillis();
FileTime ft = FileTime.fromMillis(currentTime);
Files.setLastModifiedTime(file, ft);
}
```

DOS File Attributes

DOS file attributes are also supported on file systems other than DOS, such as Samba. The following snippet uses the methods of the `DosFileAttributes` class:[104]

```
Path file = ...;
try {
    DosFileAttributes attr =
        Files.readAttributes(file, DosFileAttributes.class);
    System.out.println("isReadOnly is " + attr.isReadOnly());
    System.out.println("isHidden is " + attr.isHidden());
    System.out.println("isArchive is " + attr.isArchive());
    System.out.println("isSystem is " + attr.isSystem());
} catch (UnsupportedOperationException x) {
    System.err.println("DOS file" +
        " attributes not supported:" + x);
}
```

However, you can set a DOS attribute using the `setAttribute(Path, String, Object, LinkOption...)` method:[105]

---

104. 8/docs/api/java/nio/file/attribute/DosFileAttributes.html

105. 8/docs/api/java/nio/file/Files.html#setAttribute-java.nio.file.Path
    -java.lang.String-java.lang.Object-java.nio.file.LinkOption...-

```
Path file = ...;
Files.setAttribute(file, "dos:hidden", true);
```

POSIX File Permissions

POSIX is an acronym for Portable Operating System Interface for UNIX and is a set of IEEE and ISO standards designed to ensure interoperability among different flavors of UNIX. If a program conforms to these POSIX standards, it should be easily ported to other POSIX-compliant operating systems.

Besides file owner and group owner, POSIX supports nine file permissions: read, write, and execute permissions for the file owner, members of the same group, and "everyone else." The following code snippet reads the POSIX file attributes for a given file and prints them to standard output. The code uses the methods in the PosixFileAttributes class:[106]

```
Path file = ...;
PosixFileAttributes attr =
    Files.readAttributes(file, PosixFileAttributes.class);
System.out.format("%s %s %s%n",
    attr.owner().getName(),
    attr.group().getName(),
    PosixFilePermissions.toString(attr.permissions()));
```

11

The PosixFilePermissions[107] helper class provides several useful methods, as follows:

- The toString method, used in the previous code snippet, converts the file permissions to a string (for example, rw-r--r--).
- The fromString method accepts a string representing the file permissions and constructs a Set of file permissions.
- The asFileAttribute method accepts a Set of file permissions and constructs a file attribute that can be passed to the Path.createFile or Path .createDirectory method.

The following code snippet reads the attributes from one file and creates a new file, assigning the attributes from the original file to the new file:

```
Path sourceFile = ...;
Path newFile = ...;
PosixFileAttributes attrs =
    Files.readAttributes(sourceFile, PosixFileAttributes.class);
FileAttribute<Set<PosixFilePermission>> attr =
    PosixFilePermissions.asFileAttribute(attrs.permissions());
Files.createFile(file, attr);
```

---

106. 8/docs/api/java/nio/file/attribute/PosixFileAttributes.html
107. 8/docs/api/java/nio/file/attribute/PosixFilePermissions.html

The `asFileAttribute` method wraps the permissions as a `FileAttribute`. The code then attempts to create a new file with those permissions. Note that the umask also applies, so the new file might be more secure than the permissions that were requested.

To set a file's permissions to values represented as a hardcoded string, you can use the following code:

```
Path file = ...;
Set<PosixFilePermission> perms =
    PosixFilePermissions.fromString("rw-------");
FileAttribute<Set<PosixFilePermission>> attr =
    PosixFilePermissions.asFileAttribute(perms);
Files.setPosixFilePermissions(file, perms);
```

The Chmod[108] example recursively changes the permissions of files in a manner similar to the `chmod` utility.

Setting a File or Group Owner

To translate a name into an object you can store as a file owner or a group owner, you can use the `UserPrincipalLookupService` service.[109] This service looks up a name or group name as a string and returns a `UserPrincipal` object representing that string. You can obtain the user principal look-up service for the default file system by using the `FileSystem.getUserPrincipalLookupService` method.[110]

The following code snippet shows how to set the file owner by using the `setOwner` method:

```
Path file = ...;
UserPrincipal owner = file.GetFileSystem().getUserPrincipalLookupService()
        .lookupPrincipalByName("sally");
Files.setOwner(file, owner);
```

There is no special-purpose method in the `Files` class for setting a group owner. However, a safe way to do so directly is through the POSIX file attribute view:

```
Path file = ...;
GroupPrincipal group =
    file.getFileSystem().getUserPrincipalLookupService()
        .lookupPrincipalByGroupName("green");
Files.getFileAttributeView(file, PosixFileAttributeView.class)
    .setGroup(group);
```

---

108. `tutorial/essential/io/examples/Chmod.java`

109. `8/docs/api/java/nio/file/attribute/UserPrincipalLookupService.html`

110. `8/docs/api/java/nio/file/FileSystem.html#getUserPrincipalLookupService--`

User-Defined File Attributes

If the file attributes supported by your file system implementation aren't sufficient for your needs, you can use the UserDefinedAttributeView to create and track your own file attributes. Some implementations map this concept to features like NTFS alternative data streams and extended attributes on file systems such as ext3 and ZFS. Most implementations impose restrictions on the size of the value (e.g., ext3 limits the size to 4 kilobytes).

A file's MIME type can be stored as a user-defined attribute by using this code snippet:

```
Path file = ...;
UserDefinedFileAttributeView view = Files
    .getFileAttributeView(file, UserDefinedFileAttributeView.class);
view.write("user.mimetype",
        Charset.defaultCharset().encode("text/html"));
```

To read the MIME type attribute, you would use this code snippet:

```
Path file = ...;
UserDefinedFileAttributeView view = Files
.getFileAttributeView(file,UserDefinedFileAttributeView.class);
String name = "user.mimetype";
ByteBuffer buf = ByteBuffer.allocate(view.size(name));
view.read(name, buf);
buf.flip();
String value = Charset.defaultCharset().decode(buf).toString();
```

The Xdd[111] example shows how to get, set, and delete a user-defined attribute.

> **Note**
>
> In Linux, you might have to enable extended attributes for user-defined attributes to work. If you receive an UnsupportedOperationException when trying to access the user-defined attribute view, you need to remount the file system. The following command remounts the root partition with extended attributes for the ext3 file system. If this command does not work for your flavor of Linux, consult the documentation:
>
> ```
> $ sudo mount -o remount,user_xattr /
> ```
>
> If you want to make the change permanent, add an entry to /etc/fstab.

---

111. tutorial/essential/io/examples/Xdd.java

File Store Attributes

You can use the `FileStore` class to learn information about a file store, such as how much space is available.[112] The `getFileStore(Path)` method fetches the file store for the specified file.[113]

The following code snippet prints the space usage for the file store where a particular file resides:

```
Path file = ...;
FileStore store = Files.getFileStore(file);

long total = store.getTotalSpace() / 1024;
long used = (store.getTotalSpace() -
            store.getUnallocatedSpace()) / 1024;
long avail = store.getUsableSpace() / 1024;
```

The `DiskUsage`[114] example uses this API to print disk space information for all the stores in the default file system. This example uses the `getFileStores`[115] method in the `FileSystem` class to fetch all the file stores for the file system.

Reading, Writing, and Creating Files

This section discusses the details of reading, writing, creating, and opening files. There is a wide array of file I/O methods to choose from. To help make sense of the API, Figure 11.8 arranges the file I/O methods by complexity.

On the far left of the diagram are the utility methods, `readAllBytes` and `readAll-Lines`, and the `write` methods, designed for simple, common cases. To the right of those are the methods used to iterate over a stream or lines of text, such as `newBufferedReader`, `newBufferedWriter`, then `newInputStream` and `newOutputStream`. These methods are interoperable with the `java.io` package. To the right of those are the methods for dealing with `ByteChannels`, `SeekableByteChannels`, and `ByteBuffers`, such as the `newByteChannel` method. Finally, on the far right are the methods that use `FileChannel` for advanced applications needing file locking or memory-mapped I/O.

> **Note**
>
> The methods for creating a new file enable you to specify an optional set of initial attributes for the file. For example, on a file system that supports the POSIX set of standards (such as Solaris), you can specify a file owner, group owner, or file permissions at the time the file is created. The "Managing Metadata" section explains file attributes and how to access and set them.

---

112. `8/docs/api/java/nio/file/FileStore.html`

113. `8/docs/api/java/nio/file/Files.html#getFileStore-java.nio.file.Path-`

114. `tutorial/essential/io/examples/DiskUsage.java`

115. `8/docs/api/java/nio/file/FileSystem.html#getFileStores--`

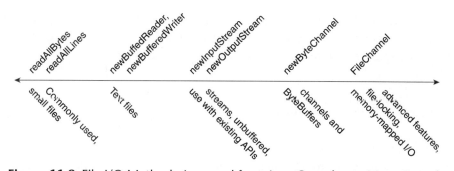

Figure 11.8 File I/O Methods Arranged from Less Complex to More Complex

The OpenOptions Parameter

Several of the methods in this section take an `OpenOptions` parameter. This parameter is optional and the API tells you what the default behavior is for the method when none is specified.

The following `StandardOpenOptions` enums are supported:

- `WRITE`. Opens the file for write access
- `APPEND`. Appends the new data to the end of the file and is used with the `WRITE` or `CREATE` options
- `TRUNCATE_EXISTING`. Truncates the file to zero bytes and is used with the `WRITE` option
- `CREATE_NEW`. Creates a new file and throws an exception if the file already exists
- `CREATE`. Opens the file if it exists or creates a new file if it does not
- `DELETE_ON_CLOSE`. Deletes the file when the stream is closed and is particularly useful for temporary files
- `SPARSE`. Hints that a newly created file will be sparse and, as an advanced option, is honored on some file systems, such as NTFS, where large files with data "gaps" can be stored in a more efficient manner where those empty gaps do not consume disk space
- `SYNC`. Keeps the file (both content and metadata) synchronized with the underlying storage device
- `DSYNC`. Keeps the file content synchronized with the underlying storage device

Commonly Used Methods for Small Files

Reading All Bytes or Lines from a File

If you have a relatively small file and you would like to read its entire contents in one pass, you can use the `readAllBytes(Path)`[116] or `readAllLines(Path,`

---

116. 8/docs/api/java/nio/file/Files.html#readAllBytes-java.nio.file.Path-

Charset)[117] method. These methods take care of most of the work for you, such as opening and closing the stream, but are not intended for handling large files. The following code shows how to use the readAllBytes method:

```
Path file = ...;
byte[] fileArray;
fileArray = Files.readAllBytes(file);
```

Writing All Bytes or Lines to a File

You can use one of the write methods to write bytes or lines to a file:

- write(Path, byte[], OpenOption...)[118]
- write(Path, Iterable<extends CharSequence>, Charset, OpenOption...)[119]

The following code snippet shows how to use a write method:

```
Path file = ...;
byte[] buf = ...;
Files.write(file, buf);
```

Buffered I/O Methods for Text Files

The java.nio.file package supports channel I/O, which moves data in buffers, bypassing some of the layers that can bottleneck stream I/O.

Reading a File by Using Buffered Stream I/O

The newBufferedReader(Path, Charset)[120] method opens a file for reading, returning a BufferedReader that can be used to read text from a file in an efficient manner. The following code snippet shows how to use the newBufferedReader method to read from a file. The file is encoded in US-ASCII:

```
Charset charset = Charset.forName("US-ASCII");
try (BufferedReader reader = Files.newBufferedReader(file, charset)) {
    String line = null;
    while ((line = reader.readLine()) != null) {
        System.out.println(line);
```

---

117. 8/docs/api/java/nio/file/Files.html#readAllLines-java.nio.file.Path
    -java.nio.charset.Charset-

118. 8/docs/api/java/nio/file/Files.html#write-java.nio.file.Path-byte:A
    -java.nio.file.OpenOption...-

119. 8/docs/api/java/nio/file/Files.html#write-java.nio.file.Path-java
    .lang.Iterable-java.nio.charset.Charset-java.nio.file.OpenOption...-

120. 8/docs/api/java/nio/file/Files.html#newBufferedReader-java.nio.file
    .Path-java.nio.charset.Charset-

```
    }
} catch (IOException x) {
    System.err.format("IOException: %s%n", x);
}
```

Writing a File by Using Buffered Stream I/O

You can use the newBufferedWriter(Path, Charset, OpenOption...)[121] method to write to a file using a BufferedWriter. The following code snippet shows how to create a file encoded in US-ASCII using this method:

```
Charset charset = Charset.forName("US-ASCII");
String s = ...;
try (BufferedWriter writer = Files.newBufferedWriter(file, charset)) {
    writer.write(s, 0, s.length());
} catch (IOException x) {
    System.err.format("IOException: %s%n", x);
}
```

Methods for Unbuffered Streams and Interoperable with java.io APIs

Reading a File by Using Stream I/O

To open a file for reading, you can use the newInputStream(Path, OpenOption...) method.[122] This method returns an unbuffered input stream for reading bytes from the file:

```
Path file = ...;
try (InputStream in = Files.newInputStream(file);
    BufferedReader reader =
      new BufferedReader(new InputStreamReader(in))) {
    String line = null;
    while ((line = reader.readLine()) != null) {
        System.out.println(line);
    }
} catch (IOException x) {
    System.err.println(x);
}
```

Creating and Writing a File by Using Stream I/O

You can create a file, append to a file, or write to a file by using the newOutputStream (Path, OpenOption...) method.[123] This method opens or creates a file for writing bytes and returns an unbuffered output stream.

---

121. 8/docs/api/java/nio/file/Files.html#newBufferedWriter-java.nio.file
     .Path-java.nio.charset.Charset-java.nio.file.OpenOption...-

122. 8/docs/api/java/nio/file/Files.html#newInputStream-java.nio.file
     .Path-java.nio.file.OpenOption...-

123. 8/docs/api/java/nio/file/Files.html#newOutputStream-java.nio.file
     .Path-java.nio.file.OpenOption...-

The method takes an optional `OpenOption` parameter. If no open options are specified and the file does not exist, a new file is created. If the file exists, it is truncated. This option is equivalent to invoking the method with the `CREATE` and `TRUNCATE_ EXISTING` options.

The following code snippet opens a log file. If the file does not exist, it is created. If the file exists, it is opened for appending:

```
import static java.nio.file.StandardOpenOption.*;

// Convert the string to a
// byte array.
String s = ...;
byte data[] = s.getBytes();

try (OutputStream out = new BufferedOutputStream(
                Files.newOutputStream(CREATE, APPEND))) {
    ...
    out.write(data, 0, data.length);
} catch (IOException x) {
    System.err.println(x);
}
```

11

Methods for Channels and ByteBuffers

Reading and Writing Files by Using Channel I/O

While stream I/O reads a character at a time, channel I/O reads a buffer at a time. The `ByteChannel` interface provides basic `read` and `write` functionality.[124] A `SeekableByteChannel` is a `ByteChannel` that has the capability to maintain a position in the channel and to change that position.[125] A `SeekableByteChannel` also supports truncating the file associated with the channel and querying the file for its size.

The capability to move to different points in the file and then read from or write to that location makes random access of a file possible. See the "Random Access Files" section for more information. There are two methods for reading and writing channel I/O:

- `newByteChannel(Path, OpenOption...)`[126]
- `newByteChannel(Path, Set<? extends OpenOption>, FileAttribute<?>...)`[127]

---

124. 8/docs/api/java/nio/channels/ByteChannel.html

125. 8/docs/api/java/nio/channels/SeekableByteChannel.html

126. 8/docs/api/java/nio/file/Files.html#newByteChannel-java.nio.file .Path-java.nio.file.OpenOption...-

127. 8/docs/api/java/nio/file/Files.html#newByteChannel-java.nio.file .Path-java.util.Set-java.nio.file.attribute.FileAttribute...-

> **Note**
>
> The `newByteChannel` methods return an instance of a `SeekableByteChannel`. With a default file system, you can cast this seekable byte channel to a `FileChannel`, providing access to more advanced features such mapping a region of the file directly into memory for faster access, locking a region of the file so other processes cannot access it, or reading and writing bytes from an absolute position without affecting the channel's current position.[128]

Both `newByteChannel` methods enable you to specify a list of `OpenOption` options. The same open options used by the `newOutputStream` methods are supported, in addition to one more option: `READ` is required because the `SeekableByteChannel` supports both reading and writing.

Specifying `READ` opens the channel for reading. Specifying `WRITE` or `APPEND` opens the channel for writing. If none of these options is specified, the channel is opened for reading.

The following code snippet reads a file and prints it to standard output:

```
// Defaults to READ
try (SeekableByteChannel sbc = Files.newByteChannel(file)) {
    ByteBuffer buf = ByteBuffer.allocate(10);

    // Read the bytes with the proper encoding for this platform.  If
    // you skip this step, you might see something that looks like
    // Chinese characters when you expect Latin-style characters.
    String encoding = System.getProperty("file.encoding");
    while (sbc.read(buf) > 0) {
        buf.rewind();
        System.out.print(Charset.forName(encoding).decode(buf));
        buf.flip();
    }
} catch (IOException x) {
    System.out.println("caught exception: " + x);
```

The following code snippet, written for POSIX file systems, creates a log file with a specific set of file permissions. This code creates a log file or appends to the log file if it already exists. The log file is created with read/write permissions for owner and read-only permissions for group:

```
import static java.nio.file.StandardCopyOption.*;

// Create the set of options for appending to the file.
Set<OpenOptions> options = new HashSet<OpenOption>();
options.add(APPEND);
options.add(CREATE);
```

---

128. 8/docs/api/java/nio/channels/FileChannel.html

```
// Create the custom permissions attribute.
Set<PosixFilePermission> perms =
    PosixFilePermissions.fromString("rw-r------");
FileAttribute<Set<PosixFilePermission>> attr =
    PosixFilePermissions.asFileAttribute(perms);

// Convert the string to a ByteBuffer.
String s = ...;
byte data[] = s.getBytes();
ByteBuffer bb = ByteBuffer.wrap(data);

try (SeekableByteChannel sbc = Files.newByteChannel(file, options, attr)) {
    sbc.write(bb);
} catch (IOException x) {
    System.out.println("exception thrown: " + x);
}
```

Methods for Creating Regular and Temporary Files

Creating Files

You can create an empty file with an initial set of attributes by using the `createFile(Path, FileAttribute<?>)` method.[129] For example, if, at the time of creation, you want a file to have a particular set of file permissions, use the `createFile` method to do so. If you do not specify any attributes, the file is created with default attributes. If the file already exists, `createFile` throws an exception.

In a single atomic operation, the `createFile` method checks for the existence of the file and creates that file with the specified attributes, which makes the process more secure against malicious code. The following code snippet creates a file with default attributes:

```
Path file = ...;
try {
    // Create the empty file with default permissions, etc.
    Files.createFile(file);
} catch (FileAlreadyExistsException x) {
    System.err.format("file named %s" +
        " already exists%n", file);
} catch (IOException x) {
    // Some other sort of failure, such as permissions.
    System.err.format("createFile error: %s%n", x);
}
```

Recall that the section "POSIX File Permissions" provides an example that uses `createFile(Path, FileAttribute<?>)` to create a file with preset permissions.

---

129. 8/docs/api/java/nio/file/Files.html#createFile-java.nio.file.Path
     -java.nio.file.attribute.FileAttribute...-

You can also create a new file by using the `newOutputStream` methods, as described in the section "Creating and Writing a File Using Stream I/O." If you open a new output stream and close it immediately, an empty file is created.

Creating Temporary Files

You can create a temporary file using one of the following `createTempFile` methods:

- `createTempFile(Path, String, String, FileAttribute<?>)`[130]
- `createTempFile(String, String, FileAttribute<?>)`[131]

The first method allows the code to specify a directory for the temporary file, and the second method creates a new file in the default temporary-file directory. Both methods allow you to specify a suffix for the file name, and the first method allows you to also specify a prefix. The following code snippet gives an example of the second method:

```
try {
    Path tempFile = Files.createTempFile(null, ".myapp");
    System.out.format("The temporary file" +
        " has been created: %s%n", tempFile)
;
} catch (IOException x) {
    System.err.format("IOException: %s%n", x);
}
```

The result of running this file would be something like the following:

```
The temporary file has been created: /tmp/509668702974537184.myapp
```

The specific format of the temporary file name is platform specific.

Random Access Files

Random access files permit nonsequential or random access to a file's contents. To access a file randomly, you open the file, seek a particular location, and read from or write to that file.

---

130. 8/docs/api/java/nio/file/Files.html#createTempFile-java.nio.file
    .Path-java.lang.String-java.lang.String-java.nio.file.attribute
    .FileAttribute...-
131. 8/docs/api/java/nio/file/Files.html#createTempFile-java.lang
    .String-java.lang.String-java.nio.file.attribute.FileAttribute...-

This functionality is possible with the `SeekableByteChannel` interface.[132] The `SeekableByteChannel` interface extends channel I/O with the notion of a current position. Methods enable you to set or query the position, and you can then read the data from or write the data to that location. The API consists of a few easy-to-use methods:

- `position`. Returns the channel's current position[133]
- `position(long)`. Sets the channel's position[134]
- `read(ByteBuffer)`. Reads bytes into the buffer from the channel[135]
- `write(ByteBuffer)`. Writes bytes from the buffer to the channel[136]
- `truncate(long)`. Truncates the file (or other entity) connected to the channel[137]

The section "Reading and Writing Files with Channel I/O" shows that the `Path.newByteChannel` methods return an instance of a `SeekableByteChannel`. On the default file system, you can use that channel as is or you can cast it to a `FileChannel`, giving you access to more advanced features, such as mapping a region of the file directly into memory for faster access, locking a region of the file, or reading and writing bytes from an absolute location without affecting the channel's current position.[138]

The following code snippet opens a file for both reading and writing by using one of the newByteChannel methods. The `SeekableByteChannel` that is returned is cast to a `FileChannel`. Then twelve bytes are read from the beginning of the file, and the string `"I was here!"` is written at that location. The current position in the file is moved to the end, and the twelve bytes from the beginning are appended. Finally, the string `"I was here!"` is appended, and the channel on the file is closed:

```
String s = "I was here!\n";
byte data[] = s.getBytes();
ByteBuffer out = ByteBuffer.wrap(data);

ByteBuffer copy = ByteBuffer.allocate(12);
```

---

132. 8/docs/api/java/nio/channels/SeekableByteChannel.html

133. 8/docs/api/java/nio/channels/SeekableByteChannel.html#position--

134. 8/docs/api/java/nio/channels/SeekableByteChannel.html#position
    -long-

135. 8/docs/api/java/nio/channels/SeekableByteChannel.html#read-java
    .nio.ByteBuffer-

136. 8/docs/api/java/nio/channels/SeekableByteChannel.html#write-java
    .nio.ByteBuffer-

137. 8/docs/api/java/nio/channels/SeekableByteChannel.html#truncate
    -long-

138. 8/docs/api/java/nio/channels/FileChannel.html

```
try (FileChannel fc = (FileChannel.open(file, READ, WRITE))) {
    // Read the first 12
    // bytes of the file.
    int nread;
    do {
        nread = fc.read(copy);
    } while (nread != -1 && copy.hasRemaining());

    // Write "I was here!" at the beginning of the file.
    fc.position(0);
    while (out.hasRemaining())
        fc.write(out);
    out.rewind();

    // Move to the end of the file.  Copy the first 12 bytes to
    // the end of the file.  Then write "I was here!" again.
    long length = fc.size();
    fc.position(length-1);
    copy.flip();
    while (copy.hasRemaining())
        fc.write(copy);
    while (out.hasRemaining())
        fc.write(out);
} catch (IOException x) {
    System.out.println("I/O Exception: " + x);
}
```

11

Creating and Reading Directories

Some of the methods previously discussed, such as delete, work on files, links, *and* directories. But how do you list all the directories at the top of a file system? How do you list the contents of a directory or create a directory?

Listing a File System's Root Directories

You can list all the root directories for a file system by using the FileSystem.get-RootDirectories method.[139] This method returns an Iterable, which enables you to use the *enhanced for* statement to iterate over all the root directories. The following code snippet prints the root directories for the default file system:

```
Iterable<Path> dirs = FileSystems.getDefault().getRootDirectories();
for (Path name: dirs) {
    System.err.println(name);
}
```

---

139. 8/docs/api/java/nio/file/FileSystem.html#getRootDirectories--

Creating a Directory

You can create a new directory by using the `createDirectory(Path, FileAttribute<?>)`[140] method. If you don't specify any `FileAttributes`, the new directory will have default attributes:

```
Path dir = ...;
Files.createDirectory(path);
```

The following code snippet creates a new directory on a POSIX file system that has specific permissions:

```
Set<PosixFilePermission> perms =
    PosixFilePermissions.fromString("rwxr-x---");
FileAttribute<Set<PosixFilePermission>> attr =
    PosixFilePermissions.asFileAttribute(perms);
Files.createDirectory(file, attr);
```

To create a directory several levels deep when one or more of the parent directories might not yet exist, you can use the convenience method, `createDirectories(Path, FileAttribute<?>)`.[141] As with the `createDirectory(Path, FileAttribute<?>)` method, you can specify an optional set of initial file attributes. The following code snippet uses default attributes:

```
Files.createDirectories(Paths.get("foo/bar/test"));
```

The directories are created, as needed, from the top down. In the `foo/bar/test` example, if the `foo` directory does not exist, it is created. Next, the `bar` directory is created, if needed, and finally, the `test` directory is created. It is possible for this method to fail after creating some but not all parent directories.

Creating a Temporary Directory

You can create a temporary directory using one of the `createTempDirectory` methods:

- `createTempDirectory(Path, String, FileAttribute<?>...)`[142]
- `createTempDirectory(String, FileAttribute<?>...)`[143]

---

140. 8/docs/api/java/nio/file/Files.html#createDirectory-java.nio.file
    .Path-java.nio.file.attribute.FileAttribute...-

141. 8/docs/api/java/nio/file/Files.html#createDirectories-java.nio.file
    .Path-java.nio.file.attribute.FileAttribute...-

142. 8/docs/api/java/nio/file/Files.html#createTempDirectory-java.nio
    .file.Path-java.lang.String-java.nio.file.attribute.FileAttribute...-

143. 8/docs/api/java/nio/file/Files.html#createTempDirectory-java.lang
    .String-java.nio.file.attribute.FileAttribute...-

The first method allows the code to specify a location for the temporary directory, and the second method creates a new directory in the default temporary file directory.

Listing a Directory's Contents

You can list all the contents of a directory by using the `newDirectoryStream(Path)` method.[144] This method returns an object that implements the `DirectoryStream` interface.[145] The class that implements the `DirectoryStream` interface also implements `Iterable` so you can iterate through the directory stream, reading all the objects. This approach scales well to very large directories.

> **Note**
>
> The returned `DirectoryStream` is a *stream*. If you are not using a `try-with-resources` statement, don't forget to close the stream in the `finally` block. The `try-with-resources` statement takes care of this for you.

The following code snippet shows how to print the contents of a directory:

```
Path dir = ...;
try (DirectoryStream<Path> stream = Files.newDirectoryStream(dir)) {
    for (Path file: stream) {
        System.out.println(file.getFileName());
    }
} catch (IOException | DirectoryIteratorException x) {
    // IOException can never be thrown by the iteration.
    // In this snippet, it can only be thrown by newDirectoryStream.
    System.err.println(x);
}
```

The `Path` objects returned by the iterator are the names of the entries resolved against the directory. So if you are listing the contents of the `/tmp` directory, the entries are returned with the form `/tmp/a`, `/tmp/b`, and so on.

This method returns the entire contents of a directory: files, links, subdirectories, and hidden files. If you want to be more selective about the contents that are retrieved, you can use one of the other `newDirectoryStream` methods, as described later in this section.

Note that if there is an exception during directory iteration, then `DirectoryIteratorException` is thrown with the `IOException` as the cause. Iterator methods cannot throw exception exceptions.

---

144. 8/docs/api/java/nio/file/Files.html#newDirectoryStream-java.nio
     .file.Path-
145. 8/docs/api/java/nio/file/DirectoryStream.html

Filtering a Directory Listing by Using Globbing

If you want to fetch only files and subdirectories where each name matches a particular pattern, you can do so by using the newDirectoryStream(Path, String)[146] method, which provides a built-in glob filter. If you are not familiar with glob syntax, see the section "What Is a Glob?"

For example, the following code snippet lists files relating to Java: .class, .java, and .jar files.

```
Path dir = ...;
try (DirectoryStream<Path> stream =
    Files.newDirectoryStream(dir, "*.{java,class,jar}")) {
    for (Path entry: stream) {
        System.out.println(entry.getFileName());
    }
} catch (IOException x) {
    // IOException can never be thrown by the iteration.
    // In this snippet, it can // only be thrown by newDirectoryStream.
    System.err.println(x);
}
```

Writing Your Own Directory Filter

Perhaps you want to filter the contents of a directory based on some condition other than pattern matching. You can create your own filter by implementing the DirectoryStream.Filter<T> interface.[147] This interface consists of one method, accept, which determines whether a file fulfills the search requirement.

For example, the following code snippet implements a filter that retrieves only directories:

```
DirectoryStream.Filter<Path> filter =
    newDirectoryStream.Filter<Path>() {
    public boolean accept(Path file) throws IOException {
        try {
            return (Files.isDirectory(path));
        } catch (IOException x) {
            // Failed to determine if it's a directory.
            System.err.println(x);
            return false;
        }
    }
};
```

146. 8/docs/api/java/nio/file/Files.html#newDirectoryStream-java.nio
     .file.Path-java.lang.String-
147. 8/docs/api/java/nio/file/DirectoryStream.Filter.html

Once the filter has been created, it can be invoked by using the `newDirectory-Stream(Path, DirectoryStream.Filter<? super Path>)` method.[148] The following code snippet uses the `isDirectory` filter to print only the directory's subdirectories to standard output:

```
Path dir = ...;
try (DirectoryStream<Path>
                    stream = Files.newDirectoryStream(dir, filter)) {
    for (Path entry: stream) {
        System.out.println(entry.getFileName());
    }
} catch (IOException x) {
    System.err.println(x);
}
```

This method is used to filter a single directory only. However, if you want to find all the subdirectories in a file tree, you would use the mechanism described in the "Walking the File Tree" section.

Links, Symbolic or Otherwise

As mentioned previously, the `java.nio.file` package, and the `Path` class in particular, is "link aware." Every `Path` method either detects what to do when a symbolic link is encountered or provides an option enabling you to configure the behavior when a symbolic link is encountered.

The discussion so far has been about symbolic or *soft* links, but some file systems also support hard links. *Hard links* are more restrictive than symbolic links, as follows:

- The target of the link must exist.
- Hard links are generally not allowed on directories.
- Hard links are not allowed to cross partitions or volumes. Therefore they cannot exist across file systems.
- A hard link looks and behaves like a regular file, so they can be hard to find.
- A hard link is, for all intents and purposes, the same entity as the original file. They have the same file permissions, time stamps, and so on. All attributes are identical.

Because of these restrictions, hard links are not used as often as symbolic links, but the `Path` methods work seamlessly with hard links.

---

148. 8/docs/api/java/nio/file/Files.html#newDirectoryStream-java.nio
     .file.Path-java.nio.file.DirectoryStream.Filter-

Creating a Symbolic Link

If your file system supports it, you can create a symbolic link by using the createSymbolicLink(Path, Path, FileAttribute<?>) method.[149] The second Path argument represents the target file or directory and may or may not exist. The following code snippet creates a symbolic link with default permissions:

```
Path newLink = ...;
Path target = ...;
try {
    Files.createSymbolicLink(newLink, target);
} catch (IOException x) {
    System.err.println(x);
} catch (UnsupportedOperationException x) {
    // Some file systems do not support symbolic links.
    System.err.println(x);
}
```

The FileAttributes vararg enables you to specify initial file attributes that are set atomically when the link is created. However, this argument is intended for future use and is not currently implemented.

Creating a Hard Link

You can create a hard (or *regular*) link to an existing file by using the createLink(Path, Path) method.[150] The second Path argument locates the existing file, and it must exist or a NoSuchFileException is thrown. The following code snippet shows how to create a link:

```
Path newLink = ...;
Path existingFile = ...;
try {
    Files.createLink(newLink, existingFile);
} catch (IOException x) {
    System.err.println(x);
} catch (UnsupportedOperationException x) {
    // Some file systems do not
    // support adding an existing
    // file to a directory.
    System.err.println(x);
}
```

---

149. 8/docs/api/java/nio/file/Files.html#createSymbolicLink-java
     .nio.file.Path-java.nio.file.Path-java.nio.file.attribute
     .FileAttribute...-

150. 8/docs/api/java/nio/file/Files.html#createLink-java.nio.file.Path
     -java.nio.file.Path-

Detecting a Symbolic Link

To determine whether a `Path` instance is a symbolic link, you can use the `isSymbolicLink(Path)` method:[151]

```
Path file = ...;
boolean isSymbolicLink =
    Files.isSymbolicLink(file);
```

For more information, see the section "Managing Metadata."

Finding the Target of a Link

You can obtain the target of a symbolic link by using the `readSymbolicLink(Path)` method, as follows:[152]

```
Path link = ...;
try {
    System.out.format("Target of link" +
        " '%s' is '%s'%n", link,
            Files.readSymbolicLink(link));
} catch (IOException x) {
    System.err.println(x);
}
```

If the `Path` is not a symbolic link, this method throws a `NotLinkException`.

Walking the File Tree

Do you need to create an application that will recursively visit all the files in a file tree? Perhaps you need to delete every `.class` file in a tree or find every file that hasn't been accessed in the last year. You can do so with the `FileVisitor` interface.[153]

The FileVisitor Interface

To walk a file tree, you first need to implement a `FileVisitor`. A `FileVisitor` specifies the required behavior at key points in the traversal process: when a file is visited, before a directory is accessed, after a directory is accessed, or when a failure occurs. The interface has four methods that correspond to these situations:

---

151. 8/docs/api/java/nio/file/Files.html#isSymbolicLink-java.nio.file
     .Path-

152. 8/docs/api/java/nio/file/Files.html#readSymbolicLink-java.nio.file
     .Path-

153. 8/docs/api/java/nio/file/FileVisitor.html

- `preVisitDirectory`. This method is invoked before a directory's entries are visited.[154]
- `postVisitDirectory`. This method is invoked after all the entries in a directory are visited.[155] If any errors are encountered, the specific exception is passed to the method.
- `visitFile`. This method is invoked on the file being visited.[156] The file's `BasicFileAttributes` is passed to the method, or you can use the file attributes package to read a specific set of attributes. For example, you can choose to read the file's `DosFileAttributeView` to determine if the file has the "hidden" bit set.
- `visitFileFailed`. This method is invoked when the file cannot be accessed.[157] The specific exception is passed to the method. You can choose whether to throw the exception, print it to the console or a log file, and so on.

If you don't need to implement all four of the `FileVisitor` methods, instead of implementing the `FileVisitor` interface, you can extend the `SimpleFileVisitor`[158] class. This class, which implements the `FileVisitor` interface, visits all files in a tree and throws an `IOError` when an error is encountered. You can extend this class and override only the methods that you require.

Here is an example that extends `SimpleFileVisitor` to print all entries in a file tree. It prints the entry whether the entry is a regular file, a symbolic link, a directory, or some other "unspecified" type of file. It also prints the size, in bytes, of each file. Any exception that is encountered is printed to the console.

The `FileVisitor` methods are shown in bold:

```
import static java.nio.file.FileVisitResult.*;

public static class PrintFiles
    extends SimpleFileVisitor<Path> {

    // Print information about
    // each type of file.
    @Override
```

154. 8/docs/api/java/nio/file/FileVisitor.html#preVisitDirectory-T-java
     .nio.file.attribute.BasicFileAttributes-

155. 8/docs/api/java/nio/file/FileVisitor.html#postVisitDirectory-T
     -java.io.IOException-

156. 8/docs/api/java/nio/file/FileVisitor.html#visitFile-T-java.nio.file
     .attribute.BasicFileAttributes-

157. 8/docs/api/java/nio/file/FileVisitor.html#visitFileFailedy-T-java
     .io.IOException-

158. 8/docs/api/java/nio/file/SimpleFileVisitor.html

```
    public FileVisitResult visitFile(Path file,
                                     BasicFileAttributes attr) {
        if (attr.isSymbolicLink()) {
            System.out.format("Symbolic link: %s ", file);
        } else if (attr.isRegularFile()) {
            System.out.format("Regular file: %s ", file);
        } else {
            System.out.format("Other: %s ", file);
        }
        System.out.println("(" + attr.size() + "bytes)");
        return CONTINUE;
    }

    // Print each directory visited.
    @Override
    public FileVisitResult postVisitDirectory(Path dir,
                                     IOException exc) {
        System.out.format("Directory: %s%n", dir);
        return CONTINUE;
    }

    // If there is some error accessing
    // the file, let the user know.
    // If you don't override this method
    // and an error occurs, an IOException
    // is thrown.
    @Override
    public FileVisitResult visitFileFailed(Path file,
                                     IOException exc) {
        System.err.println(exc);
        return CONTINUE;
    }
}
```

Kickstarting the Process

Once you have implemented your `FileVisitor`, how do you initiate the file walk?
There are two `walkFileTree` methods in the `Files` class:

- `walkFileTree(Path, FileVisitor)`[159]
- `walkFileTree(Path, Set<FileVisitOption>, int, FileVisitor)`[160]

The first method requires only a starting point and an instance of your `FileVis-itor`. You can invoke the `PrintFiles` file visitor as follows:

```
Path startingDir = ...;
PrintFiles pf = new PrintFiles();
Files.walkFileTree(startingDir, pf);
```

---

159. 8/docs/api/java/nio/file/Files.html#walkFileTree-java.nio.file.Path
    -java.nio.file.FileVisitor-

160. 8/docs/api/java/nio/file/Files.html#walkFileTree-java.nio.file.Path
    -java.util.Set-int-java.nio.file.FileVisitor-

The second `walkFileTree` method enables you to additionally specify a limit on the number of levels visited and a set of `FileVisitOption` enums.[161] If you want to ensure that this method walks the entire file tree, you can specify `Integer.MAX_VALUE` for the maximum depth argument.

You can specify the `FileVisitOption` enum, `FOLLOW_LINKS`, which indicates that symbolic links should be followed. This code snippet shows how the four-argument method can be invoked:

```java
import static java.nio.file.FileVisitResult.*;

Path startingDir = ...;

EnumSet<FileVisitOption> opts = EnumSet.of(FOLLOW_LINKS);

Finder finder = new Finder(pattern);
Files.walkFileTree(startingDir, opts, Integer.MAX_VALUE, finder);
```

Considerations When Creating a FileVisitor

A file tree is walked depth first, but you cannot make any assumptions about the iteration order that subdirectories are visited.

If your program will be changing the file system, you need to carefully consider how you implement your `FileVisitor`. For example, if you are writing a recursive delete, you first delete the files in a directory before deleting the directory itself. In this case, you delete the directory in `postVisitDirectory`.

If you are writing a recursive copy, you create the new directory in `preVisitDirectory` before attempting to copy the files to it (in `visitFiles`). If you want to preserve the attributes of the source directory (similar to the Solaris and Linux cp -p command), you need to do that *after* the files have been copied, in `postVisitDirectory`. The Copy[162] example shows how to do this.

If you are writing a file search, you perform the comparison in the `visitFile` method. This method finds all the files that match your criteria, but it does not find the directories. If you want to find both files and directories, you must also perform the comparison in either the `preVisitDirectory` or `postVisitDirectory` method. The Find[163] example shows how to do this.

You need to decide whether you want symbolic links to be followed. If you are deleting files, for example, following symbolic links might not be advisable. If you are copying a file tree, you might want to allow it. By default, `walkFileTree` does not follow symbolic links.

---

161. 8/docs/api/java/nio/file/FileVisitOption.html

162. tutorial/essential/io/examples/Copy.java

163. tutorial/essential/io/examples/Find.java

The `visitFile` method is invoked for files. If you have specified the `FOLLOW_LINKS` option and your file tree has a circular link to a parent directory, the looping directory is reported in the `visitFileFailed` method with the `FileSystemLoopException`. The following code snippet shows how to catch a circular link and is from the Copy example:

```
@Override
public FileVisitResult
    visitFileFailed(Path file,
        IOException exc) {
    if (exc instanceof FileSystemLoopException) {
        System.err.println("cycle detected: " + file);
    } else {
        System.err.format("Unable to copy:" + " %s: %s%n", file, exc);
    }
    return CONTINUE;
}
```

This case can occur only when the program is following symbolic links.

Controlling the Flow

Perhaps you want to walk the file tree looking for a particular directory and, when found, you want the process to terminate. Perhaps you want to skip specific directories.

The `FileVisitor` methods return a `FileVisitResult` value.[164] You can abort the file-walking process or control whether a directory is visited by the values you return in the `FileVisitor` methods:

- `CONTINUE`. This value indicates that the file walking should continue. If the `preVisitDirectory` method returns `CONTINUE`, then the directory is visited.

- `TERMINATE`. This value immediately aborts the file walking. No further file-walking methods are invoked after this value is returned.

- `SKIP_SUBTREE`. When `preVisitDirectory` returns this value, the specified directory and its subdirectories are skipped. This branch is "pruned out" of the tree.

- `SKIP_SIBLINGS`. When `preVisitDirectory` returns this value, the specified directory is not visited, `postVisitDirectory` is not invoked, and no further unvisited siblings are visited. If returned from the `postVisitDirectory` method, no further siblings are visited. Essentially, nothing further happens in the specified directory.

---

164. `8/docs/api/java/nio/file/FileVisitResult.html`

In this code snippet, any directory named SCCS is skipped:

```java
import static java.nio.file.FileVisitResult.*;

public FileVisitResult
    preVisitDirectory(Path dir,
        BasicFileAttributes attrs) {
    (if (dir.getFileName().toString().equals("SCCS")) {
        return SKIP_SUBTREE;
    }
    return CONTINUE;
}
```

In this code snippet, as soon as a particular file is located, the file name is printed to standard output, and the file walking terminates:

```java
import static java.nio.file.FileVisitResult.*;

// The file we are looking for.
Path lookingFor = ...;

public FileVisitResult
    visitFile(Path file,
        BasicFileAttributes attr) {
    if (file.getFileName().equals(lookingFor)) {
        System.out.println("Located file: " + file);
        return TERMINATE;
    }
    return CONTINUE;
}
```

Examples

The following examples demonstrate the file-walking mechanism:

- Find. This file recurses a file tree looking for files and directories that match a particular glob pattern. This example is discussed in the "Finding Files" section.[165]
- Chmod. This file recursively changes permissions on a file tree (for POSIX systems only).[166]
- Copy. This file recursively copies a file tree.[167]
- WatchDir. This file demonstrates the mechanism that watches a directory for files that have been created, deleted, or modified. Calling this program with the -r option watches an entire tree for changes. For more information about the file notification service, see the "Watching a Directory for Changes" section.[168]

---

165. tutorial/essential/io/examples/Find.java
166. tutorial/essential/io/examples/Chmod.java
167. tutorial/essential/io/examples/Copy.java
168. tutorial/essential/io/examples/WatchDir.java

Finding Files

If you have ever used a shell script, you have most likely used pattern matching to locate files. In fact, you have probably used it extensively. If you haven't used it, pattern matching uses special characters to create a pattern, and then file names can be compared against that pattern. For example, in most shell scripts, the asterisk (*) matches any number of characters. For example, the following command lists all the files in the current directory that end in `.html`:

```
% ls *.html
```

The `java.nio.file` package provides programmatic support for this useful feature. Each file system implementation provides a `PathMatcher`.[169] You can retrieve a file system's `PathMatcher` by using the `getPathMatcher(String)` method in the `FileSystem` class.[170] The following code snippet fetches the path matcher for the default file system:

```
String pattern = ...;
PathMatcher matcher =
    FileSystems.getDefault().getPathMatcher("glob:" + pattern);
```

The string argument passed to `getPathMatcher` specifies the syntax flavor and the pattern to be matched. This example specifies *glob* syntax. If you are unfamiliar with glob syntax, see the "What Is a Glob?" section.

Glob syntax is easy to use and flexible, but if you prefer, you can also use regular expressions, or *regex*, syntax. For further information about regex, see Chapter 14. Some file system implementations might support other syntaxes.

If you want to use some other form of string-based pattern matching, you can create your own `PathMatcher` class. The examples on this page use glob syntax.

Once you have created your `PathMatcher` instance, you are ready to match files against it. The `PathMatcher` interface has a single method, `matches`, that takes a `Path` argument and returns a `boolean`.[171] It either matches the pattern, or it does not. The following code snippet looks for files that end in `.java` or `.class` and prints those files to standard output:

```
PathMatcher matcher =
    FileSystems.getDefault().getPathMatcher("glob:*.{java,class}");
```

---

169. 8/docs/api/java/nio/file/PathMatcher.html
170. 8/docs/api/java/nio/file/FileSystem.html#getPathMatcher-java.lang
     .String-
171. 8/docs/api/java/nio/file/PathMatcher.html#matches-java.nio.file
     .Path-

```
Path filename = ...;
if (matcher.matches(filename)) {
    System.out.println(filename);
}
```

Recursive Pattern Matching

Searching for files that match a particular pattern goes hand in hand with walking a file tree. How many times have you known a file was *somewhere* on the file system but not known exactly where? Or perhaps you need to find all files in a file tree that have a particular file extension.

The `Find` example does precisely that. `Find` is similar to the Solaris and Linux `find` utility but has pared down functionality. You can extend this example to include other functionality. For example, the `find` utility supports the `-prune` flag to exclude an entire subtree from the search. You could implement that functionality by returning `SKIP_SUBTREE` in the `preVisitDirectory` method. To implement the `-L` option, which follows symbolic links, you could use the four-argument `walkFileTree` method and pass in the `FOLLOW_LINKS` enum (but make sure that you test for circular links in the `visitFile` method).

To run the `Find` application, use the following format:

```
% java Find <path> -name "<glob_pattern>"
```

The pattern is placed inside quotation marks so any wildcards are not interpreted by the shell:

```
% java Find . -name "*.html"
```

Here is the source code for the `Find` example:

```
/**
 * Sample code that finds files that match the specified glob pattern.
 * For more information on what constitutes a glob pattern, see
 * http://docs.oracle.com/javase/tutorial/essential/io/fileOps.html#glob
 *
 * The file or directories that match the pattern are printed to
 * standard out.  The number of matches is also printed.
 *
 * When executing this application, you must put the glob pattern
 * in quotes, so the shell will not expand any wild cards:
 *              java Find . -name "*.java"
 */

import java.io.*;
import java.nio.file.*;
import java.nio.file.attribute.*;
import static java.nio.file.FileVisitResult.*;
import static java.nio.file.FileVisitOption.*;
import java.util.*;
```

```java
public class Find {

    public static class Finder
        extends SimpleFileVisitor<Path> {

        private final PathMatcher matcher;
        private int numMatches = 0;

        Finder(String pattern) {
            matcher = FileSystems.getDefault()
                    .getPathMatcher("glob:" + pattern);
        }

        // Compares the glob pattern against
        // the file or directory name.
        void find(Path file) {
            Path name = file.getFileName();
            if (name != null && matcher.matches(name)) {
                numMatches++;
                System.out.println(file);
            }
        }

        // Prints the total number of
        // matches to standard out.
        void done() {
            System.out.println("Matched: "
                    + numMatches);
        }

        // Invoke the pattern matching
        // method on each file.
        @Override
        public FileVisitResult visitFile(Path file,
                BasicFileAttributes attrs) {
            find(file);
            return CONTINUE;
        }

        // Invoke the pattern matching
        // method on each directory.
        @Override
        public FileVisitResult preVisitDirectory(Path dir,
                BasicFileAttributes attrs) {
            find(dir);
            return CONTINUE;
        }

        @Override
        public FileVisitResult visitFileFailed(Path file,
                IOException exc) {
            System.err.println(exc);
            return CONTINUE;
        }
    }

    static void usage() {
        System.err.println("java Find <path>" +
```

11

```
        " -name \"<glob_pattern>\"");
      System.exit(-1);
  }

  public static void main(String[] args)
      throws IOException {

      if (args.length < 3 || !args[1].equals("-name"))
          usage();

      Path startingDir = Paths.get(args[0]);
      String pattern = args[2];

      Finder finder = new Finder(pattern);
      Files.walkFileTree(startingDir, finder);
      finder.done();
  }
}
```

Recursively walking a file tree is covered in the "Walking the File Tree" section.

Watching a Directory for Changes

Have you ever found yourself editing a file using an integrated development environment (IDE) or another editor and a dialog box appears to inform you that one of the open files has changed on the file system and needs to be reloaded? Or perhaps, like the NetBeans IDE, the application just quietly updates the file without notifying you. Figure 11.9 shows how this notification looks with the free editor jEdit.[172]

To implement this functionality, called *file-change notification*, a program must be able to detect what is happening to the relevant directory on the file system. One way to do so is to poll the file system looking for changes, but this approach is inefficient. It does not scale to applications that have hundreds of open files or directories to monitor.

The java.nio.file package provides a file change notification API called the WatchService API. This API enables you to register a directory (or directories) with the watch service. When registering, you tell the service which types of events you are interested in: file creation, file deletion, or file modification. When the service detects an event of interest, it is forwarded to the registered process. The registered process has a thread (or a pool of threads) dedicated to watching for any events it has registered for. When an event comes in, it is handled as needed.

Watch Service Overview

The WatchService API is fairly low level, allowing you to customize it. You can use it as is, or you can choose to create a high-level API on top of this mechanism so that

---

172. http://sourceforge.net/projects/jedit/

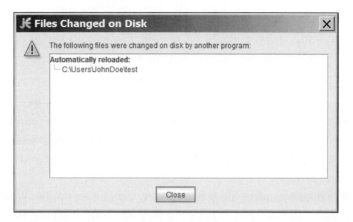

Figure 11.9 jEdit Dialog Box Showing That a Modified File Is Detected

it is suited to your particular needs. Here are the basic steps required to implement a watch service:

- Create a `WatchService` "watcher" for the file system.
- For each directory that you want monitored, register it with the watcher. When registering a directory, you specify the type of events for which you want notification. You receive a `WatchKey` instance for each directory that you register.
- Implement an infinite loop to wait for incoming events. When an event occurs, the key is signaled and placed into the watcher's queue.
- Retrieve the key from the watcher's queue. You can obtain the file name from the key.
- Retrieve each pending event for the key (there might be multiple events) and process as needed.
- Reset the key and resume waiting for events.
- Close the service. The watch service exits either when the thread exits or when it is closed (by invoking its `closed` method).

`WatchKeys` are thread safe and can be used with the `java.nio.concurrent` package. You can dedicate a thread pool to this effort, which is described in Chapter 13.

Try It Out

Because this API is more advanced, try it out before proceeding. Save the `Watch-Dir`[173] example to your computer, and compile it. Create a `test` directory that will

---

173. `tutorial/essential/io/examples/WatchDir.java`

be passed to the example. `WatchDir` uses a single thread to process all events, so it blocks keyboard input while waiting for events. Either run the program in a separate window or run it in the background, as follows:

```
java WatchDir test &
```

Play with creating, deleting, and editing files in the `test` directory. When any of these events occurs, a message is printed to the console. When you have finished, you can delete the `test` directory and `WatchDir` will exit, or if you prefer, you can manually kill the process.

You can also watch an entire file tree by specifying the `-r` option. When you specify `-r`, `WatchDir` walks the file tree, registering each directory with the watch service.

Creating a Watch Service and Registering for Events

The first step is to create a new `WatchService`[174] by using the `newWatchService`[175] method in the `FileSystem` class, as follows:

```
WatchService watcher = FileSystems.getDefault().newWatchService();
```

Next, register one or more objects with the watch service. Any object that implements the `Watchable` interface can be registered.[176] The `Path` class implements the `Watchable` interface, so each directory to be monitored is registered as a `Path` object.

As with any `Watchable`, the `Path` class implements two `register` methods. This page uses the two-argument version, `register(WatchService, WatchEvent.Kind<?>...)`.[177] (The three-argument version takes a `WatchEvent.Modifier`, which is not currently implemented.)

When registering an object with the watch service, you specify the types of events that you want to monitor. The supported `StandardWatchEventKinds` event types follow:[178]

- `ENTRY_CREATE`. A directory entry is created.
- `ENTRY_DELETE`. A directory entry is deleted.
- `ENTRY_MODIFY`. A directory entry is modified.

---

174. 8/docs/api/java/nio/file/WatchService.html
175. 8/docs/api/java/nio/file/FileSystem.html#newWatchService--
176. 8/docs/api/java/nio/file/Watchable.html
177. 8/docs/api/java/nio/file/Path.html#register-java.nio.file.WatchService
    -java.nio.file.WatchEvent.Kind...-
178. 8/docs/api/java/nio/file/StandardWatchEventKinds.html

- OVERFLOW. This indicates that events might have been lost or discarded. You do not have to register for the OVERFLOW event to receive it.

The following code snippet shows how to register a Path instance for all three event types:

```
import static java.nio.file.StandardWatchEventKinds.*;

Path dir = ...;
try {
    WatchKey key = dir.register(watcher,
                            ENTRY_CREATE,
                            ENTRY_DELETE,
                            ENTRY_MODIFY);
} catch (IOException x) {
    System.err.println(x);
}
```

Processing Events

The order of events in an event processing loop follow:

1. Get a watch key. Three methods are provided:
   - poll. This returns a queued key, if available, and returns immediately with a null value, if unavailable.[179]
   - poll(long, TimeUnit). This returns a queued key, if one is available. If a queued key is not immediately available, the program waits until the specified time. The TimeUnit argument determines whether the specified time is nanoseconds, milliseconds, or some other unit of time.[180]
   - take. This returns a queued key. If no queued key is available, this method waits.[181]
2. Process the pending events for the key. You fetch the List of WatchEvents[182] from the pollEvents[183] method.
3. Retrieve the type of event by using the kind method.[184] No matter what events the key has registered for, it is possible to receive an OVERFLOW event. You can choose to handle the overflow or ignore it, but you should test for it.

---

179. 8/docs/api/java/nio/file/WatchService.html#poll--
180. 8/docs/api/java/nio/file/WatchService.html#poll-long-java.util.concurrent .TimeUnit-
181. 8/docs/api/java/nio/file/WatchService.html#take--
182. 8/docs/api/java/nio/file/WatchEvent.html
183. 8/docs/api/java/nio/file/WatchKey.html#pollEvents--
184. 8/docs/api/java/nio/file/WatchEvent.html#kind--

4. Retrieve the file name associated with the event. The file name is stored as the context of the event, so the `context` method is used to retrieve it.[185]

5. After the events for the key have been processed, you need to put the key back into a `ready` state by invoking `reset`.[186] If this method returns `false`, the key is no longer valid and the loop can exit. This step is very *important*. If you fail to invoke `reset`, this key will not receive any further events.

A watch key has a state. At any given time, its state might be one of the following:

- `Ready` indicates that the key is ready to accept events. When first created, a key is in the ready state.

- `Signaled` indicates that one or more events are queued. Once the key has been signaled, it is no longer in the ready state until the `reset` method is invoked.[187]

- `Invalid` indicates that the key is no longer active. This state happens when one of the following events occurs:
  - ❏ The process explicitly cancels the key by using the `cancel` method.[188]
  - ❏ The directory becomes inaccessible.
  - ❏ The watch service is closed.[189]

Here is an example of an event processing loop. It is taken from the `Email`[190] example, which watches a directory, waiting for new files to appear. When a new file becomes available, it is examined to determine if it is a `text/plain` file by using the `probeContentType(Path)`[191] method. The intention is that `text/plain` files will be emailed to an alias, but that implementation detail is left to the reader.

The methods specific to the `WatchService` API are shown in bold:

```
for (;;) {

    // wait for key to be signaled
    WatchKey key;
    try {
```

185. `8/docs/api/java/nio/file/WatchEvent.html#context--`

186. `8/docs/api/java/nio/file/WatchEvent.html#reset--`

187. `8/docs/api/java/nio/file/WatchKey.html#reset--`

188. `8/docs/api/java/nio/file/WatchKey.html#cancel--`

189. `8/docs/api/java/nio/file/WatchService.html#close--`

190. `tutorial/essential/io/examples/Email.java`

191. `8/docs/api/java/nio/file/Files.html#probeContentType-java.nio.file`
     `.Path-`

```
            key = watcher.take();
    } catch (InterruptedException x) {
        return;
    }

    for (WatchEvent<?> event: key.pollEvents()) {
        WatchEvent.Kind<?> kind = event.kind();

        // This key is registered only
        // for ENTRY_CREATE events,
        // but an OVERFLOW event can
        // occur regardless if events
        // are lost or discarded.
        if (kind == OVERFLOW) {
            continue;
        }

        // The filename is the
        // context of the event.
        WatchEvent<Path> ev = (WatchEvent<Path>)event;
        Path filename = ev.context();

        // Verify that the new
        //  file is a text file.
        try {
            // Resolve the filename against the directory.
            // If the filename is "test" and the directory is "foo",
            // the resolved name is "test/foo".
            Path child = dir.resolve(filename);
            if (!Files.probeContentType(child).equals("text/plain")) {
                System.err.format("New file '%s'" +
                    " is not a plain text file.%n", filename);
                continue;
            }
        } catch (IOException x) {
            System.err.println(x);
            continue;
        }

        // Email the file to the
        //  specified email alias.
        System.out.format("Emailing file %s%n", filename);
        //Details left to reader....
    }

    // Reset the key -- this step is critical if you want to
    // receive further watch events.  If the key is no longer valid,
    // the directory is inaccessible so exit the loop.
    boolean valid = key.reset();
    if (!valid) {
        break;
    }
}
```

Retrieving the File Name

The file name is retrieved from the event context. The Email[192] example retrieves the file name with this code:

```
WatchEvent<Path> ev = (WatchEvent<Path>)event;
Path filename = ev.context();
```

When you compile the Email example, it generates the following error:

```
Note: Email.java uses unchecked or unsafe operations.
Note: Recompile with -Xlint:unchecked for details.
```

This error is a result of the line of code that casts the WatchEvent<T> to a WatchEvent<Path>. The WatchDir example avoids this error by creating a utility cast method that suppresses the unchecked warning, as follows:

```
@SuppressWarnings("unchecked")
static <T> WatchEvent<T> cast(WatchEvent<?> event) {
    return (WatchEvent<Path>)event;
}
```

If you are unfamiliar with the @SuppressWarnings syntax, see Chapter 5.

When to Use and Not Use This API

The WatchService API is designed for applications that need to be notified about file change events. It is well suited for any application, like an editor or integrated development environment (IDE), that potentially has many open files and needs to ensure that the files are synchronized with the file system. It is also well suited for an application server that watches a directory, perhaps waiting for .jsp or .jar files to drop in order to deploy them.

This API is *not* designed for indexing a hard drive. Most file system implementations have native support for file change notification. The WatchService API takes advantage of this support where available. However, when a file system does not support this mechanism, the watch service will poll the file system, waiting for events.

Other Useful Methods

A few useful methods did not fit elsewhere in this section and are covered here.

---

192. `tutorial/essential/io/examples/Email.java`

Determining MIME Type

To determine the MIME type of a file, you might find the `probeContentType(Path)` method useful:[193]

```
try {
    String type - Files.probeContentType(filename);
    if (type == null) {
        System.err.format("'%s' has an" + " unknown filetype.%n", filename);
    } else if (!type.equals("text/plain")) {
        System.err.format("'%s' is not" + " a plain text file.%n", filename);
        continue;
    }
} catch (IOException x) {
    System.err.println(x);
}
```

Note that `probeContentType` returns null if the content type cannot be determined. The implementation of this method is highly platform specific and is not infallible. The content type is determined by the platform's default file type detector. For example, if the detector determines a file's content type to be `application/x--java` based on the `.class` extension, it might be fooled.

You can provide a custom `FileTypeDetector` if the default is not sufficient for your needs.[194] The `Email` example uses the `probeContentType` method.

11

Default File System

To retrieve the default file system, use the `getDefault` method.[195] Typically this `FileSystems` method (note the plural) is chained to one of the `FileSystem` methods (note the singular) as follows:

```
PathMatcher matcher =
    FileSystems.getDefault().getPathMatcher("glob:*.*");
```

Path String Separator

The path separator for POSIX file systems is the forward slash (/) and for Microsoft Windows is the backslash (\). Other file systems might use other delimiters. To retrieve the `Path` separator for the default file system, you can use one of the following approaches:

---

193. 8/docs/api/java/nio/file/Files.html#probeContentType-java.nio.file
    .Path-

194. 8/docs/api/java/nio/file/spi/FileTypeDetector.html

195. 8/docs/api/java/nio/file/FileSystems.html#getDefault--

```
String separator = File.separator;
String separator = FileSystems.getDefault().getSeparator();
```

The getSeparator method is also used to retrieve the path separator for any available file system.[196]

File System's File Stores

A file system has one or more file stores to hold its files and directories. The *file store* represents the underlying storage device. In Solaris, Linux, and OS X operating systems, each mounted file system is represented by a file store. In Microsoft Windows, each volume is represented by a file store: C:, D:, and so on.

To retrieve a list of all the file stores for the file system, you can use the get-FileStores method.[197] This method returns an Iterable, which allows you to use the enhanced for statement described in Chapter 3 to iterate over all the root directories:

```
for (FileStore store: FileSystems.getDefault().getFileStores()) {
    ...
}
```

If you want to retrieve the file store where a particular file is located, use the getFileStore method in the Files class, as follows:[198]

```
Path file = ...;
FileStore store= Files.getFileStore(file);
```

The DiskUsage example uses the getFileStores method.

Legacy File I/O Code

Interoperability With Legacy Code

Prior to the java.nio.file package, the java.io.File class was the mechanism used for file I/O, but it had several drawbacks:

- Many methods didn't throw exceptions when they failed, so it was impossible to obtain a useful error message. For example, if a file deletion failed, the program would receive a "delete fail" but wouldn't know if it was because the file didn't exist, the user didn't have permissions, or there was some other problem.

---

196. 8/docs/api/java/nio/file/FileSystem.html#getSeparator--
197. 8/docs/api/java/nio/file/FileSystem.html#getFileStores--
198. 8/docs/api/java/nio/file/Files.html#getFileStore-java.nio.file.Path-

- The `rename` method didn't work consistently across platforms.
- There was no real support for symbolic links.
- More support for metadata was desired, such as file permissions, file owner, and other security attributes.
- Accessing file metadata was inefficient.
- Many of the `File` methods didn't scale. Requesting a large directory listing over a server could result in a hang. Large directories could also cause memory resource problems, resulting in a denial of service.
- It was not possible to write reliable code that could recursively walk a file tree and respond appropriately if there were circular symbolic links.

Perhaps you have legacy code that uses `java.io.File` and would like to take advantage of the `java.nio.file.Path` functionality with minimal impact to your code. The `java.io.File` class provides the `toPath` method, which converts an old-style `File` instance to a `java.nio.file.Path` instance, as follows:[199]

```
Path input = file.toPath();
```

You can then take advantage of the rich feature set available to the `Path` class. For example, assume you had some code that deleted a file:

```
file.delete();
```

You could modify this code to use the `Files.delete` method, as follows:

```
Path fp = file.toPath();
Files.delete(fp);
```

Conversely, the `Path.toFile` method constructs a `java.io.File` object for a `Path` object.[200]

Mapping java.io.File Functionality to java.nio.file

Because the Java implementation of file I/O has been completely redesigned, you cannot swap one method for another method. If you want to use the rich functionality offered by the `java.nio.file` package, your easiest solution is to use the `File.toPath` method, as suggested in the previous section.[201] However, if you do

---

199. 8/docs/api/java/io/File.html#toPath--
200. 8/docs/api/java/nio/file/Path.html#toFile--
201. 8/docs/api/java/io/File.html#toPath--

not want to use that approach or it is not sufficient for your needs, you must rewrite your file I/O code.

There is no one-to-one correspondence between the two APIs, but Table 11.6 gives you a general idea of what functionality in the `java.io.File` API maps to in the `java.nio.file` API and tells you where you can obtain more information.

Table 11.6 Mapping from Legacy File I/O to NIO.2

java.io.File functionality	java.nio.file functionality	Sections with more information
`java.io.File`	`java.nio.file.Path`	The Path Class
`java.io.RandomAccessFile`	The `SeekableByteChannel` functionality	Random Access Files
`File.canRead, canWrite` and `canExecute`	`Files.isReadable, Files.isWritable`, and `Files.isExecutable`. On Solaris, Linux, and OS X file systems, the "Managing Metadata" section describes the package used to check the nine file permissions.	Checking a File or Directory Managing Metadata
`File.isDirectory()`, `File.isFile()`, and `File.length()`	`Files.isDirectory(Path, LinkOption...), Files.isRegularFile(Path, LinkOption...)`, and `Files.size(Path)`	Managing Metadata
`File.lastModified()` and `File.setLastModified(long)`	`Files.getLastModifiedTime(Path, LinkOption...)` and `Files.setLastMOdifiedTime(Path, FileTime)`	Managing Metadata
The `File` methods that set various attributes: `setExecutable, setReadable, setReadOnly`, and `setWritable`	Replaced by the `Files` method `setAttribute(Path, String, Object, LinkOption...)`	Managing Metadata
`new File(parent, "newfile")`	`parent.resolve("newfile")`	Path Operations
`File.renameTo`	`Files.move`	Moving a File or Directory
`File.delete`	`Files.delete`	Deleting a File or Directory
`File.createNewFile`	`Files.createFile`	Creating Files
`File.deleteOnExit`	Replaced by the `DELETE_ON_CLOSE` option specified in the `createFile` method	Creating Files

(continued)

Table 11.6 Mapping from Legacy File I/O to NIO.2 (continued)

java.io.File functionality	java.nio.file functionality	Sections with more information
`File.createTempFile`	`Files.createTempFile(Path, String, FileAttributes<?>)`, `Files.createTempFile(Path, String, String, FileAttributes<?>)`	Creating Files Creating and Writing a File by Using Stream I/O Reading and Writing Files by Using Channel I/O
`File.exists`	`Files.exists` and `Files.notExists`	Verifying the Existence of a File or Directory
`File.compareTo` and `equals`	`Path.compareTo` and `equals`	Comparing Two Paths
`File.getAbsolutePath` and `getAbsoluteFile`	`Path.toAbsolutePath`	Converting a Path
`File.getCanonicalPath` and `getCanonicalFile`	`Path.toRealPath` or `normalize`	Converting a Path (`toRealPath`) Removing Redundancies from a Path (`normalize`)
`File.toURI`	`Path.toURI`	Converting a Path
`File.isHidden`	`Files.isHidden`	Retrieving Information about the Path
`File.list` and `listFiles`	`Path.newDirectoryStream`	Listing a Directory's Contents
`File.mkdir` and `mkdirs`	`Path.createDirectory`	Creating a Directory
`File.listRoots`	`FileSystem.getRootDirectories`	Listing a File System's Root Directories
`File.getTotalSpace`, `File.getFreeSpace`, and `File.getUsableSpace`	`FileStore.getTotalSpace`, `FileStore.getUnallocatedSpace`, `FileStore.getUsableSpace`, and `FileStore.getTotalSpace`	File Store Attributes

11

Summary

The `java.io` package contains many classes that your programs can use to read and write data. Most of the classes implement sequential access streams. The sequential access streams can be divided into two groups: those that read and write bytes and those that read and write Unicode characters. Each sequential access stream has a specialty, such as reading from or writing to a file, filtering data as its read or written, or serializing an object.

The `java.nio.file` package provides extensive support for file and file system I/O. This is a very comprehensive API, but the key entry points are as follows:

- The `Path` class has methods for manipulating a path.
- The `Files` class has methods for file operations, such as moving, copying, and deleting, and also has methods for retrieving and setting file attributes.
- The `FileSystem` class has a variety of methods for obtaining information about the file system.

More information on NIO.2 can be found on the OpenJDK: NIO[202] project web site on java.net.[203] This site includes resources for features provided by NIO.2 that are beyond the scope of this chapter, such as multicasting, asynchronous I/O, and creating your own file system implementation.

Questions and Exercises: Basic I/O

Questions

1. What class and method would you use to read a few pieces of data that are at known positions near the end of a large file?
2. When invoking `format`, what is the best way to indicate a new line?
3. How would you determine the MIME type of a file?
4. What method(s) would you use to determine whether a file is a symbolic link?

Exercises

1. Write an example that counts the number of times a particular character, such as e, appears in a file. The character can be specified at the command line. You can use `xanadu.txt` as the input file.
2. The file `datafile` begins with a single `long` that tells you the offset of a single `int` piece of data within the same file. Write a program that gets the `int` piece of data. What is the `int` data?

Answers

You can find answers to these questions and exercises at `http://docs.oracle .com/javase/tutorial/essential/io/QandE/answers.html`.

---

202. `http://openjdk.java.net/projects/nio/`
203. `http://home.java.net/`

12

Collections

Chapter Contents

Introduction to Collections   424
Interfaces   426
Aggregate Operations   471
Implementations   489
Algorithms   505
Custom Collection Implementations   509
Interoperability   513

This chapter describes the Java Collections Framework. Here you will learn what collections are and how they can make your job easier and programs better. You'll learn about the core elements—interfaces, implementations, aggregate operations, and algorithms—that comprise the Java Collections Framework.

The first section tells you what collections are and how they'll make your job easier and your programs better. You'll learn about the core elements that comprise a collections framework: *interfaces*, *implementations*, and *algorithms*.

The second section describes the *core collection interfaces*, which are the heart and soul of the Java Collections Framework. You'll learn general guidelines for effective use of these interfaces, including when to use which interface. You'll also learn idioms for each interface that will help you get the most out of the interfaces.

The third section shows how aggregate operations iterate over collections on your behalf, which enables you to write more concise and efficient code that processes elements stored in collections.

The fourth section describes the Java SE Development Kit's (JDK's) *general-purpose collection implementations* and tells you when to use which implementation.

You'll also learn about the *wrapper implementations*, which add functionality to general-purpose implementations.

The fifth section describes the *polymorphic algorithms* provided by the JDK to operate on collections. With any luck, you'll never have to write your own sort routine again!

The sixth section tells you why you might want to write your own collection implementation (instead of using one of the general-purpose implementations provided by the JDK) and how you'd go about it. It's easy with the JDK's *abstract collection implementations*!

The final section tells you how the Java Collections Framework interoperates with older Application Programming Interfaces (APIs) that predate the addition of collections to Java. It also tells you how to design new APIs so that they'll interoperate seamlessly with other new APIs.

There are questions and exercises throughout the chapter to test your knowledge.

Introduction to Collections

A *collection*—sometimes called a container—is simply an object that groups multiple elements into a single unit. Collections are used to store, retrieve, manipulate, and communicate aggregate data. Typically, they represent data items that form a natural group, such as a poker hand (a collection of cards), a mail folder (a collection of letters), or a telephone directory (a mapping of names to phone numbers). If you have used the Java programming language—or just about any other programming language—you are already familiar with collections.

What Is a Collections Framework?

A *collections framework* is a unified architecture for representing and manipulating collections. All collections frameworks contain the following:

- *Interfaces*. These are abstract data types that represent collections. Interfaces allow collections to be manipulated independently of the details of their representation. In object-oriented languages, interfaces generally form a hierarchy.
- *Implementations*. These are the concrete implementations of the collection interfaces. In essence, they are reusable data structures.
- *Algorithms*. These are the methods that perform useful computations, such as searching and sorting, on objects that implement collection interfaces. The algorithms are said to be *polymorphic*—that is, the same method can be used on many different implementations of the appropriate collection interface. In essence, algorithms are reusable functionality.

Apart from the Java Collections Framework, the best-known examples of collections frameworks are the C++ Standard Template Library (STL) and Smalltalk's collection hierarchy. Historically, collections frameworks have been quite complex, which gave them a reputation for having a steep learning curve. We believe that the Java Collections Framework breaks with this tradition, as you will learn for yourself in this chapter.

Benefits of the Java Collections Framework

The Java Collections Framework provides the following benefits:

- *Reduced programming effort*. By providing useful data structures and algorithms, the Java Collections Framework frees you to concentrate on the important parts of your program rather than on the low-level "plumbing" required to make it work. By facilitating interoperability among unrelated APIs, the Java Collections Framework frees you from writing adapter objects or conversion code to connect APIs.

- *Increased program speed and quality*. The Java Collections Framework provides high-performance, high-quality implementations of useful data structures and algorithms. The various implementations of each interface are interchangeable, so programs can be easily tuned by switching collection implementations. Because you're freed from the drudgery of writing your own data structures, you'll have more time to devote to improving programs' quality and performance.

- *Interoperability among unrelated APIs*. The collection interfaces are the vernacular by which APIs pass collections back and forth. If my network administration API furnishes a collection of node names and if your graphical user interface (GUI) toolkit expects a collection of column headings, our APIs will interoperate seamlessly, even though they were written independently.

- *Reduced effort to learn and to use new APIs*. Many APIs naturally take collections on input and furnish them as output. In the past, each such API had a small sub-API devoted to manipulating its collections. There was little consistency among these ad hoc collections sub-APIs, so you had to learn each one from scratch, and it was easy to make mistakes when using them. With the advent of standard collection interfaces, the problem went away.

- *Reduced effort to design new APIs*. This is the flip side of the previous advantage. Designers and implementers don't have to reinvent the wheel each time they create an API that relies on collections; instead, they can use standard collection interfaces.

12

- *Increased software reuse*. New data structures that conform to the standard collection interfaces are by nature reusable. The same goes for new algorithms that operate on objects that implement these interfaces.

Interfaces

The *core collection interfaces* encapsulate different types of collections, which are shown in Figure 12.1. These interfaces allow collections to be manipulated independently of the details of their representation. Core collection interfaces are the foundation of the Java Collections Framework. As you can see in Figure 12.1, the core collection interfaces form a hierarchy.

A `Set` is a special kind of `Collection`, a `SortedSet` is a special kind of `Set`, and so forth. Note also that the hierarchy consists of two distinct trees—a `Map` is not a true `Collection`.

Note that all the core collection interfaces are generic. For example, this is the declaration of the `Collection` interface:

```
public interface Collection<E>...
```

The `<E>` syntax tells you that the interface is generic. When you declare a `Collection` instance, you can *and should* specify the type of object contained in the collection. Specifying the type allows the compiler to verify (at compile time) that the type of object you put into the collection is correct, thus reducing errors at runtime. For information on generic types, see Chapter 7.

When you understand how to use these interfaces, you will know most of what there is to know about the Java Collections Framework. This chapter discusses general guidelines for effective use of the interfaces, including when to use which interface. You'll also learn programming idioms for each interface to help you get the most out of it.

To keep the number of core collection interfaces manageable, the Java platform doesn't provide separate interfaces for each variant of each collection type. (Such variants might include immutable, fixed size, and append only.) Instead, the modification operations in each interface are designated *optional*—a given implementation may elect not to support all operations. If an unsupported operation is invoked, a collection throws an `UnsupportedOperationException`.[1] Implementations are responsible for documenting which of the optional operations they support. All of the Java platform's general-purpose implementations support all of the optional operations.

The following list describes the core collection interfaces:

---

1.   8/docs/api/java/lang/UnsupportedOperationException.html

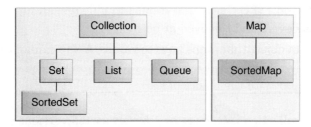

Figure 12.1 The Core Collection Interfaces

- `Collection`. This is the root of the collection hierarchy. A collection represents a group of objects known as its *elements*. The `Collection` interface is the least common denominator that all collections implement and is used to pass collections around and to manipulate them when maximum generality is desired. Some types of collections allow duplicate elements, and others do not. Some are ordered and others are unordered. The Java platform doesn't provide any direct implementations of this interface but provides implementations of more specific subinterfaces, such as `Set` and `List`.
- `Set`. This is a collection that cannot contain duplicate elements. This interface models the mathematical set abstraction and is used to represent sets, such as the cards comprising a poker hand, the courses making up a student's schedule, or the processes running on a machine.
- `List`. This is an ordered collection (sometimes called a *sequence*). `List`s can contain duplicate elements. The user of a `List` generally has precise control over where in the list each element is inserted and can access elements by their integer index (position). If you've used `Vector`, you're familiar with the general flavor of `List`.
- `Queue`. This is a collection used to hold multiple elements prior to processing. Besides basic `Collection` operations, a `Queue` provides additional insertion, extraction, and inspection operations. Queues typically but do not necessarily order elements in a FIFO (first in, first out) manner. Among the exceptions are priority queues, which order elements according to a supplied comparator or the elements' natural ordering. Whatever the ordering used, the head of the queue is the element that would be removed by a call to `remove` or `poll`. In a FIFO queue, all new elements are inserted at the tail of the queue. Other kinds of queues may use different placement rules. Every `Queue` implementation must specify its ordering properties.
- `Deque`. This is a collection used to hold multiple elements prior to processing. Besides basic `Collection` operations, a `Deque` provides additional insertion, extraction, and inspection operations. Deques can be used as both FIFO (first

in, first out) and LIFO (last in, first out). In a deque, all new elements can be inserted, retrieved, and removed at both ends.

- Map. This is an object that maps keys to values. A Map cannot contain duplicate keys; each key can map to at most one value. If you've used Hashtable, you're already familiar with the basics of Map.

The last two core collection interfaces are merely sorted versions of Set and Map:

- SortedSet. This is a Set that maintains its elements in ascending order. Several additional operations are provided to take advantage of the ordering. Sorted sets are used for naturally ordered sets, such as word lists and membership rolls.
- SortedMap. This is a Map that maintains its mappings in ascending key order. This is the Map analog of SortedSet. Sorted maps are used for naturally ordered collections of key/value pairs, such as dictionaries and telephone directories.

The Collection Interface

A Collection represents a group of objects known as its elements.[2] The Collection interface is used to pass around collections of objects where maximum generality is desired. For example, by convention, all general-purpose collection implementations have a constructor that takes a Collection argument. This constructor, known as a *conversion constructor*, initializes the new collection to contain all the elements in the specified collection, whatever the given collection's subinterface or implementation type. In other words, it allows you to *convert* the collection's type.

Suppose, for example, you have a Collection<String> c, which may be a List, a Set, or another kind of Collection. This idiom creates a new ArrayList (an implementation of the List interface), initially containing all the elements in c:

```
List<String> list = new ArrayList<String>(c);
```

You can also use the diamond operator:

```
List<String> list = new ArrayList<>(c);
```

The Collection interface contains methods that perform basic operations, such as int size(), boolean isEmpty(), boolean contains(Object

---

2.   8/docs/api/java/util/Collection.html

element), boolean add(E element), boolean remove(Object element), and Iterator<E> iterator().

It also contains methods that operate on entire collections, such as boolean containsAll(Collection<?> c), boolean addAll(Collection<? extends E> c), boolean removeAll(Collection<?> c), boolean retainAll(Collection<?> c), and void clear(). Additional methods for array operations—such as Object[] toArray() and <T> T[] toArray(T[] a)—exist as well.

In JDK 8 and later, the Collection interface also exposes methods Stream<E> stream() and Stream<E> parallelStream() for obtaining sequential or parallel streams from the underlying collection. (See the "Aggregate Operations" section for more information about using streams.)

The Collection interface does about what you'd expect, given that a Collection represents a group of objects. It has methods that tell you how many elements are in the collection (size, isEmpty), methods that check whether a given object is in the collection (contains), methods that add and remove an element from the collection (add, remove), and methods that provide an iterator over the collection (iterator).

The add method is defined generally enough so that it makes sense for collections that allow duplicates as well as those that don't. It guarantees that the Collection will contain the specified element after the call completes and returns true if the Collection changes as a result of the call. Similarly, the remove method is designed to remove a single instance of the specified element from the Collection, assuming that it contains the element to start with, and to return true if the Collection was modified as a result.

Traversing Collections

There are three ways to traverse collections: (1) by using aggregate operations, (2) with the for-each construct, and (3) by using Iterators.

Traversing Collections with Aggregate Operations

In JDK 8 and later, the preferred method of iterating over a collection is to obtain a stream and perform aggregate operations on it. Aggregate operations are often used in conjunction with lambda expressions to make programming more expressive, using less lines of code. The following code sequentially iterates through a collection of shapes and prints out the red objects:

```
myShapesCollection.stream()
.filter(e -> e.getColor() == Color.RED)
.forEach(e -> System.out.println(e.getName()));
```

Likewise, you could easily request a parallel stream, which might make sense if the collection is large enough and your computer has enough cores:

```
myShapesCollection.parallelStream()
.filter(e -> e.getColor() == Color.RED)
.forEach(e -> System.out.println(e.getName()));
```

There are many different ways to collect data with this API. For example, you might want to convert the elements of a `Collection` to `String` objects and then join them, separated by commas:

```
String joined = elements.stream()
.map(Object::toString)
.collect(Collectors.joining(", "));
```

Or perhaps you could sum the salaries of all employees:

```
int total = employees.stream()
.collect(Collectors.summingInt(Employee::getSalary)));
```

These are but a few examples of what you can do with streams and aggregate operations. For more information and examples, see the "Aggregate Operations" section later in the chapter.

The collections framework has always provided a number of so-called bulk operations as part of its API. These include methods that operate on entire collections, such as `containsAll`, `addAll`, `removeAll`, and so on. Do not confuse those methods with the aggregate operations that were introduced in JDK 8. The key difference between the new aggregate operations and the existing bulk operations (`containsAll`, `addAll`, etc.) is that the old versions are all *mutative*, meaning that they all modify the underlying collection. In contrast, the new aggregate operations *do not* modify the underlying collection. When using the new aggregate operations and lambda expressions, you must take care to avoid mutation so as to not introduce problems in the future, should your code be run later from a parallel stream.

Traversing Collections with the for-each Construct

The `for-each` construct allows you to concisely traverse a collection or array using a `for` loop. See Chapter 3, "The for Statement." The following code uses the `for-each` construct to print out each element of a collection on a separate line:

```
for (Object o : collection)
    System.out.println(o);
```

Traversing Collections with Iterators

An `Iterator` is an object that enables you to traverse through a collection and remove elements from the collection selectively, if desired.[3] You get an `Iterator` for a collection by calling its `iterator` method. The following is the `Iterator` interface:

```
public interface Iterator<E> {
    boolean hasNext();
    E next();
    void remove(); //optional
}
```

The `hasNext` method returns `true` if the iteration has more elements, and the `next` method returns the next element in the iteration. The `remove` method removes the last element that was returned by `next` from the underlying `Collection`. The `remove` method may be called only once per call to `next` and throws an exception if this rule is violated.

Note that `Iterator.remove` is the *only* safe way to modify a collection during iteration; the behavior is unspecified if the underlying collection is modified in any other way while the iteration is in progress.

Use `Iterator` instead of the `for-each` construct when you need to do the following:

- Remove the current element. The `for-each` construct hides the iterator, so you cannot call `remove`. Therefore the `for-each` construct is not usable for filtering.
- Iterate over multiple collections in parallel.

The following method shows you how to use an `Iterator` to filter an arbitrary `Collection`—that is, traverse the collection removing specific elements:

```
static void filter(Collection<?> c) {
    for (Iterator<?> it = c.iterator(); it.hasNext(); )
        if (!cond(it.next()))
            it.remove();
}
```

This simple piece of code is polymorphic, which means that it works for *any* `Collection` regardless of implementation. This example demonstrates how easy it is to write a polymorphic algorithm using the Java Collections Framework.

---

3.   8/docs/api/java/util/Iterator.html

Collection Interface Bulk Operations

Bulk operations perform an operation on an entire Collection. You could implement these shorthand operations using the basic operations, though in most cases,
such implementations would be less efficient. The following are the bulk operations:

- containsAll. This returns true if the target Collection contains all the
  elements in the specified Collection.
- addAll. This adds all the elements in the specified Collection to the target
  Collection.
- removeAll. This removes from the target Collection all its elements that
  are also contained in the specified Collection.
- retainAll. This removes from the target Collection all its elements that
  are *not* also contained in the specified Collection—that is, it retains only
  those elements in the target Collection that are also contained in the specified Collection.
- clear. This removes all elements from the Collection.

The addAll, removeAll, and retainAll methods all return true if the target
Collection was modified in the process of executing the operation.

As a simple example of the power of bulk operations, consider the following idiom
to remove *all* instances of a specified element, e, from a Collection, c:

```
c.removeAll(Collections.singleton(e));
```

More specifically, suppose you want to remove all of the null elements from a
Collection:

```
c.removeAll(Collections.singleton(null));
```

This idiom uses Collections.singleton, which is a static factory method that
returns an immutable Set containing only the specified element.

Collection Interface Array Operations

The toArray methods are provided as a bridge between collections and older APIs
that expect arrays on input. The array operations allow the contents of a Collection to be translated into an array. The simple form with no arguments creates a
new array of Object. The more complex form allows the caller to provide an array
or to choose the runtime type of the output array.

For example, suppose that c is a Collection. The following snippet dumps the contents of c into a newly allocated array of Object whose length is identical to the number of elements in c:

```
Object[] a = c.toArray();
```

Suppose that c is known to contain only strings (perhaps because c is of type Collection<String>). The following snippet dumps the contents of c into a newly allocated array of String whose length is identical to the number of elements in c:

```
String[] a = c.toArray(new String[0]);
```

The Set Interface

A Set[4] is a Collection[5] that cannot contain duplicate elements. It models the mathematical set abstraction. The Set interface contains *only* methods inherited from Collection and adds the restriction that duplicate elements are prohibited. Set also adds a stronger contract on the behavior of the equals and hashCode operations, allowing Set instances to be compared meaningfully even if their implementation types differ. Two Set instances are equal if they contain the same elements.

The Java platform contains three general-purpose Set implementations: HashSet, TreeSet, and LinkedHashSet. HashSet, which stores its elements in a hash table, is the best performing implementation; however, it makes no guarantees concerning the order of iteration.[6] TreeSet, which stores its elements in a red-black tree, orders its elements based on their values; it is substantially slower than HashSet.[7] LinkedHashSet, which is implemented as a hash table with a linked list running through it, orders its elements based on the order in which they were inserted into the set (insertion order).[8] LinkedHashSet spares its clients from the unspecified, generally chaotic ordering provided by HashSet at a cost that is only slightly higher.

Here's a simple but useful Set idiom. Suppose you have a Collection, c, and you want to create another Collection containing the same elements but with all duplicates eliminated. The following one-liner does the trick:

```
Collection<Type> noDups = new HashSet<Type>(c);
```

---

4.   8/docs/api/java/util/Set.html
5.   8/docs/api/java/util/Collection.html
6.   8/docs/api/java/util/HashSet.html
7.   8/docs/api/java/util/TreeSet.html
8.   8/docs/api/java/util/LinkedHashSet.html

12

It works by creating a `Set` (which, by definition, cannot contain duplicates) initially containing all the elements in c. It uses the standard conversion constructor described in "The Collection Interface" section.

If using JDK 8 or later, you could easily collect into a `Set` using aggregate operations:

```
c.stream()
.collect(Collectors.toSet()); // no duplicates
```

Here's a slightly longer example that accumulates a `Collection` of names into a `TreeSet`:

```
Set<String> set = people.stream()
.map(Person::getName)
.collect(Collectors.toCollection(TreeSet::new));
```

The following is a minor variant of the first idiom that preserves the order of the original collection while removing duplicate elements:

```
Collection<Type> noDups = new LinkedHashSet<Type>(c);
```

The following is a generic method that encapsulates the preceding idiom, returning a `Set` of the same generic type as the one passed:

```
public static <E> Set<E> removeDups(Collection<E> c) {
    return new LinkedHashSet<E>(c);
}
```

Set Interface Basic Operations

The `size` operation returns the number of elements in the `Set` (its *cardinality*). The `isEmpty` method does exactly what you think it would. The `add` method adds the specified element to the `Set` if it is not already present and returns a `boolean` indicating whether the element was added. Similarly, the `remove` method removes the specified element from the `Set` if it is present and returns a `boolean` indicating whether the element was present. The `iterator` method returns an `Iterator` over the `Set`.

The following `program` prints out all distinct words in its argument list. Two versions of this program are provided. The first uses JDK 8 aggregate operations. The second uses the `for-each` construct.

Here is the version that uses JDK 8 aggregate operations:

```
import java.util.*;
import java.util.stream.*;
```

```
public class FindDups {
    public static void main(String[] args) {
        Set<String> distinctWords = Arrays.asList(args).stream()
                .collect(Collectors.toSet());
        System.out.println(distinctWords.size()+
                            " distinct words: " +
                            distinctWords);
    }
}
```

Here is the version that uses the `for-each` construct:

```
import java.util.*;

public class FindDups {
    public static void main(String[] args) {
        Set<String> s = new HashSet<String>();
        for (String a : args)
            s.add(a);
            System.out.println(s.size() + " distinct words: " + s);
    }
}
```

Now run either version of the program:

```
java FindDups i came i saw i left
```

The following output is produced:

```
4 distinct words: [left, came, saw, i]
```

Note that the code always refers to the `Collection` by its interface type (`Set`) rather than by its implementation type. This is a *strongly* recommended programming practice because it gives you the flexibility to change implementations merely by changing the constructor. If either of the variables used to store a collection or the parameters used to pass it around are declared to be of the `Collection`'s implementation type rather than its interface type, *all* such variables and parameters must be changed in order to change its implementation type.

Furthermore, there's no guarantee that the resulting program will work. If the program uses any nonstandard operations present in the original implementation type but not in the new one, the program will fail. Referring to collections only by their interface prevents you from using any nonstandard operations.

The implementation type of the `Set` in the preceding example is `HashSet`, which makes no guarantees as to the order of the elements in the `Set`. If you want the program to print the word list in alphabetical order, merely change the `Set`'s implementation type from `HashSet` to `TreeSet`. Making this trivial one-line change causes the command line in the previous example to generate the following output:

```
java FindDups i came i saw i left

4 distinct words: [came, i, left, saw]
```

Set Interface Bulk Operations

Bulk operations are particularly well suited to `Sets`; when applied, they perform standard set-algebraic operations. Suppose `s1` and `s2` are sets. Here's what bulk operations do:

- `s1.containsAll(s2)`. This returns `true` if `s2` is a *subset* of `s1`. (`s2` is a subset of `s1` if set `s1` contains all the elements in `s2`.)
- `s1.addAll(s2)`. This transforms `s1` into the *union* of `s1` and `s2`. (The union of two sets is the set containing all the elements contained in either set.)
- `s1.retainAll(s2)`. This transforms `s1` into the intersection of `s1` and `s2`. (The intersection of two sets is the set containing only the elements common to both sets.)
- `s1.removeAll(s2)`. This transforms `s1` into the (asymmetric) set difference of `s1` and `s2`. (For example, the set difference of `s1` minus `s2` is the set containing all the elements found in `s1` but not in `s2`.)

To calculate the union, intersection, or set difference of two sets *nondestructively* (without modifying either set), the caller must copy one set before calling the appropriate bulk operation. The following are the resulting idioms:

```
Set<Type> union = new HashSet<Type>(s1);
union.addAll(s2);

Set<Type> intersection = new HashSet<Type>(s1);
intersection.retainAll(s2);

Set<Type> difference = new HashSet<Type>(s1);
difference.removeAll(s2);
```

The implementation type of the result `Set` in the preceding idioms is `HashSet`, which is, as already mentioned, the best all-around `Set` implementation in the Java platform. However, any general-purpose `Set` implementation could be substituted.

Let's revisit the `FindDups` program. Suppose you want to know which words in the argument list occur only once and which occur more than once, but you do not want any duplicates printed out repeatedly. This effect can be achieved by generating two sets—one containing every word in the argument list and the other containing only the duplicates. The words that occur only once are the set difference of these two sets, which we know how to compute. Here's what the resulting program looks like:

```java
import java.util.*;

public class FindDups2 {
    public static void main(String[] args) {
        Set<String> uniques = new HashSet<String>();
        Set<String> dups    = new HashSet<String>();

        for (String a : args)
            if (!uniques.add(a))
                dups.add(a);

        // Destructive set-difference
        uniques.removeAll(dups);

        System.out.println("Unique words:    " + uniques);
        System.out.println("Duplicate words: " + dups);
    }
}
```

When run with the same argument list used earlier (i came i saw i left), the program yields the following output:

```
Unique words:    [left, saw, came]
Duplicate words: [i]
```

A less common set-algebraic operation is the *symmetric set difference*—the set of elements contained in either of two specified sets but not in both. The following code calculates the symmetric set difference of two sets nondestructively:

```java
Set<Type> symmetricDiff = new HashSet<Type>(s1);
symmetricDiff.addAll(s2);
Set<Type> tmp = new HashSet<Type>(s1);
tmp.retainAll(s2);
symmetricDiff.removeAll(tmp);
```

Set Interface Array Operations

The array operations don't do anything special for `Set`s beyond what they do for any other `Collection`. These operations are described in "The Collection Interface" section.

The List Interface

A List[9] is an ordered Collection[10] (sometimes called a *sequence*). Lists may contain duplicate elements. In addition to the operations inherited from Collection, the List interface includes operations for the following:

- *Positional access.* This manipulates elements based on their numerical position in the list. This includes methods such as get, set, add, addAll, and remove.
- *Search.* This searches for a specified object in the list and returns its numerical position. Search methods include indexOf and lastIndexOf.
- *Iteration.* This extends Iterator semantics to take advantage of the list's sequential nature. The listIterator methods provide this behavior.
- *Range-view.* The sublist method performs arbitrary *range operations* on the list.

The Java platform contains two general-purpose List implementations: ArrayList,[11] which is usually the better-performing implementation, and LinkedList,[12] which offers better performance under certain circumstances.

Collection Operations

The operations inherited from Collection all do about what you'd expect them to do, assuming you're already familiar with them. If you're not familiar with them from Collection, now would be a good time to read "The Collection Interface" section. The remove operation always removes *the first* occurrence of the specified element from the list. The add and addAll operations always append the new element(s) to the *end* of the list. Thus the following idiom concatenates one list to another:

```
list1.addAll(list2);
```

Here's a nondestructive form of this idiom, which produces a third List consisting of the second list appended to the first:

```
List<Type> list3 = new ArrayList<Type>(list1);
list3.addAll(list2);
```

9.   8/docs/api/java/util/List.html
10.   8/docs/api/java/util/Collection.html
11.   8/docs/api/java/util/ArrayList.html
12.   8/docs/api/java/util/LinkedList.html

Note that the idiom, in its nondestructive form, takes advantage of `ArrayList`'s standard conversion constructor. And here's an example (JDK 8 and later) that aggregates some names into a `List`:

```
List<String> list = people.stream()
.map(Person::getName)
.collect(Collectors.toList());
```

Like the `Set`[13] interface, `List` strengthens the requirements on the `equals` and `hashCode` methods so that two `List` objects can be compared for logical equality without regard to their implementation classes. Two `List` objects are equal if they contain the same elements in the same order.

Positional Access and Search Operations

The basic positional access operations are `get`, `set`, `add`, and `remove`. (The `set` and `remove` operations return the old value that is being overwritten or removed.) Other operations (`indexOf` and `lastIndexOf`) return the first or last index of the specified element in the list.

The `addAll` operation inserts all the elements of the specified `Collection` starting at the specified position. The elements are inserted in the order they are returned by the specified `Collection`'s iterator. This call is the positional access analog of `Collection`'s `addAll` operation.

Here's a little method to swap two indexed values in a `List`:

```
public static <E> void swap(List<E> a, int i, int j) {
    E tmp = a.get(i);
    a.set(i, a.get(j));
    a.set(j, tmp);
}
```

Of course, there's one big difference. This is a polymorphic algorithm: It swaps two elements in any `List`, regardless of its implementation type. Here's another polymorphic algorithm that uses the preceding `swap` method:

```
public static void shuffle(List<?> list, Random rnd) {
    for (int i = list.size(); i > 1; i--)
        swap(list, i - 1, rnd.nextInt(i));
}
```

This algorithm, which is included in the Java platform's `Collections` class, randomly permutes the specified list using the specified source of randomness.[14] It's

---

13.   8/docs/api/java/util/Set.html

14.   8/docs/api/java/util/Collections.html

a bit subtle: it runs up the list from the bottom, repeatedly swapping a randomly selected element into the current position. Unlike most naive attempts at shuffling, it's *fair* (all permutations occur with equal likelihood, assuming an unbiased source of randomness) and *fast* (requiring exactly `list.size()-1` swaps). The following program uses this algorithm to print the words in its argument list in random order:

```
import java.util.*;

public class Shuffle {
    public static void main(String[] args) {
        List<String> list = new ArrayList<String>();
        for (String a : args)
            list.add(a);
        Collections.shuffle(list, new Random());
        System.out.println(list);
    }
}
```

In fact, this program can be made even shorter and faster. The `Arrays`[15] class has a static factory method called `asList`, which allows an array to be viewed as a `List`. This method does not copy the array. Changes in the `List` write through to the array and vice versa. The resulting `List` is not a general-purpose `List` implementation because it doesn't implement the (optional) `add` and `remove` operations: Arrays are not resizable. Taking advantage of `Arrays.asList` and calling the library version of `shuffle`, which uses a default source of randomness, you get the following tiny program, whose behavior is identical to the previous program:

```
import java.util.*;

public class Shuffle {
    public static void main(String[] args) {
        List<String> list = Arrays.asList(args);
        Collections.shuffle(list);
        System.out.println(list);
    }
}
```

Iterators

As you'd expect, the `Iterator` returned by `List`'s `iterator` operation returns the elements of the list in proper sequence. `List` also provides a richer iterator, called a `ListIterator`, that allows you to traverse the list in either direction, modify the list during iteration, and obtain the current position of the iterator.

The three methods that `ListIterator` inherits from `Iterator` (`hasNext`, `next`, and `remove`) do exactly the same thing in both interfaces. The `hasPrevious`

---

15.   8/docs/api/java/util/Arrays.html

and the `previous` operations are exact analogs of `hasNext` and `next`. The former operations refer to the element before the (implicit) cursor, whereas the latter refer to the element after the cursor. The `previous` operation moves the cursor backward, whereas `next` moves it forward.

Here's the standard idiom for iterating backward through a list:

```
for (ListIterator<Type> it = list.listIterator(list.size());
     it.hasPrevious(); ) {
    Type t = it.previous();
    ...
}
```

Note the argument to `listIterator` in the preceding idiom. The `List` interface has two forms of the `listIterator` method. The form with no arguments returns a `ListIterator` positioned at the beginning of the list; the form with an `int` argument returns a `ListIterator` positioned at the specified index. The index refers to the element that would be returned by an initial call to `next`. An initial call to `previous` would return the element whose index was `index-1`. In a list of length n, there are n+1 valid values for `index`, from 0 to n, inclusive.

Intuitively speaking, the cursor is always between two elements—the one that would be returned by a call to `previous` and the one that would be returned by a call to `next`. The n+1 valid `index` values correspond to the n+1 gaps between elements, from the gap before the first element to the gap after the last one. Figure 12.2 shows the five possible cursor positions in a list containing four elements.

Calls to `next` and `previous` can be intermixed, but you must be careful. The first call to `previous` returns the same element as the last call to `next`. Similarly, the first call to `next` after a sequence of calls to `previous` returns the same element as the last call to `previous`.

It should come as no surprise that the `nextIndex` method returns the index of the element that would be returned by a subsequent call to `next` and `previousIndex` returns the index of the element that would be returned by a subsequent call to `previous`. These calls are typically used either to report the position where something was found or to record the position of the `ListIterator` so that another `ListIterator` with an identical position can be created.

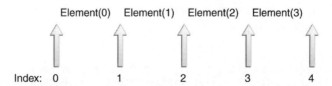

Figure 12.2 The Five Possible Cursor Positions

It should also come as no surprise that the number returned by nextIndex is always one greater than the number returned by previousIndex. This implies the behavior of the two boundary cases: (1) a call to previousIndex when the cursor is before the initial element returns −1 and (2) a call to nextIndex when the cursor is after the final element returns list.size(). To make all this concrete, the following is a possible implementation of List.indexOf:

```java
public int indexOf(E e) {
    for (ListIterator<E> it = listIterator(); it.hasNext(); )
        if (e == null ? it.next() == null : e.equals(it.next()))
            return it.previousIndex();
    // Element not found
    return -1;
}
```

Note that the indexOf method returns it.previousIndex() even though it is traversing the list in the forward direction. The reason is that it.nextIndex() would return the index of the element we are about to examine, and we want to return the index of the element we just examined.

The Iterator interface provides the remove operation to remove the last element returned by next from the Collection. For ListIterator, this operation removes the last element returned by next or previous. The ListIterator interface provides two additional operations to modify the list—set and add. The set method overwrites the last element returned by next or previous with the specified element. The following polymorphic algorithm uses set to replace all occurrences of one specified value with another:

```java
public static <E> void replace(List<E> list, E val, E newVal) {
    for (ListIterator<E> it = list.listIterator(); it.hasNext(); )
        if (val == null ? it.next() == null : val.equals(it.next()))
            it.set(newVal);
}
```

The only bit of trickiness in this example is the equality test between val and it.next. You need to check if the value of val is null to prevent a NullPointerException.

The add method inserts a new element into the list immediately before the current cursor position. This method is illustrated in the following polymorphic algorithm to replace all occurrences of a specified value with the sequence of values contained in the specified list:

```java
public static <E>
    void replace(List<E> list, E val, List<? extends E> newVals) {
    for (ListIterator<E> it = list.listIterator(); it.hasNext(); ){
        if (val == null ? it.next() == null : val.equals(it.next())) {
            it.remove();
```

```
                for (E e : newVals)
                    it.add(e);
            }
        }
    }
```

Range-View Operation

The range-view operation subList(int fromIndex, int toIndex) returns a List view of the portion of this list, whose indices range from fromIndex, inclusive, to toIndex, exclusive. This *half-open range* mirrors the typical for loop:

```
for (int i = fromIndex; i < toIndex; i++) {
    ...
}
```

As the term *view* implies, the returned List is backed up by the List on which subList was called, so changes in the former are reflected in the latter.

This method eliminates the need for explicit range operations (of the sort that commonly exist for arrays). Any operation that expects a List can be used as a range operation by passing a subList view instead of a whole List. For example, the following idiom removes a range of elements from a List:

```
list.subList(fromIndex, toIndex).clear();
```

Similar idioms can be constructed to search for an element in a range:

```
int i = list.subList(fromIndex, toIndex).indexOf(o);
int j = list.subList(fromIndex, toIndex).lastIndexOf(o);
```

Note that the preceding idioms return the index of the found element in the sub-List, not the index in the backing List.

Any polymorphic algorithm that operates on a List, such as the replace and shuffle examples, works with the List returned by subList. Here's a polymorphic algorithm whose implementation uses subList to deal a hand from a deck—that is, it returns a new List (the hand) containing the specified number of elements taken from the end of the specified List (the deck). The elements returned in the hand are removed from the deck:

```
public static <E> List<E> dealHand(List<E> deck, int n) {
    int deckSize = deck.size();
    List<E> handView = deck.subList(deckSize - n, deckSize);
    List<E> hand = new ArrayList<E>(handView);
    handView.clear();
    return hand;
}
```

12

Note that this algorithm removes the hand from the *end* of the deck. For many common `List` implementations, such as `ArrayList`, the performance of removing elements from the end of the list is substantially better than that of removing elements from the beginning.

The following is a program that uses the `dealHand` method in combination with `Collections.shuffle` to generate hands from a normal fifty-two-card deck. The program takes two command-line arguments: (1) the number of hands to deal and (2) the number of cards in each hand:

```java
import java.util.*;

public class Deal {
    public static void main(String[] args) {
        if (args.length < 2) {
            System.out.println("Usage: Deal hands cards");
            return;
        }
        int numHands = Integer.parseInt(args[0]);
        int cardsPerHand = Integer.parseInt(args[1]);

        // Make a normal 52-card deck.
        String[] suit = new String[] {
            "spades", "hearts",
            "diamonds", "clubs"
        };
        String[] rank = new String[] {
            "ace", "2", "3", "4",
            "5", "6", "7", "8", "9", "10",
            "jack", "queen", "king"
        };

        List<String> deck = new ArrayList<String>();
        for (int i = 0; i < suit.length; i++)
            for (int j = 0; j < rank.length; j++)
                deck.add(rank[j] + " of " + suit[i]);

        // Shuffle the deck.
        Collections.shuffle(deck);

        if (numHands * cardsPerHand > deck.size()) {
            System.out.println("Not enough cards.");
            return;
        }

        for (int i = 0; i < numHands; i++)
            System.out.println(dealHand(deck, cardsPerHand));
    }

    public static <E> List<E> dealHand(List<E> deck, int n) {
        int deckSize = deck.size();
        List<E> handView = deck.subList(deckSize - n, deckSize);
        List<E> hand = new ArrayList<E>(handView);
        handView.clear();
        return hand;
    }
}
```

Running the program produces output like the following:

```
% java Deal 4 5

[8 of hearts, jack of spades, 3 of spades, 4 of spades,
    king of diamonds]
[4 of diamonds, ace of clubs, 6 of clubs, jack of hearts,
    queen of hearts]
[7 of spades, 5 of spades, 2 of diamonds, queen of diamonds,
    9 of clubs]
[8 of spades, 6 of diamonds, ace of spades, 3 of hearts,
    ace of hearts]
```

Although the subList operation is extremely powerful, some care must be exercised when using it. The semantics of the List returned by subList become undefined if elements are added to or removed from the backing List in any way other than via the returned List. Thus it's highly recommended that you use the List returned by subList only as a transient object—to perform one or a sequence of range operations on the backing List. The longer you use the subList instance, the greater the probability that you'll compromise it by modifying the backing List directly or through another subList object. Note that it is legal to modify a sublist of a sublist and to continue using the original sublist (though not concurrently).

12

List Algorithms

Most polymorphic algorithms in the Collections class apply specifically to List. Having all these algorithms at your disposal makes it very easy to manipulate lists. Here's a summary of these algorithms, which are described in more detail in the "Algorithms" section:

- sort. Sorts a List using a merge sort algorithm, which provides a fast, stable sort (A *stable sort* is one that does not reorder equal elements.)
- shuffle. Randomly permutes the elements in a List
- reverse. Reverses the order of the elements in a List
- rotate. Rotates all the elements in a List by a specified distance
- swap. Swaps the elements at specified positions in a List
- replaceAll. Replaces all occurrences of one specified value with another
- fill. Overwrites every element in a List with the specified value
- copy. Copies the source List into the destination List
- binarySearch. Searches for an element in an ordered List using the binary search algorithm
- indexOfSubList. Returns the index of the first sublist of one List that is equal to another

- ▪ `lastIndexOfSubList`. Returns the index of the last sublist of one `List` that is equal to another

The Queue Interface

A `Queue` is a collection for holding elements prior to processing.[16] Besides basic `Collection` operations, queues provide additional insertion, removal, and inspection operations. The `Queue` interface follows:

```
public interface Queue<E> extends Collection<E> {
    E element();
    boolean offer(E e);
    E peek();
    E poll();
    E remove();
}
```

Each `Queue` method exists in two forms: (1) one throws an exception if the operation fails and (2) the other returns a special value if the operation fails (either `null` or `false`, depending on the operation). The regular structure of the interface is illustrated in Table 12.1.

Queues typically but do not necessarily order elements in a FIFO (first in, first out) manner. Among the exceptions are priority queues, which order elements according to their values. Whatever ordering is used, the head of the queue is the element that would be removed by a call to `remove` or `poll`. In a FIFO queue, all new elements are inserted at the tail of the queue. Other kinds of queues may use different placement rules. Every `Queue` implementation must specify its ordering properties.

It is possible for a `Queue` implementation to restrict the number of elements that it holds; such queues are known as *bounded*. Some `Queue` implementations in `java.util.concurrent` are bounded, but the implementations in `java.util` are not.

The `add` method, which `Queue` inherits from `Collection`, inserts an element unless it would violate the queue's capacity restrictions, in which case it throws `IllegalStateException`. The `offer` method, which is intended solely for use on bounded queues, differs from `add` only in that it indicates failure to insert an element by returning `false`.

The `remove` and `poll` methods both remove and return the head of the queue. Exactly which element gets removed is a function of the queue's ordering policy. The `remove` and `poll` methods differ in their behavior only when the queue is empty. Under these circumstances, `remove` throws `NoSuchElementException`, while `poll` returns `null`.

---

16. 8/docs/api/java/util/Queue.html

Table 12.1 Queue Interface Structure

Type of operation	Throws exception	Returns special value
Insert	add(e)	offer(e)
Remove	remove()	poll()
Examine	element()	peek()

The `element` and `peek` methods return but do not remove the head of the queue. They differ from one another in precisely the same fashion as `remove` and `poll`: if the queue is empty, `element` throws `NoSuchElementException`, while peek returns `null`.

`Queue` implementations generally do not allow insertion of `null` elements. The `LinkedList` implementation, which was retrofitted to implement `Queue`, is an exception. For historical reasons, it permits `null` elements, but you should refrain from taking advantage of this because `null` is used as a special return value by the `poll` and `peek` methods.

`Queue` implementations generally do not define element-based versions of the `equals` and `hashCode` methods but instead inherit the identity-based versions from `Object`. The `Queue` interface does not define the blocking queue methods, which are common in concurrent programming. These methods, which wait for elements to appear or for space to become available, are defined in the interface `java.util.concurrent.BlockingQueue`, which extends `Queue`.[17]

In the following example program, a queue is used to implement a countdown timer. The queue is preloaded with all the integer values from a number specified on the command line to zero, in descending order. Then the values are removed from the queue and printed at one-second intervals. The program is artificial in that it would be more natural to do the same thing without using a queue, but it illustrates the use of a queue to store elements prior to subsequent processing:

```java
import java.util.*;

public class Countdown {
    public static void main(String[] args) throws InterruptedException {
        int time = Integer.parseInt(args[0]);
        Queue<Integer> queue = new LinkedList<Integer>();

        for (int i = time; i >= 0; i--)
            queue.add(i);

        while (!queue.isEmpty()) {
            System.out.println(queue.remove());
            Thread.sleep(1000);
        }
    }
}
```

17. 8/docs/api/java/util/concurrent/BlockingQueue.html

In the following example, a priority queue is used to sort a collection of elements. Again, this program is artificial in that there is no reason to use it in favor of the sort method provided in `Collections`, but it illustrates the behavior of priority queues:

```
static <E> List<E> heapSort(Collection<E> c) {
    Queue<E> queue = new PriorityQueue<E>(c);
    List<E> result = new ArrayList<E>();

    while (!queue.isEmpty())
        result.add(queue.remove());

    return result;
}
```

The Deque Interface

A deque (usually pronounced *deck*) is a double-ended queue. A double-ended queue is a linear collection of elements that supports the insertion and removal of elements at both endpoints. The `Deque` interface is a richer abstract data type than both `Stack` and `Queue` because it implements both stacks and queues at the same time. The `Deque` interface defines methods to access the elements at both ends of the `Deque` instance.[18] Methods are provided to insert, remove, and examine the elements. Predefined classes like `ArrayDeque`[19] and `LinkedList`[20] implement the `Deque` interface.

Note that the `Deque` interface can be used as both last-in, first-out stacks and first-in, first-out queues. The methods given in the `Deque` interface are divided into three parts.

Insert

The `addfirst` and `offerFirst` methods insert elements at the beginning of the `Deque` instance. The methods `addLast` and `offerLast` insert elements at the end of the `Deque` instance. When the capacity of the `Deque` instance is restricted, the preferred methods are `offerFirst` and `offerLast` because `addFirst` might fail to throw an exception if it is full.

Remove

The `removeFirst` and `pollFirst` methods remove elements from the beginning of the `Deque` instance. The `removeLast` and `pollLast` methods remove elements

---

18.   8/docs/api/java/util/Deque.html
19.   8/docs/api/java/util/ArrayDeque.html
20.   8/docs/api/java/util/LinkedList.html

Table 12.2 Deque Methods

Type of operation	First element (beginning of the Deque instance)	Last element (end of the Deque instance)
Insert	addFirst(e) offerFirst(e)	addLast(e) offerLast(e)
Remove	removeFirst() pollFirst()	removeLast() pollLast()
Examine	getFirst() peekFirst()	getLast() peekLast()

from the end. The methods pollFirst and pollLast return null if the Deque is empty, whereas the methods removeFirst and removeLast throw an exception if the Deque instance is empty.

Retrieve

The methods getFirst and peekFirst retrieve the first element of the Deque instance. These methods don't remove the value from the Deque instance. Similarly, the methods getLast and peekLast retrieve the last element. The methods get-First and getLast throw an exception if the deque instance is empty, whereas the methods peekFirst and peekLast return NULL. The twelve methods for insertion, removal, and retrieval of Deque elements are summarized in Table 12.2.

In addition to these basic methods to insert, remove, and examine a Deque instance, the Deque interface also has some more predefined methods. One of these is removeFirstOccurence; this method removes the first occurrence of the specified element if it exists in the Deque instance. If the element does not exist, then the Deque instance remains unchanged. Another similar method is removeLastOccurence; this method removes the last occurrence of the specified element in the Deque instance. The return type of these methods is boolean, and they return true if the element exists in the Deque instance.

The Map Interface

A Map is an object that maps keys to values.[21] A map cannot contain duplicate keys: each key can map to at most one value. It models the mathematical *function* abstraction. The Map interface includes methods for basic operations (such as put, get, remove, containsKey, containsValue, size, and empty), bulk operations (such as putAll and clear), and collection views (such as keySet, entrySet, and values).

---

21. 8/docs/api/java/util/Map.html

The Java platform contains three general-purpose Map implementations: HashMap,[22] TreeMap,[23] and LinkedHashMap.[24] Their behavior and performance are precisely analogous to HashSet, TreeSet, and LinkedHashSet, as described in "The Set Interface" section.

The remainder of this page discusses the Map interface in detail. But, first, here are some more examples of collecting to Maps using JDK 8 aggregate operations. Modeling real-world objects is a common task in object-oriented programming, so it is reasonable to think that some programs might, for example, group employees by department:

```
// Group employees by department
Map<Department, List<Employee>> byDept = employees.stream()
    .collect(Collectors.groupingBy(Employee::getDepartment));
```

Alternately, you might compute the sum of all salaries by department:

```
// Compute sum of salaries by department
Map<Department, Integer> totalByDept = employees.stream()
    .collect(Collectors.groupingBy(Employee::getDepartment,
        Collectors.summingInt(Employee::getSalary)));
```

Or perhaps you could group students by passing or failing grades:

```
// Partition students into passing and failing
Map<Boolean, List<Student>> passingFailing = students.stream()
    .collect(Collectors.partitioningBy(s -> s.getGrade()>= PASS_THRESHOLD));
```

You could also group people by city:

```
// Classify Person objects by city
Map<String, List<Person>> peopleByCity
        = personStream.collect(Collectors.groupingBy(Person::getCity));
```

Or you could even cascade two collectors to classify people by state and city:

```
// Cascade Collectors
Map<String, Map<String, List<Person>>> peopleByStateAndCity
    = personStream.collect(Collectors.groupingBy(Person::getState,
    Collectors.groupingBy(Person::getCity)))
```

Again, these are but a few examples of how to use the new JDK 8 APIs. For in-depth coverage of lambda expressions and aggregate operations, see the "Aggregate Operations" section.

---

22. 8/docs/api/java/util/HashMap.html

23. 8/docs/api/java/util/TreeMap.html

24. 8/docs/api/java/util/LinkedHashMap.html

Map Interface Basic Operations

The basic operations of Map (put, get, containsKey, containsValue, size, and isEmpty) behave exactly like their counterparts in Hashtable. The following program generates a frequency table of the words found in its argument list. The frequency table maps each word to the number of times it occurs in the argument list:

```java
import java.util.*;

public class Freq {
    public static void main(String[] args) {
        Map<String, Integer> m = new HashMap<String, Integer>();

        // Initialize frequency table from command line
        for (String a : args) {
            Integer freq = m.get(a);
            m.put(a, (freq == null) ? 1 : freq + 1);
        }

        System.out.println(m.size() + " distinct words:");
        System.out.println(m);
    }
}
```

The only tricky thing about this program is the second argument of the put statement. That argument is a conditional expression that has the effect of setting the frequency to one if the word has never been seen before or one more than its current value if the word has already been seen. Try running this program with the following command:

```
java Freq if it is to be it is up to me to delegate
```

The program yields the following output:

```
8 distinct words:
{to=3, delegate=1, be=1, it=2, up=1, if=1, me=1, is=2}
```

Suppose you'd prefer to see the frequency table in alphabetical order. All you have to do is change the implementation type of the Map from HashMap to TreeMap. Making this four-character change causes the program to generate the following output from the same command line:

```
8 distinct words:
{be=1, delegate=1, if=1, is=2, it=2, me=1, to=3, up=1}
```

Similarly, you could make the program print the frequency table in the order the words first appear on the command line simply by changing the implementation type of the map to LinkedHashMap. Doing so results in the following output:

```
8 distinct words:
{if=1, it=2, is=2, to=3, be=1, up=1, me=1, delegate=1}
```

This flexibility provides a potent illustration of the power of an interface-based framework.

Like the Set[25] and List[26] interfaces, Map strengthens the requirements on the equals and hashCode methods so that two Map objects can be compared for logical equality without regard to their implementation types. Two Map instances are equal if they represent the same key-value mappings.

By convention, all general-purpose Map implementations provide constructors that take a Map object and initialize the new Map to contain all the key-value mappings in the specified Map. This standard Map conversion constructor is entirely analogous to the standard Collection constructor: it allows the caller to create a Map of a desired implementation type that initially contains all of the mappings in another Map, regardless of the other Map's implementation type. For example, suppose you have a Map named m. The following one-liner creates a new HashMap initially containing all the same key-value mappings as m:

```
Map<K, V> copy = new HashMap<K, V>(m);
```

Map Interface Bulk Operations

The clear operation does exactly what you would think it could do: it removes all the mappings from the Map. The putAll operation is the Map analog of the Collection interface's addAll operation. In addition to its obvious use of dumping one Map into another, it has a second, more subtle use. Suppose a Map is used to represent a collection of attribute-value pairs; the putAll operation, in combination with the Map conversion constructor, provides a neat way to implement attribute map creation with default values. The following is a static factory method that demonstrates this technique:

```
static <K, V> Map<K, V> newAttributeMap(Map<K, V>defaults, Map<K, V> overrides) {
    Map<K, V> result = new HashMap<K, V>(defaults);
    result.putAll(overrides);
    return result;
}
```

Collection Views

The Collection view methods allow a Map to be viewed as a Collection in these three ways:

---

25. 8/docs/api/java/util/Set.html

26. 8/docs/api/java/util/List.html

- keySet. This is the Set of keys contained in the Map.
- values. This is the Collection of values contained in the Map. This Collection is not a Set because multiple keys can map to the same value.
- entrySet. This is the Set of key-value pairs contained in the Map. The Map interface provides a small nested interface called Map.Entry, the type of the elements in this Set.

The Collection views provide the *only* means to iterate over a Map. This example illustrates the standard idiom for iterating over the keys in a Map with a for-each construct:

```
for (KeyType key : m.keySet())
    System.out.println(key);
```

Here is the standard idiom for iterating over the keys in a Map with an iterator:

```
// Filter a map based on some
// property of its keys.
for (Iterator<Type> it = m.keySet().iterator(); it.hasNext(); )
    if (it.next().isBogus())
        it.remove();
```

The idiom for iterating over values is analogous. The following is the idiom for iterating over key-value pairs:

```
for (Map.Entry<KeyType, ValType> e : m.entrySet())
    System.out.println(e.getKey() + ": " + e.getValue());
```

At first, many people worry that these idioms may be slow because the Map has to create a new Collection instance each time a Collection view operation is called. Rest easy: there's no reason that a Map cannot always return the same object each time it is asked for a given Collection view. This is precisely what all the Map implementations in java.util do.

With all three Collection views, calling an Iterator's remove operation removes the associated entry from the backing Map, assuming that the backing Map supports element removal to begin with. This is illustrated by the preceding filtering idiom.

With the entrySet view, it is also possible to change the value associated with a key by calling a Map.Entry's setValue method during iteration (again, assuming the Map supports value modification to begin with). Note that these are the *only* safe ways to modify a Map during iteration; the behavior is unspecified if the underlying Map is modified in any other way while the iteration is in progress.

12

The `Collection` views support element removal in all its many forms—remove, removeAll, retainAll, and clear operations, as well as the `Iterator.remove` operation. (Yet again, this assumes that the backing `Map` supports element removal.)

The `Collection` views *do not* support element addition under any circumstances. It would make no sense for the keySet and values views, and it's unnecessary for the entrySet view because the backing `Map`'s put and putAll methods provide the same functionality.

Fancy Uses of Collection Views: Map Algebra

When applied to the `Collection` views, bulk operations (containsAll, removeAll, and retainAll) are surprisingly potent tools. For starters, suppose you want to know whether one `Map` is a submap of another—that is, whether the first `Map` contains all the key-value mappings in the second. The following idiom does the trick.

```
if (m1.entrySet().containsAll(m2.entrySet())) {
    ...
}
```

Along similar lines, suppose you want to know whether two `Map` objects contain mappings for all the same keys:

```
if (m1.keySet().equals(m2.keySet())) {
    ...
}
```

Suppose you have a `Map` that represents a collection of attribute-value pairs and two `Set`s representing required attributes and permissible attributes. (The permissible attributes include the required attributes.) The following snippet determines whether the attribute map conforms to these constraints and prints a detailed error message if it doesn't:

```
static <K, V> boolean validate(Map<K, V> attrMap, Set<K> requiredAttrs, Set<K>permittedAttrs) {
    boolean valid = true;
    Set<K> attrs = attrMap.keySet();

    if (! attrs.containsAll(requiredAttrs)) {
        Set<K> missing = new HashSet<K>(requiredAttrs);
        missing.removeAll(attrs);
        System.out.println("Missing attributes: " + missing);
        valid = false;
    }
    if (! permittedAttrs.containsAll(attrs)) {
        Set<K> illegal = new HashSet<K>(attrs);
        illegal.removeAll(permittedAttrs);
        System.out.println("Illegal attributes: " + illegal);
        valid = false;
```

```
    }
    return valid;
}
```

Suppose you want to know all the keys common to two `Map` objects:

```
Set<KeyType> commonKeys = new HashSet<KeyType>(m1.keySet());
commonKeys.retainAll(m2.keySet());
```

A similar idiom gets you the common values.

All the idioms presented thus far have been nondestructive—that is, they don't modify the backing `Map`. Here are a few that do. Suppose you want to remove all the key-value pairs that one `Map` has in common with another:

```
m1.entrySet().removeAll(m2.entrySet());
```

Suppose you want to remove from one `Map` all the keys that have mappings in another:

```
m1.keySet().removeAll(m2.keySet());
```

What happens when you start mixing keys and values in the same bulk operation? Suppose you have a `Map`, `managers`, that maps each employee in a company to the employee's manager. We'll be deliberately vague about the types of the key and the value objects. It doesn't matter as long as they're the same. Now suppose you want to know who all the "individual contributors" (or nonmanagers) are. The following snippet tells you exactly what you want to know:

```
Set<Employee> individualContributors = new HashSet<Employee>(managers.keySet());
individualContributors.removeAll(managers.values());
```

Suppose you want to fire all the employees who report directly to some manager, Simon:

```
Employee simon = ... ;
managers.values().removeAll(Collections.singleton(simon));
```

Note that this idiom makes use of `Collections.singleton`, a static factory method that returns an immutable `Set` with the single, specified element.

Once you've done this, you may have a bunch of employees whose managers no longer work for the company (if any of Simon's direct-reports were themselves managers). The following code will tell you which employees have managers who no longer work for the company:

```
Map<Employee, Employee> m = new HashMap<Employee, Employee>(managers);
m.values().removeAll(managers.keySet());
Set<Employee> slackers = m.keySet();
```

This example is a bit tricky. First, it makes a temporary copy of the Map, and it removes from the temporary copy all entries whose (manager) value is a key in the original Map. Remember that the original Map has an entry for each employee. Thus the remaining entries in the temporary Map comprise all the entries from the original Map whose (manager) values are no longer employees. The keys in the temporary copy, then, represent precisely the employees that we're looking for.

There are many more idioms like the ones contained in this section, but it would be impractical and tedious to list them all. Once you get the hang of it, it's not that difficult to come up with the right one when you need it.

Multimaps

A *multimap* is like a Map, but it can map each key to multiple values. The Java Collections Framework doesn't include an interface for multimaps because they aren't used all that commonly. It's a fairly simple matter to use a Map whose values are List instances as a multimap. This technique is demonstrated in the next code example, which reads a word list containing one word per line (all lowercase) and prints out all the anagram groups that meet a size criterion. An *anagram group* is a bunch of words that all contain exactly the same letters but in a different order. The program takes two arguments on the command line: (1) the name of the dictionary file and (2) the minimum size of anagram group to print out. Anagram groups containing fewer words than the specified minimum are not printed.

There is a standard trick for finding anagram groups: For each word in the dictionary, alphabetize the letters in the word (i.e., reorder the word's letters into alphabetical order) and put an entry into a multimap, mapping the alphabetized word to the original word. For example, the word *bad* causes an entry mapping *abd* into *bad* to be put into the multimap. A moment's reflection will show that all the words to which any given key maps form an anagram group. It's a simple matter to iterate over the keys in the multimap, printing out each anagram group that meets the size constraint.

The following program is a straightforward implementation of this technique:

```
import java.util.*;
import java.io.*;

public class Anagrams {
    public static void main(String[] args) {
        int minGroupSize = Integer.parseInt(args[1]);

        // Read words from file and put into a simulated multimap
        Map<String, List<String>> m = new HashMap<String, List<String>>();

        try {
```

```
                    Scanner s = new Scanner(new File(args[0]));
                    while (s.hasNext()) {
                        String word = s.next();
                        String alpha = alphabetize(word);
                        List<String> l = m.get(alpha);
                        if (l == null)
                            m.put(alpha, l=new ArrayList<String>());
                        l.add(word);
                    }
                } catch (IOException e) {
                    System.err.println(e);
                    System.exit(1);
                }

                // Print all permutation groups above size threshold
                for (List<String> l : m.values())
                    if (l.size() >= minGroupSize)
                        System.out.println(l.size() + ": " + l);
            }

            private static String alphabetize(String s) {
                char[] a = s.toCharArray();
                Arrays.sort(a);
                return new String(a);
            }
        }
    }
```

Running this program on a 173,000-word dictionary file with a minimum ana-gram group size of eight produces the following output:

```
9: [estrin, inerts, insert, inters, niters, nitres, sinter,
     triens, trines]
8: [lapse, leaps, pales, peals, pleas, salep, sepal, spale]
8: [aspers, parses, passer, prases, repass, spares, sparse,
     spears]
10: [least, setal, slate, stale, steal, stela, taels, tales,
     teals, tesla]
8: [enters, nester, renest, rentes, resent, tenser, ternes,
     treens]
8: [arles, earls, lares, laser, lears, rales, reals, seral]
8: [earings, erasing, gainers, reagins, regains, reginas,
     searing, seringa]
8: [peris, piers, pries, prise, ripes, speir, spier, spire]
12: [apers, apres, asper, pares, parse, pears, prase, presa,
     rapes, reaps, spare, spear]
11: [alerts, alters, artels, estral, laster, ratels, salter,
     slater, staler, stelar, talers]
9: [capers, crapes, escarp, pacers, parsec, recaps, scrape,
     secpar, spacer]
9: [palest, palets, pastel, petals, plates, pleats, septal,
     staple, tepals]
9: [anestri, antsier, nastier, ratines, retains, retinas,
     retsina, stainer, stearin]
8: [ates, east, eats, etas, sate, seat, seta, teas]
8: [carets, cartes, caster, caters, crates, reacts, recast,
     traces]
```

12

Many of these words seem a bit bogus, but that's not the program's fault; they're in the dictionary file. The dictionary file we used (`dictionary.txt`) was derived from the public domain ENABLE benchmark reference word list.[27]

Object Ordering

A `List` `l` may be sorted as follows:

```
Collections.sort(l);
```

If the `List` consists of `String` elements, it will be sorted into alphabetical order. If it consists of `Date` elements, it will be sorted into chronological order. How does this happen? `String` and `Date` both implement the `Comparable`[28] interface. Comparable implementations provide a *natural ordering* for a class, which allows objects of that class to be sorted automatically. Table 12.3 summarizes some of the more important Java platform classes that implement `Comparable`.

If you try to sort a list, the elements of which do not implement `Comparable`, `Collections.sort(list)` will throw a `ClassCastException`.[29] Similarly, `Collections.sort(list, comparator)` will throw a `ClassCastException` if you try to sort a list whose elements cannot be compared to one another using the comparator. Elements that can be compared to one another are called *mutually comparable*. Although elements of different types may be mutually comparable, none of the classes listed here permit interclass comparison.

This is all you really need to know about the `Comparable` interface if you just want to sort lists of comparable elements or create sorted collections of them. The next section will be of interest to you if you want to implement your own `Comparable` type.

Writing Your Own Comparable Types

The `Comparable` interface consists of the following method:

```
public interface Comparable<T> {
    public int compareTo(T o);
}
```

The `compareTo` method compares the receiving object with the specified object and returns a negative integer, zero, or a positive integer, depending on whether the receiving object is less than, equal to, or greater than the specified object. If the

---

27. `tutorial/collections/interfaces/examples/dictionary.txt`

28. `8/docs/api/java/lang/Comparable.html`

29. `8/docs/api/java/lang/ClassCastException.html`

Table 12.3 Classes Implementing Comparable

Class	Natural ordering
Byte	Signed numerical
Character	Unsigned numerical
Long	Signed numerical
Integer	Signed numerical
Short	Signed numerical
Double	Signed numerical
Float	Signed numerical
BigInteger	Signed numerical
BigDecimal	Signed numerical
Boolean	Boolean.FALSE < Boolean.TRUE
File	System-dependent lexicographic on path name
String	Lexicographic
Date	Chronological
CollationKey	Locale-specific lexicographic

specified object cannot be compared to the receiving object, the method throws a
`ClassCastException`.

12

The following class representing a person's name implements `Comparable`:

```java
import java.util.*;

public class Name implements Comparable<Name> {
    private final String firstName, lastName;

    public Name(String firstName, String lastName) {
        if (firstName == null || lastName == null)
            throw new NullPointerException();
        this.firstName = firstName;
        this.lastName = lastName;
    }

    public String firstName() { return firstName; }
    public String lastName()  { return lastName;  }

    public boolean equals(Object o) {
        if (!(o instanceof Name))
            return false;
        Name n = (Name) o;
        return n.firstName.equals(firstName) && n.lastName.equals(lastName);
    }

    public int hashCode() {
        return 31*firstName.hashCode() + lastName.hashCode();
```

```
        }
        public String toString() {
            return firstName + " " + lastName;
        }

        public int compareTo(Name n) {
            int lastCmp = lastName.compareTo(n.lastName);
            return (lastCmp != 0 ? lastCmp : firstName.compareTo(n.firstName));
        }
    }
```

To keep the preceding example short, the class is somewhat limited: it doesn't support middle names, it demands both a first and a last name, and it is not internationalized in any way. Nonetheless, it illustrates the following important points:

- `Name` objects are *immutable*. All other things equal, immutable types are the way to go, especially for objects that will be used as elements in `Sets` or as keys in `Maps`. These collections will break if you modify their elements or keys while they're in the collection.
- The constructor checks its arguments for `null`. This ensures that all `Name` objects are well formed so that none of the other methods will ever throw a `NullPointerException`.
- The `hashCode` method is redefined. This is essential for any class that redefines the `equals` method. (Equal objects must have equal hash codes.)
- The `equals` method returns `false` if the specified object is `null` or of an inappropriate type. The `compareTo` method throws a runtime exception under these circumstances. Both of these behaviors are required by the general contracts of the respective methods.
- The `toString` method has been redefined so it prints the `Name` in human-readable form. This is always a good idea, especially for objects that are going to get put into collections. The various collection types' `toString` methods depend on the `toString` methods of their elements, keys, and values.

Since this section is about element ordering, let's talk a bit more about `Name`'s `compareTo` method. It implements the standard name-ordering algorithm, where last names take precedence over first names. This is exactly what you want in a natural ordering. It would be very confusing indeed if the natural ordering were unnatural!

Take a look at how `compareTo` is implemented, because it's quite typical. First, you compare the most significant part of the object (in this case, the last name). Often, you can just use the natural ordering of the part's type. In this case, the part is a `String` and the natural (lexicographic) ordering is exactly what's called for. If the comparison results in anything other than zero, which represents equality, you're done: you just return the result. If the most significant parts are equal, you go on to compare the next most-significant parts. In this case, there are only two parts—first name and last name. If there were more parts, you'd proceed in the obvious fashion, comparing parts until you found two that weren't equal or you were comparing the least-significant parts, at which point you'd return the result of the comparison.

Just to show that it all works, here's a program that builds a list of names and sorts them:

```
import java.util.*;

public class NameSort {
    public static void main(String[] args) {
        Name nameArray[] = {
            new Name("John", "Smith"),
            new Name("Karl", "Ng"),
            new Name("Jeff", "Smith"),
            new Name("Tom", "Rich")
        };

        List<Name> names = Arrays.asList(nameArray);
        Collections.sort(names);
        System.out.println(names);
    }
}
```

If you run this program, here's what it prints:

```
[Karl Ng, Tom Rich, Jeff Smith, John Smith]
```

There are four restrictions on the behavior of the compareTo method, which we won't go into now because they're fairly technical and boring and are better left in the API documentation. It's really important that all classes that implement Comparable obey these restrictions, so read the documentation for Comparable if you're writing a class that implements it. If your implementation fails to obey these restrictions, the behavior will be undefined when other code attempts to sort instances of your class. Technically speaking, these restrictions ensure that the natural ordering is a *total order* on the objects of a class that implements it; this is necessary to ensure that sorting is well defined.

Comparators

What if you want to sort some objects in an order other than their natural ordering? Or what if you want to sort some objects that don't implement Comparable? To do either of these things, you'll need to provide a Comparator[30]—an object that

---

30.   8/docs/api/java/util/Comparator.html

encapsulates an ordering. Like the `Comparable` interface, the `Comparator` interface consists of a single method:

```
public interface Comparator<T> {
    int compare(T o1, T o2);
}
```

The `compare` method compares its two arguments, returning a negative integer, zero, or a positive integer, depending on whether the first argument is less than, equal to, or greater than the second. If either of the arguments has an inappropriate type for the `Comparator`, the `compare` method throws a `ClassCastException`.

Much of what was said about `Comparable` applies to `Comparator` as well. Writing a `compare` method is nearly identical to writing a `compareTo` method, except the former gets both objects passed in as arguments. The `compare` method has to obey the same four technical restrictions as `Comparable`'s `compareTo` method for the same reason—a `Comparator` must induce a total order on the objects it compares.

Suppose you have a class called `Employee`, as follows:

```
public class Employee implements Comparable<Employee> {
    public Name name()     { ... }
    public int number()    { ... }
    public Date hireDate() { ... }
        ...
}
```

Let's assume that the natural ordering of `Employee` instances is `Name` ordering (as defined in the previous example) of employee names. Unfortunately, the boss has asked for a list of employees in order of seniority. This means we have to do some work but not much. The following program will produce the required list:

```
import java.util.*;
public class EmpSort {
    static final Comparator<Employee> SENIORITY_ORDER =
                                      new Comparator<Employee>() {
            public int compare(Employee e1, Employee e2) {
                return e2.hireDate().compareTo(e1.hireDate());
            }
    };

    // Employee database
    static final Collection<Employee> employees = ... ;

    public static void main(String[] args) {
        List<Employee> e = new ArrayList<Employee>(employees);
        Collections.sort(e, SENIORITY_ORDER);
        System.out.println(e);
    }
}
```

The `Comparator` in the program is reasonably straightforward. It relies on the natural ordering of `Date` applied to the values returned by the `hireDate` accessor method. Note that the `Comparator` passes the hire date of its second argument to its first, rather than vice versa. The reason is that the employee who was hired most recently is the least senior; sorting in the order of hire date would put the list in reverse seniority order. Another technique people sometimes use to achieve this effect is to maintain the argument order but to negate the result of the comparison:

```
// Don't do this!!
return -r1.hireDate().compareTo(r2.hireDate());
```

You should always use the former technique in favor of the latter because the latter is not guaranteed to work. The reason for this is that the `compareTo` method can return any negative `int` if its argument is less than the object on which it is invoked. There is one negative `int` that remains negative when negated, strange as it may seem:

```
-Integer.MIN_VALUE == Integer.MIN_VALUE
```

The `Comparator` in the preceding program works fine for sorting a `List`, but it does have one deficiency: it cannot be used to order a sorted collection, such as `TreeSet`, because it generates an ordering that is *not compatible with* equals. This means that this `Comparator` equates objects that the `equals` method does not. In particular, any two employees who were hired on the same date will compare as equal. When you're sorting a `List`, this doesn't matter; but when you're using the `Comparator` to order a sorted collection, it's fatal. If you use this `Comparator` to insert multiple employees hired on the same date into a `TreeSet`, only the first one will be added to the set; the second will be seen as a duplicate element and will be ignored.

To fix this problem, simply tweak the `Comparator` so that it produces an ordering that *is compatible with* equals. In other words, tweak it so that the only elements seen as equal when using compare are those that are also seen as equal when compared using equals. The way to do this is to perform a two-part comparison (as for `Name`), where the first part is the one we're interested in—in this case, the hire date—and the second part is an attribute that uniquely identifies the object. Here the employee number is the obvious attribute. This is the `Comparator` that results:

```
static final Comparator<Employee> SENIORITY_ORDER =
                                new Comparator<Employee>() {
    public int compare(Employee e1, Employee e2) {
        int dateCmp = e2.hireDate().compareTo(e1.hireDate());
        if (dateCmp != 0)
            return dateCmp;

        return (e1.number() < e2.number() ? -1 :
```

12

```
                    (e1.number() == e2.number() ? 0 : 1));
        }
    };
```

Note that you might be tempted to replace the final `return` statement in the `Comparator` with the simpler:

```
    return e1.number() - e2.number();
```

Don't do it unless you're *absolutely sure* no one will ever have a negative employee number! This trick does not work in general because the signed integer type is not big enough to represent the difference of two arbitrary signed integers. If `i` is a large positive integer and `j` is a large negative integer, `i - j` will overflow and will return a negative integer. The resulting `comparator` violates one of the four technical restrictions we keep talking about (transitivity) and produces horrible, subtle bugs. This is not a purely theoretical concern; people get burned by it.

The SortedSet Interface

A `SortedSet`[31] is a `Set`[32] that maintains its elements in ascending order, sorted according to the elements' natural ordering or according to a `Comparator` provided at `SortedSet` creation time. In addition to the normal `Set` operations, the `SortedSet` interface provides operations for the following:

- *Range-view*. Allows arbitrary range operations on the sorted sets
- *Endpoints*. Returns the first or last element in the sorted set
- *Comparator access*. Returns the `Comparator`, if any, used to sort the set

The code for the `SortedSet` interface follows:

```
public interface SortedSet<E> extends Set<E> {
    // Range-view
    SortedSet<E> subSet(E fromElement, E toElement);
    SortedSet<E> headSet(E toElement);
    SortedSet<E> tailSet(E fromElement);

    // Endpoints
    E first();
    E last();

    // Comparator access
    Comparator<? super E> comparator();
}
```

---

31. 8/docs/api/java/util/SortedSet.html

32. 8/docs/api/java/util/Set.html

Set Operations

The operations that `SortedSet` inherits from `Set` behave identically on sorted sets and normal sets with two exceptions:

- The `Iterator` returned by the `iterator` operation traverses the sorted set in order.
- The array returned by `toArray` contains the sorted set's elements in order.

Although the interface doesn't guarantee it, the `toString` method of the Java platform's `SortedSet` implementations returns a string containing all the elements of the sorted set, in order.

Standard Constructors

By convention, all general-purpose `Collection` implementations provide a standard conversion constructor that takes a `Collection`; `SortedSet` implementations are no exception. In `TreeSet`, this constructor creates an instance that sorts its elements according to their natural ordering. This was probably a mistake. It would have been better to check dynamically to see whether the specified collection was a `SortedSet` instance and, if so, to sort the new `TreeSet` according to the same criterion (comparator or natural ordering). Because `TreeSet` took the approach that it did, it also provides a constructor that takes a `SortedSet` and returns a new `TreeSet` containing the same elements sorted according to the same criterion. Note that it is the compile-time type of the argument, not its runtime type, that determines which of these two constructors is invoked (and whether the sorting criterion is preserved).

12

SortedSet implementations also provide, by convention, a constructor that takes a `Comparator` and returns an empty set sorted according to the specified `Comparator`. If `null` is passed to this constructor, it returns a set that sorts its elements according to their natural ordering.

Range-View Operations

The range-view operations are somewhat analogous to those provided by the `List` interface, but there is one big difference. A range-view of a sorted set remains valid even if the backing sorted set is modified directly. This is feasible because the endpoints of a range-view of a sorted set are absolute points in the element space rather than specific elements in the backing collection, as is the case for lists. A range-view of a sorted set is really just a window onto whatever portion of the set lies in the designated part of the element space. Changes to the range-view write back to the backing sorted set and vice versa. Thus it's OK to use range-views on sorted sets for long periods of time, unlike range-views on lists.

Sorted sets provide three range-view operations. The first, `subSet`, takes two endpoints, like `subList`. Rather than indices, the endpoints are objects and must be comparable to the elements in the sorted set, using the `Set`'s `Comparator` or the natural ordering of its elements—whichever the `Set` uses to order itself. Like `subList`, the range is half open, including its low endpoint but excluding the high one.

Thus the following line of code tells you how many words between `"doorbell"` and `"pickle"`, including `"doorbell"` but excluding `"pickle"`, are contained in a `SortedSet` of strings called `dictionary`:

```
int count = dictionary.subSet("doorbell", "pickle").size();
```

Similarly, the following one-liner removes all the elements beginning with the letter `f`:

```
dictionary.subSet("f", "g").clear();
```

A similar trick can be used to print a table telling you how many words begin with each letter:

```
for (char ch = 'a'; ch <= 'z'; ) {
    String from = String.valueOf(ch++);
    String to = String.valueOf(ch);
    System.out.println(from + ": " + dictionary.subSet(from, to).size());
}
```

Suppose you want to view a *closed interval*, which contains both of its endpoints, instead of an open interval. If the element type allows for the calculation of the successor of a given value in the element space, merely request the `subSet` from `lowEndpoint` to `successor(highEndpoint)`. Although it isn't entirely obvious, the successor of a string s in `String`'s natural ordering is `s + "\0"`—that is, s with a `null` character appended.

Thus the following one-liner tells you how many words between `"doorbell"` and `"pickle"`, including `"doorbell"` *and* `"pickle"`, are contained in the dictionary:

```
count = dictionary.subSet("doorbell", "pickle\0").size();
```

A similar technique can be used to view an *open interval*, which contains neither endpoint. The open-interval view from `lowEndpoint` to `highEndpoint` is the half-open interval from `successor(lowEndpoint)` to `highEndpoint`. Use the following to calculate the number of words between `"doorbell"` and `"pickle"`, excluding both:

```
count = dictionary.subSet("doorbell\0", "pickle").size();
```

The `SortedSet` interface contains two more range-view operations—`headSet` and `tailSet`—both of which take a single `Object` argument. The former returns a view of the initial portion of the backing `SortedSet`, up to but not including the specified object. The latter returns a view of the final portion of the backing `SortedSet`, beginning with the specified object and continuing to the end of the backing `SortedSet`. Thus the following code allows you to view the dictionary as two disjoint volumes (a–m and n–z):

```
SortedSet<String> volume1 = dictionary.headSet("n");
SortedSet<String> volume2 = dictionary.tailSet("n");
```

Endpoint Operations

The `SortedSet` interface contains operations to return the first and last elements in the sorted set, not surprisingly called `first` and `last`. In addition to their obvious uses, `last` allows a workaround for a deficiency in the `SortedSet` interface. One thing you'd like to do with a `SortedSet` is to go into the interior of the `Set` and iterate forward or backward. It's easy enough to go forward from the interior: Just get a `tailSet` and iterate over it. Unfortunately, there's no easy way to go backward.

The following idiom obtains the first element that is less than a specified object o in the element space:

```
Object predecessor = ss.headSet(o).last();
```

This is a fine way to go one element backward from a point in the interior of a sorted set. It could be applied repeatedly to iterate backward, but this is very inefficient, requiring a lookup for each element returned.

Comparator Accessor

The `SortedSet` interface contains an accessor method called `comparator` that returns the `Comparator` used to sort the set or `null` if the set is sorted according to the *natural ordering* of its elements. This method is provided so that sorted sets can be copied into new sorted sets with the same ordering. It is used by the `SortedSet` constructor described previously.

The SortedMap Interface

A `SortedMap`[33] is a `Map`[34] that maintains its entries in ascending order, sorted according to the keys' natural ordering or according to a `Comparator` provided at

---

33. 8/docs/api/java/util/SortedMap.html
34. 8/docs/api/java/util/Map.html

the time of the `SortedMap` creation. Natural ordering and `Comparators` are discussed in the "Object Ordering" section. The `SortedMap` interface provides operations for normal `Map` operations and for the following:

- *Range-view*. Performs arbitrary range operations on the sorted map
- *Endpoints*. Returns the first or the last key in the sorted map
- *Comparator access*. Returns the `Comparator`, if any, used to sort the map

The following interface is the `Map` analog of `SortedSet`:[35]

```
public interface SortedMap<K, V> extends Map<K, V>{
    Comparator<? super K> comparator();
    SortedMap<K, V> subMap(K fromKey, K toKey);
    SortedMap<K, V> headMap(K toKey);
    SortedMap<K, V> tailMap(K fromKey);
    K firstKey();
    K lastKey();
}
```

Map Operations

The operations `SortedMap` inherits from `Map` behave identically on sorted maps and normal maps with two exceptions:

- The `Iterator` returned by the `iterator` operation on any of the sorted map's `Collection` views traverse the collections in order.
- The arrays returned by the `Collection` views' `toArray` operations contain the keys, values, or entries in order.

Although it isn't guaranteed by the interface, the `toString` method of the `Collection` views in all the Java platform's `SortedMap` implementations returns a string containing all the elements of the view in order.

Standard Constructors

By convention, all general-purpose `Map` implementations provide a standard conversion constructor that takes a `Map`; `SortedMap` implementations are no exception. In `TreeMap`, this constructor creates an instance that orders its entries according to their keys' natural ordering. This was probably a mistake. It would have been better to check dynamically to see whether the specified `Map` instance was a `SortedMap` and, if so, to sort the new map according to the same criterion (comparator or natural ordering). Because `TreeMap` took the approach it did, it also provides a constructor that takes a `SortedMap` and returns a new `TreeMap` containing the same

---

35.   8/docs/api/java/util/SortedSet.html

mappings as the given SortedMap, sorted according to the same criterion. Note that it is the compile-time type of the argument, not its runtime type, that determines whether the SortedMap constructor is invoked in preference to the ordinary map constructor.

SortedMap implementations also provide, by convention, a constructor that takes a Comparator and returns an empty map sorted according to the specified Comparator. If null is passed to this constructor, it returns a Map that sorts its mappings according to their keys' natural ordering.

Comparison to SortedSet

Because this interface is a precise Map analog of SortedSet, all the idioms and code examples in "The SortedSet Interface" section apply to SortedMap with only trivial modifications.

Summary of Interfaces

The core collection interfaces are the foundation of the Java Collections Framework. The Java Collections Framework hierarchy consists of two distinct interface trees:

- The first tree starts with the Collection interface, which provides for the basic functionality used by all collections, such as add and remove methods. Its subinterfaces—Set, List, and Queue—provide for more specialized collections.

- The Set interface does not allow duplicate elements. This can be useful for storing collections such as a deck of cards or student records. The Set interface has a subinterface, SortedSet, that provides for ordering of elements in the set.

- The List interface provides for an ordered collection, for situations in which you need precise control over where each element is inserted. You can retrieve elements from a List by their exact position.

- The Queue interface enables additional insertion, extraction, and inspection operations. Elements in a Queue are typically ordered on a FIFO basis.

- The Deque interface enables insertion, deletion, and inspection operations at both ends. Elements in a Deque can be used in both LIFO and FIFO.

- The second tree starts with the Map interface, which maps keys and values similar to a Hashtable.

- Map's subinterface, SortedMap, maintains its key-value pairs in ascending order or in an order specified by a Comparator.

These interfaces allow collections to be manipulated independently of the details of their representation.

12

Questions and Exercises: Interfaces

Questions

1. At the beginning of this section, you learned that the core collection interfaces are organized into two distinct inheritance trees. One interface in particular is not considered a true `Collection` and therefore sits at the top of its own tree. What is the name of this interface?

2. Each interface in the collections framework is declared with the `<E>` syntax, which tells you that it is generic. When you declare a `Collection` instance, what is the advantage of specifying the type of objects that it will contain?

3. What interface represents a collection that does not allow duplicate elements?

4. What interface forms the root of the collections hierarchy?

5. What interface represents an ordered collection that may contain duplicate elements?

6. What interface represents a collection that holds elements prior to processing?

7. What interface represents a type that maps keys to values?

8. What interface represents a double-ended queue?

9. Name three different ways to iterate over the elements of a `List`.

10. True or false: Aggregate operations are mutative operations that modify the underlying collection.

Exercises

1. Write a program that prints its arguments in random order. Do not make a copy of the argument array. Demonstrate how to print out the elements using both streams and the traditional enhanced for statement.

2. Take the `FindDups` example given previously and modify it to use a `SortedSet` instead of a `Set`. Specify a `Comparator` so that case is ignored when sorting and identifying set elements.

3. Write a method that takes a `List<String>` and applies `String.trim` to each element.[36]

4. Consider the four core interfaces, `Set`, `List`, `Queue`, and `Map`. For each of the following four assignments, specify which of the four core interfaces is best suited and explain how to use it to implement the assignment:

   a. Whimsical Toys Inc. (WTI) needs to record the names of all its employees. Every month, an employee will be chosen at random from these records to receive a free toy.

---

36. `8/docs/api/java/lang/String.html#trim--`

b. WTI has decided that each new product will be named after an employee, but only first names will be used and each name will be used only once. Prepare a list of unique first names.

c. WTI decides that it only wants to use the most popular names for its toys. Count up the number of employees who have each first name.

d. WTI acquires season tickets for the local lacrosse team, to be shared by employees. Create a waiting list for this popular sport.

Answers

You can find answers to these questions and exercises at `http://docs.oracle` `.com/javase/tutorial/collections/interfaces/QandE/answers.html`.

Aggregate Operations

To better understand the concepts in this section, review Chapter 4, "Lambda Expressions," and Chapter 4, "Method References." For what do you use collections? You don't simply store objects in a collection and leave them there. In most cases, you use collections to retrieve items stored in them.

Consider again the scenario described in Chapter 4, "Lambda Expressions." Suppose that you are creating a social-networking application. You want to create a feature that enables an administrator to perform any kind of action, such as sending a message, on members of the social-networking application that satisfy certain criteria.

As before, suppose that members of this social-networking application are represented by the following Person[37] class:

```java
public class Person {

    public enum Sex {
        MALE, FEMALE
    }

    String name;
    LocalDate birthday;
    Sex gender;
    String emailAddress;

    // ...

    public int getAge() {
        // ...
    }
```

37. `tutorial/java/javaOO/examples/Person.java`

```
        public String getName() {
            // ...
        }
    }
```

The following example prints the name of all members contained in the collection `roster` with a `for-each` loop:

```
    for (Person p : roster) {
        System.out.println(p.getName());
    }
```

The following example prints all members contained in the collection `roster` but with the aggregate operation `forEach`:

```
    roster
        .stream()
        .forEach(e -> System.out.println(e.getName());
```

Although in this example the version that uses aggregate operations is longer than the one that uses a `for-each` loop, you will see that versions that use bulk-data operations will be more concise for more complex tasks. Find the code excerpts described in this section in the example `BulkDataOperationsExamples`.[38]

Pipelines and Streams

A *pipeline* is a sequence of aggregate operations. The following example prints the male members contained in the collection `roster` with a pipeline that consists of the aggregate operations `filter` and `forEach`:

```
    roster
        .stream()
        .filter(e -> e.getGender() == Person.Sex.MALE)
        .forEach(e -> System.out.println(e.getName()));
```

Compare this example to the following that prints the male members contained in the collection `roster` with a `for-each` loop:

```
    for (Person p : roster) {
        if (p.getGender() == Person.Sex.MALE) {
            System.out.println(p.getName());
        }
    }
```

---

38. `tutorial/collections/streams/examples/BulkDataOperationsExamples`
     `.java`

A pipeline contains the following components:

- *A source.* This could be a collection, an array, a generator function, or an I/O channel. In this example, the source is the collection `roster`.
- *Zero or more intermediate operations.* An intermediate operation, such as `filter`, produces a new stream. A *stream* is a sequence of elements. Unlike a collection, it is not a data structure that stores elements. Instead, a stream carries values from a source through a pipeline. This example creates a stream from the collection `roster` by invoking the method `stream`. The `filter` operation returns a new stream that contains elements that match its predicate (this operation's parameter). In this example, the predicate is the lambda expression `e -> e.getGender() == Person.Sex.MALE`. It returns the boolean value `true` if the gender field of object e has the value `Person.Sex.MALE`. Consequently, the `filter` operation in this example returns a stream that contains all male members in the collection `roster`.
- *A terminal operation.* A terminal operation, such as `forEach`, produces a non-stream result, such as a primitive value (like a double value), a collection, or in the case of `forEach`, no value at all. In this example, the parameter of the `forEach` operation is the lambda expression `e -> System.out.println(e.getName())`, which invokes the method `getName` on the object e. (The Java runtime and compiler infer that the type of the object e is `Person`.)

The following example calculates the average age of all male members contained in the collection `roster` with a pipeline that consists of the aggregate operations `filter`, `mapToInt`, and `average`:

```
double average = roster
    .stream()
    .filter(p -> p.getGender() == Person.Sex.MALE)
    .mapToInt(Person::getAge)
    .average()
    .getAsDouble();
```

The `mapToInt` operation returns a new stream of type `IntStream` (which is a stream that contains only integer values). The operation applies the function specified in its parameter to each element in a particular stream. In this example, the function is `Person::getAge`, which is a method reference that returns the age of the member. (Alternatively, you could use the lambda expression `e -> e.getAge()`.) Consequently, the `mapToInt` operation in this example returns a stream that contains the ages of all male members in the collection `roster`.

The `average` operation calculates the average value of the elements contained in a stream of type `IntStream`. It returns an object of type `OptionalDouble`. If the stream contains no elements, then the `average` operation returns an empty instance of `OptionalDouble`, and invoking the method `getAsDouble` throws a `NoSuchElementException`. The JDK contains many terminal operations such as `average` that return one value by combining the contents of a stream. These operations are called *reduction operations*; see the "Reduction" section for more information.

Differences between Aggregate Operations and Iterators

Aggregate operations, such as `forEach`, appear to be like iterators. However, they have several fundamental differences:

- *They use internal iteration*. Aggregate operations do not contain a method like `next` to instruct them to process the next element of the collection. With *internal delegation*, your application determines *what* collection it iterates, but the JDK determines *how* to iterate the collection. With *external iteration*, your application determines both what collection it iterates and how it iterates it. However, external iteration can only iterate over the elements of a collection sequentially. Internal iteration does not have this limitation. It can more easily take advantage of parallel computing, which involves dividing a problem into subproblems, solving those problems simultaneously, and then combining the results of the solutions to the subproblems. See the "Parallelism" section for more information.

- *They process elements from a stream*. Aggregate operations process elements from a stream, not directly from a collection. Consequently, they are also called *stream operations*.

- *They support behavior as parameters*. You can specify lambda expressions as parameters for most aggregate operations. This enables you to customize the behavior of a particular aggregate operation.

Reduction

The "Aggregate Operations" section describes the following pipeline of operations, which calculates the average age of all male members in the collection `roster`:

```
double average = roster
    .stream()
    .filter(p -> p.getGender() == Person.Sex.MALE)
    .mapToInt(Person::getAge)
    .average()
    .getAsDouble();
```

The JDK contains many terminal operations (such as average,[39] sum,[40] min,[41] max,[42] and count[43]) that return one value by combining the contents of a stream. These operations are called *reduction operations*. The JDK also contains reduction operations that return a collection instead of a single value. Many reduction operations perform a specific task, such as finding the average of values or grouping elements into categories. However, the JDK provides you with the general-purpose reduction operations reduce[44] and collect,[45] which this section describes in detail.

You can find the code excerpts described in this section in the example ReductionExamples.[46]

The Stream.reduce Method

The Stream.reduce[47] method is a general-purpose reduction operation. Consider the following pipeline, which calculates the sum of the male members' ages in the collection roster. It uses the Stream.sum[48] reduction operation:

```
Integer totalAge = roster
    .stream()
    .mapToInt(Person::getAge)
    .sum();
```

Compare this with the following pipeline, which uses the Stream.reduce operation to calculate the same value:

12

```
Integer totalAgeReduce = roster
    .stream()
    .map(Person::getAge)
    .reduce(
```

---

39. 8/docs/api/java/util/stream/IntStream.html#average--java/lang/ reflect/Executable.html

40. 8/docs/api/java/util/stream/IntStream.html#sum--

41. 8/docs/api/java/util/stream/Stream.html#min-java.util.Comparator-

42. 8/docs/api/java/util/stream/Stream.html#max-java.util.Comparator-

43. 8/docs/api/java/util/stream/Stream.html#count--

44. 8/docs/api/java/util/stream/Stream.html#reduce-T-java.util.function .BinaryOperator-

45. 8/docs/api/java/util/stream/Stream.html#collect-java.util.function .Supplier-java.util.function.BiConsumer-java.util.function .BiConsumer-

46. tutorial/collections/streams/examples/ReductionExamples.java

47. 8/docs/api/java/util/stream/Stream.html#reduce-T-java.util.function .BinaryOperator-

48. 8/docs/api/java/util/stream/IntStream.html#sum--

```
0,
(a, b) -> a + b);
```

The `reduce` operation in this example takes two arguments:

- `identity`. The identity element is both the initial value of the reduction and the default result if there are no elements in the stream. In this example, the identity element is 0; this is the initial value of the sum of ages and the default value if no members exist in the collection `roster`.
- `accumulator`. The accumulator function takes two parameters: a partial result of the reduction (in this example, the sum of all processed integers so far) and the next element of the stream (in this example, an integer). It returns a new partial result. In this example, the accumulator function is a lambda expression that adds two `Integer` values and returns an `Integer` value:

  ```
  (a, b) -> a + b
  ```

The `reduce` operation always returns a new value. However, the accumulator function also returns a new value every time it processes an element of a stream. Suppose that you want to reduce the elements of a stream to a more complex object, such as a collection. This might hinder the performance of your application. If your `reduce` operation involves adding elements to a collection, then every time your accumulator function processes an element, it creates a new collection that includes the element, which is inefficient. It would be more efficient for you to update an existing collection instead. You can do this with the `Stream.collect`[49] method, which the next section describes.

The Stream.collect Method

Unlike the `reduce` method, which always creates a new value when it processes an element, the `collect`[50] method modifies or mutates an existing value.

Consider how to find the average of values in a stream. You require two pieces of data: the total number of values and the sum of those values. However, like the `reduce` method and all other reduction methods, the `collect` method returns only one value. You can create a new data type that contains member variables that keep

---

49. 8/docs/api/java/util/stream/Stream.html#collect-java.util.function
    .Supplier-java.util.function.BiConsumer-java.util.function
    .BiConsumer-
50. 8/docs/api/java/util/stream/Stream.html#collect-java.util.function
    .Supplier-java.util.function.BiConsumer-java.util.function
    .BiConsumer-

track of the total number of values and the sum of those values, such as the following class, `Averager`:

```java
class Averager implements IntConsumer
{
    private int total = 0;
    private int count = 0;

    public double average() {
        return count > 0 ? ((double) total)/count : 0;
    }

    public void accept(int i) { total += i; count++; }
    public void combine(Averager other) {
        total += other.total;
        count += other.count;
    }
}
```

The following pipeline uses the `Averager` class and the `collect` method to calculate the average age of all male members:

```java
Averager averageCollect = roster.stream()
    .filter(p -> p.getGender() == Person.Sex.MALE)
    .map(Person::getAge)
    .collect(Averager::new, Averager::accept, Averager::combine);

System.out.println("Average age of male members: " +
    averageCollect.average());
```

The `collect` operation in this example takes three arguments:

- supplier. The supplier is a factory function; it constructs new instances. For the `collect` operation, it creates instances of the result container. In this example, it is a new instance of the `Averager` class.
- accumulator. The accumulator function incorporates a stream element into a result container. In this example, it modifies the `Averager` result container by incrementing the `count` variable by one and adding to the `total` member variable the value of the stream element, which is an integer representing the age of a male member.
- combiner. The combiner function takes two result containers and merges their contents. In this example, it modifies an `Averager` result container by incrementing the `count` variable by the `count` member variable of the other `Averager` instance and adding to the `total` member variable the value of the other `Averager` instance's `total` member variable.

Note the following:

- The supplier is a lambda expression (or a method reference) as opposed to a value like the identity element in the `reduce` operation.
- The accumulator and combiner functions do not return a value.
- You can use the `collect` operations with parallel streams; see the "Parallelism" section for more information. (If you run the `collect` method with a parallel stream, then the JDK creates a new thread whenever the combiner function creates a new object, such as an `Averager` object in this example. Consequently, you do not have to worry about synchronization.)

Although the JDK provides you with the `average` operation to calculate the average value of elements in a stream, you can use the `collect` operation and a custom class if you need to calculate several values from the elements of a stream.

The `collect` operation is best suited for collections. The following example puts the names of the male members in a collection with the `collect` operation:

```
List<String> namesOfMaleMembersCollect = roster
    .stream()
    .filter(p -> p.getGender() == Person.Sex.MALE)
    .map(p -> p.getName())
    .collect(Collectors.toList());
```

This version of the `collect` operation takes one parameter of type `Collector`.[51] This class encapsulates the functions used as arguments in the `collect` operation that requires three arguments (supplier, accumulator, and combiner functions).

The `Collectors` class contains many useful reduction operations, such as accumulating elements into collections and summarizing elements according to various criteria.[52] These reduction operations return instances of the class `Collector`, so you can use them as a parameter for the `collect` operation.

This example uses the `Collectors.toList`[53] operation, which accumulates the stream elements into a new instance of `List`. As with most operations in the `Collectors` class, the `toList` operator returns an instance of `Collector`, not a collection. The following example groups members of the collection `roster` by gender:

```
Map<Person.Sex, List<Person>> byGender =
    roster
        .stream()
        .collect(
            Collectors.groupingBy(Person::getGender));
```

---

51. 8/docs/api/java/util/stream/Collector.html
52. 8/docs/api/java/util/stream/Collectors.html
53. 8/docs/api/java/util/stream/Collectors.html#toList--

The groupingBy operation returns a map whose keys are the values that result from applying the lambda expression specified as its parameter (which is called a *classification function*).[54] In this example, the returned map contains two keys, Person.Sex.MALE and Person.Sex.FEMALE. The keys' corresponding values are instances of List that contain the stream elements that, when processed by the classification function, correspond to the key value. For example, the value that corresponds to key Person.Sex.MALE is an instance of List that contains all male members.

The following example retrieves the names of each member in the collection roster and groups them by gender:

```
Map<Person.Sex, List<String>> namesByGender =
    roster
        .stream()
        .collect(
            Collectors.groupingBy(
                Person::getGender,
                Collectors.mapping(
                    Person::getName,
                    Collectors.toList())));
```

The groupingBy operation in this example takes two parameters: a classification function and an instance of Collector.[55] The Collector parameter is called a *downstream collector*. This is a collector that the Java runtime applies to the results of another collector. Consequently, this groupingBy operation enables you to apply a collect method to the List values created by the groupingBy operator. This example applies the collector mapping,[56] which applies the mapping function Person::getName to each element of the stream. Consequently, the resulting stream consists of only the names of members. A pipeline that contains one or more downstream collectors, like this example, is called a *multilevel reduction*.

The following example retrieves the total age of members of each gender:

```
Map<Person.Sex, Integer> totalAgeByGender =
    roster
        .stream()
        .collect(
            Collectors.groupingBy(
```

12

54. 8/docs/api/java/util/stream/Collectors.html#groupingBy-java.util
     .function.Function-

55. 8/docs/api/java/util/stream/Collectors.html#groupingBy-java.util
     .function.Function-java.util.stream.Collector-

56. 8/docs/api/java/util/stream/Collectors.html#mapping-java.util
     .function.Function-java.util.stream.Collector-java.util.stream
     .Collector-

```
            Person::getGender,
            Collectors.reducing(
                0,
                Person::getAge,
                Integer::sum)));
```

The reducing operation takes three parameters:[57]

- identity. Like the Stream.reduce operation, the identity element is both the initial value of the reduction and the default result if there are no elements in the stream. In this example, the identity element is 0; this is the initial value of the sum of ages and the default value if no members exist.
- mapper. The reducing operation applies this mapper function to all stream elements. In this example, the mapper retrieves the age of each member.
- operation. The operation function is used to reduce the mapped values. In this example, the operation function adds Integer values.

The following example retrieves the average age of members of each gender:

```
Map<Person.Sex, Double> averageAgeByGender = roster
    .stream()
    .collect(
        Collectors.groupingBy(
            Person::getGender,
            Collectors.averagingInt(Person::getAge)));
```

Parallelism

Parallel computing involves dividing a problem into subproblems, solving those problems simultaneously (in parallel, with each subproblem running in a separate thread), and then combining the results of the solutions to the subproblems. Java SE provides the fork/join framework (discussed in Chapter 13), which enables you to more easily implement parallel computing in your applications. However, with this framework, you must specify how the problems are subdivided (partitioned). With aggregate operations, the Java runtime performs this partitioning and combining of solutions for you.

One difficulty in implementing parallelism in applications that use collections is that collections are not thread safe, which means that multiple threads cannot manipulate a collection without introducing thread interference or memory consistency errors. The Java Collections Framework provides synchronization wrappers, which add automatic synchronization to an arbitrary collection, making it thread

---

57. 8/docs/api/java/util/stream/Collectors.html#reducing-U-java.util
     .function.Function-java.util.function.BinaryOperator-

safe. However, synchronization introduces thread contention. You want to avoid thread contention because it prevents threads from running in parallel. Aggregate operations and parallel streams enable you to implement parallelism with non-thread-safe collections, provided that you do not modify the collection while you are operating on it.

Note that parallelism is not automatically faster than performing operations serially, although it can be if you have enough data and processor cores. While aggregate operations enable you to more easily implement parallelism, it is still your responsibility to determine if your application is suitable for parallelism.

You can find the code excerpts described in this section in the example `ParallelismExamples`.[58]

Executing Streams in Parallel

You can execute streams in serial or in parallel. When a stream executes in parallel, the Java runtime partitions the stream into multiple substreams. Aggregate operations iterate over and process these substreams in parallel and then combine the results.

When you create a stream, it is always a serial stream unless otherwise specified. To create a parallel stream, invoke the operation `Collection.parallelStream`.[59] Alternatively, invoke the operation `BaseStream.parallel`.[60] For example, the following statement calculates the average age of all male members in parallel:

```
double average = roster
    .parallelStream()
    .filter(p -> p.getGender() == Person.Sex.MALE)
    .mapToInt(Person::getAge)
    .average()
    .getAsDouble();
```

Concurrent Reduction

Consider again the following example (which is described in the section "Reduction") that groups members by gender. This example invokes the `collect` operation, which reduces the collection `roster` into a `Map`:

```
Map<Person.Sex, List<Person>> byGender =
    roster
        .stream()
        .collect(
            Collectors.groupingBy(Person::getGender));
```

---

58. `tutorial/collections/streams/examples/ParallelismExamples.java`

59. `8/docs/api/java/util/Collection.html#parallelStream--`

60. `8/docs/api/java/util/stream/BaseStream.html#parallel--`

The following is the parallel equivalent:

```
ConcurrentMap<Person.Sex, List<Person>> byGender =
    roster
        .parallelStream()
        .collect(
            Collectors.groupingByConcurrent(Person::getGender));
```

This is called a *concurrent reduction*. The Java runtime performs a concurrent reduction if all the following are true for a particular pipeline that contains the collect operation:

- The stream is parallel.
- The parameter of the collect operation, the collector, has the characteristic Collector.Characteristics.CONCURRENT.[61] To determine the characteristics of a collector, invoke the Collector.characteristics[62] method.
- Either the stream is unordered or the collector has the characteristic Collector. Characteristics.UNORDERED.[63] To ensure that the stream is unordered, invoke the BaseStream.unordered[64] operation.

> **Note**
>
> This example returns an instance of ConcurrentMap[65] instead of Map and invokes the groupingByConcurrent[66] operation instead of groupingBy. (See Chapter 13, "Concurrent Collections," for more information about ConcurrentMap.) Unlike the operation groupingByConcurrent, the operation groupingBy performs poorly with parallel streams. (This is because it operates by merging two maps by key, which is computationally expensive.) Similarly, the operation Collectors.toConcurrentMap[67] performs better with parallel streams than the operation Collectors.toMap.[68]

61. 8/docs/api/java/util/stream/Collector.Characteristics.html #CONCURRENT

62. 8/docs/api/java/util/stream/Collector.Characteristics.html

63. 8/docs/api/java/util/stream/Collector.Characteristics.html #UNORDERED

64. 8/docs/api/java/util/stream/BaseStream.html#unordered--

65. 8/docs/api/java/util/concurrent/ConcurrentMap.html

66. 8/docs/api/java/util/stream/Collectors.html#groupingByConcurrent -java.util.function.Function-

67. 8/docs/api/java/util/stream/Collectors.html#toConcurrentMap-java .util.function.Function-java.util.function.Function-

68. 8/docs/api/java/util/stream/Collectors.html#toMap-java.util.function .Function-java.util.function.Function-

Ordering

The order in which a pipeline processes the elements of a stream depends on whether the stream is executed in serial or in parallel, the source of the stream, and intermediate operations. For example, consider the following example that prints the elements of an instance of `ArrayList` with the `forEach` operation several times:

```
Integer[] intArray = {1, 2, 3, 4, 5, 6, 7, 8 };
List<Integer> listOfIntegers =
    new ArrayList<>(Arrays.asList(intArray));

System.out.println("listOfIntegers:");
listOfIntegers
    .stream()
    .forEach(e -> System.out.print(e + " "));
System.out.println("");

System.out.println("listOfIntegers sorted in reverse order:");
Comparator<Integer> normal = Integer::compare;
Comparator<Integer> reversed = normal.reversed();
Collections.sort(listOfIntegers, reversed);
listOfIntegers
    .stream()
    .forEach(e -> System.out.print(e + " "));
System.out.println("");

System.out.println("Parallel stream");
listOfIntegers
    .parallelStream()
    .forEach(e -> System.out.print(e + " "));
System.out.println("");

System.out.println("Another parallel stream:");
listOfIntegers
    .parallelStream()
    .forEach(e -> System.out.print(e + " "));
System.out.println("");

System.out.println("With forEachOrdered:");
listOfIntegers
    .parallelStream()
    .forEachOrdered(e -> System.out.print(e + " "));
System.out.println("");
```

This example consists of five pipelines. It prints output similar to the following:

```
listOfIntegers:
1 2 3 4 5 6 7 8
listOfIntegers sorted in reverse order:
8 7 6 5 4 3 2 1
Parallel stream:
3 4 1 6 2 5 7 8
Another parallel stream:
6 3 1 5 7 8 4 2
With forEachOrdered:
8 7 6 5 4 3 2 1
```

This example does the following:

- The first pipeline prints the elements of the list `listOfIntegers` in the order that they were added to the list.
- The second pipeline prints the elements of `listOfIntegers` after it was sorted by the method `Collections.sort`.[69]
- The third and fourth pipelines print the elements of the list in an apparently random order. Remember that stream operations use internal iteration when processing elements of a stream. Consequently, when you execute a stream in parallel, the Java compiler and runtime determine the order in which to process the stream's elements to maximize the benefits of parallel computing unless otherwise specified by the stream operation.
- The fifth pipeline uses the method `forEachOrdered`,[70] which processes the elements of the stream in the order specified by its source, regardless of whether you executed the stream in serial or parallel. Note that you may lose the benefits of parallelism if you use operations like `forEachOrdered` with parallel streams.

Side Effects

A method or an expression has a side effect if, in addition to returning or producing a value, it also modifies the state of the computer. Examples include mutable reductions (operations that use the `collect` operation, discussed in further detail in the "Reduction" section) as well as invoking the `System.out.println` method for debugging. The JDK handles certain side effects in pipelines well. In particular, the `collect` method is designed to perform the most common stream operations that have side effects in a parallel-safe manner. Operations like `forEach` and `peek` are designed for side effects; a lambda expression that returns void, such as one that invokes `System.out.println`, can do nothing but have side effects. Even so, you should use the `forEach` and `peek` operations with care; if you use one of these operations with a parallel stream, then the Java runtime may invoke the lambda expression that you specified as its parameter concurrently from multiple threads. In addition, never pass as parameters lambda expressions that have side effects in operations such as `filter` and `map`. The following sections discuss interference and stateful lambda expressions, both of which can be sources of side effects and can return inconsistent or unpredictable results, especially in parallel streams.

---

69. `8/docs/api/java/util/Collections.html#sort-java.util.List-`
70. `8/docs/api/java/util/stream/Stream.html#forEachOrdered-java.util`
     `.function.Consumer-`

However, the concept of laziness is discussed first because it has a direct effect on interference.

Laziness

All intermediate operations are *lazy*. An expression, method, or algorithm is lazy if its value is evaluated only when it is required. (An algorithm is *eager* if it is evaluated or processed immediately.) Intermediate operations are lazy because they do not start processing the contents of the stream until the terminal operation commences. Processing streams lazily enables the Java compiler and runtime to optimize how they process streams. For example, in a pipeline such as the `filter-mapToInt-average` example described in the "Aggregate Operations" section, the `average` operation could obtain the first several integers from the stream created by the `mapToInt` operation, which obtains elements from the `filter` operation. The `average` operation would repeat this process until it had obtained all required elements from the stream, and then it would calculate the average.

Interference

Lambda expressions in stream operations should not *interfere*. Interference occurs when the source of a stream is modified while a pipeline processes the stream. For example, the following code attempts to concatenate the strings contained in the `List` `listOfStrings`. However, it throws a `ConcurrentModificationException`:

```
try {
    List<String> listOfStrings =
        new ArrayList<>(Arrays.asList("one", "two"));

    // This will fail as the peek operation will attempt to add the
    // string "three" to the source after the terminal operation has
    // commenced.

    String concatenatedString = listOfStrings
        .stream()

        // Don't do this! Interference occurs here.
        .peek(s -> listOfStrings.add("three"))

        .reduce((a, b) -> a + " " + b)
        .get();

    System.out.println("Concatenated string: " + concatenatedString);

} catch (Exception e) {
    System.out.println("Exception caught: " + e.toString());
}
```

This example concatenates the strings contained in `listOfStrings` into an `Optional<String>` value with the `reduce` operation, which is a terminal operation.

However, the pipeline here invokes the intermediate operation peek, which attempts to add a new element to listOfStrings. Remember, all intermediate operations are lazy. This means that the pipeline in this example begins execution when the operation get is invoked and ends execution when the get operation completes. The argument of the peek operation attempts to modify the stream source during the execution of the pipeline, which causes the Java runtime to throw a ConcurrentModificationException.

Stateful Lambda Expressions

Avoid using *stateful lambda expressions* as parameters in stream operations. A stateful lambda expression is one whose result depends on any state that might change during the execution of a pipeline. The following example adds elements from the List listOfIntegers to a new List instance with the map intermediate operation. It does this twice, first with a serial stream and then with a parallel stream:

```
List<Integer> serialStorage = new ArrayList<>();

System.out.println("Serial stream:");
listOfIntegers
    .stream()

    // Don't do this! It uses a stateful lambda expression.
    .map(e -> { serialStorage.add(e); return e; })

    .forEachOrdered(e -> System.out.print(e + " "));
System.out.println("");

serialStorage
    .stream()
    .forEachOrdered(e -> System.out.print(e + " "));
System.out.println("");

System.out.println("Parallel stream:");
List<Integer> parallelStorage = Collections.synchronizedList(
    new ArrayList<>());
listOfIntegers
    .parallelStream()

    // Don't do this! It uses a stateful lambda expression.
    .map(e -> { parallelStorage.add(e); return e; })

    .forEachOrdered(e -> System.out.print(e + " "));
System.out.println("");

parallelStorage
    .stream()
    .forEachOrdered(e -> System.out.print(e + " "));
System.out.println("");
```

The lambda expression e -> { parallelStorage.add(e); return e; } is a stateful lambda expression. Its result can vary every time the code is run. This example prints the following:

```
Serial stream:
8 7 6 5 4 3 2 1
8 7 6 5 4 3 2 1
Parallel stream:
8 7 6 5 4 3 2 1
1 3 6 2 4 5 8 7
```

The operation forEachOrdered processes elements in the order specified by the stream, regardless of whether the stream is executed in serial or parallel. However, when a stream is executed in parallel, the map operation processes elements of the stream specified by the Java runtime and compiler. Consequently, the order in which the lambda expression e -> { parallelStorage.add(e); return e; } adds elements to the List parallelStorage can vary every time the code is run. For deterministic and predictable results, ensure that lambda expression parameters in stream operations are not stateful.

Note that this example invokes the method synchronizedList[71] so that the List parallelStorage is thread safe. Remember that collections are not thread safe. This means that multiple threads should not access a particular collection at the same time. Suppose that you do not invoke the method synchronizedList when creating parallelStorage:

```
List<Integer> parallelStorage = new ArrayList<>();
```

The example behaves erratically because multiple threads access and modify parallelStorage without a mechanism like synchronization to schedule when a particular thread may access the List instance. Consequently, the example could print output similar to the following:

```
Parallel stream:
8 7 6 5 4 3 2 1
null 3 5 4 7 8 1 2
```

Questions and Exercises: Aggregate Operations

Questions

1. A sequence of aggregate operations is known as a ___.
2. Each pipeline contains zero or more ___ operations.

---

71. 8/docs/api/java/util/Collections.html#synchronizedList-java.util
    .List-

3. Each pipeline ends with a ___ operation.

4. What kind of operation produces another stream as its output?

5. Describe one way in which the `forEach` aggregate operation differs from the enhanced `for` statement or iterators.

6. True or false: A stream is similar to a collection in that it is a data structure that stores elements.

7. Identify the intermediate and terminal operations in this code:

```
double average = roster
    .stream()
    .filter(p -> p.getGender() == Person.Sex.MALE)
    .mapToInt(Person::getAge)
    .average()
    .getAsDouble();
```

8. The code `p -> p.getGender() == Person.Sex.MALE` is an example of what?

9. The code `Person::getAge` is an example of what?

10. Terminal operations that combine the contents of a stream and return one value are known as what?

11. Name one important difference between the `Stream.reduce` method and the `Stream.collect` method.

12. If you wanted to process a stream of names, extract the male names, and store them in a new `List`, would `Stream.reduce` or `Stream.collect` be the most appropriate operation to use?

13. True or false: Aggregate operations make it possible to implement parallelism with non-thread-safe collections.

14. Streams are always serial unless otherwise specified. How do you request that a stream be processed in parallel?

Exercises

1. Write the following enhanced `for` statement as a pipeline with lambda expressions. Hint: Use the `filter` intermediate operation and the `forEach` terminal operation.

```
for (Person p : roster) {
    if (p.getGender() == Person.Sex.MALE) {
        System.out.println(p.getName());
    }
}
```

2. Convert the following code into a new implementation that uses lambda expressions and aggregate operations instead of nested `for` loops. Hint: Make

a pipeline that invokes the `filter`, `sorted`, and `collect` operations, in that order.

```
List<Album> favs = new ArrayList<>();
for (Album a : albums) {
    boolean hasFavorite = false;
    for (Track t : a.tracks) {
        if (t.rating >= 4) {
            hasFavorite = true;
            break;
        }
    }
    if (hasFavorite)
        favs.add(a);
}
Collections.sort(favs, new Comparator<Album>() {
                        public int compare(Album a1, Album a2) {
                            return a1.name.compareTo(a2.name);
                    }});
```

Answers

You can find answers to these questions and exercises at `http://docs.oracle` `.com/javase/tutorial/collections/streams/QandE/answers.html`.

Implementations

12

Implementations are the data objects used to store collections, which implement the interfaces described in the "Interfaces" section. This section describes the following kinds of implementations:

- *General-purpose implementations* are the most commonly used implementations, designed for everyday use. They are summarized in Table 12.4.

- *Special-purpose implementations* are designed for use in special situations and display nonstandard performance characteristics, usage restrictions, or behavior.

- *Concurrent implementations* are designed to support high concurrency, typically at the expense of single-threaded performance. These implementations are part of the `java.util.concurrent` package.

- *Wrapper implementations* are used in combination with other types of implementations, often the general-purpose ones, to provide added or restricted functionality.

- *Convenience implementations* are mini-implementations, typically made available via static factory methods, that provide convenient, efficient alternatives to general-purpose implementations for special collections (e.g., singleton sets).

- *Abstract implementations* are skeletal implementations that facilitate the construction of custom implementations.

The general-purpose implementations are summarized in Table 12.4.

As you can see from Table 12.4, the Java Collections Framework provides several general-purpose implementations of the Set,[72] List,[73] and Map[74] interfaces. In each case, one implementation—HashSet,[75] ArrayList,[76] and HashMap[77]—is clearly the one to use for most applications, all other things equal. Note that the SortedSet[78] and the SortedMap[79] interfaces do not have rows in the table. Each of those interfaces has one implementation (TreeSet[80] and TreeMap[81]) and is listed in the Set and the Map rows. There are two general-purpose Queue implementations—LinkedList,[82] which is also a List implementation, and PriorityQueue,[83] which is omitted from the table. These two implementations provide very different semantics: LinkedList provides FIFO semantics, while PriorityQueue orders its elements according to their values.

Each of the general-purpose implementations provides all optional operations contained in its interface. All permit null elements, keys, and values. None are synchronized (thread safe). All have *fail-fast iterators*, which detect illegal concurrent modification during iteration and fail quickly and cleanly rather than risking arbitrary, nondeterministic behavior at an undetermined time in the future. All are Serializable and all support a public clone method.

The fact that these implementations are unsynchronized represents a break with the past: the legacy collections Vector and Hashtable are synchronized. The present approach was taken because collections are frequently used when the synchronization is of no benefit. Such uses include single-threaded use, read-only use, and use as part of a larger data object that does its own synchronization. In general,

---

72. 8/docs/api/java/util/Set.html
73. 8/docs/api/java/util/List.html
74. 8/docs/api/java/util/Map.html
75. 8/docs/api/java/util/HashSet.html
76. 8/docs/api/java/util/ArrayList.html
77. 8/docs/api/java/util/HashMap.html
78. 8/docs/api/java/util/SortedSet.html
79. 8/docs/api/java/util/SortedMap.html
80. 8/docs/api/java/util/TreeSet.html
81. 8/docs/api/java/util/TreeMap.html
82. 8/docs/api/java/util/LinkedList.html
83. 8/docs/api/java/util/PriorityQueue.html

Table 12.4 General-Purpose Implementations

Interfaces	Hash table implementations	Resizable array implementations	Tree implementations	Linked list implementations	Hash table and linked list implementations
Set	HashSet		TreeSet		LinkedHashSet
List		ArrayList		LinkedList	
Queue					
Deque		ArrayDeque		LinkedList	
Map	HashMap		TreeMap		LinkedHashMap

it is good API design practice not to make users pay for a feature they don't use. Furthermore, unnecessary synchronization can result in deadlock under certain circumstances.

If you need thread-safe collections, the synchronization wrappers, described in the "Wrapper Implementations" section, allow *any* collection to be transformed into a synchronized collection. Thus synchronization is optional for general-purpose implementations, whereas it is mandatory for legacy implementations. Moreover, the `java.util.concurrent` package provides concurrent implementations of the `BlockingQueue` interface, which extends `Queue`, and of the `ConcurrentMap` interface, which extends `Map`. These implementations offer much higher concurrency than mere synchronized implementations.

As a rule, you should be thinking about the interfaces, *not* the implementations. That is why there are no programming examples in this section. For the most part, the choice of implementation affects only performance. The preferred style, as mentioned in the "Interfaces" section, is to choose an implementation when a `Collection` is created and to immediately assign the new collection to a variable of the corresponding interface type (or to pass the collection to a method expecting an argument of the interface type). In this way, the program does not become dependent on any added methods in a given implementation, leaving the programmer free to change implementations anytime that it is warranted by performance concerns or behavioral details.

The sections that follow briefly discuss the implementations. The performance of the implementations is described using terms such as *constant time*, *log*, *linear*, *n log(n)*, and *quadratic* to refer to the asymptotic upper bound on the time complexity of performing the operation. All this is quite a mouthful, and it doesn't matter much if you don't know what it means. If you're interested in knowing more, refer to any good algorithms textbook. One thing to keep in mind is that this sort of performance metric has its limitations. Sometimes the nominally slower implementation may be faster. When in doubt, measure the performance!

12

Set Implementations

The Set implementations are grouped into general-purpose and special-purpose implementations.

General-Purpose Set Implementations

There are three general-purpose Set[84] implementations—HashSet,[85] TreeSet,[86] and LinkedHashSet.[87] It is generally straightforward to determine which of these three to use. HashSet is much faster than TreeSet (constant time versus log time for most operations) but offers no ordering guarantees. If you need to use the operations in the SortedSet interface, or if value-ordered iteration is required, use TreeSet; otherwise, use HashSet. It's a fair bet that you'll end up using HashSet most of the time.

LinkedHashSet is in some sense intermediate between HashSet and TreeSet. Implemented as a hash table with a linked list running through it, it provides *insertion-ordered* iteration (least recently inserted to most recently) and runs nearly as fast as HashSet. The LinkedHashSet implementation spares its clients from the unspecified, generally chaotic ordering provided by HashSet without incurring the increased cost associated with TreeSet.

One thing worth keeping in mind about HashSet is that iteration is linear in the sum of the number of entries and the number of buckets (the *capacity*). Thus choosing an initial capacity that's too high can waste both space and time. On the other hand, choosing an initial capacity that's too low wastes time by copying the data structure each time it's forced to increase its capacity. If you don't specify an initial capacity, the default is 16. In the past, there was some advantage to choosing a prime number as the initial capacity. This is no longer true. Internally, the capacity is always rounded up to a power of two. The initial capacity is specified by using the int constructor. The following line of code allocates a HashSet whose initial capacity is 64:

```
Set<String> s = new HashSet<String>(64);
```

The HashSet class has one other tuning parameter called the *load factor*. If you care a lot about the space consumption of your HashSet, read the HashSet documentation for more information. Otherwise, just accept the default; it's almost always the right thing to do.

---

84.   8/docs/api/java/util/Set.html

85.   8/docs/api/java/util/HashSet.html

86.   8/docs/api/java/util/TreeSet.html

87.   8/docs/api/java/util/LinkedHashSet.html

If you accept the default load factor but want to specify an initial capacity, pick a number that's about twice the size to which you expect the set to grow. If your guess is way off, you may waste a bit of space, time, or both, but it's unlikely to be a big problem.

LinkedHashSet has the same tuning parameters as HashSet, but iteration time is not affected by capacity. TreeSet has no tuning parameters.

Special-Purpose Set Implementations

There are two special-purpose Set implementations—EnumSet[88] and CopyOn-WriteArraySet.[89] EnumSet is a high-performance Set implementation for enum types. All members of an enum set must be of the same enum type. Internally, it is represented by a bit vector, typically a single long. Enum sets support iteration over ranges of enum types. For example, given the enum declaration for the days of the week, you can iterate over the weekdays. The EnumSet class provides a static factory that makes it easy:

```
for (Day d : EnumSet.range(Day.MONDAY, Day.FRIDAY))
    System.out.println(d);
```

Enum sets also provide a rich, typesafe replacement for traditional bit flags:

```
EnumSet.of(Style.BOLD, Style.ITALIC)
```

CopyOnWriteArraySet is a Set implementation backed up by a copy-on-write array. All mutative operations, such as add, set, and remove, are implemented by making a new copy of the array; no locking is ever required. Even iteration may safely proceed concurrently with element insertion and deletion. Unlike most Set implementations, the add, remove, and contains methods require time proportional to the size of the set. This implementation is *only* appropriate for sets that are rarely modified but frequently iterated. It is well suited to maintaining event-handler lists that must prevent duplicates.

List Implementations

List implementations are grouped into general-purpose and special-purpose implementations.

---

88. 8/docs/api/java/util/EnumSet.html
89. 8/docs/api/java/util/concurrent/CopyOnWriteArraySet.html

General-Purpose List Implementations

There are two general-purpose List[90] implementations—ArrayList[91] and LinkedList.[92] Most of the time, you'll probably use ArrayList, which offers constant-time positional access and is just plain fast. It does not have to allocate a node object for each element in the List, and it can take advantage of System.array-copy when it has to move multiple elements at the same time. Think of ArrayList as Vector without the synchronization overhead.

If you frequently add elements to the beginning of the List or iterate over the List to delete elements from its interior, you should consider using LinkedList. These operations require constant time in a LinkedList and linear time in an ArrayList. But you pay a big price in performance. Positional access requires linear time in a LinkedList and constant time in an ArrayList. Furthermore, the constant factor for LinkedList is much worse. If you think you want to use a LinkedList, measure the performance of your application with both LinkedList and ArrayList before making your choice; ArrayList is usually faster.

ArrayList has one tuning parameter—the *initial capacity*, which refers to the number of elements the ArrayList can hold before it has to grow. LinkedList has no tuning parameters and seven optional operations, one of which is clone. The other six are addFirst, getFirst, removeFirst, addLast, getLast, and removeLast. LinkedList also implements the Queue interface.

Special-Purpose List Implementations

CopyOnWriteArrayList[93] is a List implementation backed up by a copy-on-write array. This implementation is similar in nature to CopyOnWriteArraySet. No synchronization is necessary, even during iteration, and iterators are guaranteed never to throw ConcurrentModificationException. This implementation is well suited to maintaining event-handler lists, in which change is infrequent and traversal is frequent and potentially time-consuming.

If you need synchronization, a Vector will be slightly faster than an ArrayList synchronized with Collections.synchronizedList. But Vector has loads of legacy operations, so be careful to always manipulate the Vector with the List interface, or else you won't be able to replace the implementation at a later time.

If your List is fixed in size—that is, you'll never use remove, add, or any of the bulk operations other than containsAll—you have a third option that's definitely worth considering. See Arrays.asList in the "Convenience Implementations" section for more information.

---

90.   8/docs/api/java/util/List.html

91.   8/docs/api/java/util/ArrayList.html

92.   8/docs/api/java/util/LinkedList.html

93.   8/docs/api/java/util/concurrent/CopyOnWriteArrayList.html

Map Implementations

Map implementations are grouped into general-purpose, special-purpose, and concurrent implementations.

General-Purpose Map Implementations

The three general-purpose Map[94] implementations are HashMap,[95] TreeMap,[96] and LinkedHashMap.[97] If you need SortedMap operations or key-ordered Collection-view iteration, use TreeMap; if you want maximum speed and don't care about iteration order, use HashMap; if you want near-HashMap performance and insertion-order iteration, use LinkedHashMap. In this respect, the situation for Map is analogous to Set. Likewise, everything else in the "Set Implementations" section also applies to Map implementations.

LinkedHashMap provides two capabilities that are not available with Linked-HashSet. When you create a LinkedHashMap, you can order it based on key access rather than insertion. In other words, merely looking up the value associated with a key brings that key to the end of the map. Also, LinkedHashMap provides the removeEldestEntry method, which may be overridden to impose a policy for removing stale mappings automatically when new mappings are added to the map. This makes it very easy to implement a custom cache.

For example, this override will allow the map to grow up to as many as a hundred entries, and then it will delete the eldest entry each time a new entry is added, maintaining a steady state of a hundred entries:

```
private static final int MAX_ENTRIES = 100;

protected boolean removeEldestEntry(Map.Entry eldest) {
    return size() > MAX_ENTRIES;
}
```

Special-Purpose Map Implementations

There are three special-purpose Map implementations—EnumMap,[98] WeakHashMap,[99] and IdentityHashMap.[100] EnumMap, which is internally implemented as an array, is a high-performance Map implementation for use with enum keys. This implementation

---

94. 8/docs/api/java/util/Map.html
95. 8/docs/api/java/util/HashMap.html
96. 8/docs/api/java/util/TreeMap.html
97. 8/docs/api/java/util/LinkedHashMap.html
98. 8/docs/api/java/util/EnumMap.html
99. 8/docs/api/java/util/WeakHashMap.html
100. 8/docs/api/java/util/IdentityHashMap.html

12

combines the richness and safety of the `Map` interface with a speed approaching that of an array. If you want to map an enum to a value, you should always use an `EnumMap` in preference to an array.

`WeakHashMap` is an implementation of the `Map` interface that stores only weak references to its keys. Storing only weak references allows a key-value pair to be garbage collected when its key is no longer referenced outside the `WeakHashMap`. This class provides the easiest way to harness the power of weak references. It is useful for implementing "registry-like" data structures, where the utility of an entry vanishes when its key is no longer reachable by any thread.

`IdentityHashMap` is an identity-based `Map` implementation based on a hash table. This class is useful for topology-preserving object graph transformations, such as serialization or deep copying. To perform such transformations, you need to maintain an identity-based "node table" that keeps track of which objects have already been seen. Identity-based maps are also used to maintain object-to-metainformation mappings in dynamic debuggers and similar systems. Finally, identity-based maps are useful in thwarting "spoof attacks" that are a result of intentionally perverse `equals` methods because `IdentityHashMap` never invokes the `equals` method on its keys. An added benefit of this implementation is its speed.

Concurrent Map Implementations

The `java.util.concurrent`[101] package contains the `ConcurrentMap`[102] interface, which extends `Map` with atomic `putIfAbsent`, `remove`, and `replace` methods, and the `ConcurrentHashMap`[103] implementation of that interface.

`ConcurrentHashMap` is a highly concurrent, high-performance implementation backed up by a hash table. This implementation never blocks when performing retrievals and allows the client to select the concurrency level for updates. It is intended as a drop-in replacement for `Hashtable`: in addition to implementing `ConcurrentMap`, it supports all the legacy methods peculiar to `Hashtable`. Again, if you don't need the legacy operations, be careful to manipulate it with the `ConcurrentMap` interface.

Queue Implementations

The `Queue` implementations are grouped into general-purpose and concurrent implementations.

---

101. 8/docs/api/java/util/concurrent/package-summary.html

102. 8/docs/api/java/util/concurrent/ConcurrentMap.html

103. 8/docs/api/java/util/concurrent/ConcurrentHashMap.html

General-Purpose Queue Implementations

As mentioned in the previous section, `LinkedList` implements the `Queue` interface, providing FIFO queue operations for `add`, `poll`, and so on. The `Priority-Queue` class is a priority queue based on the *heap* data structure.[104] This queue orders elements according to the order specified at construction time, which can be the elements' natural ordering or the ordering imposed by an explicit `Comparator`.

The queue retrieval operations—`poll`, `remove`, `peek`, and `element`—access the element at the head of the queue. The *head of the queue* is the least element with respect to the specified ordering. If multiple elements are tied for least value, the head is one of those elements; ties are broken arbitrarily.

`PriorityQueue` and its iterator implement all of the optional methods of the `Collection` and `Iterator` interfaces. The iterator provided in method `iterator` is not guaranteed to traverse the elements of the `PriorityQueue` in any particular order. For ordered traversal, consider using `Arrays.sort(pq.toArray())`.

Concurrent Queue Implementations

The `java.util.concurrent` package contains a set of synchronized `Queue` interfaces and classes. `BlockingQueue` extends `Queue` with operations that wait for the queue to become nonempty when retrieving an element and for space to become available in the queue when storing an element.[105] This interface is implemented by the following classes:

12

- `LinkedBlockingQueue`. An optionally bounded FIFO blocking queue backed by linked nodes[106]
- `ArrayBlockingQueue`. A bounded FIFO blocking queue backed by an array[107]
- `PriorityBlockingQueue`. An unbounded blocking priority queue backed by a heap[108]
- `DelayQueue`. A time-based scheduling queue backed by a heap[109]
- `SynchronousQueue`. A simple rendezvous mechanism that uses the `BlockingQueue` interface[110]

---

104. 8/docs/api/java/util/PriorityQueue.html

105. 8/docs/api/java/util/concurrent/BlockingQueue.html

106. 8/docs/api/java/util/concurrent/LinkedBlockingQueue.html

107. 8/docs/api/java/util/concurrent/ArrayBlockingQueue.html

108. 8/docs/api/java/util/concurrent/PriorityBlockingQueue.html

109. 8/docs/api/java/util/concurrent/DelayQueue.html

110. 8/docs/api/java/util/concurrent/SynchronousQueue.html

TransferQueue[111] is a specialized BlockingQueue in which code that adds an element to the queue has the option of waiting (blocking) for code in another thread to retrieve the element. TransferQueue has a single implementation:

- LinkedTransferQueue. An unbounded TransferQueue based on linked nodes[112]

Deque Implementations

The Deque interface represents a double-ended queue. The Deque interface can be implemented as various types of Collections. The Deque interface implementations are grouped into general-purpose and concurrent implementations.

General-Purpose Deque Implementations

The general-purpose implementations include LinkedList and ArrayDeque classes. The Deque interface supports insertion, removal, and retrieval of elements at both ends. The ArrayDeque[113] class is the resizable array implementation of the Deque interface, whereas the LinkedList[114] class is the list implementation.

The basic insertion, removal, and retrieval operations in the Deque interface are addFirst, addLast, removeFirst, removeLast, getFirst, and getLast. The method addFirst adds an element at the head, whereas addLast adds an element at the tail of the Deque instance.

The LinkedList implementation is more flexible than the ArrayDeque implementation. LinkedList implements all optional list operations; null elements are allowed in the LinkedList implementation but not in the ArrayDeque implementation.

In terms of efficiency, ArrayDeque is more efficient than the LinkedList for add and remove operations at both ends. The best operation in a LinkedList implementation is removing the current element during the iteration. LinkedList implementations are not ideal structures to iterate.

The LinkedList implementation consumes more memory than the Array-Deque implementation. For the ArrayDeque instance traversal, use any of the following.

---

111. 8/docs/api/java/util/concurrent/TransferQueue.html
112. 8/docs/api/java/util/concurrent/LinkedTransferQueue.html
113. 8/docs/api/java/util/ArrayDeque.html
114. 8/docs/api/java/util/LinkedList.html

For-Each Loop

The `for-each` loop is fast and can be used for all kinds of lists.

```
ArrayDeque<String> aDeque = new ArrayDeque<String>();

...
for (String str : aDeque) {
    System.out.println(str);
}
```

Iterator

The `Iterator` can be used for the forward traversal on all kinds of lists for all kinds of data:

```
ArrayDeque<String> aDeque = new ArrayDeque<String>();
...
for (Iterator<String> iter = aDeque.iterator(); iter.hasNext();  ) {
    System.out.println(iter.next());
}
```

The `ArrayDeque` class is used in this context to implement the `Deque` interface. The complete code of the example used here is available in `ArrayDequeSample`. Both the `LinkedList` and `ArrayDeque` classes do not support concurrent access by multiple threads.

Concurrent Deque Implementations

The `LinkedBlockingDeque` class is the concurrent implementation of the `Deque` interface.[115] If the deque is empty, then methods such as `takeFirst` and `takeLast` wait until the element becomes available and then retrieve and remove the same element.

Wrapper Implementations

Wrapper implementations delegate all their real work to a specified collection but add extra functionality on top of what this collection offers. For design pattern fans, this is an example of the *decorator* pattern. Although it may seem a bit exotic, it's really pretty straightforward.

These implementations are anonymous; rather than providing a public class, the library provides a static factory method. All these implementations are found in the `Collections`[116] class, which consists solely of static methods.

---

115. 8/docs/api/java/util/concurrent/LinkedBlockingDeque.html
116. 8/docs/api/java/util/Collections.html

Synchronization Wrappers

The synchronization wrappers add automatic synchronization (thread safety) to an arbitrary collection. Each of the six core collection interfaces—Collection,[117] Set,[118] List,[119] Map,[120] SortedSet,[121] and SortedMap[122]—has one static factory method:

```
public static <T> Collection<T> synchronizedCollection(Collection<T> c);
public static <T> Set<T> synchronizedSet(Set<T> s);
public static <T> List<T> synchronizedList(List<T> list);
public static <K,V> Map<K,V> synchronizedMap(Map<K,V> m);
public static <T> SortedSet<T> synchronizedSortedSet(SortedSet<T> s);
public static <K,V> SortedMap<K,V> synchronizedSortedMap(SortedMap<K,V> m);
```

Each of these methods returns a synchronized (thread-safe) Collection backed up by the specified collection. To guarantee serial access, *all* access to the backing collection must be accomplished through the returned collection. The easy way to guarantee this is not to keep a reference to the backing collection. Create the synchronized collection with the following trick:

```
List<Type> list = Collections.synchronizedList(new ArrayList<Type>());
```

A collection created in this fashion is every bit as thread safe as a normally synchronized collection, such as a Vector.[123]

In the face of concurrent access, it is imperative that the user manually synchronize on the returned collection when iterating over it. The reason is that iteration is accomplished via multiple calls into the collection, which must be composed into a single atomic operation. The following is the idiom to iterate over a wrapper-synchronized collection:

```
Collection<Type> c = Collections.synchronizedCollection(myCollection);
synchronized(c) {
    for (Type e : c)
        foo(e);
}
```

---

117. 8/docs/api/java/util/Collection.html

118. 8/docs/api/java/util/Set.html

119. 8/docs/api/java/util/List.html

120. 8/docs/api/java/util/Map.html

121. 8/docs/api/java/util/SortedSet.html

122. 8/docs/api/java/util/SortedMap.html

123. 8/docs/api/java/util/Vector.html

If an explicit iterator is used, the `iterator` method must be called from within the `synchronized` block. Failure to follow this advice may result in nondeterministic behavior. The idiom for iterating over a `Collection` view of a synchronized `Map` is similar. It is imperative that the user synchronize on the synchronized `Map` when iterating over any of its `Collection` views rather than synchronizing on the `Collection` view itself, as shown in the following example:

```
Map<KeyType, ValType> m = Collections.synchronizedMap(new HashMap<KeyType, ValType>());
    ...
Set<KeyType> s = m.keySet();
    ...
// Synchronizing on m, not s!
synchronized(m) {
    while (KeyType k : s)
        foo(k);
}
```

One minor downside of using wrapper implementations is that you do not have the ability to execute any *noninterface* operations of a wrapped implementation. So, for instance, in the preceding `List` example, you cannot call `ArrayList`'s `ensure-Capacity`[124] operation on the wrapped `ArrayList`.

Unmodifiable Wrappers

Unlike synchronization wrappers, which add functionality to the wrapped collection, the unmodifiable wrappers take functionality away. In particular, they take away the ability to modify the collection by intercepting all the operations that would modify the collection and throwing an `UnsupportedOperationException`. Unmodifiable wrappers have two main uses:

- *To make a collection immutable once it has been built.* In this case, it's good practice not to maintain a reference to the backing collection. This absolutely guarantees immutability.
- *To allow certain clients read-only access to your data structures.* You keep a reference to the backing collection but hand out a reference to the wrapper. In this way, clients can look but not modify, while you maintain full access.

Like synchronization wrappers, each of the six core `Collection` interfaces has one static factory method:

```
public static <T> Collection<T> unmodifiableCollection(Collection<? extends T> c);
public static <T> Set<T> unmodifiableSet(Set<? extends T> s);
```

---

124. `8/docs/api/java/util/ArrayList.html#ensureCapacity-int-`

12

```
public static <T> List<T> unmodifiableList(List<? extends T> list);
public static <K,V> Map<K, V> unmodifiableMap(Map<? extends K, ? extends V> m);
public static <T> SortedSet<T> unmodifiableSortedSet(SortedSet<? extends T> s);
public static <K,V> SortedMap<K,V> unmodifiableSortedMap(SortedMap<K, ? extends V> m);
```

Checked Interface Wrappers

The `Collections.checked` *interface* wrappers are provided for use with generic collections. These implementations return a *dynamically* type-safe view of the specified collection, which throws a `ClassCastException` if a client attempts to add an element of the wrong type. The generics mechanism in the language provides compile-time (static) type checking, but it is possible to defeat this mechanism. Dynamically type-safe views eliminate this possibility entirely.

Convenience Implementations

This section describes several mini-implementations that can be more convenient and more efficient than general-purpose implementations when you don't need their full power. All the implementations in this section are made available via static factory methods rather than `public` classes.

List View of an Array

The `Arrays.asList` method returns a `List` view of its array argument.[125] Changes to the `List` write through to the array and vice versa. The size of the collection is that of the array and cannot be changed. If the `add` or the `remove` method is called on the `List`, an `UnsupportedOperationException` will result.

The normal use of this implementation is as a bridge between array-based and collection-based APIs. It allows you to pass an array to a method expecting a `Collection` or a `List`. However, this implementation also has another use. If you need a fixed-size `List`, it's more efficient than any general-purpose `List` implementation. This is the idiom:

```
List<String> list = Arrays.asList(new String[size]);
```

Note that a reference to the backing array is not retained.

Immutable Multiple-Copy List

Occasionally you'll need an immutable `List` consisting of multiple copies of the same element. The `Collections.nCopies`[126] method returns such a list. This implementation has two main uses. The first is to initialize a newly created `List`;

---

125. 8/docs/api/java/util/Arrays.html#asList-T...-

126. 8/docs/api/java/util/Collections.html#nCopies-int-T-

for example, suppose you want an `ArrayList` initially consisting of a thousand null elements. The following incantation does the trick:

```
List<Type> list = new ArrayList<Type>(Collections.nCopies(1000, (Type)null);
```

Of course, the initial value of each element need not be null. The second main use is to grow an existing `List`. For example, suppose you want to add sixty-nine copies of the string `"fruit bat"` to the end of a `List<String>`. It's not clear why you'd want to do such a thing, but let's just suppose you did. The following is how you'd do it:

```
lovablePets.addAll(Collections.nCopies(69, "fruit bat"));
```

By using the form of `addAll` that takes both an index and a `Collection`, you can add the new elements to the middle of a `List` instead of the end of it.

Immutable Singleton Set

Sometimes you'll need an immutable *singleton* `Set`, which consists of a single, specified element. The `Collections.singleton`[127] method returns such a `Set`. One use of this implementation is to remove all occurrences of a specified element from a `Collection`:

```
c.removeAll(Collections.singleton(e));
```

A related idiom removes all elements that map to a specified value from a `Map`. For example, suppose you have a `Map`—job—that maps people to their line of work, and suppose you want to eliminate all the lawyers. The following one-liner will do the deed:

```
job.values().removeAll(Collections.singleton(LAWYER));
```

This implementation can also be used to provide a single input value to a method that is written to accept a collection of values.

Empty Set, List, and Map Constants

The `Collections`[128] class provides methods to return the empty `Set`, `List`, and `Map`— emptySet,[129] emptyList,[130] and emptyMap.[131] The main use of these constants is as

---

127. 8/docs/api/java/util/Collections.html#singleton-T-
128. 8/docs/api/java/util/Collections.html
129. 8/docs/api/java/util/Collections.html#emptySet--
130. 8/docs/api/java/util/Collections.html#emptyList--
131. 8/docs/api/java/util/Collections.html#emptyMap--

input to methods that take a `Collection` of values when you don't want to provide any values at all, as in this example:

```
tourist.declarePurchases(Collections.emptySet());
```

Summary of Implementations

Implementations are the data objects used to store collections, which implement the interfaces described in the "Interfaces" section. The Java Collections Framework provides several general-purpose implementations of the core interfaces:

- For the `Set` interface, `HashSet` is the most commonly used implementation.
- For the `List` interface, `ArrayList` is the most commonly used implementation.
- For the `Map` interface, `HashMap` is the most commonly used implementation.
- For the `Queue` interface, `LinkedList` is the most commonly used implementation.
- For the `Deque` interface, `ArrayDeque` is the most commonly used implementation.

Each of the general-purpose implementations provides all optional operations contained in its interface.

The Java Collections Framework also provides several special-purpose implementations for situations that require nonstandard performance, usage restrictions, or other unusual behavior. The `java.util.concurrent` package contains several collections implementations, which are thread safe but not governed by a single exclusion lock.

The `Collections` class (as opposed to the `Collection` interface) provides static methods that operate on or return collections, which are known as Wrapper implementations. Finally, there are several convenience implementations, which can be more efficient than general-purpose implementations when you don't need their full power. The convenience implementations are made available through static factory methods.

Questions and Exercises: Implementations

Questions

1. You plan to write a program that uses several basic collection interfaces: `Set`, `List`, `Queue`, and `Map`. You're not sure which implementations will work best, so you decide to use general-purpose implementations until you get a better idea of how your program will work in the real world. Which implementations are these?

2. If you need a `Set` implementation that provides value-ordered iteration, which class should you use?

3. Which class do you use to access wrapper implementations?

Exercise

1. Write a program that reads a text file, specified by the first command-line argument, into a `List`. The program should then print random lines from the file, with the number of lines printed specified by the second command-line argument. Write the program so that a correctly sized collection is allocated all at once instead of being gradually expanded as the file is read in. Hint: To determine the number of lines in the file, use `java.io.File.length`[132] to obtain the size of the file, then divide by an assumed size of an average line.

Answers

You can find answers to these questions and exercises at `http://docs.oracle.com/javase/tutorial/collections/implementations/QandE/answers.html`.

Algorithms

12

The *polymorphic algorithms* described here are pieces of reusable functionality provided by the Java platform. They all come from the `Collections`[133] class and take the form of static methods whose first argument is the collection on which the operation is to be performed. The great majority of the algorithms provided by the Java platform operate on `List`[134] instances, but a few of them operate on arbitrary `Collection`[135] instances.

Sorting

The `sort` algorithm reorders a `List` so that its elements are in ascending order according to an ordering relationship. Two forms of the operation are provided. The simple form takes a `List` and sorts it according to its elements' *natural ordering*. If you're unfamiliar with the concept of natural ordering, read the "Object Ordering" section.

---

132. 8/docs/api/java/io/File.html#length--
133. 8/docs/api/java/util/Collections.html
134. 8/docs/api/java/util/List.html
135. 8/docs/api/java/util/Collection.html

The `sort` operation uses a slightly optimized *merge sort* algorithm that is fast and stable:

- *Fast.* It is guaranteed to run in n log(n) time and runs substantially faster on nearly sorted lists. Empirical tests showed it to be as fast as a highly optimized quicksort. A quicksort is generally considered to be faster than a merge sort but isn't stable and doesn't guarantee n log(n) performance.
- *Stable.* It doesn't reorder equal elements. This is important if you sort the same list repeatedly on different attributes. If a user of a mail program sorts the inbox by mailing date and then sorts it by sender, the user naturally expects that the now-contiguous list of messages from a given sender will (still) be sorted by mailing date. This is guaranteed only if the second sort was stable.

The following trivial program prints out its arguments in lexicographic (alphabetical) order:

```
import java.util.*;

public class Sort {
    public static void main(String[] args) {
        List<String> list = Arrays.asList(args);
        Collections.sort(list);
        System.out.println(list);
    }
}
```

Let's run the program:

```
% java Sort i walk the line
```

The following output is produced:

```
[i, line, the, walk]
```

This program was included only to show you that algorithms really are as easy to use as they appear to be.

The second form of `sort` takes a `Comparator`[136] in addition to a `List` and sorts the elements with the `Comparator`. Suppose you want to print out the anagram groups from our earlier example in reverse order of size—largest anagram group first. The example that follows shows you how to achieve this with the help of the second form of the `sort` method.

_____

136. 8/docs/api/java/util/Comparator.html

Recall that the anagram groups are stored as values in a Map, in the form of List instances. The revised printing code iterates through the Map's values view, putting every List that passes the minimum-size test into a List of Lists. Then the code sorts this List, using a Comparator that expects List instances, and implements reverse size ordering. Finally, the code iterates through the sorted List, printing its elements (the anagram groups). The following code replaces the printing code at the end of the main method in the Anagrams example:

```
// Make a List of all anagram groups above size threshold.
List<List<String>> winners = new ArrayList<List<String>>();
for (List<String> l : m.values())
    if (l.size() >= minGroupSize)
        winners.add(l);

// Sort anagram groups according to size
Collections.sort(winners, new Comparator<List<String>>() {
    public int compare(List<String> o1, List<String> o2) {
        return o2.size() - o1.size();
    }});

// Print anagram groups.
for (List<String> l : winners)
    System.out.println(l.size() + ": " + l);
```

Running the program on the same dictionary as in "The Map Interface" section, with the same minimum anagram group size (eight), produces the following output:

```
12: [apers, apres, asper, pares, parse, pears, prase,
        presa, rapes, reaps, spare, spear]
11: [alerts, alters, artels, estral, laster, ratels,
        salter, slater, staler, stelar, talers]
10: [least, setal, slate, stale, steal, stela, taels,
        tales, teals, tesla]
9: [estrin, inerts, insert, inters, niters, nitres,
        sinter, triens, trines]
9: [capers, crapes, escarp, pacers, parsec, recaps,
        scrape, secpar, spacer]
9: [palest, palets, pastel, petals, plates, pleats,
        septal, staple, tepals]
9: [anestri, antsier, nastier, ratines, retains, retinas,
        retsina, stainer, stearin]
8: [lapse, leaps, pales, peals, pleas, salep, sepal, spale]
8: [aspers, parses, passer, prases, repass, spares,
        sparse, spears]
8: [enters, nester, renest, rentes, resent, tenser,
        ternes, treens]
8: [arles, earls, lares, laser, lears, rales, reals, seral]
8: [earings, erasing, gainers, reagins, regains, reginas,
        searing, seringa]
8: [peris, piers, pries, prise, ripes, speir, spier, spire]
8: [ates, east, eats, etas, sate, seat, seta, teas]
8: [carets, cartes, caster, caters, crates, reacts,
        recast, traces]
```

12

Shuffling

The shuffle algorithm does the opposite of what sort does, destroying any trace of order that may have been present in a List—that is, this algorithm reorders the List based on input from a source of randomness such that all possible permutations occur with equal likelihood, assuming a fair source of randomness. This algorithm is useful in implementing games of chance. For example, it could be used to shuffle a List of Card objects representing a deck. It's also useful for generating test cases.

This operation has two forms: one takes a List and uses a default source of randomness, and the other requires the caller to provide a Random[137] object to use as a source of randomness. The code for this algorithm was provided earlier in this chapter.[138]

Routine Data Manipulation

The Collections class provides five algorithms for doing routine data manipulation on List objects, all of which are pretty straightforward:

- reverse. This reverses the order of the elements in a List.
- fill. This overwrites every element in a List with the specified value. This operation is useful for reinitializing a List.
- copy. This takes two arguments, a destination List and a source List, and copies the elements of the source into the destination, overwriting its contents. The destination List must be at least as long as the source. If it is longer, the remaining elements in the destination List are unaffected.
- swap. This swaps the elements at the specified positions in a List.
- addAll. This adds all the specified elements to a Collection. The elements to be added may be specified individually or as an array.

Searching

The binarySearch algorithm searches for a specified element in a sorted List. This algorithm has two forms. The first takes a List and an element to search for (the *search key*). This form assumes that the List is sorted in ascending order according to the natural ordering of its elements. The second form takes a Comparator in addition to the List and the search key and assumes that the List is

---

137. 8/docs/api/java/util/Random.html
138. tutorial/collections/interfaces/list.html#shuffle

sorted into ascending order according to the specified `Comparator`. The `sort` algorithm can be used to sort the `List` prior to calling `binarySearch`.

The return value is the same for both forms. If the `List` contains the search key, its index is returned. If not, the return value is `(-(insertion point) - 1)`, where the insertion point is the point at which the value would be inserted into the `List` or the index of the first element greater than the value or `list.size()` if all elements in the `List` are less than the specified value. This admittedly ugly formula guarantees that the return value will be `>= 0` if and only if the search key is found. It's basically a hack to combine a `boolean` `(found)` and an integer `(index)` into a single `int` return value.

The following idiom, usable with both forms of the `binarySearch` operation, looks for the specified search key and inserts it at the appropriate position if it's not already present:

```
int pos = Collections.binarySearch(list, key);
if (pos < 0)
    l.add(-pos-1, key);
```

Composition

The frequency and disjoint algorithms test some aspect of the composition of one or more `Collections`:

- `frequency`. Counts the number of times the specified element occurs in the specified collection
- `disjoint`. Determines if two `Collections` are disjoint (i.e., they contain no elements in common)

Finding Extreme Values

The `min` and the `max` algorithms return, respectively, the minimum and maximum element contained in a specified `Collection`. Both operations come in two forms. The simple form takes only a `Collection` and returns the minimum (or maximum) element according to the elements' natural ordering. The second form takes a `Comparator` in addition to the `Collection` and returns the minimum (or maximum) element according to the specified `Comparator`.

Custom Collection Implementations

Many programmers will never need to implement their own `Collections` classes. You can go pretty far using the implementations described in the preceding sections

12

of this chapter. However, someday you might want to write your own implementation. It is fairly easy to do this with the aid of the abstract implementations provided by the Java platform. Before we discuss *how* to write an implementation, let's discuss why you might want to write one.

Reasons to Write an Implementation

The following list illustrates the sort of custom `Collections` you might want to implement. It is not intended to be exhaustive:

- *Persistent*. All the built-in `Collection` implementations reside in main memory and vanish when the program exits. If you want a collection that will still be present the next time the program starts, you can implement it by building a veneer over an external database. Such a collection might be concurrently accessible by multiple programs.

- *Application specific*. This is a very broad category. One example is an unmodifiable `Map` containing real-time telemetry data. The keys could represent locations, and the values could be read from sensors at these locations in response to the `get` operation.

- *High performance, special purpose*. Many data structures take advantage of restricted usage to offer better performance than is possible with general-purpose implementations. For instance, consider a `List` containing long runs of identical element values. Such lists, which occur frequently in text processing, can be *run-length encoded*; runs can be represented as a single object containing the repeated element and the number of consecutive repetitions. This example is interesting because it trades off two aspects of performance: it requires less space but more time than an `ArrayList`.

- *High performance, general purpose*. The Java Collections Framework's designers tried to provide the best general-purpose implementations for each interface, but many, many data structures could have been used, and new ones are invented every day. Maybe you can come up with something faster!

- *Enhanced functionality*. Suppose you need an efficient bag implementation (also known as a *multiset*): a `Collection` that offers constant-time containment checks while allowing duplicate elements. It's reasonably straightforward to implement such a collection atop a `HashMap`.

- *Convenience*. You may want additional implementations that offer conveniences beyond those offered by the Java platform. For instance, you may frequently need `List` instances representing a contiguous range of `Integers`.

- *Adapter*. Suppose you are using a legacy API that has its own ad hoc collections' API. You can write an adapter implementation that permits these collections to operate in the Java Collections Framework. An *adapter implementation* is a thin veneer that wraps objects of one type and makes them behave like objects of another type by translating operations on the latter type into operations on the former.

How to Write a Custom Implementation

Writing a custom implementation is surprisingly easy. The Java Collections Framework provides abstract implementations designed expressly to facilitate custom implementations. We'll start with the following example of an implementation of `Arrays.asList`:[139]

```
public static <T> List<T> asList(T[] a) {
    return new MyArrayList<T>(a);
}

private static class MyArrayList<T> extends AbstractList<T> {

    private final T[] a;

    MyArrayList(T[] array) {
        a = array;
    }

    public T get(int index) {
        return a[index];
    }

    public T set(int index, T element) {
        T oldValue = a[index];
        a[index] = element;
        return oldValue;
    }

    public int size() {
        return a.length;
    }
}
```

12

Believe it or not, this is very close to the implementation that is contained in `java.util.Arrays`. It's that simple! You provide a constructor and the `get`, `set`, and `size` methods, and `AbstractList` does all the rest. You get the `ListIterator`, bulk operations, search operations, hash code computation, comparison, and string representation for free.

Suppose you want to make the implementation a bit faster. The API documentation for abstract implementations describes precisely how each method is

---

139. 8/docs/api/java/util/Arrays.html#asList-T...-

implemented, so you'll know which methods to override to get the performance you want. The preceding implementation's performance is fine, but it can be improved a bit. In particular, the `toArray` method iterates over the `List`, copying one element at a time. Given the internal representation, it's a lot faster and more sensible just to clone the array:

```
public Object[] toArray() {
    return (Object[]) a.clone();
}
```

With the addition of this override and a few more like it, this implementation is exactly the one found in `java.util.Arrays`. In the interest of full disclosure, it's a bit tougher to use the other abstract implementations because you will have to write your own iterator, but it's still not that difficult. The following list summarizes the abstract implementations:

- `AbstractCollection`. This is a `Collection` that is neither a `Set` nor a `List`. At a minimum, you must provide the `iterator` and the `size` methods.[140]
- `AbstractSet`. This is a `Set`; use is identical to `AbstractCollection`.[141]
- `AbstractList`. This is a `List` backed up by a random-access data store such as an array. At a minimum, you must provide the `positional access` methods (`get` and, optionally, `set`, `remove`, and `add`) and the `size` method. The abstract class takes care of `listIterator` (and `iterator`).[142]
- `AbstractSequentialList`. This is a `List` backed up by a sequential-access data store, such as a linked list. At a minimum, you must provide the `listIterator` and `size` methods. The abstract class takes care of the positional access methods. (This is the opposite of `AbstractList`.)[143]
- `AbstractQueue`. This is a `Queue`. At a minimum, you must provide the `offer`, `peek`, `poll`, and `size` methods and an `iterator` supporting `remove`.[144]
- `AbstractMap`. This is a `Map`. At a minimum, you must provide the `entrySet` view. This is typically implemented with the `AbstractSet` class. If the `Map` is modifiable, you must also provide the `put` method.[145]

The process of writing a custom implementation follows:

---

140. 8/docs/api/java/util/AbstractCollection.html
141. 8/docs/api/java/util/AbstractSet.html
142. 8/docs/api/java/util/AbstractList.html
143. 8/docs/api/java/util/AbstractSequentialList.html
144. 8/docs/api/java/util/AbstractQueue.html
145. 8/docs/api/java/util/AbstractMap.html

1. Choose the appropriate abstract implementation class from the preceding list.
2. Provide implementations for all the abstract methods of the class. If your custom collection is modifiable, you will have to override one or more of the concrete methods as well. The API documentation for the abstract implementation class will tell you which methods to override.
3. Test and, if necessary, debug the implementation. You now have a working custom collection implementation.
4. If you are concerned about performance, read the API documentation of the abstract implementation class for all the methods whose implementations you're inheriting. If any seem too slow, override them. If you override any methods, be sure to measure the performance of the method before and after the override. How much effort you put into tweaking performance should be a function of how much use the implementation will get and how critical to performance its use is. (Often this step is best omitted.)

Interoperability

In this section, you'll learn about the following two aspects of interoperability:

- *Compatibility*. This subsection describes how collections can be made to work with older APIs that predate the addition of `Collections` to the Java platform.
- *API design*. This subsection describes how to design new APIs so that they will interoperate seamlessly with one another.

Compatibility

The Java Collections Framework was designed to ensure complete interoperability between the core collection interfaces and the types that were used to represent collections in the early versions of the Java platform: `Vector`,[146] `Hashtable`,[147] array, and `Enumeration`.[148] In this section, you'll learn how to transform old collections to the Java Collections Framework collections and vice versa.

Upward Compatibility

Suppose that you're using an API that returns legacy collections in tandem with another API that requires objects implementing the collection interfaces. To make

---

146. 8/docs/api/java/util/Vector.html
147. 8/docs/api/java/util/Hashtable.html
148. 8/docs/api/java/util/Enumeration.html

the two APIs interoperate smoothly, you'll have to transform the legacy collections into modern collections. Luckily the Java Collections Framework makes this easy.

Suppose the old API returns an array of objects and the new API requires a Collection. The Java Collections Framework has a convenience implementation that allows an array of objects to be viewed as a List. You use Arrays.asList to pass an array to any method requiring a Collection or a List:[149]

```
Foo[] result = oldMethod(arg);
newMethod(Arrays.asList(result));
```

If the old API returns a Vector or a Hashtable, you have no work to do at all because Vector was retrofitted to implement the List interface and Hashtable was retrofitted to implement Map. Therefore a Vector may be passed directly to any method calling for a Collection or a List:

```
Vector result = oldMethod(arg);
newMethod(result);
```

Similarly, a Hashtable may be passed directly to any method calling for a Map:

```
Hashtable result = oldMethod(arg);
newMethod(result);
```

Less frequently, an API may return an Enumeration that represents a collection of objects. The Collections.list method translates an Enumeration into a Collection:

```
Enumeration e = oldMethod(arg);
newMethod(Collections.list(e));
```

Backward Compatibility

Suppose you're using an API that returns modern collections in tandem with another API that requires you to pass in legacy collections. To make the two APIs interoperate smoothly, you have to transform modern collections into old collections. Again the Java Collections Framework makes this easy.

Suppose the new API returns a Collection and the old API requires an array of Object. As you're probably aware, the Collection interface contains a toArray method designed expressly for this situation:

```
Collection c = newMethod();
oldMethod(c.toArray());
```

---

149. 8/docs/api/java/util/Arrays.html#asList-T...-

What if the old API requires an array of `String` (or another type) instead of an array of `Object`? You just use the other form of `toArray`—the one that takes an array on input:

```
Collection c = newMethod();
oldMethod((String[]) c.toArray(new String[0]));
```

If the old API requires a `Vector`, the standard collection constructor comes in handy:

```
Collection c = newMethod();
oldMethod(new Vector(c));
```

The case where the old API requires a `Hashtable` is handled analogously:

```
Map m = newMethod();
oldMethod(new Hashtable(m));
```

Finally, what do you do if the old API requires an `Enumeration`? This case isn't common, but it does happen from time to time, and the `Collections.enumeration` method was provided to handle it.[150] This is a static factory method that takes a `Collection` and returns an `Enumeration` over the elements of the `Collection`:

```
Collection c = newMethod();
oldMethod(Collections.enumeration(c));
```

12

API Design

In this short but important section, you'll learn a few simple guidelines that will allow your API to interoperate seamlessly with all other APIs that follow these guidelines. In essence, these rules define what it takes to be a good "citizen" in the world of collections.

Parameters

If your API contains a method that requires a collection on input, it is of paramount importance that you declare the relevant parameter type to be one of the collection interface types. *Never* use an implementation type, because this defeats the purpose of an interface-based collections framework, which is to allow collections to be manipulated without regard to implementation details.

Further, you should always use the least-specific type that makes sense. For example, don't require a `List` or a `Set` if a `Collection` would do. It's not that

---

150. `8/docs/api/java/util/Collections.html#enumeration-java.util`
`.Collection-`

you should never require a `List` or a `Set` on input; it is correct to do so if a method depends on a property of one of these interfaces. For example, many of the algorithms provided by the Java platform require a `List` on input because they depend on the fact that lists are ordered. As a general rule, however, the best types to use on input are the most general: `Collection` and `Map`.

> **Note**
>
> Never define your own ad hoc collection class and require objects of this class on input. By doing this, you'd lose all the benefits provided by the Java Collections Framework.

Return Values

You can afford to be much more flexible with return values than with input parameters. It's fine to return an object of any type that implements or extends one of the collection interfaces. This can be one of the interfaces or a special-purpose type that extends or implements one of these interfaces.

For example, one could imagine an image-processing package, called `Image-List`, that returned objects of a new class that implements `List`. In addition to the `List` operations, `ImageList` could support any application-specific operations that seemed desirable. For example, it might provide an `indexImage` operation that returned an image containing thumbnail images of each graphic in the `ImageList`. It's critical to note that even if the API furnishes `ImageList` instances on output, it should accept arbitrary `Collection` (or perhaps `List`) instances on input.

In one sense, return values should have the opposite behavior of input parameters: It's best to return the most specific applicable collection interface rather than the most general. For example, if you're sure that you'll always return a `SortedMap`, you should give the relevant method the return type of `SortedMap` rather than `Map`. `SortedMap` instances are more time-consuming to build than ordinary `Map` instances and are also more powerful. Given that your module has already invested the time to build a `SortedMap`, it makes good sense to give the user access to its increased power. Furthermore, the user will be able to pass the returned object to methods that demand a `SortedMap` as well as those that accept any `Map`.

Legacy APIs

There are currently plenty of APIs out there that define their own ad hoc collection types. While this is unfortunate, it's a fact of life, given that there was no collections framework in the first two major releases of the Java platform. Suppose you own one of these APIs; here's what you can do about it.

If possible, retrofit your legacy collection type to implement one of the standard collection interfaces. Then all the collections you return will interoperate smoothly with other collection-based APIs. If this is impossible (e.g., because one or more of the preexisting type signatures conflict with the standard collection interfaces), define an *adapter class* that wraps one of your legacy collections objects, allowing it to function as a standard collection. (The `Adapter` class is an example of a *custom implementation*.)

Retrofit your API with new calls that follow the input guidelines to accept objects of a standard collection interface, if possible. Such calls can coexist with the calls that take the legacy collection type. If this is impossible, provide a constructor or static factory for your legacy type that takes an object of one of the standard interfaces and returns a legacy collection containing the same elements (or mappings). Either of these approaches will allow users to pass arbitrary collections into your API.

12

13

Concurrency

Chapter Contents

Processes and Threads   520
Thread Objects   521
Synchronization   527
Liveness   533
Guarded Blocks   535
Immutable Objects   539
High-Level Concurrency Objects   543
Questions and Exercises: Concurrency   555

Computer users take it for granted that their systems can do more than one thing at a time. They assume that they can continue to work in a word processor while other applications download files, manage the print queue, and stream audio. Even a single application is often expected to do more than one thing at a time. For example, that streaming audio application must simultaneously read the digital audio off the network, decompress it, manage playback, and update its display. Even the word processor should always be ready to respond to keyboard and mouse events, no matter how busy it is reformatting text or updating the display. Software that can do such things is known as *concurrent* software.

The Java platform is designed from the ground up to support concurrent programming, with basic concurrency support in the Java programming language and the Java class libraries. Since Java SE 5, the Java platform has also included high-level concurrency Application Programming Interfaces (APIs). This chapter introduces the platform's basic concurrency support and summarizes some of the high-level APIs in the `java.util.concurrent` packages.

Processes and Threads

In concurrent programming, there are two basic units of execution: *processes* and *threads*. In the Java programming language, concurrent programming is mostly concerned with threads. However, processes are also important.

A computer system normally has many active processes and threads. This is true even in systems that only have a single execution core and thus only have one thread actually executing at any given moment. Processing time for a single core is shared among processes and threads through an operating system feature called *time slicing*.

It's becoming more and more common for computer systems to have multiple processors or processors with multiple execution cores. This greatly enhances a system's capacity for concurrent execution of processes and threads—but concurrency is possible even on simple systems, without multiple processors or execution cores.

Processes

A process has a self-contained execution environment. A process generally has a complete, private set of basic runtime resources; in particular, each process has its own memory space.

Processes are often seen as synonymous with programs or applications. However, what the user sees as a single application may in fact be a set of cooperating processes. To facilitate communication between processes, most operating systems support *Inter Process Communication* (IPC) resources, such as pipes and sockets. IPC is used not just for communication between processes on the same system but for processes on different systems.

Most implementations of the Java Virtual Machine (Java VM) run as a single process. A Java application can create additional processes using a `ProcessBuilder`[1] object. Multiprocess applications are beyond the scope of this chapter.

Threads

Threads are sometimes called *lightweight processes*. Both processes and threads provide an execution environment, but creating a new thread requires fewer resources than creating a new process.

Threads exist within a process—every process has at least one. Threads share the process's resources, including memory and open files. This makes for efficient but potentially problematic communication.

---

1.   `8/docs/api/java/lang/ProcessBuilder.html`

Multithreaded execution is an essential feature of the Java platform. Every application has at least one thread—or several, if you count "system" threads that do things like memory management and signal handling. But from the application programmer's point of view, you start with just one thread, called the *main thread*. This thread has the ability to create additional threads, as we'll demonstrate in the next section.

Thread Objects

Each thread is associated with an instance of the class `Thread`.[2] There are two basic strategies for using `Thread` objects to create a concurrent application:

- To directly control thread creation and management, simply instantiate `Thread` each time the application needs to initiate an asynchronous task.
- To abstract thread management from the rest of your application, pass the application's tasks to an *executor*.

This section documents the use of `Thread` objects. Executors are discussed with other high-level concurrency objects.

Defining and Starting a Thread

An application that creates an instance of `Thread` must provide the code that will run in that thread. There are two ways to do this:

- *Provide a* `Runnable` *object.* The `Runnable`[3] interface defines a single method, run, meant to contain the code executed in the thread. The `Runnable` object is passed to the `Thread` constructor, as in the `HelloRunnable` example:

  ```
  public class HelloRunnable implements Runnable {

      public void run() {
          System.out.println("Hello from a thread!");
      }

      public static void main(String args[]) {
          (new Thread(new HelloRunnable())).start();
      }

  }
  ```

---

2.   8/docs/api/java/lang/Thread.html
3.   8/docs/api/java/lang/Runnable.html

- *Use a subclass* Thread. The Thread class itself implements Runnable, though
  its run method does nothing. An application can subclass Thread, providing
  its own implementation of run, as in the HelloThread example:

```
public class HelloThread extends Thread {

    public void run() {
        System.out.println("Hello from a thread!");
    }

    public static void main(String args[]) {
        (new HelloThread()).start();
    }

}
```

Notice that both examples invoke Thread.start in order to start the new thread.

Which of these idioms should you use? The first idiom, which employs a Runnable object, is more general because the Runnable object can subclass a class other than Thread. The second idiom is easier to use in simple applications but is limited by the fact that your task class must be a descendant of Thread. This section focuses on the first approach, which separates the Runnable task from the Thread object that executes the task. Not only is this approach more flexible; it is applicable to the high-level thread management APIs covered later.

The Thread class defines a number of methods useful for thread management. These include static methods, which provide information about or affect the status of the thread invoking the method. The other methods are invoked from other threads involved in managing the thread and Thread object. We'll examine some of these methods in the following sections.

Pausing Execution with Sleep

Thread.sleep causes the current thread to suspend execution for a specified period. This is an efficient means of making processor time available to the other threads of an application or other applications that might be running on a computer system. The sleep method can also be used for pacing, as shown in the example that follows, and waiting for another thread with duties that are understood to have time requirements, as with the SimpleThreads example in a later section.

Two overloaded versions of sleep are provided: one that specifies the sleep time to the millisecond and one that specifies the sleep time to the nanosecond. However, these sleep times are not guaranteed to be precise because they are limited by the facilities provided by the underlying operating system. Also, the sleep period can be terminated by interrupts, as we'll see in a later section. In any case, you cannot assume that invoking `sleep` will suspend the thread for precisely the time period specified.

The `SleepMessages` example uses `sleep` to print messages at four-second intervals:

```
public class SleepMessages {
    public static void main(String args[])
        throws InterruptedException {
        String importantInfo[] = {
            "Mares eat oats",
            "Does eat oats",
            "Little lambs eat ivy",
            "A kid will eat ivy too"
        };

        for (int i = 0;
             i < importantInfo.length;
             i++) {
            //Pause for 4 seconds
            Thread.sleep(4000);
            //Print a message
            System.out.println(importantInfo[i]);
        }
    }
}
```

Notice that `main` declares that it `throws InterruptedException`. This is an exception that `sleep` throws when another thread interrupts the current thread while `sleep` is active. Since this application has not defined another thread to cause the interrupt, it doesn't bother to catch `InterruptedException`.

Interrupts

An *interrupt* is an indication to a thread that it should stop what it is doing and do something else. It's up to the programmer to decide exactly how a thread responds to an interrupt, but it is very common for the thread to terminate. This is the usage emphasized in this section.

A thread sends an interrupt by invoking `interrupt`[4] on the `Thread` object for the thread to be interrupted. For the interrupt mechanism to work correctly, the interrupted thread must support its own interruption.

Supporting Interruption

How does a thread support its own interruption? This depends on what it's currently doing. If the thread is frequently invoking methods that throw an `InterruptedException`, it simply returns from the `run` method after it catches that exception. For example,

---

4.   `8/docs/api/java/lang/Thread.html#interrupt--`

suppose the central message loop in the `SleepMessages` example were in the `run` method of a thread's `Runnable` object. Then it might be modified as follows to support interrupts:

```
for (int i = 0; i < importantInfo.length; i++) {
    // Pause for 4 seconds
    try {
        Thread.sleep(4000);
    } catch (InterruptedException e) {
        // We've been interrupted: no more messages.
        return;
    }
    // Print a message
    System.out.println(importantInfo[i]);
}
```

Many methods that throw an `InterruptedException`, such as `sleep`, are designed to cancel their current operation and return immediately when an interrupt is received.

What if a thread goes a long time without invoking a method that throws `InterruptedException`? Then it must periodically invoke `Thread.interrupted`, which returns `true` if an interrupt has been received. Here is an example:

```
for (int i = 0; i < inputs.length; i++) {
    heavyCrunch(inputs[i]);
    if (Thread.interrupted()) {
        // We've been interrupted: no more crunching.
        return;
    }
}
```

In this simple example, the code simply tests for the interrupt and exits the thread if one has been received. In more complex applications, it might make more sense to throw an `InterruptedException`:

```
if (Thread.interrupted()) {
    throw new InterruptedException();
}
```

This allows interrupt handling code to be centralized in a `catch` clause.

The Interrupt Status Flag

The interrupt mechanism is implemented using an internal flag known as the *interrupt status*. Invoking `Thread.interrupt` sets this flag. When a thread checks for an interrupt by invoking the static method `Thread.interrupted`, interrupt status is cleared. The nonstatic `isInterrupted` method, which is used by one thread to query the interrupt status of another, does not change the interrupt status flag.

By convention, any method that exits by throwing an `InterruptedException` clears interrupt status when it does so. However, it's always possible that interrupt status will immediately be set again by another thread invoking `interrupt`.

Joins

The `join` method allows one thread to wait for the completion of another. If `t` is a `Thread` object whose thread is currently executing,

```
t.join();
```

causes the current thread to pause execution until `t`'s thread terminates. Overloads of `join` allow the programmer to specify a waiting period. However, as with `sleep`, `join` is dependent on the operating system for timing, so you should not assume that `join` will wait exactly as long as you specify. Like `sleep`, `join` responds to an interrupt by exiting with an `InterruptedException`.

The SimpleThreads Example

The following example brings together some of the concepts of this section. `SimpleThreads` consists of two threads. The first is the main thread that every Java application has. The main thread creates a new thread from the `Runnable` object, `MessageLoop`, and waits for it to finish. If the `MessageLoop` thread takes too long to finish, the main thread interrupts it.

The `MessageLoop` thread prints out a series of messages. If interrupted before it has printed all its messages, the `MessageLoop` thread prints a message and exits:

```java
public class SimpleThreads {

    // Display a message, preceded by
    // the name of the current thread
    static void threadMessage(String message) {
        String threadName =
            Thread.currentThread().getName();
        System.out.format("%s: %s%n",
                          threadName,
                          message);
    }

    private static class MessageLoop
        implements Runnable {
        public void run() {
            String importantInfo[] = {
                "Mares eat oats",
                "Does eat oats",
                "Little lambs eat ivy",
                "A kid will eat ivy too"
            };
```

13

```
        try {
            for (int i = 0;
                 i < importantInfo.length;
                 i++) {
                // Pause for 4 seconds
                Thread.sleep(4000);
                // Print a message
                threadMessage(importantInfo[i]);
            }
        } catch (InterruptedException e) {
            threadMessage("I wasn't done!");
        }
    }
}

public static void main(String args[])
    throws InterruptedException {

    // Delay, in milliseconds before
    // we interrupt MessageLoop
    // thread (default one hour).
    long patience = 1000 * 60 * 60;

    // If command line argument
    // present, gives patience
    // in seconds.
    if (args.length > 0) {
        try {
            patience = Long.parseLong(args[0]) * 1000;
        } catch (NumberFormatException e) {
            System.err.println("Argument must be an integer.");
            System.exit(1);
        }
    }

    threadMessage("Starting MessageLoop thread");
    long startTime = System.currentTimeMillis();
    Thread t = new Thread(new MessageLoop());
    t.start();

    threadMessage("Waiting for MessageLoop thread to finish");
    // loop until MessageLoop
    // thread exits
    while (t.isAlive()) {
        threadMessage("Still waiting...");
        // Wait maximum of 1 second
        // for MessageLoop thread
        // to finish.
        t.join(1000);
        if (((System.currentTimeMillis() - startTime) > patience)
              && t.isAlive()) {
            threadMessage("Tired of waiting!");
            t.interrupt();
            // Shouldn't be long now
            // -- wait indefinitely
            t.join();
        }
    }
}
```

```
            threadMessage("Finally!");
        }
    }
}
```

Synchronization

Threads communicate primarily by sharing access to fields and the objects reference fields refer to. This form of communication is extremely efficient but makes two kinds of errors possible: *thread interference* and *memory consistency errors*. The tool needed to prevent these errors is *synchronization*.

However, synchronization can introduce *thread contention*, which occurs when two or more threads try to access the same resource simultaneously *and* cause the Java runtime to execute one or more threads more slowly or even suspend their execution. Starvation and livelock are forms of thread contention. See the "Liveness" section for more information.

Thread Interference

Consider a simple class called Counter:

```
class Counter {
    private int c = 0;

    public void increment() {
        c++;
    }

    public void decrement() {
        c--;
    }

    public int value() {
        return c;
    }

}
```

Counter is designed so that each invocation of increment will add 1 to c and each invocation of decrement will subtract 1 from c. However, if a Counter object is referenced from multiple threads, interference between threads may prevent this from happening as expected.

Interference happens when two operations running in different threads but acting on the same data *interleave*. This means that the two operations consist of multiple steps and the sequences of steps overlap.

It might not seem possible for operations on instances of Counter to interleave, since both operations on c are single, simple statements. However, even simple statements can translate to multiple steps by the virtual machine. We won't examine the specific steps the virtual machine takes—it is enough to know that the single expression c++ can be decomposed into three steps:

1. Retrieve the current value of c.
2. Increment the retrieved value by 1.
3. Store the incremented value back in c.

The expression c-- can be decomposed the same way, except the second step decrements instead of increments. Suppose thread A invokes increment at about the same time thread B invokes decrement. If the initial value of c is 0, their interleaved actions might follow this sequence:

1. Thread A retrieves c.
2. Thread B retrieves c.
3. Thread A increments retrieved value; the result is 1.
4. Thread B decrements retrieved value; the result is –1.
5. Thread A stores result in c; c is now 1.
6. Thread B stores result in c; c is now –1.

Thread A's result is lost and overwritten by thread B. This particular interleaving is only one possibility. Under different circumstances, it might be thread B's result that gets lost, or there could be no error at all. Because they are unpredictable, thread interference bugs can be difficult to detect and fix.

Memory Consistency Errors

Memory consistency errors occur when different threads have inconsistent views of what should be the same data. The causes of memory consistency errors are complex and beyond the scope of this chapter. Fortunately, the programmer does not need a detailed understanding of these causes. All that is needed is a strategy for avoiding them.

The key to avoiding memory consistency errors is understanding the *happens-before* relationship. This relationship is simply a guarantee that memory writes by one specific statement are visible to another specific statement. To see this, consider the following example. Suppose a simple int field is defined and initialized:

```
int counter = 0;
```

The counter field is shared between two threads, A and B. Suppose thread A increments counter:

```
counter++;
```

Then, shortly afterward, thread B prints out `counter`:

```
System.out.println(counter);
```

If the two statements had been executed in the same thread, it would be safe to assume that the value printed out would be 1. But if the two statements are executed in separate threads, the value printed out might well be 0 because there's no guarantee that thread A's change to `counter` will be visible to thread B—unless the programmer has established a happens-before relationship between these two statements.

There are several actions that create happens-before relationships. One of them is synchronization, as we will see in the following sections.

We've already seen two actions that create happens-before relationships:

- When a statement invokes `Thread.start`, every statement that has a happens-before relationship with that statement also has a happens-before relationship with every statement executed by the new thread. The effects of the code that led up to the creation of the new thread are visible to the new thread.
- When a thread terminates and causes a `Thread.join` in another thread to return, then all the statements executed by the terminated thread have a happens-before relationship with all the statements following the successful join. The effects of the code in the thread are now visible to the thread that performed the join.

For a list of actions that create happens-before relationships, refer to the Summary page of the `java.util.concurrent` package.[5]

Synchronized Methods

The Java programming language provides two basic synchronization idioms: *synchronized methods* and *synchronized statements*. The more complex of the two, synchronized statements, is described in the next section. This section is about synchronized methods.

To make a method synchronized, simply add the `synchronized` keyword to its declaration:

```
public class SynchronizedCounter {
    private int c = 0;
```

---

5.   8/docs/api/java/util/concurrent/package-summary.html#MemoryVisibility

```
    public synchronized void increment() {
        c++;
    }

    public synchronized void decrement() {
        c--;
    }

    public synchronized int value() {
        return c;
    }
}
```

If count is an instance of SynchronizedCounter, then making these methods synchronized has two effects:

- First, it is not possible for two invocations of synchronized methods on the same object to interleave. When one thread is executing a synchronized method for an object, all other threads that invoke synchronized methods for the same object block (suspend execution) until the first thread is done with the object.
- Second, when a synchronized method exits, it automatically establishes a happens-before relationship with *any subsequent invocation* of a synchronized method for the same object. This guarantees that changes to the state of the object are visible to all threads.

Note that constructors cannot be synchronized; using the synchronized keyword with a constructor is a syntax error. Synchronizing constructors doesn't make sense because only the thread that creates an object should have access to it while it is being constructed.

> **Note**
> When constructing an object that will be shared between threads, be very careful that a reference to the object does not "leak" prematurely. For example, suppose you want to maintain a List called instances containing every instance of class. You might be tempted to add the following line to your constructor:
>
> ```
> instances.add(this);
> ```
>
> But then other threads can use instances to access the object before construction of the object is complete.

Synchronized methods enable a simple strategy for preventing thread interference and memory consistency errors: if an object is visible to more than one thread, all reads or writes to that object's variables are done through synchronized methods. (An important exception is that final fields, which cannot be modified after the object is constructed, can be safely read through nonsynchronized methods once the object is constructed.) This strategy is effective but can present problems with liveness, as we'll see later in this chapter.

Intrinsic Locks and Synchronization

Synchronization is built around an internal entity known as the *intrinsic lock* or *monitor lock*. (The API specification often refers to this entity simply as a "monitor.") Intrinsic locks play a role in both aspects of synchronization: enforcing exclusive access to an object's state and establishing happens-before relationships that are essential to visibility.

Every object has an intrinsic lock associated with it. By convention, a thread that needs exclusive and consistent access to an object's fields has to *acquire* the object's intrinsic lock before accessing them and then *release* the intrinsic lock when it's done with them. A thread is said to *own* the intrinsic lock between the time it has acquired the lock and released the lock. As long as a thread owns an intrinsic lock, no other thread can acquire the same lock. The other thread will block when it attempts to acquire the lock.

When a thread releases an intrinsic lock, a happens-before relationship is established between that action and any subsequent acquisition of the same lock.

Locks in Synchronized Methods

When a thread invokes a synchronized method, it automatically acquires the intrinsic lock for that method's object and releases it when the method returns. The lock release occurs even if the return was caused by an uncaught exception.

You might wonder what happens when a static synchronized method is invoked, since a static method is associated with a class, not an object. In this case, the thread acquires the intrinsic lock for the `Class` object associated with the class. Thus access to a class's static fields is controlled by a lock that's distinct from the lock for any instance of the class.

Synchronized Statements

Another way to create synchronized code is with *synchronized statements*. Unlike synchronized methods, synchronized statements must specify the object that provides the intrinsic lock:

```
public void addName(String name) {
    synchronized(this) {
        lastName = name;
        nameCount++;
    }
    nameList.add(name);
}
```

13

In this example, the addName method needs to synchronize changes to last-Name and nameCount but also needs to avoid synchronizing invocations of other objects' methods. (Invoking other objects' methods from synchronized code can create problems that are described in the "Liveness" section.) Without synchronized statements, there would have to be a separate, unsynchronized method for the sole purpose of invoking nameList.add.

Synchronized statements are also useful for improving concurrency with fine-grained synchronization. Suppose, for example, class MsLunch has two instance fields, c1 and c2, that are never used together. All updates of these fields must be synchronized, but there's no reason to prevent an update of c1 from being interleaved with an update of c2—and doing so reduces concurrency by creating unnecessary blocking. Instead of using synchronized methods or otherwise using the lock associated with this, we create two objects solely to provide locks:

```
public class MsLunch {
    private long c1 = 0;
    private long c2 = 0;
    private Object lock1 = new Object();
    private Object lock2 = new Object();

    public void inc1() {
        synchronized(lock1) {
            c1++;
        }
    }

    public void inc2() {
        synchronized(lock2) {
            c2++;
        }
    }
}
```

Use this idiom with extreme care. You must be absolutely sure that it really is safe to interleave access of the affected fields.

Reentrant Synchronization

Recall that a thread cannot acquire a lock owned by another thread but a thread *can* acquire a lock that it already owns. Allowing a thread to acquire the same lock more than once enables *reentrant synchronization*. This describes a situation where synchronized code directly or indirectly invokes a method that also contains synchronized code and both sets of code use the same lock. Without reentrant synchronization, synchronized code would have to take many additional precautions to avoid having a thread cause itself to block.

Atomic Access

In programming, an *atomic* action is one that effectively happens all at once. An atomic action cannot stop in the middle: it either happens completely or doesn't happen at all. No side effects of an atomic action are visible until the action is complete.

We have already seen that an increment expression such as c++ does not describe an atomic action. Even very simple expressions can define complex actions that can decompose into other actions. However, there are actions you can specify that are atomic:

- Reads and writes are atomic for reference variables and for most primitive variables (all types except long and double).
- Reads and writes are atomic for *all* variables declared volatile (*including* long and double variables).

Atomic actions cannot be interleaved, so they can be used without fear of thread interference. However, this does not eliminate all need to synchronize atomic actions, because memory consistency errors are still possible. Using volatile variables reduces the risk of memory consistency errors, because any write to a volatile variable establishes a happens-before relationship with subsequent reads of that same variable. This means that changes to a volatile variable are always visible to other threads. What's more, it also means that when a thread reads a volatile variable, it sees not just the latest change to the volatile but also the side effects of the code that led up to the change.

Using simple atomic variable access is more efficient than accessing these variables through synchronized code but requires more care by the programmer to avoid memory consistency errors. Whether the extra effort is worthwhile depends on the size and complexity of the application.

Some of the classes in the java.util.concurrent package provide atomic methods that do not rely on synchronization.[6] We'll discuss them in the "High-Level Concurrency Objects" section.

Liveness

A concurrent application's ability to execute in a timely manner is known as its *liveness*. This section describes the most common kind of liveness problem, deadlock, and goes on to briefly describe two other liveness problems, starvation and livelock.

---

6.   8/docs/api/java/util/concurrent/package-summary.html

Deadlock

Deadlock describes a situation where two or more threads are blocked forever, waiting for each other. Here's an example.

Alphonse and Gaston are friends and great believers in courtesy. A strict rule of courtesy is that when you bow to a friend, you must remain bowed until your friend has a chance to return the bow. Unfortunately, this rule does not account for the possibility that two friends might bow to each other at the same time. This example application, `Deadlock`, models this possibility:

```java
public class Deadlock {
    static class Friend {
        private final String name;
        public Friend(String name) {
            this.name = name;
        }
        public String getName() {
            return this.name;
        }
        public synchronized void bow(Friend bower) {
            System.out.format("%s: %s"
                + "  has bowed to me!%n",
                this.name, bower.getName());
            bower.bowBack(this);
        }
        public synchronized void bowBack(Friend bower) {
            System.out.format("%s: %s"
                + " has bowed back to me!%n",
                this.name, bower.getName());
        }
    }

    public static void main(String[] args) {
        final Friend alphonse =
            new Friend("Alphonse");
        final Friend gaston =
            new Friend("Gaston");
        new Thread(new Runnable() {
            public void run() { alphonse.bow(gaston); }
        }).start();
        new Thread(new Runnable() {
            public void run() { gaston.bow(alphonse); }
        }).start();
    }
}
```

When `Deadlock` runs, it's extremely likely that both threads will block when they attempt to invoke `bowBack`. Neither block will ever end because each thread is waiting for the other to exit `bow`.

Starvation and Livelock

Starvation and livelock are much less common than deadlock but are still problems that every designer of concurrent software is likely to encounter.

Starvation

Starvation describes a situation where a thread is unable to gain regular access to shared resources and is unable to make progress. This happens when shared resources are made unavailable for long periods by "greedy" threads. For example, suppose an object provides a synchronized method that often takes a long time to return. If one thread invokes this method frequently, other threads that also need frequent synchronized access to the same object will often be blocked.

Livelock

A thread often acts in response to the action of another thread. If the other thread's action is also a response to the action of another thread, then *livelock* may result. As with deadlock, livelocked threads are unable to make further progress. However, the threads are not blocked—they are simply too busy responding to each other to resume work. This is comparable to two people attempting to pass each other in a corridor: Alphonse moves to his left to let Gaston pass, while Gaston moves to his right to let Alphonse pass. Seeing that they are still blocking each other, Alphone moves to his right, while Gaston moves to his left. They're still blocking each other, so...

Guarded Blocks

Threads often have to coordinate their actions. The most common coordination idiom is the *guarded block*. Such a block begins by polling a condition that must be true before the block can proceed. There are a number of steps to follow in order to do this correctly.

Suppose, for example, guardedJoy is a method that must not proceed until a shared variable joy has been set by another thread. Such a method could, in theory, simply loop until the condition is satisfied, but that loop is wasteful, since it executes continuously while waiting:

```
public void guardedJoy() {
    // Simple loop guard. Wastes
    // processor time. Don't do this!
    while(!joy) {}
    System.out.println("Joy has been achieved!");
}
```

A more efficient guard invokes `Object.wait`[7] to suspend the current thread. The invocation of `wait` does not return until another thread has issued a notification that some special event may have occurred—though not necessarily the event this thread is waiting for:

```
public synchronized void guardedJoy() {
    // This guard only loops once for each special event, which may not
    // be the event we're waiting for.
    while(!joy) {
        try {
            wait();
        } catch (InterruptedException e) {}
    }
    System.out.println("Joy and efficiency have been achieved!");
}
```

> **Note**
>
> Always invoke `wait` inside a loop that tests for the condition being waited for. Don't assume that the interrupt was for the particular condition you were waiting for or that the condition is still true.

Like many methods that suspend execution, `wait` can throw an `Interrupted-Exception`. In this example, we can just ignore that exception—we only care about the value of `joy`.

Why is this version of `guardedJoy` synchronized? Suppose d is the object we're using to invoke `wait`. When a thread invokes `d.wait`, it must own the intrinsic lock for d; otherwise an error is thrown. Invoking `wait` inside a synchronized method is a simple way to acquire the intrinsic lock.

When `wait` is invoked, the thread releases the lock and suspends execution. At some future time, another thread will acquire the same lock and invoke `Object.notifyAll`,[8] informing all threads waiting on that lock that something important has happened:

```
public synchronized notifyJoy() {
    joy = true;
    notifyAll();
}
```

Some time after the second thread has released the lock, the first thread reacquires the lock and resumes by returning from the invocation of `wait`.

---

7.   8/docs/api/java/lang/Object.html#wait--

8.   8/docs/api/java/lang/Object.html#notifyAll--

> **Note**
>
> There is a second notification method, `notify`, which wakes up a single thread. Because `notify` doesn't allow you to specify the thread that is woken up, it is useful only in massively parallel applications—that is, programs with a large number of threads, all doing similar chores. In such an application, you don't care which thread gets woken up.

Let's use guarded blocks to create a *producer-consumer* application. This kind of application shares data between two threads: the *producer*, which creates the data, and the *consumer*, which does something with it. The two threads communicate using a shared object. Coordination is essential: the consumer thread must not attempt to retrieve the data before the producer thread has delivered it, and the producer thread must not attempt to deliver new data if the consumer hasn't retrieved the old data.

In this example, the data is a series of text messages that are shared through an object of type `Drop`:

```java
public class Drop {
    // Message sent from producer
    // to consumer.
    private String message;
    // True if consumer should wait
    // for producer to send message,
    // false if producer should wait for
    // consumer to retrieve message.
    private boolean empty = true;

    public synchronized String take() {
        // Wait until message is
        // available.
        while (empty) {
            try {
                wait();
            } catch (InterruptedException e) {}
        }
        // Toggle status.
        empty = true;
        // Notify producer that
        // status has changed.
        notifyAll();
        return message;
    }

    public synchronized void put(String message) {
        // Wait until message has
        // been retrieved.
        while (!empty) {
            try {
                wait();
```

13

```
            } catch (InterruptedException e) {}
        }
        // Toggle status.
        empty = false;
        // Store message.
        this.message = message;
        // Notify consumer that status
        // has changed.
        notifyAll();
    }
}
```

The producer thread, defined in `Producer`, sends a series of familiar messages. The string `"DONE"` indicates that all messages have been sent. To simulate the unpredictable nature of real-world applications, the producer thread pauses for random intervals between messages:

```
import java.util.Random;

public class Producer implements Runnable {
    private Drop drop;

    public Producer(Drop drop) {
        this.drop = drop;
    }

    public void run() {
        String importantInfo[] = {
            "Mares eat oats",
            "Does eat oats",
            "Little lambs eat ivy",
            "A kid will eat ivy too"
        };
        Random random = new Random();

        for (int i = 0;
             i < importantInfo.length;
             i++) {
            drop.put(importantInfo[i]);
            try {
                Thread.sleep(random.nextInt(5000));
            } catch (InterruptedException e) {}
        }
        drop.put("DONE");
    }
}
```

The consumer thread, defined in `Consumer`, simply retrieves the messages and prints them out until it retrieves the `"DONE"` string. This thread also pauses for random intervals:

```
import java.util.Random;

public class Consumer implements Runnable {
```

```
        private Drop drop;

        public Consumer(Drop drop) {
            this.drop = drop;
        }

        public void run() {
            Random random = new Random();
            for (String message = drop.take();
                 ! message.equals("DONE");
                 message = drop.take()) {
                System.out.format("MESSAGE RECEIVED: %s%n", message);
                try {
                    Thread.sleep(random.nextInt(5000));
                } catch (InterruptedException e) {}
            }
        }
    }
```

Finally, here is the main thread, defined in `ProducerConsumerExample`, that launches the producer and consumer threads:

```
public class ProducerConsumerExample {
    public static void main(String[] args) {
        Drop drop = new Drop();
        (new Thread(new Producer(drop))).start();
        (new Thread(new Consumer(drop))).start();
    }
}
```

13

> **Note**
>
> The `Drop` class was written in order to demonstrate guarded blocks. To avoid reinventing the wheel, examine the existing data structures in the Java Collections Framework (Chapter 12) before trying to code your own data-sharing objects. For more information, refer to the questions and exercises at the end of the chapter.

Immutable Objects

An object is considered *immutable* if its state cannot change after it is constructed. Maximum reliance on immutable objects is widely accepted as a sound strategy for creating simple, reliable code.

Immutable objects are particularly useful in concurrent applications. Since they cannot change state, they cannot be corrupted by thread interference or observed in an inconsistent state.

Programmers are often reluctant to employ immutable objects because they worry about the cost of creating a new object as opposed to updating an object in place. The impact of object creation is often overestimated and can be offset by some of the efficiencies associated with immutable objects. These include decreased overhead due to garbage collection and the elimination of code needed to protect mutable objects from corruption.

The following subsections take a class whose instances are mutable and derive a class with immutable instances from it. In doing so, they give general rules for this kind of conversion and demonstrate some of the advantages of immutable objects.

A Synchronized Class Example

The class, SynchronizedRGB, defines objects that represent colors. Each object represents the color as three integers that stand for primary color values and a string that gives the name of the color:

```java
public class SynchronizedRGB {

    // Values must be between 0 and 255.
    private int red;
    private int green;
    private int blue;
    private String name;

    private void check(int red,
                       int green,
                       int blue) {
        if (red < 0 || red > 255
            || green < 0 || green > 255
            || blue < 0 || blue > 255) {
            throw new IllegalArgumentException();
        }
    }

    public SynchronizedRGB(int red,
                           int green,
                           int blue,
                           String name) {
        check(red, green, blue);
        this.red = red;
        this.green = green;
        this.blue = blue;
        this.name = name;
    }

    public void set(int red,
                    int green,
                    int blue,
                    String name) {
        check(red, green, blue);
        synchronized (this) {
            this.red = red;
            this.green = green;
            this.blue = blue;
            this.name = name;
        }
    }
}
```

13

```
    public synchronized int getRGB() {
        return ((red << 16) | (green << 8) | blue);
    }

    public synchronized String getName() {
        return name;
    }

    public synchronized void invert() {
        red = 255 - red;
        green = 255 - green;
        blue = 255 - blue;
        name = "Inverse of " + name;
    }
}
```

SynchronizedRGB must be used carefully to avoid being seen in an inconsistent state. Suppose, for example, a thread executes the following code:

```
SynchronizedRGB color =
    new SynchronizedRGB(0, 0, 0, "Pitch Black");
...
int myColorInt = color.getRGB();        //Statement 1
String myColorName = color.getName(); //Statement 2
```

If another thread invokes color.set after statement 1 but before statement 2, the value of myColorInt won't match the value of myColorName. To avoid this outcome, the two statements must be bound together:

```
synchronized (color) {
    int myColorInt = color.getRGB();
    String myColorName = color.getName();
}
```

This kind of inconsistency is only possible for mutable objects; it will not be an issue for the immutable version of SynchronizedRGB.

A Strategy for Defining Immutable Objects

The following rules define a simple strategy for creating immutable objects. Not all classes documented as "immutable" follow these rules. This does not necessarily mean the creators of these classes were sloppy; they may have good reason for believing that instances of their classes never change after construction. However, such strategies require sophisticated analysis and are not for beginners:

1. Don't provide "setter" methods—methods that modify fields or objects referred to by fields.
2. Make all fields final and private.

3. Don't allow subclasses to override methods. The simplest way to do this is to declare the class as `final`. A more sophisticated approach is to make the constructor `private` and construct instances in factory methods.

4. If the instance fields include references to mutable objects, don't allow those objects to be changed:

   ◻ Don't provide methods that modify the mutable objects.

   ◻ Don't share references to the mutable objects. Never store references to external, mutable objects passed to the constructor; if necessary, create copies and store references to the copies. Similarly, create copies of your internal mutable objects when necessary to avoid returning the originals in your methods.

Applying this strategy to `SynchronizedRGB` results in the following steps:

1. There are two setter methods in this class. The first one, `set`, arbitrarily transforms the object and has no place in an immutable version of the class. The second one, `invert`, can be adapted by having it create a new object instead of modifying the existing one.

2. All fields are already `private`; they are further qualified as `final`.

3. The class itself is declared `final`.

4. Only one field refers to an object, and that object is itself immutable. Therefore no safeguards against changing the state of "contained" mutable objects are necessary.

After these changes, we have `ImmutableRGB`:

```
final public class ImmutableRGB {

    // Values must be between 0 and 255.
    final private int red;
    final private int green;
    final private int blue;
    final private String name;

    private void check(int red,
                       int green,
                       int blue) {
        if (red < 0 || red > 255
            || green < 0 || green > 255
            || blue < 0 || blue > 255) {
            throw new IllegalArgumentException();
        }
    }

    public ImmutableRGB(int red,
                        int green,
```

```
                            int blue,
                            String name) {
        check(red, green, blue);
        this.red = red;
        this.green = green;
        this.blue = blue;
        this.name = name;
    }


    public int getRGB() {
        return ((red << 16) | (green << 8) | blue);
    }

    public String getName() {
        return name;
    }

    public ImmutableRGB invert() {
        return new ImmutableRGB(255 - red,
                       255 - green,
                       255 - blue,
                       "Inverse of " + name);
    }
}
```

High-Level Concurrency Objects

So far this chapter has focused on the low-level APIs that have been part of the Java platform from the very beginning. These APIs are adequate for very basic tasks, but higher-level building blocks are needed for more advanced tasks. This is especially true for massively concurrent applications that fully exploit today's multiprocessor and multicore systems.

In this section we'll look at some of the high-level concurrency features, most of which are implemented in the `java.util.concurrent` packages. There are also concurrent data structures in the Java Collections Framework:

- Lock objects support locking idioms that simplify many concurrent applications.
- Executors define a high-level API for launching and managing threads. Executor implementations provided by `java.util.concurrent` provide thread-pool management suitable for large-scale applications.
- Concurrent collections make it easier to manage large collections of data and can greatly reduce the need for synchronization.
- Atomic variables have features that minimize synchronization and help avoid memory consistency errors.
- `ThreadLocalRandom` provides efficient generation of pseudorandom numbers from multiple threads.

Lock Objects

Synchronized code relies on a simple kind of reentrant lock. This kind of lock is easy to use but has many limitations. More sophisticated locking idioms are supported by the `java.util.concurrent.locks` package.[9] We won't examine this package in detail but instead will focus on its most basic interface, `Lock`.[10]

Lock objects work very much like the implicit locks used by synchronized code. As with implicit locks, only one thread can own a `Lock` object at a time. `Lock` objects also support a `wait/notify` mechanism through their associated `Condition` objects.[11]

The biggest advantage of `Lock` objects over implicit locks is their ability to back out of an attempt to acquire a lock. The `tryLock` method backs out if the lock is not available immediately or before a timeout expires (if specified). The `lockInterruptibly` method backs out if another thread sends an interrupt before the lock is acquired.

Let's use `Lock` objects to solve the deadlock problem we saw in the "Liveness" section. Alphonse and Gaston have trained themselves to notice when a friend is about to bow. We model this improvement by requiring that our `Friend` objects must acquire locks for *both* participants before proceeding with the bow. Here is the source code for the improved model, `Safelock`. To demonstrate the versatility of this idiom, we assume that Alphonse and Gaston are so infatuated with their new-found ability to bow safely that they can't stop bowing to each other:

```java
import java.util.concurrent.locks.Lock;
import java.util.concurrent.locks.ReentrantLock;
import java.util.Random;

public class Safelock {
    static class Friend {
        private final String name;
        private final Lock lock = new ReentrantLock();

        public Friend(String name) {
            this.name = name;
        }

        public String getName() {
            return this.name;
        }

        public boolean impendingBow(Friend bower) {
            Boolean myLock = false;
            Boolean yourLock = false;
```

---

9.   8/docs/api/java/util/concurrent/locks/package-summary.html

10. 8/docs/api/java/util/concurrent/locks/Lock.html

11. 8/docs/api/java/util/concurrent/locks/Condition.html

```
        try {
            myLock = lock.tryLock();
            yourLock = bower.lock.tryLock();
        } finally {
            if (! (myLock && yourLock)) {
                if (myLock) {
                    lock.unlock();
                }
                if (yourLock) {
                    bower.lock.unlock();
                }
            }
        }
        return myLock && yourLock;
    }

    public void bow(Friend bower) {
        if (impendingBow(bower)) {
            try {
                System.out.format("%s: %s has"
                    + " bowed to me!%n",
                    this.name, bower.getName());
                bower.bowBack(this);
            } finally {
                lock.unlock();
                bower.lock.unlock();
            }
        } else {
            System.out.format("%s: %s started"
                + " to bow to me, but saw that"
                + " I was already bowing to"
                + " him.%n",
                this.name, bower.getName());
        }
    }

    public void bowBack(Friend bower) {
        System.out.format("%s: %s has" +
            " bowed back to me!%n",
            this.name, bower.getName());
    }
}

static class BowLoop implements Runnable {
    private Friend bower;
    private Friend bowee;

    public BowLoop(Friend bower, Friend bowee) {
        this.bower = bower;
        this.bowee = bowee;
    }

    public void run() {
        Random random = new Random();
        for (;;) {
            try {
                Thread.sleep(random.nextInt(10));
            } catch (InterruptedException e) {}
```

13

```
                        bowee.bow(bower);
                    }
                }
            }


    public static void main(String[] args) {
        final Friend alphonse =
            new Friend("Alphonse");
        final Friend gaston =
            new Friend("Gaston");
        new Thread(new BowLoop(alphonse, gaston)).start();
        new Thread(new BowLoop(gaston, alphonse)).start();
    }
}
```

Executors

In the previous examples, there's a close connection between the task being done by a new thread, as defined by its `Runnable` object, and the thread itself, as defined by a `Thread` object. This works well for small applications, but in large-scale applications, it makes sense to separate thread management and creation from the rest of the application. Objects that encapsulate these functions are known as *executors*. The following subsections describe executors in detail:

- "Executor Interfaces" defines the three executor object types.
- "Thread Pools" are the most common kind of executor implementation.
- "Fork/Join" is a framework for taking advantage of multiple processors.

Executor Interfaces

The `java.util.concurrent` package defines three executor interfaces:

- `Executor`, a simple interface that supports launching new tasks
- `ExecutorService`, a subinterface of `Executor`, which adds features that help manage the life cycles of the individual tasks and of the executor itself
- `ScheduledExecutorService`, a subinterface of `ExecutorService`, which supports future and/or periodic execution of tasks

Typically, variables that refer to executor objects are declared as one of these three interface types, not with an executor class type.

The Executor Interface

The Executor interface provides a single method, execute, designed to be a drop-in replacement for a common thread-creation idiom.[12] If r is a Runnable object and e is an Executor object, you can replace

```
(new Thread(r)).start();
```

with

```
e.execute(r);
```

However, the definition of execute is less specific. The low-level idiom creates a new thread and launches it immediately. Depending on the Executor implementation, execute may do the same thing but is more likely to use an existing worker thread to run r or place r in a queue to wait for a worker thread to become available. (We'll describe worker threads in the "Thread Pools" section.)

The executor implementations in java.util.concurrent are designed to make full use of the more advanced ExecutorService and ScheduledExecutorService interfaces, although they also work with the base Executor interface.

The ExecutorService Interface

The ExecutorService interface supplements execute with a similar but more versatile submit method.[13] Like execute, submit accepts Runnable objects but also accepts Callable objects, which allow the task to return a value.[14] The submit method returns a Future object, which is used to retrieve the Callable return value and to manage the status of both Callable and Runnable tasks.[15]

ExecutorService also provides methods for submitting large collections of Callable objects. Finally, ExecutorService provides a number of methods for managing the shutdown of the executor. To support immediate shutdown, tasks should handle interrupts correctly.

---

12. 8/docs/api/java/util/concurrent/Executor.html

13. 8/docs/api/java/util/concurrent/ExecutorService.html

14. 8/docs/api/java/util/concurrent/Callable.html

15. 8/docs/api/java/util/concurrent/Future.html

The ScheduledExecutorService Interface

The `ScheduledExecutorService` interface supplements the methods of its parent `ExecutorService` with schedule, which executes a `Runnable` or `Callable` task after a specified delay.[16] In addition, the interface defines `scheduleAtFixed-Rate` and `scheduleWithFixedDelay`, which executes specified tasks repeatedly at defined intervals.

Thread Pools

Most of the executor implementations in `java.util.concurrent` use *thread pools*, which consist of *worker threads*. This kind of thread exists separately from the `Runnable` and `Callable` tasks it executes and is often used to execute multiple tasks.

Using worker threads minimizes the overhead due to thread creation. Thread objects use a significant amount of memory, and in a large-scale application, allocating and deallocating many thread objects creates a significant memory management overhead.

One common type of thread pool is the *fixed thread pool*. This type of pool always has a specified number of threads running; if a thread is somehow terminated while it is still in use, it is automatically replaced with a new thread. Tasks are submitted to the pool via an internal queue, which holds extra tasks whenever there are more active tasks than threads.

An important advantage of the fixed thread pool is that applications using it *degrade gracefully*. To understand this, consider a web server application where each HTTP request is handled by a separate thread. If the application simply creates a new thread for every new HTTP request and the system receives more requests than it can handle immediately, the application will suddenly stop responding to *all* requests when the overhead of all those threads exceed the capacity of the system. With a limit on the number of the threads that can be created, the application will not be servicing HTTP requests as quickly as they come in, but it will be servicing them as quickly as the system can sustain.

A simple way to create an executor that uses a fixed thread pool is to invoke the `newFixedThreadPool`[17] factory method in `java.util.concurrent.Executors`.[18] This class also provides the following factory methods:

---

16.   `8/docs/api/java/util/concurrent/ScheduledExecutorService.html`

17.   `8/docs/api/java/util/concurrent/Executors.html#newFixedThreadPool`
      `-int-`

18.   `8/docs/api/java/util/concurrent/Executors.html`

- The `newCachedThreadPool` method creates an executor with an expandable thread pool. This executor is suitable for applications that launch many short-lived tasks.[19]

- The `newSingleThreadExecutor` method creates an executor that executes a single task at a time.[20]

- Several factory methods are `ScheduledExecutorService` versions of the above executors.

If none of the executors provided by the above factory methods meet your needs, constructing instances of `java.util.concurrent.ThreadPoolExecutor`[21] or `java.util.concurrent.ScheduledThreadPoolExecutor`[22] will give you additional options.

Fork/Join

The fork/join framework is an implementation of the `ExecutorService` interface that helps you take advantage of multiple processors. It is designed for work that can be broken into smaller pieces recursively. The goal is to use all the available processing power to enhance the performance of your application.

As with any `ExecutorService` implementation, the fork/join framework distributes tasks to worker threads in a thread pool. The fork/join framework is distinct because it uses a *work-stealing* algorithm. Worker threads that run out of things to do can steal tasks from other threads that are still busy.

The center of the fork/join framework is the `ForkJoinPool` class, an extension of the `AbstractExecutorService` class.[23] `ForkJoinPool` implements the core work-stealing algorithm and can execute `ForkJoinTask` processes.[24]

Basic Use

The first step for using the fork/join framework is to write code that performs a segment of the work. Your code should look similar to the following pseudocode:

---

19. 8/docs/api/java/util/concurrent/Executors.html#newCachedThreadPool
     -int-
20. 8/docs/api/java/util/concurrent/Executors.html#newSingleThreadExecutor
     -int-
21. 8/docs/api/java/util/concurrent/ThreadPoolExecutor.html
22. 8/docs/api/java/util/concurrent/ScheduledThreadPoolExecutor.html
23. 8/docs/api/java/util/concurrent/ForkJoinPool.html
24. 8/docs/api/java/util/concurrent/ForkJoinTask.html

```
if (my portion of the work is small enough)
  do the work directly
else
  split my work into two pieces
  invoke the two pieces and wait for the results
```

Wrap this code in a `ForkJoinTask` subclass, typically using one of its more specialized types—either `RecursiveTask`[25] (which can return a result) or `RecursiveAction`.[26] After your `ForkJoinTask` subclass is ready, create the object that represents all the work to be done and pass it to the `invoke()` method of a `ForkJoinPool` instance.

Blurring for Clarity

To help you understand how the fork/join framework works, consider the following example. Suppose you want to blur an image. The original *source* image is represented by an array of integers, where each integer contains the color values for a single pixel. The blurred *destination* image is also represented by an integer array with the same size as the source.

Performing the blur is accomplished by working through the source array one pixel at a time. Each pixel is averaged with its surrounding pixels (the red, green, and blue components are averaged), and the result is placed in the destination array. Since an image is a large array, this process can take a long time. You can take advantage of concurrent processing on multiprocessor systems by implementing the algorithm using the fork/join framework. Here is one possible implementation:

```
public class ForkBlur extends RecursiveAction {
    private int[] mSource;
    private int mStart;
    private int mLength;
    private int[] mDestination;

    // Processing window size; should be odd.
    private int mBlurWidth = 15;

    public ForkBlur(int[] src, int start, int length, int[] dst) {
        mSource = src;
        mStart = start;
        mLength = length;
        mDestination = dst;
    }

    protected void computeDirectly() {
        int sidePixels = (mBlurWidth - 1) / 2;
        for (int index = mStart; index < mStart + mLength; index++) {
```

---

25. 8/docs/api/java/util/concurrent/RecursiveTask.html
26. 8/docs/api/java/util/concurrent/RecursiveAction.html

```
// Calculate average.
float rt = 0, gt = 0, bt = 0;
for (int mi = -sidePixels; mi <= sidePixels; mi++) {
    int mindex = Math.min(Math.max(mi + index, 0),
                          mSource.length - 1);
    int pixel = mSource[mindex];
    rt += (float)((pixel & 0x00ff0000) >> 16)
            / mBlurWidth;
    gt += (float)((pixel & 0x0000ff00) >>  8)
            / mBlurWidth;
    bt += (float)((pixel & 0x000000ff) >>  0)
            / mBlurWidth;
}

// Reassemble destination pixel.
int dpixel = (0xff000000      ) |
        (((int)rt) << 16) |
        (((int)gt) <<  8) |
        (((int)bt) <<  0);
mDestination[index] = dpixel;
        }
    }

    ...
```

Now you implement the abstract `compute()` method, which either performs the blur directly or splits it into two smaller tasks. A simple array length threshold helps determine whether the work is performed or split:

```
protected static int sThreshold = 100000;

protected void compute() {
    if (mLength < sThreshold) {
        computeDirectly();
        return;
    }

    int split = mLength / 2;

    invokeAll(new ForkBlur(mSource, mStart, split, mDestination),
            new ForkBlur(mSource, mStart + split, mLength - split,
                    mDestination));
}
```

If the previous methods are in a subclass of the `RecursiveAction` class, then setting up the task to run in a `ForkJoinPool` is straightforward and involves the following steps:

1. Create a task that represents all the work to be done.

```
// source image pixels are in src
// destination image pixels are in dst
ForkBlur fb = new ForkBlur(src, 0, src.length, dst);
```

2. Create the `ForkJoinPool` that will run the task.

    ```
    ForkJoinPool pool = new ForkJoinPool();
    ```

3. Run the task.

    ```
    pool.invoke(fb);
    ```

For the full source code, including some extra code that creates the destination image file, see the `ForkBlur` example.

Standard Implementations

Besides using the fork/join framework to implement custom algorithms for tasks to be performed concurrently on a multiprocessor system (such as the `ForkBlur.java` example in the previous section), there are some generally useful features in Java SE that are already implemented using the fork/join framework. One such implementation, introduced in Java SE 8, is used by the `java.util.Arrays` class for its `parallelSort()` methods.[27] These methods are similar to `sort()` but leverage concurrency via the fork/join framework. Parallel sorting of large arrays is faster than sequential sorting when run on multiprocessor systems. However, how exactly the fork/join framework is leveraged by these methods is outside the scope of this book. For this information, see the Java API documentation.

Another implementation of the fork/join framework is used by methods in the `java.util.streams` package. For more information, see Chapter 12, "Parallelism."

Concurrent Collections

The `java.util.concurrent` package includes a number of additions to the Java Collections Framework. These are most easily categorized by the collection interfaces provided:

- `BlockingQueue`[28] defines a first-in, first-out data structure that blocks or times out when you attempt to add to a full queue or retrieve from an empty queue.
- `ConcurrentMap`[29] is a subinterface of `java.util.Map`[30] that defines useful atomic operations. These operations remove or replace a key-value pair only if the key is present or add a key-value pair only if the key is absent. Making these operations atomic helps avoid synchronization. The standard general-purpose

---

27.   8/docs/api/java/util/Arrays.html
28.   8/docs/api/java/util/concurrent/BlockingQueue.html
29.   8/docs/api/java/util/concurrent/ConcurrentMap.html
30.   8/docs/api/java/util/Map.html

implementation of `ConcurrentMap` is `ConcurrentHashMap`,[31] which is a concurrent analog of `HashMap`.[32]

- `ConcurrentNavigableMap`[33] is a subinterface of `ConcurrentMap` that supports approximate matches. The standard general-purpose implementation of `ConcurrentNavigableMap` is `ConcurrentSkipListMap`,[34] which is a concurrent analog of `TreeMap`.[35]

All these collections help avoid memory consistency errors by defining a happens-before relationship between an operation that adds an object to the collection with subsequent operations that access or remove that object.

Atomic Variables

The `java.util.concurrent.atomic` package defines classes that support atomic operations on single variables.[36] All classes have `get` and `set` methods that work like reads and writes on `volatile` variables—that is, a `set` has a happens-before relationship with any subsequent `get` on the same variable. The atomic `compareAndSet` method also has these memory consistency features, as do the simple atomic arithmetic methods that apply to integer atomic variables.

To see how this package might be used, let's return to the `Counter` class we originally used to demonstrate thread interference:

```java
class Counter {
    private int c = 0;

    public void increment() {
        c++;
    }

    public void decrement() {
        c--;
    }

    public int value() {
        return c;
    }

}
```

13

---

31. 8/docs/api/java/util/concurrent/ConcurrentHashMap.html
32. 8/docs/api/java/util/HashMap.html
33. 8/docs/api/java/util/concurrent/ConcurrentNavigableMap.html
34. 8/docs/api/java/util/concurrent/ConcurrentSkipListMap.html
35. 8/docs/api/java/util/TreeMap.html
36. 8/docs/api/java/util/concurrent/atomic/package-summary.html

One way to make `Counter` safe from thread interference is to make its methods synchronized, as in `SynchronizedCounter`:

```
class SynchronizedCounter {
    private int c = 0;

    public synchronized void increment() {
        c++;
    }

    public synchronized void decrement() {
        c--;
    }

    public synchronized int value() {
        return c;
    }

}
```

For this simple class, synchronization is an acceptable solution, but for a more complicated class, we might want to avoid the liveness impact of unnecessary synchronization. Replacing the `int` field with an `AtomicInteger` allows us to prevent thread interference without resorting to synchronization, as in `AtomicCounter`:

```
import java.util.concurrent.atomic.AtomicInteger;

class AtomicCounter {
    private AtomicInteger c = new AtomicInteger(0);

    public void increment() {
        c.incrementAndGet();
    }

    public void decrement() {
        c.decrementAndGet();
    }

    public int value() {
        return c.get();
    }

}
```

Concurrent Random Numbers

The package `java.util.concurrent`[37] includes a convenience class, `Thread-LocalRandom`,[38] for applications that expect to use random numbers from multiple

---

37.   `8/docs/api/java/util/concurrent/package-summary.html`

38.   `8/docs/api/java/util/concurrent/ThreadLocalRandom.html`

threads or `ForkJoinTasks`. For concurrent access, using `ThreadLocalRan`-
`dom` instead of `Math.random()` results in less contention and ultimately better
performance.

All you need to do is call `ThreadLocalRandom.current()`, then call one of its
methods to retrieve a random number. Here is one example:

```
int r = ThreadLocalRandom.current() .nextInt(4, 77);
```

Questions and Exercises: Concurrency

Question

1. Can you pass a `Thread` object to `Executor.execute`? Would such an invoca-
    tion make sense?

Exercises

1. Compile and run `BadThreads.java`:

```
public class BadThreads {

    static String message;

    private static class CorrectorThread
        extends Thread {

        public void run() {
            try {
                sleep(1000);
            } catch (InterruptedException e) {}
            // Key statement 1:
            message = "Mares do eat oats.";
        }
    }

    public static void main(String args[])
        throws InterruptedException {

        (new CorrectorThread()).start();
        message = "Mares do not eat oats.";
        Thread.sleep(2000);
        // Key statement 2:
        System.out.println(message);
    }
}
```

The application should print out the following:

```
Mares do eat oats.
```

Is it guaranteed to always do this? If not, why not? Would it help to change the parameters of the two invocations of `Sleep`? How would you guarantee that all changes to `message` will be visible in the main thread?

2. Modify the producer-consumer example in the "Guarded Blocks" section to use a standard library class instead of the `Drop` class.

Answers

You can find answers to these questions and exercises at `http://docs.oracle .com/javase/tutorial/essential/concurrency/QandE/answers.html`.

Regular Expressions

Chapter Contents

Introduction   558
Test Harness   559
String Literals   560
Character Classes   562
Predefined Character Classes   566
Quantifiers   568
Capturing Groups   574
Boundary Matchers   576
Methods of the Pattern Class   578
Methods of the Matcher Class   583
Methods of the PatternSyntaxException Class   589
Unicode Support   591
Questions and Exercises: Regular Expressions   592

This chapter explains how to use the `java.util.regex` Application Programming Interface (API) for pattern matching with regular expressions.[1] Although the syntax accepted by this package is similar to the Perl programming language, knowledge of Perl is not a prerequisite.[2] This chapter starts with the basics and gradually builds to cover more advanced techniques.

The introductory section provides a general overview of regular expressions. It also introduces the core classes that comprise this API. The other sections do the following:

---

1.   `8/docs/api/java/util/regex/package-summary.html`

2.   `http://www.perl.com`

- Define a simple application for testing pattern matching with regular expressions.
- Introduce basic pattern matching, metacharacters, and quoting.
- Describe simple character classes, negation, ranges, unions, intersections, and subtraction.
- Describe the basic predefined character classes for white space, word, and digit characters.
- Explain greedy, reluctant, and possessive quantifiers for matching a specified expression x number of times.
- Explain how to treat multiple characters as a single unit.
- Describe line, word, and input boundaries.
- Examine other useful methods of the `Pattern` class and explore advanced features such as compiling with flags and using embedded flag expressions.
- Describe the commonly used methods of the `Matcher` class.
- Describe how to examine a `PatternSyntaxException`.

Introduction

What Are Regular Expressions?

Regular expressions are a way to describe a set of strings based on common characteristics shared by each string in the set. They can be used to search, edit, or manipulate text and data. You must learn a specific syntax to create regular expressions—one that goes beyond the normal syntax of the Java programming language. Regular expressions vary in complexity, but once you understand the basics of how they're constructed, you'll be able to decipher (or create) any regular expression.

This chapter teaches the regular expression syntax supported by the `java.util.regex` API and presents several working examples to illustrate how the various objects interact. In the world of regular expressions, there are many different flavors to choose from, such as grep, Perl, Tcl, Python, PHP, and awk. The regular expression syntax in the `java.util.regex` API is most similar to that found in Perl.

How Are Regular Expressions Represented in This Package?

The `java.util.regex` package primarily consists of three classes: `Pattern`,[3] `Matcher`,[4] and `PatternSyntaxException`.[5]

---

3.   8/docs/api/java/util/regex/Pattern.html
4.   8/docs/api/java/util/regex/Matcher.html
5.   8/docs/api/java/util/regex/PatternSyntaxException.html

- A `Pattern` object is a compiled representation of a regular expression. The `Pattern` class provides no public constructors. To create a pattern, you must first invoke one of its `public static compile` methods, which will then return a `Pattern` object. These methods accept a regular expression as the first argument; the first few sections of this chapter will teach you the required syntax.
- A `Matcher` object is the engine that interprets the pattern and performs match operations against an input string. Like the `Pattern` class, `Matcher` defines no public constructors. You obtain a `Matcher` object by invoking the `matcher` method on a `Pattern` object.
- A `PatternSyntaxException` object is an unchecked exception that indicates a syntax error in a regular expression pattern.

The last few sections of this chapter explore each class in detail, but first you must understand how regular expressions are actually constructed. Therefore, the next section introduces a simple test harness that will be used repeatedly to explore their syntax.

Test Harness

This section defines a reusable test harness, `RegexTestHarness.java`, for exploring the regular expression constructs supported by this API. The command to run this code is `java RegexTestHarness`; no command-line arguments are accepted. The application loops repeatedly, prompting the user for a regular expression and input string. Using this test harness is optional, but you may find it convenient for exploring the test cases discussed in the following pages:

```java
import java.io.Console;
import java.util.regex.Pattern;
import java.util.regex.Matcher;

public class RegexTestHarness {

    public static void main(String[] args){
        Console console = System.console();
        if (console == null) {
            System.err.println("No console.");
            System.exit(1);
        }
        while (true) {

            Pattern pattern =
            Pattern.compile(console.readLine("%nEnter your regex: "));

            Matcher matcher =
            pattern.matcher(console.readLine("Enter input string to search: "));
```

14

```
boolean found = false;
while (matcher.find()) {
    console.format("I found the text" +
        " \"%s\" starting at " +
        "index %d and ending at index %d.%n",
        matcher.group(),
        matcher.start(),
        matcher.end());
    found = true;
}
if(!found){
    console.format("No match found.%n");
}
    }
  }
}
```

Before continuing to the next section, save and compile this code to ensure that your development environment supports the required packages.

String Literals

The most basic form of pattern matching supported by this API is the match of a string literal. For example, if the regular expression is foo and the input string is foo, the match will succeed because the strings are identical. Try this out with the test harness:

```
Enter your regex: foo
Enter input string to search: foo
I found the text foo starting at index 0 and ending at index 3.
```

This match was a success. Note that while the input string is three characters long, the start index is 0 and the end index is 3. By convention, ranges are inclusive of the beginning index and exclusive of the end index, as shown in Figure 14.1.

Each character in the string resides in its own *cell*, with the index positions pointing between each cell. The string foo starts at index 0 and ends at index 3, even though the characters themselves only occupy cells 0, 1, and 2.

With subsequent matches, you'll notice some overlap; the start index for the next match is the same as the end index of the previous match:

```
Enter your regex: foo
Enter input string to search: foofoofoo
I found the text foo starting at index 0 and ending at index 3.
I found the text foo starting at index 3 and ending at index 6.
I found the text foo starting at index 6 and ending at index 9.
```

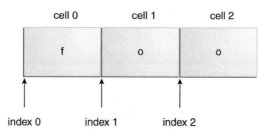

Figure 14.1 The String Literal Foo, with Numbered Cells and Index Values

Metacharacters

This API also supports a number of special characters that affect the way a pattern is matched. Change the regular expression to `cat.` and the input string to `cats`. The output will appear as follows:

```
Enter your regex: cat.
Enter input string to search: cats
I found the text cats starting at index 0 and ending at index 4.
```

The match still succeeds, even though the dot (`.`) is not present in the input string. It succeeds because the dot is a *metacharacter*—a character with special meaning interpreted by the matcher. The metacharacter `.` means *any character*, which is why the match succeeds in this example. The metacharacters supported by this API are as follows:

```
<([{\^-=$!|]})?*+.>
```

> **Note**
>
> In certain situations, the special characters listed above will *not* be treated as metacharacters. You'll encounter this as you learn more about how regular expressions are constructed. You can, however, use this list to check whether or not a specific character will ever be considered a metacharacter. For example, the characters @ and # never carry a special meaning.

There are two ways to force a metacharacter to be treated as an ordinary character:

- Precede the metacharacter with a backslash.
- Enclose it within `\Q` (which starts the quote) and `\E` (which ends it).

When using this technique, the `\Q` and `\E` can be placed at any location within the expression, provided that the `\Q` comes first.

14

Table 14.1 Character Classes

Construct	Description
[abc]	a, b, or c (simple class)
[^abc]	Any character except a, b, or c (negation)
[a-zA-Z]	a through z or A through Z, inclusive (range)
[a-d[m-p]]	a through d or m through p: [a-dm-p] (union)
[a-z&&[def]]	d, e, or f (intersection)
[a-z&&[^bc]]	a through z, except for b and c: [ad-z] (subtraction)
[a-z&&[^m-p]]	a through z, not m through p: [a-lq-z] (subtraction)

Character Classes

If you browse through the `Pattern` API documentation, you'll see tables summarizing the supported regular expression character classes. It includes Table 14.1.

The left-hand column specifies the regular expression constructs, while the right-hand column describes the conditions under which each construct will match.

> **Note**
>
> The word *class* in the phrase *character class* does not refer to a `.class` file. In the context of regular expressions, a *character class* is a set of characters enclosed within square brackets. It specifies the characters that will successfully match a single character from a given input string.

Simple Classes

The most basic form of a character class is to simply place a set of characters side by side within square brackets. For example, the regular expression [bcr]at will match the words *bat*, *cat*, or *rat* because it defines a character class (accepting either *b*, *c*, or *r*) as its first character.

```
Enter your regex: [bcr]at
Enter input string to search: bat
I found the text "bat" starting at index 0 and ending at index 3.

Enter your regex: [bcr]at
Enter input string to search: cat
I found the text "cat" starting at index 0 and ending at index 3.

Enter your regex: [bcr]at
Enter input string to search: rat
I found the text "rat" starting at index 0 and ending at index 3.
```

```
Enter your regex: [bcr]at
Enter input string to search: hat
No match found.
```

In these examples, the overall match succeeds only when the first letter matches one of the characters defined by the character class.

Negation

To match all characters *except* those listed, insert the ^ metacharacter at the beginning of the character class. This technique is known as *negation*:

```
Enter your regex: [^bcr]at
Enter input string to search: bat
No match found.

Enter your regex: [^bcr]at
Enter input string to search: cat
No match found.

Enter your regex: [^bcr]at
Enter input string to search: rat
No match found.

Enter your regex: [^bcr]at
Enter input string to search: hat
I found the text "hat" starting at index 0 and ending at index 3.
```

The match is successful only if the first character of the input string does *not* contain any characters defined by the character class.

Ranges

Sometimes you'll want to define a character class that includes a range of values, such as the letters *a* through *h* or the numbers 1 through 5. To specify a range, simply insert the – metacharacter between the first and last character to be matched, such as [1-5] or [a-h]. You can also place different ranges beside each other within the class to further expand the match possibilities. For example, [a-zA-Z] will match any letter of the alphabet: *a* to *z* (lowercase) or *A* to *Z* (uppercase). Here are some examples of ranges and negation:

```
Enter your regex: [a-c]
Enter input string to search: a
I found the text "a" starting at index 0 and ending at index 1.

Enter your regex: [a-c]
Enter input string to search: b
I found the text "b" starting at index 0 and ending at index 1.

Enter your regex: [a-c]
```

```
Enter input string to search: c
I found the text "c" starting at index 0 and ending at index 1.

Enter your regex: [a-c]
Enter input string to search: d
No match found.

Enter your regex: foo[1-5]
Enter input string to search: foo1
I found the text "foo1" starting at index 0 and ending at index 4.

Enter your regex: foo[1-5]
Enter input string to search: foo5
I found the text "foo5" starting at index 0 and ending at index 4.

Enter your regex: foo[1-5]
Enter input string to search: foo6
No match found.

Enter your regex: foo[^1-5]
Enter input string to search: foo1
No match found.

Enter your regex: foo[^1-5]
Enter input string to search: foo6
I found the text "foo6" starting at index 0 and ending at index 4.
```

Unions

You can also use *unions* to create a single character class composed of two or more separate character classes. To create a union, simply nest one class inside the other, such as [0-4[6-8]]. This particular union creates a single character class that matches the numbers 0, 1, 2, 3, 4, 6, 7, and 8:

```
Enter your regex: [0-4[6-8]]
Enter input string to search: 0
I found the text "0" starting at index 0 and ending at index 1.

Enter your regex: [0-4[6-8]]
Enter input string to search: 5
No match found.

Enter your regex: [0-4[6-8]]
Enter input string to search: 6
I found the text "6" starting at index 0 and ending at index 1.

Enter your regex: [0-4[6-8]]
Enter input string to search: 8
I found the text "8" starting at index 0 and ending at index 1.

Enter your regex: [0-4[6-8]]
Enter input string to search: 9
No match found.
```

Intersections

To create a single character class matching only the characters common to all its nested classes, use &&, as in [0-9&&[345]]. This particular intersection creates a single character class matching only the numbers common to both character classes: 3, 4, and 5:

```
Enter your regex: [0-9&&[345]]
Enter input string to search: 3
I found the text "3" starting at index 0 and ending at index 1.

Enter your regex: [0-9&&[345]]
Enter input string to search: 4
I found the text "4" starting at index 0 and ending at index 1.

Enter your regex: [0-9&&[345]]
Enter input string to search: 5
I found the text "5" starting at index 0 and ending at index 1.

Enter your regex: [0-9&&[345]]
Enter input string to search: 2
No match found.

Enter your regex: [0-9&&[345]]
Enter input string to search: 6
No match found.
```

Here's an example that shows the intersection of two ranges:

```
Enter your regex: [2-8&&[4-6]]
Enter input string to search: 3
No match found.

Enter your regex: [2-8&&[4-6]]
Enter input string to search: 4
I found the text "4" starting at index 0 and ending at index 1.

Enter your regex: [2-8&&[4-6]]
Enter input string to search: 5
I found the text "5" starting at index 0 and ending at index 1.

Enter your regex: [2-8&&[4-6]]
Enter input string to search: 6
I found the text "6" starting at index 0 and ending at index 1.

Enter your regex: [2-8&&[4-6]]
Enter input string to search: 7
No match found.
```

14

Subtraction

You can use *subtraction* to negate one or more nested character classes, such as [0-9&&[^345]]. This example creates a single character class that matches everything from 0 to 9, *except* the numbers 3, 4, and 5:

```
Enter your regex: [0-9&&[^345]]
Enter input string to search: 2
I found the text "2" starting at index 0 and ending at index 1.

Enter your regex: [0-9&&[^345]]
Enter input string to search: 3
No match found.

Enter your regex: [0-9&&[^345]]
Enter input string to search: 4
No match found.

Enter your regex: [0-9&&[^345]]
Enter input string to search: 5
No match found.

Enter your regex: [0-9&&[^345]]
Enter input string to search: 6
I found the text "6" starting at index 0 and ending at index 1.

Enter your regex: [0-9&&[^345]]
Enter input string to search: 9
I found the text "9" starting at index 0 and ending at index 1.
```

Now that we've covered how character classes are created, you may want to review Table 14.1 before continuing with the next section.

Predefined Character Classes

The `Pattern` API contains a number of useful *predefined character classes*, which offer convenient shorthands for commonly used regular expressions.

In Table 14.2, each construct in the left-hand column is shorthand for the character class in the right-hand column. For example, \d means a range of digits (zero to nine), and \w means a word character (any lowercase letter, any uppercase letter, the underscore character, or any digit). Use the predefined classes whenever possible. They make your code easier to read and eliminate errors introduced by malformed character classes.

Constructs beginning with a backslash are called *escaped constructs*. We previewed escaped constructs in the "String Literals" section, where we mentioned the use of backslash and \Q and \E for quotation. If you are using an escaped construct within a string literal, you must precede the backslash with another backslash for the string to compile:

```
private final String REGEX = "\\d"; // a single digit
```

In this example, \d is the regular expression; the extra backslash is required for the code to compile. The test harness reads the expressions directly from the console, however, so the extra backslash is unnecessary.

Table 14.2 Predefined Character Classes

Construct	Description
.	Any character (may or may not match line terminators)
\d	A digit: [0-9]
\D	A nondigit: [^0-9]
\s	A white-space character: [\t\n\x0B\f\r]
\S	A non-white-space character: [^\s]
\w	A word character: [a-zA-Z_0-9]
\W	A nonword character: [^\w]

The following examples demonstrate the use of predefined character classes:

```
Enter your regex: .
Enter input string to search: @
I found the text "@" starting at index 0 and ending at index 1.

Enter your regex: .
Enter input string to search: 1
I found the text "1" starting at index 0 and ending at index 1.

Enter your regex: .
Enter input string to search: a
I found the text "a" starting at index 0 and ending at index 1.

Enter your regex: \d
Enter input string to search: 1
I found the text "1" starting at index 0 and ending at index 1.

Enter your regex: \d
Enter input string to search: a
No match found.

Enter your regex: \D
Enter input string to search: 1
No match found.

Enter your regex: \D
Enter input string to search: a
I found the text "a" starting at index 0 and ending at index 1.

Enter your regex: \s
Enter input string to search:
I found the text " " starting at index 0 and ending at index 1.

Enter your regex: \s
Enter input string to search: a
No match found.

Enter your regex: \S
Enter input string to search:
No match found.
```

```
Enter your regex: \S
Enter input string to search: a
I found the text "a" starting at index 0 and ending at index 1.

Enter your regex: \w
Enter input string to search: a
I found the text "a" starting at index 0 and ending at index 1.

Enter your regex: \w
Enter input string to search: !
No match found.

Enter your regex: \W
Enter input string to search: a
No match found.

Enter your regex: \W
Enter input string to search: !
I found the text "!" starting at index 0 and ending at index 1.
```

In the first three examples, the regular expression is simply the dot metacharacter (`.`), which indicates *any character*. Therefore, the match is successful in all three cases (a randomly selected @ character, a digit, and a letter). The remaining examples each use a single regular expression construct from Table 14.2. You can refer to this table to figure out the logic behind each match:

- \d matches all digits.
- \s matches spaces.
- \w matches word characters.

Alternatively, a capital letter means the opposite:

- \D matches nondigits.
- \S matches nonspaces.
- \W matches nonword characters.

Quantifiers

Quantifiers allow you to specify the number of occurrences to match against. For convenience, the three sections of the `Pattern` API documentation describing greedy, reluctant, and possessive quantifiers are presented in Table 14.3. At first glance, it may appear that the quantifiers X?, X??, and X?+ do exactly the same thing, since they all promise to match "X, once or not at all." There are subtle implementation differences that will be explained near the end of this section.

Table 14.3 Greedy, Reluctant, and Possessive Quantifiers

Greedy	Reluctant	Possessive	Meaning
X?	X??	X?+	X, once or not at all
X*	X*?	X*+	X, zero or more times
X+	X+?	X++	X, one or more times
X{n}	X{n}?	X{n}+	X, exactly n times
X{n,}	X{n,}?	X{n,}+	X, at least n times
X{n,m}	X{n,m}?	X{n,m}+	X, at least n but not more than m times

Let's start our look at greedy quantifiers by creating three different regular expressions: the letter *a* followed by ?, *, or +. Let's see what happens when these expressions are tested against an empty input string " ":

```
Enter your regex: a?
Enter input string to search:
I found the text "" starting at index 0 and ending at index 0.

Enter your regex: a*
Enter input string to search:
I found the text "" starting at index 0 and ending at index 0.

Enter your regex: a+
Enter input string to search:
No match found.
```

Zero-Length Matches

In the previous example, the match is successful in the first two cases because the expressions a? and a* both allow for zero occurrences of the letter a. You'll also notice that the start and end indices are both zero, which is unlike any of the examples we've seen so far. The empty input string " " has no length, so the test simply matches nothing at index 0. Matches of this sort are known as *zero-length matches*. A zero-length match can occur in several cases: in an empty input string, at the beginning of an input string, after the last character of an input string, or in between any two characters of an input string. Zero-length matches are easily identifiable because they always start and end at the same index position.

Let's explore zero-length matches with a few more examples. Change the input string to a single letter *a* and you'll notice something interesting:

```
Enter your regex: a?
Enter input string to search: a
I found the text "a" starting at index 0 and ending at index 1.
I found the text "" starting at index 1 and ending at index 1.

Enter your regex: a*
```

```
Enter input string to search: a
I found the text "a" starting at index 0 and ending at index 1.
I found the text "" starting at index 1 and ending at index 1.

Enter your regex: a+
Enter input string to search: a
I found the text "a" starting at index 0 and ending at index 1.
```

All three quantifiers found the letter a, but the first two also found a zero-length match at index 1—that is, after the last character of the input string. Remember, the matcher sees the character a as sitting in the cell between index 0 and index 1, and our test harness loops until it can no longer find a match. Depending on the quantifier used, the presence of "nothing" at the index after the last character may or may not trigger a match.

Now change the input string to the letter a five times in a row and you'll get the following:

```
Enter your regex: a?
Enter input string to search: aaaaa
I found the text "a" starting at index 0 and ending at index 1.
I found the text "a" starting at index 1 and ending at index 2.
I found the text "a" starting at index 2 and ending at index 3.
I found the text "a" starting at index 3 and ending at index 4.
I found the text "a" starting at index 4 and ending at index 5.
I found the text "" starting at index 5 and ending at index 5.

Enter your regex: a*
Enter input string to search: aaaaa
I found the text "aaaaa" starting at index 0 and ending at index 5.
I found the text "" starting at index 5 and ending at index 5.

Enter your regex: a+
Enter input string to search: aaaaa
I found the text "aaaaa" starting at index 0 and ending at index 5.
```

The expression a? finds an individual match for each character, since it matches when a appears zero or one times. The expression a* finds two separate matches: all the letter a's in the first match, then the zero-length match after the last character at index 5. Finally, a+ matches all occurrences of the letter a, ignoring the presence of "nothing" at the last index.

At this point, you might be wondering what the results would be if the first two quantifiers encounter a letter other than a. For example, what happens if it encounters the letter b, as in $ababaaaab$?

Let's find out:

```
Enter your regex: a?
Enter input string to search: ababaaaab
I found the text "a" starting at index 0 and ending at index 1.
I found the text "" starting at index 1 and ending at index 1.
```

```
I found the text "a" starting at index 2 and ending at index 3.
I found the text "" starting at index 3 and ending at index 3.
I found the text "a" starting at index 4 and ending at index 5.
I found the text "a" starting at index 5 and ending at index 6.
I found the text "a" starting at index 6 and ending at index 7.
I found the text "a" starting at index 7 and ending at index 8.
I found the text "" starting at index 8 and ending at index 8.
I found the text "" starting at index 9 and ending at index 9.

Enter your regex: a*
Enter input string to search: ababaaaab
I found the text "a" starting at index 0 and ending at index 1.
I found the text "" starting at index 1 and ending at index 1.
I found the text "a" starting at index 2 and ending at index 3.
I found the text "" starting at index 3 and ending at index 3.
I found the text "aaaa" starting at index 4 and ending at index 8.
I found the text "" starting at index 8 and ending at index 8.
I found the text "" starting at index 9 and ending at index 9.

Enter your regex: a+
Enter input string to search: ababaaaab
I found the text "a" starting at index 0 and ending at index 1.
I found the text "a" starting at index 2 and ending at index 3.
I found the text "aaaa" starting at index 4 and ending at index 8.
```

Even though the letter b appears in cells 1, 3, and 8, the output reports a zero-length match at those locations. The regular expression a? is not specifically looking for the letter b; it's merely looking for the presence (or lack thereof) of the letter a. If the quantifier allows for a match of a zero times, anything in the input string that's not an a will show up as a zero-length match. The remaining a's are matched according to the rules discussed in the previous examples.

To match a pattern exactly n number of times, simply specify the number inside a set of braces:

```
Enter your regex: a{3}
Enter input string to search: aa
No match found.

Enter your regex: a{3}
Enter input string to search: aaa
I found the text "aaa" starting at index 0 and ending at index 3.

Enter your regex: a{3}
Enter input string to search: aaaa
I found the text "aaa" starting at index 0 and ending at index 3.
```

Here, the regular expression a{3} is searching for three occurrences of the letter a in a row. The first test fails because the input string does not have enough a's to match against. The second test contains exactly three a's in the input string, which triggers a match. The third test also triggers a match because there are exactly three a's at the beginning of the input string. Anything following that is irrelevant to the first match. If the pattern should appear again after that point, it would trigger subsequent matches:

```
Enter your regex: a{3}
Enter input string to search: aaaaaaaaa
I found the text "aaa" starting at index 0 and ending at index 3.
I found the text "aaa" starting at index 3 and ending at index 6.
I found the text "aaa" starting at index 6 and ending at index 9.
```

To require a pattern to appear at least *n* times, add a comma after the number:

```
Enter your regex: a{3,}
Enter input string to search: aaaaaaaaa
I found the text "aaaaaaaaa" starting at index 0 and ending at index 9.
```

With the same input string, this test finds only one match because the nine *a*'s in a row satisfy the need for "at least" three *a*'s.

Finally, to specify an upper limit on the number of occurrences, add a second number inside the braces:

```
Enter your regex: a{3,6} // find at least 3 (but no more than 6) a's in a row
Enter input string to search: aaaaaaaaa
I found the text "aaaaaa" starting at index 0 and ending at index 6.
I found the text "aaa" starting at index 6 and ending at index 9.
```

Here the first match is forced to stop at the upper limit of six characters. The second match includes whatever is left over, which happens to be three *a*'s—the minimum number of characters allowed for this match. If the input string were one character shorter, there would not be a second match, since only two *a*'s would remain.

Capturing Groups and Character Classes with Quantifiers

Until now, we've only tested quantifiers on input strings containing one character. In fact, quantifiers can only attach to one character at a time, so the regular expression abc+ would mean *a*, followed by *b*, followed by *c* one or more times. It would not mean *abc* one or more times. However, quantifiers can also attach to character classes and capturing groups, such as [abc]+ (*a* or *b* or *c*, one or more times) or (abc)+ (the group *abc*, one or more times).

Let's illustrate by specifying the group (dog) three times in a row:

```
Enter your regex: (dog){3}
Enter input string to search: dogdogdogdogdogdog
I found the text "dogdogdog" starting at index 0 and ending at index 9.
I found the text "dogdogdog" starting at index 9 and ending at index 18.

Enter your regex: dog{3}
Enter input string to search: dogdogdogdogdogdog
No match found.
```

Here the first example finds three matches, since the quantifier applies to the entire capturing group. Remove the parentheses, however, and the match fails because the quantifier `{3}` now applies only to the letter *g*. Similarly, we can apply a quantifier to an entire character class:

```
Enter your regex: [abc]{3}
Enter input string to search: abccabaaaccbbbc
I found the text "abc" starting at index 0 and ending at index 3.
I found the text "cab" starting at index 3 and ending at index 6.
I found the text "aaa" starting at index 6 and ending at index 9.
I found the text "ccb" starting at index 9 and ending at index 12.
I found the text "bbc" starting at index 12 and ending at index 15.

Enter your regex: abc{3}
Enter input string to search: abccabaaaccbbbc
No match found.
```

Here the quantifier `{3}` applies to the entire character class in the first example but only to the letter *c* in the second.

Differences among Greedy, Reluctant, and Possessive Quantifiers

There are subtle differences among greedy, reluctant, and possessive quantifiers. Greedy quantifiers are considered "greedy" because they force the matcher to read in, or *eat*, the entire input string prior to attempting the first match. If the first match attempt (the entire input string) fails, the matcher backs off the input string by one character and tries again, repeating the process until a match is found or there are no more characters left to back off from. Depending on the quantifier used in the expression, the last thing it will try matching against is one or zero characters.

The reluctant quantifiers, however, take the opposite approach: They start at the beginning of the input string and then reluctantly eat one character at a time looking for a match. The last thing they try is the entire input string.

Finally, the possessive quantifiers always eat the entire input string, trying once (and only once) for a match. Unlike the greedy quantifiers, possessive quantifiers never back off, even if doing so would allow the overall match to succeed. To illustrate, consider the input string xfooxxxxxxfoo:

```
Enter your regex: .*foo  // greedy quantifier
Enter input string to search: xfooxxxxxxfoo
I found the text "xfooxxxxxxfoo" starting at index 0 and ending at index 13.

Enter your regex: .*?foo  // reluctant quantifier
Enter input string to search: xfooxxxxxxfoo
I found the text "xfoo" starting at index 0 and ending at index 4.
I found the text "xxxxxxfoo" starting at index 4 and ending at index 13.

Enter your regex: .*+foo // possessive quantifier
```

```
Enter input string to search: xfooxxxxxxfoo
No match found.
```

The first example uses the greedy quantifier `.*` to find "anything," zero or more times, followed by the letters `f`, `o`, and `o`. Because the quantifier is greedy, the `.*` portion of the expression first eats the entire input string. At this point, the overall expression cannot succeed because the last three letters (`f`, `o`, and `o`) have already been consumed. So the matcher slowly backs off one letter at a time until the rightmost occurrence of `foo` has been regurgitated, at which point the match succeeds and the search ends.

The second example, however, is reluctant, so it starts by first consuming "nothing." Because `foo` doesn't appear at the beginning of the string, it's forced to swallow the first letter (an *x*), which triggers the first match at 0 and 4. Our test harness continues the process until the input string is exhausted. It finds another match at 4 and 13.

The third example fails to find a match because the quantifier is possessive. In this case, the entire input string is consumed by `.*+`, leaving nothing left over to satisfy the `foo` at the end of the expression. Use a possessive quantifier for situations where you want to seize all of something without ever backing off; it will outperform the equivalent greedy quantifier in cases where the match is not immediately found.

Capturing Groups

In the previous section, we saw how quantifiers attach to one character, character class, or capturing group at a time. Until now, we have not discussed the notion of capturing groups in any detail.

Capturing groups are a way to treat multiple characters as a single unit. They are created by placing the characters to be grouped inside a set of parentheses. For example, the regular expression (`dog`) creates a single group containing the letters d, o, and g. The portion of the input string that matches the capturing group will be saved in memory for later recall via backreferences (as discussed in the "Backreferences" section).

Numbering

As described in the `Pattern` API, capturing groups are numbered by counting their opening parentheses from left to right. In the expression `((A)(B(C)))`, for example, there are four such groups:

1. `((A)(B(C)))`
2. `(A)`

3. `(B(C))`

4. `(C)`

To find out how many groups are present in the expression, call the `groupCount` method on a matcher object. The `groupCount` method returns an `int` showing the number of capturing groups present in the matcher's pattern. In this example, `groupCount` would return the number 4, showing that the pattern contains four capturing groups.

There is also a special group, group 0, which always represents the entire expression. This group is not included in the total reported by `groupCount`. Groups beginning with `(?` are pure, *noncapturing groups* that do not capture text and do not count toward the group total. (You'll see examples of noncapturing groups later in the "Methods of the Pattern Class" section.)

It's important to understand how groups are numbered because some `Matcher` methods accept an `int`, specifying a particular group number as a parameter:

- `public int start(int group)`. Returns the start index of the subsequence captured by the given group during the previous match operation[6]
- `public int end (int group)`. Returns the index of the last character, plus one, of the subsequence captured by the given group during the previous match operation[7]
- `public String group (int group)`. Returns the input subsequence captured by the given group during the previous match operation[8]

14

Backreferences

The section of the input string matching the capturing group(s) is saved in memory for later recall via *backreference*. A backreference is specified in the regular expression as a backslash (`\`) followed by a digit indicating the number of the group to be recalled. For example, the expression `(\d\d)` defines one capturing group matching two digits in a row, which can be recalled later in the expression via the backreference `\1`.

To match any two digits followed by the exact same two digits, you would use `(\d\d)\1` as the regular expression:

```
Enter your regex: (\d\d)\1
Enter input string to search: 1212
I found the text "1212" starting at index 0 and ending at index 4.
```

6.   8/docs/api/java/util/regex/Matcher.html#start-int-

7.   8/docs/api/java/util/regex/Matcher.html#end-int-

8.   8/docs/api/java/util/regex/Matcher.html#group-int-

If you change the last two digits, the match will fail:

```
Enter your regex: (\d\d)\1
Enter input string to search: 1234
No match found.
```

For nested capturing groups, backreferencing works in exactly the same way: specify a backslash followed by the number of the group to be recalled.

Boundary Matchers

Until now, we've only been interested in whether or not a match is found *at some location* within a particular input string. We never cared about *where* in the string the match was taking place.

You can make your pattern matches more precise by specifying such information with *boundary matchers*. For example, maybe you're interested in finding a particular word, but only if it appears at the beginning or end of a line. Or maybe you want to know if the match is taking place on a word boundary or at the end of the previous match. Table 14.4 lists and explains all the boundary matchers.

The following examples demonstrate the use of boundary matchers ^ and $. As noted previously, ^ matches the beginning of a line and $ matches the end:

```
Enter your regex: ^dog$
Enter input string to search: dog
I found the text "dog" starting at index 0 and ending at index 3.

Enter your regex: ^dog$
Enter input string to search:      dog
No match found.

Enter your regex: \s*dog$
Enter input string to search:              dog
I found the text "              dog" starting at index 0 and ending at index 15.

Enter your regex: ^dog\w*
Enter input string to search: dogblahblah
I found the text "dogblahblah" starting at index 0 and ending at index 11.
```

The first example is successful because the pattern occupies the entire input string. The second example fails because the input string contains extra white space at the beginning. The third example specifies an expression that allows for unlimited white space, followed by dog on the end of the line. The fourth example requires dog to be present at the beginning of a line followed by an unlimited number of word characters.

Table 14.4 Constructs Used to Define Boundaries

Boundary construct	Description
^	The beginning of a line
$	The end of a line
\b	A word boundary
\B	A nonword boundary
\A	The beginning of the input
\G	The end of the previous match
\Z	The end of the input but for the final terminator, if any
\z	The end of the input

To check if a pattern begins and ends on a word boundary (as opposed to a substring within a longer string), just use \b on either side (e.g., \bdog\b):

```
Enter your regex: \bdog\b
Enter input string to search: The dog plays in the yard.
I found the text "dog" starting at index 4 and ending at index 7.

Enter your regex: \bdog\b
Enter input string to search: The doggie plays in the yard.
No match found.
```

To match the expression on a nonword boundary, use \B instead:

```
Enter your regex: \bdog\B
Enter input string to search: The dog plays in the yard.
No match found.

Enter your regex: \bdog\B
Enter input string to search: The doggie plays in the yard.
I found the text "dog" starting at index 4 and ending at index 7.
```

To require the match to occur only at the end of the previous match, use \G:

```
Enter your regex: dog
Enter input string to search: dog dog
I found the text "dog" starting at index 0 and ending at index 3.
I found the text "dog" starting at index 4 and ending at index 7.

Enter your regex: \Gdog
Enter input string to search: dog dog
I found the text "dog" starting at index 0 and ending at index 3.
```

Here the second example finds only one match because the second occurrence of dog does not start at the end of the previous match.

Methods of the Pattern Class

Until now, we've only used the test harness to create `Pattern` objects in their most basic form. This section explores advanced techniques such as creating patterns with flags and using embedded flag expressions. It also explores some additional useful methods that we haven't yet discussed.

Creating a Pattern with Flags

The `Pattern` class defines an alternate `compile` method that accepts a set of flags affecting the way the pattern is matched. The flags parameter is a bit mask that may include any of the following public static fields:

- `Pattern.CANON_EQ`. This enables canonical equivalence. When this flag is specified, two characters will be considered to match if and only if their full canonical decompositions match. The expression a\u030A, for example, will match the string \u00E5 when this flag is specified. By default, matching does not take canonical equivalence into account. Specifying this flag may impose a performance penalty.

- `Pattern.CASE_INSENSITIVE`. This enables case-insensitive matching. By default, case-insensitive matching assumes that only characters in the US-ASCII charset are being matched. Unicode-aware case-insensitive matching can be enabled by specifying the UNICODE_CASE flag in conjunction with this flag. Case-insensitive matching can also be enabled via the embedded flag expression (?i). Specifying this flag may impose a slight performance penalty.

- `Pattern.COMMENTS`. This permits white space and comments in the pattern. In this mode, white space is ignored and embedded comments starting with # are ignored until the end of a line. Comments mode can also be enabled via the embedded flag expression (?x).

- `Pattern.DOTALL`. This enables dotall mode. In dotall mode, the expression . matches any character, including a line terminator. By default, this expression does not match line terminators. Dotall mode can also be enabled via the embedded flag expression (?s). (The s is a mnemonic for *single-line* mode, which is what this is called in Perl.)

- `Pattern.LITERAL`. This enables literal parsing of the pattern. When this flag is specified, then the input string that specifies the pattern is treated as a sequence of literal characters. Metacharacters or escape sequences in the input sequence will be given no special meaning. The flags CASE_INSENSITIVE and UNICODE_CASE retain their impact on matching when used in conjunction with this flag. The other flags become superfluous. There is no embedded flag character for enabling literal parsing.

- `Pattern.MULTILINE`. This enables multiline mode. In multiline mode, the expressions ^ and $ match just after or just before a line terminator or the end of the input sequence, respectively. By default these expressions only match at the beginning and the end of the entire input sequence. Multiline mode can also be enabled via the embedded flag expression (`?m`).
- `Pattern.UNICODE_CASE`. This enables Unicode-aware case folding. When this flag is specified, the case-insensitive matching, when enabled by the `CASE_INSENSITIVE` flag, is done in a manner consistent with the Unicode standard. By default, case-insensitive matching assumes that only characters in the US-ASCII charset are being matched. Unicode-aware case folding can also be enabled via the embedded flag expression (`?u`). Specifying this flag may impose a performance penalty.
- `Pattern.UNIX_LINES`. This enables UNIX lines mode. In this mode, only the \n line terminator is recognized in the behavior of ., ^, and $. UNIX lines mode can also be enabled via the embedded flag expression (`?d`).

In the following steps, we will modify the test harness, `RegexTestHarness.java`, to create a pattern with case-insensitive matching.

First, modify the code to invoke the alternate version of `compile`:

```
Pattern pattern =
Pattern.compile(console.readLine("%nEnter your regex: "),
Pattern.CASE_INSENSITIVE);
```

Then compile and run the test harness to get the following results:

```
Enter your regex: dog
Enter input string to search: DoGDOg
I found the text "DoG" starting at index 0 and ending at index 3.
I found the text "DOg" starting at index 3 and ending at index 6.
```

As you can see, the string literal dog matches both occurrences, regardless of case. To compile a pattern with multiple flags, separate the flags to be included using the bitwise "or" operator, |. For clarity, the following code samples hardcode the regular expression instead of reading it from the `Console`:

```
pattern = Pattern.compile("[az]$", Pattern.MULTILINE | Pattern.UNIX_LINES);
```

You could also specify an `int` variable instead:

```
final int flags = Pattern.CASE_INSENSITIVE | Pattern.UNICODE_CASE;
Pattern pattern = Pattern.compile("aa", flags);
```

Table 14.5 Constants for Embedded Flag Expressions

Constant	Equivalent embedded flag expression
Pattern.CANON_EQ	None
Pattern.CASE_INSENSITIVE	(?i)
Pattern.COMMENTS	(?x)
Pattern.MULTILINE	(?m)
Pattern.DOTALL	(?s)
Pattern.LITERAL	None
Pattern.UNICODE_CASE	(?u)
Pattern.UNIX_LINES	(?d)

Embedded Flag Expressions

It's also possible to enable various flags using *embedded flag expressions*. Embedded flag expressions are an alternative to the two-argument version of compile and are specified in the regular expression itself. The following example uses the original test harness, RegexTestHarness.java, with the embedded flag expression (?i) to enable case-insensitive matching:

```
Enter your regex: (?i)foo
Enter input string to search: FOOfooFoOfoO
I found the text "FOO" starting at index 0 and ending at index 3.
I found the text "foo" starting at index 3 and ending at index 6.
I found the text "FoO" starting at index 6 and ending at index 9.
I found the text "foO" starting at index 9 and ending at index 12.
```

Once again, all matches succeed regardless of case.

The embedded flag expressions that correspond to Pattern's publicly accessible fields are presented in Table 14.5.

Using the matches(String,CharSequence) Method

The Pattern class defines a convenient matches method that allows you to quickly check if a pattern is present in a given input string.[9] As with all public static methods, you should invoke matches by its class name, such as Pattern.matches("\\d","1");. In this example, the method returns true because the digit 1 matches the regular expression \d.

---

9.   8/docs/api/java/util/regex/Pattern.html#matches-java.lang.String
      -java.lang.CharSequence-

Using the split(String) Method

The `split` method is a great tool for gathering the text that lies on either side of the pattern that's been matched.[10] As shown below in `SplitDemo.java`, the `split` method could extract one two three four five from the string one:two:three:four:five:

```
import java.util.regex.Pattern;
import java.util.regex.Matcher;

public class SplitDemo {

    private static final String REGEX = ":";
    private static final String INPUT =
        "one:two:three:four:five";

    public static void main(String[] args) {
        Pattern p = Pattern.compile(REGEX);
        String[] items = p.split(INPUT);
        for(String s : items) {
            System.out.println(s);
        }
    }
}
```

This example prints the following:

```
one
two
three
four
five
```

For simplicity, we've matched a string literal, the colon (:), instead of a complex regular expression. Since we're still using `Pattern` and `Matcher` objects, you can use split to get the text that falls on either side of any regular expression. Here's the same example, `SplitDemo2.java`, modified to split on digits instead:

```
import java.util.regex.Pattern;
import java.util.regex.Matcher;

public class SplitDemo2 {

    private static final String REGEX = "\\d";
    private static final String INPUT =
        "one9two4three7four1five";

    public static void main(String[] args) {
        Pattern p = Pattern.compile(REGEX);
        String[] items = p.split(INPUT);
```

---

10. 8/docs/api/java/util/regex/Pattern.html#split-java.lang.CharSequence-

```
            for(String s : items) {
                System.out.println(s);
            }
        }
    }
```

This example prints the following:

```
one
two
three
four
five
```

Other Utility Methods

You may find the following methods to be of some use as well:

- `public static String quote(String s)`. This method returns a literal pattern `String` for the specified `String`. This method produces a `String` that can be used to create a `Pattern` that would match `String` s as if it were a literal pattern. Metacharacters or escape sequences in the input sequence will be given no special meaning.[11]

- `public String toString()`. This method returns the `String` representation of this pattern. This is the regular expression from which this pattern was compiled.[12]

Pattern Method Equivalents in java.lang.String

Regular expression support also exists in `java.lang.String` through several methods that mimic the behavior of `java.util.regex.Pattern`. For convenience, key excerpts from their API are presented below:

- `public boolean matches(String regex)`. This tells whether or not the string matches the given regular expression. An invocation of this method of the form *str*`.matches(` *regex* `)` yields exactly the same result as the expression `Pattern.matches(` *regex, str* `)`.[13]

- `public String[] split(String regex, int limit)`. This splits the string around matches of the given regular expression. An invocation of this

---

11.   8/docs/api/java/util/regex/Pattern.html#quote-java.lang.String-

12.   8/docs/api/java/util/regex/Pattern.html#toString--

13.   8/docs/api/java/lang/String.html#matches-java.lang.String-

method of the form *str* .split(*regex, n*) yields the same result as the expression Pattern.compile(*regex*).split(*str, n*).[14]

- public String[] split(String regex). This splits the string around matches of the given regular expression. This method works the same as if you invoked the two-argument split method with the given expression and a limit argument of zero. Trailing empty strings are not included in the resulting array.[15]

There is also a replace method that replaces one CharSequence with another:

- public String replace(CharSequence target,CharSequence replace-ment). This replaces each substring of this string that matches the literal target sequence with the specified literal replacement sequence. The replacement proceeds from the beginning of the string to the end—for example, replacing *aa* with *b* in the string *aaa* will result in *ba* rather than *ab*.[16]

Methods of the Matcher Class

This section describes some additional useful methods of the Matcher class. For convenience, the methods listed below are grouped according to functionality.

Index Methods

Index methods provide useful index values that show precisely where the match was found in the input string:

- public int start(). Returns the start index of the previous match
- public int start(int group). Returns the start index of the subsequence captured by the given group during the previous match operation
- public int end(). Returns the offset after the last character matched
- public int end(int group). Returns the offset after the last character of the subsequence captured by the given group during the previous match operation

14

---

14. 8/docs/api/java/lang/String.html#split-java.lang.String-int-
15. 8/docs/api/java/lang/String.html#split-java.lang.String-
16. 8/docs/api/java/lang/String.html#replace-java.lang.CharSequence -java.lang.CharSequence-

Study Methods

Study methods review the input string and return a `boolean` indicating whether or not the pattern is found:

- `public boolean lookingAt()`. Attempts to match the input sequence, starting at the beginning of the region, against the pattern[17]

- `public boolean find()`. Attempts to find the next subsequence of the input sequence that matches the pattern[18]

- `public boolean find(int start)`. Resets this matcher and then attempts to find the next subsequence of the input sequence that matches the pattern, starting at the specified index[19]

- `public boolean matches()`. Attempts to match the entire region against the pattern[20]

Replacement Methods

Replacement methods are useful methods for replacing text in an input string:

- `public Matcher appendReplacement(StringBuffer sb, String replacement)`. This implements a nonterminal append-and-replace step.[21]

- `public StringBuffer appendTail(StringBuffer sb)`. This implements a terminal append-and-replace step.[22]

- `public String replaceAll(String replacement)`. This replaces every subsequence of the input sequence that matches the pattern with the given replacement string.[23]

---

17. `8/docs/api/java/util/regex/Matcher.html#lookingAt--`

18. `8/docs/api/java/util/regex/Matcher.html#find--`

19. `8/docs/api/java/util/regex/Matcher.html#find-int-`

20. `8/docs/api/java/util/regex/Matcher.html#matches--`

21. `8/docs/api/java/util/regex/Matcher.html#appendReplacement-java.lang.StringBuffer-java.lang.String-`

22. `8/docs/api/java/util/regex/Matcher.html#appendTail-java.lang.StringBuffer-`

23. `8/docs/api/java/util/regex/Matcher.html#replaceAll-java.lang.String-`

- `public String replaceFirst(String replacement)`. This replaces the first subsequence of the input sequence that matches the pattern with the given replacement string.[24]
- `public static String quoteReplacement(String s)`. This returns a literal replacement `String` for the specified `String` and produces a `String` that will work as a literal replacement s in the `appendReplacement` method of the `Matcher` class. The `String` produced will match the sequence of characters in s treated as a literal sequence. Slashes (\) and dollar signs ($) will be given no special meaning.[25]

Using the start and end Methods

Here's an example, `MatcherDemo.java`, that counts the number of times the word *dog* appears in the input string:

```
import java.util.regex.Pattern;
import java.util.regex.Matcher;

public class MatcherDemo {

    private static final String REGEX =
        "\\bdog\\b";
    private static final String INPUT =
        "dog dog dog doggie dogg";

    public static void main(String[] args) {
        Pattern p = Pattern.compile(REGEX);
        //  get a matcher object
        Matcher m = p.matcher(INPUT);
        int count = 0;
        while(m.find()) {
            count++;
            System.out.println("Match number "
                                + count);
            System.out.println("start(): "
                                + m.start());
            System.out.println("end(): "
                                + m.end());
        }
    }
}
```

---

24. 8/docs/api/java/util/regex/Matcher.html#replaceFirst-java.lang
    .String-

25. 8/docs/api/java/util/regex/Matcher.html#quoteReplacement-java
    .lang.String-

This example prints the following:

```
Match number 1
start(): 0
end(): 3
Match number 2
start(): 4
end(): 7
Match number 3
start(): 8
end(): 11
```

You can see that this example uses word boundaries to ensure that the letters d, o, g are not merely a substring in a longer word. It also gives some useful information about where in the input string the match has occurred. The start method returns the start index of the subsequence captured by the given group during the previous match operation, and end returns the index of the last character matched, plus one.

Using the matches and lookingAt Methods

The matches and lookingAt methods both attempt to match an input sequence against a pattern. The difference, however, is that matches requires the entire input sequence to be matched, while lookingAt does not. Both methods always start at the beginning of the input string. Here's the full code, MatchesLooking.java:

```java
import java.util.regex.Pattern;
import java.util.regex.Matcher;

public class MatchesLooking {

    private static final String REGEX = "foo";
    private static final String INPUT =
        "fooooooooooooooooo";
    private static Pattern pattern;
    private static Matcher matcher;

    public static void main(String[] args) {

        // Initialize
        pattern = Pattern.compile(REGEX);
        matcher = pattern.matcher(INPUT);

        System.out.println("Current REGEX is: "
                           + REGEX);
        System.out.println("Current INPUT is: "
                           + INPUT);

        System.out.println("lookingAt(): "
            + matcher.lookingAt());
        System.out.println("matches(): "
            + matcher.matches());
    }
```

```
    }
```

This example prints the following:

```
Current REGEX is: foo
Current INPUT is: foooooooooooooooooo
lookingAt(): true
matches(): false
```

Using replaceFirst(String) and replaceAll(String)

The `replaceFirst` and `replaceAll` methods replace text that matches a given regular expression. As their names indicate, `replaceFirst` replaces the first occurrence and `replaceAll` replaces all occurrences. Here's the `ReplaceDemo.java` code:

```java
import java.util.regex.Pattern;
import java.util.regex.Matcher;

public class ReplaceDemo {

    private static String REGEX = "dog";
    private static String INPUT =
        "The dog says meow. All dogs say meow.";
    private static String REPLACE = "cat";

    public static void main(String[] args) {
        Pattern p = Pattern.compile(REGEX);
        // get a matcher object
        Matcher m = p.matcher(INPUT);
        INPUT = m.replaceAll(REPLACE);
        System.out.println(INPUT);
    }
}
```

This example prints the following:

```
The cat says meow. All cats say meow.
```

In this first version, all occurrences of dog are replaced with cat. But why stop here? Rather than replace a simple literal like dog, you can replace text that matches *any* regular expression. The API for this method states that given the regular expression a*b, the input aabfooaabfooabfoob, and the replacement string –, an invocation of this method on a matcher for that expression would yield the string –foo–foo–foo–.

Here's the `ReplaceDemo2.java` code:

```java
import java.util.regex.Pattern;
import java.util.regex.Matcher;

public class ReplaceDemo2 {

    private static String REGEX = "a*b";
    private static String INPUT =
```

14

```
            "aabfooaabfooabfoob";
    private static String REPLACE = "-";

    public static void main(String[] args) {
        Pattern p = Pattern.compile(REGEX);
        // get a matcher object
        Matcher m = p.matcher(INPUT);
        INPUT = m.replaceAll(REPLACE);
        System.out.println(INPUT);
    }
}
```

This example prints the following:

```
-foo-foo-foo-
```

To replace only the first occurrence of the pattern, simply call `replaceFirst` instead of `replaceAll`. It accepts the same parameter.

Using appendReplacement(StringBuffer, String) and appendTail(StringBuffer)

The `Matcher` class also provides `appendReplacement` and `appendTail` methods for text replacement. The following example, `RegexDemo.java`, uses these two methods to achieve the same effect as `replaceAll`:

```
import java.util.regex.Pattern;
import java.util.regex.Matcher;

public class RegexDemo {

    private static String REGEX = "a*b";
    private static String INPUT = "aabfooaabfooabfoob";
    private static String REPLACE = "-";

    public static void main(String[] args) {
        Pattern p = Pattern.compile(REGEX);
        Matcher m = p.matcher(INPUT); // get a matcher object
        StringBuffer sb = new StringBuffer();
        while(m.find()){
            m.appendReplacement(sb,REPLACE);
        }
        m.appendTail(sb);
        System.out.println(sb.toString());
    }
}
```

This example prints the following:

```
-foo-foo-foo-
```

Matcher Method Equivalents in java.lang.String

For convenience, the `String` class mimics a couple of `Matcher` methods as well:

- `public String replaceFirst(String regex, String replacement)`.
  This replaces the first substring of this string that matches the given regular
  expression with the given replacement. An invocation of this method of the form
  `str.replaceFirst(regex, repl)` yields exactly the same result as the expression `Pattern.compile(regex).matcher(str).replaceFirst(repl)`.[26]
- `public String replaceAll(String regex, String replacement)`. This
  replaces each substring of this string that matches the given regular expression with the given replacement. An invocation of this method of the form `str`
  `.replaceAll(regex, repl)` yields exactly the same result as the expression
  `Pattern.compile(regex).matcher(str).replaceAll(repl)`.[27]

Methods of the PatternSyntaxException Class

A `PatternSyntaxException` is an unchecked exception that indicates a syntax
error in a regular expression pattern.[28] The `PatternSyntaxException` class provides the following methods to help you determine what went wrong:

- `public String getDescription()`. Retrieves the description of the error[29]
- `public int getIndex()`. Retrieves the error index[30]
- `public String getPattern()`. Retrieves the erroneous regular expression
  pattern[31]
- `public String getMessage()`. Returns a multiline string containing the
  description of the syntax error and its index, the erroneous regular expression
  pattern, and a visual indication of the error index within the pattern[32]

14

The following source code, `RegexTestHarness2.java`, updates our test harness
to check for malformed regular expressions:

---

26. 8/docs/api/java/lang/String.html#replaceFirst-java.lang.String
    -java.lang.String-
27. 8/docs/api/java/lang/String.html#replaceAll-java.lang.String-java
    .lang.String-
28. 8/docs/api/java/util/regex/PatternSyntaxException.html
29. 8/docs/api/java/util/regex/PatternSyntaxException.html#getDescription--
30. 8/docs/api/java/util/regex/PatternSyntaxException.html#getIndex--
31. 8/docs/api/java/util/regex/PatternSyntaxException.html#getPattern--
32. 8/docs/api/java/util/regex/PatternSyntaxException.html#getMessage--

```java
import java.io.Console;
import java.util.regex.Pattern;
import java.util.regex.Matcher;
import java.util.regex.PatternSyntaxException;

public class RegexTestHarness2 {

    public static void main(String[] args){
        Pattern pattern = null;
        Matcher matcher = null;

        Console console = System.console();
        if (console == null) {
            System.err.println("No console.");
            System.exit(1);
        }
        while (true) {
            try{
                pattern =
                Pattern.compile(console.readLine("%nEnter your regex: "));

                matcher =
                pattern.matcher(console.readLine("Enter input string to search: "));
            }
            catch(PatternSyntaxException pse){
                console.format("There is a problem" +
                            " with the regular expression!%n");
                console.format("The pattern in question is: %s%n",
                            pse.getPattern());
                console.format("The description is: %s%n",
                            pse.getDescription());
                console.format("The message is: %s%n",
                            pse.getMessage());
                console.format("The index is: %s%n",
                            pse.getIndex());
                System.exit(0);
            }
            boolean found = false;
            while (matcher.find()) {
                console.format("I found the text" +
                    " \"%s\" starting at " +
                    "index %d and ending at index %d.%n",
                    matcher.group(),
                    matcher.start(),
                    matcher.end());
                found = true;
            }
            if(!found){
                console.format("No match found.%n");
            }
        }
    }
}
```

14

To run this test, enter ?i)foo as the regular expression. This mistake is a common scenario in which the programmer has forgotten the opening parenthesis in the embedded flag expression (?i). Doing so will produce the following results:

```
Enter your regex: ?i)
There is a problem with the regular expression!
The pattern in question is: ?i)
The description is: Dangling meta character '?'
The message is: Dangling meta character '?' near index 0
?i)
^
The index is: 0
```

From this output, we can see that the syntax error is a dangling metacharacter (the question mark) at index 0. A missing opening parenthesis is the culprit.

Unicode Support

Regular expression pattern matching has expanded functionality to support Unicode 6.0.

Matching a Specific Code Point

You can match a specific Unicode code point using an escape sequence of the form \uFFFF, where FFFF is the hexadecimal value of the code point you want to match. For example, \u6771 matches the Han character for east.

Alternatively, you can specify a code point using Perl-style hex notation, \x{...}:

```
String hexPattern = "\x{" + Integer.toHexString(codePoint) + "}";
```

Unicode Character Properties

Each Unicode character, in addition to its value, has certain attributes or properties. You can match a single character belonging to a particular category with the expression \p{ prop }. You can match a single character *not* belonging to a particular category with the expression \P{ prop }. The three supported property types are scripts, blocks, and a "general" category.

Scripts

To determine if a code point belongs to a specific script, you can use either the script keyword or the sc short form (e.g., \p{script=Hiragana}). Alternatively, you can prefix the script name with the string Is, such as \p{IsHiragana}. Valid script names supported by Pattern are those accepted by UnicodeScript.forName.[33]

Blocks

A block can be specified using the block keyword or the blk short form (e.g., \p{block=Mongolian}). Alternatively, you can prefix the block name with the string In, such as \p{InMongolian}. Valid block names supported by Pattern are those accepted by UnicodeBlock.forName.

General Category

Categories can be specified with optional prefix Is. For example, IsL matches the category of Unicode letters. Categories can also be specified by using the general_ category keyword or the short form gc. For example, an uppercase letter can be matched using general_category=Lu or gc=Lu. Supported categories are those of the Unicode standard[34] in the version specified by the Character[35] class.

Questions and Exercises: Regular Expressions

Questions

1. What are the three public classes in the java.util.regex package? Describe the purpose of each.

2. Consider the string literal foo. What is the start index? What is the end index? Explain what these numbers mean.

3. What is the difference between an ordinary character and a metacharacter? Give an example of each.

4. How do you force a metacharacter to act like an ordinary character?

5. What do you call a set of characters enclosed in square brackets? What is it for?

6. Here are three predefined character classes: \d, \s, and \w. Describe each one and rewrite it using square brackets.

7. For each of \d, \s, and \w, write *two* simple expressions that match the *opposite* set of characters.

8. Consider the regular expression (dog){3}. Identify the two subexpressions. What string does the expression match?

---

33. 8/docs/api/java/lang/Character.UnicodeScript.html#forName-java
    .lang.String-

34. http://www.unicode.org/unicode/standard/standard.html

35. 8/docs/api/java/lang/Character.html

Exercise

1. Use a backreference to write an expression that will match a person's name only if that person's first name and last name are the same.

Answers

You can find answers to these questions and exercises at `http://docs.oracle .com/javase/tutorial/essential/regex/QandE/answers.html`.

14

15

The Platform Environment

Chapter Contents

Configuration Utilities   595

System Utilities   603

PATH and CLASSPATH   609

Questions and Exercises: The Platform Environment   613

An application runs in a *platform environment*, defined by the underlying operating system, the Java Virtual Machine (Java VM), the class libraries, and various configuration data supplied when the application is launched. This chapter describes some of the Application Programming Interfaces (APIs) an application uses to examine and configure its platform environment. The first section describes APIs used to access configuration data supplied when the application is deployed or by the application's user. The second section describes miscellaneous APIs defined in the System and Runtime classes. The third section describes environment variables used to configure Java SE Development Kit (JDK) tools and other applications. The chapter ends with questions and exercises to test your understanding.

Configuration Utilities

This section describes some of the configuration utilities that help an application access its start-up context.

Properties

Properties are configuration values managed as *key / value pairs*. In each pair, the key and value are both `String` values.[1] The key identifies and is used to retrieve the value, much as a variable name is used to retrieve the variable's value. For example, an application capable of downloading files might use a property named `download.lastDirectory` to keep track of the directory used for the last download.

To manage properties, create instances of `java.util.Properties`.[2] This class provides methods for the following:

- Loading key/value pairs into a `Properties` object from a stream
- Retrieving a value from its key
- Listing the keys and their values
- Enumerating over the keys
- Saving the properties to a stream

For an introduction to streams, refer to Chapter 11, "I/O Streams."

`Properties` extends `java.util.Hashtable`.[3] Some of the methods inherited from `Hashtable` support the following actions:

- Testing to see if a particular key or value is in the `Properties` object
- Getting the current number of key/value pairs
- Removing a key and its value
- Adding a key/value pair to the `Properties` list
- Enumerating over the values or the keys
- Retrieving a value by its key
- Finding out if the `Properties` object is empty

> **Note**
>
> Access to properties is subject to approval by the current security manager. The example code segments in this section are assumed to be in standalone applications, which, by default, have no security manager. The same code in an applet may not work depending on the browser in which it is running. See Chapter 18, "What Applets Can and Cannot Do," for information about security restrictions on applets.

---

1. 8/docs/api/java/lang/String.html
2. 8/docs/api/java/util/Properties.html
3. 8/docs/api/java/util/Hashtable.html

The `System` class maintains a `Properties` object that defines the configuration of the current working environment. For more about these properties, see the "System Properties" section. The remainder of this section explains how to use properties to manage application configuration.

Properties in the Application Life Cycle

Figure 15.1 illustrates how a typical application might manage its configuration data with a `Properties` object over the course of its execution:

- *Starting up*. The actions given in the first three boxes occur when the application is starting up. First, the application loads the default properties from a well-known location into a `Properties` object. Normally, the default properties are stored in a file on disk along with the `.class` and other resource files for the application. Next, the application creates another `Properties` object and loads the properties that were saved from the last time the application was run. Many applications store properties on a per-user basis, so the properties loaded in this step are usually in a specific file in a particular directory maintained by this application in the user's home directory. Finally, the application uses the default and remembered properties to initialize itself. The key here is consistency. The application must always load and save properties to the same location so that it can find them the next time it's executed.

- *Running*. During the execution of the application, the user may change some settings, perhaps in a preferences window, and the `Properties` object is updated

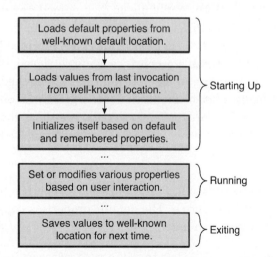

Figure 15.1 Managing Properties in an Application's Life Cycle

to reflect these changes. If the user's changes are to be remembered in future sessions, they must be saved.

- *Exiting.* Upon exiting, the application saves the properties to its well-known location, to be loaded again when the application is next started up.

Setting Up the Properties Object

The following Java code performs the first two steps described in the previous section: loading the default properties and loading the remembered properties:

```
...
// create and load default properties
Properties defaultProps = new Properties();
FileInputStream in = new FileInputStream("defaultProperties");
defaultProps.load(in);
in.close();

// create application properties with default
Properties applicationProps = new Properties(defaultProps);

// now load properties
// from last invocation
in = new FileInputStream("appProperties");
applicationProps.load(in);
in.close();
...
```

First, the application sets up a default `Properties` object. This object contains the set of properties to use if values are not explicitly set elsewhere. Then the load method reads the default values from a file on disk named `defaultProperties`.

Next, the application uses a different constructor to create a second `Properties` object, `applicationProps`, whose default values are contained in `defaultProps`. The defaults come into play when a property is being retrieved. If the property can't be found in `applicationProps`, then its default list is searched.

Finally, the code loads a set of properties into `applicationProps` from a file named `appProperties`. The properties in this file are those that were saved from the application the last time it was invoked, as explained in the next section.

Saving Properties

The following example writes out the application properties from the previous example using `Properties.store`. The default properties don't need to be saved each time because they never change:

```
FileOutputStream out = new FileOutputStream("appProperties");
applicationProps.store(out, "---No Comment---");
out.close();
```

The `store` method needs a stream to write to as well as a string that it uses as a comment at the top of the output.

Getting Property Information

Once the application has set up its `Properties` object, the application can query the object for information about various keys and values that it contains. An application gets information from a `Properties` object after start-up so that it can initialize itself based on choices made by the user. The `Properties` class has several methods for getting property information:

- `contains(Object value)` *and* `containsKey(Object key)`. These return true if the value or the key is in the `Properties` object. `Properties` inherits these methods from `Hashtable`. Thus they accept `Object` arguments, but only `String` values should be used.
- `getProperty(String key)` *and* `getProperty(String key, String default)`. These return the value for the specified property. The second version provides for a default value. If the key is not found, the default is returned.
- `list(PrintStream s)` *and* `list(PrintWriter w)`. These write all the properties to the specified stream or writer and are useful for debugging.
- `elements()`, `keys()`, *and* `propertyNames()`. These return an `Enumeration` containing the keys or values (as indicated by the method name) contained in the `Properties` object. The `keys` method only returns the keys for the object itself; the `propertyNames` method returns the keys for default properties as well.
- `stringPropertyNames()`. This is like `propertyNames` but returns a `Set` `<String>` and only returns names of properties where both key and value are strings. Note that the `Set` object is not backed by the `Properties` object, so changes in one do not affect the other.
- `size()`. This returns the current number of key/value pairs.

Setting Properties

A user's interaction with an application during its execution may impact property settings. These changes should be reflected in the `Properties` object so that they are saved when the application exits (and calls the `store` method). The following methods change the properties in a `Properties` object:

- `setProperty(String key, String value)`. Puts the key/value pair in the `Properties` object
- `remove(Object key)`. Removes the key/value pair associated with key

15

> **Note**
>
> Some of the methods described above are defined in `Hashtable` and thus accept key and value argument types other than `String`. Always use `Strings` for keys and values, even if the method allows other types. Also, do not invoke `Hashtable.set` or `Hashtable.setAll` on `Properties` objects; always use `Properties.setProperty`.

Command-Line Arguments

A Java application can accept any number of arguments from the command line. This allows the user to specify configuration information when the application is launched.

The user enters command-line arguments when invoking the application and specifies them after the name of the class to be run. For example, suppose a Java application called `Sort` sorts lines in a file. To sort the data in a file named `friends.txt`, a user would enter the following:

```
java Sort friends.txt
```

When an application is launched, the runtime system passes the command-line arguments to the application's main method via an array of `Strings`. In the previous example, the runtime system passes the command-line arguments to the `Sort` application in an array. This array contains only one value: `friends.txt`.

Echoing Command-Line Arguments

The `Echo` example displays each of its command-line arguments on a line by itself:

```java
public class Echo {
    public static void main (String[] args) {
        for (String s: args) {
            System.out.println(s);
        }
    }
}
```

The following example shows how a user might run `Echo`. User input is in italics:

```
java Echo Drink Hot Java
Drink
Hot
Java
```

Note that the application displays each word—`Drink`, `Hot`, and `Java`—on a line by itself. This is because the space character separates command-line arguments. To have `Drink`, `Hot`, and `Java` interpreted as a single argument, the user would join them by enclosing them within quotation marks:

```
java Echo "Drink Hot Java"
Drink Hot Java
```

Parsing Numeric Command-Line Arguments

If an application needs to support a numeric command-line argument, it must convert a `String` argument that represents a number, such as 34, to a numeric value. Here is a code snippet that converts a command-line argument to an `int`:

```
int firstArg;
if (args.length > 0) {
    try {
        firstArg = Integer.parseInt(args[0]);
    } catch (NumberFormatException e) {
        System.err.println("Argument" + args[0] + " must be an integer.");
        System.exit(1);
    }
}
```

`parseInt` throws a `NumberFormatException` if the format of `args[0]` isn't valid. All the `Number` classes—`Integer`, `Float`, `Double`, and so on—have `parseXXX` methods that convert a `String` representing a number to an object of their type.

Environment Variables

Many operating systems use *environment variables* to pass configuration information to applications. Like properties in the Java platform, environment variables are key/value pairs, where both the key and the value are strings. The conventions for setting and using environment variables vary between operating systems and also between command-line interpreters. To learn how to pass environment variables to applications on your system, refer to your system documentation.

15

Querying Environment Variables

On the Java platform, an application uses `System.getenv` to retrieve environment variable values.[4] Without an argument, `getenv` returns a read-only instance of `java.util.Map`, where the map keys are the environment variable names and the map values are the environment variable values. This is demonstrated in the `EnvMap` example:

```
import java.util.Map;

public class EnvMap {
    public static void main (String[] args) {
        Map<String, String> env = System.getenv();
        for (String envName : env.keySet()) {
            System.out.format("%s=%s%n",
                              envName,
```

---

4.   8/docs/api/java/lang/System.html#getenv--

```
                            env.get(envName));
        }
    }
}
```

With a `String` argument, `getenv` returns the value of the specified variable. If the variable is not defined, `getenv` returns `null`. The `Env` example uses `getenv` this way to query specific environment variables, specified on the command line:

```java
public class Env {
    public static void main (String[] args) {
        for (String env: args) {
            String value = System.getenv(env);
            if (value != null) {
                System.out.format("%s=%s%n",
                                    env, value);
            } else {
                System.out.format("%s is"
                    + " not assigned.%n", env);
            }
        }
    }
}
```

Passing Environment Variables to New Processes

When a Java application uses a `ProcessBuilder`[5] object to create a new process, the default set of environment variables passed to the new process is the same set provided to the application's virtual machine process. The application can change this set using `ProcessBuilder.environment`.

Platform Dependency Issues

There are many subtle differences in the ways environment variables are implemented on different systems. For example, Windows ignores case in environment variable names, while Solaris, Linux, and OS X do not. The way environment variables are used also varies. For example, Windows provides the user name in an environment variable called `USERNAME`, while Solaris, Linux, and OS X might provide the user name in `USER`, `LOGNAME`, or both.

To maximize portability, never refer to an environment variable when the same value is available in a system property. For example, if the operating system provides a user name, it will always be available in the system property `user.name`.

Other Configuration Utilities

Here is a summary of some other configuration utilities.

---

5.   8/docs/api/java/lang/ProcessBuilder.html

The *Preferences API* allows applications to store and retrieve configuration data in an implementation-dependent backing store. Asynchronous updates are supported, and the same set of preferences can be safely updated by multiple threads and even multiple applications. For more information, refer to the Preferences API Guide.[6]

An application deployed in a *JAR file* uses a *manifest* to describe the contents of the archive. For more information, see Chapter 16.

The configuration of a *Java Web Start application* is contained in a *Java Network Launch Protocol (JNLP) file*. For more information, see Chapter 17.

The configuration of a *Java Plug-In applet* is partially determined by the HTML tags used to embed the applet in the web page. Depending on the applet and the browser, these tags can include `<applet>`, `<object>`, `<embed>`, and `<param>`. For more information, see Chapter 18.

The class `java.util.ServiceLoader` provides a simple *service provider* facility.[7] A service provider is an implementation of a *service*—a well-known set of interfaces and (usually abstract) classes. The classes in a service provider typically implement the interfaces and subclass the classes defined in the service. Service providers can be installed as extensions. See the Extension Mechanism trail in the online tutorial for more information.[8] Providers can also be made available by adding them to the class path or by some other platform-specific means.

System Utilities

The `System` class implements a number of system utilities.[9] Some of these have already been covered in the previous section. This section covers some of the other system utilities.

Command-Line I/O Objects

`System` provides several predefined I/O objects that are useful in a Java application that is meant to be launched from the command line. These implement the standard I/O streams provided by most operating systems and also a console object that is useful for entering passwords. For more information, refer to Chapter 11, "I/O from the Command Line."

15

---

6.   `8/docs/technotes/guides/preferences/index.html`

7.   `8/docs/api/java/util/ServiceLoader.html`

8.   `tutorial/ext/index.html`

9.   `8/docs/api/java/lang/System.html`

System Properties

In the "Properties" section, we examined the way an application can use `Properties` objects to maintain its configuration. The Java platform itself uses a `Properties` object to maintain its own configuration. The `System` class maintains a `Properties` object that describes the configuration of the current working environment. System properties include information about the current user, the current version of the Java runtime, and the character used to separate components of a file path name. Table 15.1 describes some of the most important system properties.

> **Note**
>
> Access to system properties can be restricted by the security manager. This is most often an issue in applets, which are prevented from reading some system properties and from writing *any* system properties. For more on accessing system properties in applets, refer to Chapter 19, "System Properties."

Table 15.1 System Properties

Key	Meaning
file.separator	Character that separates components of a file path: / on Solaris, Linux, and OS X and \ on Windows
java.class.path	Path used to find directories and JAR files containing class files (Elements of the class path are separated by a platform-specific character specified in the path.separator property.)
java.home	Installation directory for the Java Runtime Environment (JRE)
java.vendor	JRE vendor name
java.vendor.url	JRE vendor URL
java.version	JRE version number
line.separator	Sequence used by operating system to separate lines in text files
os.arch	Operating system architecture
os.name	Operating system name
os.version	Operating system version
path.separator	Path separator character used in java.class.path
user.dir	User working directory
user.home	User home directory
user.name	User account name

15

Reading System Properties

The System class has two methods used to read system properties: getProperty and getProperties. In addition, the System class has two different versions of getProperty. Both retrieve the value of the property named in the argument list. The simpler of the two getProperty methods takes a single argument—a property key. For example, to get the value of path.separator, use the following statement:

```
System.getProperty("path.separator");
```

The getProperty method returns a string containing the value of the property. If the property does not exist, this version of getProperty returns null.

The other version of getProperty requires two String arguments: the first argument is the key to look up and the second argument is a default value to return if the key cannot be found or if it has no value. For example, the following invocation of getProperty looks up the System property called subliminal.message. This is not a valid system property, so instead of returning null, this method returns the default value provided as a second argument: Buy StayPuft Marshmallows!

```
System.getProperty("subliminal.message", "Buy StayPuft Marshmallows!");
```

The last method provided by the System class to access property values is the getProperties method, which returns a Properties object.[10] This object contains a complete set of system property definitions.

Writing System Properties

To modify the existing set of system properties, use System.setProperties. This method takes a Properties object that has been initialized to contain the properties to be set. It replaces the entire set of system properties with the new set represented by the Properties object.

> **Note**
> Changing system properties is potentially dangerous and should be done with discretion. Many system properties are not reread after start-up and are there for informational purposes. Changing some properties may have unexpected side effects.

---

10. 8/docs/api/java/util/Properties.html

The next example, `PropertiesTest`, creates a `Properties` object and initializes it from `myProperties.txt`:

```
subliminal.message=Buy StayPuft Marshmallows!
```

`PropertiesTest` then uses `System.setProperties` to install the new `Properties` objects as the current set of system properties:

```
import java.io.FileInputStream;
import java.util.Properties;

public class PropertiesTest {
    public static void main(String[] args)
        throws Exception {

        // set up new properties object
        // from file "myProperties.txt"
        FileInputStream propFile =
            new FileInputStream("myProperties.txt");
        Properties p =
            new Properties(System.getProperties());
        p.load(propFile);

        // set the system properties
        System.setProperties(p);
        // display new properties
        System.getProperties().list(System.out);
    }
}
```

Note how `PropertiesTest` creates the `Properties` object, p, which is used as the argument to `setProperties`:

```
Properties p = new Properties(System.getProperties());
```

This statement initializes the new properties object, p, with the current set of system properties, which in the case of this small application is the set of properties initialized by the runtime system. Then the application loads additional properties into p from the file `myProperties.txt` and sets the system properties to p. This has the effect of adding the properties listed in `myProperties.txt` to the set of properties created by the runtime system at start-up. Note that an application can create p without any default `Properties` object, like this:

```
Properties p = new Properties();
```

Also note that the value of system properties can be overwritten! For example, if `myProperties.txt` contains the following line, the `java.vendor` system property will be overwritten:

```
java.vendor=Acme Software Company
```

In general, be careful not to overwrite system properties.

The `setProperties` method changes the set of system properties for the current running application. These changes are not persistent—that is, changing the system properties within an application will not affect future invocations of the Java interpreter for this or any other application. The runtime system reinitializes the system properties each time it starts up. If changes to system properties are to be persistent, then the application must write the values to some file before exiting and read them in again upon start-up.

The Security Manager

A *security manager* is an object that defines a security policy for an application. This policy specifies actions that are unsafe or sensitive. Any actions not allowed by the security policy cause a `SecurityException` to be thrown.[11] An application can also query its security manager to discover which actions are allowed.

Typically, a web applet runs with a security manager provided by the browser or Java Web Start plug-in. Other kinds of applications normally run without a security manager, unless the application itself defines one. If no security manager is present, the application has no security policy and acts without restrictions.

This section explains how an application interacts with an existing security manager. For more detailed information, including information on how to design a security manager, refer to the Java Security Guide.[12]

Interacting with the Security Manager

The security manager is an object of type `SecurityManager`;[13] to obtain a reference to this object, invoke `System.getSecurityManager`:

```
SecurityManager appsm = System.getSecurityManager();
```

If there is no security manager, this method returns `null`.

Once an application has a reference to the security manager object, it can request permission to do specific things. Many classes in the standard libraries do this. For example, `System.exit`, which terminates the Java VM with an exit status, invokes `SecurityManager.checkExit` to ensure that the current thread has permission to shut down the application.

---

11. 8/docs/api/java/lang/SecurityException.html
12. 8/docs/technotes/guides/security/index.html
13. 8/docs/api/java/lang/SecurityManager.html

The `SecurityManager` class defines many other methods used to verify other kinds of operations. For example, `SecurityManager.checkAccess` verifies thread accesses and `SecurityManager.checkPropertyAccess` verifies access to the specified property. Each operation or group of operations has its own check*XXX*( ) method.

In addition, the set of check*XXX*( ) methods represents the set of operations that are already subject to the protection of the security manager. Typically an application does not have to directly invoke any check*XXX*( ) methods.

Recognizing a Security Violation

Many actions that are routine without a security manager can throw a `SecurityException` when run with a security manager. This is true even when invoking a method that isn't documented as throwing `SecurityException`. For example, consider the following code used to read a file:

```
reader = new FileReader("xanadu.txt");
```

In the absence of a security manager, this statement executes without error, provided `xanadu.txt` exists and is readable. But suppose this statement is inserted in a web applet, which typically runs under a security manager that does not allow file input. The following error messages might result:

```
appletviewer fileApplet.html
Exception in thread "AWT-EventQueue-1" java.security.AccessControlException:
  access denied (java.io.FilePermission characteroutput.txt write)
        at java.security.AccessControlContext.checkPermission(AccessControlContext.java:323)
        at java.security.AccessController.checkPermission(AccessController.java:546)
        at java.lang.SecurityManager.checkPermission(SecurityManager.java:532)
        at java.lang.SecurityManager.checkWrite(SecurityManager.java:962)
        at java.io.FileOutputStream.<init>(FileOutputStream.java:169)
        at java.io.FileOutputStream.<init>(FileOutputStream.java:70)
        at java.io.FileWriter.<init>(FileWriter.java:46)
...
```

Note that the specific exception thrown in this case, `java.security.Access-ControlException`, is a subclass of `SecurityException`.[14]

Miscellaneous Methods in System

This section describes some of the methods in `System` that aren't covered in the previous sections.

The `arrayCopy` method efficiently copies data between arrays. For more information, refer to Chapter 4.

---

14. 8/docs/api/java/security/AccessControlException.html

The `currentTimeMillis`[15] and `nanoTime`[16] methods are useful for measuring time intervals during execution of an application. To measure a time interval in milliseconds, invoke `currentTimeMillis` twice (at the beginning and end of the interval) and subtract the first value returned from the second. Similarly, invoking `nanoTime` twice measures an interval in nanoseconds.

> **Note**
>
> The accuracy of both `currentTimeMillis` and `nanoTime` is limited by the time services provided by the operating system. Do not assume that `currentTimeMillis` is accurate to the nearest millisecond or that `nanoTime` is accurate to the nearest nanosecond. Also, neither `currentTimeMillis` nor `nanoTime` should be used to determine the current time. Instead, use methods from the Date-Time API such as `LocalTime.now`;[17] see Chapter 21 for more information.

The `exit` method causes the Java VM to shut down, with an integer exit status specified by the argument.[18] The exit status is available to the process that launched the application. By convention, an exit status of zero indicates normal termination of the application, while any other value is an error code.

PATH and CLASSPATH

This section explains how to use the `PATH` and `CLASSPATH` environment variables on Microsoft Windows, Solaris, Linux, and OS X. Consult the installation instructions included with your installation of the Java Development Kit (JDK) software bundle for current information.

After installing the software, the JDK directory will have the structure shown in Figure 15.2. The `bin` directory contains both the compiler and the launcher.

Update the PATH Environment Variable (Microsoft Windows)

You can run Java applications just fine without setting the `PATH` environment variable, or you can optionally set it as a convenience. Set the `PATH` environment variable if you want to be able to conveniently run the executables (`javac.exe`, `java.exe`, `javadoc.exe`, and so on) from any directory without having to type the full

15.   `8/docs/api/java/lang/System.html#currentTimeMillis--`

16.   `8/docs/api/java/lang/System.html#nanoTime--`

17.   `8/docs/api/java/time/LocalTime.html#now--`

18.   `8/docs/api/java/lang/System.html#exit-int-`

jdk1.version.0

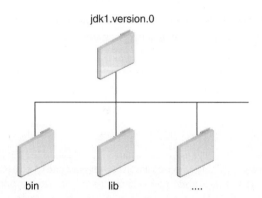

bin   lib   ....

Figure 15.2 Directory Structure after Installation of the JDK

path of the command. If you do not set the PATH variable, you need to specify the full path to the executable every time you run it:

```
C:\Java\jdk1.8.0\bin\javac MyClass.java
```

On Microsoft Windows, the PATH environment variable is a series of directories separated by semicolons (;).Windows looks for programs in the PATH directories in order, from left to right. You should have only one bin directory for the JDK in the path at a time (given that those following the first are ignored), so if one is already present, you can update that particular entry. The following is an example of a PATH environment variable:

```
C:\Java\jdk1.8.0\bin;C:\Windows\System32\;C:\Windows\;C:\Windows\System32\Wbem
```

It is useful to set the PATH environment variable permanently so it will persist after rebooting. To make a permanent change to the PATH variable, use the **System** icon in the Control Panel. The precise procedure varies depending on the version of Windows.

Windows Vista

1. From the desktop, right click the **My Computer** icon.
2. Choose **Properties** from the context menu.
3. Click the **Advanced** tab (**Advanced system settings** link in Vista).
4. Click **Environment Variables**. In the section **System Variables**, find the PATH environment variable and select it. Click **Edit**. If the PATH environment variable does not exist, click **New**.

15

5. In the **Edit System Variable** (or **New System Variable**) window, specify the value of the PATH environment variable. Click **OK**. Close all remaining windows by clicking **OK**.

Windows 7

1. From the desktop, right click the **Computer** icon.
2. Choose **Properties** from the context menu.
3. Click the **Advanced system settings** link.
4. Click **Environment Variables**. In the section **System Variables**, find the PATH environment variable and select it. Click **Edit**. If the PATH environment variable does not exist, click **New**.
5. In the **Edit System Variable** (or **New System Variable**) window, specify the value of the PATH environment variable. Click **OK**. Close all remaining windows by clicking **OK**.

> **Note**
>
> You may see a PATH environment variable similar to the following when editing it from the Control Panel:
>
> `%JAVA_HOME%\bin;%SystemRoot%\system32;%SystemRoot%;%SystemRoot%\System32\Wbem`
>
> Variables enclosed in percentage signs (%) are existing environment variables. If one of these variables is listed in the **Environment Variables** window from the Control Panel (such as JAVA_HOME), then you can edit its value. If it does not appear, then it is a special environment variable that the operating system has defined. For example, SystemRoot is the location of the Microsoft Windows system folder. To obtain the value of an environment variable, enter the following at a command prompt. (This example obtains the value of the SystemRoot environment variable.)
>
>   echo %SystemRoot%

Update the PATH Variable (Solaris, Linux, and OS X)

You can run the JDK just fine without setting the PATH variable, or you can optionally set it as a convenience. However, you should set the path variable if you want to be able to run the executables (javac, java, javadoc, etc.) from any directory without having to type the full path of the command. If you do not set the PATH variable, you need to specify the full path to the executable every time you run it:

```
% /usr/local/jdk1.8.0/bin/javac MyClass.java
```

To find out if the path is properly set, execute the following:

```
% java -version
```

This will print the version of the `java` tool if it can find it. If the version is old or you get the error `java: Command not found`, then the path is not properly set. To set the path permanently, set the path in your start-up file. For C shell (`csh`), edit the start-up file (`~/.cshrc`):

```
set path=(/usr/local/jdk1.8.0/bin $path)
```

For bash, edit the start-up file (`~/.bashrc`):

```
PATH=/usr/local/jdk1.8.0/bin:$PATH
export PATH
```

For ksh, the start-up file is named by the environment variable, ENV:

```
PATH=/usr/local/jdk1.8.0/bin:$PATH
export PATH
```

For sh, edit the profile file (`~/.profile`):

```
PATH=/usr/local/jdk1.8.0/bin:$PATH
export PATH
```

Next, load the start-up file and verify that the path is set by repeating the `java` command. For C shell (`csh`), do the following:

```
% source ~/.cshrc
% java -version
```

For ksh, bash, or sh, do the following:

```
% . /.profile
% java -version
```

Checking the CLASSPATH Variable (All Platforms)

The CLASSPATH variable is one way to tell applications, including the JDK tools, where to look for user classes. Classes that are part of the Java Runtime Environment

(JRE), Java SE Development Kit (JDK) platform, and extensions should be defined through other means, such as the bootstrap class path or the extensions directory.

The preferred way to specify the class path is by using the –cp command-line switch. This allows the CLASSPATH to be set individually for each application without affecting other applications. *Setting the CLASSPATH can be tricky and should be performed with care.*

The default value of the class path is ., meaning that only the current directory is searched. Specifying either the CLASSPATH variable or the –cp command line switch overrides this value.

To check whether CLASSPATH is set on Microsoft Windows, execute the following:

```
C:> echo %CLASSPATH%
```

On Solaris, Linux, or OS X, execute the following:

```
% echo $CLASSPATH
```

If CLASSPATH is not set, you will get a CLASSPATH: Undefined variable error (Solaris, Linux, or OS X) or simply %CLASSPATH% (Microsoft Windows). To modify the CLASSPATH, use the same procedure you used for the PATH variable.

Class path wildcards allow you to include an entire directory of .jar files in the class path without explicitly naming them individually. For more information, including an explanation of class path wildcards and a detailed description of how to clean up the CLASSPATH environment variable, see the Setting the Class Path technical note.[19]

15

Questions and Exercises: The Platform Environment

Question

1. You install a new library contained in a .jar file. In order to access the library from your code, you set the CLASSPATH environment variable to point to the new .jar file. Now you find that you get an error message when you try to launch simple applications:

   ```
   java Hello
   Exception in thread "main" java.lang.NoClassDefFoundError: Hello
   ```

---

19. 8/docs/technotes/tools/windows/classpath.html

In this case, the `Hello` class is compiled into a `.class` file in the current directory—yet the `java` command can't seem to find it. What's going wrong?

Exercise

1. Write an application, `PersistentEcho`, with the following features:
   - If `PersistentEcho` is run with command-line arguments, it prints out those arguments. It also saves the string printed out to a property and saves the property to a file called `PersistentEcho.txt`.
   - If `PersistentEcho` is run with no command-line arguments, it looks for an environment variable called `PERSISTENTECHO`. If that variable exists, `PersistentEcho` prints out its value and also saves the value in the same way it does for command-line arguments.
   - If `PersistentEcho` is run with no command-line arguments and the `PERSISTENTECHO` environment variable is not defined, it retrieves the property value from `PersistentEcho.txt` and prints that out.

Answers

You can find answers to these questions and exercises at `http://docs.oracle` `.com/javase/tutorial/essential/environment/QandE/answers.html`.

15

16

Packaging Programs in JAR Files

Chapter Contents

Using JAR Files: The Basics   616
Working with Manifest Files: The Basics   627
Signing and Verifying JAR Files   635
Using JAR-Related APIs   642
Questions and Exercises: Packaging Programs in JAR Files   648

The Java Archive (JAR) file format enables you to bundle multiple files into a single archive file. Typically a JAR file contains the class files and auxiliary resources associated with applets and applications. The JAR file format provides many benefits:

- *Security*. You can digitally sign the contents of a JAR file. Users who recognize your signature can then optionally grant your software security privileges it wouldn't otherwise have.

- *Decreased download time*. If your applet is bundled in a JAR file, the applet's class files and associated resources can be downloaded to a browser in a single HTTP transaction without the need for opening a new connection for each file.

- *Compression*. The JAR format allows you to compress your files for efficient storage.

- *Packaging for extensions*. The extensions framework provides a means by which you can add functionality to the Java core platform, and the JAR file format defines the packaging for extensions. By using the JAR file format, you can turn your software into extensions as well.

- *Package sealing*. Packages stored in JAR files can be optionally sealed so that the package can enforce version consistency. Sealing a package within a JAR file means that all classes defined in that package must be found in the same JAR file.

- *Package versioning*. A JAR file can hold data about the files it contains, such as vendor and version information.
- *Portability*. The mechanism for handling JAR files is a standard part of the Java platform's core Application Programming Interface (API).

This chapter has four sections. The first section shows you how to perform basic JAR file operations and how to run software that is bundled in JAR files. The second section explains manifest files and how to customize them so you can do such things as seal packages and set an application's entry point. The third section shows you how to digitally sign JAR files and verify the signatures of signed JAR files. The fourth section explains JAR-related APIs. The chapter ends with questions and exercises to test what you've learned about JAR files.

Using JAR Files: The Basics

JAR files are packaged with the ZIP file format, so you can use them for tasks such as lossless data compression, archiving, decompression, and archive unpacking. These tasks are among the most common uses of JAR files, and you can realize many JAR file benefits using only these basic features.

Even if you want to take advantage of advanced functionality provided by the JAR file format, such as electronic signing, you'll first need to become familiar with the fundamental operations. To perform basic tasks with JAR files, you use the Java archive tool provided as part of the Java SE Development Kit (JDK). Because the Java archive tool is invoked by using the `jar` command, this chapter refers to it as *the JAR tool*. As a synopsis and preview of some of the topics to be covered in this section, Table 16.1 summarizes common JAR file operations.

Creating a JAR File

The basic format of the command for creating a JAR file is as follows:

```
jar cf jar-file input-file(s)
```

Here are the options and arguments used in this command:

- The c option indicates that you want to *create* a JAR file.
- The f option indicates that you want the output to go to a *file* rather than to `stdout`.

- *jar-file* is the name that you want the resulting JAR file to have. You can use any file name for a JAR file. By convention, JAR file names are given a .jar extension, though this is not required.

- The *input-file(s)* argument is a space-separated list of one or more files that you want to include in your JAR file. The *input-file(s)* argument can contain the wildcard * symbol. If any of the "input-files" are directories, the contents of those directories are added to the JAR file recursively.

The c and f options can appear in either order, but there must not be any space between them. This command will generate a compressed JAR file and place it in the current directory. The command will also generate a default manifest file for the JAR archive. You can add any of the additional options presented in Table 16.2 to the cf options of the basic command.

Note

The metadata in the JAR file, such as the entry names, comments, and contents of the manifest, must be encoded in UTF-8.

Note

When you create a JAR file, the time of creation is stored in the JAR file. Therefore, even if the contents of the JAR file do not change, when you create a JAR file multiple times, the resulting files are not exactly identical. You should be aware of this when you are using JAR files in a build environment. It is recommended that you use versioning information in the manifest file, rather than creation time, to control versions of a JAR file. See the "Package Version Information" section.

16

Table 16.1 Common JAR File Operations

Operation	Command
To create a JAR file	jar cf *jar-file input-file(s)*
To view the contents of a JAR file	jar tf *jar-file*
To extract the contents of a JAR file	jar xf *jar-file*
To extract specific files from a JAR file	jar xf *jar-file archived-file(s)*
To run an application packaged as a JAR file (requires the Main-class manifest header)	java -jar *app.jar*

To invoke an applet packaged as a JAR file	```<applet
	    code="AppletClassName.class"
	    archive="JarFileName.jar"
	    width="width"
	    height="height">
	</applet>```

Table 16.2 JAR Tool Options

Option	Description
v	This produces *verbose* output on stdout while the JAR file is being built. The verbose output tells you the name of each file as it's added to the JAR file.
0 (zero)	This indicates that you don't want the JAR file to be compressed.
M	This indicates that the default manifest file should not be produced.
m	This is used to include manifest information from an existing manifest file. Here is the format for using this option: `jar cmf existing-manifest jar-file input-file(s)` See the "Modifying a Manifest File" section for more information about this option. Note that the manifest must end with a new line or carriage return. The last line will not be parsed properly if it does not end with a new line or carriage return.
–C	This is used for changing directories during execution of the command. See below for an example.

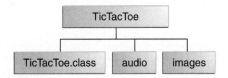

Figure 16.1 TicTacToe Folder Hierarchy

An Example

Let's look at an example, a simple TicTacToe applet. You can see the source code of this applet by downloading the JDK Demos and Samples bundle from Java SE Downloads.[1] This demo contains class files, audio files, and images with the structure depicted in Figure 16.1.

The audio and images subdirectories contain sound files and GIF images used by the applet. To package this demo into a single JAR file named TicTacToe.jar, you would run this command from inside the TicTacToe directory:

```
jar cvf TicTacToe.jar TicTacToe.class TicTacToe$1.class example1.html audio images
```

The audio and images arguments represent directories, so the JAR tool will recursively place them and their contents in the JAR file. The generated JAR file TicTacToe.jar will be placed in the current directory. Because the command used

---

1.   http://www.oracle.com/technetwork/java/javase/downloads/index.html

the v option for verbose output, you would see something similar to this output when you run the command:

```
added manifest
adding: audio/(in = 0) (out= 0)(stored 0%)
adding: audio/beep.au(in = 4032) (out= 3572)(deflated 11%)
adding: audio/ding.au(in = 2566) (out= 2055)(deflated 19%)
adding: audio/return.au(in = 6558) (out= 4401)(deflated 32%)
adding: audio/yahoo1.au(in = 7834) (out= 6985)(deflated 10%)
adding: audio/yahoo2.au(in = 7463) (out= 4607)(deflated 38%)
adding: example1.html(in = 424) (out= 238)(deflated 43%)
adding: images/(in = 0) (out= 0)(stored 0%)
adding: images/cross.gif(in = 157) (out= 160)(deflated -1%)
adding: images/not.gif(in = 158) (out= 161)(deflated -1%)
adding: TicTacToe$1.class(in = 550) (out= 369)(deflated 32%)
adding: TicTacToe.class(in = 3705) (out= 2232)(deflated 39%)
adding: TicTacToe.java(in = 9584) (out= 2973)(deflated 68%)
```

You can see from this output that the JAR file `TicTacToe.jar` is compressed. The JAR tool compresses files by default. You can turn off the compression feature by using the 0 (zero) option so that the command would look like this:

```
jar cvf0 TicTacToe.jar TicTacToe.class TicTacToe$1.class example1.html audio images
```

You might want to avoid compression in some instances (e.g., to increase the speed with which a JAR file could be loaded by a browser). Uncompressed JAR files can generally be loaded more quickly than compressed files because the need to decompress the files during loading is eliminated. However, there is a trade-off in that download time over a network may be longer for larger, uncompressed files.

The JAR tool will accept arguments that use the wildcard * symbol. As long as there weren't any unwanted files in the `TicTacToe` directory, you could have used this alternative command to construct the JAR file:

```
jar cvf TicTacToe.jar *
```

Though the verbose output doesn't indicate it, the JAR tool automatically adds a manifest file to the JAR archive with path name META-INF/MANIFEST.MF. See the "Working with Manifest Files: The Basics" section for information about manifest files.

In the above example, the files in the archive retained their relative path names and directory structure. The JAR tool provides the -C option that you can use to create a JAR file in which the relative paths of the archived files are not preserved. It's modeled after TAR's -C option.

As an example, suppose you wanted to put audio files and GIF images used by the `TicTacToe` demo into a JAR file and that you wanted all the files to be on the top level with no directory hierarchy. You could accomplish that by issuing this command from the parent directory of the images and audio directories:

```
jar cf ImageAudio.jar -C images . -C audio .
```

The −C images part of this command directs the JAR tool to go to the images directory, and the . following −C images directs the JAR tool to archive all the contents of that directory. The −C audio . part of the command then does the same with the audio directory. The resulting JAR file would have this table of contents:

```
META-INF/MANIFEST.MF
cross.gif
not.gif
beep.au
ding.au
return.au
yahoo1.au
yahoo2.au
```

By contrast, suppose that you used a command that did not employ the −C option:

```
jar cf ImageAudio.jar images audio
```

The resulting JAR file would have this table of contents:

```
META-INF/MANIFEST.MF
images/cross.gif
images/not.gif
audio/beep.au
audio/ding.au
audio/return.au
audio/yahoo1.au
audio/yahoo2.au
```

Viewing the Contents of a JAR File

The basic format of the command for viewing the contents of a JAR file is the following:

```
jar tf jar-file
```

Let's look at the options and argument used in this command:

- The t option indicates that you want to view the *table* of contents of the JAR file.
- The f option indicates that the JAR file whose contents are to be viewed is specified on the command line.
- The *jar-file* argument is the path and name of the JAR file whose contents you want to view.

The t and f options can appear in either order, but there must not be any space between them. This command will display the JAR file's table of contents to std-out. You can optionally add the verbose option, v, to produce additional information about file sizes and last-modified dates in the output.

An Example

Let's use the JAR tool to list the contents of the TicTacToe.jar file we created in the previous section:

```
jar tf TicTacToe.jar
```

This command displays the contents of the JAR file to stdout:

```
META-INF/
META-INF/MANIFEST.MF
audio/
audio/beep.au
audio/ding.au
audio/return.au
audio/yahoo1.au
audio/yahoo2.au
example1.html
images/
images/cross.gif
images/not.gif
TicTacToe$1.class
TicTacToe.class
TicTacToe.java
```

The JAR file contains the TicTacToe class file and the audio and images directory, as expected. The output also shows that the JAR file contains a default manifest file, META-INF/MANIFEST.MF, which was automatically placed in the archive by the JAR tool. For more information, see the "Understanding the Default Manifest" section.

All path names are displayed with forward slashes, regardless of the platform or operating system you're using. Paths in JAR files are always relative; you'll never see a path beginning with C:, for example.

The JAR tool will display additional information if you use the v option:

```
jar tvf TicTacToe.jar
```

For example, the verbose output for the TicTacToe JAR file would look similar to the following:

```
   0 Thu Aug 21 12:58:34 EDT 2014 META-INF/
  68 Thu Aug 21 12:58:34 EDT 2014 META-INF/MANIFEST.MF
   0 Wed Jul 30 21:42:36 EDT 2014 audio/
4032 Wed Jul 30 21:42:36 EDT 2014 audio/beep.au
```

16

```
2566 Wed Jul 30 21:42:36 EDT 2014 audio/ding.au
6558 Wed Jul 30 21:42:36 EDT 2014 audio/return.au
7834 Wed Jul 30 21:42:36 EDT 2014 audio/yahoo1.au
7463 Wed Jul 30 21:42:36 EDT 2014 audio/yahoo2.au
 424 Wed Jul 30 21:42:36 EDT 2014 example1.html
   0 Wed Jul 30 21:42:36 EDT 2014 images/
 157 Wed Jul 30 21:42:36 EDT 2014 images/cross.gif
 158 Wed Jul 30 21:42:36 EDT 2014 images/not.gif
 550 Wed Jul 30 21:42:36 EDT 2014 TicTacToe$1.class
3705 Wed Jul 30 21:42:36 EDT 2014 TicTacToe.class
9584 Wed Jul 30 21:42:36 EDT 2014 TicTacToe.java
```

Extracting the Contents of a JAR File

The basic command to use for extracting the contents of a JAR file is

```
jar xf jar-file [archived-file(s)]
```

Let's look at the options and arguments in this command:

- The x option indicates that you want to *extract* files from the JAR archive.
- The f options indicates that the JAR *file* from which files are to be extracted is specified on the command line, rather than through `stdin`.
- The `jar-file` argument is the file name (or path and file name) of the JAR file from which to extract files.
- `archived-file(s)` is an optional argument consisting of a space-separated list of the files to be extracted from the archive. If this argument is not present, the JAR tool will extract all the files in the archive.

16

As usual, the order in which the x and f options appear in the command doesn't matter, but there must not be a space between them.

When extracting files, the JAR tool makes copies of the desired files and writes them to the current directory, reproducing the directory structure that the files have in the archive. The original JAR file remains unchanged.

> **Note**
> When it extracts files, the JAR tool will overwrite any existing files having the same path name as the extracted files.

An Example

Let's extract some files from the `TicTacToe` JAR file we've been using in previous sections. Recall that the contents of `TicTacToe.jar` are as follows:

```
META-INF/
META-INF/MANIFEST.MF
audio/
audio/beep.au
audio/ding.au
audio/return.au
audio/yahoo1.au
audio/yahoo2.au
example1.html
images/
images/cross.gif
images/not.gif
TicTacToe$1.class
TicTacToe.class
TicTacToe.java
```

Suppose you want to extract the `TicTacToe` class file and the `cross.gif` image file. To do so, you can use this command:

```
jar xf TicTacToe.jar TicTacToe.class images/cross.gif
```

This command does two things:

- It places a copy of `TicTacToe.class` in the current directory.
- It creates the directory `images`, if it doesn't already exist, and places a copy of `cross.gif` within it.

The original `TicTacToe` JAR file remains unchanged.

As many files as desired can be extracted from the JAR file in the same way. When the command doesn't specify which files to extract, the JAR tool extracts all files in the archive. For example, you can extract all the files in the `TicTacToe` archive by using this command:

```
jar xf TicTacToe.jar
```

Updating a JAR File

The JAR tool provides a u option, which you can use to update the contents of an existing JAR file by modifying its manifest or by adding files.

The basic command for adding files has this format:

```
jar uf jar-file input-file(s)
```

Here are the options and arguments in this command:

- The u option indicates that you want to *update* an existing JAR file.
- The f option indicates that the JAR file to update is specified on the command line.

16

- *jar-file* is the existing JAR file that is to be updated.
- *input-file(s)* is a space-delimited list of one or more files that you want to add to the JAR file.

Any files already in the archive having the same path name as a file being added will be overwritten.

When creating a new JAR file, you can optionally use the -C option to indicate a change of directory. For more information, see the "Creating a JAR File" section.

Examples

Recall that `TicTacToe.jar` has these contents:

```
META-INF/
META-INF/MANIFEST.MF
audio/
audio/beep.au
audio/ding.au
audio/return.au
audio/yahoo1.au
audio/yahoo2.au
example1.html
images/
images/cross.gif
images/not.gif
TicTacToe$1.class
TicTacToe.class
TicTacToe.java
```

Suppose that you want to add the file `images/new.gif` to the JAR file. You could accomplish that by issuing this command from the parent directory of the `images` directory:

```
jar uf TicTacToe.jar images/new.gif
```

The revised JAR file would have this table of contents:

```
META-INF/
META-INF/MANIFEST.MF
audio/
audio/beep.au
audio/ding.au
audio/return.au
audio/yahoo1.au
audio/yahoo2.au
example1.html
images/
images/cross.gif
images/new.gif
images/not.gif
```

```
TicTacToe$1.class
TicTacToe.class
TicTacToe.java
```

You can use the −C option to "change directories" during execution of the command. Here's an example:

```
jar uf TicTacToe.jar -C images new.gif
```

This command would change to the images directory before adding new.gif to the JAR file. The images directory would not be included in the path name of new.gif when it's added to the archive, resulting in a table of contents that looks like this:

```
META-INF/
META-INF/MANIFEST.MF
audio/
audio/beep.au
audio/ding.au
audio/return.au
audio/yahoo1.au
audio/yahoo2.au
example1.html
images/
images/cross.gif
images/not.gif
new.gif
TicTacToe$1.class
TicTacToe.class
TicTacToe.java
```

Running JAR-Packaged Software

Now that you have learned how to create JAR files, how do you actually run the code you packaged? Consider these scenarios:

- Your JAR file contains an applet that is to be run inside a browser.
- Your JAR file contains an application that is to be started from the command line.
- Your JAR file contains code that you want to use as an extension.

This section will cover the first two situations. See the online tutorial on the use of JAR files as extensions.[2]

---

2.   `tutorial/ext/index.html`

Applets Packaged in JAR Files

To start any applet from an HTML file for running inside a browser, you can use the `applet` tag. For more information about other ways to deploy applets, see Chapter 18. If the applet is bundled as a JAR file, the only thing you need to do differently is to use the *archive* parameter to specify the relative path to the JAR file.

As an example, use the `TicTacToe` demo applet. The `applet` tag in the HTML file that displays the applet can be marked up like this:

```
<applet code="TicTacToe.class"
        width="120" height="120">
</applet>
```

If the `TicTacToe` demo was packaged in a JAR file named `TicTacToe.jar`, you can modify the `applet` tag with the addition of an `archive` parameter:

```
<applet code="TicTacToe.class"
        archive="TicTacToe.jar"
        width="120" height="120">
</applet>
```

The `archive` parameter specifies the relative path to the JAR file that contains `TicTacToe.class`. For this example, it is assumed that the JAR file and the HTML file are in the same directory. If they are not, you must include the JAR file's relative path in the `archive` parameter's value. For example, if the JAR file was one directory below the HTML file in a directory called `applets`, the `applet` tag would look like this:

```
<applet code="TicTacToe.class"
        archive="applets/TicTacToe.jar"
        width="120" height="120">
</applet>
```

JAR Files as Applications

You can run JAR packaged applications with the Java launcher (`java` command). Here is the basic command:

```
java -jar jar-file
```

The `-jar` flag tells the launcher that the application is packaged in the JAR file format. You can only specify one JAR file, which must contain all the application-specific code. Before you execute this command, make sure that the runtime environment has information about which class within the JAR file is the application's entry point. To indicate which class is the application's entry point, you must add a `Main-Class` header to the JAR file's manifest. The header takes the following form:

```
Main-Class: classname
```

The header's value, *classname*, is the name of the class that is the application's entry point. For more information, see the "Setting an Application's Entry Point" section.

When the `Main-Class` is set in the manifest file, you can run the application from the command line:

```
java -jar app.jar
```

To run the application from the JAR file that is in another directory, you must specify the path of that directory: `java -jar path/app.jar`.

Working with Manifest Files: The Basics

JAR files support a wide range of functionality, including electronic signing, version control, package sealing, and others. What gives a JAR file this versatility? The answer is the JAR file's *manifest*.

The manifest is a special file that can contain information about the files packaged in a JAR file. By tailoring this "meta" information that the manifest contains, you enable the JAR file to serve a variety of purposes. This section will explain the contents of the manifest file and show you how to work with it, with examples for the basic features.

Understanding the Default Manifest

When you create a JAR file, it automatically receives a default manifest file. There can be only one manifest file in an archive, and it always has the following path name:

```
META-INF/MANIFEST.MF
```

When you create a JAR file, the default manifest file simply contains the following:

```
Manifest-Version: 1.0
Created-By: 1.8.0_20 (Oracle Corporation)
```

These lines show that a manifest's entries take the form of "header: value" pairs. The name of a header is separated from its value by a colon. The default manifest conforms to version 1.0 of the manifest specification and was created by the 1.8.0_20 version of the JDK.

The manifest can also contain information about the other files that are packaged in the archive. Exactly which file information should be recorded in the manifest depends on how you intend to use the JAR file. The default manifest makes no assumptions about what information it should record about other files.

Digest information is not included in the default manifest. To learn more about digests and signing, see the "Signing and Verifying JAR Files" section.

16

Modifying a Manifest File

You use the m command-line option to add custom information to the manifest during the creation of a JAR file. This section describes the m option.

The JAR tool automatically puts a default manifest with the path name META-INF/MANIFEST.MF into any JAR file you create. You can enable special JAR file functionality, such as package sealing, by modifying the default manifest. Typically, modifying the default manifest involves adding special-purpose *headers* to the manifest that allow the JAR file to perform a particular desired function.

To modify the manifest, you must first prepare a text file containing the information you wish to add to the manifest. You then use the JAR tool's m option to add the information in your file to the manifest.

> **Note**
>
> The text file from which you are creating the manifest must end with a new line or carriage return. The last line will not be parsed properly if it does not end with a new line or carriage return.

The basic command has this format:

```
jar cfm jar-file manifest-addition input-file(s)
```

Let's look at the options and arguments used in this command:

- The c option indicates that you want to *create* a JAR file.
- The f option indicates that you want the output to go to a *file* (the JAR file you're creating) rather than to standard output.
- The m option indicates that you want to merge information from an existing file into the manifest file of the JAR file you're creating.
- *jar-file* is the name that you want the resulting JAR file to have.
- *manifest-addition* is the name (or path and name) of the existing text file whose contents you want to add to the contents of JAR file's manifest.
- The *input-file(s)* argument is a space-separated list of one or more files that you want to be placed in your JAR file.

The f and m options must be in the same order as the corresponding arguments.

> **Note**
>
> The contents of the manifest must be encoded in UTF-8.

The remaining sections of this chapter demonstrate specific modifications you may want to make to the manifest file.

Setting an Application's Entry Point

If you have an application bundled in a JAR file, you need some way to indicate which class within the JAR file is your application's entry point. You provide this information with the `Main-Class` header in the manifest, which has the general form:

```
Main-Class: classname
```

The value `classname` is the name of the class that is your application's entry point.

Recall that the entry point is a class having a method with the signature `public static void main(String[] args)`. After you have set the `Main-Class` header in the manifest, you then run the JAR file using the following form of the `java` command:

```
java -jar JAR-name
```

The `main` method of the class specified in the `Main-Class` header is executed.

An Example

We want to execute the `main` method in the class `MyClass` in the package `MyPackage` when we run the JAR file. We first create a text file named `Manifest.txt` with the following contents:

```
Main-Class: MyPackage.MyClass
```

> **Note**
> The text file must end with a new line or carriage return. The last line will not be parsed properly if it does not end with a new line or carriage return.

16

We then create a JAR file named `MyJar.jar` by entering the following command:

```
jar cfm MyJar.jar Manifest.txt MyPackage/*.class
```

This creates the JAR file with a manifest with the following contents:

```
Manifest-Version: 1.0
Created-By: 1.8.0_20 (Oracle Corporation)
Main-Class: MyPackage.MyClass
```

When you run the JAR file with the following command, the `main` method of `MyClass` executes:

```
java -jar MyJar.jar
```

Setting an Entry Point with the JAR Tool

The *e* flag (for *entry point*) creates or overrides the manifest's `Main-Class` attribute. It can be used while creating or updating a JAR file. Use it to specify the application entry point without editing or creating the manifest file.

For example, this command creates `app.jar` where the `Main-Class` attribute value in the manifest is set to `MyApp`:

```
jar cfe app.jar MyApp MyApp.class
```

You can directly invoke this application by running the following command:

```
java -jar app.jar
```

If the entry-point class name is in a package, it may use a dot character (`.`) as the delimiter. For example, if `Main.class` is in a package called `foo`, the entry point can be specified in the following way:

```
jar cfe Main.jar foo.Main foo/Main.class
```

Adding Classes to the JAR File's Class Path

You may need to reference classes in other JAR files from within a JAR file. For example, in a typical situation, an applet is bundled in a JAR file whose manifest references a different JAR file or several different JAR files that serve as utilities for the purposes of that applet.

You specify classes to include in the `Class-Path` header field in the manifest file of an applet or application. The `Class-Path` header takes the following form:

```
Class-Path: jar1-name jar2-name directory-name/jar3-name
```

By using the `Class-Path` header in the manifest, you can avoid having to specify a long `-classpath` flag when invoking Java to run your application.

> **Note**
>
> The `Class-Path` header points to classes or JAR files on the local network, not JAR files within the JAR file or classes accessible over Internet protocols. To load classes in JAR files within a JAR file into the class path, you must write custom code to load those classes. For example, if `MyJar.jar` contains another JAR file called `MyUtils.jar`, you cannot use the `Class-Path` header in `MyJar.jar`'s manifest to load classes in `MyUtils.jar` into the class path.

An Example

We want to load classes in `MyUtils.jar` into the class path for use in `MyJar.jar`. These two JAR files are in the same directory.

We first create a text file named `Manifest.txt` with the following contents:

```
Class-Path: MyUtils.jar
```

> **Note**
>
> The text file must end with a new line or carriage return. The last line will not be parsed properly if it does not end with a new line or carriage return.

We then create a JAR file named `MyJar.jar` by entering the following command:

```
jar cfm MyJar.jar Manifest.txt MyPackage/*.class
```

This creates the JAR file with a manifest with the following contents:

```
Manifest-Version: 1.0
Class-Path: MyUtils.jar
Created-By: 1.8.0_20 (Oracle Corporation)
```

The classes in `MyUtils.jar` are now loaded into the class path when you run `MyJar.jar`.

Setting Package Version Information

You may need to include package version information in a JAR file's manifest. You provide this information with the headers presented in Table 16.3.

16

Table 16.3 Headers in a Manifest

Header	Definition
Name	The name of the specification
Specification-Title	The title of the specification
Specification-Version	The version of the specification
Specification-Vendor	The vendor of the specification
Implementation-Title	The title of the implementation
Implementation-Version	The build number of the implementation
Implementation-Vendor	The vendor of the implementation

One set of such headers can be assigned to each package. The versioning headers should appear directly beneath the `Name` header for the package. This example shows all the versioning headers:

```
Name: java/util/
Specification-Title: Java Utility Classes
Specification-Version: 1.2
Specification-Vendor: Example Tech, Inc.
Implementation-Title: java.util
Implementation-Version: build57
Implementation-Vendor: Example Tech, Inc.
```

For more information about package version headers, see the Package Versioning specification.[3]

An Example

We want to include the headers in the example above in the manifest of `MyJar.jar`. We first create a text file named `Manifest.txt` with the following contents:

```
Name: java/util/
Specification-Title: Java Utility Classes
Specification-Version: 1.2
Specification-Vendor: Example Tech, Inc.
Implementation-Title: java.util
Implementation-Version: build57
Implementation-Vendor: Example Tech, Inc.
```

> **Note**
>
> The text file must end with a new line or carriage return. The last line will not be parsed properly if it does not end with a new line or carriage return.

16

We then create a JAR file named `MyJar.jar` by entering the following command:

```
jar cfm MyJar.jar Manifest.txt MyPackage/*.class
```

This creates the JAR file with a manifest with the following contents:

```
Manifest-Version: 1.0
Created-By: 1.8.0_20 (Oracle Corporation)
Name: java/util/
Specification-Title: Java Utility Classes
Specification-Version: 1.2
Specification-Vendor: Example Tech, Inc.
Implementation-Title: java.util
```

---

3.   8/docs/technotes/guides/versioning/spec/versioning2.html#wp89936

```
Implementation-Version: build57
Implementation-Vendor: Example Tech, Inc.
```

Sealing Packages within a JAR File

Packages within JAR files can be optionally sealed, which means that all classes defined in that package must be archived in the same JAR file. You might want to seal a package for several reasons (e.g., to ensure version consistency among the classes in your software).

You seal a package in a JAR file by adding the `Sealed` header in the manifest, which has the following general form:

```
Name: myCompany/myPackage/
Sealed: true
```

The value `myCompany/myPackage/` is the name of the package to seal. Note that the package name must end with a `/`.

An Example

We want to seal two packages, `firstPackage` and `secondPackage`, in the JAR file `MyJar.jar`. We first create a text file named `Manifest.txt` with the following contents:

```
Name: myCompany/firstPackage/
Sealed: true

Name: myCompany/secondPackage/
Sealed: true
```

> **Note**
>
> The text file must end with a new line or carriage return. The last line will not be parsed properly if it does not end with a new line or carriage return.

We then create a JAR file named `MyJar.jar` by entering the following command:

```
jar cfm MyJar.jar Manifest.txt MyPackage/*.class
```

This creates the JAR file with a manifest with the following contents:

```
Manifest-Version: 1.0
Created-By: 1.8.0_20 (Oracle Corporation)
Name: myCompany/firstPackage/
Sealed: true
```

16

```
Name: myCompany/secondPackage/
Sealed: true
```

Sealing JAR Files

If you want to guarantee that all classes in a package come from the same code source, use JAR sealing. A sealed JAR specifies that all packages defined by that JAR are sealed unless overridden on a per-package basis.

To seal a JAR file, use the `Sealed` manifest header with the value `true`:

```
Sealed: true
```

This specifies that all packages in this archive are sealed unless explicitly overridden for particular packages with the `Sealed` attribute in a manifest entry.

Enhancing Security with Manifest Attributes

The following JAR file manifest attributes are available to help ensure the security of your applet or Java Web Start application. Only the `Permissions` attribute is required:

- The `Permissions` attribute is used to ensure that the application requests only the level of permissions that is specified in the applet tag or Java Network Launch Protocol (JNLP) file used to invoke the application. Use this attribute to help prevent someone from redeploying an application that is signed with your certificate and running it at a different privilege level. This attribute is required in the manifest for the main JAR file. See Permissions Attribute[4] in the Java Platform Standard Edition Deployment Guide for more information.

- The `Codebase` attribute is used to ensure that the code base of the JAR file is restricted to specific domains. Use this attribute to prevent someone from redeploying your application on another web site for malicious purposes. See Codebase Attribute[5] in the Java Platform Standard Edition Deployment Guide for more information.

- The `Application-Name` attribute is used to provide the title that is shown in the security prompts for signed applications. See Application-Name Attribute[6] in the Java Platform Standard Edition Deployment Guide for more information.

---

4.   8/docs/technotes/guides/deploy/manifest.html#JSDPG896
5.   8/docs/technotes/guides/deploy/manifest.html#JSDPG897
6.   8/docs/technotes/guides/deploy/manifest.html#JSDPG899

- The `Application-Library-Allowable-Codebase` attribute is used to identify the locations where your application is expected to be found. Use this attribute to reduce the number of locations shown in the security prompt when the JAR file is in a different location than the JNLP file or the HTML page. See Application-Library-Allowable-Codebase Attribute[7] in the Java Platform Standard Edition Deployment Guide for more information.

- The `Caller-Allowable-Codebase` attribute is used to identify the domains from which JavaScript code can make calls to your application. Use this attribute to prevent unknown JavaScript code from accessing your application. See Caller-Allowable-Codebase Attribute[8] in the Java Platform Standard Edition Deployment Guide for more information.

- The `Entry-Point` attribute is used to identify the classes that are allowed to be used as entry points to your RIA. Use this attribute to prevent unauthorized code from being run from other available entry points in the JAR file. See Entry-Point Attribute[9] in the Java Platform Standard Edition Deployment Guide for more information.

- The `Trusted-Only` attribute is used to prevent untrusted components from being loaded. See Trusted-Only Attribute[10] in the Java Platform Standard Edition Deployment Guide for more information.

- The `Trusted-Library` attribute is used to allow calls between privileged Java code and sandbox Java code without prompting the user for permission. See Trusted-Library Attribute[11] in the Java Platform Standard Edition Deployment Guide for more information.

See the "Modifying a Manifest File" section for information on adding these attributes to the manifest file.

Signing and Verifying JAR Files

You can optionally sign a JAR file with your electronic "signature." Users who verify your signature can grant your JAR-bundled software security privileges that it wouldn't ordinarily have. Conversely, you can verify the signatures of signed JAR

---

7.   8/docs/technotes/guides/deploy/manifest.html#JSDPG900

8.   8/docs/technotes/guides/deploy/manifest.html#JSDPG901

9.   8/docs/technotes/guides/deploy/manifest.html#JSDPG902

10. 8/docs/technotes/guides/deploy/manifest.html#JSDPG903

11. 8/docs/technotes/guides/deploy/manifest.html#JSDPG904

files that you want to use. This section shows you how to use the tools provided in the JDK to sign and verify JAR files.

Understanding Signing and Verification

The Java platform enables you to digitally sign JAR files. You digitally sign a file for the same reason you might sign a paper document with pen and ink—to let readers know that you wrote the document or at least that the document has your approval.

When you sign a letter, for example, everyone who recognizes your signature can confirm that you wrote the letter. Similarly, when you digitally sign a file, anyone who "recognizes" your digital signature knows that the file came from you. The process of "recognizing" electronic signatures is called *verification*.

When the JAR file is signed, you also have the option of time stamping the signature. Similar to putting a date on a paper document, time stamping the signature identifies when the JAR file was signed. The time stamp can be used to verify that the certificate used to sign the JAR file was valid at the time of signing.

The ability to sign and verify files is an important part of the Java platform's security architecture. Security is controlled by the security *policy* that's in effect at runtime. You can configure the policy to grant security privileges to applets and to applications. For example, you could grant permission to an applet to perform normally forbidden operations such as reading and writing local files or running local executable programs. If you have downloaded some code that's signed by a trusted entity, you can use that fact as a criterion in deciding which security permissions to assign to the code.

Once you (or your browser) have verified that an applet is from a trusted source, you can have the platform relax security restrictions to let the applet perform operations that would ordinarily be forbidden. A trusted applet can have freedoms as specified by the *policy file* in force.

The Java platform enables signing and verification by using special numbers called public and private *keys*. Public keys and private keys come in pairs, and they play complementary roles.

The private key is the electronic "pen" with which you can sign a file. As its name implies, your private key is known only to you so that no one else can "forge" your signature. A file signed with your private key can be verified only by the corresponding public key.

Public and private keys alone, however, aren't enough to truly verify a signature. Even if you've verified that a signed file contains a matching key pair, you still need some way to confirm that the public key actually comes from the signer that it purports to come from.

One more element, therefore, is required to make signing and verification work. That additional element is the *certificate* that the signer includes in a signed JAR file. A certificate is a digitally signed statement from a recognized *certification authority* that indicates who owns a particular public key. Certification authorities are entities (typically firms specializing in digital security) that are trusted throughout the industry to sign and issue certificates for keys and their owners. In the case of signed JAR files, the certificate indicates who owns the public key contained in the JAR file.

When you sign a JAR file, your public key is placed inside the archive along with an associated certificate so that it's easily available for use by anyone wanting to verify your signature.

To summarize digital signing, the signer signs the JAR file using a private key. The corresponding public key is then placed in the JAR file, together with its certificate, so that it is available for use by anyone who wants to verify the signature.

Digests and the Signature File

When you sign a JAR file, each file in the archive is given a digest entry in the archive's manifest. Here's an example of what such an entry might look like:

```
Name: test/classes/ClassOne.class
SHA1-Digest: TD1GZt8G11dXY2p4o1SZPc5Rj64=
```

The digest values are hashes or encoded representations of the contents of the files as they were at the time of signing. A file's digest will change if and only if the file itself changes.

When a JAR file is signed, a *signature* file is automatically generated and placed in the JAR file's META-INF directory, the same directory that contains the archive's manifest. Signature files have file names with an .SF extension. Here is an example of the contents of a signature file:

```
Signature-Version: 1.0
SHA1-Digest-Manifest: h1yS+K9T7DyHtZrtI+LxvgqaMYM=
Created-By: 1.8.0_20 (Oracle Corporation)

Name: test/classes/ClassOne.class
SHA1-Digest: fcav7ShIG6i86xPepmitOVo4vWY=

Name: test/classes/ClassTwo.class
SHA1-Digest: xrQem9snnPhLySDiZyclMlsFdtM=

Name: test/images/ImageOne.gif
SHA1-Digest: kdHbE7kL9ZHLgK7akHttYV4XIa0=

Name: test/images/ImageTwo.gif
SHA1-Digest: mFOD5zpk68R4oaxEqoS9Q7nhm60=
```

16

As you can see, the signature file contains digest entries for the archive's files that look similar to the digest-value entries in the manifest. However, while the digest values in the manifest are computed from the files themselves, the digest values in the signature file are computed from the corresponding entries in the manifest. Signature files also contain a digest value for the entire manifest (see the SHA1-Digest-Manifest header in the above example).

When a signed JAR file is being verified, the digests of each of its files are recomputed and compared with the digests recorded in the manifest to ensure that the contents of the JAR file haven't changed since it was signed. As an additional check, digest values for the manifest file itself are recomputed and compared against the values recorded in the signature file. You can read additional information about signature files on the Manifest Format[12] page of the JDK documentation.

The Signature Block File

In addition to the signature file, a *signature block* file is automatically placed in the META-INF directory when a JAR file is signed. Unlike the manifest file or the signature file, signature block files are not human readable.

The signature block file contains two elements essential for verification:

- The digital signature for the JAR file that was generated with the signer's private key
- The certificate containing the signer's public key, to be used by anyone wanting to verify the signed JAR file

Signature block file names typically will have a .DSA extension indicating that they were created by the default Digital Signature Algorithm. Other file name extensions are possible if keys associated with some other standard algorithm are used for signing.

Related Documentation

For additional information about keys, certificates, and certification authorities, see the following:

- The JDK Security Tools[13]
- X.509 Certificates[14]

---

12. 8/docs/technotes/guides/jar/jar.html#JAR_Manifest

13. 8/docs/technotes/tools/index.html#security

14. 8/docs/technotes/guides/security/cert3.html

For more information about the Java platform's security architecture, see this related documentation:

- Security Features in Java SE[15]
- Java SE Security[16]
- Security Tools[17]

Signing JAR Files

You use the JAR Signing and Verification Tool to sign JAR files and time stamp the signature. You invoke the JAR Signing and Verification Tool by using the `jarsigner` command, so we'll refer to it as the *Jarsigner tool* for short.

To sign a JAR file, you must first have a private key. Private keys and their associated public-key certificates are stored in password-protected databases called *keystores*. A keystore can hold the keys of many potential signers. Each key in the keystore can be identified by an *alias*, which is typically the name of the signer who owns the key. The key belonging to Rita Jones might have the alias *rita*, for example.

Here is the basic form of the command for signing a JAR file:

```
jarsigner jar-file alias
```

This command includes the following elements:

- `jar-file` is the path name of the JAR file that's to be signed.
- `alias` is the alias identifying the private key that's to be used to sign the JAR file and the key's associated certificate.

The Jarsigner tool will prompt you for the passwords for the keystore and alias.

This basic form of the command assumes that the keystore to be used is in a file named `.keystore` in your home directory. It will create signature and signature block files with names x.SF and x.DSA, respectively, where x is the first eight letters of the alias, all converted to uppercase. This basic command will *overwrite* the original JAR file with the signed JAR file.

In practice, you might want to use one or more of the command options that are available. For example, time stamping the signature is encouraged so that any tool

---

15. `tutorial/security/index.html`

16. `http://www.oracle.com/technetwork/java/javase/tech/index-jsp-136007`
     `.html`

17. `8/docs/technotes/tools/index.html#security`

used to deploy your application can verify that the certificate used to sign the JAR file was valid at the time that the file was signed. A warning is issued by the Jar-signer tool if a time stamp is not included.

Options precede the `jar-file` path name. Table 16.4 describes the options that are available.

Example

Let's look at a couple of examples of signing a JAR file with the Jarsigner tool. In these examples, we will assume the following:

- Your alias is *johndoe*.
- The keystore you want to use is in a file named *mykeys* in the current working directory.

Table 16.4 Jarsigner Tool Options

Option	Description
`-keystore url`	This specifies a keystore to be used if you don't want to use the `.keystore` default database.
`-storepass password`	This allows you to enter the keystore's password on the command line rather than be prompted for it.
`-keypass password`	This allows you to enter your alias's password on the command line rather than be prompted for it.
`-sigfile file`	This specifies the base name for the `.SF` and `.DSA` files if you don't want the base name to be taken from your alias; `file` must be composed only of uppercase letters (A–Z), numerals (0–9), a hyphen (-), and an underscore (_).
`-signedjar file`	This specifies the name of the signed JAR file to be generated if you don't want the original unsigned file to be overwritten with the signed file.
`-tsa url`	This generates a time stamp for the signature using the time stamping authority (TSA) identified by the URL.
`-tsacert alias`	This generates a time stamp for the signature using the TSA's public key certificate identified by *alias*.
`-altsigner class`	This indicates that an alternative signing mechanism be used to time stamp the signature. The fully qualified class name identifies the class used.
`-altsignerpath classpathlist`	This provides the path to the class identified by the `altsigner` option and any JAR files that the class depends on.

16

- The keystore's password is *abc123*.
- The TSA that you want to use to time stamp the signature is located at `http://example.tsa.url`.

Under these assumptions, you could use this command to sign a JAR file named `app.jar`:

```
jarsigner -keystore mykeys -storepass abc123 -tsa http://example.tsa.url app.jar johndoe
```

You will be prompted for the keystore password. Because this command doesn't make use of the -sigfile option, the .SF and .DSA files it creates would be named JOHNDOE.SF and JOHNDOE.DSA. Because the command doesn't use the -signedjar option, the resulting signed file will overwrite the original version of app.jar.

Let's look at what would happen if you used a different combination of options:

```
jarsigner -keystore mykeys -sigfile SIG -signedjar SignedApp.jar
          -tsacert testalias app.jar johndoe
```

This time, you would be prompted to enter the passwords for both the keystore and your alias because the passwords aren't specified on the command line. The signature and signature block files would be named SIG.SF and SIG.DSA, respectively, and the signed JAR file SignedApp.jar would be placed in the current directory. The original unsigned JAR file would remain unchanged. Also, the signature would be time stamped with the TSA's public key certificate, identified as testalias.

Additional Information

Complete reference pages for the JAR Signing and Verification Tool are online in the Summary of Security Tools section.[18]

16

> **Note**
> When a certificate is self-signed, UNKNOWN will be displayed as the publisher of the application.[19]

Verifying Signed JAR Files

Typically, verification of signed JAR files will be the responsibility of your Java Runtime Environment (JRE). Your browser will verify signed applets that it downloads. Signed applications invoked with the -jar option of the interpreter will be verified by the runtime environment.

---

18. `8/docs/technotes/guides/security/SecurityToolsSummary.html`

19. `http://www.java.com/en/download/faq/self_signed.xml`

However, you can verify signed JAR files yourself by using the Jarsigner tool. You might want to do this, for example, to test a signed JAR file that you've prepared.

The basic command to use for verifying a signed JAR file is as follows:

```
jarsigner -verify jar-file
```

This command will verify the JAR file's signature and ensure that the files in the archive haven't changed since it was signed. You'll see the following message if the verification is successful:

```
jar verified.
```

If you try to verify an unsigned JAR file, the following message results:

```
jar is unsigned. (signatures missing or not parsable)
```

If the verification fails, an appropriate message is displayed. For example, if the contents of a JAR file have changed since the JAR file was signed, a message similar to the following will result if you try to verify the file:

```
jarsigner: java.lang.SecurityException: invalid SHA1
signature file digest for test/classes/Manifest.class
```

Using JAR-Related APIs

The Java platform contains several classes for use with JAR files. Here are some of these APIs:

- The java.util.jar package[20]
- The java.net.JarURLConnection class[21]
- The java.net.URLClassLoader class[22]

To give you an idea of the possibilities that are opened up by these new APIs, this section guides you through the inner workings of a sample application called JarRunner.

---

20.   8/docs/api/java/util/jar/package-summary.html
21.   8/docs/api/java/net/JarURLConnection.html
22.   8/docs/api/java/net/URLClassLoader.html

An Example: The JarRunner Application

`JarRunner` enables you to run an application that's bundled in a JAR file by specifying the JAR file's URL on the command line. For example, if an application called `TargetApp` were bundled in a JAR file at `http://www.example.com/TargetApp` `.jar`, you could run the application using this command:

```
java JarRunner http://www.example.com/TargetApp.jar
```

In order for `JarRunner` to work, it must be able to perform the following tasks, all of which are accomplished by using the new APIs:

- Access the remote JAR file and establish a communications link with it.
- Inspect the JAR file's manifest to see which of the classes in the archive is the main class.
- Load the classes in the JAR file.

The `JarRunner` application consists of two classes, `JarRunner` and `JarClassLoader`. `JarRunner` delegates most of the JAR-handling tasks to the `JarClassLoader` class. `JarClassLoader` extends the `java.net.URLClassLoader` class. You can browse the source code for the `JarRunner`[23] and `JarClassLoader`[24] classes before proceeding with the section.

The JarClassLoader Class

The `JarClassLoader` class extends `java.net.URLClassLoader`. As its name implies, `URLClassLoader` is designed to be used for loading classes and resources that are accessed by searching a set of URLs. The URLs can refer either to directories or to JAR files.

In addition to subclassing `URLClassLoader`, `JarClassLoader` also makes use of features in two other new JAR-related APIs: the `java.util.jar` package and the `java.net.JarURLConnection` class. In this section, we'll look in detail at the constructor and two methods of `JarClassLoader`.

---

23. `tutorial/deployment/jar/examples/JarRunner.java`

24. `tutorial/deployment/jar/examples/JarClassLoader.java`

The JarClassLoader Constructor

The constructor takes an instance of `java.net.URL` as an argument. The URL passed to this constructor will be used elsewhere in `JarClassLoader` to find the JAR file from which classes are to be loaded:

```
public JarClassLoader(URL url) {
    super(new URL[] { url });
    this.url = url;
}
```

The `URL` object is passed to the constructor of the superclass, `URLClassLoader`, which takes a `URL[]` array, rather than a single `URL` instance, as an argument.

The getMainClassName Method

Once a `JarClassLoader` object is constructed with the URL of a JAR-bundled application, it's going to need a way to determine which class in the JAR file is the application's entry point. That's the job of the `getMainClassName` method:

```
public String getMainClassName() throws IOException {
    URL u = new URL("jar", "", url + "!/");
    JarURLConnection uc = (JarURLConnection)u.openConnection();
    Attributes attr = uc.getMainAttributes();
    return attr != null
                    ? attr.getValue(Attributes.Name.MAIN_CLASS)
                    : null;
}
```

You may recall that a JAR-bundled application's entry point is specified by the `Main-Class` header of the JAR file's manifest. To understand how `getMainClass-Name` accesses the `Main-Class` header value, let's look at the method in detail, paying special attention to the new JAR-handling features that it uses.

16

The JarURLConnection class and JAR URLs

The `getMainClassName` method uses the JAR URL format specified by the `java.net.JarURLConnection` class. The syntax for the URL of a JAR file is as in this example:

```
jar:http://www.example.com/jarfile.jar!/
```

The terminating `!/` separator indicates that the URL refers to an entire JAR file. Anything following the separator refers to specific JAR file contents, as in this example:

```
jar:http://www.example.com/jarfile.jar!/mypackage/myclass.class
```

The first line in the `getMainClassName` method is as follows:

```
URL u = new URL("jar", "", url + "!/");
```

This statement constructs a new `URL` object representing a JAR URL, appending the `!/` separator to the URL that was used in creating the `JarClassLoader` instance.

The java.net.JarURLConnection class

This class represents a communications link between an application and a JAR file. It has methods for accessing the JAR file's manifest. The second line of `getMainClassName` is as follows:

```
JarURLConnection uc = (JarURLConnection)u.openConnection();
```

In this statement, the `URL` instance created in the first line opens a `URLConnection`. The `URLConnection` instance is then cast to `JarURLConnection` so it can take advantage of `JarURLConnection`'s JAR-handling features.

Fetching Manifest Attributes: java.util.jar.Attributes

With a `JarURLConnection` open to a JAR file, you can access the header information in the JAR file's manifest by using the `getMainAttributes` method of `JarURLConnection`. This method returns an instance of `java.util.jar.Attributes`, a class that maps header names in JAR file manifests with their associated string values. The third line in `getMainClassName` creates an `Attributes` object:

```
Attributes attr = uc.getMainAttributes();
```

To get the value of the manifest's `Main-Class` header, the fourth line of `getMainClassName` invokes the `Attributes.getValue` method:

```
return attr != null
             ? attr.getValue(Attributes.Name.MAIN_CLASS)
             : null;
```

The method's argument, `Attributes.Name.MAIN_CLASS`, specifies that it's the value of the `Main-Class` header that you want. (The `Attributes.Name` class also provides static fields such as `MANIFEST_VERSION`, `CLASS_PATH`, and `SEALED` for specifying other standard manifest headers.)

The invokeClass Method

We've seen how `JarURLClassLoader` can identify the main class in a JAR-bundled application. The last method to consider, `JarURLClassLoader.invokeClass`, enables that main class to be invoked to launch the JAR-bundled application:

```
public void invokeClass(String name, String[] args)
    throws ClassNotFoundException,
           NoSuchMethodException,
           InvocationTargetException
{
    Class c = loadClass(name);
    Method m = c.getMethod("main", new Class[] { args.getClass() });
    m.setAccessible(true);
    int mods = m.getModifiers();
    if (m.getReturnType() != void.class || !Modifier.isStatic(mods) ||
        !Modifier.isPublic(mods)) {
        throw new NoSuchMethodException("main");
    }
    try {
        m.invoke(null, new Object[] { args });
    } catch (IllegalAccessException e) {
        // This should not happen, as we have disabled access checks
    }
}
```

The `invokeClass` method takes two arguments: the name of the application's entry-point class and an array of string arguments to pass to the entry-point class's `main` method. First, the main class is loaded:

```
Class c = loadClass(name);
```

The `loadClass` method is inherited from `java.lang.ClassLoader`.

Once the main class is loaded, the Reflection API of the `java.lang.reflect` package is used to pass the arguments to the class and launch it. You can refer to the online tutorial on Reflection API[25] for a review of reflection.

The JarRunner Class

The `JarRunner` application is launched with a command of this form:

```
java JarRunner url [arguments]
```

In the previous section, we saw how `JarClassLoader` is able to identify and load the main class of a JAR-bundled application from a given URL. To complete the Jar-Runner application, therefore, we need to be able to take a URL and any arguments

25. tutorial/reflect/index.html

from the command line and pass them to an instance of `JarClassLoader`. These tasks belong to the `JarRunner` class, the entry point of the `JarRunner` application.

It begins by creating a `java.net.URL` object from the URL specified on the command line:

```
public static void main(String[] args) [
    if (args.length < 1) {
        usage();
    }
    URL url = null;
    try {
        url = new URL(args[0]);
    } catch (MalformedURLException e) {
        fatal("Invalid URL: " + args[0]);
    }
```

If `args.length < 1`, that means no URL was specified on the command line, so a usage message is printed. If the first command-line argument is a good URL, a new URL object is created to represent it.

Next, `JarRunner` creates a new instance of `JarClassLoader`, passing to the constructor the URL that was specified on the command line:

```
JarClassLoader cl = new JarClassLoader(url);
```

As we saw in the previous section, it's through `JarClassLoader` that `JarRunner` taps into the JAR-handling APIs.

The URL that's passed to the `JarClassLoader` constructor is the URL of the JAR-bundled application that you want to run. `JarRunner` next calls the class loader's `getMainClassName` method to identify the entry-point class for the application:

```
String name = null;
try {
    name = cl.getMainClassName();
} catch (IOException e) {
    System.err.println("I/O error while loading JAR file:");
    e.printStackTrace();
    System.exit(1);
}
if (name == null) {
    fatal("Specified jar file does not contain a 'Main-Class'" +
            " manifest attribute");
}
```

16

The key statement is highlighted in bold. The other statements are for error handling.

Once `JarRunner` has identified the application's entry-point class, only two steps remain: passing any arguments to the application and actually launching the application. `JarRunner` performs these steps with this code:

```
// Get arguments for the application
String[] newArgs = new String[args.length - 1];
System.arraycopy(args, 1, newArgs, 0, newArgs.length);
// Invoke application's main class
try {
    cl.invokeClass(name, newArgs);
} catch (ClassNotFoundException e) {
    fatal("Class not found: " + name);
} catch (NoSuchMethodException e) {
    fatal("Class does not define a 'main' method: " + name);
} catch (InvocationTargetException e) {
    e.getTargetException().printStackTrace();
    System.exit(1);
}
```

Recall that the first command-line argument was the URL of the JAR-bundled application. Any arguments to be passed to that application are therefore in element 1 and beyond in the `args` array. `JarRunner` takes those elements and creates a new array called `newArgs` to pass to the application (bold in the previous example). `JarRunner` then passes the entry point's class name and the new argument list to the `invokeClass` method of `JarClassLoader`. As we saw in the previous section, `invokeClass` will load the application's entry-point class, pass it any arguments, and launch the application.

Questions and Exercises: Packaging Programs in JAR Files

Questions

1. How do you invoke an applet that is packaged as a JAR file?
2. What is the purpose of the `-e` option in a `jar` command?
3. What is the significance of the manifest in a JAR file?
4. How do you modify a JAR's manifest file?

Answers

You can find answers to these questions and exercises at `http://docs.oracle` `.com/javase/tutorial/deployment/jar/QandE/answers.html`.

16

17

Java Web Start

Chapter Contents

Developing a Java Web Start Application   650
Deploying a Java Web Start Application   653
Displaying a Customized Loading Progress Indicator   656
Running a Java Web Start Application   660
Java Web Start and Security   661
Common Java Web Start Problems   662
Questions and Exercises: Java Web Start   663

Java Web Start software provides the power to launch full-featured applications with a single click. Users can download and launch applications, such as a complete spreadsheet program or an Internet chat client, without going through lengthy installation procedures.

With Java Web Start software, users can launch a Java application by clicking a link in a web page. The link points to a Java Network Launch Protocol (JNLP) file, which instructs Java Web Start software to download, cache, and run the application.

Java Web Start software provides Java developers and users with many deployment advantages:

- With Java Web Start software, you can place a single Java application on a web server for deployment to a wide variety of platforms, including Windows, Linux, and Solaris.

- Java Web Start software supports multiple, simultaneous versions of the Java platform. An application can request a specific version of the Java Runtime Environment (JRE) software without conflicting with the needs of other applications.

- Users can create a desktop shortcut to launch a Java Web Start application outside a browser.
- Java Web Start software takes advantage of the inherent security of the Java platform. By default, applications have restricted access to local disk and network resources.
- Applications launched with Java Web Start software are cached locally for improved performance.
- Updates to a Java Web Start application are automatically downloaded when the application is run standalone from the user's desktop.

Java Web Start software is installed as part of the JRE software. Users do not have to install Java Web Start software separately or perform additional tasks to use Java Web Start applications.

Additional References

This chapter is intended to get you started with Java Web Start technology and does not include all available documentation. For more information about Java Web Start technology, see the following:

- Java Web Start Guide[1]
- Java Web Start FAQ[2]
- JNLP Specification[3]
- `javax.jnlp` API Documentation[4]
- Java Web Start Developers Site[5]

Developing a Java Web Start Application

Software designed by using a component-based architecture can easily be developed and deployed as a Java Web Start application. Consider the example of a Java Web Start application with a Swing-based graphical user interface (GUI). With component-based design, the GUI can be built with smaller building blocks or components. The following general steps are used to create an application's GUI:

---

1.   8/docs/technotes/guides/javaws/developersguide/contents.html
2.   8/docs/technotes/guides/javaws/developersguide/faq.html
3.   http://jcp.org/en/jsr/detail?id=56
4.   8/docs/jre/api/javaws/jnlp/index.html
5.   http://www.oracle.com/technetwork/java/javase/javawebstart/index
     .html

- Create a `MyTopJPanel` class that is a subclass of `JPanel`. Lay out your application's GUI components in the constructor of the `MyTopJPanel` class.
- Create a class called `MyApplication` that is a subclass of the `JFrame` class.
- In the `main` method of the `MyApplication` class, instantiate the `MyTopJPanel` class and set it as the content pane of the `JFrame`.

The following sections explore these steps in greater detail by using the Dynamic Tree Demo application,[6] which uses Swing GUI components; see Creating a GUI with Swing[7] for more information.

Creating the Top JPanel Class

Create a class that is a subclass of `JPanel`. This top `JPanel` acts as a container for all your other user interface components. In the following example, the `Dynamic-TreePanel` class is the topmost `JPanel`. The constructor of the `DynamicTreePanel` class invokes other methods to create and lay out the user interface controls properly:

```java
public class DynamicTreePanel extends JPanel implements ActionListener {
    private int newNodeSuffix = 1;
    private static String ADD_COMMAND = "add";
    private static String REMOVE_COMMAND = "remove";
    private static String CLEAR_COMMAND = "clear";

    private DynamicTree treePanel;

    public DynamicTreePanel() {
        super(new BorderLayout());

        //Create the components.
        treePanel = new DynamicTree();
        populateTree(treePanel);

        JButton addButton = new JButton("Add");
        addButton.setActionCommand(ADD_COMMAND);
        addButton.addActionListener(this);

        JButton removeButton = new JButton("Remove");
        ....

        JButton clearButton = new JButton("Clear");
        ...

        //Lay everything out.
        treePanel.setPreferredSize(
            new Dimension(300, 150));
        add(treePanel, BorderLayout.CENTER);

        JPanel panel = new JPanel(new GridLayout(0,3));
```

17

---

6. `tutorial/deployment/webstart/examplesIndex.html`

7. `tutorial/uiswing/index.html`

```
            panel.add(addButton);
            panel.add(removeButton);
            panel.add(clearButton);
            add(panel, BorderLayout.SOUTH);
        }
        // ...
    }
```

Creating the Application

For an application that has a Swing-based GUI, create a class that is a subclass of `javax.swing.JFrame`.

Instantiate your top `JPanel` class and set it as the content pane of the `JFrame` in the application's `main` method. The `main` method of the `DynamicTreeApplication` class invokes the `createGUI` method in the AWT Event Dispatcher thread:[8]

```
    package webstartComponentArch;

    import javax.swing.JFrame;

    public class DynamicTreeApplication extends JFrame {
        public static void main(String [] args) {
            DynamicTreeApplication app = new DynamicTreeApplication();
            app.createGUI();
        }

        private void createGUI() {
            //Create and set up the content pane.
            DynamicTreePanel newContentPane = new DynamicTreePanel();
            newContentPane.setOpaque(true);
            setContentPane(newContentPane);
            setDefaultCloseOperation(JFrame.EXIT_ON_CLOSE);
            pack();
            setVisible(true);
        }
    }
```

17

Benefits of Separating Core Functionality from the Final Deployment Mechanism

Another way to create an application is to just remove the layer of abstraction (separate top `JPanel`) and lay out all the controls in the application's `main` method itself. The downside to creating the GUI directly in the application's `main` method is that it will be more difficult to deploy your functionality as an applet if you choose to do so later.

---

8.   `tutorial/uiswing/concurrency/dispatch.htm`

In the Dynamic Tree Demo example, the core functionality is separated into the `DynamicTreePanel` class. It is now trivial to drop the `DynamicTreePanel` class into a `JApplet` and deploy it as an applet.

Hence, to preserve portability and keep deployment options open, follow component-based design as described in this topic.

Retrieving Resources

Use the `getResource` method to read resources from a JAR file. For example, the following code retrieves images from a JAR file:

```
// Get current classloader
ClassLoader cl = this.getClass().getClassLoader();
// Create icons
Icon saveIcon  = new ImageIcon(cl.getResource("images/save.gif"));
Icon cutIcon   = new ImageIcon(cl.getResource("images/cut.gif"));
```

This example assumes that the following entries exist in the application's JAR file:

- `images/save.gif`
- `images/cut.gif`

Deploying a Java Web Start Application

To deploy your Java Web Start application, first compile the source code, package it as a JAR file, and sign the JAR file. Java Web Start applications are launched using the Java Network Launch Protocol (JNLP). Hence you must create a JNLP file to deploy your application.

The Deployment Toolkit script contains useful JavaScript functions that can be used to deploy Java Web Start applications on a web page. If you are unfamiliar with these deployment technologies, see Chapter 20 before proceeding.

Here are some step-by-step instructions to package and deploy your application. The Dynamic Tree Demo application[9] is used to illustrate the deployment of Java Web Start applications. You might want to build scripts to execute some of the following steps:

1. Compile your application's Java code and make sure that all class files and resources such as images are in a separate directory. In the Dynamic Tree Demo application, the compiled classes are placed in the `build/classes/webstartComponentArch` directory.

---

9.   `tutorial/deployment/webstart/examples/zipfiles/webstart_ComponentArch`
     `_DynamicTreeDemo.zip`

2. Create a text file that contains any JAR file manifest attributes that your applet needs. For the Dynamic Tree Demo applet, create a file named `mymanifest.txt` in the `build/classes` directory and add the `Permissions`, `Codebase`, and `Application-Name` attributes. The applet does not require access to the user's system resources, so use `sandbox` for the permissions. Use the domain from which you will load the sample for the code base (e.g., `myserver.com`). Add the following attributes to the `mymanifest.txt` file:

```
Permissions: sandbox
Codebase: myserver.com
Application-Name: Dynamic Tree Demo
```

Other manifest attributes are available to restrict an applet to using only trusted code and to provide security for applets that need to make calls between privileged Java code and sandbox Java code or have JavaScript code that calls the applet. See Chapter 16, "Enhancing Security with Manifest Attributes," to learn more about the manifest attributes that are available.

3. Create a JAR file containing your application's class files and resources. Include the manifest attributes in the `mymanifest.txt` file that you created in the previous step. For example, the following command creates a JAR file with the class files in the `build/classes/webstartComponentArch` directory and the manifest file in the `build/classes` directory:

```
% cd build/classes
% jar cvfm  DynamicTreeDemo.jar  mymanifest.txt webstartComponentArch
```

See Chapter 16 to learn more about creating and using JAR files.

4. Sign the JAR file for your applet and time stamp the signature. Use a valid, current code-signing certificate issued by a trusted certificate authority to assure your users that it is safe to run the applet. See Chapter 16, "Signing JAR Files," for more information. If you want to use a signed JNLP file for security, create the JNLP file as described in the next step and include it in the JAR file before the JAR file is signed. See Signed JNLP Files[10] in the Java Platform Standard Edition Deployment Guide for information.

5. Create a JNLP file that describes how your application should be launched. Here is the JNLP file that is used to launch the Dynamic Tree Demo application. Permissions are not requested for this application, so it runs in the security sandbox. The source for `dynamictree_webstart.jnlp` follows:

```
<?xml version="1.0" encoding="UTF-8"?>
<jnlp spec="1.0+" codebase=
"http://docs.oracle.com/javase/tutorialJWS/samples/deployment/
   webstart_ComponentArch_DynamicTreeDemo"
```

---

10. `8/docs/technotes/guides/deploy/signed_jnlp.html`

```
        href="dynamictree_webstart.jnlp">
    <information>
        <title>Dynamic Tree Demo</title>
        <vendor>Dynamic Team</vendor>
    </information>
    <resources>
        <!-- Application Resources -->
        <j2se version="1.7+"
              href="http://java.sun.com/products/autodl/j2se"/>
        <jar href="DynamicTreeDemo.jar"
            main="true" />

    </resources>
    <application-desc
        name="Dynamic Tree Demo Application"
        main-class=
          "webstartComponentArch.DynamicTreeApplication"
        width="300"
        height="300">
     </application-desc>
     <update check="background"/>
</jnlp>
```

Chapter 20, "Structure of the JNLP File," describes the JNLP file syntax and options.

Note

The `codebase` and `href` attributes are optional when deploying Java Web Start applications that will run on at least the Java SE 6 update 18 release or later. You must specify the `codebase` and `href` attributes when deploying Java Web Start applications that will run with previous releases of the JRE software.

---

6. Create the HTML page from which your application will be launched. Invoke Deployment Toolkit functions to deploy the Java Web Start application. In the example, the Dynamic Tree Demo application is deployed in `JavaWebStart-AppPage.html`:

```
    <body>
        <!-- ... -->
        <script src=
          "https://www.java.com/js/deployJava.js"></script>
        <script>
            // using JavaScript to get location of JNLP
            // file relative to HTML page
            var dir = location.href.substring(0,
                location.href.lastIndexOf('/')+1);
            var url = dir + "dynamictree_webstart.jnlp";
            deployJava.createWebStartLaunchButton(url, '1.7.0');
        </script>
```

```
    <!-- ... -->
</body>
```

If you are not sure whether your end users will have the JavaScript interpreter enabled in their browsers, you can deploy the Java Web Start application directly by creating a link to the JNLP file as follows:

```
<a href="/absolute path to JNLP file/dynamictree_webstart.jnlp">
    Launch Notepad Application
</a>
```

If you deploy the Java Web Start application with a direct link, you cannot take advantage of the additional checks that the Deployment Toolkit functions provide. See Chapter 20, "Deploying a Java Web Start Application," for details.

7. Place the application's JAR file, JNLP file, and HTML page in the appropriate folders. For this example, place `DynamicTreeDemo.jar`, `dynamictree_webstart.jnlp`, and `JavaWebStartAppPage.html` in the same directory on the local machine or a web server. A web server is preferred. To run from the local machine, you must add your application to the exception site list, which is managed from the **Security** tab of the Java Control Panel.

8. Open the application's HTML page in a browser to view the application. Agree to run the application when prompted. Check the Java Console log for error and debugging messages.

Setting Up a Web Server

You might need to configure your web server to handle Java Network Launch Protocol (JNLP) files. If the web server is not set up properly, the Java Web Start application will not launch when you click on the link to the JNLP file. Configure the web server so that files with the `.jnlp` extension are set to the `application/x-java-jnlp-file` MIME type.

The specific steps to set up the JNLP MIME type will vary depending on the web server. As an example, to configure an Apache web server, you should add the following line to the `mime.types` file:

```
application/x-java-jnlp-file JNLP
```

For other web servers, check the documentation for instructions on setting MIME types.

Displaying a Customized Loading Progress Indicator

A Java Web Start application can display a customized loading progress indicator that shows the progress of download of the application's resources. Consider the

Java Web Start Application with Customized Loading Progress Indicator example[11] and the CustomProgress class to understand how to implement a customized loading progress indicator for a Java Web Start application. For the purpose of demonstrating a large and prolonged download, this Java Web Start application's JAR file has been artificially inflated and the customprogress_webstart.jnlp file specifies additional JAR files as resources.

Developing a Customized Loading Progress Indicator

To develop a customized loading progress indicator for your Java Web Start application, create a class that implements the DownloadServiceListener interface.[12] The constructor of the loading progress indicator class should not have any parameters:

```
import javax.jnlp.DownloadServiceListener;
import java.awt.Container;
import java.applet.AppletStub;
import netscape.javascript.*;
// ...
public class CustomProgress
        implements DownloadServiceListener {
    JFrame frame = null;
    JProgressBar progressBar = null;
    boolean uiCreated = false;

    public CustomProgress() {
    }
...
}
```

The following code snippet shows how to build the user interface for the loading progress indicator:

```
private void create() {
    JPanel top = createComponents();
    frame = new JFrame(); // top level custom progress
                          // indicator UI
    frame.getContentPane().add(top,
                         BorderLayout.CENTER);
    frame.setBounds(300,300,400,300);
    frame.pack();
    updateProgressUI(0);
}

private JPanel createComponents() {
    JPanel top = new JPanel();
    top.setBackground(Color.WHITE);
```

17

---

11. tutorial/deployment/webstart/examplesIndex.html

12. 8/docs/jre/api/javaws/jnlp/javax/jnlp/DownloadServiceListener.html

```
    top.setLayout(new BorderLayout(20, 20));

    String lblText =
        "<html><font color=green size=+2" +
        ">JDK Documentation</font><br/> " +
        "The one-stop shop for Java enlightenment! <br/></html>";
    JLabel lbl = new JLabel(lblText);
    top.add(lbl, BorderLayout.NORTH);
    ...
    progressBar = new JProgressBar(0, 100);
    progressBar.setValue(0);
    progressBar.setStringPainted(true);
    top.add(progressBar, BorderLayout.SOUTH);

    return top;
}
```

Create and update the loading progress indicator in the following methods based on the `overallPercent` argument. These methods are invoked regularly by the Java Web Start software to communicate the progress of the application's download. Java Web Start software will always send a message when download and validation of resources is 100% complete:

```
public void progress(URL url, String version, long readSoFar,
                     long total, int overallPercent) {
    updateProgressUI(overallPercent);

}

public void upgradingArchive(java.net.URL url,
            java.lang.String version,
            int patchPercent,
            int overallPercent) {
    updateProgressUI(overallPercent);
}

public void validating(java.net.URL url,
            java.lang.String version,
            long entry,
            long total,
            int overallPercent) {
    updateProgressUI(overallPercent);
}

private void updateProgressUI(int overallPercent) {
    if (overallPercent > 0 && overallPercent < 99) {
        if (!uiCreated) {
            uiCreated = true;
            // create custom progress indicator's
            // UI only if there is more work to do,
            // meaning overallPercent > 0 and
            // < 100 this prevents flashing when
            // RIA is loaded from cache
            create();
        }
```

```
                    progressBar.setValue(overallPercent);
                    SwingUtilities.invokeLater(new Runnable() {
                        public void run() {
                            frame.setVisible(true);
                        }
                    });
            } else {
                // hide frame when overallPercent is
                // above 99
                SwingUtilities.invokeLater(new Runnable() {
                    public void run() {
                        frame.setVisible(false);
                        frame.dispose();
                    }
                });
            }
        }
    }
```

Compile the loading progress indicator class and build a JAR file with all the resources needed to display the loading progress indicator. Include the *<your JRE directory>*/lib/javaws.jar file in your classpath to enable compilation. The loading progress indicator class is now ready for use. The next step is to specify this loading progress indicator JAR file as your Java Web Start application's progress indicator.

Specifying a Customized Loading Progress Indicator for a Java Web Start Application

To specify a customized loading progress indicator for a Java Web Start application, include the following information in the application's JNLP file:

- jar tag with the download="progress" attribute
- progress-class attribute with the fully qualified name of the customized loading progress class.

The following code snippet from the customprogress_webstart.jnlp file displays the usage of the download="progress" and progress-class attributes:

```
<jnlp spec="1.0+" codebase=
  "http://docs.oracle.com/javase/tutorialJWS/samples/deployment"
  href="customprogress_webstartJWSProject/customprogress_webstart.jnlp">
  <!-- ... -->
  <resources>
    <j2se version="1.7+"/>
    <jar href=
     "webstart_AppWithCustomProgressIndicator/webstart_AppWithCustomProgressIndicator.jar" />
    <jar href=
     "webstart_CustomProgressIndicator/webstart_CustomProgressIndicator.jar"
        download="progress" />
```

17

```
  <jar href=
    "webstart_AppWithCustomProgressIndicator/lib/IconDemo.jar" />
  <jar href=
    "webstart_AppWithCustomProgressIndicator/lib/SplitPaneDemo.jar" />
  <jar href=
    "webstart_AppWithCustomProgressIndicator/lib/SplitPaneDemo2.jar" />
  <jar href=
    "webstart_AppWithCustomProgressIndicator/lib/TextBatchPrintingDemo.jar" />
  <jar href=
    "webstart_AppWithCustomProgressIndicator/lib/ToolBarDemo.jar" />
  <jar href=
    "webstart_AppWithCustomProgressIndicator/lib/ToolBarDemo2.jar" />
  <jar href=
    "webstart_AppWithCustomProgressIndicator/lib/SwingSet2.jar" />
</resources>
<application-desc
    main-class="customprogressindicatordemo.Main"
    progress-class="customprogressindicator.CustomProgress"
/>
<!-- ... -->
</jnlp>
```

See Chapter 19, "Customizing the Loading Experience," for more information about customizing the rich Internet application (RIA) loading experience.

Running a Java Web Start Application

Users can run Java Web Start applications in the following ways.

> **Note**
>
> To run applications deployed with Java Web Start technology, you must have a compatible version of the Java Runtime Environment (JRE) software. The complete Java Development Kit (JDK) is not required.

17

Running a Java Web Start Application from a Browser

You can run a Java Web Start application from a browser by clicking a link to the application's JNLP file. The following text is an example of a link to a JNLP file:

```
<a href="/some/path/Notepad.jnlp">Launch Notepad Application</a>
```

Java Web Start software loads and runs the application based on instructions in the JNLP file.

Running a Java Web Start Application from the Java Cache Viewer

You can run a Java Web Start application through the Java Cache Viewer. When Java Web Start software first loads an application, information from the application's

JNLP file is stored in the local Java Cache Viewer. To launch the application again, you do not need to return to the web page where you first launched it; you can launch it from the Java Cache Viewer.

To open the Java Cache Viewer, use the following steps:

1. Open the Control Panel.
2. Double click the **Java** icon. The Java Control Panel opens.
3. Select the **General** tab.
4. Click **View**. The Java Cache Viewer opens.

The application is listed on the Java Cache Viewer screen (Figure 17.1). To run the application, select it and click the **Run** icon or double click the application. The application starts just as it did from the web page.

Running a Java Web Start Application from the Desktop

You can add a desktop shortcut to a Java Web Start application. Select the application in the Java Cache Viewer. Right click and select **Install Shortcuts** or click the **Install** icon. A shortcut is added to the desktop. You can then launch the Java Web Start application just as you would launch any native application.

Java Web Start and Security

This section describes the basics of security for applications deployed through Java Web Start. Applications launched with Java Web Start are, by default, run in a restricted environment known as a *sandbox*. In this sandbox, Java Web Start does the following:

17

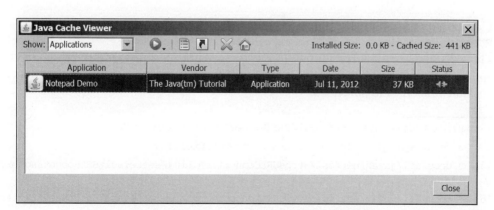

Figure 17.1 Java Cache Viewer Application

- Protects users against malicious code that could affect local files
- Protects enterprises against code that could attempt to access or destroy data on networks

Sandbox applications that are launched by Java Web Start remain in this sandbox, meaning they cannot access local files or the network. See Chapter 18, "Security in Rich Internet Applications," for information.

Dynamic Downloading of HTTPS Certificates

Java Web Start dynamically imports certificates as browsers typically do. To do this, Java Web Start sets its own `https` handler, using the `java.protocol.handler.pkgs` system properties, to initialize defaults for the `SSLSocketFactory`[13] and `HostnameVerifier`.[14] It sets the defaults with the methods `HttpsURLConnection.setDefaultSSLSocketFactory`[15] and `HttpsURLConnection.setDefaultHostnameVerifier`.[16]

If your application uses these two methods, ensure that they are invoked after the Java Web Start initializes the `https` handler; otherwise your custom handler will be replaced by the Java Web Start default handler.

You can ensure that your own customized `SSLSocketFactory` and `HostnameVerifier` are used by doing one of the following:

- Install your own `https` handler to replace the Java Web Start `https` handler.
- In your application, invoke `HttpsURLConnection.setDefaultSSLSocketFactory` or `HttpsURLConnection.setDefaultHostnameVerifier` only after the first `https URL` object is created, which executes the Java Web Start `https` handler initialization code first.

Common Java Web Start Problems

This section covers some common problems that you might encounter when developing and deploying Java Web Start applications. After each problem is a list of possible reasons and solutions.

---

13. `8/docs/api/javax/net/ssl/SSLSocketFactory.html`

14. `8/docs/api/javax/net/ssl/HostnameVerifier.html`

15. `8/docs/api/javax/net/ssl/HttpsURLConnection.html#setDefaultSSLSocketFactory`
    `-javax.net.ssl.SSLSocketFactory-`

16. `8/docs/api/javax/net/ssl/HttpsURLConnection.html#setDefaultHostnameVerifier`
    `-javax.net.ssl.HostnameVerifier-`

"My Browser Shows the Java Network Launch Protocol (JNLP) File for My Application as Plain Text"

Most likely, your web server is not aware of the proper MIME type for JNLP files. See the "Setting Up a Web Server" section for more information. Furthermore, if you are using a proxy server, ensure that the update versions of the files are returned by updating the time stamp of the resources on the web server such that the proxies will update their caches.

"When I Try to Launch My JNLP File, I Get the Following Error"

```
MissingFieldException[ The following required field is missing from the launch
    file: (<application-desc>|<applet-desc>|<installer-desc>|<component-desc>)]
        at com.sun.javaws.jnl.XMLFormat.parse(Unknown Source)
        at com.sun.javaws.jnl.LaunchDescFactory.buildDescriptor(Unknown Source)
        at com.sun.javaws.jnl.LaunchDescFactory.buildDescriptor(Unknown Source)
        at com.sun.javaws.jnl.LaunchDescFactory.buildDescriptor(Unknown Source)
        at com.sun.javaws.Main.launchApp(Unknown Source)
        at com.sun.javaws.Main.continueInSecureThread(Unknown Source)
        at com.sun.javaws.Main.run(Unknown Source)
        at java.lang.Thread.run(Unknown Source)
```

Often this error occurs when your XML is malformed. You can stare at the code until you figure it out, but it is easier to run an XML syntax checker over the file. (NetBeans IDE and jEdit both provide XML syntax checkers.)

However, this error can occur in other situations, and the above was caused by the following line in an otherwise well-formed XML file:

```
<description kind="short">Demonstrates choosing the drop location in the
    target <code>TransferHandler</code></description>
```

The error was caused by the illegal embedded `code` tags.

Questions and Exercises: Java Web Start

Questions

1. In a link that is to run a Java Web Start application, which file is specified as the a tag's `href` attribute?

2. Which MIME type must a Web server recognize in order for it to host Java Web Start applications?

3. In an application's `JNLP` file, which two elements must be specified within the `resources` element?

4. Which interface provides the ability to control how the Java Web Start application's resources are cached?

     a. BasicService

     b. DownloadService

     c. PersistenceService

     d. ExtendedService

5. True or false: Java Web Start applications run in a secure sandbox by default.

6. True or false: If a Java Web Start application is running in a secure sandbox, JAR files for the application can reside on different servers.

7. For a Java Web Start application to support operations outside the secure sandbox, what must you do?

Exercises

1. Write the XML code you would add to a JNLP file in order to request that the application have complete access to the client system.

2. For a Java Web Start application, you have two icons, one.gif and two.gif, in the images directory in a JAR file. Write the application code you would use to access these images.

Answers

You can find answers to these questions and exercises at `http://docs.oracle` `.com/javase/tutorial/deployment/webstart/QandE/answers.html`.

18

Applets

Chapter Contents

Getting Started with Applets   666
Doing More with Applets   677
Solving Common Applet Problems   707
Questions and Exercises: Applets   708

This chapter discusses the basics of Java applets, how to develop applets that interact richly with their environment, and how to deploy applets.

A Java applet is a special kind of Java program that a browser enabled with Java technology can download from the Internet and run. An applet is typically embedded inside a web page and runs in the context of a browser. An applet must be a subclass of the `java.applet.Applet`[1] class. The `Applet` class provides the standard interface between the applet and the browser environment.

Swing[2] provides a special subclass of the `Applet` class called `javax.swing.JApplet`.[3] The `JApplet` class should be used for all applets that use Swing components to construct their graphical user interfaces (GUIs).

The browser's Java Plug-In software manages the life cycle of an applet.

Use a web server to test the examples in this chapter. The use of local applets is not recommended, and local applets are blocked when the security level setting in the Java Control Panel is set to High or Very High.

---

1.   `8/docs/api/java/applet/Applet.html`
2.   `tutorial/uiswing/index.html`
3.   `8/docs/api/javax/swing/JApplet.html`

> **Note**
>
> Some features of Java applets may not work as described on OS X. This is because of the way the Java Plug-In software interfaces with browsers on OS X.

Getting Started with Applets

The Hello World applet[4] is a Java class that displays the string "Hello World." Here is the source code for the Hello World applet:

```java
import javax.swing.JApplet;
import javax.swing.SwingUtilities;
import javax.swing.JLabel;

public class HelloWorld extends JApplet {
    //Called when this applet is loaded into the browser.
    public void init() {
        //Execute a job on the event-dispatching thread; creating this applet's GUI.
        try {
            SwingUtilities.invokeAndWait(new Runnable() {
                public void run() {
                    JLabel lbl = new JLabel("Hello World");
                    add(lbl);
                }
            });
        } catch (Exception e) {
            System.err.println("createGUI didn't complete successfully");
        }
    }
}
```

An applet such as this is typically managed and run by the Java Plug-In software in the browser.

Defining an Applet Subclass

Every Java applet must define a subclass of the `Applet` or `JApplet` class. In the Hello World applet, shown in the previous section, this subclass is called `HelloWorld`.

Java applets inherit significant functionality from the `Applet` or `JApplet` class, including the capabilities to communicate with the browser and present a GUI to the user. An applet that will be using GUI components from Swing (Java's GUI toolkit) should extend the `javax.swing.JApplet` base class, which provides the best integration with Swing's GUI facilities.

---

4.   `tutorial/deployment/applet/examples/zipfiles/applet_HelloWorld.zip`

JApplet provides a root pane, which is the same top-level component structure as Swing's JFrame and JDialog components, whereas Applet provides just a basic panel. An applet can extend the java.applet.Applet class when it does not use Swing's GUI components.

Methods for Milestones

The Applet class provides a framework for applet execution, defining methods that the system calls when milestones occur. Milestones are major events in an applet's life cycle. Most applets override some or all of these methods to respond appropriately to milestones.

init Method

The init method is useful for one-time initialization that doesn't take very long. The init method typically contains the code that you would normally put into a constructor. The reason applets don't usually have constructors is that they aren't guaranteed to have a full environment until their init method is called. Keep the init method short so that your applet can load quickly.

start Method

Every applet that performs tasks after initialization (except in direct response to user actions) must override the start method. The start method starts the execution of the applet. It is good practice to return quickly from the start method. If you need to perform computationally intensive operations, it might be better to start a new thread for this purpose.

stop Method

Most applets that override the start method should also override the stop method. The stop method should suspend the applet's execution so that it doesn't take up system resources when the user isn't viewing the applet's page. For example, an applet that displays an animation should stop trying to draw the animation when the user isn't viewing it.

destroy Method

Many applets don't need to override the destroy method because their stop method (which is called before destroy) will perform all tasks necessary to shut down the applet's execution. However, the destroy method is available for applets that need to release additional resources.

18

> **Note**
> Keep implementations of the `destroy` method as short as possible, because there is no guarantee that this method will be completely executed. The Java Virtual Machine (Java VM) might exit before a long `destroy` method has completed.

Life Cycle of an Applet

An applet can react to major events in the following ways:

- It can *initialize* itself.
- It can *start* running.
- It can *stop* running.
- It can perform a *final cleanup* in preparation for being unloaded.

This section introduces a new applet, `Simple`, that uses all of these methods. Unlike Java applications, applets do *not* need to implement a `main` method.

The following is the source code for the `Simple` applet.[5] This applet displays a descriptive string whenever it encounters a major milestone in its life, such as when the user first visits the page the applet is on:

```java
import java.applet.Applet;
import java.awt.Graphics;

//No need to extend JApplet, since we don't add any components;
//we just paint.
public class Simple extends Applet {

    StringBuffer buffer;

    public void init() {
        buffer = new StringBuffer();
        addItem("initializing... ");
    }

    public void start() {
        addItem("starting... ");
    }

    public void stop() {
        addItem("stopping... ");
    }

    public void destroy() {
        addItem("preparing for unloading...");
    }
```

---

5.   `tutorial/deployment/applet/examples/applet_Simple/src/Simple.java`

```
    private void addItem(String newWord) {
        System.out.println(newWord);
        buffer.append(newWord);
        repaint();
    }

    public void paint(Graphics g) {
        //Draw a Rectangle around the applet's display area.
        g.drawRect(0, 0,
                   getWidth() - 1,
                   getHeight() - 1);

        //Draw the current string inside the rectangle.
        g.drawString(buffer.toString(), 5, 15);
    }
}
```

Note

In this example, the `Applet` class is extended, not the Swing `JApplet` class, as Swing components do not need to be added to this applet.

Loading the Applet

As a result of the applet being loaded, you should see the text `initializing...` `starting....` When an applet is loaded, here's what happens:

- An instance of the applet's controlling class (an `Applet` subclass) is created.
- The applet initializes itself.
- The applet starts running.

Leaving and Returning to the Applet's Page

When the user leaves the page (e.g., to go to another page), the browser stops and destroys the applet. The state of the applet is not preserved. When the user returns to the page, the browser initializes and starts a new instance of the applet.

Reloading the Applet

When you refresh or reload a browser page, the current instance of the applet is stopped and destroyed and a new instance is created.

Quitting the Browser

When the user quits the browser, the applet has the opportunity to stop itself and perform a final cleanup before the browser exits. Download source code for the Simple Applet example to experiment further.[6]

---

6. `tutorial/deployment/applet/examples/zipfiles/applet_Simple.zip`

Applet's Execution Environment

A Java applet runs in the context of a browser. The Java Plug-In software in the browser controls the launch and execution of Java applets. The browser also has a JavaScript interpreter, which runs the JavaScript code on a web page.

Java Plug-In

The Java Plug-In software creates a worker thread for every Java applet. It launches an applet in an instance of the Java Runtime Environment (JRE) software. Normally, all applets run in the same instance of the JRE. The Java Plug-In software starts a new instance of the JRE in the following cases:

- An applet requests to be executed in a specific version of the JRE.
- An applet specifies its own JRE start-up parameters (e.g., the heap size). A new applet uses an existing JRE if its requirements are a subset of an existing JRE; otherwise, a new JRE instance is started.

An applet will run in an existing JRE if the following conditions are met:

- The JRE version required by the applet matches an existing JRE.
- The JRE's start-up parameters satisfy the applet's requirements.

Figure 18.1 shows how applets are executed in the JRE.

Java Plug-In and JavaScript Interpreter Interaction

Java applets can invoke JavaScript functions present in the web page. JavaScript functions are also allowed to invoke methods of an applet embedded on the same web page. The Java Plug-In software and the JavaScript interpreter orchestrate calls from Java code to JavaScript code and calls from JavaScript code to Java code.

The Java Plug-In software is multithreaded, while the JavaScript interpreter runs on a single thread. Hence to avoid thread-related issues, especially when multiple applets are running simultaneously, keep the calls between Java code and JavaScript code short and avoid round trips, if possible. See the "Invoking JavaScript Code from an Applet" and "Invoking Applet Methods from JavaScript Code" sections in this chapter for more information.

Developing an Applet

An application designed using component-based architecture can be developed into a Java applet. Consider the example of a Java applet with a Swing-based GUI. With

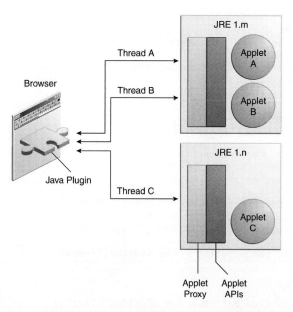

Figure 18.1 Java Plug-In Running Applets on Different JRE Versions

component-based design, the GUI can be built with smaller building blocks or components. The following general steps are used to create an applet GUI:

- Create a class `MyTopJPanel` that is a subclass of `javax.swing.JPanel`. Lay out your applet's GUI components in the constructor of the `MyTopJPanel` class.
- Create a class called `MyApplet` that is a subclass of `javax.swing.JApplet`.
- In the `init` method of `MyApplet`, instantiate `MyTopJPanel` and set it as the applet's content pane.

The following sections explore these steps in greater detail by using the Dynamic Tree Demo applet.[7]

Creating the Top JPanel Class

Create a class that is a subclass of `JPanel`. This top `JPanel` acts as a container for all your other user interface components. In the following example, the `Dynamic-TreePanel` class is the topmost `JPanel`. The constructor of the `Dynamic-TreePanel` class invokes other methods to create and lay out the user interface controls properly:

18

---

7. `tutorial/deployment/applet/examples/zipfiles/applet_ComponentArch`
    `_DynamicTreeDemo.zip`

```java
public class DynamicTreePanel extends JPanel implements ActionListener {
    private int newNodeSuffix = 1;
    private static String ADD_COMMAND = "add";
    private static String REMOVE_COMMAND = "remove";
    private static String CLEAR_COMMAND = "clear";

    private DynamicTree treePanel;

    public DynamicTreePanel() {
        super(new BorderLayout());

        //Create the components.
        treePanel = new DynamicTree();
        populateTree(treePanel);

        JButton addButton = new JButton("Add");
        addButton.setActionCommand(ADD_COMMAND);
        addButton.addActionListener(this);

        JButton removeButton = new JButton("Remove");

        // ...

        JButton clearButton = new JButton("Clear");

        // ...

        //Lay everything out.
        treePanel.setPreferredSize(
            new Dimension(300, 150));
        add(treePanel, BorderLayout.CENTER);

        JPanel panel = new JPanel(new GridLayout(0,3));
        panel.add(addButton);
        panel.add(removeButton);
        panel.add(clearButton);
        add(panel, BorderLayout.SOUTH);
    }
    // ...
}
```

Creating the Applet

For a Java applet that has a Swing-based GUI, create a class that is a subclass of
`javax.swing.JApplet`. An applet that does not contain a Swing-based GUI can
extend the `java.applet.Applet` class.

Override the applet's `init` method to instantiate your top `JPanel` class and create the applet's GUI. The `init` method of the `DynamicTreeApplet` class invokes
the `createGUI` method in the AWT Event Dispatcher thread:[8]

---

8. `tutorial/uiswing/concurrency/dispatch.htm`

```
package appletComponentArch;

import javax.swing.JApplet;
import javax.swing.SwingUtilities;

public class DynamicTreeApplet extends JApplet {
    //Called when this applet is loaded into the browser.
    public void init() {
        //Execute a job on the event-dispatching thread; creating this applet's GUI.
        try {
            SwingUtilities.invokeAndWait(new Runnable() {
                public void run() {
                    createGUI();
                }
            });
        } catch (Exception e) {
            System.err.println("createGUI didn't complete successfully");
        }
    }

    private void createGUI() {
        //Create and set up the content pane.
        DynamicTreePanel newContentPane = new DynamicTreePanel();
        newContentPane.setOpaque(true);
        setContentPane(newContentPane);
    }
}
```

Benefits of Separating Core Functionality from the Final Deployment Mechanism

Another way to create an applet is to just remove the layer of abstraction (separate top JPanel) and lay out all the controls in the applet's init method itself. The downside to creating the GUI directly in the applet is that it will now be more difficult to deploy your functionality as a Java Web Start application if you choose to do so later.

In the Dynamic Tree Demo example, the core functionality resides in the Dynamic-TreePanel class. It is now trivial to drop the DynamicTreePanel class into a JFrame and deploy as a Java Web Start application.

Hence, to preserve portability and keep deployment options open, follow component-based design as described on this page.

Deploying an Applet

To deploy your Java applet, first compile the source code, package it as a JAR file, and sign the JAR file. Java applets can be launched in two ways:

- You can launch your applet by using Java Network Launch Protocol (JNLP). Applets launched by using JNLP have access to powerful JNLP Application Programming Interfaces (APIs) and extensions.

- Alternatively, you can launch an applet by specifying the applet's launch properties directly in the applet tag. However, this old way of deploying applets imposes severe security restrictions on the applet.

The Deployment Toolkit script contains useful JavaScript functions that can be used to deploy applets in a web page. If you are unfamiliar with these deployment technologies, review Chapter 20 before proceeding further.

Here are some step-by-step instructions to package and deploy your applet. The Dynamic Tree Demo applet is used to illustrate applet deployment. You might want to set up build scripts to execute some of the following steps:

1. Compile your applet's Java code and make sure all class files and resources such as images are in a separate directory. In the case of the Dynamic Tree Demo applet, the compiled classes are placed in the `build/classes/applet-ComponentArch` directory.

2. Create a text file that contains any JAR file manifest attributes that your applet needs. For the Dynamic Tree Demo applet, create a file named `mymanifest.txt` in the `build/classes` directory and add the `Permissions`, `Codebase`, and `Application-Name` attributes. The applet does not require access to the user's system resources, so use `sandbox` for the permissions. Use the domain from which you will load the sample for the code base (e.g., `myserver.com`). Add the following attributes to the `mymanifest.txt` file:

   ```
   Permissions: sandbox
   Codebase: myserver.com
   Application-Name: Dynamic Tree Demo
   ```

   Other manifest attributes are available to restrict an applet to using only trusted code and to provide security for applets that need to make calls between privileged Java code and sandbox Java code or have JavaScript code that calls the applet. See Chapter 16, "Enhancing Security with Manifest Attributes," to learn more about the manifest attributes that are available.

3. Create a JAR file containing your applet's class files and resources. Include the manifest attributes in the `mymanifest.txt` file that you created in the previous step. For example, the following command creates a JAR file with the class files in the `build/classes/appletComponentArch` directory and the manifest file in the `build/classes` directory.

   ```
   % cd build/classes
   % jar cvfm DynamicTreeDemo.jar mymanifest.txt appletComponentArch
   ```

   See Chapter 16 to learn more about creating and using JAR files.

4. Sign the JAR file for your applet and time stamp the signature. Use a valid, current code-signing certificate issued by a trusted certificate authority to provide your users with assurance that it is safe to run the applet. See Chapter 16, "Signing JAR Files," for more information. If you want to use a signed JNLP file for security, create the JNLP file as described in the next step and include it in the JAR file before the JAR file is signed. See Signed JNLP Files[9] in the Java Platform Standard Edition Deployment Guide for information.

5. Create a JNLP file that describes how your applet should be launched. Here is the JNLP file used to launch the Dynamic Tree Demo applet. The source for `dynamictree_applet.jnlp` follows:

```xml
<?xml version="1.0" encoding="UTF-8"?>
<jnlp spec="1.0+" codebase="" href="">
    <information>
        <title>Dynamic Tree Demo</title>
        <vendor>Dynamic Team</vendor>
    </information>
    <resources>
        <!-- Application Resources -->
        <j2se version="1.7+"
            href="http://java.sun.com/products/autodl/j2se" />
        <jar href="DynamicTreeDemo.jar" main="true" />

    </resources>
    <applet-desc
        name="Dynamic Tree Demo Applet"
        main-class="components.DynamicTreeApplet"
        width="300"
        height="300">
    </applet-desc>
    <update check="background"/>
</jnlp>
```

Note that the security element for requesting additional permissions is not present in the JNLP file; therefore the applet runs only in the security sandbox. See Chapter 20, "Structure of the JNLP File," which describes JNLP file syntax and options.

6. Create the HTML page that will display the applet. Invoke Deployment Toolkit functions to deploy the applet. In our example, the Dynamic Tree Demo applet is deployed in `AppletPage.html`:

```html
<body>
    <!-- ... -->
    <script src="https://www.java.com/js/deployJava.js"></script>
    <script>
        var attributes = {
            code:'components.DynamicTreeApplet', width:300, height:300} ;
        var parameters = {jnlp_href: 'dynamictree_applet.jnlp'} ;
```

18

9.   `8/docs/technotes/guides/deploy/signed_jnlp.html`

```
            deployJava.runApplet(attributes, parameters, '1.7+');
        </script>
        <!-- ... -->
    </body>
```

7. Place the applet's JAR file, JNLP file, and HTML page in the appropriate folder(s). For this example, place `DynamicTreeDemo.jar`, `dynamictree_applet.jnlp`, and `AppletPage.html` in the same directory on the local machine or a web server. A web server is preferred. To run from the local machine, you must add your application to the exception site list, which is managed from the **Security** tab of the Java Control Panel.

8. Open the applet's HTML page in a browser to view the applet. Agree to run the applet when prompted. Check the Java Console log for error and debugging messages.

Deploying with the Applet Tag

If you are not sure whether your end users' browsers will have the JavaScript interpreter enabled, you can deploy your Java applet by manually coding the `<applet>` HTML tag, instead of using the Deployment Toolkit functions. Depending on the browsers you need to support, you may need to deploy your Java applet using the `<object>` or `<embed>` HTML tag. Check the W3C HTML Specification for details on the usage of these tags.[10] You can launch your applet using Java Network Launch Protocol (JNLP) or specify the launch attributes directly in the `<applet>` tag.

Preparing for Deployment

Follow the steps described in the "Deploying an Applet" section to compile your source code, create and sign the JAR file, and create the JNLP file if necessary. The overall steps for deployment are still relevant. Only the contents of your HTML page containing the applet will change.

Manually Coding Applet Tag, Launching Using JNLP

The `AppletPage_WithAppletTag.html` page deploys the Dynamic Tree Demo applet with an `<applet>` tag that has been manually coded (meaning the applet is not deployed using the Deployment Toolkit, which automatically generates the required HTML). The applet is still launched using JNLP. The JNLP file is specified in the `jnlp_href` attribute.

```
<applet code = 'appletComponentArch.DynamicTreeApplet'
        jnlp_href = 'dynamictree_applet.jnlp'
        width = 300
        height = 300 />
```

---

10. `http://www.w3.org/TR/1999/REC-html401-19991224/`

Manually Coding Applet Tag, Launching without JNLP

Using JNLP is the preferred way to deploy an applet; however, you can also deploy your applet without a JNLP file. The `AppletPage_WithAppletTagNoJNLP.html` deploys the Dynamic Tree Demo applet as shown in the following code snippet:

```
<applet code = 'appletComponentArch.DynamicTreeApplet'
    archive = 'DynamicTreeDemo.jar'
    width = 300
    height = 300>
    <param name="permissions" value="sandbox" />
</applet>
```

where

- `code` is the name of the applet class.
- `archive` is the name of the JAR file containing the applet and its resources.
- `width` is the width of the applet.
- `height` is the height of the applet.
- `permissions` indicates if the applet runs in the security sandbox. Specify `sandbox` for the value to run in the sandbox. Specify `all-permissions` to run outside the sandbox. If the `permissions` parameter is not present, signed applets default to `all-permissions` and unsigned applets default to `sandbox`.

Doing More with Applets

The Java applet API enables you to take advantage of the close relationship that applets have with browsers. The API is provided by the `javax.swing.JApplet` class and the `java.applet.AppletContext` interface. The applet execution architecture enables applets to interact with their environment to produce a rich user experience. An applet can manipulate its parent web page, interact with JavaScript code in the web page, find other applets running in the same web page, and much more.

Advanced capabilities of Java applets are explored in subsequent topics. See Chapter 19 for further information on advanced topics that are common to applets and Java Web Start applications (such as setting arguments and properties using the Java Network Launch Protocol [JNLP] API).

Finding and Loading Data Files

Whenever a Java applet needs to load data from a file that is specified with a relative URL (a URL that doesn't completely specify the file's location), the applet usually uses either the code base or the document base to form the complete URL.

18

The code base, returned by the JApplet getCodeBase method, is a URL that specifies the directory from which the applet's classes were loaded. For locally deployed applets, the getCodeBase method returns null.

The document base, returned by the JApplet getDocumentBase method, specifies the directory of the HTML page that contains the applet. For locally deployed applets, the getDocumentBase method returns null.

Unless the <applet> tag specifies a code base, both the code base and document base refer to the same directory on the same server. Data that the applet might need or needs to rely on as a backup is usually specified relative to the code base. Data that the applet developer specifies, often by using parameters, is usually specified relative to the document base.

> **Note**
>
> For security reasons, browsers limit the URLs from which untrusted applets can read. For example, most browsers don't allow untrusted applets to use .. to access directories above the code base or document base. Also, because untrusted applets cannot read files except for those files on the applet's originating host, the document base is generally not useful if the document and the untrusted applet reside on different servers.

The JApplet class defines convenient forms of image-loading and sound-loading methods that enable you to specify images and sounds relative to a base URL. For example, assume an applet is set up with one of the directory structures shown in Figure 18.2.

To create an Image object that uses the a.gif image file under imgDir, the applet can use the following code:

```
Image image = getImage(getCodeBase(), "imgDir/a.gif");
```

Defining and Using Applet Parameters

Parameters are to Java applets what command-line arguments are to applications. They enable the user to customize the applet's operation. By defining parameters, you can increase your applet's flexibility, making your applet work in multiple situations without recoding and recompiling it.

Specifying an Applet's Input Parameters

You can specify an applet's input parameters in the applet's JNLP file or in the <parameter> element of the <applet> tag. It is usually better to specify the parameters in the applet's JNLP file so that the parameters can be supplied consistently even if the applet is deployed on multiple web pages. If the applet's parameters will

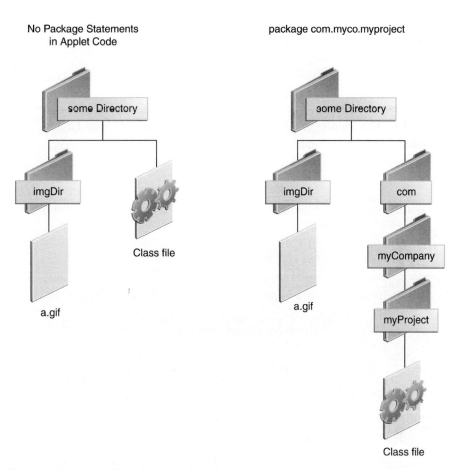

Figure 18.2 Code Directory Structures with and without Package Statements

vary by web page, then you should specify the parameters in the `<parameter>` element of the `<applet>` tag. If you are unfamiliar with JNLP, see Chapter 20, "Java Network Launch Protocol," for more information.

Consider an applet that takes three parameters. The `paramStr` and `paramInt` parameters are specified in the applet's JNLP file, `applettakesparams.jnlp`:

```
<?xml version="1.0" encoding="UTF-8"?>
<jnlp spec="1.0+" codebase="" href="">
    <!-- ... -->
    <applet-desc
        name="Applet Takes Params"
        main-class="AppletTakesParams"
        width="800"
        height="50">
            <param name="paramStr"
```

18

```
               value="someString"/>
           <param name="paramInt" value="22"/>
      </applet-desc>
      <!-- ... -->
  </jnlp>
```

The `paramOutsideJNLPFile` parameter is specified in the `parameters` variable passed to the Deployment Toolkit script's `runApplet` function in `Applet-Page.html`:

```html
<html>
  <head>
    <title>Applet Takes Params</title>
    <meta http-equiv="Content-Type" content="text/html;
      charset=windows-1252">
  </head>
  <body>
    <h1>Applet Takes Params</h1>

    <script
      src="https://www.java.com/js/deployJava.js"></script>
    <script>
        var attributes = { code:'AppletTakesParams.class',
            archive:'applet_AppletWithParameters.jar',
            width:800, height:50 };
        var parameters = {jnlp_href: 'applettakesparams.jnlp',
            paramOutsideJNLPFile: 'fooOutsideJNLP' };
        deployJava.runApplet(attributes, parameters, '1.7');
    </script>

  </body>
</html>
```

See Chapter 20, "Deploying an Applet," for more information about the `runApplet` function.

Retrieving the Applet's Input Parameters

You can retrieve the applet's input parameters by using the `getParameter`[11] method of the `Applet` class. The `AppletTakesParams.java` applet[12] retrieves and displays all its input parameters (`paramStr`, `paramInt`, and `paramOutsideJNLPFile`):

```java
import javax.swing.JApplet;
import javax.swing.SwingUtilities;
import javax.swing.JLabel;

public class AppletTakesParams extends JApplet {
```

---

11. `8/docs/api/java/applet/Applet.html#getParameter-java.lang.String-`
12. `tutorial/deployment/applet/examples/zipfiles/applet_AppletWithParameters`
    `.zip`

```
    public void init() {
        final String  inputStr = getParameter("paramStr");
        final int inputInt = Integer.parseInt(getParameter("paramInt"));
        final String inputOutsideJNLPFile = getParameter("paramOutsideJNLPFile");

        try {
            SwingUtilities.invokeAndWait(new Runnable() {
                public void run() {
                    createGUI(inputStr, inputInt, inputOutsideJNLPFile);
                }
            });
        } catch (Exception e) {
            System.err.println("createGUI didn't successfully complete");
        }
    }
    private void createGUI(String inputStr, int inputInt, String inputOutsideJNLPFile) {
        String text = "Applet's parameters are -- inputStr: " + inputStr +
                ",    inputInt: " + inputInt +
                ",    paramOutsideJNLPFile: " + inputOutsideJNLPFile;
        JLabel lbl = new JLabel(text);
        add(lbl);
    }
}
```

Displaying Short Status Strings

All browsers allow Java applets to display a short status string. All Java applets on the page, as well as the browser itself, share the same status line.

Never put crucial information in the status line. If a significant number of users might need the information, display that information within the applet area. If only a few, sophisticated users might need the information, consider sending the information to standard output (see the "Writing Diagnostics to Standard Output and Error Streams" section).

The status line is not usually very prominent, and it can be overwritten by other applets or by the browser. For these reasons, it is best used for incidental, transitory information. For example, an applet that loads several image files might display the name of the image file it is currently loading.

Applets display status lines with the showStatus method, inherited in the JApplet class from the Applet class.[13] Here is an example of its use:

```
showStatus("MyApplet: Loading image file " + file);
```

Note

Don't put scrolling text in the status line. Browser users find such behavior highly annoying.

18

---

13. 8/docs/api/java/applet/Applet.html#showStatus-java.lang.String-

Displaying Documents in the Browser

A Java applet can load a web page in a browser window using the `showDocument` methods in the `java.applet.AppletContext` class.[14] Here are the two forms of `showDocument`:

```
public void showDocument(java.net.URL url)
public void showDocument(java.net.URL url, String targetWindow)
```

The one-argument form of `showDocument` simply instructs the browser to display the document at the specified URL without specifying the window in which to display the document. The two-argument form of `showDocument` lets you specify the window or HTML frame in which to display the document. The second argument can have one of the following values:

- `"_blank"`. This displays the document in a new, nameless window.
- `" windowName "`. This displays the document in a window named *windowName*. This window is created if necessary.
- `"_self"`. This displays the document in the window and frame that contain the applet.
- `"_parent"`. This displays the document in the parent frame of the applet's frame. If the applet frame has no parent frame, this acts the same as `"_self"`.
- `"_top"`. This displays the document in the top-level frame. If the applet's frame is the top-level frame, this acts the same as `"_self"`.

> **Note**
>
> In this discussion, *frame* refers not to a Swing `JFrame` but to an HTML frame within a browser window.

18

The `ShowDocument` applet enables you try every argument of both forms of `showDocument`. The applet opens a window that lets you type in a URL and choose an option for the `targetWindow` argument. When you press **Return** or click the **Show Document** button, the applet calls `showDocument`.

The following is the applet code that calls `showDocument`[15]:

---

14. 8/docs/api/java/applet/AppletContext.html

15. tutorial/deployment/applet/examples/zipfiles/applet_ShowDocument
     .zip

```
        .../In an Applet subclass:
        urlWindow = new URLWindow(getAppletContext());
        ...

class URLWindow extends Frame {
    ...
    public URLWindow(AppletContext appletContext) {
        ...
        this.appletContext = appletContext;
        ...
    }
    ...
    public boolean action(Event event, Object o) {
        ...
        String urlString =
            /* user-entered string */;
        URL url = null;
        try {
            url = new URL(urlString);
        } catch (MalformedURLException e) {
            .../Inform the user and return...
        }

        if (url != null) {
            if (/* user doesn't want to specify
                    the window */) {
                appletContext.showDocument(url);
            } else {
                appletContext.showDocument(url,
                    /* user-specified window */);
            }
        }
    }
    ...
```

Invoking JavaScript Code from an Applet

Java applets can invoke JavaScript functions present in the same web page as the applet. The LiveConnect Specification describes details about how JavaScript code communicates with Java code.[16]

The `netscape.javascript.JSObject` class enables Java applets to retrieve a reference to JavaScript objects and interact with the web page. The Data Summary applet (in the Invoking JavaScript Code from Applet example[17]) described next invokes JavaScript code to retrieve information from the web page and writes a data summary back to the web page.

---

16. http://www.oracle.com/technetwork/java/javase/plugin2-142482.html
     #LIVECONNECT

17. tutorial/deployment/applet/examples/zipfiles/applet
     _InvokingAppletMethodsFromJavaScript.zip

Assume you have a web page with a few JavaScript functions. The example `AppletPage.html` has JavaScript functions to retrieve age, address, and phone numbers. There is also a variable called `userName` that has no value at the outset:

```
<head>
<title>Data Summary Applet Page - Java to JavaScript LiveConnect</title>
<meta http-equiv="Content-Type" content="text/html; charset=windows-1252"/>
<script language="javascript">
    var userName = "";

    // returns number
    function getAge() {
        return 25;
    }
    // returns an object
    function address() {
        this.street = "1 Example Lane";
        this.city = "Santa Clara";
        this.state = "CA";
    }
    // returns an array
    function getPhoneNums() {
        return ["408-555-0100", "408-555-0102"];
    }
    function writeSummary(summary) {
        summaryElem =
            document.getElementById("summary");
        summaryElem.innerHTML = summary;
    }
    </script>

    <!-- ... -->
</head>
<body>
    <script src =
      "https://www.java.com/js/deployJava.js"></script>
    <script>
        <!-- ... -->
        deployJava.runApplet(attributes, parameters, '1.6');
    </script>
    <!-- ... -->
    <p id="summary"/>  // this HTML element contains
                       // the summary
    <!-- ... -->
</body>
```

Next, consider an applet class called `DataSummaryApplet`. The `DataSummaryApplet` class performs the following operations:

- Invokes the `JSObject`'s `setMember` method to set the `userName` variable to *John Doe*
- Retrieves the age, address, and phone numbers and builds a string containing a summary of this data

- Invokes the `writeSummary` JavaScript function to write the summary back to the web page

This applet first needs to retrieve a reference to `JSObject` as follows:

```
...
JSObject window = JSObject.getWindow(this);
...
```

Put the preceding statement in a `try` block to handle `netscape.javascript.JSException`. Now that the applet has a reference to `JSObject`, it can invoke the relevant JavaScript functions by using the `eval` and `call` methods of `JSObject`:

```java
package javatojs;

import java.applet.Applet;
import netscape.javascript.*; // add plugin.jar to classpath during compilation

public class DataSummaryApplet extends Applet {
    public void start() {
        try {
            JSObject window = JSObject.getWindow(this);

            String userName = "John Doe";

            // set JavaScript variable
            window.setMember("userName", userName);

            // invoke JavaScript function
            Number age = (Number) window.eval("getAge()");

            // get a JavaScript object and retrieve its contents
            JSObject address = (JSObject) window.eval("new address();");
            String addressStr = (String) address.getMember("street") + ", " +
                    (String) address.getMember("city") + ", " +
                    (String) address.getMember("state");

            // get an array from JavaScript and retrieve its contents
            JSObject phoneNums = (JSObject) window.eval("getPhoneNums()");
            String phoneNumStr = (String) phoneNums.getSlot(0) + ", " +
                    (String) phoneNums.getSlot(1);

            // dynamically change HTML in page; write data summary
            String summary = userName + " : " + age + " : " +
                    addressStr + " : " + phoneNumStr;
            window.call("writeSummary", new Object[] {summary})    ;
        } catch (JSException jse) {
            jse.printStackTrace();
        }
    }
}
```

18

To compile Java code that has a reference to classes in the `netscape.javascript` package, include *<your JDK path>*`/jre/lib/plugin.jar` in your class path. At runtime, the Java Plug-In software automatically makes these classes available to applets.

The Data Summary applet displays the following result on the web page:

```
Result of applet's Java calls to JavaScript on this page

John Doe : 25 : 1 Example Lane, Santa Clara, CA : 408-555-0100, 408-555-0102
```

Invoking Applet Methods from JavaScript Code

JavaScript code on a web page can interact with Java applets embedded on the page. JavaScript code can perform operations such as the following:

- Invoke methods on Java objects
- Get and set fields in Java objects
- Get and set Java array elements

The LiveConnect Specification describes details about how JavaScript code communicates with Java code.[18]

Security warnings are shown when JavaScript code makes calls to a Java applet. To suppress these warnings, add the `Caller-Allowable-Codebase` attribute to the JAR file manifest. Specify the location of the JavaScript code that is allowed to make calls to the applet. See JAR File Manifest Attributes for Security for information about the `Caller-Allowable-Codebase` attribute.[19]

This topic explores JavaScript code to Java applet communication using the Math applet example (in the Invoking JavaScript Code from Applet example[20]). The `MathApplet` class and supporting `Calculator` class provide a set of public methods and variables. The JavaScript code on the web page invokes and evaluates these public members to pass data and retrieve calculated results.

Math Applet and Related Classes

Here is the source code for the `MathApplet` class. The `getCalculator` method returns a reference to the `Calculator` helper class:

---

18. http://www.oracle.com/technetwork/java/javase/plugin2-142482.html
     #LIVECONNECT

19. 8/docs/technotes/guides/deploy/manifest.html

20. tutorial/deployment/applet/examples/zipfiles/applet
     _InvokingAppletMethodsFromJavaScript.zip

```
package jstojava;
import java.applet.Applet;

public class MathApplet extends Applet{

    public String userName = null;

    public String getGreeting() {
        return "Hello " + userName;
    }

    public Calculator getCalculator() {
        return new Calculator();
    }

    public DateHelper getDateHelper() {
        return new DateHelper();
    }

    public void printOut(String text) {
        System.out.println(text);
    }
}
```

The methods in the `Calculator` class let the user set two values, add numbers, and retrieve the numbers in a range:

```
package jstojava;

public class Calculator {
    private int a = 0;
    private int b = 0; // assume b > a

    public void setNums(int numA, int numB) {
        a = numA;
        b = numB;
    }

    public int add() {
        return a + b;
    }

    public int [] getNumInRange() {
        int x = a;
        int len = (b - a) + 1;
        int [] range = new int [len];
        for (int i = 0; i < len; i++) {
            range[i]= x++;
            System.out.println("i: " + i + " ; range[i]: " + range[i]);
        }
        return range;
    }
}
```

The `getDate` method of the `DateHelper` class returns the current date:

```
package jstojava;
import java.util.Date;
import java.text.SimpleDateFormat;

public class DateHelper {

    public static String label = null;

    public String getDate() {
        return label + " " + new SimpleDateFormat().format(new Date());
    }

}
```

Deploying the Applet

When deploying the applet, make sure that you specify an id for the applet. Deploy the applet in a web page, `AppletPage.html`. The applet id is used later to obtain a reference to the applet object:

```
<script src=
  "https://www.java.com/js/deployJava.js"></script>
<script>
    <!-- applet id can be used to get a reference to
    the applet object -->
    var attributes = { id:'mathApplet',
        code:'jstojava.MathApplet',  width:1, height:1} ;
    var parameters = { jnlp_href: 'math_applet.jnlp'} ;
    deployJava.runApplet(attributes, parameters, '1.6');
</script>
```

Next, add some JavaScript code to the `AppletPage.html` web page. The JavaScript code can use the applet id as a reference to the applet object and invoke the applet's methods. In the next example, the JavaScript code sets the applet's public member variables, invokes public methods, and retrieves a reference to another object referenced by the applet (`Calculator`). The JavaScript code is able to handle primitive, array, and object return types:

```
<script language="javascript">
    function enterNums(){
        var numA = prompt('Enter number \'a\'?','0');
        var numB = prompt(
            'Enter number \'b\' (should be greater than number \'a\' ?','1');
        // set applet's public variable
        mathApplet.userName = "John Doe";

        // invoke public applet method
        var greeting = mathApplet.getGreeting();

        // get another class referenced by applet and
        // invoke its methods
        var calculator = mathApplet.getCalculator();
        calculator.setNums(numA, numB);
```

```
        // primitive datatype returned by applet
        var sum = calculator.add();

        // array returned by applet
        var numRange = calculator.getNumInRange();

        // check Java console log for this message
        mathApplet.printOut("Testing printing to System.out");

        // get another class, set static field and invoke its methods
        var dateHelper = mathApplet.getDateHelper();
        dateHelper.label = "Today\'s date is: ";
        var dateStr = dateHelper.getDate();
        <!-- ... -->
</script>
```

The Math applet displays the following results on the web page when the input is a = 0 and b = 5:

```
Results of JavaScript to Java Communication

Hello John Doe

a = 0 ; b = 5

Sum: 5

Numbers in range array: [ 0, 1, 2, 3, 4, 5 ]

Today's date is: 5/28/13 4:12 PM //shows current date
```

Open `AppletPage.html` in a browser to view the Math applet. Check security restrictions placed on applets invoked by JavaScript code.

> **Note**
>
> If you don't see the applet running, you might need to enable the JavaScript interpreter in your browser so that the Deployment Toolkit script can function properly.

18

Handling Initialization Status with Event Handlers

An applet cannot handle requests from JavaScript code in the web page until the applet has been initialized. A call to an applet method or access to an applet variable from JavaScript code will be blocked until the applet's `init()` method is complete or the applet first invokes JavaScript code from the web page in which it is deployed. As the JavaScript implementation is single-threaded in many browsers, the web page may appear frozen during applet start-up.

You can check the `status` variable of the applet while it is loading to determine if the applet is ready to handle requests from JavaScript code. You can also register event handlers that will automatically be invoked during various stages of applet initialization. To leverage this functionality, the applet should be deployed with the `java_status_events` parameter set to `true`.

In the Status and Callback applet, JavaScript code registers an `onLoad` handler with the applet.[21] The `onLoad` handler is automatically invoked by the Java Plug-In software when the applet has been initialized. The `onLoad` handler invokes other methods of the applet to draw the graph on the web page. The `init` method of the `DrawingApplet` class sleeps for two seconds to simulate a long applet initialization period.

The following steps describe how to register event handlers and check an applet's status. For a complete list of applet status values and applet events for which event handlers can be registered, see Applet Status and Event Handlers.[22]

1. Create a JavaScript function to register event handlers. The following code snippet shows the `registerAppletStateHandler` function that registers an `onLoad` event handler if the applet has not already loaded:

```
<script>
<!-- ... -->
    var READY = 2;
    function registerAppletStateHandler() {
        // register onLoad handler if applet has
        // not loaded yet
        if (drawApplet.status < READY)  {
            drawApplet.onLoad = onLoadHandler;
        } else if (drawApplet.status >= READY) {
            // applet has already loaded or there
            // was an error
            document.getElementById("mydiv").innerHTML =
                "Applet event handler not registered because applet status is: "
                + drawApplet.status;
        }
    }

    function onLoadHandler() {
        // event handler for ready state
        document.getElementById("mydiv").innerHTML =
            "Applet has loaded";
        draw();
    }
<!-- ... -->
</script>
```

2. Invoke the previously created `registerAppletStateHandler` function in the body tag's `onload` method. This ensures that the HTML tag for the applet

---

21. `tutorial/deployment/applet/examples/zipfiles/applet_StatusAndCallback.zip`

22. `8/docs/technotes/guides/deploy/applet_dev_guide.html#JSDPG719`

has been created in the Document Object Model (DOM) tree of the web page before the applet's event handlers are registered.

```
<body onload="registerAppletStateHandler()">
```

3. Deploy the applet with the `java_status_events` parameter set to `true`:

```
<script src=
  "https://www.java.com/js/deployJava.js"></script>
<script>
    // set java_status_events parameter to true
    var attributes = { id:'drawApplet',
        code:'DrawingApplet.class',
        archive: 'applet_StatusAndCallback.jar',
        width:600, height:400} ;
        var parameters = {java_status_events: 'true', permissions:'sandbox' } ;
        deployJava.runApplet(attributes, parameters, '1.7');
</script>
```

Manipulating DOM of Applet's Web Page

Every web page is composed of a series of nested objects. These objects make up the Document Object Model (DOM). A Java applet can traverse and modify objects of its parent web page using the Common DOM API.[23]

Consider an example of a Java applet that dumps the contents of its parent web page (in the DOM Dump example).[24] In order to traverse and manipulate the DOM tree, you must first obtain a reference to the `Document` object for the web page. You can do so by using the `getDocument` method in the `com.sun.java.browser.plugin2.DOM` class. Here is a code snippet that retrieves a reference to a `Document` object in the DOMDump applet's `start` method. See inline comments in the code:

```
public void start() {
    try {
        // use reflection to get document
        Class c =
          Class.forName("com.sun.java.browser.plugin2.DOM");
        Method m = c.getMethod("getDocument",
          new Class[] { java.applet.Applet.class });

        // cast object returned as HTMLDocument;
        // then traverse or modify DOM
        HTMLDocument doc = (HTMLDocument) m.invoke(null,
            new Object[] { this });
        HTMLBodyElement body =
            (HTMLBodyElement) doc.getBody();
        dump(body, INDENT);
    } catch (Exception e) {
```

23. `8/docs/jre/api/plugin/dom/index.html`

24. `tutorial/deployment/applet/examples/zipfiles/applet_TraversingDOM
     .zip`

```
            System.out.println("New Java Plug-In not available");
            // In this case, you could fallback to the old
            // bootstrapping mechanism available in the
            // com.sun.java.browser.plugin.dom package
        }
    }
```

Now that you have a reference to the Document object, you can traverse and
modify the DOM tree using the Common DOM API. The DOMDump applet traverses
the DOM tree and writes its contents to the Java Console log:

```
private void dump(Node root, String prefix) {
    if (root instanceof Element) {
        System.out.println(prefix +
            ((Element) root).getTagName() +
            " / " + root.getClass().getName());
    } else if (root instanceof CharacterData) {
        String data =
            ((CharacterData) root).getData().trim();
        if (!data.equals("")) {
            System.out.println(prefix +
                "CharacterData: " + data);
        }
    } else {
        System.out.println(prefix +
            root.getClass().getName());
    }
    NamedNodeMap attrs = root.getAttributes();
    if (attrs != null) {
        int len = attrs.getLength();
        for (int i = 0; i < len; i++) {
            Node attr = attrs.item(i);
            System.out.print(prefix + HALF_INDENT +
                "attribute " + i + ": " +
                attr.getNodeName());
            if (attr instanceof Attr) {
                System.out.print(" = " +
                    ((Attr) attr).getValue());
            }
            System.out.println();
        }
    }

    if (root.hasChildNodes()) {
        NodeList children = root.getChildNodes();
        if (children != null) {
            int len = children.getLength();
            for (int i = 0; i < len; i++) {
                dump(children.item(i), prefix +
                    INDENT);
            }
        }
    }
}
```

Displaying a Customized Loading Progress Indicator

A Java applet can display a customized loading progress indicator that shows the progress of the download of the applet's resources as well as other applet specific data. Consider the Weather applet and the `CustomProgress` class (in the Applet with Customized Loading Progress Indicator example[25]) to understand how to implement a customized loading progress indicator for a Java applet. For the purpose of demonstrating a large and prolonged download, this applet's JAR file has been artificially inflated and the `customprogress_applet.jnlp` file specifies additional JAR files as resources.

Developing a Customized Loading Progress Indicator

To develop a customized loading progress indicator for your applet, create a class that implements the `DownloadServiceListener` interface.[26] The constructor of the loading progress indicator class will vary depending on how the user interface should be displayed and the capabilities needed by the class. The following guidelines should be applied:

- To display the loading progress indicator in a separate top level window, create a constructor that does not have any parameters.
- To display the loading progress indicator for an applet in the applet's container, create a constructor that takes an `Object` as a parameter. The `Object` argument can be type cast to an instance of the `java.awt.Container` class.[27]
- If the loading progress indicator class needs to access the applet's parameters, create two constructors as follows:
  - Create a constructor that takes an `Object` as a parameter as described previously.
  - Create a constructor that takes two parameters of type `Object`. The first argument can be type cast to an instance of the `java.awt.Container`[28] class and the second argument can be type cast to an instance of the `java.applet.AppletStub`[29] class. The Java Plug-In software will invoke the

---

25. `tutorial/deployment/applet/examples/zipfiles/applet` `_AppletWithCustomProgressIndicator.zip`, `tutorial/deployment/applet/` `examples/zipfiles/applet_CustomProgressIndicator.zip`, and `tutorial/deployment/` `webstart/examples/zipfiles/webstart_AppWithCustomProgressIndicator.zip`

26. `8/docs/jre/api/javaws/jnlp/javax/jnlp/DownloadServiceListener.html`

27. `8/docs/api/java/awt/Container.html`

28. `8/docs/api/java/awt/Container.html`

29. `8/docs/api/java/applet/AppletStub.html`

appropriate constructor depending on the capabilities of the JRE software
on the client machine:

```
import javax.jnlp.DownloadServiceListener;
import java.awt.Container;
import java.applet.AppletStub;
import netscape.javascript.*;

// ...

public class CustomProgress implements DownloadServiceListener {
    Container surfaceContainer = null;
    AppletStub appletStub = null;
    JProgressBar progressBar = null;
    JLabel statusLabel = null;
    boolean uiCreated = false;

    public CustomProgress(Object surface) {
        init(surface, null);
    }

    public CustomProgress(Object surface, Object stub) {
        init(surface, stub);
    }

    public void init(Object surface, Object stub) {
        try {
            surfaceContainer = (Container) surface;
            appletStub = (AppletStub) stub;
        } catch (ClassCastException cce) {
            // ...
        }
    }
    // ...
}
```

The following code snippet shows how to build the user interface for the loading
progress indicator. Use the instance of the `java.applet.AppletStub`[30] class to
retrieve the applet's parameters. Invoke the `JSObject.getWindow(null)` method
to obtain a reference to the applet's parent web page and invoke JavaScript code on
that page:

```
private void create() {
    JPanel top = createComponents();
    if (surfaceContainer != null) {
        // lay out loading progress UI in the given
        // Container
        surfaceContainer.add(top, BorderLayout.NORTH);
        surfaceContainer.invalidate();
        surfaceContainer.validate();
    }
}
```

---

30. 8/docs/api/java/applet/AppletStub.html

```
private JPanel createComponents() {
    JPanel top = new JPanel();
    // ...
    // get applet parameter using an instance of the
    // AppletStub class "tagLine" parameter specified
    // in applet's JNLP file
    String tagLine = "";
    if (appletStub !- null) {
        tagLine = appletStub.getParameter("tagLine");
    }
    String lblText = "<html><font color=red size=+2>JDK
        Documentation</font><br/>" +
        tagLine + " <br/></html>";
    JLabel lbl = new JLabel(lblText);
    top.add(lbl, BorderLayout.NORTH);

    // use JSObject.getWindow(null) method to retrieve
    // a reference to the web page and make JavaScript
    // calls. Duke logo displayed if displayLogo variable
    // set to "true" in the web page
    String displayLogo = "false";
    JSObject window = JSObject.getWindow(null);
    if (window != null) {
        displayLogo = (String)window.getMember("displayLogo");
    }
    if (displayLogo.equals("true")) {
        lbl = new JLabel();
        ImageIcon logo = createImageIcon("images/DukeWave.gif", "logo");
        lbl.setIcon(logo);
        top.add(lbl, BorderLayout.EAST);
    }

    statusLabel = new JLabel(
        "html><font color=green size=-2>" +
        "Loading applet...</font></html>");
    top.add(statusLabel, BorderLayout.CENTER);

    // progress bar displays progress
    progressBar = new JProgressBar(0, 100);
    progressBar.setValue(0);
    progressBar.setStringPainted(true);
    top.add(progressBar, BorderLayout.SOUTH);

    return top;
}
```

18

Create and update the progress indicator in the following methods based on the `overallPercent` argument. These methods are invoked regularly by the Java Plug-In software to communicate progress of the applet's download. Java Plug-In software will always send a message when download and validation of resources is 100% complete:

```
public void progress(URL url, String version,
                     long readSoFar, long total,
                     int overallPercent) {
```

```
        // check progress of download and update display
        updateProgressUI(overallPercent);
    }

    public void upgradingArchive(java.net.URL url,
                     java.lang.String version,
                     int patchPercent,
                     int overallPercent) {
        updateProgressUI(overallPercent);
    }

    public void validating(java.net.URL url,
              java.lang.String version,
              long entry,
              long total,
              int overallPercent) {
        updateProgressUI(overallPercent);
    }

    private void updateProgressUI(int overallPercent) {
        if (!uiCreated && overallPercent > 0
            && overallPercent < 100) {
            // create custom progress indicator's
            // UI only if there is more work to do,
            // meaning overallPercent > 0 and
            // < 100 this prevents flashing when
            // RIA is loaded from cache
            create();
            uiCreated = true;
        }
        if (uiCreated) {
            progressBar.setValue(overallPercent);
        }
    }
}
```

Compile the loading progress indicator class and build a JAR file with all the resources needed to display the loading progress indicator. Include the following JAR files in your `classpath` to enable compilation:

- *<your JRE directory>*/lib/javaws.jar
- *<your JRE directory>*/lib/plugin.jar (This JAR file is required only if your loading progress indicator class uses the JSObject.getWindow method to invoke JavaScript code in the applet's parent web page.)

The loading progress indicator class is now ready for use. The next step is to specify this loading progress indicator JAR file as your applet's loading progress indicator.

Specifying a Loading Progress Indicator for an Applet

To specify a customized loading progress indicator for an applet, include the following information in the applet's JNLP file:

- jar tag with the `download="progress"` attribute
- `progress-class` attribute with the fully qualified name of the loading progress class

The following code snippet from the `customprogress_applet.jnlp` file displays the usage of the `download="progress"` and `progress-class` attributes:

```
<jnlp spec="1.0+"
  codebase="tutorial/deployment"
  href="">
  <!-- ... -->
  <resources>
    <!-- ... -->
    <jar
      href="applet/examples/dist/applet_AppletWithCustomProgressIndicator"
      main="true" />
    <jar
      href="applet/examples/dist/applet_CustomProgressIndicator/applet_CustomProgressIndicator.jar"
      download="progress" />
  </resources>
  <applet-desc
      name="customprogressindicatordemo.WeatherApplet"
      main-class="customprogressindicatordemo.WeatherApplet"
      progress-class="customprogressindicator.CustomProgress"
      width="600"
      height="200">
      <param
        name="tagLine"
        value="Information straight from the horse's mouth!"/>
  </applet-desc>
<!-- ... -->
</jnlp>
```

Deploy the applet in a web page. Open `AppletPage.html` in a web browser to view the loading progress indicator for the Weather applet.

Integrating the Loading Progress Indicator with the Applet User Interface

You can also integrate the loading progress indicator into the applet's user interface. Open `AppletPage.html` in a web browser to view the loading progress indicator integrated into the Weather applet's user interface. View the `IntegratedProgressIndicator.java` class (in the Applet with Integrated Progress Indicator example[31]) and the inline comments for more information. See Chapter 19,

18

---

31. `tutorial/deployment/applet/examples/zipfiles/applet` `_AppletWithIntegratedProgressIndicator.zip` and `tutorial/deployment/` `webstart/examples/zipfiles/webstart_AppWithCustomProgressIndicator` `.zip`

"Customizing the Loading Experience," for more information about customizing the rich Internet application (RIA) loading experience.

Writing Diagnostics to Standard Output and Error Streams

A Java applet can write messages to the standard output and standard error streams. Writing diagnostics to standard output can be an invaluable tool when you are debugging a Java applet. The following code snippet writes messages to the standard output stream and the standard error stream:

```
// Where instance variables are declared:
boolean DEBUG = true;
// ...
// Later, when we want to print some status:
if (DEBUG) {
    try {
        // ...
        //some code that throws an exception
        System.out.
            println("Called someMethod(" + x + "," + y + ")");
    } catch (Exception e) {
        e.printStackTrace()
    }
}
```

Check the Java Console log for messages written to the standard output stream or standard error stream. To store messages in a log file, enable logging in the Java Control Panel. Messages will be written to a log file in the user's home directory (e.g., on Windows, the log file might be in C:\Documents and Settings\someuser\ Application Data\Sun\Java\Deployment\log).

Note

Be sure to disable all debugging output before you release your applet.

18

Developing Draggable Applets

A Java applet that is deployed by specifying the draggable parameter can be dragged outside the browser and dynamically transformed into a Java Web Start application. The Java applet can be dragged by pressing the **Alt** key and the left mouse button and dragging the mouse. When the drag operation begins, the applet is removed from its parent container (Applet or JApplet) and placed in a new undecorated top-level window (Frame or JFrame). A small floating **Close** button is displayed next to the dragged applet. When the floating **Close** button is clicked, the applet is placed back in the browser. Java applets that can be dragged out of the browser shall henceforth be referred to as *draggable applets*.

You can customize the behavior of a draggable applet in the following ways:

- You can change the keystroke and mouse button sequence that is used to drag the applet outside the browser.
- You can add a desktop shortcut that can be used to launch your application outside the browser.
- You can define how the applet should be closed after it has been dragged outside the browser.

The following sections describe how to implement and customize a draggable applet. The `MenuChooserApplet` class (from the Draggable Applet example[32]) is used to demonstrate the development and deployment of draggable applets. Open `AppletPage.html` in a browser to view the Menu Chooser applet on a new page.

Enabling the Capability to Drag an Applet

You can enable the capability to drag an applet by setting the `draggable` parameter to `true` when deploying the applet, as shown in the following code snippet:

```
<script src="https://www.java.com/js/deployJava.js"></script>
<script>
    var attributes = { code:'MenuChooserApplet', width:900, height:300 };
    var parameters = { jnlp_href: 'draggableapplet.jnlp', draggable: 'true' };
    deployJava.runApplet(attributes, parameters, '1.6');
</script>
```

Changing the Keystroke and Mouse Button Sequence That Is Used to Drag an Applet

You can change the keystroke and mouse button sequence that is used to drag an applet by implementing the `isAppletDragStart` method. In the following code snippet, the applet can be dragged by pressing the left mouse button and dragging the mouse:

```
public boolean isAppletDragStart(MouseEvent e) {
        if(e.getID() == MouseEvent.MOUSE_DRAGGED) {
            return true;
        } else {
            return false;
        }
    }
```

Enabling the Addition of a Desktop Shortcut When the Applet Is Disconnected from the Browser

If the user closes the browser window or navigates away from the page after dragging an applet outside the page, the applet is said to be *disconnected* from the

18

32. `tutorial/deployment/applet/examples/zipfiles/applet_Draggable.zip`

browser. You can create a desktop shortcut for the applet when the applet is disconnected from the browser. The desktop shortcut can be used to launch the application
outside the browser. To enable the creation of a desktop shortcut, add the `offline-`
`allowed` and `shortcut` tags to the applet's JNLP file:

```
<information>
    <!-- ... -->
    <offline-allowed />
    <shortcut online="false">
        <desktop />
    </shortcut>
</information>
```

Note

Depending on the setting for Shortcut Creation in the user's Java Control Panel, the user
might be prompted for confirmation before the shortcut is created.

Defining How the Applet Should Be Closed

You can define how your applet can be closed. For example, your Swing applet could
have a `JButton` to close the applet instead of relying on the default floating **Close**
button.

The Java Plug-In software gives the applet an instance of the `ActionListener`
class. This instance of the `ActionListener` class, also referred to as the *close lis-*
tener, can be used to modify the default close behavior of the applet.

To define how the applet should be closed, implement the `setAppletCloseLis-`
`tener` and `appletRestored` methods in your applet. In the following code snippet,
the `MenuChooserApplet` class receives the close listener and passes it on to the
instance of the `MenuItemChooser` class:

```
MenuItemChooser display = null;
// ...
display = new MenuItemChooser();
// ...
public void setAppletCloseListener(ActionListener cl) {
    display.setCloseListener(cl);
}

public void appletRestored() {
    display.setCloseListener(null);
}
```

The `MenuItemChooser` class is responsible for controlling the applet's user
interface. The `MenuItemChooser` class defines a `JButton` labeled **Close**. The following code is executed when the user clicks this **Close** button:

```
private void close() {
    // invoke actionPerformed of closeListener received
    // from the Java Plug-in software.
    if (closeListener != null) {
        closeListener.actionPerformed(null);
    }
}
```

Requesting and Customizing Applet Decoration

When deploying an applet, you can specify that the window of dragged applet should be decorated with the default or customized window title. To enable window decoration of a dragged applet, specify the `java_decorated_frame` parameter with a value of true. To enable a customized window title, specify the `java_applet_title` parameter also. The value of this parameter should be the text of the window title:

```
<script src="https://www.java.com/js/deployJava.js"></script>
<script>
    var attributes =
        { code:'SomeDraggableApplet', width:100, height:100 };
    var parameters =
        { jnlp_href: 'somedraggableapplet.jnlp',
            java_decorated_frame: 'true',
            java_applet_title: 'A Custom Title'
        };
    deployJava.runApplet(attributes, parameters, '1.7');
</script>
```

The `java_decorated_frame` and `java_applet_title` parameters can also be specified in the applet's JNLP file, as shown in the following code snippet:

```
<applet-desc main-class="SayHello" name="main test" height="150" width="300">
    <param name="java_decorated_frame" value="true" />
    <param name="java_applet_title" value="" />
</applet-desc>
```

Communicating with Other Applets

18

A Java applet can communicate with other Java applets by using JavaScript functions in the parent web page. JavaScript functions enable communication between applets by receiving messages from one applet and invoking methods of other applets. See the "Invoking JavaScript Code from an Applet" and "Invoking Applet Methods from JavaScript Code" sections in this chapter for more information about the interaction between Java code and JavaScript code.

You should avoid using the following mechanisms to find other applets and share data between applets:

- Avoid using static variables to share data between applets.
- Do not use the `getApplet` and `getApplets` methods of the `AppletContext`[33] class to find other applets. These methods only find applets that are running in the same instance of the JRE software.

Note that applets must originate from the same directory on the server in order to communicate with each other.

The Sender and Receiver applets are discussed next.[34] When a user clicks the button to increment the counter, the Sender applet invokes a JavaScript function to send a request to the Receiver applet. Upon receiving the request, the Receiver applet increments a counter variable and displays the value of the variable.

To enable communication with another applet, obtain a reference to an instance of the `netscape.javascript.JSObject` class. Use this instance to invoke JavaScript functions. The `Sender` applet uses an instance of the `netscape.javascript.JSObject` class to invoke a JavaScript function called `sendMsgToIncrementCounter`:

```
try {
    JSObject window = JSObject.getWindow(this);
    window.eval("sendMsgToIncrementCounter()");
} catch (JSException jse) {
    // ...
}
```

Note

To compile Java code that has a reference to classes in the `netscape.javascript` package, include `<your JDK path>`/`jre/lib/plugin.jar` in your class path. At runtime, the Java Plug-In software automatically makes these classes available to applets.

Write the JavaScript function that will receive requests from one applet and invoke methods of another applet on the web page. The `sendMsgToIncrement-Counter` JavaScript function invokes the Receiver applet's `incrementCounter` method:

```
<script>
    function sendMsgToIncrementCounter() {
        var myReceiver = document.getElementById("receiver");
        myReceiver.incrementCounter();
    }
</script>
```

18

---

33. 8/docs/api/java/applet/AppletContext.html
34. tutorial/deployment/applet/examples/zipfiles/applet_SenderReceiver
     .zip

Note that the JavaScript code uses the name `receiver` to obtain a reference to the Receiver applet on the web page. This name should be the same as the value of the `id` attribute that is specified when you deploy the Receiver applet. The Receiver applet's `incrementCounter` method is shown next:

```
public void incrementCounter() {
    ctr++;
    String text = " Current Value Of Counter: "
        + (new Integer(ctr)).toString();
    ctrLbl.setText(text);
}
```

Deploy the applets on the web page as shown in the following code snippet. You can view the Sender and Receiver applets and associated JavaScript code in `AppletPage.html`:

```
<!-- Sender Applet -->
<script src="https://www.java.com/js/deployJava.js"></script>
<script>
    var attributes = { code:'Sender.class',
        archive:'examples/dist/applet_SenderReceiver/applet_SenderReceiver.jar',
        width:300, height:50} ;
    var parameters = { permissions:'sandbox' };
    deployJava.runApplet(attributes, parameters, '1.6');
</script>

<!-- Receiver Applet -->
<script>
    var attributes = { id:'receiver', code:'Receiver.class',
        archive:'examples/dist/applet_SenderReceiver/applet_SenderReceiver.jar',
        width:300, height:50} ;
    var parameters = { permissions:'sandbox' };
    deployJava.runApplet(attributes, parameters, '1.6');
</script>
```

Working with a Server-Side Application

Java applets, like other Java programs, can use the API defined in the `java.net` package to communicate across the network. A Java applet can communicate with server applications that run on the same host as the applet. This communication does not require any special setup on the server.

18

> **Note**
>
> Depending on the networking environment that an applet is loaded into and depending on the browser that runs the applet, an applet might be unable to communicate with its originating host. For example, browsers running on hosts inside firewalls often cannot obtain much information about the world outside the firewall. As a result, some browsers might not allow applet communication to hosts outside the firewall.

When the applet is deployed to a web server, use the `Applet getCodeBase` method and the `java.net.URL getHost` method to determine which host the applet came from, as follows:

```
String host = getCodeBase().getHost();
```

If the applet is deployed locally, the `getCodeBase` method returns null. Use of a web server is recommended.

> **Note**
>
> Not all browsers support all networking code flawlessly. For example, one widely used browser compatible with Java technology doesn't support posting to a URL.

For an example of implementing an applet that is a network client, see the "Network Client Applet Example" section.

Network Client Applet Example

The `QuoteClientApplet` class allows you to fetch quotations from a server-side application that runs on the same host as this applet. This class also displays the quotation received from the server.

The `QuoteServer.java` and `QuoteServerThread.java` classes make up the server-side application that returns quotations. The text file `one-liners.txt` contains a number of quotations. Perform the following steps to test `QuoteClientApplet`:

1. Download and save the following files to your local machine:
   - `QuoteClientApplet.java`[35]
   - `QuoteServer.java`[36]
   - `QuoteServerThread.java`[37]
   - `one-liners.txt`[38]
   - `quoteApplet.html`[39]

2. Include the following HTML code in a web page to deploy `QuoteClientApplet`:
   ```
   <script src=
     "https://www.java.com/js/deployJava.js"></script>
   ```

---

35. `tutorial/deployment/applet/examples/QuoteClientApplet.java`
36. `tutorial/deployment/applet/examples/QuoteServer.java`
37. `tutorial/deployment/applet/examples/QuoteServerThread.java`
38. `tutorial/deployment/applet/examples/one-liners.txt`
39. `tutorial/deployment/applet/examples/quoteApplet.html`

```
<script>
    var attributes =
      { code:'QuoteClientApplet.class',  width:500, height:100} ;
    var parameters =
      { codebase_lookup:'true', permissions:'sandbox' };
    deployJava.runApplet(attributes, parameters, '1.6');
</script>
```

Alternatively, you can use the quoteApplet.html page that already contains this HTML code.

3. Compile the QuoteClientApplet.java class. Copy the generated class files to the same directory where you saved your web page.

4. Compile the classes for the server-side application, QuoteServer.java and QuoteServerThread.java.

5. Copy the file one-liners.txt to the directory that has the class files for the server-side application (generated in the previous step).

6. Start the server-side application.

```
java QuoteServer
```

You should see a message with the port number, as shown in the following example. Note the port number.

```
QuoteServer listening on port:3862
```

7. Open the web page containing your applet in a browser by entering the URL of the web page. The host name in the URL should be the same as the name of the host on which the server-side application is running. For example, if the server-side application is running on a machine named JohnDoeMachine, you should enter a similar URL. The exact port number and path will vary depending on your web server setup.

```
http://JohnDoeMachine:8080/quoteApplet/quoteApplet.html
```

The QuoteClientApplet will be displayed on the web page.

8. Enter the port number of your server-side application in the applet's text field and click **OK**. A quotation is displayed.

What Applets Can and Cannot Do

Java applets are loaded on a client when the user visits a page containing an applet. The security model behind Java applets has been designed with the goal of protecting the user from malicious applets.

Applets are either sandbox applets or privileged applets. Sandbox applets are run in a security sandbox that allows only a set of safe operations. Privileged applets can run outside the security sandbox and have extensive capabilities to access the client.

18

Applets that are not signed are restricted to the security sandbox and run only if the user accepts the applet. Applets that are signed by a certificate from a recognized certificate authority either can run only in the sandbox or can request permission to run outside the sandbox. In either case, the user must accept the applet's security certificate; otherwise the applet is blocked from running.

It is recommended that you launch your applet using JNLP to leverage expanded capabilities and improve user experience. See the "Deploying an Applet" section for step-by-step instructions on applet deployment.

It is recommended that you deploy your applets to a web server, even for testing. To run applets locally, add the applets to the exception site list, which is managed from the **Security** tab of the Java Control Panel.

Now we will discuss the security restrictions and capabilities of applets.

Sandbox Applets

Sandbox applets are restricted to the security sandbox and can perform the following operations:

- They can make network connections to the host and port they came from. Protocols must match, and if a domain name is used to load the applet, the domain name must be used to connect back to the host, not the IP address.
- They can easily display HTML documents using the `showDocument` method of the `java.applet.AppletContext` class.
- They can invoke public methods of other applets on the same page.
- Applets that are loaded from the local file system (from a directory in the user's `CLASSPATH`) have none of the restrictions that applets loaded over the network do.
- They can read secure system properties. See Chapter 19, "System Properties," for a list of secure system properties.
- When launched by using JNLP, sandbox applets can also perform the following operations:
  - They can open, read, and save files on the client.
  - They can access the shared system-wide clipboard.
  - They can access printing functions.
  - They can store data on the client, decide how applets should be downloaded and cached, and much more. See Chapter 19, "JNLP API," for more information about developing applets by using the JNLP API.

Sandbox applets *cannot* perform the following operations:

- They cannot access client resources such as the local file system, executable files, system clipboard, and printers.
- They cannot connect to or retrieve resources from any third-party server (any server other than the server it originated from).
- They cannot load native libraries.
- They cannot change the security manager.
- They cannot create a class loader.
- They cannot read certain system properties. See Chapter 19, "System Properties," for a list of forbidden system properties.

Privileged Applets

Privileged applets do not have the security restrictions that are imposed on sandbox applets and can run outside the security sandbox.

> **Note**
> JavaScript code is treated like unsigned code. When a privileged applet is accessed from JavaScript code in an HTML page, the applet is executed *within* the security sandbox. This implies that the privileged applet essentially behaves likes a sandbox applet.

See Chapter 19, "Security in Rich Internet Applications," for information on how to work with applets.

Additional Information

For more information about applet security dialog boxes, see Exploring Security Warning Functionality.[40]

Solving Common Applet Problems

This section covers some common problems that you might encounter when writing Java applets. After each problem is a list of possible reasons and solutions.

"My Applet Does Not Display"

- Check the Java Console log for errors.
- Check the syntax of the applet's JNLP file. Incorrect JNLP files are the most common reason for failures without obvious errors.

---

40. http://www.oracle.com/technetwork/articles/javase/appletwarning-135102.html

- Check the JavaScript syntax if deploying using the `runApplet` function of the Deployment Toolkit. See Chapter 20, "Deploying an Applet," for details.

"The Java Console Log Displays java.lang.ClassNotFoundException"

- Make sure your Java source files compiled correctly.
- If deploying using the `<applet>` tag, check that the path to the applet JAR file is specified accurately in the `archive` attribute.
- If launching using a JNLP file, check the path in the `jar` tag in the JNLP file.
- Make sure the applet's JAR file, JNLP file, and web page are located in the correct directory and reference each other accurately.

"I Was Able to Build the Code Once, but Now the Build Fails Even Though There Are No Compilation Errors"

- Close your browser and run the build again. The browser most likely has a lock on the JAR file, because of which the build process is unable to regenerate the JAR file.

"When I Try to Load a Web Page That Has an Applet, My Browser Redirects Me to www.java.com without Any Warning"

- The applet on the web page is most likely deployed using the Deployment Toolkit script. The applet may require a later version of the JRE software than the version that currently exists on the client. Check the `minimumVersion` parameter of the `runApplet` function in the applet's web page. See Chapter 20, "Deploying an Applet," for details.

"I Fixed Some Bugs and Rebuilt My Applet's Source Code. When I Reload the Applet's Web Page, My Fixes Are Not Showing Up"

- You may be viewing a previously cached version of the applet. Close the browser. Open the Java Control Panel and delete temporary Internet files. This will remove your applet from cache. Try viewing your applet again.

Questions and Exercises: Applets

Questions

1. Which classes can an applet extend?
2. For what do you use the `start()` method?

3. True or false: An applet can make network connections to any host on the Internet.

4. How do you get the value of a parameter specified in the JNLP file from within the applet's code?

5. Which class enables applets to interact with JavaScript code in the applet's web page?

6. True or false: Applets can modify the contents of the parent web page.

Exercise

1. The `Exercise` applet's parent web page has a JavaScript variable called `memberId`. Write the code to set the value of the `memberId` equal to "123489" in the applet's `start` method.

Answers

You can find answers to these questions and exercises at `http://docs.oracle.com/javase/tutorial/deployment/applet/QandE/answers.html`. In addition, try the following online quiz about Java applets: `http://docs.oracle.com/javase/tutorialJWS/flash/AppletQuiz/AppletQuiz.html`.

18

19

Doing More with Java Rich Internet Applications

Chapter Contents

Setting Trusted Arguments and Secure Properties   711
JNLP API   714
Cookies   719
Customizing the Loading Experience   722
Security in Rich Internet Applications   722
Guidelines for Securing RIAs   724
Questions and Exercises: Doing More with Rich Internet Applications   726

Applets launched by using the Java Network Launch Protocol (JNLP) have capabilities similar to those of Java Web Start applications. This chapter contains topics common to the development and deployment of applets and Java Web Start applications (together known as rich Internet applications, or RIAs). If you are unfamiliar with applets or Java Web Start applications, you can learn more in the following chapters:

- To learn more about the development and deployment of Java Web Start applications, see Chapter 17.
- To learn more about applet development and deployment, see Chapter 18.

Setting Trusted Arguments and Secure Properties

You can set certain Java Virtual Machine (Java VM) arguments and secure properties for your rich Internet application (RIA) in the RIA's JNLP file. For applets, you can also set arguments in the `java_arguments` parameter of the `<applet>` tag. Although there is a predefined set of secure properties, you can also define new secure properties by prefixing the property name with `jnlp.` or `javaws.`. Properties can be retrieved in your RIA by using the `System.getProperty` method.

Consider the Properties and Arguments Demo applet.[1] The following Java VM arguments and properties are set in the applet's JNLP file, `appletpropsargs.jnlp`:

- `-Xmx`. A secure argument set equal to `256M`
- `sun.java2d.noddraw`. A predefined secure property set equal to `true`
- `jnlp.myProperty`. A user-defined secure property set equal to a user-defined property

```xml
<?xml version="1.0" encoding="UTF-8"?>
<jnlp spec="1.0+" codebase="" href="">
    <information>
        <title>Properties and Arguments Demo Applet</title>
        <vendor>Dynamic Team</vendor>
    </information>
    <resources>
        <!-- Application Resources -->
        <j2se version="1.6+"
            href="http://java.sun.com/products/autodl/j2se"
            <!-- secure java vm argument -->
            java-vm-args="-Xmx256M"/>
        <jar href="applet_PropertiesAndVMArgs.jar"
            main="true" />
            <!-- secure properties -->
        <property name="sun.java2d.noddraw"
            value="true"/>
        <property name="jnlp.myProperty"
            value="a user-defined property"/>
    </resources>
    <applet-desc
        name="Properties and Arguments Demo Applet"
        main-class="PropertiesArgsDemoApplet"
        width="800"
        height="50">
    </applet-desc>
    <update check="background"/>
</jnlp>
```

The `PropertiesArgsDemoApplet` class uses the `System.getProperty` method to retrieve the `java.version` property and other properties that are set in the JNLP file. The `PropertiesArgsDemoApplet` class also displays the properties:

```java
import javax.swing.JApplet;
import javax.swing.SwingUtilities;
import javax.swing.JLabel;

public class PropertiesArgsDemoApplet extends JApplet {
```

1. `tutorial/deployment/doingMoreWithRIA/examples/zipfiles/applet_PropertiesAndVMArgs.zip`

```
public void init() {
    final String javaVersion = System.getProperty("java.version");
    final String  swing2dNoDrawProperty = System.getProperty("sun.java2d.noddraw");
    final String  jnlpMyProperty = System.getProperty("jnlp.myProperty");

    try {
        SwingUtilities.invokeAndWait(new Runnable() {
            public void run() {
                createGUI(javaVersion, swing2dNoDrawProperty, jnlpMyProperty);
            }
        });
    } catch (Exception e) {
        System.err.println("createGUI didn't successfully complete");
    }
}
private void createGUI(String javaVersion, String swing2dNoDrawProperty, String jnlpMyProperty) {
    String text = "Properties: java.version = " + javaVersion +
            ",  sun.java2d.noddraw = " + swing2dNoDrawProperty +
            ",   jnlp.myProperty = " + jnlpMyProperty;
    JLabel lbl = new JLabel(text);
    add(lbl);
}
}
```

See the following section for a complete set of system properties that can be accessed by RIAs.

System Properties

This section lists system properties that can be accessed by RIAs that are restricted to the security sandbox and are launched with or without JNLP. Some system properties cannot be accessed by sandbox RIAs.

Secure System Properties Accessible by All RIAs

All RIAs can retrieve the following secure system properties:

- `java.class.version`
- `java.vendor`
- `java.vendor.url`
- `java.version`
- `os.name`
- `os.arch`
- `os.version`
- `file.separator`
- `path.separator`
- `line.separator`

19

Secure System Properties Accessible by RIAs Launched by Using JNLP

RIAs launched by using JNLP can set and retrieve the following secure properties:

- `awt.useSystemAAFontSettings`
- `http.agent`
- `http.keepAlive`
- `java.awt.syncLWRequests`
- `java.awt.Window.locationByPlatform`
- `javaws.cfg.jauthenticator`
- `javax.swing.defaultlf`
- `sun.awt.noerasebackground`
- `sun.awt.erasebackgroundonresize`
- `sun.java2d.d3d`
- `sun.java2d.dpiaware`
- `sun.java2d.noddraw`
- `sun.java2d.opengl`
- `swing.boldMetal`
- `swing.metalTheme`
- `swing.noxp`
- `swing.useSystemFontSettings`

Forbidden System Properties

Sandbox RIAs cannot access the following system properties:

- `java.class.path`
- `java.home`
- `user.dir`
- `user.home`
- `user.name`

19

JNLP API

RIAs can use the JNLP Application Programming Interface (API) to perform extensive operations on the user's environment. When launched by using JNLP, even unsigned RIAs can perform the following operations with the user's permission:

- They can use the `FileOpenService`[2] and `FileSaveService`[3] API to access the user's file system.
- They can use the `ClipboardService`[4] API to access the shared system-wide clipboard.
- They can use the `PrintService`[5] API to access printing functions
- They can use the `PersistenceService`[6] API to access persistence storage.
- They can use the `DownloadService`[7] API to control how the RIA is downloaded and cached.
- They can use the `DownloadServiceListener`[8] API to determine the progress of the RIA's download.
- They can use the `SingleInstanceService`[9] API to decide how to handle arguments when multiple instances of the RIA are launched.
- They can use the `ExtendedService`[10] API to request permission to open certain files that have not been opened before.

Check the JNLP API documentation[11] to see the complete list of the functionality available to RIAs that are launched by using JNLP.

Accessing the Client Using the JNLP API

When launched using JNLP, RIAs can access the client with the user's permission. Consider the Text Editor applet example to understand how to use JNLP API-based services.[12] The Text Editor has a text area and buttons labeled **Open**, **Save**, and **SaveAs**. The Text Editor can be used to open an existing text file, edit it, and save it back to disk.

---

2.   `8/docs/jre/api/javaws/jnlp/javax/jnlp/FileOpenService.html`

3.   `8/docs/jre/api/javaws/jnlp/javax/jnlp/FileSaveService.html`

4.   `8/docs/jre/api/javaws/jnlp/javax/jnlp/ClipboardService.html`

5.   `8/docs/jre/api/javaws/jnlp/javax/jnlp/PrintService.html`

6.   `8/docs/jre/api/javaws/jnlp/javax/jnlp/PersistenceService.html`

7.   `8/docs/jre/api/javaws/jnlp/javax/jnlp/DownloadService.html`

8.   `8/docs/jre/api/javaws/jnlp/javax/jnlp/DownloadServiceListener.html`

9.   `8/docs/jre/api/javaws/jnlp/javax/jnlp/SingleInstanceService.html`

10. `8/docs/jre/api/javaws/jnlp/javax/jnlp/ExtendedService.html`

11. `8/docs/jre/api/javaws/jnlp/javax/jnlp/package-summary.html`

12. `tutorial/deployment/doingMoreWithRIA/examples/zipfiles/applet_JNLP _API.zip`

19

The TextEditor and TextEditorApplet classes lay out the user interface and display it as an applet. The FileHandler class contains the core functionality with respect to using JNLP API-based services. (Remember, the techniques described in this section apply to Java Web Start applications as well.)

To make use of a JNLP service, first retrieve a reference to the service. The initialize method of the FileHandler class retrieves references to JNLP services as shown in the following code snippet:

```
private static synchronized void initialize() {
    ...
    try {
        fos = (FileOpenService)
            ServiceManager.lookup("javax.jnlp.FileOpenService");
        fss = (FileSaveService)
            ServiceManager.lookup("javax.jnlp.FileSaveService");
    } catch (UnavailableServiceException e) {
        ...
    }
}
```

After you have a reference to the required services, invoke methods on the service to perform the necessary operations. The open method of the FileHandler class invokes the openFileDialog method of the FileOpenService class to display a file chooser. The open method returns the contents of the selected file:

```
public static String open() {
    initialize();
    try {
        fc = fos.openFileDialog(null, null);
        return readFromFile(fc);
    } catch (IOException ioe) {
        ioe.printStackTrace(System.out);
        return null;
    }
}
```

Similarly, the save and saveAs methods of the FileHandler class invoke corresponding methods of the FileSaveService class to enable the user to select a file name and save the contents of the text area to disk:[13]

```
public static void saveAs(String txt) {
    initialize();
    try {
        if (fc == null) {
            // If not already saved.
            // Save-as is like save
            save(txt);
```

---

13. 8/docs/jre/api/javaws/jnlp/javax/jnlp/FileSaveService.html

```
            } else {
                fc = fss.saveAsFileDialog(null, null,
                                              fc);
                save(txt);
            }
        } catch (IOException ioe) {
            ioe.printStackTrace(System.out);
        }
    }
```

At runtime, when the RIA attempts to open or save a file, users see a security dialog asking them if they want to allow the action. The operation will proceed only if users allow the RIA to access their environment.

Here is the complete source of the `FileHandler` class:[14]

```java
// add javaws.jar to the classpath during compilation
import javax.jnlp.FileOpenService;
import javax.jnlp.FileSaveService;
import javax.jnlp.FileContents;
import javax.jnlp.ServiceManager;
import javax.jnlp.UnavailableServiceException;
import java.io.*;

public class FileHandler {

    static private FileOpenService fos = null;
    static private FileSaveService fss = null;
    static private FileContents fc = null;

    // retrieves a reference to the JNLP services
    private static synchronized void initialize() {
        if (fss != null) {
            return;
        }
        try {
            fos = (FileOpenService) ServiceManager.lookup("javax.jnlp.FileOpenService");
            fss = (FileSaveService) ServiceManager.lookup("javax.jnlp.FileSaveService");
        } catch (UnavailableServiceException e) {
            fos = null;
            fss = null;
        }
    }

    // displays open file dialog and reads selected file using FileOpenService
    public static String open() {
        initialize();
        try {
            fc = fos.openFileDialog(null, null);
            return readFromFile(fc);
        } catch (IOException ioe) {
            ioe.printStackTrace(System.out);
```

19

---
14. tutorial/deployment/doingMoreWithRIA/examples/applet_JNLP_API/src/
     FileHandler.java

```
                return null;
          }
    }

    // displays saveFileDialog and saves file using FileSaveService
    public static void save(String txt) {
          initialize();
          try {
                // Show save dialog if no name is already given
                if (fc == null) {
                      fc = fss.saveFileDialog(null, null,
                            new ByteArrayInputStream(txt.getBytes()), null);
                      // file saved, done
                      return;
                }
                // use this only when filename is known
                if (fc != null) {
                      writeToFile(txt, fc);
                }
          } catch (IOException ioe) {
                ioe.printStackTrace(System.out);
          }
    }

    // displays saveAsFileDialog and saves file using FileSaveService
    public static void saveAs(String txt) {
          initialize();
          try {
                if (fc == null) {
                      // If not already saved. Save-as is like save
                      save(txt);
                } else {
                      fc = fss.saveAsFileDialog(null, null, fc);
                      save(txt);
                }
          } catch (IOException ioe) {
                ioe.printStackTrace(System.out);
          }
    }

    private static void writeToFile(String txt, FileContents fc) throws IOException {
          int sizeNeeded = txt.length() * 2;
          if (sizeNeeded > fc.getMaxLength()) {
                fc.setMaxLength(sizeNeeded);
          }
          BufferedWriter os = new BufferedWriter(new OutputStreamWriter(fc.getOutputStream(true)));
          os.write(txt);
          os.close();
    }

    private static String readFromFile(FileContents fc) throws IOException {
          if (fc == null) {
                return null;
          }
          BufferedReader br = new BufferedReader(new InputStreamReader(fc.getInputStream()));
          StringBuffer sb = new StringBuffer((int) fc.getLength());
          String line = br.readLine();
```

```
      while (line != null) {
          sb.append(line);
          sb.append("\n");
          line = br.readLine();
      }
      br.close();
      return sb.toString();
   }
}
```

> **Note**
>
> To compile Java code that has a reference to classes in the `javax.jnlp` package, include `<your JDK path>`/`jre/lib/javaws.jar` in your class path. At runtime, the Java Runtime Environment (JRE) software automatically makes these classes available to RIAs.

Cookies

Web applications are typically a series of Hypertext Transfer Protocol (HTTP) requests and responses. As HTTP is a stateless protocol, information is not automatically saved between HTTP requests. Web applications use cookies to store state information on the client. Cookies can be used to store information about the user, the user's shopping cart, and so on.

Types of Cookies

There are two types of cookies:

- *Session cookies*. Session cookies are stored in memory and are accessible as long as the user is using the web application. Session cookies are lost when the user exits the web application. Such cookies are identified by a session ID and are most commonly used to store details of a shopping cart.

- *Permanent cookies*. Permanent cookies are used to store long-term information such as user preferences and user identification information. Permanent cookies are stored in persistent storage and are not lost when the user exits the application. Permanent cookies are lost when they expire.

Cookie Support in RIAs

RIAs (applets and Java Web Start applications) support session and permanent cookies. The underlying cookie store depends on the browser and the operating system on the client. To learn more about cookies, see the following:

19

- Working with Cookies[15] in the online tutorial
- API Documentation for `CookieManager`[16] and related classes

Accessing Cookies

You can set and retrieve cookies in your RIA. Cookies can enhance the capabilities of your RIA. For example, consider the scenario where you have applets on various web pages. An applet on a web page cannot directly access or share information with an applet on another web page. In this scenario, cookies provide an important connection between applets and help one applet pass information to another applet on a different web page. Java Web Start applications can also use cookies to store information on the client. The Cookie Applet example[17] has a `CookieAccessor`[18] class that retrieves and sets cookies.

Retrieving Cookies

The following code snippet shows the `getCookieUsingCookieHandler` method of the `CookieAccessor` class:

```
public void getCookieUsingCookieHandler() {
    try {
        // Instantiate CookieManager;
        // make sure to set CookiePolicy
        CookieManager manager = new CookieManager();
        manager.setCookiePolicy(CookiePolicy.ACCEPT_ALL);
        CookieHandler.setDefault(manager);

        // get content from URLConnection;
        // cookies are set by web site
        URL url = new URL("http://host.example.com");
        URLConnection connection = url.openConnection();
        connection.getContent();

        // get cookies from underlying
        // CookieStore
        CookieStore cookieJar =  manager.getCookieStore();
        List <HttpCookie> cookies =
            cookieJar.getCookies();
        for (HttpCookie cookie: cookies) {
          System.out.println("CookieHandler retrieved cookie: " + cookie);
        }
```

---

15. `tutorial/networking/cookies/index.html`

16. `8/docs/api/java/net/CookieManager.html`

17. `tutorial/deployment/doingMoreWithRIA/examples/zipfiles/applet`
    `_AccessingCookies.zip`

18. `tutorial/deployment/doingMoreWithRIA/examples/applet_AccessingCookies/`
    `src/CookieAccessor.java`

```
        } catch(Exception e) {
            System.out.println("Unable to get cookie using CookieHandler");
            e.printStackTrace();
        }
    }
```

The `CookieManager` class is the main entry point for cookie management.[19] Create an instance of the `CookieManager` class and set its `CookiePolicy`.[20] Set this instance of the `CookieManager` as the default `CookieHandler`.[21] Open a `URLConnection` to the web site of your choice.[22] Next, retrieve cookies from the underlying `CookieStore` by using the `getCookies` method.[23]

Setting Cookies

The following code snippet shows the `setCookieUsingCookieHandler` method of the `CookieAccessor` class:

```
public void setCookieUsingCookieHandler() {
    try {
        // instantiate CookieManager
        CookieManager manager = new CookieManager();
        CookieHandler.setDefault(manager);
        CookieStore cookieJar =  manager.getCookieStore();

        // create cookie
        HttpCookie cookie = new HttpCookie("UserName", "John Doe");

        // add cookie to CookieStore for a
        // particular URL
        URL url = new URL("http://host.example.com");
        cookieJar.add(url.toURI(), cookie);
        System.out.println("Added cookie using cookie handler");
    } catch(Exception e) {
        System.out.println("Unable to set cookie using CookieHandler");
        e.printStackTrace();
    }
}
```

As shown in the "Retrieving Cookies" section, the `CookieManager` class is the main entry point for cookie management. Create an instance of the `CookieManager` class and set the instance as the default `CookieHandler`.

19

---

19. 8/docs/api/java/net/CookieManager.html

20. 8/docs/api/java/net/CookiePolicy.html

21. 8/docs/api/java/net/CookieHandler.html

22. 8/docs/api/java/net/URLConnection.html

23. 8/docs/api/java/net/CookieStore.html

Create the desired `HttpCookie` with the necessary information. In our example, we have created a new `HttpCookie` that sets the `UserName` as `John  Doe`. Next, add the cookie to the underlying cookie store.

Running the Cookie Applet Example

To access cookies, you must sign your RIA JAR file and request permission to run outside the security sandbox. See the documentation for the `jarsigner`[24] tool to learn how to sign JAR files. See the "Security in Rich Internet Applications" section for information on requesting permissions.

Customizing the Loading Experience

RIAs may take a few seconds to load, depending on factors such as network speed and resources required by the RIA. Customize the RIA loading experience by providing a splash screen or a customized loading progress indicator to engage the end user during the loading process and to communicate measurable progress information.

While the overall mechanisms to customize the loading experience for applets and Java Web Start applications are similar, there are subtle differences in syntax and implementation. See the following sections for step-by-step instructions and conceptual information about customizing the RIA loading experience:

- Customizing the Loading Experience in the Java Platform Standard Edition Deployment Guide[25]
- Chapter 17, "Displaying a Customized Loading Progress Indicator for Java Web Start Applications"
- Chapter 18, "Displaying a Customized Loading Progress Indicator for Applets"
- Chapter 20, "Customizing the Loading Screen"

Security in Rich Internet Applications

The security model behind RIAs works to protect the user from malicious Internet applications. This section discusses security aspects that are common to applets and Java Web Start applications. See the following sections for more information:

---

24. `8/docs/technotes/tools/index.html#security`
25. `8/docs/technotes/guides/deploy/customized_loading.html`

- Chapter 17, "Java Web Start and Security"
- Chapter 18, "What Applets Can and Cannot Do"

RIAs can be restricted to the Java security sandbox or request permission to access resources outside the sandbox. The first time an RIA is launched, the user is prompted for permission to run. The dialog shown provides information about the signer's certificate and indicates if the RIA requests permission to run outside the sandbox. The user can then make an informed decision about running the application.

Apply the following guidelines to help secure your RIAs:

- Sign the JAR file of the RIA with a certificate from a recognized certificate authority. For more information, see Chapter 15, "Signing and Verifying JAR Files."
- If the RIA requires access outside the security sandbox, specify the `all-permissions` element in the JNLP file for the RIA. Otherwise, let the RIA default to running in the security sandbox. The following code snippet shows the `all-permissions` element in the RIA's JNLP file:

```
<security>
    <all-permissions/>
</security>
```

If the applet tag is used, see Chapter 18, "Deploying with the Applet Tag," for information on setting the permissions level.

- A JNLP file can only include JAR files signed by the same certificate. If you have JAR files that are signed using different certificates, specify them in separate JNLP files. In the RIA's main JNLP file, specify the `component-desc` element to include the other JNLP files as component extensions. See Chapter 20, "Structure of the JNLP File," for information.
- The security model for RIAs does not allow JavaScript code from a web page to invoke security-sensitive code in a signed JAR file unless you explicitly enable this. In the signed JAR file, wrap the section of code that you want JavaScript code to be able to invoke in an `AccessController.doPrivileged` block.[26] This allows the JavaScript code to run with elevated permissions when executing the code in the `doPrivileged` code block.
- Avoid mixing privileged and sandbox components in an RIA, if possible, as they can raise security warnings about mixed code. For more information, see Mixing Privileged Code and Sandbox Code.[27]

---

26.   8/docs/api/java/security/AccessController.html
27.   8/docs/technotes/guides/deploy/mixed_code.html

- Include the `Permissions` and `Codebase` attributes in the JAR file manifest to ensure that your RIA requests only the permissions you specify and that the RIA is accessed from the correct location. For more information, see JAR File Manifest Attributes for Security.[28]

- JAR file manifest attributes enable you to restrict access to your RIA and help to ensure that your code is not tampered with. See Chapter 16, "Enhancing Security with Manifest Attributes," for information on all the JAR file manifest attributes that are available.

Guidelines for Securing RIAs

The following guidelines provide steps you can take to reduce the vulnerability of the RIAs that you provide to users.

Follow Secure Coding Guidelines

Follow the recommendations in the Secure Coding Guidelines for the Java Programming Language.[29] Section 4, "Accessibility and Extensibility," describes how to limit accessibility to classes and packages, which reduces the vulnerability of your code.

JavaScript code is considered insecure and is restricted to the security sandbox by default. Minimize interactions between your RIA and JavaScript code. Use the `AccessController.doPrivileged` block with care because it allows access from any HTML page or JavaScript code.

Test with the Latest Version of the JRE

Make sure that your RIA runs on the latest, secure version of the JRE. The Java platform supports the ability for RIAs to specify the Java version that is needed to run the RIA; however, requiring users to maintain more than one version of the JRE, especially older, insecure versions, is a security risk for the user.

One of the benefits of RIAs is that updated versions of the RIA are automatically downloaded to a user's system. Test your RIA against each update of the JRE, and make sure that it works. If changes are needed, update your RIA on the server so that users can install the latest JRE and still run the RIA.

---

28. `8/docs/technotes/guides/deploy/manifest.html`

29. `http://www.oracle.com/technetwork/java/seccodeguide-139067.html`

Include Manifest Attributes

Add attributes to the JAR file manifest that describe the properties of the RIA. Values in the JNLP file or the `applet` tag are compared to values in the manifest to verify that the correct code is run.

Request sandbox permissions when your RIA does not require access beyond the security sandbox. The Java sandbox provides additional protections for users, and users might not run a privileged application if they do not understand why it requests unrestricted access to their system.

Manifest attributes can also be used to identify the locations from which your RIA can be accessed. This includes locations from which JavaScript code can call your RIA and locations of JNLP files or applet tags that can start your RIA. See Chapter 16, "Enhancing Security with Manifest Attributes," for information on the manifest attributes that are available.

Use a Signed JNLP File

If your RIA needs to access nonsecure system properties or Java VM arguments, use a signed JNLP. If some variation between the external and internal JNLP files is required, use JNLP templates. For more information, see Signed JNLP Files in the Java Platform Standard Edition Deployment Guide.[30]

To access nonsecure system properties or Java VM arguments, include the property or argument in the JNLP file as described in the "Setting Trusted Arguments and Secure Properties" section.

Sign and Time Stamp JAR Files

Obtain a code-signing certificate from a trusted certificate authority and use it to sign the JAR files for your RIA. Deploy to users only RIAs that are signed with a valid certificate.

When you sign your JAR file, also time stamp the signature. Time stamping verifies that the certificate was valid at the time that the JAR was signed, so the RIA is not automatically blocked when the certificate expires. See Chapter 16, "Signing JAR Files," for information on signing and time stamping.

Self-signed and unsigned RIAs are considered unsafe and are not allowed to run unless an exception site list or deployment rule set is set up to allow specific applications. However, self-signing can be useful for testing purposes. To

19

---

30. 8/docs/technotes/guides/deploy/signed_jnlp.html

test using your self-signed RIA, you can import the self-signed certificate into the trusted keystore.

Use the HTTPS Protocol

Use the HTTPS protocol for the web server from which users get your RIAs. The HTTPS protocol is encrypted and validated by the server, making it more difficult for anyone to tamper with your RIAs.

Avoid Local RIAs

Local RIAs are not intended for use in production. To ensure that users run the code that you intend for them to run, host your RIAs on an application server.

For testing, the use of a web server is recommended. Another option is to add your application to the exception site list, which is managed in the **Security** tab of the Java Control Panel.

Questions and Exercises: Doing More with Rich Internet Applications

Questions

1. True or false: RIAs can set secure properties by prefixing the property name with `jnlp`.

2. True or false: Only signed RIAs can use the JNLP API to access files on the client.

Exercise

1. In the following JNLP file, add a secure property called `jnlp.foo` and set its value to `true`:

```
<?xml version="1.0" encoding="UTF-8"?>
<jnlp spec="1.0+" codebase="" href="">
    <information>
        <title>Dynamic Tree Demo</title>
        <vendor>Dynamic Team</vendor>

    </information>
    <resources>
        <!-- Application Resources -->
        <j2se version="1.6+" href=
            "http://java.sun.com/products/autodl/j2se" />
        <jar href="DynamicTreeDemo.jar" main="true" />
    </resources>
    <applet-desc
      name="Dynamic Tree Demo Applet"
```

19

```
                main-class="components.DynamicTreeApplet"
                width="300"
                height="300">
            </applet-desc>
            <update check="background"/>
        </jnlp>
```

Answers

You can find answers to these questions and exercises at `http://docs.oracle`
`.com/javase/tutorial/deployment/doingMoreWithRIA/QandE/answers`
`.html`.

Deployment in Depth

Chapter Contents

User Acceptance of RIAs   729
Deployment Toolkit   731
Java Network Launch Protocol   739
Deployment Best Practices   748
Questions and Exercises: Deployment in Depth   753

Rich Internet application (RIA) deployment involves various technologies and tools such as the Java Network Launch Protocol (JNLP), Deployment Toolkit, `pack200`, `jarsigner`, and so on. This chapter explores how these technologies and tools help developers deploy RIAs (applets and Java Web Start applications).

Here are the main components that are involved in RIA deployment:

- The HTML page in which the RIA will be deployed
- The JNLP file for the RIA
- The JAR file containing the class files and resources of the RIA

These components are referred to in subsequent topics.

User Acceptance of RIAs

For security, users are prompted for permission to run an RIA before launching for the first time, even if the application is signed or doesn't require access outside the security sandbox. The prompt includes the following information, depending on the RIA being run:

- Name of the RIA or notification that the application is unsigned
- Information about the publisher if the app is signed with a certificate from a trusted authority (If the certificate is expired, a warning is included; if the application is self-signed, the publisher is shown as UNKNOWN.)
- Warnings if the certificate is expired or revoked or the revocation status cannot be checked
- Location from which the application is accessed
- Level of access required by the application (Limited access restricts the application to the security sandbox; unrestricted access provides the application with access to resources on the user's system.)
- Warning about missing JAR file manifest attributes if recommended attributes are not present
- For unsigned or self-signed applications, a check box that the user must select to accept the application
- In some cases, the option to not show the prompt again

For a description of the prompts, see What Should I Do When I See a Security Prompt from Java?[1]

Users are also warned if they are running an out-of-date Java Runtime Environment (JRE) and are given the opportunity to update to the latest version before running an application. Users can also choose to run with the JRE on their system or to block the application from running.

The security level setting in the Java Control Panel determines if users are given the opportunity to run RIAs. The default setting of High prompts users for permission to run applications that are signed with a valid certificate and include the Permissions attribute in the manifest for the main JAR file. If the revocation status of an application cannot be checked, the application is also allowed to run with the user's permission.

Signing your RIA provides the user with a level of trust. Consider the following when preparing your application for deployment:

- The best user experience is provided by an application that is signed with a certificate issued by a recognized certificate authority.
- Self-signed and unsigned applications are not allowed to be run unless an exception site list or deployment rule set has been created to explicitly allow the application to run.

---

1.   http://java.com/faq-securityprompts

- Signed applications can be either privileged applications or sandbox applications. Privileged applications are provided unrestricted access to resources on the user's system. Sandbox applications are restricted to the Java security sandbox. Unsigned applications are restricted to the sandbox.

Deployment Toolkit

The Deployment Toolkit script is a set of JavaScript functions that can help developers deploy RIAs consistently across various browser and operating system configurations. The Deployment Toolkit script evaluates the underlying browser and operating system and deploys the RIA with the correct HTML. This script can also ensure that the required version of the JRE software is present on the client machine.

Location of Deployment Toolkit Script

The Deployment Toolkit script exists at the following web addresses:

- `http://www.java.com/js/deployJava.js`
- `https://www.java.com/js/deployJava.js` (When deploying your applet on a secure page, use the Deployment Toolkit script from this secure location to avoid mixed content warnings when the page is loaded.)

> **Note**
>
> The `http://www.java.com/js/deployJava.js` web address is being phased out. Use the `https://www.java.com/js/deployJava.js` web address to launch all apps.

The JavaScript code in this location has been minimized so that it can load quickly. You can view the human-readable version of the JavaScript code with associated comment blocks at `https://www.java.com/js/deployJava.txt`.[2]

> **Note**
>
> The JavaScript interpreter should be enabled in the client's browser so that the Deployment Toolkit script can run and deploy your RIA properly.

20

---

2.   `https://www.java.com/js/deployJava.txt`

Deploying an Applet

You can deploy applets by using the `runApplet` function of the Deployment Toolkit script. The `runApplet` function ensures that the required minimum version of the JRE software exists on the client and then runs the applet. The `runApplet` function generates an HTML `<applet>` tag with the information provided.

> **Note**
>
> Depending on the type of browser, you might be unable to view the HTML generated by the Deployment Toolkit script when you try to view the source for the web page. To view the generated HTML, try saving the HTML page after it has been loaded or use a tool such as Firebug (a Mozilla Firefox add-on).

You can deploy applets by specifying the deployment options as attributes and parameters of the `<applet>` tag. You can also specify deployment options in a JNLP file to take advantage of advanced features. See the "Java Network Launch Protocol" section for more information about this protocol.

> **Note**
>
> If the client does not have the required minimum version of the JRE software, the Deployment Toolkit script redirects the browser to `http://www.java.com` to allow users to download the latest JRE software. On some platforms, users might be redirected before they can view the web page containing the applet.

The parameters of the `runApplet` function vary depending on whether you are using JNLP. The next section shows how to use the `runApplet` function in the HTML page that will display the applet. The following usage scenarios are described:

- Specifying deployment options as attribute and parameter name-value pairs
- Using the `jnlp_href` parameter to specify deployment options in a JNLP file

Here is the function signature: `runApplet: function(attributes, parameters, minimumVersion)`. Here are the parameters:

- `attributes`. The names and values of the attributes of the generated `<applet>` tag
- `parameters`. The names and values of the `<param>` tags in the generated `<applet>` tag
- `minimumVersion`. The minimum version of the JRE software that is required to run this applet

When using the `jnlp_href` parameter to specify deployment options in a JNLP file, the attributes and parameters (`jnlp_href` in this case) passed as name-value pairs are written out as attributes and nested `<param>` tags in the generated `<applet>` tag. It is better to specify the applet's width and height as attributes as follows:

```
<script src="https://www.java.com/js/deployJava.js"></script>
<script>
    var attributes = { code:'java2d.Java2DemoApplet', width:710, height:540 };
    var parameters = { jnlp_href: 'java2d.jnlp' };
    deployJava.runApplet(attributes, parameters, '1.6');
</script>
```

The following guidelines are helpful if some deployment options have different values in the attribute name-value pairs and in the JNLP file:

- Specify `width` and `height` as attribute name-value pairs (not in the JNLP file).
- Specify parameters such as `image` and `boxbgcolor` as parameter name-value pairs (not in the JNLP file). These parameters are needed early on in the applet start-up process.
- In the JNLP file, leave the `codebase` attribute empty or specify an absolute URL. When the `codebase` attribute is left empty, it defaults to the directory containing the JNLP file.
- If the applet is launched using a JNLP file, the values for the `code`, `codebase`, and `archive` attributes are taken from the JNLP file. If these attributes are also specified separately as attribute name-value pairs, the attribute name-value pairs are ignored.

Customizing the Loading Screen

A default loading screen is displayed when an applet is being loaded in the web page. You can display a customized splash screen by specifying the following parameters when you deploy the applet:

- `image`. The image to be displayed in the splash screen
- `boxbgcolor`. The background color of the area in which the applet will be displayed
- `boxborder`. Whether the applet should have a border; defaults to `true`
- `centerimage`. The position of the image; defaults to `false`

The splash screen can display a static image or an animated GIF.

The code snippet from `AppletPage.html` shows how to customize the splash screen to display an animation of Duke, the Java mascot:

20

```
<script src="https://www.java.com/js/deployJava.js"></script>
<script>
  var attributes = {code:'SwingSet2Applet.class',
      archive:'SwingSet2.jar', width:695, height:525} ;
    <!-- customize splash screen display options -->
  var parameters = {jnlp_href: 'SwingSet2.jnlp',
                      image: 'dukeanimated.gif',
                      boxbgcolor: 'cyan',
                      boxborder: 'true',
                      centerimage: 'true'
                      };
  deployJava.runApplet(attributes, parameters, '1.6');
</script>
```

See Chapter 18, "Displaying a Customized Loading Progress Indicator," for information about displaying a customized loading progress indicator when the applet's resources are being downloaded.

Embedding the JNLP File in the Applet Tag

When applets are deployed by using the JNLP, the Java Plug-In software launches the applet after downloading the JNLP file from the network. You can reduce the time it takes for applets to launch by embedding the JNLP file in the web page itself so that an additional network request can be avoided the first time the applet is loaded. This will result in applets launching quickly on the web browser.

A Base64 encoded JNLP file can be embedded in the `jnlp_embedded` parameter when deploying an applet in a web page. The attributes of the `<jnlp>` element should meet the following restrictions:

- The `href` attribute should contain a relative path.
- The `codebase` attribute should not be specified. This implies that the code base will be derived from the URL of the web page in which the applet is loaded.

The following steps describe how to embed a JNLP file in a web page to deploy an applet:

1. Create a JNLP file for your applet. A sample file is shown next.

```
<?xml version="1.0" encoding="UTF-8"?>
<!-- href attribute contains relative path;
     codebase attribute not specified -->
<jnlp href="dynamictree_applet.jnlp">
    <information>
        <title>Dynamic Tree Demo</title>
        <vendor>Dynamic Team</vendor>
    </information>
    <resources>
        <!-- Application Resources -->
        <j2se version="1.7+" />
```

```
                        <jar href=
                            "dist/applet_ComponentArch_DynamicTreeDemo/DynamicTreeDemo.jar"
                            main="true" />
                    </resources>
                    <applet-desc
                        name="Dynamic Tree Demo Applet"
                        main-class="appletComponentArch.DynamicTreeApplet"
                        width="300"
                        height="300">
                    </applet-desc>
                    <update check="background"/>
                </jnlp>
```

2. Encode the contents of the JNLP file using the Base64 scheme. You can use
    any Base64 encoding tool to encode the JNLP file. Check the usage of the tool
    to create a string with Base64 encoding. Some examples of tools and web sites
    that may be used are as follows:

    ▫ Solaris and Linux commands—`base64`, `uuencode`
    ▫ Web sites—Base64 Encode and Decode,[3] Base64 Encoder[4]

3. When deploying the applet in a web page, specify the `jnlp_embedded` param-
    eter with its value set to the Base64 encoded JNLP string. Make sure to include
    only the actual Base64 bytes without any encoding tool specific headers or
    footers.

```
<script src="https://www.java.com/js/deployJava.js"></script>
<script>
    var attributes = {} ;
    <!-- Base64 encoded string truncated below for readability -->
    var parameters = {jnlp_href: 'dynamictree_applet.jnlp',
        jnlp_embedded: 'PCEtLSANCi8qDQogKiBDb ... bmxwPg=='
    } ;
    deployJava.runApplet(attributes, parameters, '1.6');
</script>
```

Some encoding tools may wrap the encoded string into several 76-column lines.
To use this multiline attribute value in JavaScript code, specify the attribute
value as a set of concatenated strings. You can include the multiline attribute
value as is if the applet is deployed directly with the <applet> HTML tag.

Deploying a Java Web Start Application

20

You can deploy Java Web Start applications by using the `createWebStartLaunch-`
`Button` function of the Deployment Toolkit script. Java Web Start applications are
launched using JNLP. The `createWebStartLaunchButton` function generates a
link (HTML anchor tag, `<a>`) to the Java Web Start application's JNLP file.

---

3. http://base64encode.org/
4. http://www.opinionatedgeek.com/dotnet/tools/base64encode/

This generated anchor tag is the Java Web Start application's Launch button. When the end user clicks the Launch button, the Deployment Toolkit script ensures that the appropriate JRE software is installed and then launches the Java Web Start application.

> **Note**
>
> Depending on the type of browser, you might be unable to view the HTML generated by the Deployment Toolkit script when you try to view the source for the web page. To view the generated HTML, try saving the HTML page after it has been loaded or use a tool such as Firebug (a Mozilla Firefox add-on). Also, if the client does not have the required minimum version of the JRE software, the Deployment Toolkit script redirects the browser to `http://www.java.com` to allow users to download the latest JRE software.

Here is the function signature: `createWebStartLaunchButton:` `function` `(jnlp, minimumVersion)` or `createWebStartLaunchButton: function(jnlp)`. Here are the parameters:

- `jnlp`. The URL of the JNLP file containing deployment information for the Java Web Start application; should be an absolute path
- `minimumVersion`. The minimum version of JRE software required to run this application

Here are some usage scenarios:

- Specifying a minimum version of JRE software that is required to run the application requires the following:

```
<script src="https://www.java.com/js/deployJava.js"></script>
<script>
    var url = "http://java.sun.com/javase/technologies/desktop/javawebstart/apps/notepad.jnlp";
    deployJava.createWebStartLaunchButton(url, '1.6.0');
</script>
```

- When enabling a Java Web Start application to run on any JRE software version, use the `createWebStartLaunchButton: function(jnlp)` function if your application does not have a minimum JRE software version requirement.

> **Note**
>
> When deploying by using any of the previously described `createWebStartLaunchButton` functions, you must specify an absolute code base in the Java Web Start application's JNLP file. This enables the Java Web Start application to be launched from the command line with the `javaws <path/to/local JNLP file>` command.

Changing the Launch Button

You can change your Java Web Start application's Launch button image if you don't like the default Launch button or if you have another image that you have standardized on. Use the `deployJava.launchButtonPNG` variable to point to the location of your Launch button's image. In this example, the Notepad application's Launch button is now an image of Duke waving:

```
<script src="https://www.java.com/js/deployJava.js"></script>
<script>
    deployJava.launchButtonPNG='tutorial/images/DukeWave.gif';
    var url = "tutorialJWS/deployment/webstart/examples/Notepad.jnlp";
    deployJava.createWebStartLaunchButton(url, '1.6.0');
</script>
```

Deploying without Codebase

You do not have to specify an absolute path for the `codebase` attribute in the Java Web Start application's JNLP file. You can develop and test your applications in different environments without having to modify the path in the `codebase` attribute. If no code base is specified, the Java Web Start software assumes that the code base is relative to the web page from which the Java Web Start application is launched.

The following functions of the Deployment Toolkit script can be used to deploy Java Web Start applications in a web page when the JNLP file does not contain the `codebase` attribute:

- `launchWebStartApplication`. Use this function in an HTML link to deploy your Java Web Start application.
- `createWebStartLaunchButtonEx`. Use this function to create a Launch button for your Java Web Start application.

Here is the function signature: `launchWebStartApplication: function(jnlp)`. The parameter is the path to the JNLP file containing deployment information for the Java Web Start application. This path can be relative to the web page in which the Java Web Start application is deployed.

In the following example, the `launchWebStartApplication` function is invoked in the `href` attribute of an HTML anchor (`<a>`) tag. The `dynamictree_webstart_no_codebase.jnlp` JNLP file is used to deploy the Dynamic Tree Demo application:

```
<script src="https://www.java.com/js/deployJava.js"></script>
<a href=
  "javascript:deployJava.launchWebStartApplication('dynamictree_webstart_no_codebase.jnlp');"
>Launch</a>
```

20

The Java Web Start application is launched when the user clicks the resulting HTML link. The function signature is `createWebStartLaunchButtonEx:` `function(jnlp)`. Again, the parameter is the path to the JNLP file containing deployment information for the Java Web Start application. This path can be relative to the web page in which the Java Web Start application is deployed.

The following example shows the usage of the `createWebStartLaunchButtonEx` function. The `dynamictree_webstart_no_codebase.jnlp` JNLP file is used to deploy the Dynamic Tree Demo application.

```
<script src="https://www.java.com/js/deployJava.js"></script>
<script>
    var jnlpFile = "dynamictree_webstart_no_codebase.jnlp";
    deployJava.createWebStartLaunchButtonEx(jnlpFile);
</script>
```

The Java Web Start application is launched when the user clicks the resulting Launch button.

Checking the Client JRE Software Version

There are many reasons to check if a particular version of the JRE software is available on a client machine. For example, you might want to launch a different version of your RIA or redirect the user to a different page depending on the client's JRE software version.

Use the Deployment Toolkit script's `versionCheck` function to check if a particular version or range of JRE versions is installed on the client. The function signature is `versionCheck: function(versionPattern)`. The parameter, `versionPattern`, is a string specifying the version or range of versions to check for, such as 1.4, 1.5.0* (1.5.x family), and 1.6.0_02+ (any version greater than or equal to 1.6.0_02).

In this example, a Launch button is created for the Notepad application only if the version of JRE software on the client is greater than or equal to 1.6. If not, the browser redirects them to `oracle.com`:

```
<script src="https://www.java.com/js/deployJava.js"></script>
<script>
    if (deployJava.versionCheck('1.6+')) {
        var url = "tutorialJWS/deployment/webstart/examples/Notepad.jnlp";

        <!-- you can also invoke deployJava.runApplet here -->
        deployJava.createWebStartLaunchButton(url, '1.6.0');
    } else {
        document.location.href="http://oracle.com";
    }
</script>
```

20

> **Note**
> Depending on the client's operating system and version of the Java platform, you might be able to verify version information for JRE software at the major version level (e.g., 1.6) or at a finer update level (e.g., 1.6.0_10).

Java Network Launch Protocol

JNLP enables an application to be launched on a client desktop by using resources that are hosted on a remote web server. Java Plug-In software and Java Web Start software are considered JNLP clients because they can launch remotely hosted applets and applications on a client desktop. See the Java Network Launching Protocol and API Specification Change Log[5] for details.

Improvements in deployment technologies enable us to launch RIAs by using JNLP. Both applets and Java Web Start applications can be launched using this protocol. RIAs that are launched by using JNLP also have access to the JNLP API. The JNLP API allows the RIAs to access the client desktop with the user's permission.

JNLP is enabled by an RIA's JNLP file. The JNLP file describes the RIA. The JNLP file specifies the name of the main JAR file, the version of JRE software that is required to run the RIA and name and display information, optional packages, runtime parameters, system properties, and so on.

You can find more information about deploying RIAs by using JNLP in the next section and also the following:

- Chapter 17, "Deploying a Java Web Start Application"
- Chapter 18, "Deploying an Applet"
- Chapter 19, "JNLP API"

Structure of the JNLP File

This topic describes the syntax of the JNLP file for RIAs. The following code snippet shows a sample JNLP file for a Java Web Start application:

```
<?xml version="1.0" encoding="UTF-8"?>
<jnlp spec="1.0+" codebase="" href="">
    <information>
        <title>Dynamic Tree Demo</title>
```

20

---

5. http://www.oracle.com/technetwork/java/javase/jnlp-spec-log-139509
    .html

```
                <vendor>Dynamic Team</vendor>
                <icon href="sometree-icon.jpg"/>
                <offline-allowed/>
        </information>
        <resources>
            <!-- Application Resources -->
            <j2se version="1.6+" href=
                "http://java.sun.com/products/autodl/j2se"/>
            <jar href="DynamicTreeDemo.jar"
                main="true" />

        </resources>
        <application-desc
            name="Dynamic Tree Demo Application"
            main-class="webstartComponentArch.DynamicTreeApplication"
            width="300"
            height="300">
        </application-desc>
        <update check="background"/>
    </jnlp>
```

Table 20.1 describes the elements and attributes commonly used in JNLP files.

> **Note**
>
> Table 20.1 does not include all possible contents of the JNLP file. For more information, see the Java Network Launching Protocol and API Specification Change Log.

Encoding JNLP Files

Java Web Start software supports encoding of JNLP files in any character encoding supported by the Java platform. For more information about character encoding in the Java platform, see the Supported Encodings Guide.[6] To encode a JNLP file, specify an encoding in the XML prolog of that file. For example, the following line indicates that the JNLP file is encoded in UTF-16:

```
<?xml version="1.0" encoding="utf-16"?>
```

> **Note**
>
> The XML prolog itself must be UTF-8-encoded.

20

---

6.   8/docs/technotes/guides/intl/encoding.doc.html

Table 20.1 Commonly Used Elements and Attributes in a JNLP File

Element	Attributes	Description	Required
jnlp		The topmost xml element for a JNLP file	Yes
	spec	Value of the attribute can be 1.0, 1.5, or 6.0 or can use wildcards such as 1.0+; denotes the minimum version cf the JNLP Specification that this JNLP file can work with	
	codebase	The base location for all relative URLs specified in href attributes in the JNLP file	
	href	The URL of the JNLP file itself	
	version	The version of the RIA being launched as well as the version of the JNLP file itself	
information		Contains other elements that describe the RIA and its source	Yes
	os	The operating system for which this information element should be considered	
	arch	The architecture for which this information element should be considered	
	platform	The platform for which this information element should be considered	
	locale	The locale for which this information element should be considered	
title		The title of the RIA	Yes
vendor		The provider of the RIA	Yes
homepage		The homepage of the RIA	
	href	A URL pointing to where more information about this RIA can be found	Yes
description		A short statement describing the RIA	

(continued)

20

Table 20.1 Commonly Used Elements and Attributes in a JNLP File (continued)

Element	Attributes	Description	Required
	kind	An indicator as to the type of description; legal values are `one-line`, `short`, and `tooltip`.	
icon		An icon that can be used to identify the RIA to the user	
	href	A URL pointing to the icon file; can be in one of the following formats: `gif`, `jpg`, `png`, `ico`	Yes
	kind	Indicates the suggested use of the icon can be `default`, `selected`, `disabled`, `rollover`, `splash`, or `short-cut`	
	width	Can be used to indicate the resolution of the image	
	height	Can be used to indicate the resolution of the image	
	depth	Can be used to indicate the resolution of the image	
offline-allowed		Indicates that this RIA can operate when the client system is disconnected from the network	
shortcut		Can be used to indicate the RIA's preferences for desktop integration.	
	online	Can be used to describe the RIA's preference for creating a shortcut to run online or offline	
desktop		Can be used to indicate the RIA's preference for putting a shortcut on the user's desktop	
menu		Can be used to indicate the RIA's preference for putting a menu item in the user's start menus	
	sub-menu	Can be used to indicate the RIA's preference for where to place the menu item	

`association`		Can be used to hint to the JNLP client that the RIA wants to be registered with the operating system as the primary handler of certain extensions and a certain MIME type; if this element is included, either the `offline-allowed` element must also be included or the `href` attribute must be set for the `jnlp` element.	
	`extensions`	A list of file extensions (separated by spaces) that the RIA requests it be registered to handle	
	`mime-type`	The MIME type that the RIA requests it be registered to handle	
`related-content`		An additional piece of related content that can be integrated with the RIA	
	`href`	A URL pointing to the related content	Yes
`update`		The preferences for how RIA updates should be handled by the JNLP client	
	`check`	The preference for when the JNLP client should check for updates; value can be `always`, `timeout`, or `background`.	
	`policy`	The preference for how the JNLP client should handle a RIA update when a new version is available before the RIA is launched; value can be `always`, `prompt-update`, or `prompt-run`.	
`security`		Can be used to request enhanced permissions; if this element is not included, the application is run in the security sandbox.	
	`all-permissions`	Requests that the RIA be run with all permissions	
	`j2ee-application-client-permissions`	Requests that the RIA be run with a permission set that meets the security specifications of the J2EE application client environment	

(continued)

20

Table 20.1 Commonly Used Elements and Attributes in a JNLP File (continued)

Element	Attributes	Description	Required
resources		Describes all the resources that are needed for the RIA	Yes
	os	The operating system for which the resources element should be considered	
	arch	The architecture for which the resources element should be considered	
	locale	The locales for which the resources element should be considered	
java or j2se		Versions of Java software to run the RIA with	
	version	Ordered list of version ranges to use	Yes
	href	The URL denoting the supplier of this version of Java software and from where it can be downloaded	
	java-vm-args	An additional set of standard and nonstandard virtual machine arguments that the RIA would prefer the JNLP client use when launching the JRE software	
	initial-heap-size	The initial size of the Java heap	
	max-heap-size	The maximum size of the Java heap	
jar		A JAR file that is part of the RIA's class path	Yes
	href	The URL of the JAR file	Yes
	version	The requested version of the JAR file; requires using the version-based download protocol	
	main	Indicates if this JAR file contains the class containing the main method of the RIA	
	download	Indicates that this JAR file can be downloaded lazily, or when needed	
	size	The downloadable size of the JAR file in bytes	

20

	part	Can be used to group resources together so that they are downloaded at the same time	
nativelib		A JAR file that contains native libraries in its root directory	
	href	The URL of the JAR file	Yes
	version	The requested version of the JAR file; requires using the version-based download protocol	
	download	Can be used to indicate this JAR file can be downloaded lazily	
	size	The downloadable size of the JAR file in bytes	
	part	Can be used to group resources together so they will be downloaded at the same time	
extension		A pointer to an additional component-desc or installer-desc to be used with this RIA	
	href	The URL to the additional extension JNLP file	Yes
	version	The version of the additional extension JNLP file	
	name	The name of the additional extension JNLP file	
ext-download		Can be used in an extension element to denote the parts contained in a component extension	
	ext-part	The name of a part that can be expected to be found in the extension	Yes
	download	Can be used to indicate this extension can be download-ed eagerly or lazily	
	part	Denotes the name of a part in this JNLP file in which to include the extension	
package		Can be used to indicate to the JNLP client which packages are implemented in which JAR files	
	name	Package name contained in the JAR files of the given part	Yes

(continued)

20

Table 20.1 Commonly Used Elements and Attributes in a JNLP File (continued)

Element	Attributes	Description	Required
	part	Part name containing the JAR files that include the given package name	Yes
	recursive	Can be used to indicate that all package names, beginning with the given name, can be found in the given part	
property		Defines a system property that will be available through the System.getProperty and System.getProperties methods	
	name	Name of the system property	Yes
	value	Value of the system property	Yes
		Note: A JNLP file must contain one of the following: application-desc, applet-desc, component-desc, or installer-desc.	Yes
application-desc		Denotes this is the JNLP file for an application	
	main-class	The name of the class containing the public static void main(String[]) method of the application	Yes
argument		Each argument contains (in order) an additional argument to be passed to the main method.	
applet-desc		Denotes this is the JNLP file for an applet	

20

	main-class	The name of the main applet class	Yes
	documentbase	The document base for the applet as a URL	
	name	Name of the applet	Yes
	width	The width of the applet in pixels	Yes
	height	The height of the applet in pixels	Yes
param		A set of parameters that can be passed to the applet	
	name	The name of this parameter	Yes
	value	The value of this parameter	Yes
component-desc		Denotes this is the JNLP file for a component extension	
installer-desc		Denotes this is the JNLP file for an installed extension	
	main-class	The name of the class containing the public static void main(String[]) method of the installer	Yes

20

Deployment Best Practices

You can improve the user experience of your RIA using the following best practices:

- Sign the RIA using a certificate from a recognized certificate authority. Make sure that all artifacts are signed and that the certificate has not expired. See Chapter 16, "Signing and Verifying JAR Files," for information on signing.
- Request the minimum level of permissions that is needed. If the RIA does not require unrestricted access to a user's system, request that the RIA run in the security sandbox. See Chapter 19, "Security in Rich Internet Applications," for more security guidelines.
- Optimize the size of JAR files and related resources so that your RIA can load quickly. See the "Reducing the Download Time" section for optimization techniques.
- Enable the version download protocol and use background update checks to enable your RIA to start quickly. See the "Avoiding Unnecessary Update Checks" section to learn more about the version download protocol and update checks.
- Make sure that the client has the required version of the JRE software. See the "Ensuring the Presence of the JRE Software" section for details on how the Deployment Toolkit script can be used for this purpose.
- Embed the contents of your applet's JNLP file in the `<applet>` tag to avoid loading the JNLP file from the network. See the "Embedding JNLP File in Applet Tag" section to learn how to embed the contents of the applet's JNLP file in the web page.
- Preload your Java Web Start application, if possible. If you plan to deploy your RIA as a Java Web Start application in an enterprise where you have some administrative control, you can preload your application to various clients so that it is cached and ready to use. Use the following command to preload your Java Web Start application:

```
javaws -import -silent <jnlp url>
```

Reducing the Download Time

RIAs are downloaded from a web site when the user tries to access them. (RIAs can be cached after the initial download to improve performance.) The time taken to download an RIA depends on the size of the RIA's JAR file. Larger JAR files take longer to download.

You can reduce the download time of your RIA by applying the following techniques:

- Compress your RIA's JAR file by using the pack200 tool.[7]

---

7.   8/docs/technotes/tools/windows/pack200.html

- Remove unnecessary white space from the JNLP file and the JavaScript files.
- Optimize images and animation.

The following steps describe how to create and deploy a compressed JAR file for a signed RIA:

1. Normalize the JAR file using the `--repack` option. This step ensures that the security certificate and JAR file will pass verification checks when the RIA is launched:

   ```
   pack200 --repack DynamicTreeDemo.jar
   ```

2. Sign the normalized JAR file, where `myKeyStore` is the name of the keystore and me is the alias for the keystore:

   ```
   jarsigner -keystore myKeyStore DynamicTreeDemo.jar me
   ```

3. Pack the signed JAR file:

   ```
   pack200 DynamicTreeDemo.jar.pack.gz DynamicTreeDemo.jar
   ```

4. Set the `jnlp.packEnabled` property to `true` in the RIA's JNLP file:

   ```
   <resources>
       <j2se version="1.6+"
           href="http://java.sun.com/products/autodl/j2se"
               max-heap-size="128m" />
       <jar href="DynamicTreeDemo.jar"
           main="true"/>
       <property name="jnlp.packEnabled"
           value="true"/>
       <!-- ... -->
   </resources>
   ```

When the `jnlp.packEnabled` property is set in the JNLP file, the Java Plug-In software looks for the compressed JAR file with the `.pack.gz` extension (e.g., `DynamicTreeDemo.jar.pack.gz`). If found, the Java Plug-In software automatically unpacks and loads the JAR file. If a file with the `.pack.gz` extension is not found, then the Java Plug-In software attempts to load the regular JAR file (e.g., `DynamicTreeDemo.jar`).

> **Note**
> You need to deploy your RIA on a web server to test the `jnlp.packEnabled` property.

20

Avoiding Unnecessary Update Checks

RIAs are cached locally to improve start-up time. However, before launching a RIA, the launch software checks to make sure that every JAR file referenced in the RIA's JNLP file is up-to-date. In other words, the launch software makes sure that you are running the latest version of the RIA and not an older cached copy. These update checks can take up to a few hundred milliseconds depending on the number of JAR files and network speed. Use the techniques described in this section to avoid unnecessary update checks and to enhance the start-up time of your RIA.

> **Note**
>
> The term *launch software* is used here to collectively refer to the Java Plug-In software and the Java Web Start software. The Java Plug-In software launches applets while the Java Web Start software launches Java Web Start applications.

Leveraging the Version Download Protocol

You can leverage the *version download protocol* to eliminate unnecessary version checks. See the following steps to enable this protocol:

1. Rename the JAR files to include a version number suffix with the following naming convention:

   ```
   <JAR file name>__V<version number>.jar
   ```

   For example, `DynamicTreeDemo.jar` would be `DynamicTreeDemo__V1.0.jar`.

2. In the JNLP file, specify a version for every JAR file and set the `jnlp.versionEnabled` property to `true`.

   ```
   <resources>
       <!-- Application Resources -->
       <j2se version="1.6+"
           href="http://java.sun.com/products/autodl/j2se"
               max-heap-size="128m" />
       <jar href="DynamicTreeDemo.jar"
           main="true" version="1.0"/>
       <jar href="SomeOther.jar" version="2.0"/>
       <property name="jnlp.versionEnabled"
           value="true"/>
       <!-- ... -->
   </resources>
   ```

When the `jnlp.versionEnabled` property is enabled, the launch software performs only *one* update check to make sure that the JNLP file is up-to-date. The software compares the version numbers that are specified in the JNLP file with the corresponding JAR file versions (according to the naming convention mentioned in step 1) and updates only the outdated JAR files. This approach is efficient because only the update check for the JNLP file occurs over the network. All other version checks occur locally. If a file with the correct version number is not found, the launch software attempts to load the default JAR file (e.g., `DynamicTreeDemo.jar`).

Performing Update Checks in the Background

If it is not critical for the user to immediately run the latest version of your RIA, you can specify that all update checks should occur in the background. In this case, the launch software launches the locally cached copy for immediate usage and downloads a newer version of the RIA in the background. The newer version of the RIA will be launched the next time the user attempts to use your RIA. To enable background update checks, add the following line to your JNLP file:

```
<update check='background'/>
```

The following code snippet shows a sample JNLP file with the background update check enabled:

```
<?xml version="1.0" encoding="UTF-8"?>
<jnlp spec="1.0+" codebase="" href="">
    <information>
        <title>Applet Takes Params</title>
        <vendor>Dynamic Team</vendor>
    </information>
    <resources>
        <!-- Application Resources -->
        <j2se version="1.6+" href=
            "http://java.sun.com/products/autodl/j2se"/>
        <jar href="applet_AppletWithParameters.jar"
            main="true" />
    </resources>
    <applet-desc
        name="Applet Takes Params"
        main-class="AppletTakesParams"
        width="800"
        height="50">
            <param name="paramStr" value="someString"/>
            <param name="paramInt" value="22"/>
    </applet-desc>
    <update check="background"/>
</jnlp>
```

Ensuring the Presence of the JRE Software

RIAs usually need a minimum version of the JRE software to be present on the client machine. When deploying a RIA, you need to ensure that client machines have the required version of the JRE software so that your RIA can function well. With the Deployment Toolkit script, you have at least two ways to handle this requirement:

- You can check the version of client JRE software as soon as users access your web site and install the latest version if necessary.
- You can let users navigate the web site and check and install the latest JRE only when they attempt to use your RIA.

20

Checking and Installing the Latest JRE Software When the User Accesses Your Web Site

The following example checks if a user has at least version 1.6.0_13 of the JRE software installed. If not, the code installs the latest JRE software. See inline comments in the code:

```
<script src="https://www.java.com/js/deployJava.js"></script>
<script>

    // check if current JRE version is greater than 1.6.0
    alert("versioncheck " + deployJava.versionCheck('1.6.0_10+'));
    if (deployJava.versionCheck('1.6.0_10+') == false) {
        userInput = confirm(
            "You need the latest Java(TM) Runtime Environment. " +
            "Would you like to update now?");
        if (userInput == true) {

            // Set deployJava.returnPage to make sure user comes back to
            // your web site after installing the JRE
            deployJava.returnPage = location.href;

            // Install latest JRE or redirect user to another page to get JRE
            deployJava.installLatestJRE();
        }
    }
</script>
```

Installing the Correct JRE Software Only When the User Attempts to Use Your RIA

When you specify the minimum version of the JRE software in the `runApplet` or `createWebStartLaunchButton` function, the Deployment Toolkit script makes sure that the required version of the JRE software exists on the client before running your RIA.

Use the `runApplet` function to deploy an applet, as shown in the following example. The last parameter of the `runApplet` function is the minimum version that is required to run your applet (version 1.6):

```
<script src="https://www.java.com/js/deployJava.js"></script>
<script>
    var attributes = { code:'components.DynamicTreeApplet',
        width:300, height:300};
    var parameters = {jnlp_href: 'dynamictree_applet.jnlp'};
    deployJava.runApplet(attributes, parameters, '1.6');
</script>
```

To deploy a Java Web Start application, use the `createWebStartLaunchButton` function with the correct minimum version parameter (version 1.6):

```
<script src="https://www.java.com/js/deployJava.js"></script>
<script>
```

20

```
        var url = "dynamictree_applet.jnlp";
        deployJava.createWebStartLaunchButton(url, '1.6.0');
</script>
```

The `runApplet` and `createWebStartLaunchButton` functions check the client's version of the JRE software. If the minimum version is not installed, the functions install the latest version of the JRE software.

Questions and Exercises: Deployment in Depth

Questions

1. What script contains functions to deploy applets and Java Web Start applications?
2. True or false: You should always sign your RIA just to be sure it will always work.

Exercise

1. Write the JavaScript code to deploy the `Exercise` applet using the `ex.jnlp` file.

Answers

You can find answers to these questions and exercises at `http://docs.oracle .com/javase/tutorial/deployment/deploymentInDepth/QandE/answers .html`.

20

21

Date-Time

Chapter Contents

Date-Time Overview   756
Date-Time Design Principles   756
The Date-Time Packages   757
Method Naming Conventions   758
Standard Calendar   759
Overview   759
DayOfWeek and Month Enums   760
Date Classes   762
Date and Time Classes   764
Time Zone and Offset Classes   766
Instant Class   770
Parsing and Formatting   772
The Temporal Package   774
Period and Duration   780
Clock   783
Non-ISO Date Conversion   784
Legacy Date-Time Code   787
Summary   789
Questions and Exercises: Date-Time   791

The Date-Time package, `java.time`,[1] introduced in the Java SE 8 release, provides a comprehensive model for date and time and was developed under the JSR 310 Date and Time API.[2] Although `java.time` is based on the International Organization for

---

1.   `8/docs/api/java/time/package-summary.html`

2.   `http://jcp.org/en/jsr/detail?id=310`

Standardization (ISO) calendar system, commonly used global calendars are also supported. This chapter covers the fundamentals of using the ISO-based classes to represent date and time and to manipulate date and time values.

Date-Time Overview

Time seems to be a simple subject; even an inexpensive watch can provide a reasonably accurate date and time. However, with closer examination, you realize the subtle complexities and many factors that affect your understanding of time. For example, the result of adding one month to January 31 is different for a leap year than for other years. Time zones also add complexity. For example, a country may go in and out of daylight saving time at short notice or more than once a year or it may skip daylight saving time entirely for a given year.

The Date-Time API uses the calendar system defined in ISO-8601[3] as the default calendar. This calendar is based on the Gregorian calendar system and is used globally as the de facto standard for representing date and time. The core classes in the Date-Time API have names such as `LocalDateTime`, `ZonedDateTime`, and `OffsetDateTime`. All of these use the ISO calendar system. If you want to use an alternative calendar system, such as Hijrah or Thai Buddhist, the `java.time.chrono` package allows you to use one of the predefined calendar systems. Or you can create your own.

The Date-Time API uses the Unicode Common Locale Data Repository (CLDR).[4] This repository supports the world's languages and contains the world's largest collection of locale data available. The information in this repository has been localized to hundreds of languages. The Date-Time API also uses the Time Zone Database (TZDB).[5] This database provides information about every time zone change globally since 1970, with history for primary time zones since the concept was introduced.

Date-Time Design Principles

The Date-Time API was developed using several design principles.

Clear

The methods in the API are well defined and their behavior is clear and expected. For example, invoking a Date-Time method with a `null` parameter value typically triggers a `NullPointerException`.

---

3.   `http://www.iso.org/iso/home/standards/iso8601.htm`

4.   `http://cldr.unicode.org`

5.   `http://www.iana.org/time-zones`

Fluent

The Date-Time API provides a fluent interface, making the code easy to read. Because most methods do not allow parameters with a `null` value and do not return a `null` value, method calls can be chained together and the resulting code can be quickly understood:

```
LocalDate today = LocalDate.now();
LocalDate payday = today.with(TemporalAdjusters.lastDayOfMonth()).minusDays(2);
```

Immutable

Most of the classes in the Date-Time API create objects that are immutable, meaning that after the object is created, it cannot be modified. To alter the value of an immutable object, a new object must be constructed as a modified copy of the original. This also means that the Date-Time API is, by definition, thread safe. This affects the API in that most of the methods used to create date or time objects are prefixed with `of`, `from`, or `with`, rather than constructors, and there are no `set` methods:

```
LocalDate dateOfBirth = LocalDate.of(2012, Month.MAY, 14);
LocalDate firstBirthday = dateOfBirth.plusYears(1);
```

Extensible

The Date-Time API is extensible wherever possible. For example, you can define your own time adjusters and queries or build your own calendar system.

The Date-Time Packages

The Date-Time API consists of the primary package, `java.time`, and multiple subpackages:

- `java.time`. This is the core of the API for representing date and time. It includes classes for date, time, date and time combined, time zones, instants, duration, and clocks. These classes are based on the calendar system defined in ISO-8601 and are immutable and thread safe.
- `java.time.chrono`. This is the API for representing calendar systems other than the default ISO-8601. You can also define your own calendar system. This chapter does not cover this package in any detail.
- `java.time.format`. These are classes for formatting and parsing dates and times.
- `java.time.temporal`. This is an extended API, primarily for framework and library writers, allowing interoperations between the date and time classes,

21

querying, and adjustment. Fields (`TemporalField` and `ChronoField`) and units (`TemporalUnit` and `ChronoUnit`) are defined in this package.

- `java.time.zone`. These are classes that support time zones, offsets from time zones, and time zone rules. If working with time zones, most developers will need to use only (1) `ZonedDateTime` and (2) `ZoneId` or `ZoneOffset`.

Method Naming Conventions

The Date-Time API offers a rich set of methods within a rich set of classes. The method names are made consistent between classes wherever possible. For example, many of the classes offer a now method that captures the date or time values of the current moment that are relevant to that class. There are `from` methods that allow conversion from one class to another.

There is also standardization regarding the method name prefixes. Because most of the classes in the Date-Time API are immutable, the API does not include `set` methods. (After its creation, the value of an immutable object cannot be changed. The immutable equivalent of a `set` method is `with`.) Table 21.1 lists the commonly used prefixes.

Table 21.1 Method Name Prefixes

Prefix	Method type	Use
`of`	static factory	Creates an instance where the factory is primarily validating the input parameters, not converting them
`from`	static factory	Converts the input parameters to an instance of the target class, which may involve losing information from the input
`parse`	static factory	Parses the input string to produce an instance of the target class
`format`	instance	Uses the specified formatter to format the values in the temporal object to produce a string
`get`	instance	Returns a part of the state of the target object
`is`	instance	Queries the state of the target object
`with`	instance	Returns a copy of the target object with one element changed; this is the immutable equivalent to a `set` method on a JavaBean.
`plus`	instance	Returns a copy of the target object with an amount of time added
`minus`	instance	Returns a copy of the target object with an amount of time subtracted
`to`	instance	Converts this object to another type
`at`	instance	Combines this object with another

21

Standard Calendar

The core of the Date-Time API is the `java.time` package.[6] The classes defined in `java.time` base their calendar system on the ISO calendar, which is the world standard for representing date and time. The ISO calendar follows the proleptic Gregorian rules. The Gregorian calendar was introduced in 1582; in the *proleptic* Gregorian calendar, dates are extended backward from that time to create a consistent, unified timeline and to simplify date calculations.

Overview

There are two basic ways to represent time. One way represents time in human terms, referred to as *human time*, such as year, month, day, hour, minute, and second. The other way, *machine time*, measures time continuously along a timeline from an origin, called the *epoch*, in nanosecond resolution. The Date-Time package provides a rich array of classes for representing date and time. Some classes in the Date-Time API are intended to represent machine time, and others are more suited to representing human time.

First determine which aspects of date and time you require, and then select the class or classes that fulfill those needs. When choosing a temporal-based class, you first decide whether you need to represent human time or machine time. You then identify what aspects of time you need to represent. Do you need a time zone? Date *and* time? Date only? If you need a date, do you need month, day, *and* year or a subset?

> **Definition**
>
> The classes in the Date-Time API that capture and work with date or time values, such as `Instant`, `LocalDateTime`, and `ZonedDateTime`, are referred to as *temporal-based* classes (or types) throughout this chapter. Supporting types, such as the `TemporalAdjuster` interface or the `DayOfWeek` enum, are not included in this definition.

For example, you might use a `LocalDate` object to represent a birth date, because most people observe their birthday on the same day, whether they are in their birth city or across the globe on the other side of the International Date Line. If you are tracking astrological time, then you might want to use a `LocalDateTime` object to represent the date and time of birth or a `ZonedDateTime`, which also includes the time zone.

21

---

6. `8/docs/api/java/time/package-summary.html`

If you are creating a time stamp, then you will most likely want to use an `Instant`, which allows you to compare one instantaneous point on the timeline to another.

Table 21.2 summarizes the temporal-based classes in the `java.time` package that store date and/or time information or that can be used to measure an amount of time. An "X" in a column indicates that the class uses that particular type of data, and the "toString Output" column shows an instance printed using the `toString` method. The "Where Discussed" column indicates the relevant section in this chapter.

DayOfWeek and Month Enums

The Date-Time API provides enums for specifying days of the week and months of the year.

DayOfWeek

The `DayOfWeek` enum consists of seven constants that describe the days of the week: `MONDAY` through `SUNDAY`.[7] The integer values of the `DayOfWeek` constants range from 1 (Monday) through 7 (Sunday). Using the defined constants (`DayOf-Week.FRIDAY`) makes your code more readable.

This enum also provides a number of methods, similar to the methods provided by the temporal-based classes. For example, the following code adds three days to `MONDAY` and prints the result. The output is `THURSDAY`:

```
System.out.printf("%s%n", DayOfWeek.MONDAY.plus(3));
```

By using the `getDisplayName(TextStyle, Locale)` method, you can retrieve a string to identify the day of the week in the user's locale.[8] The `TextStyle` enum enables you to specify what sort of string you want to display: `FULL`, `NARROW` (typically a single letter), or `SHORT` (an abbreviation).[9] The `STANDALONE TextStyle` constants are used in some languages where the output is different when used as part of a date than when it is used by itself. The following example prints the three primary forms of the `TextStyle` for `MONDAY`:

```
DayOfWeek dow = DayOfWeek.MONDAY;
Locale locale = Locale.getDefault();
System.out.println(dow.getDisplayName(TextStyle.FULL, locale));
System.out.println(dow.getDisplayName(TextStyle.NARROW, locale));
System.out.println(dow.getDisplayName(TextStyle.SHORT, locale));
```

21

---

7. 8/docs/api/java/time/DayOfWeek.html

8. 8/docs/api/java/time/DayOfWeek.html#getDisplayName-java.time.format
    .TextStyle-java.util.Locale-

9. 8/docs/api/java/time/format/TextStyle.html

Table 21.2 Temporal-Based Date-Time Classes

Class or enum	Year	Month	Day	Hours	Minutes	Seconds*	Zone offset	Zone ID	toString output	Where discussed
Instant						X			2013-08-20T15:16:26.355Z	"Instant Class"
LocalDate	X	X	X						2013-08-20	"Date Classes"
LocalDateTime	X	X	X	X	X	X			2013-08-20T08:16:26.937	"Date and Time Classes"
ZonedDateTime	X	X	X	X	X	X	X	X	2013-08-21T00:16:26.941+09:00 [Asia/Tokyo]	"Time Zone and Offset Classes"
LocalTime				X	X	X			08:16:26.943	"Date and Time Classes"
MonthDay		X	X						--08-20	"Date Classes"
Year	X								2013	"Date Classes"
YearMonth	X	X							2013-08	"Date Classes"
Month		X							AUGUST	"DayOfWeek and Month Enums"
OffsetDateTime	X	X	X	X	X	X	X		2013-08-20T08:16:26.954-07:00	"Time Zone and Offset Classes"
OffsetTime				X	X	X	X		08:16:26.957-07:00	"Time Zone and Offset Classes"
Duration			**	**	**	X			PT20H (20 hours)	"Period and Duration"
Period	X	X	X				***	***	P10D (10 days)	"Period and Duration"

* Seconds are captured to nanosecond precision.

** This class does not store this information but has methods to provide time in these units.

*** When a Period is added to a ZonedDateTime, daylight saving time or other local time differences are observed.

21

This code has the following output for the en locale:

```
Monday
M
Mon
```

Month

The Month enum includes constants for the twelve months, JANUARY through DECEM-BER.[10] As with the DayOfWeek enum, the Month enum is strongly typed, and the integer value of each constant corresponds to the ISO range from 1 (January) through 12 (December). Using the defined constants (Month.SEPTEMBER) makes your code more readable.

The Month enum also includes a number of methods. The following line of code uses the maxLength method to print the maximum possible number of days in the month of February. The output is 29:

```
System.out.printf("%d%n", Month.FEBRUARY.maxLength());
```

The Month enum also implements the getDisplayName(TextStyle, Locale) method to retrieve a string to identify the month in the user's locale using the specified TextStyle.[11] If a particular TextStyle is not defined, then a string representing the numeric value of the constant is returned. The following code prints the month of August using the three primary text styles:

```
Month month = Month.AUGUST;
Locale locale = Locale.getDefault();
System.out.println(month.getDisplayName(TextStyle.FULL, locale));
System.out.println(month.getDisplayName(TextStyle.NARROW, locale));
System.out.println(month.getDisplayName(TextStyle.SHORT, locale));
```

This code has the following output for the en locale:

```
August
A
Aug
```

Date Classes

The Date-Time API provides four classes that deal exclusively with date information, without respect to time or time zone. The use of these classes is suggested by the class names: LocalDate, YearMonth, MonthDay, and Year.

---

10.   8/docs/api/java/time/Month.html

11.   8/docs/api/java/time/Month.html#getDisplayName-java.time.format
      .TextStyle-java.util.Locale-

LocalDate

A `LocalDate` represents year, month, day in the ISO calendar and is useful for representing a date without a time.[12] You might use a `LocalDate` to track a significant event, such as a birth date or wedding date. The following examples use the `of` and `with` methods to create instances of `LocalDate`:

```
LocalDate date = LocalDate.of(2000, Month.NOVEMBER, 20);
LocalDate nextWed = date.with(TemporalAdjusters.next(DayOfWeek.WEDNESDAY));
```

For more information about the `TemporalAdjuster` interface, see the "Temporal Adjuster" section.

In addition to the usual methods, the `LocalDate` class offers get methods for obtaining information about a given date. The `getDayOfWeek` method returns the day of the week that a particular date falls on.[13] For example, the following line of code returns MONDAY:

```
DayOfWeek dotw = LocalDate.of(2012, Month.JULY, 9).getDayOfWeek();
```

The following example uses a `TemporalAdjuster` to retrieve the first Wednesday after a specific date:

```
LocalDate date = LocalDate.of(2000, Month.NOVEMBER, 20);
TemporalAdjuster adj = TemporalAdjusters.next(DayOfWeek.WEDNESDAY);
LocalDate nextWed = date.with(adj);
System.out.printf("For the date of %s, the next Wednesday is %s.%n",
                  date, nextWed);
```

Running the code produces the following:

```
For the date of 2000-11-20, the next Wednesday is 2000-11-22.
```

The "Period and Duration" section also has examples using the `LocalDate` class.

YearMonth

The `YearMonth` class represents the month of a specific year.[14] The following example uses the `YearMonth.lengthOfMonth()` method to determine the number of days for several year and month combinations.

21

---

12. 8/docs/api/java/time/LocalDate.html
13. 8/docs/api/java/time/LocalDate.html#getDayOfWeek--
14. 8/docs/api/java/time/YearMonth.html

```
YearMonth date = YearMonth.now();
System.out.printf("%s: %d%n", date, date.lengthOfMonth());

YearMonth date2 = YearMonth.of(2010, Month.FEBRUARY);
System.out.printf("%s: %d%n", date2, date2.lengthOfMonth());

YearMonth date3 = YearMonth.of(2012, Month.FEBRUARY);
System.out.printf("%s: %d%n", date3, date3.lengthOfMonth());
```

The output from this code looks like the following:

```
2013-06: 30
2010-02: 28
2012-02: 29
```

MonthDay

The `MonthDay` class represents the day of a particular month, such as New Year's Day on January 1.[15] The following example uses the `MonthDay.isValidYear` method to determine if February 29 is valid for the year 2010.[16] The call returns `false`, confirming that 2010 is not a leap year:

```
MonthDay date = MonthDay.of(Month.FEBRUARY, 29);
boolean validLeapYear = date.isValidYear(2010);
```

Year

The `Year`[17] class represents a year. The following example uses the `Year.isLeap` method to determine if the given year is a leap year.[18] The call returns `true`, confirming that 2012 is a leap year:

```
boolean validLeapYear = Year.of(2012).isLeap();
```

Date and Time Classes

LocalTime

The `LocalTime` class is similar to the other classes whose names are prefixed with `Local` but deals in time only.[19] This class is useful for representing human-based

---

21

15. 8/docs/api/java/time/MonthDay.html

16. 8/docs/api/java/time/MonthDay.html#isValidYear#isValidYear-int-

17. 8/docs/api/java/time/Year.html

18. 8/docs/api/java/time/Year.html#isLeap--

19. 8/docs/api/java/time/LocalTime.html

times of day, such as movie times or the opening and closing times of the local library. It could also be used to create a digital clock, as shown in the following example:

```
LocalTime thisSec;

for (;;) {
    thisSec = LocalTime.now();

    // implementation of display code is left to the reader
    display(thisSec.getHour(), thisSec.getMinute(), thisSec.getSecond());
}
```

The `LocalTime` class does not store time zone or daylight saving time information.

LocalDateTime

The class that handles both date and time, without a time zone, is `LocalDateTime`, one of the core classes of the Date-Time API.[20] This class is used to represent date (month, day, year) together with time (hour, minute, second, nanosecond) and is, in effect, a combination of `LocalDate` with `LocalTime`. This class can be used to represent a specific event, such as the first race for the Louis Vuitton Cup Finals in the America's Cup Challenger Series, which began at 1:10 p.m. on August 17, 2013. Note that this means 1:10 p.m. in local time. To include a time zone, you must use a `ZonedDateTime` or an `OffsetDateTime`, as discussed in "Time Zone and Offset Classes."

In addition to the now method that every temporal-based class provides, the `Local-DateTime` class has various `of` methods (or methods prefixed with `of`) that create an instance of `LocalDateTime`. There is a `from` method that converts an instance from another temporal format to a `LocalDateTime` instance. There are also methods for adding or subtracting hours, minutes, days, weeks, and months. The following example shows a few of these methods. The date-time expressions are in bold:

```
System.out.printf("now: %s%n", LocalDateTime.now());

System.out.printf("Apr 15, 1994 @ 11:30am: %s%n",
                  LocalDateTime.of(1994, Month.APRIL, 15, 11, 30));

System.out.printf("now (from Instant): %s%n",
                  LocalDateTime.ofInstant(Instant.now(), ZoneId.systemDefault()));

System.out.printf("6 months from now: %s%n",
                  LocalDateTime.now().plusMonths(6));

System.out.printf("6 months ago: %s%n",
                  LocalDateTime.now().minusMonths(6));
```

21

20.   8/docs/api/java/time/LocalDateTime.html

This code produces output that will look similar to the following:

```
now: 2013-07-24T17:13:59.985
Apr 15, 1994 @ 11:30am: 1994-04-15T11:30
now (from Instant): 2013-07-24T17:14:00.479
6 months from now: 2014-01-24T17:14:00.480
6 months ago: 2013-01-24T17:14:00.481
```

Time Zone and Offset Classes

A *time zone* is a region of the earth where the same standard time is used. Each time zone is described by an identifier and usually has the format *region/city* (Asia/ Tokyo) and an offset from Greenwich/UTC time. For example, the offset for Tokyo is +09:00.

ZoneId and ZoneOffset

The Date-Time API provides two classes for specifying a time zone or an offset:

- ZoneId specifies a time zone identifier and provides rules for converting between an Instant and a LocalDateTime.

- ZoneOffset specifies a time zone offset from Greenwich/UTC time.

Offsets from Greenwich/UTC time are usually defined in whole hours, but there are exceptions. The following code, from the TimeZoneId example, prints a list of all time zones that use offsets from Greenwich/UTC that are not defined in whole hours:

```
Set<String> allZones = ZoneId.getAvailableZoneIds();
LocalDateTime dt = LocalDateTime.now();

// Create a List using the set of zones and sort it.
List<String> zoneList = new ArrayList<String>(allZones);
Collections.sort(zoneList);

...

for (String s : zoneList) {
    ZoneId zone = ZoneId.of(s);
    ZonedDateTime zdt = dt.atZone(zone);
    ZoneOffset offset = zdt.getOffset();
    int secondsOfHour = offset.getTotalSeconds() % (60 * 60);
    String out = String.format("%35s %10s%n", zone, offset);

    // Write only time zones that do not have a whole hour offset
    // to standard out.
    if (secondsOfHour != 0) {
        System.out.printf(out);
```

```
    }
      ...
  }
```

This example produces the following output:

```
         America/Caracas      -04:30
       America/St_Johns      -02:30
         Asia/Calcutta       +05:30
         Asia/Colombo        +05:30
          Asia/Kabul         +04:30
        Asia/Kathmandu       +05:45
        Asia/Katmandu        +05:45
         Asia/Kolkata        +05:30
         Asia/Rangoon        +06:30
          Asia/Tehran        +04:30
      Australia/Adelaide     +09:30
   Australia/Broken_Hill     +09:30
      Australia/Darwin       +09:30
       Australia/Eucla       +08:45
        Australia/LHI        +10:30
     Australia/Lord_Howe     +10:30
       Australia/North       +09:30
       Australia/South       +09:30
   Australia/Yancowinna      +09:30
    Canada/Newfoundland      -02:30
         Indian/Cocos        +06:30
             Iran            +04:30
           NZ-CHAT           +12:45
       Pacific/Chatham       +12:45
      Pacific/Marquesas      -09:30
       Pacific/Norfolk       +11:30
```

The `TimeZoneId` example also prints a list of all time zone IDs to a file called `timeZones`.

The Date-Time Classes

The Date-Time API provides three temporal-based classes that work with time zones:

- `ZonedDateTime` handles a date and time with a corresponding time zone with a time zone offset from Greenwich/UTC.
- `OffsetDateTime` handles a date and time with a corresponding time zone offset from Greenwich/UTC, without a time zone ID.
- `OffsetTime` handles time with a corresponding time zone offset from Greenwich/UTC, without a time zone ID.

When would you use `OffsetDateTime` instead of `ZonedDateTime`? If you are writing complex software that models its own rules for date and time calculations

21

based on geographic locations, or if you are storing time stamps in a database that track only absolute offsets from Greenwich/UTC time, then you might want to use `OffsetDateTime`. Also, XML and other network formats define date-time transfer as `OffsetDateTime` or `OffsetTime`.

Although all three classes maintain an offset from Greenwich/UTC time, only `ZonedDateTime` uses the `ZoneRules`,[21] part of the `java.time.zone` package, to determine how an offset varies for a particular time zone. For example, most time zones experience a gap (typically of one hour) when moving the clock forward to daylight saving time and a time overlap when moving the clock back to standard time and the last hour before the transition is repeated. The `ZonedDateTime` class accommodates this scenario, whereas the `OffsetDateTime` and `OffsetTime` classes, which do not have access to the `ZoneRules`, do not.

ZonedDateTime

The ZonedDateTime[22] class, in effect, combines the `LocalDateTime`[23] class with the `ZoneId`[24] class. It is used to represent a full date (year, month, day) and time (hour, minute, second, nanosecond) with a time zone (region/city, such as `Europe/Paris`).

The following code, from the `Flight`[25] example, defines the departure time for a flight from San Francisco to Tokyo as a `ZonedDateTime` in the America/Los Angeles time zone. The `withZoneSameInstant` and `plusMinutes` methods are used to create an instance of `ZonedDateTime` that represents the projected arrival time in Tokyo after the 650-minute flight. The `ZoneRules.isDaylightSavings` method determines whether it is daylight saving time when the flight arrives in Tokyo.

A `DateTimeFormatter` object is used to format the `ZonedDateTime` instances for printing:

```
DateTimeFormatter format = DateTimeFormatter.ofPattern("MMM d yyyy hh:mm a");

// Leaving from San Francisco on July 20, 2013, at 7:30 p.m.
LocalDateTime leaving = LocalDateTime.of(2013, Month.JULY, 20, 19, 30);
ZoneId leavingZone = ZoneId.of("America/Los_Angeles");
ZonedDateTime departure = ZonedDateTime.of(leaving, leavingZone);

try {
    String out1 = departure.format(format);
    System.out.printf("LEAVING: %s (%s)%n", out1, leavingZone);
} catch (DateTimeException exc) {
    System.out.printf("%s can't be formatted!%n", departure);
    throw exc;
```

21

21. 8/docs/api/java/time/zone/ZoneRules.html

22. 8/docs/api/java/time/ZonedDateTime.html

23. 8/docs/api/java/time/LocalDateTime.html

24. 8/docs/api/java/time/ZoneId.html

25. tutorial/datetime/iso/examples/Flight.java

```
}

// Flight is 10 hours and 50 minutes, or 650 minutes
ZoneId arrivingZone = ZoneId.of("Asia/Tokyo");
ZonedDateTime arrival = departure.withZoneSameInstant(arrivingZone)
                                 .plusMinutes(650);

try {
    String out2 = arrival.format(format);
    System.out.printf("ARRIVING: %s (%s)%n", out2, arrivingZone);
} catch (DateTimeException exc) {
    System.out.printf("%s can't be formatted!%n", arrival);
    throw exc;
}

if (arrivingZone.getRules().isDaylightSavings(arrival.toInstant()))
    System.out.printf(" (%s daylight saving time will be in effect.)%n",
                      arrivingZone);
else
    System.out.printf(" (%s standard time will be in effect.)%n",
                      arrivingZone);
```

This produces the following output:

```
LEAVING: Jul 20 2013 07:30 PM (America/Los_Angeles)
ARRIVING: Jul 21 2013 10:20 PM (Asia/Tokyo)
  (Asia/Tokyo standard time will be in effect.)
```

OffsetDateTime

The `OffsetDateTime`[26] class, in effect, combines the `LocalDateTime`[27] class with the `ZoneOffset`[28] class. It is used to represent a full date (year, month, day) and time (hour, minute, second, nanosecond) with an offset from Greenwich/UTC time (+/-hours:minutes, such as +06:00 or –08:00).

The following example uses `OffsetDateTime` with the `TemporalAdjuster.lastDay` method to find the last Thursday in July 2013.

```
// Find the last Thursday in July 2013.
LocalDateTime localDate = LocalDateTime.of(2013, Month.JULY, 20, 19, 30);
ZoneOffset offset = ZoneOffset.of("-08:00");

OffsetDateTime offsetDate = OffsetDateTime.of(localDate, offset);
OffsetDateTime lastThursday =
        offsetDate.with(TemporalAdjusters.lastInMonth(DayOfWeek.THURSDAY));
System.out.printf("The last Thursday in July 2013 is the %sth.%n",
                  lastThursday.getDayOfMonth());
```

21

The code produces the following output:

---

26. 8/docs/api/java/time/OffsetDateTime.html

27. 8/docs/api/java/time/LocalDateTime.html

28. 8/docs/api/java/time/ZoneOffset.html

The last Thursday in July 2013 is the 25th.

OffsetTime

The `OffsetTime`[29] class, in effect, combines the `LocalTime`[30] class with the `ZoneOffset`[31] class. It is used to represent time (hour, minute, second, nanosecond) with an offset from Greenwich/UTC time (+/-hours:minutes, such as +06:00 or –08:00).

The `OffsetTime` class is used in the same situations as the `OffsetDateTime` class when tracking the date is not needed.

Instant Class

One of the core classes of the Date-Time API is the `Instant` class, which represents the start of a nanosecond on the timeline.[32] This class is useful for generating a time stamp to represent machine time:

```
import java.time.Instant;

Instant timestamp = Instant.now();
```

A value returned from the `Instant` class counts time beginning from the first second of January 1, 1970 (1970-01-01T00:00:00Z), also called the EPOCH.[33] An instant that occurs before the epoch has a negative value, and an instant that occurs after the epoch has a positive value.

The other constants provided by the `Instant` class are MIN,[34] representing the smallest possible (far past) instant, and MAX,[35] representing the largest (far future) instant. Invoking `toString` on an `Instant` produces output like the following:

```
2013-05-30T23:38:23.085Z
```

This format follows the ISO-8601 standard for representing date and time.[36]

---

29. 8/docs/api/java/time/OffsetTime.html
30. 8/docs/api/java/time/LocalTime.html
31. 8/docs/api/java/time/ZoneOffset.html
32. 8/docs/api/java/time/Instant.html
33. 8/docs/api/java/time/Instant.html#EPOCH
34. 8/docs/api/java/time/Instant.html#MIN
35. 8/docs/api/java/time/Instant.html#MAX
36. http://www.iso.org/iso/home/standards/iso8601.htm

The `Instant` class provides a variety of methods for manipulating an `Instant`. There are `plus` and `minus` methods for adding or subtracting time. The following code adds one hour to the current time:

```
Instant oneHourLater = Instant.now().plusHours(1);
```

There are methods for comparing instants, such as `isAfter`[37] and `isBefore`.[38] The `until` method returns how much time exists between two `Instant` objects.[39] The following line of code reports how many seconds have occurred since the beginning of the Java epoch:

```
long secondsFromEpoch = Instant.ofEpochSecond(0L).until(Instant.now(),
                        ChronoUnit.SECONDS);
```

The `Instant` class does not work with human units of time, such as years, months, or days. If you want to perform calculations in those units, you can convert an `Instant` to another class, such as `LocalDateTime` or `ZonedDateTime`, by binding the `Instant` with a time zone. You can then access the value in the desired units. The following code converts an `Instant` to a `LocalDateTime` object using the `ofInstant`[40] method and the default time zone and then prints out the date and time in a more readable form:

```
Instant timestamp;
...
LocalDateTime ldt = LocalDateTime.ofInstant(timestamp, ZoneId.systemDefault());
System.out.printf("%s %d %d at %d:%d%n", ldt.getMonth(), ldt.getDayOfMonth(),
                  ldt.getYear(), ldt.getHour(), ldt.getMinute());
```

The output is similar to the following:

```
MAY 30 2013 at 18:21
```

Either a `ZonedDateTime` or an `OffsetTimeZone` object can be converted to an `Instant` object, as each maps to an exact moment on the timeline. However, the reverse is not true. Converting an `Instant` object to a `ZonedDateTime` or an `OffsetDateTime` object requires time zone or time zone offset information.

---

37. 8/docs/api/java/time/Instant.html#isAfter-java.time.Instant-
38. 8/docs/api/java/time/Instant.html#isBefore-java.time.Instant-
39. 8/docs/api/java/time/Instant.html#until-java.time.temporal.Temporal
    -java.time.temporal.TemporalUnit-
40. 8/docs/api/java/time/LocalDateTime.html#ofInstant-java.time.Instant
    -java.time.ZoneId-

21

Parsing and Formatting

The temporal-based classes in the Date-Time API provide `parse` methods for parsing a string that contains date and time information. These classes also provide `format` methods for formatting temporal-based objects for display. In both cases, the process is similar: you provide a pattern to the `DateTimeFormatter` to create a formatter object. This formatter is then passed to the `parse` or `format` method.

The `DateTimeFormatter` class provides numerous predefined formatters, or you can define your own.[41] The `parse` and the `format` methods throw an exception if a problem occurs during the conversion process. Therefore, your parse code should catch the `DateTimeParseException` error and your format code should catch the `DateTimeException` error. For more information on exception handing, see Chapter 10, "Catching and Handling Exceptions."

The `DateTimeFormatter` class is both immutable and thread safe; it can (and should) be assigned to a static constant where appropriate.

> **Note**
>
> The `java.time` date-time objects can be used directly with `java.util.Formatter` and `String.format` by using the familiar pattern-based formatting that was used with the legacy `java.util.Date` and `java.util.Calendar` classes.

Parsing

The one-argument `parse(CharSequence)` method in the `LocalDate` class uses the `ISO_LOCAL_DATE` formatter.[42] To specify a different formatter, you can use the two-argument `parse(CharSequence, DateTimeFormatter)` method.[43] The following example uses the predefined `BASIC_ISO_DATE` formatter, which uses the format `19590709` for July 9, 1959:

```
String in = ...;
LocalDate date = LocalDate.parse(in, DateTimeFormatter.BASIC_ISO_DATE);
```

You can also define a formatter using your own pattern. The following code, from the `Parse` example, creates a formatter that applies a format of `MMM d yyyy`. This format specifies three characters to represent the month, one digit to represent day of the month, and four digits to represent the year. A formatter created using this

21

---

41. `8/docs/api/java/time/format/DateTimeFormatter.html#predefined`

42. `8/docs/api/java/time/LocalDate.html#parse-java.lang.CharSequence-`

43. `8/docs/api/java/time/LocalDate.html#parse-java.lang.CharSequence`
     `-java.time.format.DateTimeFormatter-`

pattern would recognize strings such as `Jan 3 2003` or `Mar 23 1994`. However, to specify the format as `MMM dd yyyy`, with two characters for day of the month, then you would have to always use two characters, padding with a zero for a one-digit date: `Jun 03 2003`.

```
String input = ...;
try {
    DateTimeFormatter formatter =
                    DateTimeFormatter.ofPattern("MMM d yyyy");
    LocalDate date = LocalDate.parse(input, formatter);
    System.out.printf("%s%n", date);
}
catch (DateTimeParseException exc) {
    System.out.printf("%s is not parsable!%n", input);
    throw exc;        // Rethrow the exception.
}
// 'date' has been successfully parsed
```

The documentation for the `DateTimeFormatter` class specifies the full list of symbols that you can use to specify a pattern for formatting or parsing.[44] The `StringConverter` example in the "Non-ISO Date Conversion" section provides another example of a date formatter.

Formatting

The `format(DateTimeFormatter)` method converts a temporal-based object to a string representation using the specified format.[45] The following code, from the `Flight` example, converts an instance of `ZonedDateTime` using the format `"MMM d yyyy hh:mm a"`. The date is defined in the same manner as was used for the previous parsing example, but this pattern also includes the hour, minutes, and a.m. and p.m. components.

```
ZoneId leavingZone = ...;
ZonedDateTime departure = ...;

try {
    DateTimeFormatter format = DateTimeFormatter.ofPattern("MMM d yyyy hh:mm a");
    String out = departure.format(format);
    System.out.printf("LEAVING: %s (%s)%n", out, leavingZone);
}
catch (DateTimeException exc) {
    System.out.printf("%s can't be formatted!%n", departure);
    throw exc;
}
```

21

---

44. `8/docs/api/java/time/format/DateTimeFormatter.html#patterns`

45. `8/docs/api/java/time/LocalDate.html#format-java.time.format`
    `.DateTimeFormatter-`

The output for this example, which prints both the arrival and departure times, is as follows:

```
LEAVING: Jul 20 2013 07:30 PM (America/Los_Angeles)
ARRIVING: Jul 21 2013 10:20 PM (Asia/Tokyo)
```

The Temporal Package

The `java.time.temporal` package provides a collection of interfaces, classes, and enums that support date and time code and, in particular, date and time calculations.[46] These interfaces are intended to be used at the lowest level. Typical application code should declare variables and parameters in terms of the concrete type, such as `LocalDate` or `ZonedDateTime`, and not in terms of the `Temporal` interface. This is exactly the same as declaring a variable of type `String` and not of type `CharSequence`.

Temporal and TemporalAccessor

The `Temporal` interface provides a framework for accessing temporal-based objects and is implemented by the temporal-based classes, such as `Instant`, `LocalDate-Time`, and `ZonedDateTime`.[47] This interface provides methods to add or subtract units of time, making time-based arithmetic easy and consistent across the various date and time classes. The `TemporalAccessor` interface provides a read-only version of the `Temporal` interface.[48]

Both `Temporal` and `TemporalAccessor` objects are defined in terms of fields, as specified in the `TemporalField` interface.[49] The `ChronoField` enum is a concrete implementation of the `TemporalField` interface and provides a rich set of defined constants, such as `DAY_OF_WEEK`, `MINUTE_OF_HOUR`, and `MONTH_OF_YEAR`.[50]

The units for these fields are specified by the `TemporalUnit`[51] interface. The `ChronoUnit` enum implements the `TemporalUnit` interface. The field `Chrono-Field.DAY_OF_WEEK` is a combination of `ChronoUnit.DAYS` and `ChronoUnit.WEEKS`. The `ChronoField` and `ChronoUnit` enums are discussed in the following sections.

---

46. 8/docs/api/java/time/temporal/package-summary.html
47. 8/docs/api/java/time/temporal/Temporal.html
48. 8/docs/api/java/time/temporal/TemporalAccessor.html
49. 8/docs/api/java/time/temporal/TemporalField.html
50. 8/docs/api/java/time/temporal/ChronoField.html
51. 8/docs/api/java/time/temporal/TemporalUnit.html

The arithmetic-based methods in the `Temporal` interface require parameters defined in terms of `TemporalAmount` values.[52] The `Period` and `Duration` classes (discussed in the "Period and Duration" section) implement the `TemporalAmount` interface.

ChronoField and IsoFields

The `ChronoField` enum, which implements the `TemporalField` interface, provides a rich set of constants for accessing date and time values.[53] A few examples are CLOCK_HOUR_OF_DAY, NANO_OF_DAY, and DAY_OF_YEAR. This enum can be used to express conceptual aspects of time, such as the third week of the year, the eleventh hour of the day, or the first Monday of the month. When you encounter a `Temporal` of unknown type, you can use the `TemporalAccessor.isSupported(TemporalField)` method to determine if the `Temporal` supports a particular field.[54] The following line of code returns `false`, indicating that LocalDate does not support ChronoField.CLOCK_HOUR_OF_DAY:

```
boolean isSupported = LocalDate.now().isSupported(ChronoField.CLOCK_HOUR_OF_DAY);
```

Additional fields, specific to the ISO-8601 calendar system, are defined in the `IsoFields` class.[55] The following examples show how to obtain the value of a field using both `ChronoField` and `IsoFields`:

```
time.get(ChronoField.MILLI_OF_SECOND)
int qoy = date.get(IsoFields.QUARTER_OF_YEAR);
```

Two other classes define additional fields that may be useful: `WeekFields`[56] and `JulianFields`.[57]

ChronoUnit

The `ChronoUnit`[58] enum implements the `TemporalUnit` interface and provides a set of standard units based on date and time, from milliseconds to millennia. Note that not all `ChronoUnit` objects are supported by all classes. For example,

---

52. 8/docs/api/java/time/temporal/TemporalAmount.html
53. 8/docs/api/java/time/temporal/ChronoField.html
54. 8/docs/api/java/time/temporal/TemporalAccessor.html#isSupported
     -java.time.temporal.TemporalField-
55. 8/docs/api/java/time/temporal/IsoFields.html
56. 8/docs/api/java/time/temporal/WeekFields.html
57. 8/docs/api/java/time/temporal/JulianFields.html
58. 8/docs/api/java/time/temporal/ChronoUnit.html

the `Instant` class does not support `ChronoUnit.MONTHS` or `ChronoUnit.YEARS`. Classes in the Date-Time API contain the method `isSupported(TemporalUnit)`, which can be used to verify whether an instance of a class supports a particular time unit. The following call to `isSupported` returns `false`, confirming that the `Instant` class does not support `ChronoUnit.MONTHS`:

```
Instant instant = Instant.now();
boolean isSupported = instant.isSupported(ChronoUnit.MONTHS);
```

Temporal Adjuster

The `TemporalAdjuster` interface, in the `java.time.temporal` package, provides methods that take a `Temporal` value and return an adjusted value.[59] The adjusters can be used with any of the temporal-based types. If an adjuster is used with a `ZonedDateTime`, then a new date is computed that preserves the original time and time zone values.

Predefined Adjusters

The `TemporalAdjusters` class (note the plural) provides a set of predefined adjusters for finding the first or last day of the month, the first or last day of the year, the last Wednesday of the month, or the first Tuesday after a specific date, to name a few examples.[60] The predefined adjusters are defined as static methods and are designed to be used with the static import statement.

The following example uses several `TemporalAdjusters` methods, in conjunction with the `with` method defined in the temporal-based classes, to compute new dates based on the original date of 15 October 2000:

```
LocalDate date = LocalDate.of(2000, Month.OCTOBER, 15);
DayOfWeek dotw = date.getDayOfWeek();
System.out.printf("%s is on a %s%n", date, dotw);

System.out.printf("first day of Month: %s%n",
            date.with(TemporalAdjusters.firstDayOfMonth()));
System.out.printf("first Monday of Month: %s%n",
            date.with(TemporalAdjusters.firstInMonth(DayOfWeek.MONDAY)));
System.out.printf("last day of Month: %s%n",
            date.with(TemporalAdjusters.lastDayOfMonth()));
System.out.printf("first day of next Month: %s%n",
            date.with(TemporalAdjusters.firstDayOfNextMonth()));
System.out.printf("first day of next Year: %s%n",
            date.with(TemporalAdjusters.firstDayOfNextYear()));
System.out.printf("first day of Year: %s%n",
```

59.   8/docs/api/java/time/temporal/TemporalAdjuster.html

60.   8/docs/api/java/time/temporal/TemporalAdjusters.html

```
                     date.with(TemporalAdjusters.firstDayOfYear()));
```

This produces the following output:

```
2000-10-15 is on a SUNDAY
first day of Month: 2000-10-01
first Monday of Month: 2000 10 02
last day of Month: 2000-10-31
first day of next Month: 2000-11-01
first day of next Year: 2001-01-01
first day of Year: 2000-01-01
```

Custom Adjusters

You can also create your own custom adjuster. To do this, you create a class that implements the `TemporalAdjuster` interface with an `adjustInto(Temporal)`[61] method. The `PaydayAdjuster` class from the `NextPayday` example is a custom adjuster. The `PaydayAdjuster` evaluates the passed-in date and returns the next payday, assuming that payday occurs twice a month: on the fifteenth and again on the last day of the month. If the computed date occurs on a weekend, then the previous Friday is used. The current calendar year is assumed:

```
/**
 * The adjustInto method accepts a Temporal instance
 * and returns an adjusted LocalDate. If the passed in
 * parameter is not a LocalDate, then a DateTimeException is thrown.
 */
public Temporal adjustInto(Temporal input) {
    LocalDate date = LocalDate.from(input);
    int day;
    if (date.getDayOfMonth() < 15) {
        day = 15;
    } else {
        day = date.with(TemporalAdjusters.lastDayOfMonth()).getDayOfMonth();
    }
    date = date.withDayOfMonth(day);
    if (date.getDayOfWeek() == DayOfWeek.SATURDAY ||
        date.getDayOfWeek() == DayOfWeek.SUNDAY) {
        date = date.with(TemporalAdjusters.previous(DayOfWeek.FRIDAY));
    }

    return input.with(date);
}
```

The adjuster is invoked in the same manner as a predefined adjuster, using the `with` method. The following line of code is from the `NextPayday` example:

21

61. 8/docs/api/java/time/temporal/TemporalAdjuster.html#adjustInto-java
     .time.temporal.Temporal-

```
LocalDate nextPayday = date.with(new PaydayAdjuster());
```

In 2013, both June 15 and June 30 occur on the weekend. Running the `NextPay-day` example with the respective dates of June 3 and June 18 (in 2013) gives the following results:

```
Given the date: 2013 Jun 3
the next payday: 2013 Jun 14

Given the date: 2013 Jun 18
the next payday: 2013 Jun 28
```

Temporal Query

A `TemporalQuery` can be used to retrieve information from a temporal-based object.[62]

Predefined Queries

The `TemporalQueries` class (note the plural) provides several predefined queries, including methods that are useful when the application cannot identify the type of temporal-based object.[63] As with the adjusters, the predefined queries are defined as static methods and are designed to be used with the static import statement.

The `precision`[64] query, for example, returns the smallest `ChronoUnit` that can be returned by a particular temporal-based object. The following example uses the `precision` query on several types of temporal-based objects:

```
TemporalQueries query = TemporalQueries.precision();
System.out.printf("LocalDate precision is %s%n",
                  LocalDate.now().query(query));
System.out.printf("LocalDateTime precision is %s%n",
                  LocalDateTime.now().query(query));
System.out.printf("Year precision is %s%n",
                  Year.now().query(query));
System.out.printf("YearMonth precision is %s%n",
                  YearMonth.now().query(query));
System.out.printf("Instant precision is %s%n",
                  Instant.now().query(query));
```

The output looks like the following:

```
LocalDate precision is Days
LocalDateTime precision is Nanos
```

21

---

62. 8/docs/api/java/time/temporal/TemporalQuery.html

63. 8/docs/api/java/time/temporal/TemporalQueries.html

64. 8/docs/api/java/time/temporal/TemporalQueries.html#precision--

```
Year precision is Years
YearMonth precision is Months
Instant precision is Nanos
```

Custom Queries

You can also create your own custom queries. One way to do this is to create a class that implements the `TemporalQuery` interface with the `queryFrom(TemporalAccessor)` method.[65] The `CheckDate` example implements two custom queries. The first custom query can be found in the `FamilyVacations` class, which implements the `TemporalQuery` interface.[66] The `queryFrom` method compares the passed-in date against scheduled vacation dates and returns TRUE if it falls within those date ranges:

```java
// Returns true if the passed-in date occurs during one of the
// family vacations. Because the query compares the month and day only,
// the check succeeds even if the Temporal types are not the same.
public Boolean queryFrom(TemporalAccessor date) {
    int month = date.get(ChronoField.MONTH_OF_YEAR);
    int day = date.get(ChronoField.DAY_OF_MONTH);

    // Disneyland over Spring Break
    if ((month == Month.APRIL.getValue()) && ((day >= 3) && (day <= 8)))
        return Boolean.TRUE;

    // Smith family reunion on Lake Saugatuck
    if ((month == Month.AUGUST.getValue()) && ((day >= 8) && (day <= 14)))
        return Boolean.TRUE;

    return Boolean.FALSE;
}
```

The second custom query is implemented in the `FamilyBirthdays` class. This class provides an `isFamilyBirthday` method that compares the passed-in date against several birthdays and returns TRUE if there is a match.

```java
// Returns true if the passed-in date is the same as one of the
// family birthdays. Because the query compares the month and day only,
// the check succeeds even if the Temporal types are not the same.
public static Boolean isFamilyBirthday(TemporalAccessor date) {
    int month = date.get(ChronoField.MONTH_OF_YEAR);
    int day = date.get(ChronoField.DAY_OF_MONTH);

    // Angie's birthday is on April 3.
    if ((month == Month.APRIL.getValue()) && (day == 3))
        return Boolean.TRUE;

    // Sue's birthday is on June 18.
```

21

---

65. `8/docs/api/java/time/temporal/TemporalQuery.html#queryFrom-java`
    `.time.temporal.TemporalAccessor-`

66. `8/docs/api/java/time/temporal/TemporalQuery.html`

```
        if ((month == Month.JUNE.getValue()) && (day == 18))
            return Boolean.TRUE;

        // Joe's birthday is on May 29.
        if ((month == Month.MAY.getValue()) && (day == 29))
            return Boolean.TRUE;

        return Boolean.FALSE;
    }
```

The `FamilyBirthday` class does not implement the `TemporalQuery` interface and can be used as part of a lambda expression. The following code, from the `Check-Date` example, shows how to invoke both custom queries.

```
// Invoking the query without using a lambda expression.
Boolean isFamilyVacation = date.query(new FamilyVacations());

// Invoking the query using a lambda expression.
Boolean isFamilyBirthday = date.query(FamilyBirthdays::isFamilyBirthday);

if (isFamilyVacation.booleanValue() || isFamilyBirthday.booleanValue())
    System.out.printf("%s is an important date!%n", date);
else
    System.out.printf("%s is not an important date.%n", date);
```

Period and Duration

When you write code to specify an amount of time, use the class or method that best meets your needs: the `Duration`[67] class, `Period`[68] class, or the `ChronoUnit`. `between`[69] method. A `Duration` measures an amount of time using time-based values (seconds, nanoseconds). A `Period` uses date-based values (years, months, days).

> **Note**
>
> A `Duration` of one day is *exactly* twenty-four hours. A `Period` of one day, when added to a `ZonedDateTime`, may vary according to the time zone (e.g., if it occurs on the first or last day of daylight saving time).

21

67. 8/docs/api/java/time/Duration.html
68. 8/docs/api/java/time/Period.html
69. 8/docs/api/java/time/temporal/ChronoUnit.html#between-java.time
     .temporal.Temporal-java.time.temporal.Temporal-

Duration

A Duration is most suitable in situations that measure machine-based time, such as code that uses an Instant object. A Duration object is measured in seconds or nanoseconds and does not use date-based constructs such as years, months, and days, though the class provides methods that convert to days, hours, and minutes. A Duration can have a negative value if it is created with an end point that occurs before the start point.

The following code calculates, in nanoseconds, the duration between two instants:

```
Instant t1, t2;
...
long ns = Duration.between(t1, t2).toNanos();
```

The following code adds ten seconds to an Instant:

```
Instant start;
...
Duration gap = Duration.ofSeconds(10);
Instant later = start.plus(gap);
```

A Duration is not connected to the timeline, in that it does not track time zones or daylight saving time. Adding a Duration equivalent to one day to a Zoned-DateTime results in exactly twenty-four hours being added, regardless of daylight saving time or other time differences that might result.

ChronoUnit

The ChronoUnit enum, discussed in "The Temporal Package" section, defines the units used to measure time. The ChronoUnit.between method is useful when you want to measure an amount of time in a single unit of time only, such as days or seconds. The between method works with all temporal-based objects, but it returns the amount in a single unit only. The following code calculates the gap, in milliseconds, between two time stamps:

```
import java.time.Instant;
import java.time.temporal.Temporal;
import java.time.temporal.ChronoUnit;

Instant previous, current, gap;
...
current = Instant.now();
if (previous != null) {
    gap = ChronoUnit.MILLIS.between(previous,current);
}
...
```

21

Period

To define an amount of time with date-based values (years, months, days), use the Period[70] class. The Period class provides various get methods, such as getMonths,[71] getDays,[72] and getYears,[73] so that you can extract the amount of time from the period.

The total period of time is represented by all three units together: months, days, and years. To present the amount of time measured in a single unit of time, such as days, you can use the ChronoUnit.between method.

The following code reports how old you are, assuming that you were born on January 1, 1960. The Period class is used to determine the time in years, months, and days. The same period, in total days, is determined by using the ChronoUnit. between method and is displayed in parentheses:

```
LocalDate today = LocalDate.now();
LocalDate birthday = LocalDate.of(1960, Month.JANUARY, 1);

Period p = Period.between(birthday, today);
long p2 = ChronoUnit.DAYS.between(birthday, today);
System.out.println("You are " + p.getYears() + " years, " + p.getMonths() +
                " months, and " + p.getDays() +
                " days old. (" + p2 + " days total)");
```

The code produces output similar to the following:

```
You are 53 years, 4 months, and 29 days old. (19508 days total)
```

To calculate how long it is until your next birthday, you could use the following code from the Birthday example. The Period class is used to determine the value in months and days. The ChronoUnit.between method returns the value in total days and is displayed in parentheses:

```
LocalDate birthday = LocalDate.of(1960, Month.JANUARY, 1);

LocalDate nextBDay = birthday.withYear(today.getYear());

//If your birthday has occurred this year already, add 1 to the year.
if (nextBDay.isBefore(today) || nextBDay.isEqual(today)) {
    nextBDay = nextBDay.plusYears(1);
}
```

21

---

70. 8/docs/api/java/time/Period.html

71. 8/docs/api/java/time/Period.html#getMonths--

72. 8/docs/api/java/time/Period.html#getDays--

73. 8/docs/api/java/time/Period.html#getYears--

```
Period p = Period.between(today, nextBDay);
long p2 = ChronoUnit.DAYS.between(today, nextBDay);
System.out.println("There are " + p.getMonths() + " months, and " +
                    p.getDays() + " days until your next birthday. (" +
                    p2 + " total)");
```

The code produces output similar to the following:

```
There are 7 months, and 2 days until your next birthday. (216 total)
```

These calculations do not account for time zone differences. If you were, for example, born in Australia but currently live in Bangalore, this slightly affects the calculation of your exact age. In this situation, use a `Period` in conjunction with the `ZonedDateTime` class. When you add a `Period` to a `ZonedDateTime`, the time differences are observed.

Clock

Most temporal-based objects provide a no-argument `now()` method that provides the current date and time using the system clock and the default time zone. These temporal-based objects also provide a one-argument `now(Clock)` method that allows you to pass in an alternative `Clock`.[74]

The `Clock` class provides access to the current instant, date, and time using a time zone. Because the `Clock` class is abstract, you cannot create an instance of it. Instead, use one of the the `Clock` class's factory methods, which include the following:

- `Clock.offset(Clock, Duration)` returns a clock that is offset by the specified `Duration`.[75]

- `Clock.systemUTC()` returns a clock representing the Greenwich/UTC time zone.[76]

- `Clock.fixed(Instant, ZoneId)` always returns the same `Instant`. For this clock, time stands still.[77]

---

74. `8/docs/api/java/time/Clock.html`
75. `8/docs/api/java/time/Clock.html#offset-java.time.Clock-java.time.Duration-`
76. `8/docs/api/java/time/Clock.html#systemUTC--`
77. `8/docs/api/java/time/Clock.html#fixed-java.time.Instant-java.time.ZoneId-`

21

You don't have to use the `Clock` class if you want to obtain just the current date and time. However, if you are creating a globalized application or want to test your code with other time zones, use the `Clock` class to ensure that the date and time are created with the desired time zone. A fixed clock (a `Clock` obtained from the method `Clock.fixed`) enables you to test your code with a specific date and time.

Non-ISO Date Conversion

This chapter does not discuss the `java.time.chrono`[78] package in any detail. However, it might be useful to know that this package provides several predefined chronologies that are not ISO-based, such as Japanese, Hijrah, Minguo, and Thai Buddhist. You can also use this package to create your own chronology. This section shows you how to convert between an ISO-based date and a date in one of the other predefined chronologies.

Converting to a Non-ISO-Based Date

You can convert an ISO-based date to a date in another chronology by using the `from(TemporalAccessor)` method, such as `JapaneseDate.from(TemporalAccessor)`.[79] This method throws a `DateTimeException` if it is unable to convert the date to a valid instance. The following code converts a `LocalDateTime` instance to several predefined non-ISO calendar dates:

```
LocalDateTime date = LocalDateTime.of(2013, Month.JULY, 20, 19, 30);
JapaneseDate jdate     = JapaneseDate.from(date);
HijrahDate hdate       = HijrahDate.from(date);
MinguoDate mdate       = MinguoDate.from(date);
ThaiBuddhistDate tdate = ThaiBuddhistDate.from(date);
```

The `StringConverter` example converts from a `LocalDate` to a `ChronoLocalDate` to a `String` and back. The `toString` method takes an instance of `LocalDate` and a `Chronology` and returns the converted string by using the provided `Chronology`. The `DateTimeFormatterBuilder` is used to build a string that can be used for printing the date:

```
/**
 * Converts a LocalDate (ISO) value to a ChronoLocalDate date
 * using the provided Chronology, and then formats the
 * ChronoLocalDate to a String using a DateTimeFormatter with a
 * SHORT pattern based on the Chronology and the current Locale.
```

---

78. 8/docs/api/java/time/chrono/package-summary.html

79. 8/docs/api/java/time/chrono/JapaneseDate.html#from-java.time.temporal
     .TemporalAccessor-

```
 *
 * @param localDate - the ISO date to convert and format.
 * @param chrono - an optional Chronology. If null, then IsoChronology is used.
 */
public static String toString(LocalDate localDate, Chronology chrono) {
    if (localDate != null) {
        Locale locale = Locale.getDefault(Locale.Category.FORMAT);
        ChronoLocalDate cDate;
        if (chrono == null) {
            chrono = IsoChronology.INSTANCE;
        }
        try {
            cDate = chrono.date(localDate);
        } catch (DateTimeException ex) {
            System.err.println(ex);
            chrono = IsoChronology.INSTANCE;
            cDate = localDate;
        }
        DateTimeFormatter dateFormatter =
            DateTimeFormatter.ofLocalizedDate(FormatStyle.SHORT)
                            .withLocale(locale)
                            .withChronology(chrono)
                            .withDecimalStyle(DecimalStyle.of(locale));
        String pattern = "M/d/yyyy GGGGG";
        return dateFormatter.format(cDate);
    } else {
        return "";
    }
}
```

The method is invoked with the following date for the predefined chronologies:

```
LocalDate date = LocalDate.of(1996, Month.OCTOBER, 29);
System.out.printf("%s%n",
    StringConverter.toString(date, JapaneseChronology.INSTANCE));
System.out.printf("%s%n",
    StringConverter.toString(date, MinguoChronology.INSTANCE));
System.out.printf("%s%n",
    StringConverter.toString(date, ThaiBuddhistChronology.INSTANCE));
System.out.printf("%s%n",
    StringConverter.toString(date, HijrahChronology.INSTANCE));
```

The output looks like this:

```
10/29/0008 H
10/29/0085 1
10/29/2539 B.E.
6/16/1417 1
```

21

Converting to an ISO-Based Date

You can convert from a non-ISO date to a `LocalDate` instance using the static `LocalDate.from`[80] method, as shown in the following example:

```
LocalDate date = LocalDate.from(JapaneseDate.now());
```

Other temporal-based classes also provide this method, which throws a `DateTime-Exception` if the date cannot be converted.

The `fromString` method, from the `StringConverter` example, parses a `String` containing a non-ISO date and returns a `LocalDate` instance.

```
/**
 * Parses a String to a ChronoLocalDate using a DateTimeFormatter
 * with a short pattern based on the current Locale and the
 * provided Chronology, then converts this to a LocalDate (ISO)
 * value.
 *
 * @param text - the input date text in the SHORT format expected
 *               for the Chronology and the current Locale.
 *
 * @param chrono - an optional Chronology. If null, then IsoChronology
 *                 is used.
 */
public static LocalDate fromString(String text, Chronology chrono) {
    if (text != null && !text.isEmpty()) {
        Locale locale = Locale.getDefault(Locale.Category.FORMAT);
        if (chrono == null) {
            chrono = IsoChronology.INSTANCE;
        }
        String pattern = "M/d/yyyy GGGGG";
        DateTimeFormatter df = new DateTimeFormatterBuilder().parseLenient()
                            .appendPattern(pattern)
                            .toFormatter()
                            .withChronology(chrono)
                            .withDecimalStyle(DecimalStyle.of(locale));
        TemporalAccessor temporal = df.parse(text);
        ChronoLocalDate cDate = chrono.date(temporal);
        return LocalDate.from(cDate);
    }
    return null;
}
```

The method is invoked with the following strings:

```
System.out.printf("%s%n", StringConverter.fromString("10/29/0008 H",
    JapaneseChronology.INSTANCE));
System.out.printf("%s%n", StringConverter.fromString("10/29/0085 1",
    MinguoChronology.INSTANCE));
System.out.printf("%s%n", StringConverter.fromString("10/29/2539 B.E.",
```

---

80. 8/docs/api/java/time/LocalDate.html#from-java.time.temporal
     .TemporalAccessor-

```
    ThaiBuddhistChronology.INSTANCE));
  System.out.printf("%s%n", StringConverter.fromString("6/16/1417 1",
    HijrahChronology.INSTANCE));
```

The printed strings should all convert back to October 29, 1996:

```
1996-10-29
1996-10-29
1996-10-29
1996-10-29
```

Legacy Date-Time Code

Prior to the Java SE 8 release, the Java date and time mechanism was provided by the `java.util.Date`,[81] `java.util.Calendar`,[82] and `java.util.TimeZone`[83] classes, as well as their subclasses, such as `java.util.GregorianCalendar`.[84] These classes had several drawbacks, including the following:

- The `Calendar` class was not type safe.
- Because the classes were mutable, they could not be used in multithreaded applications.
- Bugs in application code were common due to the unusual numbering of months and the lack of type safety.

Interoperability with Legacy Code

Perhaps you have legacy code that uses the `java.util` date and time classes and you would like to take advantage of the `java.time` functionality with minimal changes to your code.

Added to the JDK 8 release are several methods that allow conversion between `java.util` and `java.time` objects:

- `Calendar.toInstant()` converts the `Calendar` object to an `Instant`.[85]
- `GregorianCalendar.toZonedDateTime()` converts a `GregorianCalendar` instance to a `ZonedDateTime`.[86]

---

81. 8/docs/api/java/util/Date.html
82. 8/docs/api/java/util/Calendar.html
83. 8/docs/api/java/util/TimeZone.html
84. 8/docs/api/java/util/GregorianCalendar.html
85. 8/docs/api/java/util/Calendar.html#toInstant--
86. 8/docs/api/java/util/GregorianCalendar.html#toZonedDateTime--

21

- `GregorianCalendar.from(ZonedDateTime)` creates a `GregorianCalendar` object using the default locale from a `ZonedDateTime` instance.[87]
- `Date.from(Instant)` creates a `Date` object from an `Instant`.[88]
- `Date.toInstant()` converts a `Date` object to an `Instant`.[89]
- `TimeZone.toZoneId()` converts a `TimeZone` object to a `ZoneId`.[90]

The following example converts a `Calendar` instance to a `ZonedDateTime` instance. Note that a time zone must be supplied to convert from an `Instant` to a `ZonedDateTime`:

```
Calendar now = Calendar.getInstance();
ZonedDateTime zdt = ZonedDateTime.ofInstant(now.toInstant(),
ZoneId.systemDefault());
```

The following example shows conversion between a `Date` and an `Instant`:

```
Instant inst = date.toInstant();

Date newDate = Date.from(inst);
```

The following example converts from a `GregorianCalendar` to a `ZonedDate-Time` and then from a `ZonedDateTime` to a `GregorianCalendar`. Other temporal-based classes are created using the `ZonedDateTime` instance:

```
GregorianCalendar cal = ...;

TimeZone tz = cal.getTimeZone();
int tzoffset = cal.get(Calendar.ZONE_OFFSET);

ZonedDateTime zdt = cal.toZonedDateTime();

GregorianCalendar newCal = GregorianCalendar.from(zdt);

LocalDateTime ldt = zdt.toLocalDateTime();
LocalDate date = zdt.toLocalDate();
LocalTime time = zdt.toLocalTime();
```

Mapping java.util Date and Time Functionality to java.time

Because the Java implementation of date and time has been completely redesigned in the Java SE 8 release, you cannot swap one method for another method. If you

21

---

87. 8/docs/api/java/util/GregorianCalendar.html#from-java.time.ZonedDateTime-

88. 8/docs/api/java/util/Date.html#from-java.time.Instant-

89. 8/docs/api/java/util/Date.html#toInstant--

90. 8/docs/api/java/util/TimeZone.html#toZoneId--

want to use the rich functionality offered by the `java.time` package, your easiest solution is to use the `toInstant` or `toZonedDateTime` methods listed in the previous section. However, if you do not want to use that approach or it is not sufficient for your needs, then you must rewrite your date-time code.

Table 21.2 is a good place to begin evaluating which `java.time` classes meet your needs. There is no one-to-one mapping correspondence between the two APIs, but Table 21.3 gives you a general idea of which functionality in the `java.util` date and time classes maps to the `java.time` APIs.

Date and Time Formatting

Although the `java.time.format.DateTimeFormatter` provides a powerful mechanism for formatting date and time values, you can also use the `java.time` temporal-based classes directly with `java.util.Formatter` and `String.format`, using the same pattern-based formatting that you use with the `java.util` date and time classes.

Summary

The `java.time` package contains many classes that your programs can use to represent time and date. This is a very rich API. The key entry points for ISO-based dates are as follows:

- The `Instant` class provides a machine view of the timeline.
- The `LocalDate`, `LocalTime`, and `LocalDateTime` classes provide a human view of date and time without any reference to time zone.
- The `ZoneId`, `ZoneRules`, and `ZoneOffset` classes describe time zones, time zone offsets, and time zone rules.
- The `ZonedDateTime` class represents date and time with a time zone. The `OffsetDateTime` and `OffsetTime` classes represent date and time or time, respectively. These classes take a time zone offset into account.
- The `Duration` class measures an amount of time in seconds and nanoseconds.
- The `Period` class measures an amount of time using years, months, and days.

Other non-ISO calendar systems can be represented using the `java.time.chrono` package. This package is beyond the scope of this book, though the "Non-ISO Date Conversion" section provides information about converting an ISO-based date to another calendar system.

21

Table 21.3 Mapping between java.util and java.time Classes

java.util functionality	java.time functionality	Comments
java.util.Date	java.time.Instant	The Instant and Date classes are similar. Each class does the following: 1. Represents an instantaneous point of time on the timeline (UTC) 2. Holds a time independent of a time zone 3. Is represented as epoch-seconds (since 1970-01-01T00:00:00Z) plus nanoseconds The Date.from(Instant) and Date.toInstant() methods allow conversion between these classes.

java.util.GregorianCalendar	java.time.ZonedDateTime	The ZonedDateTime class is the replacement for GregorianCalendar. It provides the following similar functionality.
		Human time representation is as follows:
		  LocalDate: year, month, day
		  LocalTime: hours, minutes, seconds, nanoseconds
		  ZoneId: time zone
		  ZoneOffset: current offset from GMT
		The GregorianCalendar.from(ZonedDateTime) and GregorianCalendar.to(ZonedDateTime) methods facilitate conversions between these classes.

java.util.TimeZone	java.time.ZoneId or java.time.ZoneOffset	The ZoneId class specifies a time zone identifier and has access to the rules used for each time zone. The ZoneOffset class specifies only an offset from Greenwich/UTC. For more information, see the "Time Zone and Offset Classes" section.
GregorianCalendar with the date set to 1970-01-01	java.time.LocalTime	Code that sets the date to 1970-01-01 in a GregorianCalendar instance in order to use the time components can be replaced with an instance of LocalTime.
GregorianCalendar with time set to 00:00	java.time.LocalDate	Code that sets the time to 00:00 in a GregorianCalendar instance in order to use the date components can be replaced with an instance of LocalDate. (This GregorianCalendar approach was flawed, as midnight does not occur in some countries once a year due to the transition to daylight saving time.)

21

The Date-Time API was developed as part of the Java community process under the designation of JSR 310. For more information, see JSR 310: Date and Time API.[91]

Questions and Exercises: Date-Time

Questions

1. Which class would you use to store your birthday in years, months, days, seconds, and nanoseconds?
2. Given a random date, how would you find the date of the previous Thursday?
3. What is the difference between a `ZoneId` and a `ZoneOffset`?
4. How would you convert an `Instant` to a `ZonedDateTime`? How would you convert a `ZonedDateTime` to an `Instant`?

Exercises

1. Write an example that, for a given year, reports the length of each month within that year.
2. Write an example that, for a given month of the current year, lists all the Mondays in that month.
3. Write an example that tests whether a given date occurs on Friday the thirteenth.

Answers

You can find answers to these questions and exercises at `http://docs.oracle .com/javase/tutorial/datetime/iso/QandE/answers.html`.

21

---

91. `http://jcp.org/en/jsr/detail?id=310`

22

Introduction to JavaFX

JavaFX is a set of graphics and media packages that enables developers to design, create, test, debug, and deploy rich client applications that operate consistently across diverse platforms.

With JavaFX, you can build many types of applications. Typically, they are network-aware applications that are deployed across multiple platforms and display information in a high-performance modern user interface that features audio, video, graphics, and animation.

Because the JavaFX library is written as a Java Application Programming Interface (API), JavaFX application code can reference APIs from any Java library. For example, JavaFX applications can use Java API libraries to access native system capabilities and connect to server-based middleware applications.

You can customize the look and feel of JavaFX applications with cascading style sheets (CSSs) that separate appearance and style from implementation so that you can concentrate on coding. Graphic designers can easily customize the appearance and style of your application through the CSS. If you have a web design background or if you would like to separate the user interface and the back-end logic, then you can develop the presentation aspects of the user interface in the FXML scripting language and use Java code for the application logic. If you prefer to design user interfaces without writing code, then use JavaFX Scene Builder. As you design the user interface, Scene Builder creates FXML markup that can be ported to an integrated development environment (IDE) so that developers can add the business logic.

The JavaFX APIs are available as a fully integrated feature of the Java SE Runtime Environment (JRE) and the Java Development Kit (JDK). Because the JDK is available for all major desktop platforms (Windows, OS X, and Linux), JavaFX applications compiled to JDK 8 and later also run on all the major desktop plat-forms. Support for ARM platforms has also been made available with JavaFX 8. JDK for ARM includes the base, graphics, and control components of JavaFX.

The cross-platform compatibility enables a consistent runtime experience for JavaFX applications developers and users. Oracle ensures synchronized releases and updates on all platforms and offers an extensive support program for compa-nies that run mission-critical applications.

If you are developer of Swing applications, you can enrich Swing applications by adding JavaFX functionality and embed Swing components in JavaFX applications.

See the Java SE Client Technologies documentation for more information about JavaFX, which includes tutorials and reference documentation.[1]

22

---

1.   8/javase-clienttechnologies.htm

Appendix

Preparation for Java Programming Language Certification

Chapter Contents

Programmer Level I Exam   795
Programmer Level II Exam   801
Java SE 8 Upgrade Exam   801

Oracle provides certification examinations and certificates for Java SE 8 programmers. This book can be a valuable resource to help you prepare for the certification exams.

For more information on Oracle Java Certification and Oracle Java Training, including information on classes, exams, and prerequisites, go to oracle.com and click the **Training** tab. This appendix describes these exams; it lists the sections of this book and external resources that contain pertinent and valuable information to use when preparing for these exams.

Programmer Level I Exam

This section discusses topics covered in the Java SE 8 Programmer I exam. This exam is associated with the "Oracle Certified Associate, Java SE 8 Programmer" certificate and includes nine topics.

Section 1: Java Basics

Item 1: Define the scope of variables.

- Chapter 3: Variables

Item 2: Define the structure of a Java class.

- Chapter 1: A Closer Look at the "Hello World!" Application
- Chapter 4: Classes

Item 3: Create executable Java applications with a main method; run a Java program from the command line, including working with console output.

- Chapter 1: A Closer Look at the "Hello World!" Application
- Chapter 1: "Hello World!" for Microsoft Windows
- Chapter 1: "Hello World!" for the NetBeans IDE
- Chapter 1: "Hello World!" for Solaris and Linux

Item 4: Import other Java packages to make them accessible in your code.

- Chapter 8: Creating and Using Packages
- Chapter 8: Using Package Members

Item 5: Compare the features and components of Java such as platform independence, object orientation, and encapsulation.

- Chapter 1: The Java Technology Phenomenon
- Chapter 2: What Is an Object?

Section 2: Working with Java Data Types

Item 1: Declare and initialize variables (including casting of primitive data types).

- Chapter 3: Variables
- Chapter 4: Initializing Fields

Item 2: Differentiate between object reference variables and primitive variables.

- Chapter 3: Primitive Data Types
- Chapter 9: The Numbers Classes

Item 3: Know how to read or write to object fields.

- Chapter 4: Declaring Member Variables
- Chapter 4: Using Objects

A

- Chapter 6: Inheritance

Item 4: Explain an object's life cycle (creation, "dereference by reassignment," and garbage collection).

- Chapter 4: Creating Objects
- Chapter 4: Objects
- Chapter 4: Using Objects

Item 5: Use call methods on user-created wrapper class objects.

- Chapter 4: Using Objects

Section 3: Using Operators and Decision Constructs

Item 1: Use Java operators, including parentheses to override operator precedence.

- Chapter 3: Assignment, Arithmetic, and Unary Operators
- Chapter 3: Bitwise and Bit Shift Operators
- Chapter 3: Equality, Relational, and Conditional Operators
- Chapter 3: Expressions, Statements, and Blocks
- Chapter 3: Operators

Item 2: Test equality between strings and other objects using the == operator and the `equals` method.

- Chapter 6: Object as a Superclass

Item 3: Create if, if/else, and ternary constructs.

- Chapter 3: The if-then and if-then-else Statements

Item 4: Use a `switch` statement.

- Chapter 3: The switch Statement

Section 4: Creating and Using Arrays

Item 1: Declare, instantiate, initialize, and use a one-dimensional array.

- Chapter 3: Arrays

A

Item 2: Declare, instantiate, initialize, and use a multidimensional array.

- Chapter 3: Arrays

Section 5: Using Loop Constructs

Item 1: Create and use `while` loops.

- Chapter 3: The while and do-while Statements

Item 2: Create and use `for` loops including the enhanced `for` loop.

- Chapter 3: The for Statement

Item 3: Create and use `do-while` loops.

- Chapter 3: The while and do-while Statements

Item 4: Compare loop constructs.

- Chapter 3: Summary of Control Flow Statements

Item 5: Use `break` and `continue` statements.

- Chapter 3: Branching Statements

Section 6: Working with Methods and Encapsulation

Item 1: Create methods with arguments and return values, including overloaded methods.

- Chapter 4: Returning a Value from a Method

Item 2: Apply the `static` keyword to methods and fields.

- Chapter 3: Variables
- Chapter 4: Understanding Class Members

Item 3: Create and overload constructors, including impact on default constructors.

- Chapter 4: Defining Methods

Item 4: Apply access modifiers.

- Chapter 4: Providing Constructors for Your Classes

A

Item 5: Apply encapsulation principles to a class.

- Chapter 4: Controlling Access to Members of a Class

Item 6: Determine the effect of object references and primitive values when they are passed into methods that change their values.

- Chapter 4: Inner Class Example
- Chapter 4: Nested Classes
- Chapter 6: Inheritance

Section 7: Working with Inheritance

Item 1: Describe the hierarchy of implementing inheritance.

- Chapter 6: Inheritance
- Chapter 6: Overriding and Hiding Methods

Item 2: Develop code that demonstrates the use of polymorphism, including overriding and object type versus reference type.

- Chapter 6: Polymorphism

Item 3: Determine when casting is necessary.

- Chapter 6: Inheritance

Item 4: Use super and this to access objects and constructors.

- Chapter 4: Using the this Keyword
- Chapter 6: Using the Keyword super

Item 5: Use abstract classes and interfaces.

- Chapter 6: Abstract Methods and Classes
- Chapter 6: Defining an Interface
- Chapter 6: Implementing an Interface

Section 8: Handling Exceptions

Item 1: Differentiate among checked exceptions, unchecked exceptions, and errors.

- Chapter 10: The Catch or Specify Requirement

A

Item 2: Create a `try-catch` block and determine how exceptions alter normal program flow.

- Chapter 10: Catching and Handling Exceptions
- Chapter 10: The catch Blocks
- Chapter 10: The try Block

Item 3: Describe the advantages of exception handling.

- Chapter 10: Advantages of Exceptions
- Chapter 10: What Is an Exception?

Item 4: Create and invoke a method that throws an exception.

- Chapter 11: Catching Exceptions

Item 5: Recognize common exception classes (such as `NullPointerException`, `ArithmeticException`, `ArrayIndexOutOfBoundsException`, and `ClassCastException`).

Section 9: Working with Selected Classes from the Java API

Item 1: Manipulate data using the `StringBuilder` class and its methods.

- Chapter 9: The StringBuilder Class

Item 2: Create and manipulate `String` objects.

- Chapter 9: Strings

Item 3: Create and manipulate calendar data using these classes from the `java.time` package: `LocalDateTime`, `LocalDate`, `LocalTime`, `DateTimeFormatter`, and `Period`.

- Chapter 21: Date-Time Overview
- Chapter 21: Date Classes
- Chapter 21: Date and Time Classes
- Chapter 21: Instant Class
- Chapter 21: Period and Duration

Item 4: Declare and use an `ArrayList` of a given type.

- Chapter 12: The List Interface

A

Item 5: Write a simple lambda expression that consumes a lambda predicate expression.

- Chapter 4: Lambda Expressions

Programmer Level II Exam

The Java SE 8 Programmer II exam is associated with the "Oracle Certified Professional, Java SE 8 Programmer" certificate. At the time of publication of this book, the details of this exam are not available. See `http://education.oracle.com` for more information about this exam.

Java SE 8 Upgrade Exam

This section discusses topics covered in the Update to Java SE 8 Programmer exam. This exam is associated with the "Oracle Certified Professional, Java SE 8 Programmer" certificate and includes nine topics.

Section 1: Lambda Expressions

Item 1: Describe Java inner classes and develop the code that uses Java inner classes (such as nested classes, static classes, local classes, and anonymous classes).

- Chapter 4: Anonymous Classes
- Chapter 4: Local Classes
- Chapter 4: Nested Classes

Item 2: Define and write functional interfaces.

- Chapter 4: Lambda Expressions

Item 3: Describe a lambda expression, including type inference and target typing; refactor code that uses an anonymous inner class to use a lambda expression.

- Chapter 4: Lambda Expressions

Section 2: Using Built-In Lambda Types

You can find most information about these topics in Chapter 4, "Lambda Expressions" and Chapter 4, "Method References."

A

Item 1: Describe the built-in interfaces included in Java SE 8 in the `java.util. function` package.[1]

Item 2: Develop code that uses the `Function` interface.[2]

Item 3: Develop code that uses the `Consumer` interface.[3]

Item 4: Develop code that uses the `Supplier` interface.[4]

Item 5: Develop code that uses the `UnaryOperator` interface.[5]

Item 6: Develop code that uses the `Predicate` interface.[6]

Item 7: Develop code that uses primitive and binary variations of base interfaces of the `java.util.function` package.[7]

Item 8: Develop code that uses method references, including refactoring code that uses lambda expressions to use method references.

Section 3: Filtering Collections with Lambdas

Item 1: Develop code that iterates a collection by using the `forEach` method, including method chaining.

- Chapter 12: Aggregate Operations

Item 2: Describe the `Stream` interface and pipelines.

- Chapter 12: Aggregate Operations

Item 3: Filter a collection using lambda expressions.

- Chapter 12: Aggregate Operations

Item 4: Identify lambda operations that are lazy.

- Chapter 12: Parallelism

---

1.   8/docs/api/java/util/function/package-summary.html
2.   8/docs/api/java/util/function/Function.html
3.   8/docs/api/java/util/function/Consumer.html
4.   8/docs/api/java/util/function/Supplier.html
5.   8/docs/api/java/util/function/UnaryOperator.html
6.   8/docs/api/java/util/function/Predicate.html
7.   8/docs/api/java/util/function/package-summary.html

A

Section 4: Collection Operations with Lambda

Item 1: Develop code to extract data from an object using the `Map` interface.

- Chapter 12: The Map Interface

Item 2: Search for data using search methods in the `Stream` interfaces, including `findFirst`, `findAny`, `anyMatch`, `allMatch`, and `noneMatch`.[8]
Item 3: Describe the unique characteristics of the `Optional` classes.[9]
Item 4: Perform calculations using the methods `count`, `max`, `min`, `average`, and `sum`.

- Chapter 6: Default Methods
- Chapter 12: Reduction

Item 5: Sort a collection using lambda expressions.

- Chapter 6: Default Methods
- Chapter 12: Parallelism

Item 6: Save results to a collection by using the `collect` method (in the `Stream` classes) and the `Collector`[10] class, including using methods such as `averagingDouble`, `groupingBy`, `joining`, and `partitioningBy`.

- Chapter 12: Reduction

Section 5: Parallel Streams

Item 1: Develop code that uses parallel streams.

- Chapter 12: Parallelism

Item 2: Implement decomposition and reduction in streams.

- Chapter 12: Reduction

---

8.   8/docs/api/java/util/stream/Stream.html
9.   8/docs/api/java/util/Optional.html
10. 8/docs/api/java/util/stream/Collector.html

A

Section 6: Lambda Cookbook

Item 1: Develop code that uses Java SE 8 collection improvements: `Collection.removeIf`,[11]`List.replaceAll`,[12]`Map.computeIfAbsent`[13]and`computeIfPresent`,[14] and `Map.forEach`.[15]

Item 2: Read files using lambda improvements in the `Files` class: `find`, `lines`, and `walk`.[16]

Item 3: Use the `Map.merge` and `flatMap` (in the `Optional` and `Stream` classes) methods on a collection.[17]

Item 4: Describe other stream sources such as `Arrays.stream`[18] and `IntStream.range`.[19]

Section 7: Method Enhancements

Item 1: Add static methods to interfaces.

- Chapter 6: Static Methods

Item 2: Define and use a default method of a interface; describe the inheritance rules for a default method.

- Chapter 6: Default Methods

Section 8: Use Java SE 8 Date/Time API

Item 1: Create and manage date-based and time-based events, including combination of date and time into a single object using the classes `LocalDate`, `LocalTime`, `LocalDateTime`, `Instant`, `Period`, and `Duration`.

---

11. `8/docs/api/java/util/Collection.html#removeIf-java.util.function.Predicate-`

12. `8/docs/api/java/util/List.html#replaceAll-java.util.function.UnaryOperator-`

13. `8/docs/api/java/util/Map.html#computeIfAbsent-K-java.util.function.Function-`

14. `8/docs/api/java/util/Map.html#computeIfPresent-K-java.util.function.BiFunction-`

15. `8/docs/api/java/util/Map.html#forEach-java.util.function.BiConsumer-`

16. `8/docs/api/java/nio/file/Files.html`

17. `8/docs/api/java/util/Map.html#merge-K-V-java.util.function.BiFunction-`

18. `8/docs/api/java/util/Arrays.html#stream-T:A-`

19. `8/docs/api/java/util/stream/IntStream.html#range-int-int-`

A

- Chapter 21: Date-Time Overview
- Chapter 21: Date Classes
- Chapter 21: Date and Time Classes
- Chapter 21: Instant Class
- Chapter 21: Period and Duration

Item 2: Work with dates and times across time zones and manage changes resulting from daylight saving time.

- Time Zone and Offset Classes[20]

Item 3: Define and create time stamps, periods, and durations; apply formatting to local and zoned dates and times.

- Instant Class[21]
- Parsing and Formatting[22]

Section 9: JavaScript on Java with Nashorn

See the *Java Platform, Standard Edition, Nashorn User's Guide* for more information.[23]
Item 1: Develop JavaScript code that creates and uses Java members such as Java objects, methods, JavaBeans, arrays, collections, and interfaces.
Item 2: Develop code that evaluates JavaScript in Java, passes Java objects to JavaScript, invokes JavaScript functions, and calls methods on JavaScript objects.

---

20. `tutorial/datetime/iso/timezones.html`
21. `tutorial/datetime/iso/instant.html`
22. `tutorial/datetime/iso/format.html`
23. `8/docs/technotes/guides/scripting/nashorn/toc.html`

A

Index

Symbols

- (minus sign)
    operator, 59–62, 279
    in regular expressions, 562–64
-- operator, 59, 61, 62
_ (underscore)
    in constant names, 114
    in numeric literals, 50–51
    in package names, 263
    in predefined character classes, 566
    in variable names, 45–46
, (comma)
    in numbers, 50, 276, 278
    in regular expressions, 572
; (semicolon)
    in class paths, 212, 269, 610
    declaring abstract methods, 159
    listing enum types, 159
    in statements, 28, 70, 319
    terminating method signatures, 176, 178
: (colon), in class paths, 269
! operator, 59
!/ separator, 644, 645
!= operator, 59, 63, 66
? (question mark)
    in regular expressions, 236, 372–73
?: operator, 64, 67
/ (forward slash)
    file name separator, 267, 360, 417, 621
    operator, 59–60, 279–80
// in comments, 12, 25
/* in comments, 24
/** in comments, 24

/= operator, 59
. (dot)
    in class paths, 364, 612
    in JAR file commands, 620, 630
    in method invocations, 87, 104–7
    in numbers, 278, 287, 299
    in regular expressions, 561, 568
    in variable names, 105
... (ellipsis), 96–97
^ (caret)
    operator, 59, 66–67
    in regular expressions, 563, 576–77, 579
^= operator, 59
~ operator, 59, 65
' (single quote), escape sequence for, 50, 288
" (double quote)
    escape sequence for, 50, 288
    in literals, 288
() (parentheses)
    in declarations, 92, 106, 317
    in expressions, 69, 797
    in generics, 222
    in interfaces, 133
    in regular expressions, 573–74
[] (square brackets)
    in arrays, 53–54
    in regular expressions, 373, 568, 592
{} (braces)
    in blocks, 71, 72, 117, 127
    in declarations, 89–90, 90–92, 127–28
    in lambda expressions, 147
    in methods, 44
    in regular expressions, 373, 571–72

@ (at)
in annotations, 164, 166
in Javadoc, 167
$ (dollar sign)
in `DecimalFormat` patterns, 278
in variable names, 45
* (asterisk)
in `import` statements, 264
operator, 59
in regular expressions, 372, 407
*/ in comments, 24
*= operator, 59
\ (backslash)
in escape sequences, 50, 288–89, 360, 566
file name separator, 267, 417
in regular expressions, 373, 561
& (ampersand) operator, 59, 66–67
&& operator, 59, 63, 66–67
&= operator, 59
(pound sign)
in `DecimalFormat` patterns, 278
in regular expressions, 561
% (percent sign)
format specifier, 275, 350
operator, 59, 279–80
%= operator, 59
+ (plus sign)
operator, 59, 66–67, 279–80
in regular expressions, 561
++ operator, 59, 61–62, 66–67, 70
+= operator, 59
< operator, 59, 62–63
<< operator, 59, 66–67
<<= operator, 59
<= operator, 59, 62–63, 66–67
<> (angle brackets), 141, 221, 223, 224–27, 232
= operator, 59
-= operator, 59
== operator, 59, 62–63, 66–67
> operator, 59, 62–63, 66–67
>= operator, 59, 62–63, 66–67
>> operator, 59, 66–67
>>= operator, 59
>>> operator, 59, 66–67
>>>= operator, 59
-> (arrow token), 147, 487
| (vertical bar)
in exception handling, 316
operator, 59, 66–67
in regular expressions, 579
|= operator, 59
|| operator, 59, 63, 66–67

A

`abs` method, 280
abstract classes, 212–14
example, 214–15
as an implementation of a service, 603
implementations, 512
methods, 212–13
numeric wrapper classes, 272
versus interfaces, 213–14
Abstract Window Toolkit (AWT), 265
AWT Event Dispatcher, 652, 672
`AbstractMap` class, 214
access control list (ACL), 380
access modifiers
classes and, 90–95, 111
constants and, 178
default, 110–11
fields and, 196
interfaces and, 177–78
levels of, 110–12
methods and, 92, 196, 206
package-private, 111
`private` keyword, 89, 110–11, 196–97
`protected`, 111–12
`public`, 89, 110–11, 196–97
`AccessControlException`, 608
accessor methods, 290, 295, 296, 381, 382, 467
accumulator function, 476–77
`acos` method, 282–83
`add` method, 429, 434, 442, 446
`addAll` method
in the `Collection` interface, 428–29, 430, 432, 452
in the `List` interface, 438, 439
in the `Map` interface, 452
`addFirst` method, 448–49, 494, 498
`addLast` method, 448–49, 494, 498
aggregate operations, xxiv, 145–46, 450, 471–72
bulk operations vs., 430–31
iterators vs., 474
side effects of, 484–87
traversing collections with, 429–30
algorithms (collections), 423–25, 500–509
in the `Collections` class, 508–9
composition, 509
finding extreme values with, 509
generic, 220, 229
listing data, 445
polymorphism, defined, 424
routine data manipulation, 508
searching data, 508–9
shuffling data, 508

sorting data, 505–8
work stealing, 549
ampersand. *See* &
Anagrams example, 456, 507
angle brackets. *See* <>
annotations, 163–74
cardinality of type, 173
container, 172
declaring, 165–67, 172
design considerations, 173
elements and, 164
formatting of, 164–65
legacy code, 173
meta-annotations, 169–70
predefined, 165, 167–70
repeating, 164–65, 171–73
retrieving, 173
type. *See* type annotations
used by the Java language, 167–68
where to use, 165
anonymous classes, 131–36
declaring and accessing, 131–34
examples of, 134–36
GUI applications and, 134
specifying search criteria code in, 140
syntax of, 132–33
when to use, 155
APIs (Application Programming Interfaces), 138
array-based versus collection-based, 502
compatibility of, 513–15
design of, 515–17
interfaces as, 177
JAR-related, 642–648
Java core, 4, 34, 40
logging, 328
Reflection API, 173
append method, 253, 302–4
appendReplacement method, 584–85, 588
appendTail method, 584, 588
Applet class, 665, 667, 672, 680–81, 684
applet tag, 626, 673–76
deploying with, 676
JAR files and, 626
JNLP and, 676, 734–35, 748
manually coding, 676
AppletContext interface, 677, 682–83, 702, 706
applets, 665–709
API of, 677
background color of, 733
common problems, 707–8
communicating with other applets, 701–3
core functionality versus deployment
mechanism, 673–74

debugging, 698
defining and using applet parameters, 678–80
deploying, 673–76, 733–35
developing, 670–73
directories of, 673–75, 678
displaying documents, 682–83
displaying short status strings, 681
draggable, 698–701
event handling and, 689–90
execution environment of, 670
finding and loading data files, 677
GUIs in, 671
JavaScript functions and, 670, 676–77, 701–3
leaving and returning to web pages, 669
life cycle of, 668–69
loading, 669
milestones, 667–68
packing in JAR files, 673–75
parameters in, 668–670
qualified names, 659, 697
quitting the browser, 669
reloading, 669
sandbox, 706–7
security and, 596, 634, 677
server-side applications, 703–5
signed, 31, 654
threads in, 670
appletviewer application, 608
Application-Library-Allowable-Codebase
attribute, 635
Application-Name attribute, 634
applications. *See* rich Internet applications (RIAs)
archive attribute, 708, 733
args variable, 45, 274–75, 601, 646–47
arguments
arbitrary number of, 96–97
command-line. *See* command-line arguments
glob, 372–73
number of, 95
primitive data types, 96, 98
reference data types, 98
versus parameters, 95
arithmetic operators, 59–60, 61, 66
ArithmeticDemo example, 60, 68
ArrayBlockingQueue class, 497
arraycopy method, 55–56, 608, 648
ArrayCopyDemo example, 55–56
ArrayDemo example, 52–54, 55
ArrayDeque class, 498
arrays, 51–57
assigning values to, 54
of characters, 288–89
comparing, 56

arrays (*continued*)
  copying, 55–56
  creating, 54–55
  filling, 56
  List view of, 502
  looping through, 85
  multidimensional, 54–55
  searching, 56
  sorting, 57
arrow token. *See* ->
asin method, 282
  as a convenience implementation, 502
  upward compatibility and, 513
  writing a custom implementation, 511
asList method, 237–38, 440
assert statement, 120
assignments
  checking with assert, 120
  compound, 61, 67
  conditional operators and, 63–64
asterisk. *See* *
at. *See* @
at prefix, 758
atan method, 282–83
atomic file operations, 372, 377, 392, 496, 500
  access, 533
  actions, 533
  methods, 496
  synchronization, 500–501, 533, 553–54
  variables, 553–54
ATOMIC_MOVE enum, 372, 377
AtomicCounter example, 554
AtomicInteger class, 272, 554
Attributes class, 645
autoboxing, 223, 253, 271–72, 283–84, 285, 288
AutoCloseable interface, 317, 320
autoflush, 346

B
backslash. *See* \
backspace, 50, 289
BadThreads example, 555
BasicMathDemo example, 279
BasicService interface, 664
between method, 781
BicycleDemo example, 37
BigDecimal class, 47, 272, 347, 357, 359
BigInteger class, 272, 347, 459
binary numbers, 49, 273–74
binarySearch method, 56, 445, 508–9
bit shift operators, 65, 67, 797
BitDemo example, 65–66

bitwise operators, 65, 67, 579, 797
  precedence, 58
BlockDemo example, 71
BlockingQueue implementation, 447, 497,
    498, 552
blocks, 68, 128–29
boolean data type, 47
  default value of, 48
  unary operations on, 61
BorderLayout class, 651–52, 657–58, 672,
    694–95
boxing. *See* autoboxing; unboxing
braces. *See* {}
branching statements, 43, 72, 82–85, 798
break statements, 75–76, 82–83
BreakDemo example, 82
BreakWithLabelDemo example, 82–83
brittle applications, 138
browsers. *See* web browsers
BufferedInputStream class, 345, 356
BufferedOutputStream class, 345, 355, 390
BufferedReader class, 317–18, 344–48, 386–89, 718
BufferedWriter class, 318–20, 345, 370–71,
    386, 389, 718
buffers, 345–46
bugs. *See* errors
byte data type, 46
  data streams and, 390
  default value of, 49
  switch statement and, 74
byte streams, 340–42
  buffered, 346
  character streams and, 342–43
  classes, 348–49
  closing, 341–42
  I/O streams and, 352, 354–55
  standard streams and, 352
  using, 341
  when not to use, 342
bytecodes, 2, 5, 7, 16, 18, 20
  in the HelloWorld example, 13, 16, 18, 20,
    29–30
  type erasure and, 244–45
byteValue method, 273, 286

C
CA. *See* Signer Certificate Authority (CA)
    keystore
Calendar class, 358
call stack
  exception handling, 310–11, 315, 321, 323
  propagating errors up, 332–33

Callable objects, 547–48
Caller-Allowable-Codebase attribute, 635, 686
capturing groups, 572–73
cascading style sheets (CSSs), 793
catch blocks, 315–16, 321, 336, 370, 800
Catch or Specify Requirement, 309–12, 330, 799
   bypassing, 312
cd command, 18, 21–22, 29–30
ceil method, 280
char data type, 47
character and string literals, 50, 288–90
   converting to strings, 288–90
   in data streams, 354–55
   default value of, 48
   escape sequences in, 50, 288–90
   generic methods and bounded type
      parameters, 229
   getting by index, 295
   translating individual tokens, 347–48
   wrapper class. See Character class
Character class, 287–89, 306
   implementing Comparable, 459
   restrictions on generics, 252–56
   switch statement and, 74
   useful methods in, 289
   as a wrapper class, 287
character classes, 564–68
   intersections of, 565
   negation of, 563
   predefined, 566–68
   quantifiers and, 572–73
   ranges of, 563–64
   regular expressions and, 562, 567
   simple, 562–63
   subtractions of, 565–66
   unions of, 564–65
character streams, 342–45
charAt method, 84, 290, 305, 307
CharSequence interface, 192–93, 296–98, 303,
      388, 581–83, 772, 774
Checker Framework, 171
ChessAlgorithm example, 212
ChronoField enum, 774–75
ChronoUnit enum, 774–76, 778, 781
Class class, 216–17
class files, 19, 28, 30, 125, 267–68
class library. See Java Application Programming
      Interface (API)
class paths, 268, 269, 603–4, 613, 630–31, 686,
      702, 719
class variables. See fields, static

ClassCastException, 248–50, 252, 458–59, 462,
      502, 694, 800
classes, 36–38, 88–89, 118–19. See also
      inheritance; nested classes
   abstract, 212–16
   access modifiers and, 90–91
   adapter, 517
   base or parent. See superclasses
   child, derived, or extended. See subclasses
   constructors for, 94–95
   declaring, 89–90, 127–28
   final, 212
   hierarchy of, 194
   inner, 130–31. See also inner classes
   instantiating, 101
   interfaces implemented by, 90, 178
   local, 127–31, 139–40, 155
   methods and, 92–94
   naming, 92
   numbers, 272–74
   passing information, 95–99
   static initialization blocks in, 117
   variables (static fields), 44, 57
   wrapper, 272, 283–87, 306, 797
ClassNotFoundException, 357, 646, 648, 708
CLASSPATH system variable, 29–30, 268–69, 595,
      609, 611–13, 706
ClipboardService interface, 715
Clock class, 783
clone method, 209, 490
Cloneable interface, 209, 213–14
CloneNotSupportedException, 208–9
close method, 319–20, 347, 370
Closeable interface, 313, 317, 320, 370
cmd command, 17
code
   case sensitivity in, 12, 17, 22, 45
   error handling, 331–32
   error-prone, 76, 107, 171, 335
   platform-independent, 4, 31
   readability of, 31, 64, 94, 122, 155, 267, 311,
      329, 346
Codebase attribute, manifest file, 634, 724
codebase attribute, JNLP file, 733, 734, 737
CollationKey class, 459
collect method, 476–80
Collection interface, 428–29, 432
   array operations, 432–33
   backward compatibility and, 514
   bulk operations, 432
   implementations of, 502

Collection interface (*continued*)
  views, 452–54
  wrappers for, 499–500
collections, 423–517
  concurrent, 552–53
  hierarchy of, 265
  internal delegation and, 474
  older APIs and, 225, 432–33, 512–13
  ordered, 427, 438, 469, 495
  read-only access to, 490
  synchronized, 490, 500–501
  traversing, 429–30
Collections class, 224, 230, 439, 445, 504, 508–9
  backward compatibility and, 224–25, 230–31
  methods in, 499–500
  polymorphic algorithms in, 424
Collectors class, 478–79
colon. *See* :
combiner function, 477
comma. *See* ,
command-line arguments, 292–93, 600–601
  analogies to applet parameters, 678
  echoing, 600
  numeric, 601
  test harnesses and, 559–60
  URLs and, 646–47
comments, 24
  annotations and, 165–67
  Pattern class methods, 578, 580
Comparable interface, 369, 458, 462
Comparator interface, 189–92, 461–64, 497, 506–7, 509, 796, 798
compare method, 462
compareTo method
  custom uses, 458–61
  for objects, 369
  for primitive data types, 273
  for strings, 301
compareToIgnoreCase method, 154, 301
ComparisonDemo example, 63
comparisons
  between classes, 459
  of numbers, 59–62
  of object, 64–65
compatibility, 513–15
  backward, 514–15
  binary, 183, 187
  cross-platform, 794
  upward, 513–14
compile method, 559, 578
compilers, 124, 198, 234
  information for, 163
ComputeResult class, 307

concat method, 291
ConcatDemo example, 61
concurrency, 519–56
  collections, 552–53
  high-level objects, 543–55
  random numbers, 554
ConcurrentHashMap implementation, 214, 496, 553
ConcurrentMap interface, 482, 491, 496, 552–53
ConcurrentNavigableMap interface, 553
ConcurrentSkipListMap interface, 553
conditional operators, 62–64, 67, 797
ConditionalDemo1 example, 63
ConditionalDemo2 example, 64
constants, 115
  compile-time, 115
  data streams and, 354–55
  embedded flag expressions, 580
  empty, 503–4
  enum types and, 157–61
  importing, 265–66
  interfaces and, 176, 177–78
  naming, 45–46, 157–58
  numbers and, 278–79, 286
  for upper and lower bounds, 238–39, 272
  variables, 130–31
constructors, 87–89, 95–99
  calling, 108–10
  chaining, 208
  conversion, 428–29
  declaring, 89, 94–95
  default, 95
  for enum types, 159
  generic, 234
  inheritance and, 194, 207–8
  methods and, 95, 212
  no-argument, 95, 104, 110, 207, 783
  synchronization and, 530
Consumer interface, 142–43, 146
containers. *See* collections
contains method, 296, 297, 428, 599
containsAll method, 429, 430, 430–32, 454, 494
containsKey method, 449, 451, 599
containsValue method, 214, 449, 451
continue statements, 83–84
ContinueDemo example, 83
ContinueWithLabelDemo example, 84
control flow statements, 72–86
  branching, 82–85
  decision-making, 72
controlling access. *See* access modifiers
converters, 275–76

Cookie Applet Example, 722
cookies
    accessing, 719–22
    kinds of, 719
    rich Internet applications (RIAs) and, 719–20,
        722
copy method, 243, 376
CopyBytes example, 341–42, 343
CopyCharacters example, 343–44, 345
CopyLines example, 344–45
copyOfRange method, 56
CopyOnWriteArrayList implementation, 494
CopyOnWriteArraySet implementation,
        493–94
core collection interfaces, 423, 426–28, 469–70,
        500–501, 513. See also by individual type
    compatibility of, 513–14
    hierarchy of, 265
    implementations of, 499–502
cos method, 266, 279
Countdown example, 447
Counter example, 527
CreateObjectDemo example, 99–100, 105–6
createTempFile method, 393, 421
currentTimeMillis method, 609
customized loading screens
    in applets, 722
    in Java Web Start applications, 656–61

D
data encapsulation, 33, 35
data types, 46–51, 95–96, 341–42. See also by
        individual type
    reference, 95–96
    returned by expressions, 68–69, 91–92
    switch statement and, 74
DataInput interface, 355–57
DataInputStream class, 355–56
DataOutput interface, 355, 356, 357
DataOutputStream class, 355, 356
DataStreams example, 355–57
dates, 153, 621. See also Date-Time package
Date-Time package, xxiv, 755–91
    basic representations of time, 759–60
    calendar systems, xxiv, 755–56, 759, 788
    clarity in, 756
    clocks, 783–84
    date-time classes, 764–70
    design principles, 756–57
    duration, 781
    epochs, 759, 770
    extensibility of, 757
    fluent interface of, 757

    formatting 773–74
    human vs. machine time, 770
    immutability of, 757
    Instant class and, 770–71
    legacy date-time code, 787–90
    method naming conventions, 758
    non-ISO date conversions, 784–87
    packages, 757–58, 774–80
    parsing 772–73
    period, 782–83
    temporal-based classes, 760–61
    time zone and offset classes, 766–70
DateTimeFormatter class, 772
DayOfWeek enum, 760–62
Deadlock example, 534
deadlocks, 491, 533–35, 544
Deal example, 444–45
decimal number system, 48, 49, 273
DecimalFormat class, 272, 277–78
declaration statements, 70, 317
declarations. See by individual type
decode method, 274
default keyword, 185
default methods, xxiii, 182–92
    binary compatibility, 183
    defining implementations for, 182–84
    defining new methods as, 182
    extending interfaces that contain, 185–86
    integrating into existing libraries, 187–92
DelayQueue class, 497
delete method, 304, 375, 419
deleteOnExit method, 420
deployment, 729–53
    applets, 673–77
    best practices, 748
    Java Web Start applications, 653–56
Deployment Toolkit, 653–56, 673–76
@Deprecated annotation type, 167–68
@deprecated Javadoc tag, 167
Deque interface, 448–49
    basic operations, 498
    concurrent implementations, 499
    implementations of, 498–99
    methods, 448–49
destroy method, 668
diamond, 223–24, 233–34, 428
dir command, 18, 29
directories
    changing, 17–19, 27
    checking, 374–75
    copying, 376–77
    creating, 20–22, 395–96
    deleting, 375

directories (*continued*)
    delimiters, 360
    error messages involving, 29
    filtering, 398
    moving, 377–78
    packages, 267–68
    root, 363, 395
    temporary, 396–97
    verifying the existence of, 375
    watching for changes, 410–16
documentation, 165–66
    source code comments, 24
@Documented annotation type, 167, 169
dollar sign. *See* $
dot. *See* .
double data type, 47
double quote. *See* "
doubleValue method, 237, 273
do-while statements, 53, 72, 79, 82–83, 85, 798
DoWhileDemo example, 79
DownloadService interface, 657, 664, 693,
      694, 715
DownloadServiceListener interface, 657,
      693–94, 715
Duration object, 780–81
Dynamic Tree Demo applet, 654, 674

E
E
    constant, 279
    in scientific notation, 49
    as type parameter naming convention, 221
Echo example, 600
element method, 438
elements (in collections), 427–28
    adding, 428–29, 432, 438–39
    checking, 431
    counting, 433–34, 447
    cursor position and, 441–442
    not duplicated, 433–434
    null, 432
    ordering, 427, 433–434
    removing, 429–432, 435–436
    searching, 435–436
    sequence of, 145
    swapping, 439–440
ellipsis. *See* ...
emacs text editor, 20
emptyList method, 235, 503
emptyMap method, 503
emptySet method, 503
EmptyStackException, 325

encapsulation, 33, 35, 91, 122, 155, 796, 799
end method, 583
endsWith method, 301, 369
EnhancedForDemo example, 81
ensureCapacity method, 303, 501
Entry-Point attribute, 635
entrySet method, 449, 453–55, 512
enum keyword, 157
enum types, 87, 157–61, 493
    constructors for, 159
    naming, 157–58
enumerated types. *See* enum types
Enumeration collection, 259, 513, 514, 515, 599
    compatibility and, 513–15
EnumMap implementation, 495
EnumSet implementation, 493
EnumTest example, 158
Env example, 602
environment, 595–614
    properties of, 596–99
    restricted, 661
environment variables, 601–2, 609–13
    CLASSPATH, 29, 30, 609
    common problems with, 29
    passing to new processes, 602
    PATH, 609–12
    platform dependency issues, 602
    querying, 601–2
EnvMap example, 601–2
EOFException, 335, 356
epochs, 759, 770
equality operators. *See* comparisons
equals method, 56, 208, 210–11, 460, 463, 496
equalsIgnoreCase method, 301
Error class, 326
error messages, 313–15
    legacy file I/O code, 418
    Microsoft Windows, 27, 29–30
    Solaris and Linux, 27–28, 30–31
    unchecked, 225–26
    using to check assignments, 120
    wildcard capture and, 241
errors
    compiler, 28, 58, 101, 105, 107, 201, 229, 241,
      255, 264, 330
    compile-time, 48, 95, 172, 197, 203, 207, 220,
      228, 239, 244, 253–56, 284
    grouping and differentiating types, 334–35
    memory consistency, 527, 528–29, 530–31, 533,
      543, 553
    propagating in, 332–34
    runtime, 29–31

semantic, 29
syntax, 28
escape sequences, 50, 288–89
in regular expressions, 578, 582
in Unicode, 50, 591
EventHandler interface, 134–35, 146
exception classes, 309, 324–29
creating, 328–29
grouping errors, 334–35
hierarchy, 329
PatternSyntaxException class, 589–91
exception handlers, 45, 310–17
associating with try blocks, 314–15
catching more than one exception type, 316
catching multiple exceptions, 319
constructing, 320–23
exceptions, 309–37
advantages of, 329–30
catching, 313–23
chained, 326–28
checked, 312
class hierarchy of, 329
creating exception classes, 328
external. See errors
in file operations, 370–71
kinds of, 311–12
logging, 328, 698
specifying by method, 323–24
suppressed, 319–20
throwing, 324–30
unchecked, 329–30
exclamation sign. See !
Executor interface, 546–48, 549
ExecutorService interface, 546–49
exit method, 609
exp method, 281
ExponentialDemo example, 281
exponents, 266
expression statements, 70–71
expressions, 68–70
ExtendedService interface, 664, 715
extends keyword, 38, 227, 236, 238
extensions, 603, 613, 615, 625, 638, 673, 723

F

F or f in 32-bit float literals, 47
fields, 35–38, 206, 796. See also variables
declaring, 117
default values of, 48
final, 530
hiding, 206
inherited, 196

initializing, 116–18, 796
members versus, 45
nonstatic, 44, 57
private, 196
qualified names, 98
referencing, 104–5
shadowing, 97, 123–24
static, 44, 112–14, 216, 254, 531, 578, 645
static final. See constants
synchronization and, 527, 531
FIFO (first-in, first out), 427, 446, 469, 490, 497
File class, 359
file descriptors, 211
file operations, 370–74
atomic, 372
catching exceptions, 370–71
method chaining, 372
releasing system resources, 370
varargs in, 371–72
file paths, 359–62
checking symbolic links, 375–76
comparing, 369
converting, 366–67
creating, 363
creating a path between two, 368
joining two, 367
relative versus absolute, 360–61
removing redundancies from, 364–66
retrieving information about, 363–64
symbolic links and, 361–62
FileInputStream class, 341, 343, 356, 598, 606
Filename class, 298
FilenameDemo example, 299
FileNotFoundException, 312, 334–35
FileOpenService interface, 715–17
FileOutputStream class, 341, 344, 355, 598, 608
FileReader class, 311–12, 317–18, 343–48, 608
files
accessibility of, 376
basic attributes, 381
checking, 374–75
copying, 376–77
creating, 389–90, 392–93
deleting, 375
DOS attributes, 378
file stores, 418
finding, 407–8
I/O and, 359–420
moving, 377–78
POSIX file permissions, 383–84
random access, 339, 359, 390, 393, 420

files (*continued*)
    reading, 389–90
    setting ownership, 384
    temporary, 393
    time stamps, 382
    user-defined attributes, 385
    verifying the existence of, 375
    writing, 389–90
FileSaveService interface, 715–18
FileSystem class, 373, 386, 407, 412, 422
FileVisitor interface, 401–5
FileWriter class, 313–14, 316, 320–23, 343–45,
        608
fill method, 56
final
    catch parameter, 316
    class, 212
    class variable, 44, 115
    constants, 115
    effectively, 129, 133, 149-150
    immutable objects, 541, 542
    method, 118, 212
final modifier, 115, 178
finalize method, 208, 210–11
finally block, 309, 316–17
find method, 584
FindDups example, 435–37, 470
FindDups2 example, 437
first method, 448
float data type, 47
    default value of, 48
floatValue method, 273, 293
floor method, 280
flush method, 346
for statement, 80–82, 85
    enhanced, 81, 395, 418, 470, 488, 798
    nested, 82
    skipping the current iteration, 84–85
    terminating, 80
ForDemo example, 80–81
for-each construct, 159, 429, 430, 434, 435,
        472–73, 499
fork/join framework, 480, 546, 549–50, 552
form feed, 50
Format example, 352
format method, 274–75, 278, 350, 758, 772
format specifiers, 275, 350–51, 644, 772
format strings, 275, 292, 349–50
Formatter class, 350
formatting
    numeric print output, 274–78
    stream objects, 346, 349–52

forward slash. *See* /
frequency method, 451–52
from method, 758
functional interface, 141–42
@FunctionalInterface annotation type, 169
functions. *See* methods
Future object, 547
FXML scripting language, 793

G

garbage collection, 5, 106–7, 119, 120, 208, 210,
        496, 540, 797
    empty references and, 208
    immutable objects and, 539–40
    memory leaks and, 5
    weak references and, 496
generic methods, 226–27
generic objects, 219–58
    bounded type parameters and, 227
    erasure of, 244–46
    instantiating, 222, 233–34
    invoking, 222
    subtyping and, 230–31
    type inference and, 232–35
generic types, 141–42, 220–26, 239, 245, 249,
        252, 426
get method, 211, 313–14, 363, 758
getAbsolutePath method, 421
getApplet method, 683, 702
getCanonicalPath method, 421
getCause method, 327
getChars method, 291
getClass method, 208, 211, 216, 227
getCodeBase method, 678, 704
getDescription method, 589–90
getEnv method, 601–2
getFields method, 211
getFirst method, 449, 494, 498
getHost method, 704
getImage method, 678
getIndex method, 589–90
getInterfaces method, 211
getLast method, 449, 494, 498
getMainAttributes method, 644–45
getMainClassName method, 644–45
getMessage method, 371, 589, 590
getName method, 365
getParameter method, 680–81
getParent method, 364–66
getPattern method, 589
getProperty method, 599, 605, 711–13
getResource method, 653

getSecurityManager method, 607
getSimpleName method, 211
getStackTrace method, 327
getSuperclass method, 211
getValue method, 645
globbing, 372–74
    filtering a directory listing, 398
    finding files, 407–10
graphical user interfaces (GUIs), 4, 40–41,
        99–100, 134, 146–47, 425, 650–52, 665–67,
        670–73
groupCount method, 575
groupingBy operation, 479, 482
groupingByConcurrent operation, 482
guarded blocks, 535–39

H
hard links, 359, 399
hashCode method, 189, 191, 208, 210–11, 433,
        439, 447, 452, 459–60
HashMap implementation, 214, 234, 451–52, 491,
        495–96, 504
HashSet implementation, 433–37, 450, 454–55,
        490–93
Hashtable collection, 428, 451, 496, 513–15,
        596, 599–600
    compatibility and, 513–14
    concurrency through ConcurrentHashMap, 496
    synchronization and, 490–91
hasNext method, 431, 441
headSet method, 464–67
heap pollution, 250
HelloRunnable example, 521–22
HelloThread example, 522
HelloWorld, 6–24, 656–66
    applet, 665–66
    JavaFX example, 146
    for Microsoft Windows, 15–20
    for Solaris and Linux, 20–23
    for the NetBeans IDE, 6–15
hexadecimal number system, 49, 51, 211, 273–74,
        286, 351, 591
HTML. *See also* web browsers; web pages
    generated code, 732, 736
    specification, 676
HTTP requests, 548, 719
HTTPS certificates, 662, 726

I
IDE projects, 7–9, 14–15
identity element, 476, 480
IdentityHashMap implementation, 495–96

IfElseDemo example, 73
if-then statements, 72–73, 85, 797
if-then-else statements, 73, 85, 797
IllegalAccessException, 646
IllegalStateException, 446
immutable objects, 539–43
    defining, 541–43
immutable singleton set, 503
ImmutableRGB example, 542–43
implementations, 489–505
    abstract, 490, 510–13
    adapter, 510–11
    anonymous, 499
    concurrent, 489, 491, 498–99
    convenience, 489, 502–4
    custom, 509–13
    documenting, 426
    general purpose, 489, 490, 491, 498, 502, 504,
            510, 553
        multiple inheritance of, 198
    special purpose, 489, 493, 504
    wrapper, 424, 499–502
    writing, 510–13
implements keyword, 39, 89, 178
import statement, 264–66, 776
indexOf method, 299, 438–39, 442
indexOfSubList method, 445–46
information hiding, 36
inheritance, 38–39, 193–217, 797, 799
    example, 195–96
    multiple, 159, 198–99, 214
@Inherited annotation type, 170
init method, 667, 671–73, 690
initCause method, 327
initializer blocks, 117–18
inner classes, 87, 122, 123–27
    accessing members of, 128–29
    anonymous, 123
    compatibility issues, 125
    controlling access to, 122
    example, 125–27
    instantiating, 123
    local, 127–31
    serialization of, 124–25
InputStream class, 343–44
InputStreamReader class, 344, 352–53, 389, 718
insert method, 302
instance members, 87, 117–18, 122, 130
instance methods
    interface methods vs., 200–202
instance variables, 44, 57, 87, 112–19, 122, 698

instanceof operator, 59, 64–67, 198, 250, 254,
    405, 459, 692
InstanceofDemo example, 64
instances, 36, 44, 101–2, 112–13
    class members and, 112–16
    inner classes and, 123
    testing, 64–65
Instant class, 770–71
int data type, 46
    default value of, 48
    switch statement and, 74
Integer class, 228, 273–74
interfaces, 39–40, 176–93
    abstract classes and, 213–14, 799
    as APIs, 177
    body, 178
    collection. *See* core collection interfaces
    defining, 177–78
    evolving, 181–82
    functional, 141–42
    implementing, 178–80
    as a type, 180–81
International Organization for Standardization
    (ISO) calendar system, xxiv, 755–56, 759
internationalization, 342–43
Internet domain names, 262–63, 267
Internet Explorer. *See* web browsers
interoperability, 513–17
    API design, 515–17
    compatibility, 513–15
    with legacy code, 418–21, 420–21
interprocess communication (IPC) resources, 520
interrupt mechanism, 423–24
interrupt status, 525–25
interrupted method, 524–25
InterruptedException, 447, 523–26, 536–39,
    545, 555
intValue method, 228, 273, 284
invokeClass method, 646–48
I/O, 339–422
    atomic, 372
    binary, 354–55
    buffered, 345–46
    channel, 390–92, 393–94
    closing, 210–11, 341–42
    from the command line, 352–57
    command-line objects, 603
    exceptions, 334–35, 370–71
    interoperability, 418–19
    line oriented, 344–45
    memory mapped, 386
    method chaining, 372, 802
    NIO.2, 339–422

    of objects, 357
    of primitive data type values, 354–55
    random access, 393–94
    scanning and formatting, 246–352
    streams, 339–40, 603. *See* streams, I/O
IOError, 312, 402
IOException, 313–23
is prefix, 758
isAfter method, 771
isAnnotation method, 211
isBefore method, 771
isEmpty method, 428–39, 434, 447–48, 451, 786
isInterface method, 211
isInterrupted method, 524
isLetter method, 289
isLowerCase method, 289
ISO-86013. *See* International Organization for
    Standardization (ISO) calendar system
IsoFields class, 775
isUpperCase method, 289
isWhitespace method, 289, 346
Iterator class, 428–34, 438–39, 440–42, 453, 465,
    468, 474, 488, 490, 494, 497, 499, 501, 512
iterator method, 125, 244–45, 369, 397, 431,
    434, 438, 441, 501
Iterator object, 431
iterators, 428–34
    aggregate operations vs., 474
    fail-fast, 490

J

JApplet class, 653, 665–69, 671–73, 677, 678,
    680–81, 698, 712
JApplet getCodeBase method, 678
JApplet getDocumentBase method, 678
JAR tool, 616, 618–23, 628, 630
    setting entry points, 630
JarClassLoader class, 643–48
JarRunner example, 643–46
jarsigner tool, 722
JarURLConnection class, 642–45
Java 2D, 4
Java Application Programming Interface
    (API), 3–5, 34, 40–41, 793. *See also* APIs
    (Application Programming Interfaces)
    hierarchy of packages, 265
    legacy, 224–25
    raw types and, 224–25
    runtime exceptions and, 312, 326, 330
Java Archive (JAR) files, 615–48. *See also* security
    adding classes class path, 630–31
    applets packaged in, 626
    as applications, 626–27

benefits of, 615–16
creating, 616–20
extracting contents of, 622–23
manifest files, 627–35, 654, 674, 686, 724
paths in, 621
running JAR packaged software, 625–27
sealing, 634
signing, 639–41, 654, 722, 725–26
time stamping and, 654, 675, 725–26
uncompressed, 619
updating, 623–25
using, 616–27
using JAR-related APIs, 642–48
verifying, 635–42
viewing contents of, 620–22
Java Archive Tool. *See* JAR tool
Java Cache Viewer, 660–61
Java Collections Framework. *See* collections
Java Database Connectivity (JDBC) API, 4
Java HotSpot virtual machine, 2
Java Interactive Data Language (IDL) API, 4
`java` launcher tool, 2, 4, 626
Java Naming and Directory Interface (JNDI)
      API, 4
Java Network Launching Protocol. *See* JNLP files
Java platform, 2–4, 595–14
   API specification. *See* Java Application
         Programming Interface (API)
   command-line arguments, 600–601
   configuration utilities, 595–603
   environment variables, 601–3
   language, 2–4
   properties, 596–600, 604–7
   supported encodings on. *See* Unicode encoding
   system utilities, 603–9
Java Plug-In software, 670, 693, 700–702, 734,
      739, 749, 750
Java Programming Language Certification,
      795–805
   Java SE 8 Upgrade Exam, 801–5
   Programmer Level I Exam, 795–801
   Programmer Level II Exam, 801–5
Java Remote Invocation (RMI), 4
Java Remote Method Invocation over Internet
      Inter-ORB Protocol (Java RMI-IIOP), 4
Java SE Development Kit 8. *See* JDK 8 (Java SE
      Development Kit 8)
Java SE Runtime Environment. *See* JRE (Java
      SE Runtime Environment)
Java Virtual Machine (Java VM), 2–3, 268–70
Java Web Start applications, 650–56
   changing the launch button of, 737
   common problems, 662–63

deploying, 653–56, 735–38
deploying without `codebase` attribute, 737–38
developing, 650–53
displaying customized loading progress
      indicator, 656–60
Java Cache Viewer, 660–61
retrieving resources, 653
running, 660–61
security and, 661–62
separating core functionality from final
      deployment mechanism, 652–53
setting up web servers for, 656
signed, 31, 654
`java.awt` packages, 262, 265, 657, 668, 693–94,
      714
JavaBeans, 5
`javac` compiler, 2, 4, 7
   case sensitivity in, 12
`javadoc` tool, 24
JavaFX, xxiv, 4, 134, 793–94
   `HelloWorld.java` example, 146
   Scene Builder, 793
`java.io` package, 274, 339, 386, 389, 421
`java.lang.Character` API, 288
JavaScript
   applets and, 670, 673–89
   Deployment Toolkit scripts, 653, 673–74
   interpreter, 670, 689, 731
`java.time`, 757. *See* Date-Time package
`java.time.chrono` package, 757
`java.time.format` package, 757
`java.time.temporal` package, 757–58, 774
`java.time.zone` package, 758
`java.util.Arrays` class, 56, 552
`java.util.concurrent.atomic` package,
      553–54
`java.util.concurrent.locks` package, 544
`java.util.function`, 141
`java.util.jar` package, 642–43, 645
`java.util.regex` package, 551, 557–58,
      581–88, 590, 592
`javax.jnlp` package, 650, 657, 716–17, 719
`javax.swing.JApplet` class, 666, 671–73, 677,
      680, 712
JButton, 651, 672, 700
JDialog, 667
JDK 8 (Java SE Development Kit 8), xxiii–xxiv, 4, 6
   adding to platform list, 9
   aggregate operations. *See* aggregate operations
   concurrency in, 552
   concurrent random numbers, 554–55
   default manifest, 627
   default methods. *See* default methods

JDK 8 (Java SE Development Kit 8) (*continued*)
    directory structure, 609–13
    generics and, 224
    high-level concurrency objects and, 543
    JAR tool in, 616
    lambda expressions. *See* lambda expressions
    local classes. *See* local classes
    repeating annotations and, 165. *See also*
        annotations; type annotations
    target typing and, 236
    ThreadLocalRandom, 543, 555
    TransferQueue implementation, 498
JFrame class, 651
JNLP files, 739–48
    API, 650, 706, 711, 714–17, 739
    common errors, 662–63
    commonly used elements and attributes,
        741–47
    deployment options with jnlp_href, 733
    embedding in Applet tag, 734–35
    encoding, 740
    rich Internet applications (RIAs) and, 714–19
    security and, 634
    signed, 725
    structure of, 740–47
join method, 525
JPanel class, 651–52, 671–72
JProgressBar object, 657, 658, 694, 695
JRE (Java SE Runtime Environment), 604
    checking client version of, 738–39
    ensuring the presence of, 751–53
JSR 310 Date and Time API. *See* Date-Time
    package

K

keys method, 599
keySet method, 453–56
keywords, 90. *See also* by individual type

L

lambda expressions, xxiii, 136–55
    aggregate operations that accept, 145–46
    as anonymous methods, 147
    as arguments, 190
    classification function, 479
    errors, 149
    example use, 137
    generic types and, 141–42, 144–45
    GUI applications and, 146–47
    interference and, 484–85
    in pipelines and streams, 478
    shadowing and, 148

specifying search criteria code in, 141
    stateful, 486–87
    stream operations and, 486
    syntax of, 147
    using throughout an application, 142–44, 155–56
last method, 605, 646
lastIndexOf method, 296–99, 438–39
lastIndexOfSubList method, 446
laziness, 485–86
length method, 290, 302
line feed, 50, 344
line terminators, 344, 364, 567, 578
link awareness, 374
LinkedBlockingDeque class, 499
LinkedBlockingQueue class, 497
LinkedHashMap implementation, 450, 451, 491,
    495
LinkedHashSet implementation, 433–34, 450,
    491, 492, 493
LinkedList implementation, 498
links
    hard, 359, 399
    symbolic, 361, 364, 367, 374–77, 379, 381,
        399–405, 408, 419, 422
Linux. *See* Solaris/Linux
List interface, 468–46
    algorithms, 445–46
    collection operations, 375, 386, 394, 553
    implementations, 493–94
    iterators, 440–43
    method, 513–14
    positional acccess and search operations,
        439–40
    range view operations, 443–45
listIterator method, 438, 440–42, 512
ListOfNumbers example, 313–14, 320, 322,
    323, 337
listRoots method, 421
lists, 138
    cursor positions in, 441–42
    iterating backward, 441
literals, 43, 48–51, 291, 557, 560–61, 566
    character and string, 50
    class, 50
    floating point, 49
    integer, 48–49
    using underscore characters, 50–51
LiveConnect Specification, 683–84, 686
local classes, 127–31
    specifying search criteria code in, 139–40
    when to use, 155
LocalDate class, 763

LocalDateTime class, 765–66
locales, 342, 347–48
LocalTime class, 764–65
lockInterruptibly method, 544
locks, 531–32, 544
    deadlocks, 491, 533–35, 544
    intrinsic, 531, 536
    livelocks, 527, 533, 535
    starvation, 527, 533, 535
    synchronization and, 531–32
logarithms, 178, 279, 281, 286
logical operators, 58–68
Long class, 273, 286, 292–93, 459
long data type, 47
    default value of, 48
longValue method, 273
lookingAt method, 584, 586–87
loops, 80–84, 798
    infinite, 79–81, 86, 411
    nested, 84
    test harness, 559–60, 570
ls command, 22, 23, 238, 254, 407

M

main method, 24–26
manifest files, 616, 619, 627–35
    default, 627
    digest entries, 637–638
    fetching attributes, 645
    modifying, 628–629
    setting application entry point, 629–630
    setting package version information, 631–633
    signature block files, 638, 641
    signature files, 637–38
Map interface, 214, 449–58, 469, 482, 486, 491,
        496, 504, 507, 803
    basic operations, 451–52
    bulk operations, 452
    implementations of, 495–96
    viewing as a Collection, 452–54
mapper element, 480
Matcher class, 557–58, 583, 585, 587–88
MatcherDemo example, 585–86
MatchesLooking example, 586–87
Math class, 266, 279, 281–82, 286
MAX_VALUE constant, 286, 404
members, 45
    controlling access to, 110–11, 799
memory
    allocating sufficient, 101
    consistency errors, 528–29
    error-handling, 331–32

garbage collection, 106–7
    leaks, 5
    locations, 12
    saving in large arrays, 46–47
metadata, 378–86
method references, 152–55
    to a constructor, 154–55
    to an instance method of a particular object,
        154
    to an instance method of an arbitrary object of
        a particular type, 154
    in pipelines and streams, 478
    to a static method, 154
method signatures, 92
    in interface declarations, 177–78
    in method declarations, 92
    overloaded methods and, 92
    type erasure and, 248–49
methods, 34–36. *See also* by individual type
    abstract, 184–86, 212–16
    access modifiers and, 90, 95, 213, 798
    accessor, 290, 295–96, 381–82, 467
    applet milestone, 667–68
    atomic, 496
    bridge, 245–49
    chaining, 372
    class, 114, 118, 122, 273, 286, 292, 294
    default, 182–92
    defining, 92–94
    final, 212
    generic, 226–27
    hiding, 199–203
    instance, 199, 200–201
    interface, 200–201
    naming, 93, 758
    overloaded, 93–94
    overriding, 199–203
    package-private, 111
    qualified names, 119
    returning a class or interface, 108–9
    returning values from, 107–8
    static, 186–87
    synchronized, 529–31
    wildcards, 240–43
Microsoft Windows
    access control list (ACL), 380
    CLASSPATH in, 612
    common errors, 27–28
    environment variables on, 602
    file name separators on, 267
    HelloWorld, 15–19
    log files, 698

Microsoft Windows (*continued*)
   PATH in, 362–70
   path separators on, 296
   root directories on, 359–60
   system file stores, 417–18
MIME types, 380, 385, 417, 422, 656, 663
minus prefix, 758, 771
MIN_VALUE constant, 272, 286, 463
modifiers. *See* access modifiers
modularity, 36
monitor locks. *See* locks, intrinsic
Month enum, 760, 762
MonthDay class, 764
Mozilla Firefox add-ons, 732, 736
MultiDimArrayDemo example, 54, 55
multimaps, 456
multiple inheritance, 198–99
multisets, 510

N

NameSort example, 461
nanoTime method, 609
nCopies method, 502–3
NegativeArraySizeException, 326
nested classes, 121–57
   controlling access and, 196
   importing, 264–65
   inheritance and, 195
   inner. *See* inner classes
   nonstatic, 121–22, 156
   static, 122–23, 156
   when to use, 156
NetBeans IDE, 1, 5–10, 14–15, 31, 410, 663, 796
   HelloWorld application, 6–15
new keyword, 48, 101, 132, 222, 289
newCachedThreadPool method, 549
newFixedThreadPool method, 548
newline. *See* line terminators
newSingleThreadExecutor method, 549
next method, 431
nextIndex method, 441–42
NIO.2, 339–422
NonNull module, 171
NoSuchElementException, 446–47, 474
NoSuchMethodError, 30–31
Notepad demo, 656, 660, 736–38
Notepad text editor, 16–17
notifyAll method, 208, 536–38
now method, 758, 783
null parameter, 756–57
null value, 50, 342, 413
NullPointerException, 78, 171, 312, 330, 442,
   459–60, 756, 800

Number class, 271, 273, 286, 601
number systems, 48–49
   converting between, 273
   decimal, 47, 49
   hexidecimal, 49, 211, 273–74, 286, 351, 591
   octal, 273–74
NumberFormatException, 526, 601
numbers, 271–87
   converting between strings and, 292–95
   formatting, 274–78
   random, 283

O

Object class, 175, 208–16, 237, 243
   as a superclass, 208–12
object ordering, 458–64
object references, 59, 87, 105–7, 113–14, 122,
   209–10, 248, 342, 358, 688, 796, 799
ObjectInput interface, 357
ObjectInputStream class, 357
object-oriented programming, 33–41, 203
ObjectOutput interface, 357
ObjectOutputStream class, 357
objects, 34–36, 99–107, 118–19
   calling methods, 105–6
   casting, 197–98
   creating, 100–104
   declaring variables to refer to, 101
   hash codes of, 208, 211, 460
   immutable, 539–43
   initializing, 102–4
   lock, 544–46
   referencing fields, 104–5
ObjectStreams example, 357
octal number system, 273–74
of prefix, 758
offer method, 446
offerFirst method, 448–49
offerLast method, 448–49
OffsetDateTime class, 767, 769–70
operation element, 480
operators, 58–68. *See also* by individual type
   assignment, 59
   precedence of, 59, 69, 797
   prefix/postfix, 59, 62
OutputStream class, 340–41, 343–45, 718
OutputStreamWriter class, 344, 718
@Override annotation class, 168, 199

P

package members, 263
   package importing, 264

package referring to, 263–64
package using, 263–67
package-private, 111
package statements, 261–62, 264, 269, 679
packages, 4, 33, 34, 40, 259–70, 796
  apparent hierarchies of, 265
  creating, 261–62
  importing, 264–65
  name ambiguities, 265–66
  naming, 262–63
  qualified names, 262–67
  using package members, 263–67
pages. *See* web pages
Panel class, 651
parallelism, 480–81
parallelSort method, 57, 552
parameterized types, 224
  assigning raw types, 224–25
  backward compatibility and, 224
  bounded, 227–28
  casting, 254
  generic, 252
  heap pollution and, 250, 251
  primitive, 252–53
  restrictions, 252–56
  type erasure and, 244–45
  type inference and, 233–34
  varargs methods and, 249–50
parameters, 45
  naming, 97
  types, 96
parentheses. *See* ( )
parse methods, 758, 772
parseXXX methods, 294, 601
PassPrimitiveByValue class, 98
Password example, 353–54
passwords, 353, 603, 639–40, 641
Path class, 362–70
PATH variable, 27, 29, 610–13
Pattern class, 557–59, 575, 578–79, 581. *See also* regular expressions
PatternSyntaxException, 589–91
peek method, 447, 449
percent sign. *See* %
Period class, 780
Perl, 557, 558, 578, 591
permissions
  Permissions attribute, 31, 634, 724
  sandbox, 654, 674
PI constant, 266
pipelines, 145, 472–74. *See also* streams
  collections vs., 473
  components of, 473

downstream collectors, 479
  ordering, 483–84
  parallel execution of, 481
  terminal operations, 473, 475. *See also* reduction operations
Planet class, 159–60
pluggable type systems, xxiii, 170–71. *See also* type annotations
plus method, 758, 771
poll method, 410, 416, 446–47
polymorphism, 203–6, 245, 249, 799
pound sign. *See* #
pow method, 95, 281
precision query, 778
Predicate interface, 141–42
Preferences API, 603
PrePostDemo example, 62, 68
primitive data types, 46–51. *See also by individual type*; numbers
print method, 349–50
printf method, 97, 274–76
println method, 349–50
PriorityBlockingQueue class, 497
PriorityQueue implementation, 490, 497
problems. *See* errors
ProcessBuilder object, 520, 602
processElements method, 145–46
processes, 520
  lightweight. *See* threads
Producer example, 538
ProducerConsumerExample example, 539
programs. *See* applications
properties
  managing, 597
  saving, 599–600
  setting, 599–600
  system, 605–7, 713–14
PropertiesTest example, 606
propertyNames method, 599
protected modifier, 111
public modifier, 91, 111, 178, 185, 187
put method, 512
putAll method, 449, 452, 454
pwd command, 22, 30

Q
qualified names
  in applets, 659, 697
  for fields, 97
  for instance variables, 118
  for methods, 118
  for packages, 262–63
quantifiers, 573

question mark. *See* ?
Queue implementations, 427, 446–47, 490, 496–97
Queue interface, 446–48, 469, 491, 494, 497, 504
queues, 446–48
    bounded, 446
    priority, 427
QuoteClientApplet applet, 704–5
quoteReplacement method, 585
QuoteServer applet, 704–5

R

radians, 282–83
random access files, 339, 390, 393–95
random method, 283
random numbers, 283, 286, 543, 554–55
RandomAccessFile class, 337, 420
raw types, 224–25, 234, 248, 249, 250
readDouble method, 355–56
readInt method, 355–56
readObject method, 357–59
readPassword method, 353–54
readUTF method, 355–56
Receiver applet, 702–3
reduction operations, 474–80
    concurrent, 481–82
    multilevel reduction in streams, 479
    mutable, 484
RegexTestHarness example, 559, 579–80
RegexTestHarness2 example, 589–90
regionMatches method, 300–301
RegionMatchesDemo example, 300
regular expressions, 557–93
    backreferences in, 574–75
    boundary matchers in, 576–77
    capturing groups in, 572–76
    character classes in, 557–58, 562–67
    greedy quantifiers, 569, 573–74
    intersections, 558–65
    Matcher class, 583–89
    metacharacters in, 561–62
    negation, 563
    Pattern class, 578–83
    PatternSyntaxException class, 589–91
    possessive quantifiers, 573
    quantifiers in, 568–74
    ranges, 563–64
    reluctant quantifiers, 573
    string literals, 560–62
    subtraction, 565–66
    test harness, 559–60
    Unicode support, 591–92
    zero-length matches in, 569–72

Relatable interface, 178–80
relational operators. *See* comparisons
remove method, 429, 431, 434, 469, 502
removeAll method, 430, 432–37, 454–56, 503
removeDups method, 434
removeEldestEntry method, 495
removeFirst method, 448, 494, 498
removeFirstOccurence method, 449
removeLast method, 449, 498
removeLastOccurence method, 449 [*]
renameTo method, 420
@Repeatable annotation type, 170, 172
replace method, 496
replaceAll method, 298, 445, 584, 587–89
ReplaceDemo example, 587
ReplaceDemo2 example, 587–88
REPLACE_EXISTING enum, 376–78
replaceFirst method, 298, 585, 587–89
reserved words. *See* keywords
retainAll method, 436–37, 454, 455
@Retention annotation type, 169
return statements, 85, 107, 147, 151, 464
return types, 92–94
    constructors, 102
    covariant, 109, 199
rich Internet applications (RIAs), xxiv, 711–27
    cookies and, 719–22
    customizing the loading experience in, 722
    entry points, 635
    local, 726
    security in, 722–26
    setting secure properties, 711–14
    setting trusted arguments, 711–14
    signing, 730–31
    system properties, 713–14
    testing, 724
    user acceptance of, 729–31
    using the JNLP API, 714–19
Root example, 349–50
Root2 example, 350
round method, 280
run method, 522, 523
runtime, 2, 26
    checks at, 197
    errors, 29–31
    examining annotations at, 163
RuntimeException, 309, 312, 326, 329–30

S

Safelock example, 544–46
@SafeVarargs annotation type, 169

sandbox, 635, 661–62, 722–25, 729–31, 748
  applets, 705–7, 713–14
  permissions, 654, 674, 677, 691, 703
Scanner class, 346–48, 457
scanning, 345–46
ScanSum example, 348
ScanXan example, 346–47
ScheduledExecutorService interface, 546,
    548, 549
ScheduledThreadPoolExecutor class, 549
security, xxiv
  applets and, 596, 677–78
  coding guidelines, 724
  digitally signed files, 31, 637
  JAR files, 31, 615, 635–42
  Java Control Panel settings, 31, 730
  Java versions and, 724, 730
  Java Web Start applications and, 661–62
  keystores and, 31, 639
  legacy file I/O code and, 418–19
  managers, 607–8, 707
  manifest attributes and, 634–35
  password entry and, 353
  public and private keys, 636, 639
  rich Internet applications (RIAs) and, 722–24
  sandbox, 706–7
  time stamping and, 654, 675, 725–26
  TOCTTOU, 375
  violations, 608
  web browsers and, 697
SecurityException, 172, 607, 608
SecurityManager class, 607–8
semicolon. See ;
Sender applet, 702–3
sequences. See collections, ordered
Serializable interface, 214, 232, 357, 490
serialization, 152, 214
servers, 664, 678. See web servers
ServiceLoader class, 603
Set implementations, 492–93
Set interface, 433–37, 469, 504
  array operations of, 437
  basic operations of, 434–35
  bulk operations of, 436–37
set method, 553, 757–58
setDefaultHostnameVerifier method, 662
setDefaultSSLSocketFactory method, 662
setLastModified method, 420–21
setLayout method, 379
setLength method, 302, 303
setProperties method, 605–7
setProperty method, 599–600

shadowing, 123–24
  fields, 123–24
  lambda expressions and, 148
  local classes and, 129
Short class, 74, 273, 285, 293, 459
short data type, 46
  default value of, 46
  switch statement and, 74
shortValue method, 273, 286
ShowDocument applet, 682
showDocument method, 682–83, 706
showStatus method, 681
Shuffle example, 440, 444
signature block files, 638
signature files, 637–38
Signer Certificate Authority (CA) keystore, 31
Simple applet, 668
SimpleThreads example, 522, 525–26
single quote. See '
singleton method, 432, 455, 489, 503
size method, 511–12
slash. See /
sleep method, 522–23
SleepMessages example, 523–24
Smalltalk's collection hierarchy, 425
Socket class, 40
sockets, 40, 520
software. See applications
Solaris/Linux
  HelloWorld, 20–23
  paths in, 360–67
  updating PATH variable, 611–12
sort method, 56, 189–90, 448, 506
SortedMap interface, 428, 467–69, 490, 495, 500,
    502, 516
  Sorted comparison to SortedSet, 468
  Sorted map operations, 468
  Sorted standard conversion constructor in, 468
SortedSet interface, 426, 428, 464–67, 468–69,
    490, 492, 500
  Sorted comparison to SortedMap, 469
  Sorted endpoint operations in, 467
  Sorted range-view operations, 465–67
  Sorted set operations, 465
  Sorted standard conversion constructors, 434
split method, 550, 581, 583
SplitDemo example, 581
SplitDemo2 example, 581–82
sqrt method, 97, 281, 349–50
square brackets. See [ ]
square root, 266, 281, 349–50
SSLSocketFactory class, 662

`Stack` interface, 448
stack trace, 248, 312, 327–28, 335
`StackOfInts` class, 263
standard error, 352, 698
standard input, 352–53
`start` method, 586, 667, 691, 699, 709
`startsWith` method, 301, 369
statements, 70. *See also* by individual type
    synchronized, 529, 531–532
static import statement, 266–67
static initialization blocks, 117
static keyword, 130–31, 186–87
static modifier, 44, 57, 112, 114–15
stop method, 667
`Stream.collect` method, 476–80
`Stream.reduce` method, 475–76
streams, 145, 473
    parallel, 481–84
    pipelines and, 472–74
streams, I/O, 339–59. *See also* by individual type
    buffered, 345–46
    byte, 340–42
    character, 342–45
    closing, 341–42
    creating a file using, 389
    data, 354–57
    flushing, 346
    object, 357–59
    reading a file using, 389
    unbuffered, 345
string builders, 302–6
`String` class, 48, 57, 74, 212, 271, 288, 289, 290, 291, 292, 295–98, 300, 302, 306–7, 588
`StringBuilder` class, 271, 302–7, 800
`StringDemo` example, 290, 294, 305
`StringIndexOutOfBoundsException`, 299
`stringPropertyNames` method, 599
strings, 288–308
    capacity of, 302
    comparing portions of, 300, 301
    concatenating, 291–92
    converting between numbers and, 292–95
    creating, 289
    creating format strings, 292
    length, 302
    manipulating characters in, 295–300
    replacing characters in, 296
    searching within, 296
`StringSwitchDemo` example, 77–78
subclasses, 38–39, 88–90, 111, 118, 194, 787
    abstract methods and, 212–16
    access levels and, 111

    capabilities of, 196
    constructors, 207–8
    creating, 38–39
    final methods and, 117–18
    inheritance and, 38–39
    polymorphism in, 203–4
    returning, 108
`subList` method, 438, 443–46, 466
`submit` method, 547
`subSequence` method, 55, 297, 363, 575, 583–86
`subSet` method, 264, 436, 464, 466, 670, 759
`substring` method, 295–96, 299
subtyping, 203–31, 239, 249
super keyword, 202, 207, 238
superclasses, 33, 168, 175, 198–99, 209, 216, 334
    accessing, 206–7
    choosing, 329
    constructors for, 95, 207
    declaring, 89–90
    inheritance and, 38–39, 193–94, 216
    `Object` class, 208–12
    private members in, 196–97
`supplier` argument, 477
`@SuppressWarnings` annotation type, 165, 167–68, 226, 252, 416
`swap` method, 439–40, 445, 508, 788
Swing, 4, 210, 794. *See* graphical user interfaces
    (GUIs)
switch block, 74–75
switch statements, 74–79
`SwitchDemo` example, 74
`SwitchDemo2` example, 76–77
`SwitchDemoFallThrough` example, 75–76
symbolic links, 361–62, 364, 374–77, 379, 381, 399–405, 408, 419, 422
synchronization, 527–33
    atomic access, 533
    intrinsic locks and, 531
    reentrant, 532
    synchronized class example, 540–41
synchronized keyword, 529–30
`synchronizedCollection` method, 500–501
`SynchronizedCounter` example, 529–30, 554
`synchronizedList` method, 486–87, 494
`synchronizedMap` method, 500–501
`SynchronizedRGB` example, 540–42
`synchronizedSet` method, 500
`synchronizedSortedMap` method, 500
`synchronizedSortedSet` method, 500
`SynchronousQueue` class, 497
synthetic constructs, 124–25
`System` class, 26, 55–56, 597, 603–5

`System.console`, 353, 559, 590
`System.err`, 349, 352–53
`System.in`, 352–53
`System.out`, 274, 348, 352

T
tab, 289
`tailSet` method, 464, 467
`@Target` annotation type, 170
target typing, 150–51, 235–36
`Temporal` interface, 774–75
`TemporalAccessor` interface, 774–75
`TemporalAdjuster` interface, 776–80
    custom, 779–80
    predefined, 778–79
`TemporalQuery` method, 778–80
`TemporalUnit` interface, 774
ternary operators, 59, 64, 67, 797
test harness, 559–60
`TestFormat` example, 276–77
`TextField` class, 135
`this` keyword, 87, 98, 109–10, 799
`Thread` class, 522
thread pools, 411, 546–49
`ThreadLocalRandom`, 543, 554–55
`ThreadPoolExecutor` class, 549
threads, 520–21
    in applets, 670
    contention, 481
    defining, 521–22
    guarded blocks and, 535–39
    interference, 485–86, 527
    interrupts, 523–25
    joins, 525
    locks and, 534–35
    multithreaded applications, 272
    pausing, 522–23
    starting, 523–24
    synchronization of, 527–33
    thread objects, 521–27
    thread pools, 548–49
    thread safe, 306
`throw` statement, 324–25, 335
`Throwable` class, 255, 315, 325–26, 335
`throws` keyword, 324
`TicTacToe` example, 618–26
time. *See* Date-Time package
Time Zone Database (TZDB), 756
to prefix, 758
`toArray` method, 429–33, 465, 468, 497, 512, 514–15
TOCTTOU, 375

`toDegrees` method, 282–83
tokens, 346–47
`toLowerCase` method, 77–78, 289, 297, 306
`toRadians` method, 282–83
`toString` method, 211–12
`ToStringDemo` example, 294–95
`toUpperCase` method, 289, 297, 306
`TransferQueue` implementation, 498
`TreeMap` implementation, 450, 451, 468, 490–91, 495, 553
`TreeSet` implementation, 433–35, 450, 463, 465, 490–93
`TrigonometricDemo` example, 282
trigonometry, 272, 282–83, 286
`trim` method, 297, 470
troubleshooting. *See* errors
`Trusted-Library` attribute, 635
`Trusted-Only` attribute, 635
`try` blocks, 314–16, 318–22, 336, 370, 685, 800
`tryLock` method, 544–45
try-with-resources statement, 313, 317–20, 370, 397
type annotations, xxiii, 165. *See also* annotations
    pluggable type systems and, 170–71
type erasure, 244–52, 256
    bridge methods and, 247–49
    effects of, 247–49
type inference, 219, 223, 227, 232–34, 241, 801
type parameters, 98, 141, 221–30, 233–35, 237, 245–46, 249, 253–57
type variables, 221–22, 228
types. *See also* by individual type
    multiple inheritance of, 198–99
    nonreifiable, 227–27
    parameterized. *See* parameterized types
    raw, 224–26
    supertypes with common ancestors, 201
    type-checking, 170–71
TZDB. *See* Time Zone Database (TZDB)

U
unary operators, 59, 61–62, 66, 797
`UnaryDemo` example, 61
unboxing, 253, 271–72, 283–86, 288
underscore. *See* _
Unicode encoding
    character properties, 591–92
    regular expressions and, 591–92
    UTF-8, 356, 617, 628, 740
    UTF-16, 50, 740
UNIX. *See* Solaris/Linux
unset CLASSPATH, 30, 269

UnsupportedOperationException, 382, 385, 400, 426, 501–2
URLClassLoader implementation, 642–44, 646
useDelimiter method, 347
UTF. *See* Unicode encoding

V

valueOf method, 286, 293, 294
ValueOfDemo example, 287, 293–94
values method, 159
varargs, 96
    potential vulnerabilities of, 250–52
    preventing warnings from, 252
variables, 44–57. *See also* by individual type; fields
    atomic, 553–54
    class. *See* fields, static
    constant, 130–31
    environment, 601–2, 609–13
    instance. *See* instance variables
    local, 42, 44, 133–34, 148–49
    naming conventions, 45–46, 90, 92
    referring to objects, 101
Vector collection, 490, 494, 514
    compared to ArrayList, 494
vertical bar. *See* |
vi text editor, 20
volatile keyword, 533, 553

W

wait method, 208
warning messages, 225
    deprecation, 168
    security, 686
    suppressing, 686
    unchecked, 168
WarningDemo example, 225
watch keys, 413–14
WatchService API, 410–16
WeakHashMap implementation, 495–96
web browsers
    displaying documents in, 682–83
    frames in, 682–83
    security in, 677–78
web pages
    HTML frames, 682–83
    invoking applets, 674–76, 704–5
    Java applications, 654–56. *See* Java Web Start applications

web servers
    applets and, 31, 453–54
    JNLP errors in, 663
    placing applications on, 649, 656
    setting up, 656, 731–32
    testing, 31, 749–50
while statement, 79–80, 85–86
WhileDemo example, 79
white space
    allowing, 577–78
    character construct for, 567
    cleaning up, 749
    disallowed, 45
    leading, 576–77
    tokens and, 308, 347–48
    trailing, 296–97
wildcards, 236–44
    capture and, 240–43
    guidelines for using, 243–44
    helper methods and, 240–43
    lower-bounded, 238–39
    subtyping and, 239–40
    unbounded, 237–38
    upper-bounded, 236–37
Windows. *See* Microsoft Windows
with method, 758
wrappers, 344, 480, 491, 500–502
    checked interface, 502
    implementations of, 489–90, 499–502
    synchronization, 480–81, 489, 491, 500–501
    unmodifiable, 502
write method, 349, 386–88
writeDouble method, 355–56
writeInt method, 355–56
writeObject method, 358–59
writer method, 353
writeUTF method, 355–56

Y

Year class, 764
YearMonth class, 763–64

Z

ZIP archives, 616
ZonedDateTime object, 767–69
ZoneId class, 766–67
ZoneOffset class, 766–67